www.wadsworth.com

www.wadsworth.com is the World Wide Web site for Thomson Wadsworth and is your direct source to dozens of online resources.

At *www.wadsworth.com* you can find out about supplements, demonstration software, and student resources. You can also send e-mail to many of our authors and preview new publications and exciting new technologies.

www.wadsworth.com
Changing the way the world learns®

IN MIXED COMPANY

Communicating in Small Groups and Teams

Sixth Edition

J. Dan Rothwell
Cabrillo College

THOMSON ™

WADSWORTH

Australia • Brazil • Canada • Mexico • Singapore • Spain
United Kingdom • United States

THOMSON
™
WADSWORTH

In Mixed Company: Communicating in Small Groups and Teams,
Sixth Edition
J. Dan Rothwell

Communication Editor: Jaime Perkins

Publisher: Holly J. Allen

Assistant Editor: John Gahbauer

Editorial Assistant: Laura Localio

Senior Technology Project Manager: Jeanette Wiseman

Senior Marketing Manager: Kimberly Russell

Marketing Assistant: Alexandra Tran

Senior Marketing Communications Manager: Shemika Britt

Project Manager, Editorial Production: Christine Sosa

Creative Director: Rob Hugel

Executive Art Director: Maria Epes

Print Buyer: Karen Hunt

Permissions Editor: Joohee Lee

Production Service and Compositor: G&S Book Services

Text Designer: Gopa

Photo Researcher: Rebecca Seggel

Copy Editor: Joan Harris

Illustrator: G&S Book Services

Cover Designer: Gopa & Ted2, Inc.

Cover Image: Martin Müller/Altendo Images/Getty Images

Cover Printer: Phoenix Color Corp

Printer: Courier Corporation/Kendallville

Library of Congress Control Number: 2005927697

Student Edition: ISBN 0-495-00726-9

Thomson Higher Education
10 Davis Drive
Belmont, CA 94002-3098
USA

For more information about our products, contact us at:
Thomson Learning Academic Resource Center
1-800-423-0563
For permission to use material from this text or product, submit a request online at **http://www.thomsonrights.com**. Any additional questions about permissions can be submitted by e-mail to **thomsonrights@thomson.com**.

Brief Contents

Contents

CHAPTER EIGHT: GROUP DISCUSSION: EFFECTIVE DECISION MAKING AND PROBLEM SOLVING

Preface

IN *MIXED COMPANY* continues to show substantial increases in popularity and acclaim with each successive edition. More than 150,000 students at hundreds of colleges and universities have used it. I am profoundly grateful to all who have helped make *In Mixed Company* such a great success. For the sixth edition, I have preserved the essence of previous versions. The central unifying theme, that cooperation in small groups is usually superior to competition, has been maintained but updated with the addition of **recent research on constructive competition.** The communication competence model continues to guide discussions of key small group concepts and processes. The model is one of the communication discipline's unique contributions to understanding and improving human behavior. It is thoroughly integrated throughout the text. Systems theory also remains as a key theoretical component of the text, providing a conceptual framework for analysis and insights. Finally, the unique focus on power in groups remains. Power is a central underlying element in small group conflict, teamwork, decision making, problem solving, normative behavior, roles, and leadership. I strongly believe that it deserves careful analysis, not simply obligatory mention.

In addition, **I continue to place great emphasis on *readability.*** Textbooks are not meant to read like spy thrillers, but neither should they induce a coma by reading like instructions for filling out your income tax forms. Unlike calculus, which I have no idea how to make interesting, group communication, because of its relevance to your lives, should stir your interest. I have made a concerted effort to stimulate, not sedate you.

The risk in telling you this, obviously, is that you may respond, "And that's the best you could do?" Alas, yes. Whatever the shortcomings of this work, I was ever mindful of my audience. I have searched in obvious and not-so-obvious places for the precise example, the amusing illustration, the poignant instance, and the dramatic case to enhance your reading enjoyment. I have employed a more narrative or storytelling style than is usual in textbook writing. Research also confirms that the narrative style increases comprehension and recall of information (Fernald, 1987). The Closer Looks, vivid examples, and personal experiences are narrative in nature. I also have attempted to enliven and personalize the writing style by incorporating colorful language and lively metaphors that bring interesting images to mind, and to depart from standard academic practice by employing the "perpendicular pronoun" **I**. Occasional use of first-person singular speaks more directly and personably to readers than the more impersonal style of writing commonly used in textbooks ("this author's view"). Although it has been suggested that I employ the "editorial we" instead of the first-person singular, I tend to agree with Mark Twain, who said that "people with tapeworms have the right to use the editorial 'we'" but others should avoid it. I could use the passive voice and avoid the first-person singular, but that makes copy editors twitch.

Cosmetic Changes

Although the essence of previous editions of *In Mixed Company* has been preserved, this sixth edition provides both significant cosmetic and substantive changes. **The principal cosmetic change is the addition of full color.** Because *In Mixed Company* has become a market leader, producing this edition in full color is possible. This is no small change. Color makes a text more attractive and visually interesting to readers. Reviewers have often requested it. Color also helps combat the textbooks-are-boring appearance. The downside, however, is that adding color is expensive. As a faculty member who sits on a campus committee that is exploring ways to hold the line on textbook prices, I am hypersensitive to increasing the price of *In Mixed Company* despite the obvious advantages of introducing this new edition in color. I am pleased to report that Thomson Wadsworth is absorbing the additional cost of producing this text in full color.

A second cosmetic change is the addition of snappier subheads. These subheads attempt to accomplish three purposes: (1) to draw attention to key concepts and processes, (2) to create interest in the material discussed, and (3) to help clarify concepts and processes at a glance.

A third cosmetic change is the addition of a few carefully selected cartoons and many new photographs. Well-chosen photographs are important to enhance "the look" of a text and to offer instructive insights. Thus, you won't see staged photos of people sitting around a table feigning a meaningful group discussion. I look for engaging photos that draw your interest and sometimes make a point better than a paragraph of explanation.

Substantive Changes

The accusation is often made that new editions of textbooks offer mostly cosmetic changes (a few new photos or an occasional new example or reference). This is emphatically not the case for *In Mixed Company*. I feel an ethical obligation to provide significant substantive changes to warrant a new edition. Numerous substantive changes have been made for this edition. They are:

1. *A new chapter on virtual groups and technology* has been added. Expanding *In Mixed Company* to 11 chapters was a topic of lengthy discussion and debate. Although technology is an issue discussed throughout the text, a separate chapter was deemed desirable primarily because of the ubiquity of new technologies that influence small group communication and because of the increased popularity of virtual teams. **Despite the addition of a new chapter, the overall text word count has increased only slightly compared to the previous edition. Nevertheless, page count has increased primarily because of layout changes and the addition of lengthy self-quizzes, video case studies, and cartoons.**

2. An exciting new *customizing option* for instructors is offered. Upon request and given enough interest and demand to warrant the effort, I will write a new chapter or craft a substantial segment on important topics to meet the unique needs of certain programs and courses. This customized material would then be placed online at the website for *In Mixed Company* (http://communication.wadsworth .com/rothwell6). Students would have easy access to this material at no additional cost to them. Any instructor interested in this option need only contact the author or publisher to discuss the possibility and procedure.

3. *Self-assessment tests* appear in many chapters. These assessment tests have been carefully crafted to be of maximum usefulness and interest to students. If I couldn't compose a meaningful assessment test for a particular chapter, none was included merely for show. Thus, some chapters have no assessment test.

4. All chapters have been thoroughly *updated.* More than 150 recent references have been added and many older references have been expunged. New, sharper examples have replaced shopworn illustrations. In all subject areas I have searched energetically for the very latest research and insights. I have also included numerous recent events to illustrate key points and to give the text a contemporary feel.

5. *Additional theories, models, and concepts* have been included. The Collective Effort Model, dynamic equilibrium, social compensation, the norm of group interest, symbolic convergence, media richness and media synchronicity theories are some examples.

6. Most chapters have been slightly *reorganized,* and several Closer Looks were moved from boxed asides to the main text. Chapter 4 (group climate), in particular, has undergone a substantial reorganization with a lengthy section on constructive competition added and a careful discussion of intragroup compared to intergroup competition addressed. **Concepts of collaborative interdependence, individual accountability, equal reward systems, and meaningful participation as means to induce cooperation have been moved to Chapter 6 on teambuilding and teamwork.** Chapter 10 (conflict) was flabby and needed slimming, so it has been trimmed.

7. A new feature called *Video Case Studies* appears at the end of every chapter. As students, you are asked to choose one of the movies listed and answer criti-

cal thinking questions that require understanding and application of chapter material.

8. Discussions of *gender and culture* continue to be updated and expanded. In some cases, boxed material (Focus on Gender and Culture) on these important topics has been moved into the main text primarily because it seemed to improve the flow of the chapter and it integrated well with prime subject matter. Reviewers have suggested that I include separate chapters on gender and culture. They have also suggested separate chapters on verbal and nonverbal communication, listening, parliamentary procedure, and technology. Although I welcome and respect reviewers' suggestions, I have resisted adding new chapters to the core text except for one on virtual groups and technology. I want the clear focus of *In Mixed Company* to be small group communication. All of these topics are covered extensively throughout the text in relationship to group concepts and processes (see the table of contents and the index), except for parliamentary procedure, a topic that seems more appropriate for large groups and organizations, not small groups and teams. Nevertheless, **the customizing option explained already might be a suitable choice for some who prefer chapter-size coverage of certain topics.**

9. The subject of *ethics* in small group and team communication has received increased attention. Besides many shorter discussions of ethics throughout the text, ethical leadership has been addressed more extensively and directly.

Continued Features

Several acclaimed features of previous editions have been maintained. They include:

1. *Closer Look segments* have been updated where warranted and a few no-longer-relevant segments have been deleted.

2. Tables, each called a *Second Look,* act as succinct summaries of complicated and/or detailed material. These can be useful when studying for exams.

3. A **glossary** of key terms for quick reference appears at the end of the text. Terms that are **boldfaced** in each chapter are included in the glossary.

4. An opportunity for students to use **InfoTrac® College Edition**, an online library with extensive material on communication, has been provided. InfoTrac College Edition offers access to complete articles from more than 5,000 scholarly and popular periodicals. Suggestions for InfoTrac College Edition research and critical thinking are provided at the end of each chapter.

5. *Self-quizzes* for each chapter appear on the *In Mixed Company* website at http://communication.wadsworth.com/rothwell6. These quizzes provide practice before taking exams.

6. A comprehensive *Instructor's Manual* with a test bank has been revised. One innovative testing feature highlighted in the Instructor's Manual is the Cooperative Exam in both objective and essay form. A Cooperative Group Examination is one way simultaneously to test students and to apply the text material on building cooperation.

7. I have also produced a *videotape entitled Working Together,* shot in documentary style, which illustrates several key classroom activities (e.g., "Power Carnival," "Building Blocks"). This video can serve either as a substitute for having students do the activities or as a visual guide showing how to conduct these very successful innovative exercises in class. The videotape is available as an ancillary to the text.

Text Organization

Although there is no ideal organizational pattern, my schema for the sequence of chapters is quite simple. A theoretical foundation is discussed first (Chapters 1 and 2), followed by how groups are formed and developed (Chapter 3). Then a discussion of how to establish the proper climate for the group to work effectively is presented (Chapter 4). This is followed by an explanation and analysis of what roles group members are likely to play (Chapter 5). Then how to build teams and instill effective teamwork in groups is addressed (Chapter 6). This is followed by a discussion of decision making/problem solving—the primary work to be performed by most groups, with special focus on critical thinking (Chapters 7 and 8). The close connection between power and conflict is then explored (Chapters 9 and 10). Finally, virtual groups and technology are addressed. I can see other ways of organizing this same material, but the order I have chosen works well for me, students seem satisfied with the sequence of topics, and reviewers have praised the organization.

Acknowledgments

My sincere thanks are extended to all those who reviewed this edition of *In Mixed Company.* They are Daniel DuBray, Cosumnes River College; Daniel S. Fox, Monterey Peninsula College; Gayle Martin, Ferris State University; Juliann C. Scholl, Texas Tech University; Susan D. Sheane, University of Alaska Fairbanks; Roaxane Sutherland, Clark College; and Scott D. Wells, St. Cloud State University. I also wish to extend a sincere thanks to all those who reviewed previous editions of *In Mixed Company,* now too numerous to include their names here.

A special thanks goes to Georg Romero, reference librarian at Cabrillo College, who located references and material that would have remained forever hidden from me if I hadn't benefited from his herculean efforts. I'm told that I still own the record for the most interlibrary loan requests.

My considerable gratitude is also extended to my editor, Annie Mitchell, whose idea it was to produce this edition in full color. Her steadfast faith in this project was welcomed. Unfortunately for me, Annie proved to be so enormously capable that she was promoted to a well-deserved vice-presidential position just prior to the completion of this revision. I wish her continued success. The editorial challenge was quickly picked up by Jaime Perkins who expertly guided the project's completion. To the entire Thomson Wadsworth team, I express my deep appreciation for a job well done. My thanks go to Holly J. Allen, Aarti Jayaraman, Trina Enriquez, John Gahbauer, Jeanette Wiseman, Kimberly Russell, Alexandra Tran, Shemika Britt, Jennifer Klos, Karen Hunt, and Joohee Lee. Thanks also to Jamie Armstrong and Leah McAleer at G&S Book Services, Rebecca Seggel, and Gopa. It is a pleasure to work with such capable and pleasant professionals.

I also express my heartfelt gratitude to my colleagues in the communication studies department at Cabrillo College. You are a continuing source of inspiration for me and you demonstrate daily that cooperation and teamwork can be practical realities, not merely wishful thinking.

Finally, to my wife, Marcy, a special thanks for being so understanding and loving when I spent hundreds of hours isolated in my home office working on two textbooks simultaneously. I remained sane in no small part because of you.

About the Author

J. Dan Rothwell is chair of the Communication Studies Department at Cabrillo College. He has a B.A. in American History from the University of Portland (Oregon), an M.A. in Rhetoric and Public Address, and a Ph.D. in Communication Theory. His M.A. and Ph.D. are both from the University of Oregon. He is the author of three other books: *In the Company of Others: An Introduction to Communication, Telling It Like It Isn't: Language Misuse and Malpractice,* and (with James Costigan) *Interpersonal Communication: Influences and Alternatives.*

He is currently co-authoring a general psychology textbook with Terry Fetterman and David Douglass, psychology professors at Cabrillo College. During his extensive teaching career, Dr. Rothwell has received a dozen teaching awards.

Professor Rothwell encourages feedback and correspondence from both students and instructors regarding *In Mixed Company.* Anyone so inclined may communicate with him by e-mail at darothwe@cabrillo.edu or by snail-mail care of the Communication Studies Department, Cabrillo College, Aptos, CA 95003. Dr. Rothwell may also be reached by phone at 1-831-479-6511.

1 Communication Competence in Groups

I F YOU WANT TO FIND OUT what people think about groups, ask them. I have. Periodically, I pass out a questionnaire in some of my small group communication classes. The results are quite revealing. The great majority of students seem to view working in groups with the same fondness they have for undergoing a root canal or wisdom teeth removal. Comments include: "If God had ordered a committee to create the world, it would still be discussing proposals." "For every group I've enjoyed, there have been a dozen groups looking to make my life miserable—and succeeding." "Working in groups is like eating tofu. I'm told it's good for me, but it makes me gag." "I hate groups. I hate group assignments. I hate teachers who require group assignments. Take the hint." As two communication experts note, "Students arrive at college with an opinion of group decision making that is often negative and distrustful." They typically find groups "to be slow, often ill-informed, and uneven in participation" (McMillan & Harriger, 2002, p. 244).

Surveys in the business world duplicate the reactions of students (Alexander, 1989; Lippincott, 1999; F. Stone, 1997; Tuck, 1996). Executives spend approximately a third of their time trapped in group meetings, and they consider about half of these meetings to be a waste of time. Avid baseball fan and conservative columnist George Will, commenting on what he dislikes about football, remarks, "Football combines the two worst features of American life. It is violence punctuated by committee meetings" (Fitzhenry, 1993, p. 426).

Sorensen (1981) coined the term **grouphate** to describe how troublesome the group experience is for many people. The most interesting result of her research, however, **shows a direct relationship between the grouphate phenomenon and communication competence.** Those individuals with the most instruction in effective group communication have the most positive attitude about working in groups. Unfortunately, most people do not receive the requisite training, so grouphate flourishes. With grouphate comes an understandable desire to avoid group work, making any improvement in our attitudes about groups unlikely.

Virtually everyone can point to positive group experiences, including some that are profoundly rewarding. The rewards include: a feeling of belonging and affection gained from **primary groups** (family and friends); social support in difficult times, acquired from self-help and **support groups** (Alcoholics Anonymous, cancer survivors groups); satisfaction from solving challenging problems by working in

project groups (task forces, self-managing work teams); enhanced knowledge from participating in **learning groups** (class study groups, college seminar groups, Bible study groups, mock trial teams); thrills and entertainment from participating in **activities groups** (chess clubs, sports teams); a sense of community from **neighborhood groups** (homeowners associations, PTA); an identity and pleasure from helping others through **social and service groups** (fraternities, sororities, Rotary, Lions, and Kiwanis clubs); and a creative outlet in **music and artistic groups** (bands, choirs, quilting circles). Of course, a single group may provide many of these benefits and more.

The most successful groups are composed of members who love working in groups and who experience the rewards (Goleman, 1989). The least successful groups are composed of members who dislike working in groups and who see primarily the disadvantages (Keyton et al., 1996). Participating in successful groups—those that achieve desirable goals and reap valued rewards—improves one's attitude about groups (Isaksen, 1988). Because communication plays such a central role in achieving this group success and producing rewarding experiences, **there's no substitute for competent communication as a means of counteracting grouphate.**

Whatever the degree of your satisfaction or dissatisfaction with groups, there is no escaping them, unless you plan to live your life alone in a cave like some out-of-touch survivalist. Reliance on groups will increase, not diminish, in the future (LaFasto & Larson, 2001). By the end of the 1990s, four-fifths of both Fortune 1000 companies and manufacturing organizations were using self-managing work teams (Thoms et al., 2002). Advances in computers and electronic technology will boost the reliance on **virtual teams**—groups whose members are connected by the Internet, video, fax, and phone (Godar & Ferris, 2004). The American Association for the Advancement of Science, The National Council of Teachers of English, the National Council of Teachers of Mathematics, and the National Communication Association all recommend frequent group activity in the college classroom.

Maximizing the benefits of our unavoidable group experiences seems like a worthy goal. **The central purpose of this textbook, then, is to teach you how to be a competent communicator in groups.** This purpose presupposes, of course, that there is much for you to learn. Because we all have participated in many groups, it may be tempting to conclude that these experiences leave relatively little for you to learn. Experience, however, isn't always an effective teacher. Sometimes experience teaches us bad habits and misinformation (note the myths discussed in the next section). I will not presume to tell you what you know and don't know about small group communication. That is for you to assess, perhaps with the help of your instructor.

When making this initial self-assessment, however, please consider this: most Americans have a common tendency to overestimate their communication proficiency in groups. One study asked 144 business managers to rate their listening skills. Ninety-four percent saw themselves as "good" or "very good" listeners and no one chose "poor" or "very poor." More than half of their employees, however, rated these managers' listening skills as "poor." Only a few managers' listening skills were rated highly (Brownell, 1990). A long-term study of 600 teams and 6,000 team members in a wide variety of organizations found that assessments of leaders by team members were a whopping *50% lower* than the leaders' self-assessments (LaFasto & Larson, 2001). These same team members also noted the serious communication deficiencies of teams as a whole. Ironically, it is the poorest communicators who inflate their self-assessments the most (Kruger & Dunning, 1999).

No one is a perfect communicator, so everyone can improve his or her communication in groups. **The primary purpose of this chapter is to establish the theoretical groundwork for a communication competence approach to groups.** There are four chapter objectives:

1. to correct some common misconceptions regarding the human communication process,
2. to explain what communication is and isn't,
3. to identify broadly what constitutes competent communication, and
4. to discuss general ways to achieve communication competence.

Myths about Communication

Before tackling the question "What is communication?" and then, more specifically, "What is competent communication?" let's sweep out some of the musty misconceptions many people have stored in their intellectual attics regarding the communication process. As American humorist Will Rogers once remarked, "It isn't what we don't know that gives us trouble, it's what we know that ain't so" (Fitzhenry, 1993, p. 243). Foolishness springs from holding firmly to indefensible myths. Consider four of them.

MYTH 1: COMMUNICATION IS A PANACEA

Communication is not the magical answer to all our woes. Sometimes more communication aggravates differences between people and exposes qualities in others we may find unappealing. Active listening may reveal truths that make it impossible for us to remain in a group. Sometimes groups dismantle, not because the communication is poor, but because members have personalities or values that severely clash or because they have contradictory visions for the group.

Communication is a tool that, in the possession of someone knowledgeable and skillful, can be used to help solve most problems that arise in groups. **Communication, however, is not an end in itself but merely a means to an end.** You will not solve every conceivable problem in groups by learning to communicate more effectively, because not all group problems are communication based.

MYTH 2: COMMUNICATION CAN BREAK DOWN

Communication does not break down. Machines break down; they quit, and if they belong to me they do so with amazing regularity. Human beings continue to communicate even when they may wish not to do so. Behaviors such as not showing up for a group meeting, remaining silent during group discussions, or walking out in the middle of a group discussion without saying a word don't stop communication. Group members infer messages from these nonverbal acts—perhaps incorrect messages, but potentially important ones nonetheless.

The view that communication can break down comes partly from the recognition that we do not always achieve our goals through communication; the group may disband in failure. But failure to achieve our group goals may occur even when communication between the parties in conflict is exemplary. So where's the breakdown?

We sometimes draw the mistaken conclusion that disagreement constitutes a communication breakdown because our ability to influence group members stops working. Group members may understand our message(s) perfectly; they may simply dislike what they're hearing. In this case there is a difference of opinion, not a communication breakdown.

MYTH 3: EFFECTIVE COMMUNICATION IS MERELY SKILL BUILDING

The skills orientation to communication assumes that if you learn a few magical communication skills, you will become a much better communicator. **Without understanding the complexities of the communication process, no amount of skills training will be meaningful, and it may be harmful.** Merely teaching the skill of assertiveness to a battered woman, for example, without addressing the volatile and often unpredictable circumstances of abusive relationships in families, could prove fatal for the abused woman and her children (O'Leary et al., 1985). Assertiveness with your boss or team leader may get you fired or demoted to a position equivalent to cleaning up after parading elephants. One skill doesn't fit all circumstances.

Teaching communication skills without knowledge, without a well-researched theoretical map guiding our behavior, is like constructing a house without a carefully developed set of blueprints. All the skills necessary to build a house won't be very useful without a thoughtful plan to guide the construction and prevent collapse of the structure. The blueprint I offer is the communication competence model presented later in this chapter.

MYTH 4: EFFECTIVE COMMUNICATION IS JUST COMMON SENSE

Consider **hindsight bias** (Worthington et al., 2002). This is the "I-knew-it-already" effect. We tend to overestimate our prior knowledge once we have been told the correct answers. Anything can seem like mere common sense when you've been given the correct answers, or as psychologist David Myers (2002) observes, "How easy it is to seem wise when drawing the bull's-eye after the arrow has struck" (p. 89). Everybody knows that opposites attract, right? When told this by Myers, most students find this conclusion unsurprising. But wait! When college students are told the *opposite* ("Birds of a feather flock together"), most also find this result unsurprising and merely common sense (D. G. Myers, 2002).

The hindsight bias may influence us to view competent communication as mere common sense once we have received communication training. If, however, it is just common sense, why does miscommunication occur so often? For example, there is a "leadership failure rate in the range of 50% to 60%" in groups large and small (Hogan et al., 1994, p. 497). Competent communication is the core of effective leadership, so failure is directly linked to miscommunication (M. Hackman & Johnson, 2004). Between half and three-quarters of teams in organizations fail to achieve their goals (Ju & Cushman, 1995), and between 80% and 90% of teams have significant difficulty performing effectively (Buzaglo & Wheelan, 1999). A principal reason that most teams struggle is lack of communication training in how to make teams work effectively (Goleman, 1998).

The simple way to test whether we knew it all along is to pose questions before training is received. I regularly quiz my students at the beginning of each term on general knowledge of group communication (see Box 1.1). I do not ask technical questions or definitions of concepts (making this the least challenging test of the term). Typical questions include: True or False? "Competition motivates higher achievement and performance in groups for most people" and "There is a strong relationship between intelligence and effective group leadership." Consistently, students do very poorly on this quiz. Such results are not surprising, or cause for ridicule. I would be foolish to expect my students to do well on this exam before they've taken the class.

Learning requires a degree of humility, a willingness to recognize and address our shortcomings. To paraphrase Alfred Korzybski, no one knows everything about anything. Everyone has more to learn. You are invited to approach this text not with an attitude of contentment with your knowledge and skills (whatever their level), but with a strong desire to learn more and to improve your communication in groups. This improvement comes not just from knowing the right answers on tests

BOX 1.1 HINDSIGHT TEST

MULTIPLE CHOICE
(More than one answer could be correct)

1. In general, competition
   a. increases motivation to perform at peak levels for most group members
   b. is embraced by all cultures as a natural aspect of our biological makeup as human beings
   c. encourages cheating and dishonesty
   d. enhances social relationships with group members.

2. Increasing the size of a group
   a. is almost always constructive because it increases the group's resources
   b. usually increases the pressure to conform to group norms and opinions
   c. usually makes decision making more complex and difficult
   d. often produces an increasing number of nonparticipating group members

3. Leaders in groups must _____ to be effective.
   a. be highly intelligent
   b. be highly competitive
   c. use the democratic leadership style (members participate in decision making)
   d. be flexible in their communication with group members

4. Intergroup (between two groups) competition has which of the following effects on competing groups?
   a. It often produces hypercompetitiveness.
   b. It increases friction and hostility.
   c. It often increases intragroup (within each group) cohesiveness (bonding among members).
   d. Intergroup interactions are far more competitive than interactions between individuals.

5. Which of the following are effective strategies for dealing with difficult group members (disruptive troublemakers)?
   a. Provide opportunities for the difficult group member to air his/her disagreement, allowing whatever amount of time is necessary.
   b. Permit the difficult member to interrupt the group proceedings so he/she can "blow off some steam."
   c. Encourage a competitive group climate where everyone is free to argue, disagree, and attempt to win points with the group.
   d. Confront the difficult group member directly; if the entire group is affected, then the group as a whole should confront the troublemaker.

TRUE-FALSE

1. Groups should never close off communication, because remaining open to others is a key principle of competent communication.

2. Compromising should be the ultimate and most desired goal when we try to resolve conflicts in groups.

3. Venting your anger, not holding it in, is a constructive and productive way to manage your anger because it allows you to "blow off steam" before it builds to an explosive point.

4. Reward systems that stress individual achievement, such as merit pay plans where the highest performing group members receive bonuses or pay increases, work well to boost motivation and performance of most group members.

5. Competition builds character and teaches most group members how to accept defeat gracefully.

6. If you are highly intelligent, have excellent speaking skills, and are physically attractive, you are highly likely to be an effective group leader.

7. A group can never have too much information when trying to make high-quality decisions.

8. The greater the harmony within a group the better will be the decisions made by the group.

9. Achieving a consensus (unanimity) is always possible in groups if members try hard enough and are skillful in their communication.

10. Some group members can be completely powerless.

Answers are given on page 36.

of your knowledge of group communication, but also from demonstrating an ability to put this knowledge into skillful practice in a wide variety of challenging group situations.

Communication Defined

Thus far, I have indicated what communication is not but not what it is. What communication is can be ascertained clearly by first considering several fundamental principles.

▶ Focus Questions

1. How are the content and the relationship dimensions of messages different from each other?
2. "Communication is a process." What does this mean?

COMMUNICATION AS TRANSACTIONAL: THE FOUR-LEGGED PERSPECTIVE

Wendall Johnson once defined human communication as a process with four legs. Merely sending a message does not constitute communication; there also has to be a receiver. But communication is more than a mere transmission of information from sender to receiver and back again, like Ping-Pong balls batted to and fro. Communication is a **transaction.** This means essentially two things. First, **each person communicating is both a sender and a receiver simultaneously, not merely a sender or a receiver.** As you speak, you receive feedback (responses), mostly nonverbal, from listeners; this, in turn, influences the messages that you continue to send. Skillful communicators read feedback accurately and adjust their ensuing message appropriately.

Second, **communication as a transaction also means that all parties influence each other.** You don't communicate in quite the same manner with your parents as you do with a group of close friends. Your team leader may have his Donald Trump act in high gear, exhibiting an imperious, scowling demeanor that is intimidating. If so, your communication is probably more measured and stiff than it would be with a different leader who manifests a more relaxed, less fearsome style.

You can see this mutual-influence process clearly by examining the two dimensions of a message—content and relationship (Watzlawick et al., 1967). The **content dimension** refers to the information transmitted. The **relationship dimension** refers to how messages define or redefine the relationship between group members.

Consider the following transactional dialogue:

Anne: We need to meet to prepare our group presentation.

Benny: I can't meet until Wednesday night after 6:30. I work.

Charise: Wednesday, say about 7:00, works fine for me. How about the rest of you?

David: No can do! I'm busy.

Eduardo: Well, get *un*busy because our project is due in a week and we're way behind schedule.

David: Hey, Hitler's spawn, come up with another time. Wednesday night doesn't work for me.

Benny: Come on people, let's not get snotty.

Anne: Exactly how busy are you on Wednesday night, David? Can't you change your plans?

David: I'm busy! Let's leave it at that.

Eduardo: Well, because you're causing the problem, why don't you come up with a time that works with your "busy" schedule?

Charise: How about next Monday evening?

Anne: Now I've got a schedule conflict.

The content of this group transaction is the need to schedule a group meeting and the schedule conflicts that exist. The relationship dimension, however, is far more complex. Group members are not merely identifying scheduling difficulties; they're maneuvering for power positions in the group. Who gets to tell whom what to do is a subtext (the meaning is derived not from a literal interpretation of the words, but from how the words are used). How messages are spoken (sarcastically or as a request) influences group members' responses. Whether group members are being cooperative or competitive with each other is a concern affecting the discussion.

When we are in a group, every utterance, choice, and action continually defines and redefines who we are in relation to other group members and who they are in relation to us. This is ongoing and unavoidable. Individuals affect the group and the group influences the individual. Communication in groups is a continuous series of transactions.

COMMUNICATION AS A PROCESS: THE CONTINUOUS FLOW

Identifying communication as a process recognizes that nothing stands still, or as the bumper sticker proclaims, "Change is inevitable—except from a vending machine." Communication reveals the dynamic nature of relationships and events.

Communication is a process because changes in events and relationships are part of a continuous flow. You can't understand the ocean by freezing a single wave on film. The ocean is understood only in its dynamism—its tides, currents, waves in motion, plant and animal life interacting symbiotically, and so forth. Similarly, communication makes sense, not by isolating a word, sentence, gesture, facial expression, or exclamation, but by looking at currents of thought and feelings expressed verbally and nonverbally as a whole.

Students, for instance, affect the quality of instruction they receive by their attitudes and degree of interest in the subject matter. Great lectures may fall flat with students who don't care or have an antagonistic relationship with the instructor. Conversely, mediocre presentations by instructors can be made more dynamic by the enthusiastic participation of students. Students may be bored one minute and attentive the next. Relationships between teachers and students may change in the short span of a single class period or in the flash of an ill-chosen phrase, especially when controversial material is presented.

We cannot freeze relationships in time. Every conversation is a point of departure for an ensuing conversation. Every communication experience is the result of the accumulation of experiences preceding the present one. Each new experience affects future transactions. Human communication is a process.

COMMUNICATION AS SHARING MEANING: MAKING SENSE

Our world becomes meaningful through communication with others. You do not establish meaning in social isolation. Sharing ideas, feelings, ruminations, and experiences with others is part of the process of constructing meaning, of determining connections and patterns in our minds, of making sense of our world.

Verbal Communication: Telling It Like It Isn't We share meaning verbally with language. **Language** is a structured system of symbols for sharing meaning. **Symbols** are representations of *referents*—whatever the symbol refers to. Because symbols represent referents but are not the objects, ideas, events, or relationships represented, symbols have no meaning apart from us. The story of a psychiatrist giving a Rorschach inkblot test to a client demonstrates this point. When asked to identify the meaning of each inkblot, the client responds to the first, "a couple making love," to the second, "a nude woman silhouetted behind a shower curtain," and to the third, "a couple walking naked hand in hand." The psychiatrist pauses, then remarks, "Mr. Smith, you seem obsessed with sex." Mr. Smith indignantly retorts, "What do you mean? You're the one showing me the dirty pictures." Meaning is in the mind of the beholder. There is no inherent meaning in any inkblot anymore than there is inherent meaning in any word. Words are symbols, so meaning is not contained in words. We aren't "telling it like it is" (identifying objective reality); we're telling others with words what our subjective view of the world is. Meaning is derived from the associations or connections each of us makes when we interpret these words.

Comedian Stephen Wright asks, "Why is it that when you transport something by car it's called a shipment but when you transport something by ship it's called cargo?" and "Why are they called apartments when they are all stuck together?" The simple answer is that **the meaning of words depends on common agreement.** As a speech community, English speakers tacitly agree to certain meanings for words. We can also invent new words, such as *arachnidiot* (a person who, having wandered into an "invisible" spider web, begins flailing wildly) or *stupiphany* (a seemingly brilliant idea, until you start to tell it to someone) or *downloafing* (surfing the Internet when you should be working), all found on the *Unwords.com* website. Members of the speech community, however, must agree to use these invented words with their corresponding meanings to make them functional. **This common agreement, however, doesn't always avoid misunderstandings because words can be ambiguous; they can have double or multiple common meanings.** A *booty call* could be an invitation to a treasure hunt, or a search for something quite different. Actual newspaper headlines reported by the *Columbia Journalism Review* illustrate this ambiguity: "Dog Rules on Agenda in Old Orchard"; "Prostitutes Appeal to Pope"; and "Kids Make Nutritious Snacks."

I've observed several group discussions at my own campus on the issue of *diversity*. The term may seem straightforward, but it is far more ambiguous than one might realize. Some college campuses have relatively few white students. At University of California, Berkeley, for example, white students make up less than a third of the total student body (Ralston, 2001). Does diversity mean more white students should be recruited? In fall 2002, 8.3 million women and 6.4 million men enrolled in college, a trend that had been growing for several years (Goodman, 2002). Does

Language can have ambiguous meanings.

diversity mean that more men should be recruited to close this gender gap? Does diversity mean only including more students and faculty from historically underrepresented groups in the national population, or also from underrepresented local populations?

Verbal misunderstandings are further complicated by culture. The emergence of virtual teams has created an international challenge for most of the world's team members. Increasingly, virtual teams (especially in the realm of international business) are composed of members from various nations, many of whom speak English as a second language. English is the dominant language of the Internet, and it has been proposed as the global language of business (Crystal, 1997). Inevitably, however, the nuances and complexities of mastering a language such as English lead to problems of interpretation and even translation (Rad & Levin, 2003). For example, should the e-mail from your team leader saying that the team project "is fine" be interpreted as damning (with faint praise), or as giving a genuine thumbs-up for a job well done? Electrolux, a Scandinavian vacuum cleaner manufacturer, once used the sales slogan in the United States, "Nothing sucks like an Electrolux." The slogan was quickly pulled once the misunderstanding was revealed. Clairol Corporation marketed its "Mist Stick" curling iron in Germany before realizing that *mist* is a German slang term meaning "manure." It is unlikely that a "manure stick" would be a real hot seller. The NBC *Today* show reported that during the opening baseball game at the 2000 Olympics in Sydney, Australia, many fans giggled during a group rendition

The mixture of language and culture can lead to misunderstandings.

of "Take Me Out to the Ballgame." The lyric "root, root, root for the home team" was the source of the amusement. *Root* to the Australian fans is equivalent to *shagging* (having sex) in England. *Rooting* in Australia for your home team is taking fan support a tad far.

When we assume that everyone has the same meaning for a word, it is called **bypassing.** You counteract bypassing by recognizing that meaning is not in a word, so the meaning you have in your head for key words should be clearly specified at the outset of any group discussion to avoid confusion and misunderstanding. Nevertheless, some misunderstandings will occur because language can be complex and ambiguous even with the best effort to avoid bypassing.

Nonverbal Communication: Wordless Meaning We share meaning nonverbally as well as verbally. **Nonverbal communication** is sharing meaning with others without using words. Our facial expressions, eye contact, personal appearance, tone of voice, gestures, posture, touch, and use of space and time all have the potential to communicate messages to group members. When we compete with group members, for example, we tend to sit across from each other or increase distance between each other, but when we cooperate we tend to sit side by side or corner to corner at a table (Forsyth, 1990). Cooperating group members tend to mirror (copy) posture, whereas competing members tend to exhibit the opposite posture pattern (Ketrow, 1999). Seating patterns and posture can signal whether group members are focused on competing or cooperating. Business meetings in U.S. culture are expected to begin on time. Even small delays of 5–10 minutes can be offensive and irritating, but most Latin American, southern European, African, and Middle Eastern cultures are not nearly as time sensitive. Delays of 15 minutes or even as long as a day are viewed as acceptable and nonoffensive (Trompenaars, 1994).

Nonverbal communication, like verbal communication, is often ambiguous. When group members look down for several minutes while you are speaking, does it mean they are bored, uncomfortable with your message, not listening, carefully considering your message, or devising a plan to exit the meeting early? When a group member frowns, is he or she showing confusion, taking offense at something said, or contemplating something unrelated to the discussion? Jury consultant Howard Varinsky notes that attempting to decipher a jury's verdict by observing whether jurors look at or avoid eye contact with the defendant before the pronouncement of guilt or innocence is silly. "Who they look at when they come into the courtroom—you can interpret looks 50 different ways." Rich Matthews, a jury consultant with Decision Analysis in San Francisco, also states that it is "practically impossible and it's just dangerous to interpret facial expressions and gestures and reactions" during a trial (quoted in Sulek, 2004a, p. 9A).

Even though nonverbal communication can be ambiguous and difficult to read accurately, it can nevertheless have a big impact on our impressions of others. In 2004, Scott Peterson was found guilty of murdering his pregnant wife and unborn child. Jurors revealed after the trial that they chose the death penalty as his punishment partly because, as juror Richelle Nice put it, "For me, a big part of it was at the end—the verdict—no emotion. No anything. That spoke a thousand words—loud and clear. Today—the giggle at the table. Loud and clear." Jury foreman Steve Cardosi echoed this reaction: "He lost his wife and his child and it didn't seem to faze him" (quoted in Sulek, 2004b, p. 16A).

Unlike verbal communication, nonverbal communication is continuous, not discrete (P. Andersen, 1999). Verbal communication has identifiable, discrete beginnings and endings. We speak and verbal communication begins; we stop speaking and verbal communication ends. Nonverbal communication, however, continues to

AFP/Getty Images

Is Robert Noel communicating "nothing" to you, or do you form an impression from his facial expression?

send messages to those who are aware of our behavior. We can't stop our facial expressions. Even a blank face communicates. Showing no eye contact can signal respect, intimidation, boredom, or insult. You can't stop the nonverbal leakage.

In 2002, a jury convicted Robert Noel, the owner of a dog that viciously mauled and killed Diane Whipple, of involuntary manslaughter. Noel apparently was oblivious to the continuous nature of nonverbal communication. Staring stoically into space for most of the trial, Noel responded after the verdict to jurors' characterization of him as unremorseful and unpleasant in his demeanor: "I made up my mind not to react one way or another. I'm sitting there just watching what was going on, making notes for the attorneys . . . And it's just amazing that I could just sit there doing nothing and that gets twisted into, 'Oh, he's a cold-hearted son of a bitch'" (P. May, 2002, p. 18A). When others are observing us, we always communicate something.

Verbal and Nonverbal Interconnectedness: Joined at the Hip Although we commonly discuss them as though they were completely separate, verbal and nonverbal communication are interconnected. Nonverbal cues that accompany language can be as or more important than the words spoken. For example, an interesting verbal message can be made boring by a glacially slow speaking pattern, monotonous voice, poor eye contact, expressionless face, and frequent hesitations.

Mixed messages also show the connection between verbal and nonverbal communication. A **mixed message** occurs when there is positive verbal and negative nonverbal communication, or vice versa. A group member may verbally endorse the group's decision but nonverbally exhibit disagreement, even contempt. It is easier to hide our real feelings verbally than it is nonverbally. For example, attempting to wipe an opinion off your face is a real challenge.

One of the difficulties with communicating in virtual groups is the absence of nonverbal cues that typically accompany verbal messages (Wallace, 1999). The tone of an online message can easily be misinterpreted as hostile, impersonal, or disagreeable because vocal tone, facial expressions, posture, gestures, and the normal array of nonverbal cues are missing. **Emoticons**—typed icons or combinations of punctuation marks meant to indicate emotional tone—help but are still limited, and using them often can interrupt the flow of messages. Individuals may also be hesitant to use emoticons in business communication for fear of appearing too informal and unprofessional.

Context: The Communication Environment Every communication transaction has a **context,** or an environment in which meaning emerges. Context consists of *who* (sender) communicates *what* (message) to *whom* (receiver), *why* (purpose) the communicator does it, *where* (setting), *when* (time), and *how* (way) it is done. **Context is a central element of verbal communication.** Little notice may be given to obscene words and phrases used unthinkingly when talking with a group of friends. If used during a job interview, however, they would probably be highly objectionable and cause for rejection of an applicant.

Context is also central to nonverbal communication. For instance, in 1997 a Newton, Massachusetts, jury found Louise Woodward, a British teenager employed as a nanny by an American couple, guilty of manslaughter for the death of the couple's infant cared for by Woodward. Why did the jury not believe Woodward's testimony that the infant's death was an accident, and would a British jury have made the same verdict? Jonathon Raban (1997), a British author living in the United States and present at the trial, concluded, "My English eyes saw one thing; my American-resident eyes saw something else altogether" (p. 53). Raban's "English eyes" saw a Louise Woodward with "shoulders hunched submissively forward, eyes lowered, voice a humble whisper. Ms. Woodward made a good impression as an English church mouse. Her posture announced that she knew her place; that she acknowledged the superior authority of the court; that she was a nobody." He concluded, "I thought she was telling the truth." Raban's "American-resident eyes," however, saw something quite different. "My second pair of eyes saw Ms. Woodward as sullen, masked, affectless, dissembling. Her evasive body language clearly bespoke the fact that she was keeping something of major importance hidden from the court." He concluded, "I thought she was telling lies" (p. 55). Raban's dual-culture perspective emphasizes the ambiguity of nonverbal communication and the influence of context (e.g., American or British culture) on interpreting nonverbal messages. This trial was watched with great interest in Britain, where, according to CNN, most believed Woodward was innocent.

Verbal and nonverbal communication is discussed in much greater detail later. Such subjects as gender styles of communicating, boundary control, defensive and supportive communication patterns, false dichotomies, collective inferential error, verbal and nonverbal indicators of power, low-context and high-context communication, and assertiveness explore ways verbal and nonverbal communication influence group transactions.

I have thus far discussed what communication is not and, conversely, what communication is. To summarize by way of definition, **communication** is a transactional process of sharing meaning with others. The intricacies of sharing meaning with others in group situations will become more apparent when I discuss what constitutes competent communication, the next topic for consideration.

Communication Competence

Knowing what constitutes human communication does not tell you how to engage in the process in a competent manner. To accomplish this goal, it helps to understand what it means to communicate competently—the objective of this next section. **Communication competence** is engaging in communication with others that is both effective and appropriate. This definition requires brief elaboration.

▶ **Focus Questions**

1. How do you determine communication competence?
2. Does appropriate communication require unswerving conformity to group rules and standards?
3. Does being a competent communicator mean never engaging in poor communication practices?

EFFECTIVENESS: ACHIEVING GOALS

Communication competence is predicated on results. Consequently, **effectiveness** is defined as how well we have progressed toward the achievement of goals. Effectiveness is a litmus test of competence (Spitzberg & Cupach, 1989). Someone who knows the changes in communication behavior that need to be made, and who wants to make these changes but never does, can hardly be deemed a competent communicator.

A Matter of Degree: From Deficiency to Proficiency Communication effectiveness is a relative concept—a matter of degree (Spitzberg & Cupach, 1989). We speak of communicators along a continuum, from highly proficient in achieving goals to woefully deficient, with designations in between such as ordinary and average. All of us have our communication strengths and weaknesses in certain situations and circumstances. Some individuals are at ease in social situations such as parties or gatherings of strangers, but they would rather be dipped in molasses and strapped to an anthill than confront conflict in their own group. We can be highly proficient in one circumstance but minimally skillful or depressingly ineffective in another situation. Therefore, the label "competent communicator" is a judgment of an individual's degree of proficiency in achieving goals in a particular context, not an inherent characteristic of any individual.

We (Not Me) Oriented: Primacy of Groups In groups, our primary attention is on the group (we), not the individual (me). Zander (1982) even goes so far as to claim, "A body of people is not a group if the members are primarily interested in individual accomplishment" (p. 2). This, however, is not the same as saying that groups should always supersede individual interests. Nevertheless, trying to achieve your individual goals at the expense of the group's goals usually produces unsatisfactory outcomes for both you and the group. As very successful NBA coach Pat Riley (1994) notes in his book *The Winner Within,* some group members develop the

Individualism versus Collectivism: A Basic Cultural Difference

A POLL OF 131 business people, scholars, government officials, and professionals in eight East Asian countries and the United States showed glaring differences in the value placed on order and personal rights and freedoms (as cited in Simons & Zielenziger, 1996). When asked the question "Which of the following are critically important to your people?" the results were as follows:

	Asians	Americans
An orderly society	70%	11%
Personal freedom	32%	82%
Individual rights	29%	73%

All cultures vary in the degree of emphasis they place on individuals exploring their uniqueness and independence versus maintaining their conformity and interdependence. **This individualism–collectivism dimension is thought by some scholars to be the most important, deep-seated value that distinguishes one culture from another** (Hui & Triandis, 1986). It has provoked voluminous research. The individualism–collectivism dimension is at the center of the communication competence model's We-orientation perspective.

The autonomy of the individual is of paramount importance in individualist cultures, hence, the emphasis placed on self-actualization and personal growth. Words such as independence, self, privacy, and rights imbue cultural conversations. Individualist cultures have an "I" consciousness. Competition, not cooperation, is encouraged. Decision making is predicated on what benefits the individual, even if this jeopardizes the group welfare. Individual achievement and initiative are stressed (Samovar & Porter, 2004). Self-promotion is expected, even encouraged.

In collectivist cultures, by contrast, commitment to the group is paramount. Words such as loyalty, responsibility (to the group welfare), and community imbue collectivist cultural conversations. Collectivist cultures have a "We" consciousness. Cooperation within valued groups (family, friends, coworkers) is strongly emphasized, although transactions with groups perceived as outsiders (foreigners, strangers) can become competitive (Yu, 1998). Individuals often downplay personal goals in favor of advancing the goals of a valued group (Samovar & Porter, 2004). Self-promotion is discouraged.

All cultures have both individualist and collectivist influences, but one tends to predominate over the other (Gudykunst, 1991). A worldwide study of 50 countries and three geographic areas ranks the United States as the number one individualistic country (see also Acuff, 1997). The United States is followed by other Western countries such as Australia, Great Britain, Canada, Netherlands, and New Zealand in that order. Latin American, Asian,

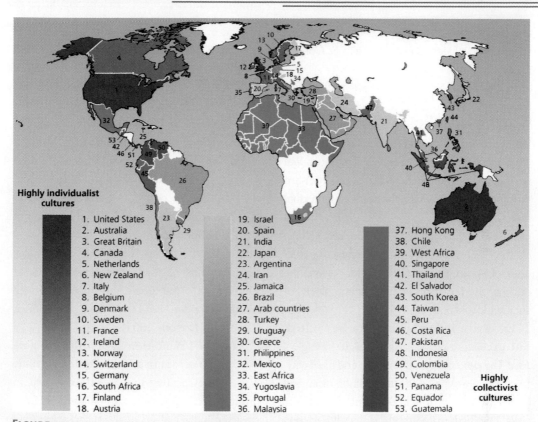

FIGURE 1.1
Map of individualist and collectivist cultures.
From *In the Company of Others*, Second Edition, by J. Dan Rothwell. © 2004 McGraw-Hill Companies, Inc.
Reprinted with permission of The McGraw-Hill Companies.

Highly individualist cultures

1. United States
2. Australia
3. Great Britain
4. Canada
5. Netherlands
6. New Zealand
7. Italy
8. Belgium
9. Denmark
10. Sweden
11. France
12. Ireland
13. Norway
14. Switzerland
15. Germany
16. South Africa
17. Finland
18. Austria
19. Israel
20. Spain
21. India
22. Japan
23. Argentina
24. Iran
25. Jamaica
26. Brazil
27. Arab countries
28. Turkey
29. Uruguay
30. Greece
31. Philippines
32. Mexico
33. East Africa
34. Yugoslavia
35. Portugal
36. Malaysia
37. Hong Kong
38. Chile
39. West Africa
40. Singapore
41. Thailand
42. El Salvador
43. South Korea
44. Taiwan
45. Peru
46. Costa Rica
47. Pakistan
48. Indonesia
49. Colombia
50. Venezuela
51. Panama
52. Equador
53. Guatemala

Highly collectivist cultures

and West and East African countries rank high on collectivism. Guatemala is the most collectivist. Ecuador, Panama, Venezuela, Colombia, Indonesia, Taiwan, and Singapore are also among the most collectivist (Hofstede, 1991) (see Figure 1.1). Approximately 70% of the world's population lives in collectivist cultures (Triandis, 1990).

Despite strong cultural pressure, no population uniformly accepts its culture's values (see Box 1.2 to check your degree of individualism or collectivism). A review of 35 studies involving thousands of participants showed that African Americans are significantly more individualistic than European Americans (white respondents), but both are substantially more individualistic than are Asian Americans (Oyserman et al., 2002). Even different regions of the United States vary. Individualism is strongest in the Mountain West

▶

and Great Plains states, but collectivism is quite strong in the Deep South (Vandello & Cohen, 1999).

In the United States, the preoccupation with individualism has drawn fire. Psychologist Carol Tavris (1989) argues that individualism in the United States has become excessive, producing what she terms the "Imperial I." The individual is king, regal in importance. Groups often are thought to exist to satisfy the needs of individual members, not to advance the greater social welfare. Sociologist Charles Derber (1996) claims, "As individualism intensifies, the balance of commitment can tilt so far toward the self that the family and other building blocks of society decompose" (p. 111).

Excessive individualism can be faulted, but excessive collectivism has its dangers too. The perils of group pressure and blind conformity to groups, issues that will be discussed at length later in this book, remind us of the risks involved from excessive loyalty to any group. Collectivist cultures require a level of conformity and restrictive rules that are unacceptable to most Americans. Singapore, for example, levies heavy fines on anyone littering, spitting, smoking in public places, or failing to flush public toilets—actions that are monitored by government employees (Bordewich, 1995; En-Lai, 2003). Requiring students to take drug tests is a routine practice and groups of five individuals or more cannot meet on the street without police permission. Video cameras are set up at busy intersections to monitor compliance with traffic laws; heavy censorship of printed material, CDs, and motion pictures is widespread; only the police can own guns; and political opposition to the government is a risky undertaking, often resulting in fines and imprisonment for dissidents (Huckshorn, 1996).

Individualist and collectivist cultures exhibit glaring differences in their perceptions of the world and how people should behave. **Individualist and collectivist values, however, do not always conflict** (Schwartz, 1990). When an individual learns conflict management skills or improves interpersonal communication skills, the group benefits as well as the group member. Nevertheless, if groups are to succeed, individual goals and agendas should be of secondary, not primary, importance (LaFasto & Larson, 2001).

The We-orientation is a difficult perspective to accept in a Me-oriented culture. The We-perspective that is so necessary to group success, however, can be learned. Contrast the individualism of track sensation Carl Lewis 1996 with the collectivism of the U.S. women's soccer team at the 1999 World Cup.

When Lewis won the long jump for the fourth straight Olympics, he had tied for the most Olympic gold medals ever won by a single individual—nine total. Immediately he began lobbying for a place on the men's 4 × 100-meter relay team, to get one last chance to earn another gold medal and go down in history as the most decorated Olympian ever. Interviewed on CNN, Lewis implored viewers to "call the Olympic people" and "make your voice heard" (cited in Purdy, 1996, p. 1D).

▶

Lewis had not qualified for the relay team at the Olympic Trials because he finished last in the 100-meter final. Placing Lewis on the relay team meant pulling off one of the U.S. sprinters who had qualified for the team, thus ending that runner's Olympic dream. Apparently, that seemed less important to Lewis than personal glory. Lewis had been invited to work out with the relay team as an alternate, to be used if a team member was injured. Lewis had declined. The U.S. relay team had the fastest qualifying time but lost to the Canadian team in the finals. The distraction of the Lewis controversy may or may not have contributed to the second-place finish; there is no way to determine this. Nevertheless, Carl Lewis clearly showed the individualist philosophy at work in a not-so-noble finish to his phenomenal Olympic career.

In stark contrast, the U.S. women's soccer team exhibited noteworthy We-orientation (not Me-orientation) during their drive to win the 1999 World Cup. Mia Hamm, the internationally recognized star of the team, refused to accept any individualistic notoriety. She appeared for clinics, autograph sessions, and promotions, but she steadfastly refused photo shoots for numerous high-profile publications during the World Cup. "This isn't all about me,"

Getty Images

The 1999 U.S. Women's World Cup soccer championship was a model of teamwork.

she noted. "Everything I am I owe to this team" (Starr & Brant, 1999, pp. 52–53). Self*lessness* reigned supreme. Starters, even some players who were star performers on the 1996 gold medal Olympic team, accepted diminished roles without complaint. Shannon MacMillan came off the bench to score a goal and two assists in a game against North Korea. She could have cajoled team coach, Tony DiCicco, to put her in a starting position. She didn't. "I'm going to do anything I'm asked for this team. My heart and soul is with it" (Starr & Brant, 1999, p. 53). Even a television ad taped by team members exhibited the We-orientation. A player comes out of the dentist's examination room and announces to fellow team members that she needs two fillings. Players sitting in the waiting room, one by one, stand up and announce, "Then I will have two fillings."

Carl Lewis demonstrated how difficult it is to put aside individualism, even when collectivism is clearly required; the women's soccer team demonstrated that even in a highly individualist culture, collectivist behavior is possible and

rewarding. Embracing the We-orientation and de-emphasizing the Me-orientation in the United States will not come quickly or easily. **The United States does not have to become a collectivist culture where the group is supreme, but teamwork and putting the group ahead of individual needs and goals are often appropriate and important.** As Larson and LaFasto (1989) pointedly state:

> The potential for collective problem-solving is so often unrealized and the promise of collective achievement so often unfulfilled, that we exhibit what seems to be a developmental disability in the area of social competence. . . .
>
> Clearly, if we are to solve the enormous problems facing our society, we need to learn how to collaborate more effectively. We need to set aside individual agendas. (pp. 13–14)

Emphasizing team building and collaborative effort can prove beneficial to both individuals and society.

Questions for Thought

1. Do you agree that the United States has become excessively Me-oriented? Explain.
2. Singapore has low crime, safe cities, low unemployment, and few homeless citizens. The United States has the opposite. Should we strive to become collectivist and emulate the Singaporeans?
3. Could the United States ever become a collectivist nation, given our individualist history?

BOX 1.2   BE YE INDIVIDUALIST OR COLLECTIVIST?

How closely do you personally reflect individualist or collectivist values of your culture or coculture? Consider the following statements and, using a scale from 1 (strongly disagree) to 9 (strongly agree), indicate your degree of agreement or disagreement with each statement.*

1. I prefer to be direct and forthright when I talk with people.

2. I would do what would please my family, even if I detested that activity.

3. I enjoy being unique and different from others in many ways.

4. I usually sacrifice my self-interest for the benefit of my group.

5. Children should be taught to place duty before pleasure.

6. I like my privacy.

7. I hate to disagree with others in my group.

8. Before taking a major trip, I consult with most members of my family and many friends.

9. When I succeed, it is usually because of my abilities.

10. We should keep our aging parents with us at home.

Total your score for all odd-numbered statements (1, 3, etc.) then total your score for even-numbered statements (2, 4, etc.). All odd-numbered statements reflect individualism and all even-numbered statements reflect collectivism. Which are you? Overall, do you agree more with individualist statements (higher score on odd-numbered statements) than with collectivist statements (lower score on even-numbered statements)? If so, you reflect the prevailing individualist values of American culture.

*For the entire 63-statement measuring instrument, see Triandis (1995).

"disease of me." He describes it this way: "They develop an overpowering belief in their own importance. Their actions virtually shout the claim, 'I'm the one'" (p. 41). Riley concludes that the "disease of me" inevitably produces "the defeat of us" (p. 52).

There are potential dividends when group members assume a We-orientation. Usually, helping others satisfy their goals creates an environment conducive to the satisfaction of your own goals. For instance, one way for women and ethnic minorities to overcome bias that prevents them from achieving high status in a group is to act in a group-oriented, not a self-oriented, manner (Ridgeway, 1982). A We-orientation requires concern for others, not merely concern for self. Consequently, communication competence in groups necessitates behavior that is both effective and appropriate.

APPROPRIATENESS: FOLLOWING THE RULES

The appropriateness of a person's communication is determined by examining the context. Thus, **appropriateness** means complying with rules and their accompanying expectations (Spitzberg & Cupach, 1989). A **rule** is a prescription that indicates what you should or shouldn't do in specific contexts (Shimanoff, 1980). One study examined fundamental social interaction rules in four cultures (Great Britain, Hong Kong, Italy, and Japan). All four cultures shared the same basic rules: an individual should be polite, friendly, and pleasant, and no one should attempt to make another person feel embarrassed or small (Argyle & Henderson, 1985). Sustaining strong relationships in a group is partly dependent on following such basic rules (Kline & Stafford, 2004).

The difficulty in determining appropriateness can be seen readily from the following intercultural example:

> An American college student, while having a dinner party with a group of foreigners, learns that her favorite cousin has just died. She bites her lip, pulls herself up, and politely excuses herself from the group. The interpretation given to this behavior will vary with the culture of the observer. The Italian student thinks, "How insincere; she doesn't even cry." The Russian student thinks, "How unfriendly; she didn't care enough to share her grief with her friends." The fellow American student thinks, "How brave; she wanted to bear her burden by herself." (DeVito, 1990, p. 218)

The appropriateness of your communication cannot be determined by merely examining a message that is isolated from the rich complexity of context. For instance, you may self-disclose intimate information about yourself to members of some groups but not others. If you attend a therapy group on marriage, self-disclosing will be expected and encouraged because it is compatible with the group's purpose. If, however, you are talking to a meeting of the Student Senate or the Dormitory Advisory Committee, intimate self-disclosure will likely make members squirm in their chairs and wish for an earthquake. The purpose of these groups is not therapeutic, so the expectations regarding what constitutes appropriate communication in these contexts are different from expectations found at meetings of Alcoholics Anonymous or Marriage Encounter.

Communication becomes inappropriate if it violates rules of the group when such violations could have been avoided, without sacrificing a goal, by choosing different communication behaviors (Getter & Nowinski, 1981). In short, inappropriateness is usually the result of being clueless or clumsy.

Achieving Communication Competence

Defining communication competence identifies what it is, but not how to achieve it. **There are five general ways to improve your effectiveness and appropriateness in groups:** You can acquire knowledge, hone communication skills, improve your sensitivity, redouble your commitment, and apply ethical standards to your communication choices (see Figure 1.2).

KNOWLEDGE: LEARNING THE RULES

I have already noted the centrality of appropriateness and effectiveness to the definition of communication competence. Both require knowledge. **Knowledge** means learning the rules and understanding what is required to be appropriate and effective in your communication.

Communication may be appropriate but not effective, and vice versa. Knowledge of the context tells you which is most likely. Consider the following example:

> Brian Holtz is a U.S. businessperson assigned by his company to manage its office in Thailand. Mr. Thani, a valued assistant manager in the Bangkok office, has recently been arriving late for work. Holtz has to decide what to do about this problem. After carefully thinking about his options, he decides there are four possible strategies: (1) Go privately to Mr. Thani, ask him why he has been arriving late, and tell him that he needs to come to work on time. (2) Ignore the problem. (3) Publicly reprimand Mr. Thani the next time he is late. (4) In a private discussion, suggest seeking Mr. Thani's assistance in dealing with employees in the company who regularly arrive late for work, and solicit his suggestions about what should be done. (Lustig & Koester, 2003, p. 65)

What choice would you make? The first option is often the way Americans would handle this type of situation. It is direct, and it probably would be effective in getting

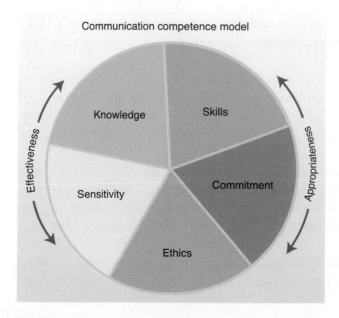

FIGURE 1.2
Communication
competence model.

Mr. Thani to arrive at work on time. Nevertheless, considering the Thai culture (context), where one person does not directly criticize another person, this choice would be very inappropriate, even disastrous. Conversely, the second choice would be appropriate but hardly effective, because Mr. Thani would likely persist in his tardiness. The third choice would be neither appropriate nor effective. Public humiliation would likely induce Mr. Thani, a valuable employee, to resign in shame. Thus, the fourth choice is best because it is both appropriate and effective (Lustig & Koester, 2003). Mr. Thani would receive the message indirectly that he must arrive at work on time, yet he could save face. He can respond affirmatively to the indirect request that he change his behavior from tardiness to punctuality, without suffering public humiliation.

Knowledge in any communication situation is critical, whether the context is our culture's or another culture's. **We cannot determine what is appropriate and effective without knowing the rules operating in a given situation.**

We don't always make the wisest communication choices, but we are likely to make a fair number of foolish ones if our limited knowledge shields us from appropriate alternatives. In communicative matters, a little knowledge is like the dim flicker of a candle flame in a dark mine shaft. There's just enough illumination to see choices, but not enough light to provide effective direction. If you are uncertain what is expected or required in a given situation, you should seek knowledge from those who are likely to know and who can enhance your understanding.

SKILLS: SHOWING, NOT JUST KNOWING

Communication competence encompasses the ability to apply your knowledge in actual situations. **To be effective, you have to combine knowledge with skill.** One study of undergraduate women (Christensen et al., 1980) found that even when subjects were told in advance the appropriate communication behavior in an interview situation, half still couldn't do it.

A communication **skill** is "the successful performance of a communication behavior . . . [and] the ability to repeat such a behavior" (Spitzberg & Hecht, 1984, p. 577). Practice, of course, is essential to the mastery of any communication skill. Group members who are trained and practice together acquire skills and improve group performance (Hollingshead, 1998).

There is abundant evidence that links communication skills with success or failure in the workplace. Ninety-eight percent of 253 personnel interviewers at businesses large and small reported that oral communication skills significantly affect hiring decisions (Peterson, 1997). Communication ability was deemed the most desirable quality of college graduates by 480 companies and organizations looking to hire employees (cited in Morreale, 1999). A study by the National Association of Colleges and Employers ranked communication skills as most important and teamwork skills as third most desirable on a list of 20 employee skills ("What Employers Want," 2003). "Successful communication is critical in business" (Hansen & Hansen, 2005). Employers want to hire skillful communicators who can work in teams and make decisions in groups.

Communication competence, of course, is not simply a matter of learning a single skill or even a set of skills. As indicated earlier, skills without knowledge of when and how to use them are mostly useless, even harmful. **The key is learning many skills and using them flexibly, with the proper knowledge of what's appropriate for a given context.**

SENSITIVITY: RECEPTIVE ACCURACY

Having the knowledge to determine what constitutes appropriate communication in a specific context and having the skills to be effective is great, but what if you don't have your antenna extended to pick up signals that indicate inappropriateness? What if you aren't attentive to signals from group members that indicate hostility, tension, anger, irritation, disgust, or uneasiness? In addition to knowledge and skills, the competent communicator needs sensitivity. **Sensitivity** is receptive accuracy whereby you can detect, decode, and comprehend signals sent within groups (Bernieri, 2001). **Failure to attend to and comprehend signals can severely affect our relationships with group members** (J. A. Hall & Bernieri, 2001). Problems that lie just below the surface go unattended by groups and magnify difficulties unless members are sensitive to the nuances and subtleties of communication transactions between members. Fortunately, sensitivity can be learned (J. A. Hall & Bernieri, 2001). One of the functions of this text is to assist you in developing greater sensitivity by identifying patterns of communication that pose problems in group transactions and by providing solutions for these dysfunctional patterns.

COMMITMENT: A PASSION FOR EXCELLENCE

Effectiveness requires commitment. **Commitment** is the conscious decision to invest time, energy, thought, and feeling to improve yourself or your relationships with others. Little that is worthwhile comes without commitment. Do you want to be a great athlete? Then you must commit yourself to the hard work necessary to achieve greatness. The U.S. women's soccer team didn't achieve international glory by half-hearted commitment (see Focus on Culture: "Individualism versus Collectivism"). They made big individual sacrifices, labored untold hours, and planned strategies carefully. Do you want to receive an academic scholarship, earn good grades, and finish a degree? It won't happen by listless attention in class and lackluster attendance. You have to want it, work for it, have a passion to achieve it—you must be committed.

The predominant motivation of the competent communicator is the desire to avoid previous mistakes and to find better ways of communicating with group members. Someone who makes the same mistakes repeatedly and shows little interest in altering his or her behavior is a nuisance, or worse, a deadweight that can sink a group. Such anemic commitment is a frequent source of frustration in groups, and it can fester into grouphate. It is easily the most frequent complaint I hear from my group communication students each term. Who wants to deal with a lethargic member who can't be counted on to produce and doesn't seem to care? In sports, they are booted off the team; in business, they are fired; in politics, they are voted out of office; in college, they are invited to leave.

Commitment to improving your communication effectiveness requires self-monitoring. When you interact in groups you have to be a **participant–observer.** You assume a detached view of yourself. You analyze your communication behavior, looking for areas to improve, while noting successes. Ultimately, the competent communicator considers it a personal responsibility to interact with group members as effectively and productively as possible.

ETHICS: THE RIGHT AND WRONG OF COMMUNICATION

A 1997 survey of 1,324 workers by the Ethics Officer Association revealed that 48% of respondents admitted they had engaged in one or more unethical communication behaviors in the past year. Workers covered up unethical or illegal incidents; lied or deceived customers, coworkers, or supervisors; or took credit for a coworker's idea. More recently, a survey of workers by the Ethics Resource Center showed that 36% of workers called in sick when they weren't ill and 12% of executives inflated their resumes with bogus information (MacIntyre, 2005). Three quarters of 747 companies surveyed by the Ethics Resource Center have ethics codes for all workers ("Cheating at Work," 1997). American culture cares about ethics, but we don't always communicate ethically.

Why should anyone care about ethics in communication? The very definition of communication competence requires it. **Appropriateness and the We-orientation make ethics important.** Competent communicators concern themselves with more than what works for them personally. Stealing someone's idea and taking credit raises the issue of right and wrong because another person is adversely affected. The theft of an idea is inappropriate and self-centered.

Ethics is a set of standards for judging the moral correctness of our behavior. Five essential values, based on the 1999 "Credo for Ethical Communication" adopted by the National Communication Association (http://www.natcom.org), can serve as an ethical guide for our communication in groups:

1. *Honesty.* The American culture presumes that honesty is valued and dishonesty is wrong (Bok, 1978). Accuse a person of lying and immediately they become

defensive. All ethical systems condemn lying (Jaksa & Pritchard, 1994). Imagine trying to keep a family together when everyone lies regularly and no one can be trusted.

2. *Respect.* Relationships in groups fall apart, and groups can't function effectively when members show disrespect for each other. From an ethical viewpoint, respect is right and disrespect is wrong even if showing respect to others works against a group goal (such as defeating a team). We are expected to show respect to group members only if it provides some tangible reward or advantage. "Some form of the golden rule is embraced by virtually all of the major religious and moral systems" (Jaksa & Pritchard, 1994, p. 101).

3. *Fairness.* Prejudice treats people unfairly. Bigots want different rules for themselves than those applied to a disfavored group. Bigotry should have no place in the communication arena. Students recognize immediately how unfair it would be if an instructor gave an advantage to some students in class and penalized others based on their sex, ethnicity, age, or lifestyle. Cheating on an exam gives an unfair advantage to the cheater. Although some students may cheat, few would be proud to announce it to others. (See Callahan, 2004, for a detailed discussion of cheating.)

4. *Choice.* Freedom to choose for oneself without threat of force or intimidation is a basic ethical value (Jaksa & Pritchard, 1994). It is why most nations have outlawed torture. Coercion prevents choice. There is no real option presented. Choice goes hand in hand with honesty. If you fear reprisals for telling the truth, then your freedom to choose truthfulness instead of deceit is compromised.

5. *Responsibility.* Ethical communication is We oriented. Every group member and the group as a whole have a responsibility, a duty, to be concerned about more than merely what works to achieve personal or even group goals. How goals are achieved is also a vital consideration. As the rash of corporate scandals showed, our ethical responsibility encompasses more than effectiveness.

When considered as general ethical guidelines, all five values are easy to justify. Group communication is so complex, however, that any list of standards used to judge members' communication ethics, applied absolutely, would immediately create problems. Ethical communication is a matter of context. A lie that accuses your roommate of stealing college property that a friend of yours actually stole is different from a lie that covers up an embarrassing family secret. Exceptions also will inevitably surface. Students don't have complete freedom to choose what they want to learn and how they want to learn it, nor should they. Few would freely take a public speaking course unless mandated by general education requirements, because most people fear giving speeches. Honesty, respect, fairness, choice, and responsibility, however, are strong values in most cultures, and they act as basic standards for our communication behavior.

Gender and Communication Competence

"WHY IS IT GOOD that there are female astronauts? When the crew gets lost in space, at least the woman will ask for directions." "When do women stop advocating equality? When they have to kill large, hairy spiders." "Give a man an inch and he thinks he's a ruler." "How do you impress a woman? Compliment her, cuddle her, caress her, love her, listen to her, support her, and spend money on her. How do you impress a man? Show up naked. Bring beer." Take a moment and consider these jokes found on the Internet. Amusing? Offensive? (They are tame samples compared to many truly tasteless and mean-spirited jokes found on numerous websites.) These attempts at humor reflect a belief that men and women communicate differently.

John Gray has popularized these gender differences with his *Men Are from Mars, Women Are from Venus* book and subsequent Mars/Venus materials that morphed from this best seller. Are men and women really so different that we appear to live in two separate worlds? One communication expert likens gender differences in communication to North and South Dakota—men and women live in neighboring places with much in common (Dindia, 1997). One review of numerous studies found that, in aggregate, men and women are 99% similar and only 1% different in their communication (Canary & Hause, 1993). Others, however, disagree (Mulac, 1998; Wood & Dindia, 1998). **Some major differences have been supported by research.** For example, women are far better than men at accurately perceiving verbal and nonverbal cues; however, men express greater confidence in *their* ability to read signals from others (Costanzo, 1992). Women smile and laugh more than men, especially in groups (Provine, 2000). Men more often prefer jokes that ridicule women, are aggressive, and involve sexual innuendo. Women, on the other hand, tend to favor jokes based on wordplay ("A man walks into a bar with a piece of tarmac under his arm. He says to the bartender: 'A pint for me, and one for the road.'") (Wiseman, 2003). Women cry more at work, whereas men express their anger or frustration in the workplace with outbursts of yelling and rage (Domagalski, 1998). Women are more inclined than men to talk about their relationships, and women are better caregivers than men (Wood & Dindia, 1998).

Deborah Tannen (1990), in her provocative book *You Just Don't Understand,* argues that gender differences in communication are significant. She explains, as do others (Bruess & Pearson, 1996; Noller, 1993; Wood, 2000), that for most women, talk is primarily a means to "establish connections and negotiate relationships"; for most men, "talk is primarily a means to preserve independence and negotiate and maintain status in a hierarchical social order" (p. 77). According to Tannen, both

▶

men and women are concerned about the dual dimensions of status and connection during conversation, but **status is usually given far more relative weight by men and connection is usually given far more relative weight by women** (see also Coates, 1993; Wood, 1997b). The status dimension is very different from the connection dimension, as indicated below. Therefore, each produces very different communication expectations and patterns.

Status	Connection
Independence (separateness)	Interdependence (intimacy)
Competition (contest)	Cooperation (consensus)
Power (control)	Empowerment (choices)

In mixed-sex groups, men's speech consists mostly of task-oriented, instrumental communication that consists of giving information, opinions, and suggestions (James & Drakich, 1993). Men usually see talk as a contest, an opportunity to establish or increase status in the eyes of group members. Thus, men report their knowledge to the group. They talk more than women, tell more jokes, impart more information and advice, and offer more solutions to problems. Why? Because this spotlights them as experts and raises their status in a group.

Conversely, **women's speech in mixed-sex groups consists more of supportive and facilitative communication** such as agreeing,

indicating interest in what others are saying, and encouraging others to participate in group discussions (James & Drakich, 1993). Women try to connect with other speakers, share feelings, and listen intently to establish rapport (Tannen, 1990). Displaying interest in other group members and offering encouragement to them establishes a connection.

So are men jerks for seeing conversation as an opportunity to enhance status? Are women meek and emotional for seeing conversation as an opportunity to bond with others? Such interpretations are extremely limiting and simplistic. Consider the tendency of women to encourage member participation in group discussions, whereas men rarely show such a tendency. How should this be interpreted? From the connection perspective, women appear to be highly sensitive, caring group members and men seem to be insensitive clods. From the status perspective, however, women may appear to be the insensitive ones. Inviting a man into a conversation may diminish his status. It calls attention to his nonparticipation, making him appear unassertive. He may have little or no knowledge on the subject of conversation. Spotlighting his lack of knowledge in front of the group could be embarrassing. When men and women approach simple conversation from conflicting perspectives, it is not surprising that misunderstanding and ridicule result.

Not all men and women will follow the male and female patterns outlined by Tannen. Mostly, however, men and women exhibit recognizable, documented patterns of

▶

communication that manifest differences between the sexes when they engage in group discussion.

Tannen's model of gender differences in communication has received two main criticisms. First, **Tannen is accused of seriously underemphasizing the role of unequal power.** That is, women's style of communication is typical of relatively powerless people (Freed, 1992; Tavris, 1992). This is partly true, but not the entire explanation for gender differences in communication (Mulac & Bradac, 1995; Noller, 1993). As Tannen (1990) explains: "Male dominance is not the whole story. It is not sufficient to account for everything that happens to women and men in conversation, especially in conversations in which both are genuinely trying to relate to each other with attention and respect" (p. 18).

Second, **some communication experts argue that contrary to the different communication styles perspective of Tannen or the dominance of men perspective, gender differences in communication occur primarily because of skills deficiencies.** "Members of each sex tend to specialize in some skills while having comparative deficits in other skills" (Kunkel & Burleson, 1998, p. 118). Men may exhibit poor listening skills. Women may exhibit lack of assertiveness skills. Again, this does not explain all of the communication differences between men and women. When a person displays knowledge during a group discussion (enhancing status) or listens intently (inducing connection), these behaviors are not usually perceived as skill deficiencies. They may be effective and appropriate communication depending on the context, but men tend to do the former and women tend to do the latter more often. Men and women may have the skill to do either, but merely choose what they are most accustomed to doing (communication styles).

Given their differences, how do men and women communicate competently with each other? They have to allow for differences, combat dominance, and correct deficiencies. This can be accomplished in a number of ways. First, **knowledge of the different conversational assumptions made by men and women has to be broadened.** Applying the

Definition of a Group

I've defined and discussed both communication and communication competence. In this section, I define the main focus of this text, namely a group, and I distinguish it from interpersonal communication and public speaking.

GROUPS: MORE THAN PEOPLE STANDING AT A BUS STOP

A **group** is a human communication system composed of three or more individuals, interacting for the achievement of some common goal(s), who influence and are influenced by each other. A group is different from a mere collection of individuals

standards of one group to the behavior of the other can create misunderstanding (Tannen, 1990). Women will continue to misjudge men if they apply the single standard of connection to all conversations, and men will continue to misjudge women if they continue to apply the single standard of status to all conversations. Both status and connection are legitimate standards for assessing conversations, but we all can look silly to the other sex when only one standard is applied.

Second, **adaptation to each other's style of conversation would display skills proficiency, and thus, be beneficial.** Men could make fewer interruptions that seize conversational control, be more attentive listeners, ask more questions to clarify points or seek information, and encourage women to join the group discussion when appropriate. These adaptations show flexibility and a concern for connection without the appearance of subservience. Women who learn assertiveness skills expand their opportunities to be heard during group discussion and taken seriously (enhancing status) without losing their sensitivity to the importance of connection.

Third, **equalizing power imbalances that often put women at a disadvantage will diminish some of the gender differences in communication.** How this can be done is discussed in Chapter 9.

Questions for Thought

1. Can you think of additional ways men and women can adjust their conversational styles to reduce misunderstandings and increase effectiveness?
2. Do the typical male–female patterns of conversation identified by Tannen correspond with your experience of communicating in mixed-sex groups?
3. Do you think the criticism of Tannen's model is justified? Apply your own experiences.

called an **aggregation** (Goldhaber, 1990). Twenty-five people standing in line to buy tickets for a movie are not a group, but simply an aggregation. Because they do not interact with and influence each other to achieve a common goal (strangers standing in line are not there expressly to help each other secure tickets), they do not qualify as a group. The same holds for a crowd shopping in a mall or waiting for a plane departure delayed by fog. In both cases, the presence of other people is irrelevant to the achievement of the specific goal (buying clothes or traveling from point A to point B). To be called a group, a collection of individuals must succeed or fail as a unit in a quest to achieve a common goal(s). Crowds, of course, can become groups if they satisfy the definition provided.

The transactional view of communication posits that each participant influences the other, so it should not be surprising that my definition of a group includes the influence group members have on each other. This aspect of the definition of a group is explored extensively in later chapters when norms, roles, leadership, and power are discussed. Explaining how a group is a human communication system, another aspect of the definition of groups, is the subject of the next chapter.

This text will focus on *small* groups, with special emphasis in Chapters 7 and 8 given to decision-making and problem-solving groups. **Trying to draw a clear line between small and large groups, however, can prove to be fruitless.** When does the addition of one more member transform a small group into a large one? Over the years, some communication theorists have set the upper limit of small groups at between 12 and 20 members, with 15 often cited. Other theorists identify a small group as comprising few enough members to enable treating each other in a personal manner and to allow specific impressions of each other to be formed (Pavitt & Curtis, 1994). When you attend a group meeting and you can't remember afterwards whether some members were even present, you've probably reached large group status. When groups grow to the point where problems of coordination emerge and formal rules for discussion and debate (parliamentary procedure) during meetings become necessary, the group can reasonably be designated as large. To borrow the words of Sir Francis Bacon, when members' "faces are but a gallery of pictures, and talk but a tinkling cymbal" *small* doesn't seem like an appropriate designation for a group.

INTERPERSONAL COMMUNICATION AND PUBLIC SPEAKING: UNGROUPS

You may have noticed that the definition of a group sets the minimum number of participants at three. That is because communication between only two individuals is usually referred to as **interpersonal communication.** As every couple experiences, interpersonal communication between spouses is massively changed with the addition of a child. In such cases, three individuals seem like many more than two.

▶●● SECOND LOOK

GROUPS VERSUS AGGREGATIONS

GROUPS	AGGREGATIONS
Crowd doing "the wave"	Crowd in a shopping mall
Cheerleading squad	Individuals waiting for cheerleader tryouts
Crossing guard leading children across street	Children waiting at stop signal
Jury	Individuals waiting for jury duty assignment

Communication between two individuals is far less complex than the complicated network of transactions found in groups of three or more. As the old saying goes, "Two's company, three's a crowd." Thus, the unit of analysis is structurally different when focusing on three or more individuals, not just two (see the next chapter for more detailed discussion). Conventional terminology also refers to a two-person transaction as a couple or, in academic circles, a **dyad.** Transactions of three or more persons are usually referred to as a group. I doubt that anyone reading this text would find it unusual to refer to a family as a group, but many might think it odd to label a married couple a group.

Group communication is also distinct from **public speaking.** With public speaking, the speaker and the audience are clearly indicated, and the speaking situation is far more formal than what is usually found in group discussions. Verbal feedback is often delayed in public speaking events, but during group discussions verbal feedback often is almost immediate. Public speakers usually prepare remarks in advance and speak from notes or even a manuscript. Group members usually don't make formal preparations to speak during group discussions, but may do so when participating on group panels, symposiums, or public forums (see Appendix A for details).

In summary, human communication is a transactional process of sharing meaning with others. Communication competence, a recurring theme throughout this book, is communicating effectively and appropriately in a given context. It is achieved through knowledge, skills, sensitivity, commitment, and ethics. Learning to communicate competently in groups is of vital importance to all of us. With this as a backdrop, let's explore how groups function as systems. ● ●

Questions for Critical Thinkers

1. Are there any circumstances in which a Me-orientation becomes necessary when participating in a small group?
2. Does competent communication ever necessitate dishonesty? Explain.
3. When you are a member of a group, should you always exhibit commitment to the group or are there exceptions? Explain.

InfoTrac College Edition

Log onto InfoTrac College Edition.
1. Type "individualism" in the keywords search window. Choose an article to read and critique. SUGGESTION: Article A90164205 by Maxim Voronov and Jefferson A. Singer entitled "The myth of individualism—collectivism: A critical review."

2. Type "communication competence" in the search window. Choose an article to critique. SUGGESTION: Article A89079476 "As ugly and painful as it was, it was effective: Individuals' unique assessment of communication competence during aggressive conflict episodes" by Loreen N. Olson.

Video Case Studies

This activity presents video case studies from a variety of films for you to analyze. A movie rating (PG-13, R, etc.) and critics' rating (* for "turkey" to ***** for "excellent") provided by Martin and Porter (2006) are included to help you decide which movies are suitable for your viewing. A brief plot summary is provided in Martin and Porter's video guide if you care to check this before viewing the movie. You are asked to analyze each video case study, applying key material presented in each chapter.

*Home for the Holidays (1995). Comedy/Drama; PG-13; **1/2*

Uneven, but ultimately entertaining movie about a family that experiences a stressful Thanksgiving weekend. Analyze family members' communication competence, especially during the disastrous dinner segment. What rules operate during the dinner? Which ones are violated? Does any family member exhibit effective and appropriate communication? Explain.

*The Insider (1999). Drama; R; ****1/2*

Russell Crowe plays a tobacco-industry scientist (based on a real character) who has secrets to tell. Analyze the issue of communication ethics by applying the five ethical standards (honesty, respect, fairness, choice, and responsibility).

*Return to Paradise (1998). Drama; R; ***1/2*

Underrated film about a harrowing ethical dilemma involving three friends who vacationed in Malaysia. You'll be contemplating what action you would take in the same circumstances. Analyze this film from a communication ethics perspective. Is Anne Heche's character justified in lying to the Vince Vaughn character? Does Vince Vaughn's character have a choice, or is he being coerced unethically? Does he have a responsibility to return to save his friend?

MULTIPLE CHOICE
1, c; 2, c, d; 3, d; 4, a, b, c, d; 5, d.

TRUE-FALSE
All false.

Each multiple-choice question is worth 4 points; each true-false 2 points. Deduct 1 point for each incorrect multiple-choice answer; deduct 2 points for each incorrect true-false answer. Total possible points = 40.

2 Groups as Systems

I N ONE OF MY SMALL GROUP communication courses, six women formed a project group. During their first meeting in class, their communication was warm, friendly, and task oriented. They accomplished a great deal in a short period of time: deciding which of the five project options they would pursue, dividing labor to develop the project, and setting deadlines for accomplishment of specified tasks. They told me that they all were very pleased with their new group.

During the next week, the six women met one more time for a lengthy session, and again they were pleased by their progress on the project and increasingly comfortable with their harmonious interactions. Then a male student who had missed a week of class and had no project group approached me and asked which of the four class groups he should join. I told him to join the all-women group for two reasons: I typically encourage mixed-sex, not same-sex, groups (there were far more women than men in the class), and the other groups had seven members already. From the moment he joined the six women he transformed this harmonious, task-effective group into a frustrating experience for every group member. His opening introductory remark upon joining the group of women was, "I hope PMS won't be a problem for us." He guffawed loudly at his supposed humor, but all six women seemed stunned. During the group meeting he made sexist remarks, offered derogatory comments about the choice of project already decided by the women, and made a complete nuisance of himself. As he left class, he loudly proclaimed to everyone that he was "leader of a chicks group."

All six women bolted to the front of the class and begged me to assign this disruptive individual to another group. I gently but firmly explained that moving him to another group would make the other groups too large and would merely pass the problem to another group, not solve it.

The problem became more complex because at midterm I have students form new project groups. Nobody wanted this disruptive individual as a group member. When he joined a new group, a woman in that group immediately shot out of her chair and confronted me with the ultimatum: "Either you move that guy to another group or I'm dropping this class." With no small effort I managed to convince her to remain in the class.

This example illustrates that every group is a system. A **system** is a set of interconnected parts working together to form a whole in the context of a changing environment (Infante et al., 1997; Littlejohn, 1999). In general, a system is composed of input, throughput, and output (Katz & Kahn, 1978). **Input** consists of resources that come from outside the system, such as energy (sunlight, electricity), information (Internet, books), and people (a new group member). **If input ceases, a system deceases.** A system inevitably wears down without continuous input. This wearing-down process is called **entropy**—a measure of a system's movement toward disorganization and eventual termination. All living systems combat entropy with input. No group, for example, can survive without new members. The group will dismantle because current members will lose interest and leave, join different groups, or the members themselves will eventually die. Consider the religious sect called the Shakers (members shook to rid themselves of evil). This group splintered from a Quaker community in Manchester, England, in 1747 and came to New York in 1774. Now near extinction, their inevitable demise is foreordained by three Shaker decisions: a belief in celibacy, a complete withdrawal from mainstream society, and a group decision in 1965 to admit no new members (Melton, 1992). From a peak membership of 6,000 in the 1830s, there are only a few women remaining at the Sabbath Day Lake, Maine, community (Harlan, 2001). Contrary to the Shakers' difficult-to-understand aversion to new members, interjecting "new blood" into a group can bring new information, new ideas, new experiences, new energy, and even different values and perspectives. New members can thwart entropy.

Throughput is the process of transforming input into output to keep the system functioning. Input is transformed in a group by its members engaging in activities such as group discussion and creative problem solving. The throughput process involves roles, rules, norms, power distribution, discussion procedures, and conflict management strategies (all subjects for later development).

Output comprises the continual results of the group's throughput (transformation of input). Group outputs include decisions made, solutions to problems created and implemented, projects completed, group procedures modified, team member cohesiveness enhanced, member relationships improved, and so forth. Again, these outputs are discussed in detail in ensuing chapters.

As my colleague Mark Murphy has noted, if groups mess up their input, throughput, and output, they're going to be kaput. **My principal purpose in this chapter is to avoid such an outcome by explaining and discussing systems theory and how it can be applied to groups.** This is not merely an abstract exercise for the intellectually curious. Understanding at least the basics of systems theory provides very useful insights into why some small groups succeed and others fail.

There are three chapter objectives:

1. to explain interconnectedness of parts in a system,
2. to discuss how groups must adapt to a changing environment, and
3. to explore the influence of size on a group's ability to function effectively.

Interconnectedness of Parts

▶ **Focus Questions**

1. What is the ripple effect and how does it affect groups?
2. What is synergy? What is negative synergy?

Every system is a whole composed of a collection of integrated parts. All parts interconnect and work together. A group is composed of individual members interrelating with each other. The behavior of one member affects the entire group, especially if the behavior is disruptive. In the opening case presented, the six women could not ignore their obnoxious individual. They had to adapt to the jarring change that occurred once he joined their group. Ultimately, it worked out reasonably well. How the group handled this disruptive member is discussed in this section, which explains the ripple effect and synergy (see Box 2.1: "The Difficult Group Member" to assess your own behavior).

RIPPLE EFFECT: A CHAIN REACTION

In a system, one part can have a significant impact on the whole. This **ripple effect** or chain reaction spreads across the entire system, much like a pebble tossed into a pond disturbs the water and forces adjustments.

This ripple effect can be plainly seen from a historical example. The influenza pandemic of 1918–19 began in Europe but quickly rippled throughout the world. It sickened over *one billion* people, half the world's total population at the time, and left 21 million people dead worldwide (half a million in the United States). This was equivalent to the total deaths from both world wars of the twentieth century. So virulent was the virus that there was an instance reported of women boarding a New York subway in Coney Island feeling mild fatigue and being found dead when the subway train pulled into Columbus Circle some 45 minutes later. Nearly 20% of the Western Samoa population died from the disease, and entire Inuit villages in isolated parts of Alaska were decimated (Garrett, 1994). This flu pandemic rippled through every part of society. Enormous stress was placed on healthcare systems that nursed the sick and on economic systems that struggled with a major portion of the workforce incapacitated. Even social relations were affected. People avoided contact with each other or, when forced to interact, commonly wore cloth masks across their faces, which they hoped would protect them from the virus (Kolata, 1999). This pandemic ripple effect is precisely why the World Health Organization in February 2005 warned that an outbreak in several Asian countries of bird flu posed the "gravest possible danger of a pandemic" and was "an imminent threat" worldwide (V. Miller, 2005).

BOX 2.1 THE DIFFICULT GROUP MEMBER

Instructions: Answer the questions below honestly. Then ask fellow class or team members to complete this same assessment about you. If team members are hesitant, encourage them to complete the assessment without identifying themselves in the questionnaire (ideally, all team members should complete the assessment to preserve anonymity). Compare the results by following the scoring system at the end of this assessment.

1. When a topic of great interest to me is discussed in my group, I tend to talk much longer and more forcefully than I know I should

   ALWAYS   NEVER
   5   4   3   2   1

2. During group discussions I typically remain silent, exhibiting lack of interest in the proceedings

   ALWAYS   NEVER
   5   4   3   2   1

3. When my group attempts to work on a task, especially one that interests me little, I prefer to joke around and be comical instead of focusing on the task

   ALWAYS   NEVER
   5   4   3   2   1

4. When I oppose what my group decides, I am inclined to reintroduce the issue already decided even though I know there is little chance the group will change its decision

   ALWAYS   NEVER
   5   4   3   2   1

5. I often quarrel openly with group members by raising my voice, interrupting other members to forcefully interject my own opinion, and criticizing those who disagree with me

   ALWAYS   NEVER
   5   4   3   2   1

6. I have strong opinions that often color my participation during group discussions, and I attempt to convert group members to my way of thinking even if they are unresponsive

   ALWAYS   NEVER
   5   4   3   2   1

7. I'm inclined to predict failure of the group, especially if a risk is involved, and I tend to focus on what will go wrong, not on what will go right with my group's decisions

   ALWAYS   NEVER
   5   4   3   2   1

Total your responses for all seven of your answers (maximum score = 35; minimum score = 7). Determine your average score (total score divided by 7). If your average score is 3.0 or higher, you tend toward being a difficult group member. Any single answer that you gave that is 3, 4, or 5 indicates trouble for your group on that particular behavior.

A small part of a huge system can generate an enormous ripple effect. There was an immense ripple effect when 9,200 workers at two General Motors (GM) parts plants in Flint, Michigan, went out on strike in June 1998. This choked off the supply of critical car parts such as fenders, odometers, air filters, and hoods, and 26 of GM's 29 assembly plants in the United States, Canada, and Mexico were shut down.

More than 161,000 workers, most of whom were not on strike, were idled. GM lost more than $1 billion and workers suffered from lost wages (Sandoval, 1998). Both sides debated the justification for the strike, but there is no debate about the impact one small part can have on an entire system.

The ripple effect, of course, does not have to be a negative experience. When a parent gets a job promotion or a significant raise in pay, all members of the family stand to gain from the good fortune. If a child wins a scholarship to a major university, the entire family potentially benefits from the news. Accomplishments of individual family members may motivate others in the group to seek similar goals. When a group leader who provokes dislike comparable to a skunk in your clothes closet is replaced with a competent, well-liked leader, optimism and enthusiasm can spread throughout a group.

Recognizing the significance of the ripple effect means paying close attention to your own impact on groups. Your level of communication proficiency or deficiency can mean success or failure of the entire group. "The power of one" should not be underestimated (see Closer Look: "Dealing with Difficult Group Members").

AP/Wide World Photos

The SARS epidemic prompted people in China to wear gauze masks to prevent the ripple effect.

DEALING WITH DIFFICULT GROUP MEMBERS

THIS CHAPTER OPENED with a narrative about a difficult group member. One troublesome member's inappropriate behavior can ripple throughout the group, causing disharmony and dissension, preventing a group from operating as a cohesive, fully functioning team. Jerry Talley of Edgewise Consulting in Mountain View, California, estimates that dealing with difficult individuals consumes a minimum of 10% of a company's time, and can easily grow to 30–40% if the company is truly dysfunctional (Townsend, 1999a). Most group members in decision-making and problem-solving groups feel ill equipped to handle disruptive behavior (Gouran, 1988). There are several fundamental steps that should be taken by the group when dealing with a difficult member.

First, **make certain the group climate is cooperative.** Chapter 4 discusses group climate in depth. Most difficult people are created by a competitive system (Aguayo, 1990). If your group creates a ruthlessly competitive, politicized climate where decision making is influenced by rumor-mongering, backstabbing, deal making, and sabotaging of coworkers' efforts, then difficult group members will appear like flies at a summer picnic (Lafasto & Larson, 2001). The group of six women in this chapter's opening example had established a very cooperative group climate, so this was not what precipitated their troublemaker's offensive behavior. Nevertheless, they did make some mis-

takes, as we'll see—some that they corrected, and others that they didn't.

Second, **change your communication in relation to a difficult person's behavior,** such as:

a. *Don't placate the troublemaker.* Laughing nervously when the disrupter cracks sexist or racist jokes or makes offensive remarks about group members merely encourages further moronic behavior. Permitting frequent interruptions from the offending party—enduring this ploy for conversational control—is a strategy of appeasement with little potential for success. Allowing the disrupter to manipulate the group so an illusion of harmony can be maintained rewards the troublemaker for objectionable behavior. Initially, all six women laughed nervously at their troublemaker's sexist "jokes" and comments, and they let him dominate conversations. Soon, they stopped laughing and wouldn't let him interrupt, as he was prone to do. They began saying to him, "Please wait; I'm not finished speaking."

b. *Refuse to be goaded into a reciprocal pattern.* Don't counter abusive remarks with abusive remarks of your own. Be unconditionally constructive (Ury, 1993). Disrupters thrive on provoking retaliation. Becoming aggressive with aggressors escalates into intractable power struggles. So don't take the bait. Keep telling

▶

yourself that if you do, you're engaging them on their terms and on their familiar ground, to your disadvantage. As Nancy Heischman, director of the Conflict Resolution Center in Aptos, California, notes, "You're not going to win if you enter into a competition with these people" (Townsend, 1999a, p. C2). Fighting fire with fire produces a firestorm. Resist the temptation. This requires self-control (and in some cases deserves a medal of commendation). In some extreme cases it won't be possible. To their great credit, none of the six women reciprocated the inappropriate behavior of their tormenter.

c. *Have an out-of-body experience* (Lulofs, 1994). Remove yourself mentally from the conflict. Listen to the disrupter as if you were an uninvolved third party with no energy in the outcome. Picture yourself as a mediator whose job it is to resolve the problem.

d. *Don't provide a soapbox for the troublemaker.* On two occasions in my teaching career, I have had a disruptive student interrupt me in the middle of a lecture/discussion to complain about the class. On the first occasion, I handled the situation poorly. My difficult student blurted out in a loud voice, "Can we do something relevant for a change? I'm tired of discussing other people's problems." I mistakenly took the bait and tried justifying what I had been doing in the class. Not surprisingly, he was unmoved by my response and undeterred in his obnoxious behavior. He was more than happy to mount the soapbox and focus attention on his personal agenda. The rest of the class became restless and annoyed with this interruption. I felt angry and ineffectual.

On the second occasion, my disrupter demanded to know why I was "wasting so much time on the relationship between gender and communication patterns." In this instance, I immediately deferred to the entire class, "Do the rest of you agree that this is a waste of time?" When they indicated that they did not, I then asked the class, "Do you want to take class time to discuss his complaint?" They again indicated that they did not. With the support of the group, I then deferred a confrontation with this student until the class was over. He was ill prepared to challenge the entire group. Notice, however, that I said I *deferred* the confrontation. You can't ignore disruptive behavior, especially when it becomes chronic.

Third, **attempt to convert disruption into a constructive contribution** (Gouran, 1988). Suppose in the middle of a group discussion your disrupter blurts out, "That's a completely stupid suggestion." You could reply in kind, thereby setting in motion a reciprocal pattern of derision. Instead, you could attempt to divert the disrupter away from abusive remarks and toward constructive contributions to the group by responding, "Perhaps you could provide a better suggestion." This response does not invite your obnoxious member to mount a soapbox and launch into an irrelevant monologue. You are requesting a pertinent contribution. Research indicates that substantive comments in a group discussion encourage a focus on content, not on relationship conflicts (Bell, 1974). Disrupters are less likely to continue their abuse when they are focused on the substance of the discussion. If the disrupter does not respond appropriately to your invitation to be constructive, then you can proceed to the next step.

▶

Fourth, **confront the difficult person directly.** If the entire group is upset by the behavior of the difficult person, then the *group* should confront the disrupter. Even truly abrasive individuals whose behavior seems to indicate a complete lack of regard for the group will find it tough to ignore pressure from group members. Be descriptive. State what behavior is offensive and encourage more constructive behavior. For example: "Your comments about women offend me. Please stop." Do not get abusive or nasty with the troublemaker. I strongly encouraged the six women to confront their troublemaker as a group. I presented this as an opportunity to experiment with communication strategies for dealing with difficult members. Unfortunately, they never directly confronted him.

Fifth, **separate yourself from the difficult person if all else fails.** Communication is not a panacea for every problem that comes up in groups. Some individuals leave no other option except removal from the group. This was the initial choice favored by the six women who were offended by their sexist troublemaker. Interesting, albeit difficult, lessons were learned, however, by not permitting this choice. Group members learned that they should have immediately confronted their difficult individual about his objectionable behavior. Their difficult member also learned a lesson. At the end of the first class project, I passed out a questionnaire asking members to indicate how much each individual in their group displayed specific group roles. There was one section listing disruptive roles (see Chapter 5). All six women indicated that their difficult member had played every disruptive role, often.

When these feedback forms were distributed, their troublemaker was stunned. He had no antenna extended to pick up the obvious signals from his group members indicating that his behavior was not appreciated. When he changed to a new group, he was immediately confronted about his boorish behavior and notified that such behavior would not be tolerated. A transformation occurred. He settled down and became not an exemplary group member, but one that no longer caused trouble. As a result of this experience, I now give groups the option to expel a troublemaker from their group as a last resort, provided that they have made a serious attempt without success to use other strategies outlined here.

If the difficult person is powerful, expulsion may not be an option. In this case, try putting physical distance between you and the problem person. Stay out of each other's way whenever possible. Keep interactions to a minimum. In a few instances, you may have to leave the group to restore your sanity. Some jobs, for instance, are just not worth keeping when abuse is heaped on you daily by an individual with more power than you have.

So how did the six women do on their project with the added challenge of dealing with a difficult member? They all performed wonderfully, giving an excellent presentation to the class. Their troublemaker, however, missed several group meetings outside of class and his enthusiasm for the project was underwhelming. It showed. He embarrassed himself by performing poorly during his presentation. His presentation on a second project with a different group, however, was much improved.

I have presented you with a rational model for handling troublemakers. Try these methods. They will work well for you in most situations. Nevertheless, we are not strictly rational beings. Difficult people can provoke intense anger and deep frustration from group members. In my own experience, I have found that even if I lost my temper and let my emotions get the better of me, this response is not as problematic as simply ignoring or enduring the disruptive behavior. Even if your anger translates into personal attacks (not a good choice), at the very least you have served notice on the troublesome group member that his or her pattern of behavior is unacceptable and will not be suffered in silence.

Questions for Thought

1. What are some possible disadvantages of expelling a difficult group member? Why should this be a last resort, not a first choice?
2. Have you ever had to deal with a difficult group member? What seemed to work best to manage this challenge?

SYNERGY: ONE PLUS ONE EQUALS A TON

The whole is not necessarily equal to the sum of its parts. It may be greater than the sum of its individual parts. This effect is called synergy. **Synergy** (*syn* = together + *ergon* = work) occurs when group performance from joint action of members exceeds expectations based on perceived abilities and skills of individual members (Salazar, 1995).

The synergistic quality of group decision making is analogous to mixing drugs or chemicals. Some combinations of drugs, such as those used in chemotherapy, can produce more effective results than two or more drugs taken separately. Combining some pesticides can dramatically increase potency. One study at Tulane University found that mixing two common pesticide chemicals, endosulfan and dieldrin, didn't just double the potency of each—it increased their potency by as much as 1,600 times. As endocrinologist John A. McLachlan, who led the Tulane University team that did the study, explains, "Instead of one plus one equaling two, we found that one plus one equals a thousandfold" (cited in "Playing Havoc," 1996, p. 14A).

A June 23, 1998, *NBC News at Sunrise* report provides an apt example of group synergy. A Little League team in Tucson, Arizona, called the Diamondbacks, consisted of players thought to be too unskilled to play for other teams. These castoffs finished the season with a perfect 18–0 team win–loss record, and they won the league championship. The group effort far exceeded expectations of success based on the individual abilities of the players.

Habitat for Humanity is a case study in synergy. Habitat was begun in 1968 by Millard Fuller. Habitat builds modest homes for poor people around the world. It has become one of the largest homebuilders in the United States. It has 1,900 chapters in 64 countries. In 2005, Habitat finished its two hundred thousandth home ("Habitat for Humanity," 2005). Habitat work crews composed of volunteers divide

An all-woman construction team works cooperatively to build a Habitat home.

the labor, with each small subgroup erecting portions of the total structure a section at a time. Most volunteers who build Habitat homes have no expertise in such tasks. In fact, one Habitat construction team in Bend, Oregon, called itself Chris's Bad Girls and advertised on the Internet, encouraging women from ages 16 to 100, "experienced or inexperienced, walking or in a wheelchair, sighted or unsighted," to volunteer their labor to build Habitat homes. On their first project, women from ages 16 to 84 volunteered to build a Habitat home constructed entirely by women (at the time, only the third such all-female construction project of its kind in the United States). With the exception of Chris, who was the leader of the group and a general contractor, none of the women were builders. The second-in-command was picked because she had once built a doghouse. Nevertheless, they successfully constructed a Habitat home by working together.

Synergy is produced only when group members work in a cooperative, interconnected way. If group members work independently by completing individual assignments on their own and the group merely compiles the results without the benefit of group discussion and interaction, no synergy will occur (Fandt, 1991). For instance, if your group took an essay test and each member was assigned one question to answer, no synergistic benefit would occur if group members did not discuss rough draft answers with the whole group and make improvements prior to a final draft.

Negative Synergy: Results beyond Bad

Systems don't always produce synergy. Sometimes they produce negative synergy. **Negative synergy** occurs when group members working together produce a worse result than expected based on perceived individual skills and abilities of members (Salazar, 1995). The whole is worse than the sum of its parts. Negative synergy is like mixing alcohol and tranquilizers, causing suicidal effects. When group members

Sometimes groups produce negative synergy.

know little about a subject, compete against each other (Me-orientation), resist change, or share a collective bias or mindset, the result of mixing their individual contributions can produce decisions beyond bad.

One such instance occurred in the early 1980s. The Federal Emergency Management Agency (FEMA) published a booklet that stated, "With reasonable protective measures, the United States could survive nuclear attack and go on to recovery within a relatively few years" (cited in Scheer, 1983, p. 111). FEMA compounded this widely recognized absurdity with plans to evacuate whole cities (as if an aggressor would provide a week's warning in advance of an attack). Incredibly, FEMA also instructed survivors to fill out change-of-address cards with their post offices following the nuclear attack (apparently so the IRS could still collect taxes from traumatized survivors). FEMA presumed that life would return to something approaching normality soon after nuclear bombs had decimated a substantial portion of the human species (not to mention most post offices).

FEMA's *Alice-in-Wonderland* civil defense plan makes as much sense as satirical advice given in the "Meet Mr. Bomb" spoof of the plan, edited by Tony Hendra (1982). It advises citizens to prepare for the 4,000-degree centigrade temperature at ground zero by spending 10–15 minutes a day in a clothes dryer.

In February, 2003, the Department of Homeland Security encouraged Americans to seal a "safe room" in their homes with plastic sheeting and duct tape. This protection against a bioterrorist attack seemed to ignore the downside of this recommendation: oxygen deprivation leading to death.

On a less global scale, negative synergy can be seen in a group dialogue recorded by one researcher (Hirokawa, 1987). The group is deliberating a winter survival task whereby items must be ranked according to their utility in improving the group's survival in a wilderness area. Here, the actual process of negative synergy becomes apparent.

B: This may sound crazy, but I say we go for the radio.

A: Why the radio? It's broken.

B: I know, I know . . . but that doesn't mean we can't use it.

C: I don't understand.

A: I think I do . . . but go ahead.

B: OK, like here's what I'm thinking. I remember, like I'm a fan of *Star Trek,* right . . . anyway, like on one show, Spock and Kirk are being held prisoners and they make this makeshift radio to call for help. So, like here's what I was thinking we could do . . . we could use the parts to build our own transmitter.

A: Right . . . like we could take the antenna and place it on a high tree . . . run wires down, and start building a transmitter, maybe then send Morse codes. We wouldn't have to talk.

B: What about power, though?

A: We could use the battery from the plane.

B: But that's not on the list here and we were told not to assume other things aside from the list.

C: We could use solar power.

B: Yeah, the sun . . . or electrical power . . . build our own generator . . . like on *Gilligan's Island,* remember where he was on a stationary bicycle?

A: Do we know codes?

C: I know SOS . . . three dots, three dashes, three dots . . .

B: Anyway, no matter. Just keep sending signals—any signals. . . .

C: So we go with the radio?

B: Yeah, I bet no one else thought of it. (p. 22)

In this illustration, there is no indication that any of the group members knows anything about building a transmitter or generator. The success of such a venture would be doubtful at best, even if MacGyver (to continue the group's reference to classic television shows) were available. Bad ideas in this group are simply compounded one upon the other—negative synergy at work.

Adaptability to Change

Systems are never in a static state. They are in a constant state of becoming until they terminate. You do not have a choice between change and no change. The relevant choice is, can a system (group) adapt to the inevitable changes that are certain to occur? Every system reacts to change in its own way. For instance, two groups that begin at the same point and experience similar environmental conditions may turn out very differently. Conversely, two groups that begin at very different points and experience dissimilar environmental conditions may turn out very similarly. In other words, groups with a similar or identical final goal (e.g., financial security) may reach that end in highly diverse ways (called **equifinality** in the somewhat ponderous systems lingo). In this section, the process of adapting to change in a system is discussed.

▶ **Focus Questions**

1. What relationship does stability and change have in groups?
2. Why do groups establish boundaries? How do they control boundaries?
3. Can groups ever become too open? Too closed?
4. Is it better for a group to be more open than closed?

DYNAMIC EQUILIBRIUM: MANAGING STABILITY AND CHANGE

All systems attempt to maintain stability and to achieve a state of equilibrium (*homeostasis*) by resisting change, but no system can avoid inevitable change (Wood, 1997). Too much stability can produce stagnation and tedium. Too much change can produce chaos and group disintegration. There is no perfect balance point between stability and change in any system, but there is a range in which systems can manage change effectively to promote growth and success without pushing the system to disaster. This range is called **dynamic equilibrium.** A system sustains dynamic equilibrium when it regulates the *degree, rate,* and *desirability* of change, allowing stability and change to coexist.

Consider what happens when the three variables of change are not sufficiently regulated. As the owner of a small business, a friend of mine decided to go high tech and computerize his office with the very latest, most sophisticated equipment. At the same time, he embarked on an office renovation project. To add to the disruption, he moved in a new partner. His office staff went berserk. Staff members hadn't been trained to run the sophisticated computer programs and equipment. They resented the renovation, which displaced them from their normal work areas and created a huge mess that interfered with their efficiency. The new partner turned out to be a very demanding individual who expected instant results from the beleaguered staff. His favorite saying, posted on the wall of his office, was "Impossible is a word found only in a fool's dictionary." The final change, however, that toppled this house of horrors was my friend's insistence that his staff work half-days on weekends until the office was returned to a more normal state. Three of the four members of his staff quit, and they were spitting fire as they stomped out of the office, never to return. They left a gift for my friend's partner—a thesaurus renamed with black marker pen *Fool's Dictionary* with words such as *idiot, pompous, twit, jerk,* and *moron* highlighted. The business had to be shut down for 2 weeks, resulting in a substantial loss of revenue.

Too much change (degree) was required in too concentrated a period of time (rate) without a concerted effort to persuade the staff of the value (desirability) of the changes demanded. Groups can often adapt even to large changes if given sufficient time to absorb them and if members are convinced the changes have merit. **In some instances, of course, the dismantling of an ineffective system may be necessary to replace it with a better system—one that institutes wholesale change and radical departure from the way things were.** The San Francisco 49ers, following a dismal 2004 football season of 2 wins 14 losses, "cleaned house" by replacing their coach, their general manager, and most of the assistant coaches. Sometimes, to rebuild a dysfunctional team you have to tear it apart and resurrect it from the ground up.

BOUNDARY CONTROL: REGULATING INPUT

Openness and change go hand in hand in a system. Openness refers to the degree of continuous interchange with the outside environment. As systems open to the outside, new input enters the system, inevitably disturbing it. Admit women into a previously all-male club, boardroom, or law firm and change is inevitable. A group must adapt to change or suffer strife, even possible demise. **Adaptability** to change is the adjustment of group boundaries in response to changing conditions.

Boundaries regulate input and consequent exposure to change in a system. When groups establish boundaries, they regulate the degree, rate, even the desirability of change. This **boundary control** determines the amount of access a group has to input, and thus influence, from outsiders.

Every group maintains boundary control to some extent. It is a critical group function. The cast of the television sitcom *Friends* showed keen awareness of the necessity of maintaining boundaries (Chin, 2000). Matthew Perry, the self-deprecating Chandler Bing character in the series, became addicted to painkillers following a Jet Ski accident, and he subsequently lost a shocking amount of weight. Fellow cast members became intensely protective and supportive of Perry during his recovery, offering little information to the press and public about his ordeal. They erected strict boundary control to maintain group solidarity and personal friendships among cast members.

Boundaries, however, are permeable. They leak. No group can close off so completely to its environment that no change is possible. There is always some interchange with the environment that leaks through the boundaries (see Closer Look: "Cult Boundary Control").

METHODS OF BOUNDARY CONTROL: ERECTING BARRIERS

Groups establish boundaries by erecting physical, psychological, and linguistic barriers, and by establishing rules, roles, and networks.

Physical Barriers: Protecting Group Space There are many possible physical barriers that can establish group boundaries. They include locking group meeting rooms, choosing an inconvenient location in a building to discourage people from just dropping by and disturbing a group meeting, and placing a board of supervisors on a raised stage or roping off audience members from direct access to board members during public meetings. Physical boundaries are not always quite so obvious. Gangs may designate a few city blocks as their turf (Conquerwood, 1994). Graffiti painted on signs or buildings serve as markers of a gang's turf. Rev. Gregory J. Boyle, a Jesuit priest, has presided at the funerals of 70 young gang members in Los Angeles. Many of those who were killed died because graffiti scrawlings were removed or painted over by rival gang members in turf wars (Terry, 2000). Cyberbanging, the high-tech tagging on thousands of gang-related websites, creates virtual turf warfare (Carreon, 2005). Rival gang members exchange threats and "throw up" gang numbers and names on sites operated by the Crips, Bloods, Nortenos, Surenos, and various Asian and lesser known gangs. In May 2004, cyberbanging produced a street brawl in a suburb of Dallas. Maintaining a group's physical boundaries, even boundaries that only appear on a computer screen, can be serious business.

Psychological Barriers: Member in Name Only Groups can make an individual feel that they do not belong in the group. When this occurs the group is erecting a psychological barrier. Such barriers occur when members' contributions are ignored or they are treated as outcasts. They may even be told that they are not wanted in the group. Women and ethnic minorities historically have been made to feel like outsiders and tokens when first joining mostly white, male groups.

Linguistic Barriers: Having to Speak the Language Groups erect linguistic barriers when members use a private vocabulary, or **argot,** peculiar to a specific group. Those who understand the argot are presumed to be group members. Those who don't are clearly outsiders. Imagine if you heard this statement in an elevator from one business executive to another: "You could bring in a good athlete, but there's always the chance he or she could hit the windshield. Because you're worried that your VC partners have short arms, you're wondering whether to wake the giant. In any case, you're out of bandwidth: You're thinking about putting a ribbon on it and moving into sell mode. It's the living dead and about to become plankton." Translation? "You

© Greg Smith/CORBIS

Group boundaries are permeable, as illustrated by this "immigrant wall," erected to prevent border crossings. Can you see ways to penetrate the barrier?

could bring in a talented executive from another field, but there's always a chance that he or she could fail. Because you're worried that your Venture Capitalist partners won't participate in a second round of funding, you're wondering whether to talk to Microsoft. In any case, you're out of time and exhausted. You're thinking about firing the engineers and selling the company. It's stagnant and about to be a small company swallowed by a larger one" (Herbold, 1998, p. 26A). This is an example of the argot of venture capitalists, the high-risk deal makers in the business world.

Rules: Permission Not Granted Membership rules establish who can join a group and who is barred. They also define appropriate behaviors in specified social situations. Rules may specify who can talk to whom, thus controlling input from outside. Within organizations there is usually a chain-of-command rule. You do not

CLOSER LOOK

CULT BOUNDARY CONTROL: BOUND AND GAGGED

FROM THE MANSON FAMILY and the Heaven's Gate Cybergroup to the Moonies and the Branch Davidians, cults small and large have emerged in the United States. Some have disintegrated in violent clashes with law enforcement or in mass suicides, while others continue to troll the waters of the disenchanted and dispossessed for new converts.

Depending on the definition, there are between 3,000 and 5,000 cults in the United States with between two and five million members (Singer, 1995). These are rough estimates at best because there is no precise way to make a membership head count. These numbers do not include the millions of relatives and friends profoundly affected by individuals' membership in cults. Thus, although cults are typically viewed as "fringe groups," their impact stretches far beyond the actual number of cults or size of cult membership. **Ultimately, however, the value of examining cults here is to illustrate the process of group boundary control taken to excess. All groups need to heed the potential for disaster when boundaries are regulated too stringently.**

Singer (1995) defines a **cult** as "a group that forms around a person who claims he or she has a special mission or knowledge, which will be shared with those who turn over most of their decision making to that self-appointed leader" (p. xx). There are four important characteristics of cults that separate them from other religious, political, or social groups (Galanter, 1999; Pratkanis & Aronson, 2001; Singer, 1995). These four characteristics are as follows:

1. Cults have strong, charismatic leaders who exercise control in an authoritarian power structure.
2. Cults have a shared belief system whose adherents accept that they alone are gifted with the revealed truth.
3. Cults insist on regimented behavior of followers, strict obedience to authority figures, and unquestioning acceptance of the group's norms and beliefs.
4. Cults create rigid boundary control.

It is this last cult characteristic that I'll explore here.

▶

---

normally leapfrog your immediate supervisor and communicate directly with the president of the company. To prevent information overload and inefficiency, the Big Cheese will want you to talk to the Cheez Whiz.

Roles: Staying in Bounds A **role** is a pattern of expected behavior associated with parts we play in groups. The expectations attached to group roles specify appropriate behavior, thereby fostering predictability and controlling variability. Once the pattern of behavior is associated with a group member, a boundary is set.

Cults exercise boundary control in the same ways that other groups do, just with greater enthusiasm and extremity. First, they create physical isolation. The most obvious examples are the Jonestown complex in Guyana and the Branch Davidian fortress in Waco, Texas. Reverend Jim Jones, dubbed the "Messiah from Ukiah" by the media, awash in his paranoid delusions and threatened by a series of exposés in newspapers and magazines, moved the bulk of the membership in his People's Temple from San Francisco to the jungles of Guyana, South America. There, in splendid isolation, Jones ruled his cult followers with an iron fist until it came to an end with the mass murder/suicide of 912 people, 276 of whom were children. David Koresh followed a similar pattern to Jones. Followers of this Branch Davidian leader built a 77-acre fortress of isolation in the middle of Texas. The Koresh cult also ended tragically in a 1993 fiery battle with federal authorities.

Physical isolation is also achieved through secrecy, in some instances. The manual of the Free Militia, a Midwest paramilitary cult, reads in part:

> The identities of cell members are known only within the cell and by their immediate superior. . . . All codes, passwords, and telephone networks are determined by and held in confidence within the cell. All fortified positions are determined, prepared, and concealed by the cell. . . .

The cell leader easily conveys clear orders to a small group of men. [Cell members] can communicate freely and openly while shrouding the particulars of their tactics, positions, and signals to everyone outside the group. These cells, or subterranean secret units, are reserved for hardcore insurgent operations. (Conway & Siegelman, 1995, pp. 344, 354)

A second way cults maintain rigid boundaries is through information control. As Galanter (1999) explains, if a cult "is to maintain a system of shared beliefs markedly at variance with that of the surrounding culture, members must sometimes be rigidly isolated from consensual information from the general society that would unsettle this belief system" (p. 105). Working hand in hand with physical isolation, information control is exercised partly by creating closed networks that prevent outsiders such as parents, friends, and the media (unbelievers) from entering the cult's premises. A member's support network (family) is severed. Access to outside information is cut off. Cult members are encouraged to read cult literature. Of course, the best means of information control is self-censorship (Pratkanis & Aronson, 2001). Information that is not "of the cult" is labeled "of the devil," "lies of the government," and so forth. Members are made to feel guilt and shame for showing interest in such information.

In the United States, managers are expected to respect the boundary between an employee's work life and private life. Commenting on a female employee's lack of a husband and informing her that she will be attending a luncheon to meet an eligible male would be viewed as clearly overstepping the boundaries separating supervisor and employee. The same reaction may not occur, however, in India, where a leadership style called *paternal authoritativeness* is often preferred. Indians expect that someone in a supervisory leadership role, typically a male, will act like a father who

Cult followers are also fed a diet of misinformation (Singer, 1995). Sheltered from outside information, the only reality for members of Jonestown, for instance, was what Jim Jones and his band of cohorts created for the group. Jonestown members were told that Los Angeles had been abandoned due to severe drought, that the Ku Klux Klan was boldly marching through the streets of San Francisco, and that the U.S. government was preparing to destroy Jonestown and kill its inhabitants. So restricted was the information entering Jonestown that even misinformation served to control the membership and create a paranoid atmosphere.

A third method of cult boundary control is the use of a group argot incomprehensible to outsiders. How, for example, are outsiders to know that *the devil disguise, just flesh relationships,* and *pollution* are derogatory terms for parents (Singer, 1995)? *Being too horizontal* is being too sympathetic to peers. Moonies refer to all relationships between people as either a *Cain–Abel* (superior–subordinate) or a *chapter 2* (sexuality) problem (Hassan, 1988). The Divine Light Mission refers to their services as *satsang* and *darshan* (Pratkanis & Aronson, 2001). Deceptive fundraising practices are referred to by some cults as *transcendental trickery*. This **group-speak** or cult jargon shuts down members' critical thinking. "Eventually, speaking in cult jargon is

second nature, and talking with outsiders becomes energy-consuming and awkward. Soon enough, members find it most comfortable to talk only among themselves in the new vocabulary. To reinforce this, all kinds of derogatory names are given to outsiders: wogs, systemites, reactionaries, unclean, of Satan" (Singer, 1995, p. 70).

A fourth method of cult boundary control involves erecting psychological barriers. This practice is most clearly evident in the "them versus us" in-group/out-group mentality that fosters either/or thinking within cults. You're *either* "with us" and right, redeemed, saved, *or* you're "against us" and therefore wrong, evil, unenlightened, doomed (Singer, 1995). To be an in-group member is to be a chosen one. Those in the out-group are hated or feared as enemies (Pratkanis & Aronson, 2001). The beast in David Koresh's worldview was the U.S. government—also the object of virulent hatred from various militia cults in the United States (Conway & Siegelman, 1995). The Heaven's Gate group believed that Earth was controlled by demonic extraterrestrial "Luciferians" (Goodstein, 1997). "Fearfulness of outsiders, or xenophobia, a common characteristic of cults, is an important manifestation of boundary control. It holds groups together but it can reach the dimension of outright paranoia" (Galanter, 1999, p. 107).

▶

cares about a family member. Going to the trouble of arranging a luncheon for a female employee to meet an eligible male would likely be perceived as showing personal interest and concern for the employee's welfare (Brislin, 1993). The employee would likely appreciate the gesture (and attend the luncheon), whereas in the United States charges of sexual harassment might be filed. **Role boundaries and culture are inseparably interconnected.**

Networks: Controlling Information Flow Groups set boundaries by establishing networks. **Networks** control the access and flow of information within the

Cults also erect psychological barriers against "bad thoughts." Questions that might arise in a member's mind that indicate less than total acceptance of the belief system of the cult are forcefully discouraged. These are "disagreeable thoughts," "evil," or "the work of Satan" (Pratkanis & Aronson, 2001). Members become their own mind police trying to clear their heads of Orwellian thought crimes.

Finally, cult boundary control is created by rigid rules. There are dress codes, dietary restrictions, and rules governing with whom a member may associate, marry, or talk. Some cults have rules stipulating whether members may raise their own children and where they may live (Singer, 1995). Gag rules that prohibit gossiping or "nattering," where members might express doubts or misgivings about the cult and the cult leaders, are commonplace. Members are instructed to report any violations of the gag rule.

Although cults have extremely tight boundary control, no group can exist as a totally closed system. Boundaries are permeable even for cults. Seeking new converts requires some interaction with the outside world. The Branch Davidians, although isolated in their fortress, equipped their compound with a satellite dish; some members, including Koresh, regularly jogged through Waco neighborhoods and shopped in local stores ("Cult Compound," 1993). Members of the Heaven's Gate cult designed Internet websites for San Diego businesses and used their own websites to recruit members and proselytize their beliefs.

All groups exercise boundary control, but cults make boundary control a top priority, sometimes an obsession. This rigid boundary control is self-protective and has the effect of maintaining stability within the group and stifling change, but it can also produce tragic consequences.

Questions for Thought

1. Although cults are often religious or quasi-religious in nature, can cults be secular?
2. Why do you think individuals join cults?
3. How are cults different from the U.S. Marine Corps? The Catholic Church? The Mormon Church? The CIA?

group, and they may also isolate the group from outside influences. A network is a structured pattern of information flow and personal contact. The more open the network, the more accessible information is to a broad range of individuals. Open networks encourage change; closed networks emphasize stability and permanence.

In some cases, becoming a link in the network is the hard part. In a study of African Americans in the banking industry (Irons & Moore, 1985), 75% of the respondents rated not being included in the network as the most serious problem to

CBS via Getty Images

Unreality TV programs such as "Survivor" loosen boundaries and create extreme openness to the probing eyes of viewers.

advancement in their jobs. Other studies of Asian Americans found similar barriers to upward mobility (see Morrison & Von Glinow, 1990).

BOUNDARY CONTROL AND GROUP EFFECTIVENESS: OPEN AND CLOSED SYSTEMS

Although all groups set boundaries, there is a strong bias in American culture that encourages openness, or loose boundaries, and discourages closedness, or rigid boundaries. We preach the value of fostering an open society and maintaining an open mind. Having a closed mind is linked to an authoritarian personality and dogmatism. A closed society is likened to China or North Korea. Highly closed, isolated groups are often referred to as cults (see Closer Look: "Cult Boundary Control"). The fact that cults are controversial groups that are excessively closed, however, shouldn't prompt a desire for unrestricted openness. The belief that openness is always good and closedness is always bad is a faulty one (Klapp, 1978). No group can long endure unless it closes off to *some* outside influences and restricts access to *some* information (Galanter, 1999). This is why boundary control is an essential group function.

A group must close off when both the quantity and type of input place undue stress on the group and/or prevent it from accomplishing its task. There are times, for instance, when a family seeks advice and counsel from friends and relatives (input), but there are also times when a family should close itself off to intrusion

> ●● SECOND LOOK

OPENNESS AND GROUP BOUNDARY CONTROL

TYPES OF GROUP BOUNDARIES REGULATING CHANGE

Physical Barriers	Psychological Barriers
Linguistic Barriers	Rules
Roles	Networks

BOUNDARY CONTROL AND GROUP EFFECTIVENESS

- Signs of Excessive Openness or Closedness:

Debilitating Stress	Divisive Conflicts
Boredom	Malaise
Poor Productivity	

- Adjust boundaries when signs of excessive openness/closedness occur.

from outsiders. In-laws who are overly free with advice and criticism impose stress on the family. Permitting even well-intentioned relatives and friends to hammer immediate family members with unsolicited counsel can easily lead to bickering, increased tension, conflict, and even family disintegration.

The Voyeur Dorm website became a controversial issue in Tampa, Florida, in August 1999 (Blumner, 1999). For $34 a month, customers, mostly men, could observe seven female college students in their home. The women occupied a residential house wired with 34 video cameras that covered almost every part of the house. The Tampa Variance Review Board discovered this live "Truman Show" and ruled that the Voyeur Dorm was not a legitimate home occupation but an adult-use business, a position rejected by the Eleventh Circuit Court of Appeals in 2001 and tacitly rejected by the U.S. Supreme Court in 2002 when it refused to hear the appeal. Despite what you might think of this bizarre business venture, imagine what it would be like living under the constant view of strangers in your own home. Taking a shower would be a public event. Although there was a no-sex policy in the Voyeur Dorm, practically every other personal activity was paraded before the peeping eyes of website subscribers. Clearly, this would be far too much openness for the vast majority of people, as was made evident in the movie *EDtv*.

Despite the popularity of shows such as *Survivor, Big Brother,* and *The Apprentice* and their billing as "reality television," participants do not act naturally when cameras and microphones record their every move and conversation. It's too intrusive. Competing for huge prize money also makes for "unreality television." We need our boundaries to live our lives without the increased stress from probing eyes of strangers.

Group members should watch for signs of excessive openness or closedness, such as when groups experience debilitating stress and tension, divisive conflicts, boredom and malaise, and poor productivity. Loosening or tightening boundaries may be in order. Knowing whether to relax or tighten boundaries depends on whether the group is already very closed or very open.

Influence of Size

Size is a central element in any human system. Fluctuations in size have enormous influence on the structure and function of a group.

▶ **Focus Questions**

1. What is the most appropriate size for a decision-making group?
2. What distinguishes a small group from a large one?
3. How are groups and organizations different?

GROUP SIZE AND COMPLEXITY

As groups increase in numerical size, complexity increases. Try scheduling a meeting for a group of 15 or 20 members. Consider how difficult it would be finding a time that doesn't conflict with at least one or more members' personal schedules and preferences. There are numerous complications that increased complexity produces. This section discusses these complications.

Quantitative Complexity: Exponentially Complicated As the size of a group increases, the possible number of interactions between group members increases exponentially (Bostrom, 1970). The calculations are as follows:

Number in Group	Interactions Possible
2	2
3	9
4	28
5	75
6	186
7	441
8	1,056

In a dyad, only two relationships are possible, namely, person A to person B, and vice versa. A and B may not have the same perception of their relationship. Person A may perceive the relationship with B as a close friendship, whereas B sees the relationship with A as merely acquaintanceship. In a triad, or three-member group, there are nine possibilities:

1. A to B   4. C to A   7. A to B and C
2. B to A   5. B to C   8. B to A and C
3. A to C   6. C to B   9. C to A and B

Adding even a single member to a group enormously complicates the group dynamics. In a study investigating why groups fail, one notable factor was the difficulty of scheduling meetings when groups grew to eight members (Fiechtner & Davis, 1992).

Imagine the difficulty Diane and Stanley Cook experience raising their ever-expanding family (McLaughlin, 2004). As college sweethearts they began dreaming of raising a large family. Their wish was granted—in a big way. They raised five biological children and *106 foster children!* Many of the foster children were developmentally disabled, physically or mentally. Now in their senior years, this amazing couple has adopted 13 of these foster children. Living in a 2,000-square-foot home, "only" 13 children lived under the same roof at the same time. Nevertheless, preventing sheer chaos would be a substantial challenge. "It was organized," Diane Cook explains. "Everybody chipped in" (p. 19A).

Complexity and Group Transactions: Size Matters Variations in size affect group transactions in several specific ways. First, **larger groups typically have more nonparticipants than smaller groups.** This occurs partly because in larger groups there is more intense competition to seize the floor (Carletta et al., 1998).

More reticent members are apt to sit quietly rather than fight to be heard. This also means that the more talkative members are likely to emerge as leaders of larger groups because influence on the group comes partly from speaking (Kolb, 1997).

A long-term study by Jeremy Finn, a professor at the University of Buffalo Graduate School of Education, followed 12,000 students in kindergarten through third grade. These students were from urban, rural, and inner-city backgrounds, randomly assigned to small classes of 13 to 17 students or regular-size classes of 22 to 25 students. Finn followed their progress for 12 years. Those children who began in smaller classes had higher on-time high school graduation rates and attained more honors than students who began in the larger classes (Elley, 2001). Larger classes provide less personal attention from teachers, and more students are likely to become nonparticipants.

Second, **smaller groups inhibit overt disagreement and signs of dissatisfaction more than larger groups.** Smaller groups can apply more intense pressure to conform to majority opinion than can be applied in larger groups (Bettinghaus & Cody, 1987). Splinter groups and factions are more likely to emerge in larger groups. In a six-person group there may be only a single deviant who must stand alone against the group. In a 12-person group, however, two or more deviants may more easily emerge, forming a supportive faction. Having an ally makes nonconformity easier to sustain.

In the movie *Twelve Angry Men,* only one juror votes "not guilty" on the first vote. Hailed by many as a dramatization of the importance of one person standing against the many in a fight for truth and justice, one scene is often overlooked. The lone holdout debates with fellow jurors for a while, but eventually indicates that he is unwilling to continue if no other juror will support his position. He makes a deal with the jury. If no other juror votes not guilty on the next ballot, then he will join the majority and also vote for conviction, thereby sending the defendant to death row. When he gains an ally, the fight is continued to its dramatic conclusion. Non-conformity is easier when you don't have to stand alone against the group.

Third, **group size affects levels of cooperation** (Benenson et al., 2000; Stahelski & Tsukuda, 1990). When groups of 12 to 30 members were compared, the smallest groups were found to be the most cooperative, meaning they worked together on tasks more interdependently, engaged in collaborative effort, and exhibited consensus leadership. As groups increased in size, cooperation decreased. This resulted in diminished task effectiveness, unmet goals, and increased conflicts. Other studies have found that larger groups encourage formation of **cliques** or small, narrowly focused subgroups (factions) that create a competitive atmosphere. These cliques diminish overall group performance (Carron & Spink, 1995).

Fourth, **group members tend to be less satisfied with groups of 10 or more** (Carter & West, 1998). The overall group climate often deteriorates when groups become large. Cooperation is more difficult in larger groups (De Cremer & Leonardelli, 2003). Tasks become more complex to perform, tension mounts, and dominant group members can trigger interpersonal disharmony by becoming too aggressive and forceful with other members while trying to impose order (Pavitt & Curtis, 1994).

So what is the ideal size for a group? There is no specific number. **The best size for a group is the smallest size capable of performing the task effectively** (J. Hackman, 1987; Sundstrom et al., 1990). This admittedly is somewhat imprecise advice, but there is a trade-off between quality and speed when trying to determine ideal group size (Pavitt & Curtis, 1994). If the primary group goal is the quality of the decision, then a moderately sized group of 7 to 10 is advisable. (Groups larger than this, especially substantially larger, can easily become unwieldy and inefficient.) Moderate-sized groups are especially effective if there is little overlap of knowledge and skills among group members and the group task requires substantial diversity in knowledge and skills (Valacich et al., 1994). If the primary goal of the group is speed, however, then groups of three or four members are advisable. Larger groups typically slow down decision making and problem solving, sometimes maddeningly so. In a comparison of 6-member and 12-member mock juries, the larger juries took much longer to deliberate and they took more votes (Davis et al., 1997).

Because juries are faced with momentous choices that significantly affect people's lives, the 12-member jury has been the norm. If your freedom depended on a jury verdict, you would certainly want the primary group goal to be the quality and not the speed of the decision. Consensus (unanimous agreement) becomes difficult and majority vote is often used to make final decisions when groups are large. Some research (see Pavitt & Curtis, 1994) suggests five-member groups are a nice compromise when both quality and speed are important group goals. **Ultimately, there is no magic number that constitutes the ideal-sized group.** Even five-member groups can circumvent high-quality deliberations by a quick majority vote. Contextual factors (politics, legal requirements, institutional norms, availability of members, task complexity, etc.) may necessitate groups larger in size than 5 or even 10. Competent communicators can work effectively in larger groups, although increased size magnifies the challenges.

AN ORGANIZATION: A GROUP OF GROUPS

When groups grow, they reach a point where they may become organizations with bureaucracies. For instance, suppose you and two friends decide to open a small business together. Let's say you call it New Age Repair & Care (NARC for short). Your business specializes in "holistic healing of automobiles" in addition to conventional automotive services.

In its initial stages, the structure of your group is informal and the division of labor is most likely equal. Since the three of you work at the establishment, communication is not hampered by cumbersome chains of command, middle managers, and the paper chase of a large formal organization. Standards of operation and procedures for decision making are informally negotiated among the three of you as situations occur.

If your little enterprise booms, employees will have to be hired, thus expanding the business and increasing the complexity of the entire operation. Work schedules will have to be coordinated. Standardized codes of dress and conduct on the job may be required. Some training in New Age automotive techniques may be necessary. Formal grievance procedures may also be required to settle disputes. You may decide to open additional NARC outlets, and even become a chain, selling franchises around the country. Now you must hire managers, accountants, and lawyers; establish a board of directors; sell stock in the company; and become business executives. What began as a small enterprise can grow into a large organization.

When small groups grow into larger groups, finally graduating into complex organizations, the structure and function of these human systems change. **With increasing group size comes greater formality.** Small groups are more personal than large organizations. Small groups usually can function well as a committee of the whole, with relatively equal distribution of power. Large organizations become hierarchical, with clearly demarcated power structures and lines of authority, although recently there has been a trend toward *flattening the hierarchy* by moving away from tightly defined roles of superiors and subordinates and placing greater emphasis on teamwork. The company becomes more important than any single individual. Employees in the organization can be replaced with relative ease, whereas in a small intimate group, loss of a single member may bring about the demise of the group.

The flow of information is one of the most important differences between small groups and complex organizations. Normally, little negative information from below reaches the top of the corporate hierarchy, or, if it does, it is delayed (Conrad, 1990). Who wants to be the bearer of bad tidings? They often shoot (figuratively) the messenger who brings bad news. In the spring of 1995, software producer Intuit, Inc., confessed that there were bugs in its tax-preparation software. Those using the software would likely file erroneous income tax returns with the IRS. Intuit's tax-preparation programs were the market leaders, and the timing of the announcement that the programs were defective came just 6 weeks prior to the April 15 income tax deadline—too late for eager beavers who filed an early return. Intuit President Scott Cook admitted at a news conference that the firm's technical support team knew about the software bugs in December 1994, but didn't pass the information up the corporate ladder for many weeks. Cook sheepishly explained, "This one is particularly embarrassing because we didn't know we knew about it. I am very disappointed that we did not act more quickly on this. We really let our customers down" (cited in Gomes, 1995, p. 4C).

Bad decision making cannot be hidden easily when the group is small. Almost any blunder will become incandescent when the black hole of bureaucracy is not present to shroud it. If you have three people running a small business and one of the three does something boneheaded that affects the enterprise, your choices immediately narrow to two possibilities (unless, of course, you are guilty but playing dumb). One of your two partners has to be the culprit.

Information distortion usually is a bigger problem in organizations than in smaller groups. Managers act as gatekeepers, screening messages, selecting which ones will be brought to the attention of higher-ups. By the time a message from below reaches top executives in an organization, it can easily become unrecognizable nonsense. Similarly, information from the top can be distorted by the time it filters down to the bottom of the organization (Conboy, 1976).

In smaller groups, the communication is usually more direct, with fewer opportunities for distortion, because messages are transmitted serially through several people. If the message is communicated to the entire group at the same time—a comparatively easy task if the gathering is small—then the problems of message distortion are reduced.

Although organizations are not emphasized in this text, I include examples from organizational settings because many of you can relate meaningfully to such an

In large organizations, negative information often does not reach the top of the corporate hierarchy.

▷ ●● SECOND LOOK

EFFECTS OF INCREASING GROUP SIZE

INCREASES

- Complexity
- Factionalism/cliques
- Formality—more hierarchical
- Information distortion
- Quality decision making (unless group becomes too large and unwieldy)
- Difficulty achieving consensus/ majority vote often substituted
- Likelihood talkative members become leaders

DECREASES

- Participation in group discussion
- Cooperation (in very large groups)
- Pressure to conform—coalitions likely to form in opposition to group norms
- Member satisfaction with group experience (10 or more)
- Access to information
- Flow of negative information to top of hierarchy
- Speed of decision making

environment. Virtually all of what is discussed is immediately relevant to enhancing communication competence in organizations. After all, "an organization itself may be viewed as a group of groups" (Haslett et al., 1992, p. 103). Work is often performed in teams (subsystems) within the larger organizational system, a subject for later discussion in Chapter 6.

In summary, groups are systems. The three main elements of a system are interconnectedness of parts, adaptability to change, and the influence of size. A small group is defined in terms of function, and the ideal size for most decision-making and problem-solving groups is the smallest group capable of performing the task effectively. Having now laid the theoretical foundation for analyzing small groups, I will discuss the process of group development in the next chapter. ● ●

Questions for Critical Thinkers

1. How does the effect of a disruptive group member demonstrate the interconnectedness element of a system?
2. In groups that you belong to, what boundaries are erected?
3. Have you experienced group boundaries that are too rigid in any groups in which you belong? How can you tell that the boundaries are too rigid?
4. What's the largest group that you've ever belonged to that didn't experience serious problems because of its size?

InfoTrac College Edition

Log onto InfoTrac College Edition.

1. Type "group size" in the search window. Choose an article to critique. SUGGESTIONS: (a) Article A75950671, "The influence of group size on children's competitive behavior" by Joyce F. Benenson, Catherine Nicholson, Angela Waite, Rosanne Roy, and Anna Simpson; (b) Article A55877231, "Interactions on an elementary school playground: Variations by age, gender, group size, and playground area" by Tracey E. Lewis and Leslie C. Phillipsen; and (c) Article A19532473, "The impact of group size and proportion of shared information on the exchange and integration of information in groups" by Michael G. Cruz, Franklin J. Boster, and Jose I. Rodriguez.
2. Type "change" in the search window. Choose an article to critique. SUGGESTIONS: (a) Article A89436078, "Seven keys to making change work for you" (no author given) and (b) Article A86650422, "Who moved my beer?" by Karl Edmunds.

Video Case Studies

October Sky (1999). Drama; PG-13; ****

This is the fact-based story of Homer Hickam, a West Virginia coal miner's son who becomes a rocket scientist. Analyze the four "rocket boys" as a system. Consider all three main elements of a system: interconnectedness of parts, adaptability to change, and influence of size.

What's Cooking (2000). Comedy/Drama; PG-13; ***1/2

Four multicultural families are unexpectedly interconnected in this story of conflict surrounding Thanksgiving celebrations. Conduct a systems analysis of each family.

Miracle (2004). Drama; PG; ***1/2

Faithful and involving re-creation of the 1980 "Miracle on Ice" performed by the U.S. Olympic hockey team when they defeated a far more talented team from the Soviet Union and went on to capture the gold medal. Focus your analysis on synergy and boundary control. Were there any difficult group members?

3 Group Development

O N APRIL 24, 1997, the board of directors for Delta Air Lines announced the unanimous decision not to renew the contract of Delta's chairman, Ronald Allen. Despite helping to pull Delta out of a tailspin in the early 1990s, during which heavy financial losses were recorded, Allen was forced out because, as one board member put it, there was "an accumulation of abrasions over time" (Brannigan, 1997, p. A8). So what were these "abrasions" that led the board to replace Allen despite Delta's turnaround from near financial collapse? In a memo released to Delta employees, the board, without making direct reference to Allen, stated that it placed "a high value on Delta's culture of respect, unity and deep regard for our heritage." The board went on to say that it intended "to select a person as our next leader who will work well within this culture we all value so highly" (cited in Brannigan, 1997, p. A8). Ronald Allen clearly did not engender respect, unity, and a deep regard for the worker-friendly, family atmosphere valued by the board.

Allen had a caustic management style that concentrated on the financial "bottom line" at the expense of relationships with workers. He developed a reputation for berating employees in front of other workers. He was known as autocratic, intolerant, and harsh (Brannigan, 1997). When Hollis Harris revealed to Allen that he was resigning as Delta's president to head Continental Airlines, Allen demanded that Harris relinquish the keys to his company car on the spot, leaving him stranded without transportation home. Allen cut thousands of jobs. Employees were extremely upset with this cost-cutting measure and the heavy-handed way in which it was done. Allen acknowledged that workers were upset with his slash-and-burn tactics, but his glib response was "so be it." Soon, buttons reading "So Be It" began appearing on the chests of pilots, flight attendants, and mechanics. Worker morale plunged. An exodus of senior managers began. Many experienced workers were laid off or quit. Delta service, once the envy of the airline industry, rapidly deteriorated. Dirty planes and frustrated flight attendants became the norm. On-time performance of flights sank from the top to the bottom of the industry. Passengers began joking that Delta stood for "**D**oesn't **E**ver **L**eave **T**he **A**irport." Tough measures were necessary to save Delta when Allen took over, but, as Wayne Horvitz, a Washington, D.C., labor relations consultant notes, "You don't have to be an SOB to be tough" (Brannigan, 1997, p. A1). Allen had "broken the spirit" of this once proud company. His narrow focus on the task of returning Delta to profitability ignored the vital role interpersonal relations play in group success.

This example highlights the strong connection between the task and social dimensions of groups. Put simply, how group members are treated and the quality of their relationships within a group can markedly affect task accomplishment. As groups move through phases of development, this relationship between these two key dimensions of every group can become a critical factor in achieving success or experiencing failure. **The primary purpose of this chapter is to explore this interconnectedness of task and social dimensions through phases of group development.** There are three related chapter objectives:

1. to explain the connection between task and social dimensions of a group,
2. to discuss task and social dimensions within the periodic phases of group development, and
3. to discuss how newcomers affect task and social dimensions of groups, with strategies offered for newcomer acceptance into groups.

Primary Dimensions of Groups

▶ **Focus Questions**

1. How do the task and social dimensions of groups interconnect?
2. How are the task and social dimensions integral to both the formation and development of decision-making groups?
3. How does a group build cohesiveness?

The Ronald Allen case study illustrates the importance of social relations on group performance and effectiveness. This is not a unidirectional process, however. Social relations in groups affect the task, but the reverse is also true. In this section, the interconnection between the two primary dimensions of groups, task and social, are explored.

TASK AND SOCIAL DIMENSIONS: WORKING AND SOCIALIZING

All decision-making groups have both task and social dimensions. The **task dimension** is the work performed by the group. The **social dimension** is the relationships that form between members in the group and their impact on the group as a whole. Because groups are systems, the task and social dimensions are interconnected. Thus, degree of concern for a task affects the social or relationship aspects.

Conversely, degree of concern for relationships in the group affects the accomplishment of the task.

The output from a group's task dimension is productivity. **Productivity** is the result of the efficient and effective accomplishment of a group task. **The output from the social dimension is cohesiveness.** **Cohesiveness** is the degree to which members feel a part of the group, wish to stay in the group, and are committed to each other and to the group's work (Lanfred, 1998; Wech et al., 1998). Cohesiveness is produced primarily by attention to social relationships.

Neither the task nor the social dimension can be ignored for a decision-making group to be successful. Too much attention to productivity can diminish cohesiveness by producing stress and conflict. Ronald Allen's single-minded focus on the task of returning Delta Air Lines to profitability disrupted the interpersonal harmony within the company. This disruption ultimately led to poor service, diminished worker morale, loss of valuable employees, and a negative image within the industry and among passengers. Conversely, too much emphasis on cohesiveness can produce a group of socializers who like each other a great deal but accomplish nothing in particular (see Closer Look: "The Case of Hormones with Feet"). This is a problem unless, of course, the purpose of the group is merely to have a good time and no task needs to be accomplished, in which case knock yourself out.

In general, cohesiveness enhances group productivity unless overemphasized (Evans & Dion, 1991; Gammage et al., 2001). This relationship, however, is stronger in small groups than in larger ones, for ongoing natural groups than for artificially created groups, and for cooperative groups than for competitive groups (Klein, 1996). The nature of the task also affects the relationship between cohesiveness and productivity. The more interdependent group members must be to accomplish a task (e.g., flying a passenger jet, performing surgery, playing team basketball) the stronger is the cohesiveness–productivity relationship (Gully et al., 1995).

BUILDING COHESIVENESS: BRINGING US TOGETHER

So how do groups build cohesiveness? The main strategies are:

1. *Encourage compatible membership.* When group members enjoy each other's company and share an attraction for one another, cohesiveness can be easily built. When difficult, disruptive individuals join the group, cohesiveness can suffer. Of course, a group doesn't always have the luxury of choosing who can join. Sometimes membership is mandated from outside (e.g., by an institution or corporation).

2. *Develop shared goals.* One aspect of cohesiveness is sharing a common vision. When all group members are pulling together to achieve a goal valued by all, cohesiveness increases.

CLOSER LOOK

THE CASE OF "HORMONES WITH FEET"

ANXIOUS TO MAKE FRIENDS and not infrequently hopeful that romance is in the offing, students preparing group symposium presentations in my classes often become sidetracked. They devote disproportionate energy toward cultivating interpersonal relationships at the expense of the group's overall performance. Sometimes this involves only certain members, and other times the total membership becomes involved in pursuing a good time at the expense of task accomplishment.

I would never wish to thwart burgeoning romance nor interfere with blossoming friendship, but there is a time and place for everything. I still remember with some amusement the couple in one group a few years back who aptly illustrated Mark Twain's definition of an adolescent as "hormones with feet." This couple's group was desperately attempting to put together a symposium presentation on some issue of national importance. Meanwhile, these overheated lovers were fixated with each other. Their conversation gushed with honey-coated affection. Meaningful squeezes, tender hugs, starry-eyed gazes, the entire repertoire of longing for each other was amply demonstrated for all to observe.

I'm confident that you can predict the reaction of other group members to this overt display of adolescent behavior. At first, group members were uncomfortable, and then mildly amused, irritated, exasperated, and finally just plain hostile. Two group members self-absorbed in promoting a social relationship while ignoring the task at hand can seriously undermine the entire group's ability to function productively. In other circumstances, I am certain the entire group membership would have applauded this couple's newly discovered love for each other. In this particular context, however, members viewed the couple's behavior as disruptive. This couple did not exhibit communication competence. Both individuals showed insensitivity to the needs of the group, a pronounced Me-orientation, and no commitment to group goals. They put their agenda ahead of the group's.

When whole groups decide that it is better to socialize than to work, task accomplishment obviously suffers. It is not unusual for a group to waste valuable time socializing with each other, only to realize too late that deadlines are fast approaching and sufficient work has not been completed.

Questions for Thought

1. How do you know when the group as a whole has become excessively social?
2. Have you experienced a similar case of over-socializing to the detriment of task accomplishment?

3. *Accomplish tasks.* Productive groups usually become more cohesive as a result of task accomplishment. If group members feel good about work accomplished, this often pulls the group together and promotes team spirit. As a rule, successful teams exhibit harmony. Unsuccessful teams, however, frequently manifest frustration and disappointment by sniping, sniveling, and finger-pointing (Van Oostrum & Rabbie, 1995). Poor productivity can lead to group disintegration.

4. *Develop a positive history of cooperation.* If group members work together cooperatively rather than competitively, cohesiveness can flourish (Klein, 1996). Constructing cooperation in small groups is discussed in Chapter 4.

5. *Promote acceptance of group members.* Make each other feel valued and welcomed in the group. Make an effort to engage in friendly conversation.

The task and social dimensions are integral to both the formation and development of decision-making groups. Just where these two dimensions fit into the life of a group can be ascertained by exploring the periodic phases of group development.

Periodic Phases of Group Development

Tuckman (1965) describes the four phases of group development as forming, storming, norming, and performing (see also Wheelan et al., 2003). These phases, however, should not be viewed as sequential. Groups do not necessarily pass through these phases of development in linear fashion like a person does when growing older (i.e., youth, middle age, old age). Groups tend to be far messier than this, sometimes cycling back around to a previous phase that was seemingly completed (Hare, 1994). (Unhappily, such cycling back is not possible with aging.)

Admittedly, group development can be classified in terms of an initial phase where individuals join together for some reason (forming), a tension phase (storming), a standards and rules of conduct for members phase (norming), and a phase where effort is targeted toward goal achievement (performing). These phases, however, can be periodic, meaning that they are apt to appear, disappear, reappear, and even overlap. Forming, storming, norming, and performing are also global phases of group development relevant to groups in general, large or small. Specific phases relevant to the process of decision emergence in small groups are discussed in Chapter 8.

▶ **Focus Questions**

1. Does why we join a group make any difference to the group?
2. Is tension in a group undesirable?
3. Where do group norms come from? Why do we conform to group norms?
4. Under what conditions do groups outperform individuals?

FORMING: WHY WE JOIN GROUPS

The reasons we join groups act as catalysts for group formation. We join groups to satisfy some need (Shaw, 1981). This need satisfaction divides into six principal categories discussed in this section.

Need to Belong: No One's an Island Humans are communal beings. We have a powerful need to belong, one that is as much an imperative as the need for food. This innate need is universal, not specific to any culture (Baumeister & Leary, 1995). It has survival value for humans. Forming social bonds with group members can provide protection from outside threats to one's person and possessions. Group membership can stave off the "lethal poison" of chronic loneliness (Lynch, 2000). We find mates by joining groups (e.g., Parents Without Partners), and we satisfy our desire for affection from family and groups of friends. American culture lauds individualism, but, as evolutionary biologist George Gaylord Simpson (1994) observes, "The quest to be alone is indeed a futile one, never successfully followed in the history of life." Joining a group provides an opportunity to satisfy our deep need to belong.

Interpersonal Attraction: The Drawing Power of Others We join a group because we are drawn to its members. We seem drawn to others who are similar in personality, attitudes and beliefs, ethnic origin, sexual orientation, and economic status (Aboud & Mendelson, 1998; Berscheid & Reis, 1998). Many campus clubs and support groups are attractive because of member similarity. Physical attractiveness may also draw us to join a group. We may have no other reason to join a group than that we'd like to get to know a particular attractive group member. Although there is a popular belief that physical attractiveness is more important to men than it is to women as a factor influencing interpersonal attraction, reviews of hundreds of studies show otherwise (Langlois et al., 2000).

Attraction to Group Activities: Joining for Fun and Frolic Sometimes we join groups to participate in the group's activities. This is a primary motivation for joining most college athletic teams, fraternities, and sororities. Joining a group because you are attracted to the group's activities doesn't preclude the additional draw from social connection among members. When I coached intercollegiate debate, students joined primarily for the competition. Secondary motivations, however, developed along the way, such as traveling around the country, cultivating friendships, falling in love, and engaging in the inevitable social activities that are attached to debating. Softball leagues are frequently rated A, B, and C so the hard-core athletes can be separated from the Budweiser crowd. Some players are drawn to the physical activity, and others are drawn more to the social activities.

Attraction to Group Goals: A Purpose-Driven Membership Another reason why we join groups and wish to remain as members is an attraction to the group's goals. Political groups gain members because individuals are drawn to the cause or the candidate. We join most volunteer groups because we are attracted to the groups' goals.

When you join a group for a worthy cause, you don't have the luxury of interacting only with members that you'd enjoy inviting to dinner. You're stuck adapting to the various personalities and quirks of fellow members. Your commitment to the goal of the group, however, may be enough to keep you coming back.

Establishment of Meaning and Identity: Groups-R-Us We sometimes join groups to make sense of our world. Consider cults, for instance. Making sense of the world is the fundamental basis of cult conversions. Individuals who join cults are in the throes of an identity crisis. They are searching for meaning in their lives, and cults offer such meaning and identity. Social psychologist George Cvetkovich notes that studies of ex-cult members reveal that 75% are recruited during an identity crisis and 25% had always been in an identity crisis (cited in Valdez, 1983, p. 7). When situations are ambiguous, and we're looking for answers, we often join groups as a means of better understanding ourselves, our world, and others who cross our paths (Goethals & Darley, 1987). A study of youth violence by former Massachusetts Commissioner of Public Health Deborah Prothrow-Stith (1991) draws this comparison between antisocial groups such as gangs and prosocial groups such as fraternities: "They provide young people with goals and objectives, a world view, and a place where they are valued (p. 97)." Personal and group identity merge.

Fulfillment of Unrelated Needs: Our Miscellaneous Reasons Finally, we join groups to satisfy needs that are unrelated to the group's task, goals, members, or even our desire to belong. We may become group members to enhance our résumé or establish business contacts. Sometimes we join a group because other members familiar to us have joined, removing some of the uncertainty associated with group formation (Arrow & Crosson, 2003). In some cases we are told by persons in authority to join a group. You may be summoned for jury duty. It is wise to comply. The instructor of your class may put you into a group of people who interest you very little. If you are pragmatic, you will make the best of a less-than-satisfactory situation because your grade may depend on it.

The reasons individuals join groups have noticeable effects on the productivity and cohesiveness of those groups. If they join because they are attracted to the other members, the likelihood of cohesiveness in the group is certainly more probable than if they join to meet self-oriented needs. If they join because they are attracted to the group's goals, productivity is likely to be enhanced. If they join groups

▶ ● ● SECOND LOOK

WHY WE JOIN GROUPS
- Need to belong
- Interpersonal attraction (we are drawn to members of the group)
- Attraction to the activities of the group
- Attraction to group goals
- Establishment of meaning and identity
- Attraction to the fulfillment of needs outside of the group

for personal gain only, they'll likely end up as deadweight and drag down the entire group.

The competent communicator can show sensitivity to the needs of the group during the forming phase in the following ways (J. Andersen, 1988):

1. *Express positive attitudes and feelings.* Avoid disagreement and disagreeableness. This phase is the getting-acquainted stage of group development. This is not an appropriate time to be deviant (e.g., displaying embarrassing lapses in social etiquette, making abrasive remarks or provocative statements, or wearing outrageous dress). Don't put your foot in your mouth. Put your best foot forward.
2. *Appear friendly, open, and interested.* Be approachable by establishing eye contact with group members, initiating conversation, and responding warmly to interactions from others.

STORMING: FEELING THE TENSION

All groups experience some social tension because change in any system can be an ordeal. Tension can be a positive force. We are usually at our best when we experience some tension. Athletes perform best when they find the proper balance between complete relaxation and crippling anxiety. Excessive tension, however, can produce damaging conflict that may split the group apart. The relative absence of tension in a group can result in lethargy, haphazard attention to the task, and weak productivity. **Finding both the level of tension that solidifies the group and effectively managing group tension are important factors in successful group development.**

There are two types of social tension: primary and secondary (Bormann, 1990). All long-term groups experience both types.

Primary Tension: Initial Uneasiness When you first gather in a group, you normally feel some jitters and uneasiness called **primary tension.** Instructors meeting classes for the first time usually experience some primary tension. When you initially meet roommates, classmates, or teammates, primary tension occurs. Even groups that have a lengthy history can experience primary tension at the outset of every meeting. This is especially true if groups such as the PTA, homeowners associations, or Student Senate meet infrequently.

There are many signs of primary tension. Group members may become cautious and hesitant in their communication. Long periods of uncomfortable silence and tentative statements are all indicators of primary tension. Group members are often overly polite and careful to avoid controversy. Interruptions normally invoke immediate apologies.

Primary tension is a natural dynamic of group life. In most instances it tends to be short-lived and cause for little concern. With time, you become comfortable with the group and your primary tension diminishes. **Joking, laughing, and chatting about your interests, experiences, and beliefs on noncontroversial subjects all serve to reduce primary tension.** You're not trying to "Free Tibet," "Save the Whales," or "Convert the Unbelievers." Your purpose is to become acquainted with other group members. As you get to know each other better, there is less perceived threat and, consequently, less primary tension.

If a group is too anxious to get down to business and foregoes the small talk, however, primary tension is likely to create an atmosphere of formality, stiffness, and insecurity. Communication will be stilted and hesitant. The ability of the group to work on a task will be hindered by excessive and persistent primary tension.

Engaging in small talk to relieve primary tension has cultural variations. In the United States, we tend to view small talk as wasting time, especially if our primary focus is on a task (e.g., finalizing a business agreement). Many Asian (e.g., Japanese, Chinese, and Korean), Middle Eastern (e.g., Saudi Arabian), and Latin American (e.g., Mexican, Brazilian, and Chilean) cultures, however, view small talk as a necessary ritual engaged in over many cups of coffee or tea for several hours, or several meetings, during which the group's task may not even be mentioned (Samovar & Porter, 2004). Ethiopians attach prestige to tasks that require a great deal of time to complete. Lengthy small talk, viewed by most Americans anxious to do business as "doing nothing," is considered highly significant and purposeful.

Secondary Tension: Later Stress and Strain The stress and strain that occur within the group later in its development is called **secondary tension.** Having to make decisions produces secondary tension. Disagreements and conflicts—storming—inevitably emerge when group members struggle to define their status and roles in the group. Tight deadlines for task completion can induce tension. Whatever the causes, you should expect some secondary tension in a long-term group. Low levels of secondary tension may mean that the group is highly harmonious. It may also mean that group members are unmotivated, apathetic, and bored.

Signs of secondary tension include a sharp outburst, a sarcastic barb, hostile and antagonistic exchanges between members, or shouting matches. Extreme secondary tension is unpleasant for the group. If it is left uncontrolled, the group's existence may be threatened.

Secondary tension has become an issue in jury deliberations (Finkelstein, 2001). This is particularly true in cases involving controversial statutes such as "three strikes" and death penalty laws. Even in relatively minor cases, however, secondary tension can produce juror warfare. For example, during a Manhattan, New York, jury deliberation involving a man charged with selling a $10 bag of heroin, jurors yelled at each other, and after 4 days of antagonistic debate a note was sent to the judge complaining about the lone holdout juror. It read: "Tension is high, nerves are frayed and all minds are not sound" (Finkelstein, 2001). In other instances, court officers have broken up fistfights, jurors have flung chairs through windows, and some jurors have screamed so loudly that they could be heard on other floors of the courthouse. Jurors have been caught wandering away from the jury room, and in one case a juror tried to escape the deliberations permanently by leaping off the jury bus. Courts all around the United States have begun providing booklets to jurors detailing how to deliberate while remaining courteous and even-tempered.

The goal is not to eliminate secondary tension in groups. Most decision-making groups experience secondary tension. Within tolerable limits, such tension can be a positive force. **Tension can energize a group, challenge the members to think creatively, and bring the group together.** Trying to avoid or to camouflage secondary tension, however, merely tricks us into believing that the group is functioning well. Beneath the surface, the group may be disintegrating or the decisions coming from the group may be ill conceived, even disastrous.

The real challenge facing competent communicators is to manage secondary tension within tolerable limits. But how do we know when tension exceeds the limits? There is no mathematical formula for such a determination. Some groups can tolerate a great deal of disagreement and conflict. Other groups are more vulnerable to disintegration because members are more thin-skinned or insecure and view disagreements as personal repudiations and attacks.

A group's inability to accomplish tasks and to maintain a satisfying social climate is a general rule of thumb for determining excessive tension in a group (G. Wilson & Hanna, 1990). In a Los Angeles trial of defendants charged with seriously beating a trucker named Reginald Denny, jurors clearly experienced excessive tension. One juror was dismissed by the judge at the request of the other 11 exasperated jurors for "failure to deliberate." One female member of the sequestered jury became so upset about not being able to see her boyfriend that she ran down a hallway of the courthouse yelling, "I can't take it anymore" (Kramer, 1993, p. 1A). The judge gave jurors the weekend off from their deliberations to recharge their batteries and to reduce the tension so they could finish their task.

A competent communicator can handle secondary tension as follows (J. Andersen, 1988):

1. *Tolerate, even encourage, disagreement.* Suppressing differences of opinion will likely increase tension and exacerbate conflict. The trick is to keep the disagreement within tolerable limits. One way to do this is to focus the disagreements on the task (unless, of course, the conflict is social in nature). Resist the temptation to drift into irrelevant side issues, especially contentious ones.
2. *Keep a civil tongue.* Disagree without being disagreeable. You want to foster a cooperative, not a competitive, atmosphere for discussion. You can express opinions with conviction and exuberance without going psycho on those who do not agree with you.
3. *Be an active listener.* Encourage all group members to express their opinions and feelings. Clarify significant points that are confusing. Resist the temptation to interrupt, especially if this produces defensive behavior from group members. Make an honest effort to understand the point of view that is in opposition to your own.

There are numerous sources of conflict within a group that raise the level of tension. Reasons for stormy transactions in groups and strategies for effectively managing them will be discussed in greater detail in later chapters. For now, recognize that conflict and tension are a normal part of the group experience. Dealing with tension may be smooth sailing for some groups and white-water rafting for others.

NORMING: REGULATING THE GROUP

In groups, rules that establish standards of appropriate behavior are called **norms.** In this section, types of norms, their purpose and development, and conformity and nonconformity to norms are discussed.

Types of Norms: Explicit and Implicit There are two types of norms: explicit and implicit. **Explicit norms** are rules that expressly identify acceptable behavior. Such rules are codified in constitutions and bylaws of fraternal organizations, religious orders, and the like. All laws in our society act as explicit norms. Most norms in small groups, however, are not so obvious. **Implicit norms** are rules that are indirectly indicated by uniformities in the behavior and expressed attitudes of members.

A college seminar illustrates the difference between explicit and implicit norms. If participating in a seminar qualifies as a new experience for you, group norms could be determined in several ways. Usually, the professor teaching the seminar will provide a syllabus explicitly specifying what students are expected to do during the term. Such norms as "Refrain from tardiness and absenteeism," "All assignments must be turned in on time," "All papers must be typed—no exceptions," and "Active participation in class discussions is expected" are some of the possible explicit rules.

The implicit rules for the seminar class might be such things as "Don't interrupt the professor when he or she is speaking," "Sit in chairs stationed around the rectangular table," "Be polite when disagreeing with classmates," and "Don't hide the professor's notes, even in jest" (it happens). These norms are ascertained by observing the behavior of your classmates and the professor.

Purpose and Sources of Norms: Achieving Group Goals **The general purpose of norms is to achieve group goals.** Consider the group Overeaters Anonymous (Shimanoff, 1992). Change (i.e., losing weight) is regulated by rules, one of which is that members are permitted to talk about food only in generic terms (carbohydrates, protein, etc.) but not in terms of specific foods (Twinkies, burgers, cookies). The rule is based on the assumption that references to particular foods will stimulate a craving for those foods and make goal achievement more difficult, while references to foods in generic terms will produce no such cravings. Apparently you won't hear the refrigerator calling your name when merely talking about carbohydrates, but mention Häagen-Dazs and there better be a clear path to the Frigidaire or someone is going to get trampled.

The norming process takes place almost immediately in groups. When a group is formed, members cast about trying to determine what behavior will be acceptable and what will be unacceptable. Part of the primary tension in a group may stem from this concern for proper group etiquette.

There are three principal sources of norms in small groups. **The first source of norms is from systems outside the small group.** Standards of excellence and specific norms of performance for work teams within organizations often are externally influenced by management outside of the team (Sundstrom et al., 1990). Charters and bylaws of local chapters of fraternal organizations, therapeutic groups, and others are usually set by parent organizations or agencies.

A second source of small group norms is the influence of a single member. Research shows that a single person can influence the group to accept higher standards of behavior and performance than would exist without the influence of this member. Even when that influential member leaves the group, the norm typically remains (MacNeil & Sherif, 1976). Sometimes these influential individuals are designated group leaders and sometimes they are newcomers joining an established group.

A third source of small group norms is the group itself (Jetten et al., 1996). Small group norms most often develop from transactions within the group. Sometimes this is explicitly negotiated (e.g., juries deciding what procedures will be used to arrive at a verdict), but most often it emerges implicitly from trial and error ("Oops, the group is looking at me like I just suggested euthanizing all family pets; guess I shouldn't share every thought that comes into my head.").

Degree of Conformity: Strength of Group Pressure Solomon Asch (1955) found that when a group composed of confederates of the experimenter unanimously judged the length of a line incorrectly, naive participants unaware of the setup chose the obviously erroneous group judgment 35% of the time. Most of these same participants (75%) conformed to the group error at least once during the study. Social psychologist Anthony Pratkanis of the University of California Santa Cruz replicated this study for *Dateline NBC* in August 1997. In his study, 9 of 16 college students studied fell in line with the unanimous choice made by 6 other group members, even though the choice was clearly incorrect. Ironically, one participant interviewed beforehand characterized himself as a nonconformist. During the study he conformed earlier and more often than any other student. **Conformity** is the adherence to group norms by group members, in this case "following the crowd" by choosing the wrong answer.

Although the degree of conformity in the United States is fairly high (Baron et al., 1996; Jetten et al., 1996), **it is significantly higher in other cultures.** A review of 133 conformity studies found significantly higher rates of conformity in collectivist cultures compared to individualist cultures (R. Bond & Smith, 1996). This, of course, makes sense. Collectivist cultures place greater emphasis on group harmony and on individuals blending into groups than do individualist cultures.

The serious negative consequences of conformity can be seen from a Harvard School of Public Health study of binge drinking (cited in Kalb & McCormick, 1998). Defined as "five or more drinks at one sitting for men, and four or more drinks for women," the study found that almost half of college students in the United States binge drink. More than 80% of students living in fraternities and sororities report binge drinking. Aside from the health risks, binge drinking diminishes sound judgment. In the Harvard study, 37% of binge drinkers reported that they had done something they regretted afterwards (e.g., argued with friends, engaged in unprotected sex). Drinking to excess is encouraged by group norms. A Zogby International poll reported that 56% of 1,005 college students surveyed felt group pressure to drink ("Poll," 2000).

Conformity isn't always a negative experience. Group pressure can be applied for pro-social reasons. At Shaker Heights High School in Ohio, a group of black upperclassmen dressed in shirts and ties march conspicuously down the hallway to the auditorium, where underachieving black underclassmen wait to explain their poor

© Barbara Stitzer/Photo Edit

Stockbyte/Getty Images

Conformity to norms, in this case the style of dress, is found in all cultures and groups to some degree.

© A. Ramey/Photo Edit

grades. "You think Ds and Fs are funny?" a senior says to a grinning 15-year-old student. "This is mediocre," claims another, flashing a report card in front of a clearly uncomfortable underclassman. The Minority Achievement Committee (MAC), a group of high-achieving African American male students, is working to establish the norm that being smart and doing well in school is cool, not "acting white." Junior Justin Taylor reflects the committee's point of view, "What, only white people study? That's just plain stupid and insulting" (Clemetson, 1999, p. 37). Students must earn at least a 2.8 GPA to gain membership into the MAC. Weekly MAC meetings begin with a firm handshake and the MAC credo, "I pledge to uphold the name of the African American man. I will do so by striving for academic excellence." Raji Bey, a senior, comments on the MAC effort, "These guys have the grades, the respect *and* the girls. Who wouldn't want to be like them?" (Clemetson, 1999, p. 37). Cullen Buie, a MAC scholar, puts it this way, "We create positive peer pressure. We make success seem like something real" (p. 37). According to the Minority Student Achievement Network, this highly regarded peer-mentoring program has been expanded to include female students ("District Updates," 2004).

Why We Conform: Fitting In So why do we conform to norms, especially in a society as individualistic as the United States? We conform for two principal reasons. First, **we conform to norms to be *liked*. We want social acceptance, support, companionship, and recognition** (Baumeister & Leary, 1995; Cotterell et al., 1992). We must "go along to get along." (See Closer Look: "High School Cliques.") Loyalty to the group is manifested in conformity to group norms and is rewarded with approval from the members. Norms create solidarity with group members. Our natural desire to belong and to be liked makes such solidarity attractive. Individual goals, such as making friends or increasing social activities, can be satisfied by conforming to group norms. As Walter Kirn (1997) notes, college students don't usually binge drink just to get drunk and feel the buzz, "They think they are doing something more meaningful: vowing their loyalty to new friends, winning the respect of others, building a zany memory they'll cherish. Fraternities and selective social clubs exploit students' desperate hunger to fit in" (p. A11).

Second, **we conform to norms because we want to be *right*** (Baron et al., 1996). Acting incorrectly can be embarrassing and humiliating. Group norms identify correct behavior. In this case, we may not want to be liked by group members as much as we want to avoid social disapproval by being ridiculed or harassed. Few people enjoy appearing to be a fool.

Conditions for Conformity: When We Bow to Group Pressure There is greater conformity to group norms when certain conditions exist. First and foremost, **the**

CLOSER LOOK

HIGH SCHOOL CLIQUES: A LESSON IN CONFORMITY

WHEN THE SCHOOL LUNCH BELL rings at high schools across the country, kids pour out of their classrooms and almost instantly sort themselves into small groups or cliques. In a field investigation of cliques at three Santa Cruz county, California, high schools, students split into a myriad of small groups—jocks, preps, dirts, surfers, skaters, Goths, nerds, and a variety of ethnic groupings (Townsend, 1999b). We all remember cliques in high school. For some of you it may still be a fresh memory.

Students join cliques because the pressure to belong, to be accepted by peers, is intense. In some cases, the outcasts rejected by more established cliques form their own group. As one girl at Soquel High School revealed, "We're outcasts, but at least we're outcasts together" (Townsend, 1999b, p. A8). As Margarita Azmitia, professor of developmental psychology at University of California Santa Cruz notes, "Some kids don't want to be in deviant cliques, but that's their only option" (Townsend, 1999b, p. A8). The clique gives them an identity, and some protection from harassment by more favored cliques on campus.

High school cliques typically divide into a competitive hierarchy, with jocks on top and nerds on the bottom. This competitive hierarchy often leads to in-group versus out-group hostility. Name-calling, threats, water balloons, and food rain down on those who belong to the less popular cliques.

"They throw stuff at us all the time" says one 18-year-old male student, indicating a collection of surfers, jocks, and popular kids. "I've had yogurt thrown at me, apples, oranges," says another student dressed entirely in black. "They call me dirt, faggot, queer" (Townsend, 1999b, p. A1). A student athlete, one of the popular kids at Aptos High School, looks across the open quad where cliques have fanned out like ripples on a pond and says, "I hate 'em, I don't care." Another jock adds, "They smell . . . and they don't wear shoes." A 15-year-old female student expresses her anguish regarding the abuse heaped on her by competing cliques, "A lot of people yell at us. They say, 'You freak of nature. You Satanist.' We've had people harass us to tears. I've come back crying. They yell, 'Go back to hell, no one wants you.' It hurts." "It's almost as bad as racism," says an 18-year-old male student who is one of the objects of jock derision. "We are who we are, and we can't be someone else" (Townsend, 1999b, p. A8). Misery loves miserable company, so the outcasts and the derided join cliques for identity and for self-protection.

Conformity to the norms of the clique is strong. At least there is some protection from harassment when you aren't facing it alone. Some students are so desperate to fit in that they will do almost anything to gain membership and to remain in a clique. Professor Azmitia explains that cliques are typically only 10–12 members in size. This sets up an intense competition to get into the cliques, especially the most favored ones, and to remain members once admitted. Even minor deviance from clique norms, such as wearing the wrong clothes, hanging with someone from an outcast clique, or missing a clique party can get a member ousted. As a ninth grader at Aptos High confessed, "I wasn't comfortable with myself, so I tried to conform. I felt pressure to look a certain way. To party, to use drugs and alcohol." She would get "weird looks" when she wore a colorful scarf wrapped around her short blond hair. "They were too uptight about everything" (Townsend, 1999b, p. A8). Eventually she left her popular clique, but she quickly joined an outcast group.

Cliques can provide social acceptance, support, companionship, and recognition for members. Friendships can blossom from participation in cliques. Nevertheless, cliques can also encourage blind, desperate conformity, especially when intergroup competition erupts into hostility and abuse.

Questions for Thought

1. Do you remember your experiences with cliques? Were your experiences mostly positive or negative?
2. Did you experience an intense pressure to conform as a clique member? Did intergroup rivalry exist that produced harassment of members from other cliques?
3. Are there ethical issues involved in joining cliques and rejecting others from joining? Apply the five criteria for ethical communication discussed in Chapter 1.

stronger the cohesiveness in the group, the greater is the conformity to group norms (Prapavessis & Carron, 1997). The relationship between cohesiveness and conformity is hardly surprising. Cohesiveness, by definition, is the degree of attraction we have to a group and our desire to be a member. If there is minimal attraction to the group and nebulous desire to be a member, then there is scant reason to adhere to the rules of behavior. A group has little leverage against apathetic or scornful members. Conversely, individuals who are strongly attracted to the group and wish to remain members in good standing are much more likely to conform and to bow to pressure for uniformity of opinion and behavior. (See Closer Look: "Hazing Rituals.")

Second, **conformity increases as the task importance increases** (Baron et al., 1996). When accurately performing the group task assumes great importance, we tend to conform even when other group members confess to a general lack of confidence in the accuracy of their own judgments (Baron et al., 1996).

Third, **conformity is greater when individuals expect to be group members for a long time** (M. Smith, 1982). After all, you must live with this group. Why make

CLOSER LOOK

HAZING RITUALS: FROM WATER TORTURE TO LIVER SWALLOWING

IN THE WEE HOURS of the morning of February 2, 2005, Matthew Carrington, a student at Chico State University in northern California, was pronounced dead from a fraternity hazing ritual that turned lethal (M. May, 2005). Carrington died from hyponatremia, a deadly drop in sodium levels in the bloodstream caused by drinking massive quantities of water in a short period of time—in this case five gallons in a few hours. Pledging Chi Tau, a fraternity kicked off the Chico State campus in 2002 for serving alcohol to minors, Carrington was not the first college student to become a victim of this bizarre hazing ritual. Walter Dean Jennings, a freshman at the State University of New York, suffered the same fate in September 2003 while pledging the Psi Epsilon Chi fraternity (Foderaro, 2003). In Jennings's case, he was prodded into drinking water in such quantities that he would vomit. He endured this water torture on and off for 10 days before dying.

Recognizing the strong link between cohesiveness and conformity to norms, groups will sometimes go to dangerous extremes to foster cohesiveness. Hazing is an example. Hazing, or an initiation rite, is defined as "any humiliating or dangerous activity expected of you to join a group, regardless of your willingness to participate" (Hoover & Pollard, 2000, p. 2). According to an Alfred University national study of hazing, almost 2 million high school students, 48% of all students who join high school groups, are hazed. Of these 2 million students, more than 800,000 were hazed when they joined sports teams; almost 560,000 were hazed by a peer group or gang; almost 300,000 were hazed when they joined a music, art, or theater group; and almost 250,000 students were hazed when they joined a church group (Hoover & Pollard, 2000). A 1999 study of hazing in college conducted by Alfred University and the National Collegiate Athletic Association (NCAA) found that more than 80% of college athletes had experienced some form of hazing (cited in R. Myers, 2000).

Hazing purposely subjects prospective group members to a series of activities, often ludicrous and sometimes dangerous, designed to test the limits of physical exertion, psychological strain, and social embarrassment. The list of silly, stupid, dangerous, illegal, and even lethal activities actually required by some groups as a rite of passage into groups is long. Examples include forcing students to swallow quarter-pound hunks of raw liver slathered with oil; abandoning students on mountaintops or in remote areas in bitter cold conditions without suitable clothing; repeatedly punching the stomach and kidneys of students who forget parts of ritual incantations; incarcerating initiates in a locked storage closet for 2 days with only salty foods, no liquids, and only a small plastic cup to catch urine; requiring initiates to consume a mix-

▶

ture of urine, spoiled milk, and eggs; forcing initiates to steal; forcing initiates to abuse alcohol or illegal drugs; and requiring initiates to engage in unprotected sex or sex with multiple partners (Cialdini, 1993; Hoover & Pollard, 2000).

Dangerous hazing activities are prevalent among both high school students (22%) and college athletes (21%). Surprisingly, students in church groups were more apt to engage in dangerous hazing activities than students in most other groups except gangs, fraternities, and cheerleaders (Hoover & Pollard, 2000). Almost a quarter of high school students abused alcohol or illegal drugs during hazing, and half of college students did likewise (Hoover & Pollard, 2000). Almost three-quarters of students reported negative consequences from hazing, such as fighting, injuring themselves or others, arguing with parents, feeling angry or embarrassed, and losing sleep and appetite for food (Hoover & Pollard, 2000).

Hazing raises serious ethical questions. Is it respectful to treat those hazed by torturing, humiliating, and shaming them? Is endangering their lives responsible behavior even if the intentions are worthwhile? If membership in a highly desirable group is dependent on debasing oneself or engaging in high-risk or illegal activities, does this not remove choice from the equation? Hazing works to create group cohesiveness and conformity, but that's hardly the important point. Is it ethical?

Forty-four states have outlawed hazing ("State Anti-hazing Laws," 2005). Numerous colleges and universities have followed suit. Stopping hazing, however, is not easy. When Richard Swanson, a University of Southern California student, gagged on an oil-soaked hunk of liver, then choked to death before anyone could help him, the university applied stringent rules to initiation practices. Students rioted in protest. Outlawing hazing is more likely to drive it underground than to eliminate the practice.

Why do groups insist on such harsh and risky membership rituals? There are several reasons (Moreland & Levine, 1987). First, **the harder it is to get into a group, the greater will be the loyalty and commitment to the group once membership has been attained.** We tend to place greater value on that which is difficult to achieve than that which requires minimal effort (Prapavessis & Carron, 1997). The more severe the hazing ritual, the more desirable a group appears to be. In one experiment, the more electric shock a woman received as part of the hazing ritual, the more she convinced herself that the group and its activities were valuable, interesting, and desirable despite the clear effort of the experimenters to make the

▶

your life unpleasant by not conforming, particularly in job situations in which economic considerations may make job switching impractical? Melanie Singer, a Los Angeles Highway Patrol officer, was called to testify on behalf of the accused officers in the second Rodney King trial in 1993. She admitted on the witness stand that she didn't give medical assistance to the hogtied, bleeding King following his horrific beating by fellow officers because she didn't want her peers on the police force to

group appear uninteresting and worthless (Gerard & Mathewson, 1966). Another study of 54 tribal groups found that those with the most severe and difficult initiation rituals had the greatest group solidarity (Young, 1965).

If you had to swallow a slimy, oil-soaked slab of raw liver, freeze off the south side of your anatomy, or risk your life to gain membership, chances are quite good that you would slavishly conform to the norms of the group once you were admitted as a member. Deviance is not likely to emerge from a tight-knit group bonded by ordeals.

Second, **a harsh initiation provides the group with valuable information about the newcomers.** If newcomers refuse to be initiated, fail the initiation tasks, or participate in the rites of passage grudgingly, then this informs the group that such newcomers are not likely to fit in with the group. They probably will not conform to group norms.

Third, **a harsh initiation discourages newcomers who have a weak commitment to the group or have a half-hearted desire to join the group.** The sooner such individuals leave before becoming members, the less trouble they are likely to pose for group members. Troublemakers can destroy the cohesiveness of the group.

Fourth, **a harsh initiation may convince newcomers how dependent they are on longtime members (old-timers).** The old-timers make the decisions regarding who is granted membership and who is not. The old-timers must be convinced that the newcomers are worthy of that membership.

Questions for Thought

1. Have you ever participated in hazing, either as the perpetrator or the recipient? Was it for the reasons stated above?
2. Should hazing rituals, especially the high-risk ones, be outlawed? Would outlawing such practices ever stop them?
3. Are all hazing rituals unethical? Is it possible to have hazing rituals that are not dangerous, illegal, or abusive and still serve the purpose of creating cohesiveness and subsequent conformity in the group?

start heckling her ("Fearing Heckling," 1993). When your life's profession forces you to live with a certain group, you tend to conform to implicit norms of behavior even when your conscience may dictate otherwise.

Fourth, **conformity is greater when individuals perceive that they have somewhat lower status in the group than other members or that they are not completely accepted by the group** (M. Smith, 1982). Higher-status members have earned the right to dissent, but lower-status members must still earn that right to occasional nonconformity. Lower-status members also feel a greater need to prove themselves to the group, to show fealty.

Addressing Nonconformity: When Groups Get Tough Because behavior in groups is governed by rules, a violation of a norm can be quite disturbing for group members. Groups usually do not appreciate nonconformity except within fairly limited boundaries. There are four communication strategies groups typically use to command conformity from nonconforming members (Leavitt, 1964). These strategies tend to follow a sequential order, although there may be variation in some circumstances.

First, **group members attempt to *reason* with the deviant.** The quantity of talk aimed at the nonconformist initially increases substantially (Schachter, 1951). Groups show an intense interest in convincing nonconforming members of their folly. Clearly, groups expect their troublesome members to change their point of view and behavior.

Second, **if reason fails to sway a nonconforming member, a group will often try** *seduction.* This is usually a ploy to make the deviant feel guilty or uncomfortable because the group is made to look bad in the eyes of outsiders. Telling the nonconformist that his or her efforts are wasted and will accomplish nothing is another form of the seduction strategy. "You won't get anywhere anyway, so why cause such turmoil?" is the seduction strategy at work. Offers of promotions, perquisites, monetary incentives, and the like in exchange for conformity are other examples of seduction.

The third line of defense against nonconformists is *coercion.* This is where groups begin to get rough. Communication turns abusive and threatening. Groups attempt to force conformity by using nasty and unpleasant tactics. In one study, 55 whistle-blowers were followed over a period of several years (Glazer & Glazer, 1986). Whistle-blowers are individuals who expose to the light of public scrutiny such abuses as waste, fraud, corruption, and dangerous practices in corporations and organizations. In the study, coercive tactics against these whistle-blowers included threats of firing and sometimes actual terminations. In addition, some were transferred to undesirable jobs and locations, demoted, harassed, and intimidated by supervisors and peers. On December 10, 1993, CNN, reporting on a study of whistle-blowers, noted that 88% of whistle-blowers had suffered personal reprisals for their defiance. Workers file, on average, more than 2,000 complaints each year charging that they were fired, demoted, or penalized for reporting health and safety violations to employers or to the government (Pear, 1999). The movie *The Insider* dramatically depicts the true story of a tobacco-industry scientist who revealed the darkest secrets of his employers for the TV program *60 Minutes.* His whistle-blowing effort provoked danger for himself and his family.

The final stage of group pressure to induce conformity is *ostracism.* This strategy ignores or excludes a member by giving the silent treatment or isolating the member from social interaction with the group. It is a kind of social death that produces significant psychological pain (A. Smith & Williams, 2004). Ostracism is "an exceptionally potent form of social influence" (Williams et al., 2000, p. 760). A member's sense of belonging to the group is severed. When coercion doesn't gain conformity from whistle-blowers, for example, ostracism is often the next strategy used (Miceli & Near, 1992). When an opportunity arises to get back into the good graces of the group, members will often seize that opportunity by conforming to group norms (Williams & Sommer, 1997).

Studies show that even **cyberostracism,** a remote form of ostracism that occurs on the Internet, can be quite potent (A. Smith & Williams, 2004; Williams et al., 2000). Acts of cyberostracism occur when a group of online team members or chat room users deliberately ignore a member who violates the group's norms (e.g., by incorrect use of technology, straying from the topic, using profanity, flaming, etc.). Even when the ostracism isn't clearly deliberate, the negative effects occur.

Shannon Faulkner's effort under court order to become the first female cadet at the Citadel, a military academy in Charleston, South Carolina, illustrates coercion and ostracism in action. Faulkner was violating the long-standing norm of the institution: "No women allowed." In this instance, the way to regain group conformity was to

© Mitchell Smith/Corbis Sygma

Male cadets react to the news that Shannon Faulkner quit the Citadel. Standing against the group can be enormously difficult.

drive away Faulkner and any other woman contemplating enrolling at the Citadel, because barring their enrollment outright was illegal. Her mere presence disturbed male cadets. She became the campus leper. Faulkner was "booed, mooed, hissed at and scorned as 'Shrew Shannon' and 'Mrs. Doubtgender'" (Goldstein, 1994, p. 13A). Bumper stickers advocating "Save the Males" and "Shave Shannon's Head" appeared. Except for derision, Faulkner was given the silent treatment. One teacher observed that Faulkner was wise to sit in the front of her class so she couldn't see the looks from boys sitting behind her.

Those who defended Faulkner's attempt to crack the all-male brotherhood at the Citadel received similar treatment. Faulkner's mother, Sandra, a social studies teacher, was ostracized by some of her colleagues. Faulkner's father, Ed, saw his fence company business suffer. A black student, Von Mickle, defended Faulkner because it reminded him that African Americans were not welcome at the Citadel until 1966. He was "spoken to" by other students and was ridiculed in the student newspaper.

▶●● SECOND LOOK

THE NORMING PROCESS

TYPES OF NORMS
   Explicit—preferences and prohibitions specifically stated in some form
   Implicit—preferences and prohibitions determined from observation

SOURCES OF NORMS
   Other larger systems outside the small group
   Influence of a single member
   Transactions within the group

WHY GROUP MEMBERS CONFORM TO NORMS
   Desire to be liked
   Desire to be right

CONDITIONS FOR CONFORMITY TO NORMS
   The stronger the cohesiveness, the greater the conformity
   Greater conformity when individuals expect to be group members for a long time
   Greater conformity when individuals perceive they have lower status in groups

ADDRESSING NONCONFORMITY
   Reason
   Seduction
   Coercion
   Ostracism

Faulkner's attempt to become the first female graduate from the Citadel ultimately failed. She left the Citadel in her first week as a cadet. Other women, however, followed her lead and were successful.

The norming periodic phase of group development provides a structure for appropriate and effective communication. A competent communicator should do the following during the norming phase of group development to be appropriate and effective:

1. *Adapt communication to the norms of the group.* As previously noted, communication becomes inappropriate when, without sacrificing goals, violation of norms could be averted by more prudent action.
2. *Encourage change when norms are excessively rigid.* Norms are not sacrosanct. Some norms can be suffocatingly rigid—too closed to permit adaptation to change in the system. Norm rigidity fosters nonconformity and disruption. Violating the norm is one avenue of change if rational argument proves unsuccessful, but expect backlash from the group. Leaving the group is certainly an option. Failure to loosen norms from within may require intervention from without, such as court suits and protests.
3. *Encourage change when norms are too elastic.* Excessive openness in a system can be counterproductive. Apply the same guidelines for changing overly rigid norms.

PERFORMING: GROUP OUTPUT

If I had a dollar for every time I have been told that a camel is a horse designed by a committee, I'd be downing dark beers on a white sand beach in the tropics, enjoying a blissful state of very early retirement. Then there is the equally moth-eaten description of a committee as "a group of people who can do nothing individually but, as a group, can gather and decide that nothing can be done." Along the same line is this anonymous offering: "Trying to solve a problem through group discussion is like trying to clear up a traffic jam by honking your horn." Winston Churchill, always armed with his sardonic wit, fired this salvo: "A committee is the organized result of a group of the incompetent who have been appointed by the uninformed to accomplish the unnecessary." On my own campus, committees metastasize like cancer, eating up professors' and administrators' time and sucking the lifeblood from the institution. There was even a recent proposal to establish a committee on committees, ostensibly to bring this energy-sucking monster under control, but nothing ever came of the proposal.

In terms of performance, groups as decision-making units are in need of better public relations. Too many people are inclined to believe that groups are assembled to stymie progress and to serve as roadblocks to decision making, not to produce better alternatives. Grouphate is real.

So, are groups as inept as the moldy jokes and caustic criticisms indicate? Berg's (1967) study of 124 discussion groups is not very encouraging. He found that groups pursued their discussion topics for an average of only *58 seconds* at a time before diverting to an irrelevant topic. The range varied from a low of 28 seconds to a high of 118 seconds. One group leader in this study described his job as "chairman of the bored." Other studies support Berg's results. "Whether groups were composed of women in a Lebanese college, Japanese graduate students, university undergraduates, first-line managers at IBM, or educators in public-health nursing, the average attention span for all the groups was about one minute" (Bormann & Bormann, 1988, p. 120).

Although the tired jokes about groups and the research on the group attention span suggest that groups hinder effective decision making and problem solving, the evidence is far more mixed. One of the most researched areas of group communication is the comparison of individual to group performance. The key issue from this research is not whether individuals or groups are superior performers, **but rather, under what conditions groups outperform individuals and vice versa.** Since grouphate is often a result of poor group productivity, group versus individual performance seems to be a significant issue to explore.

Motivation to Perform: Social Loafing and Social Compensation Undoubtedly, you have participated in groups in which your enthusiasm for a group task has been blunted by the lifeless response from other group members. Grouphate is fueled by this all too common experience. Why are some group members strongly motivated to work hard on a task, but other members are not? The **Collective Effort Model** (CEM) suggests that group members are strongly motivated to perform well in a group if they are convinced that their individual effort will likely help in attaining valued results (Hart et al., 2001). **If members view the task as unimportant or meaningless (mere busy work) or a member's effort is expected to have little effect on the group outcome even when the outcome is highly valued (a person of low ability working with high-ability members), then social loafing will likely occur.**

Social loafing is the tendency of a group member to exert less effort on a task when working in a group than when working individually (Karau & Hart, 1998). Members display social loafing by missing group meetings, showing up late to meetings, performing and participating in a lackluster manner, or failing to start or complete individual tasks requested by the group. Please note here that reticence to participate during group discussions because of shyness does not constitute social loafing. Loafers put out little effort because of poor motivation, disinterest, or a bad attitude.

Social loafing is more common in individualist cultures than in collectivist cultures (Early, 1989; Gabreyna et al., 1985). Personal efforts and achievements are less visible in a group and more likely to go unrecognized, so social loafing is more likely in an individualist culture. In a collectivist culture, social striving or the desire to produce for the group because group membership is highly valued is strong.

So what can you do about social loafers? Here are several steps that can be taken to address the problem (see also Lumsden & Lumsden, 1993):

1. *Choose meaningful tasks.* Groups can't always choose their tasks, and sometimes they are given unchallenging tasks to perform by those with higher authority. If required to choose a project from a list of several options, however, choose the option most interesting to the group as a whole, not the option interesting to only one or two relatively dominant members.

2. *Establish a group responsibility norm.* Emphasize individual responsibility to the team and the importance of every member contributing a fair share to the successful completion of a task. Fairness and responsibility are important ethical concerns.

3. *Note the critical importance of each member's effort.* Impress upon all members that their individual effort is special and essential to the group's success. When group members believe that their contribution is indispensable to group success, they typically exert greater effort (Henningsen et al., 2000; D. W. Johnson, 2003). This is especially true if the task is difficult (J. M. Jackson & Williams, 1985; Matsui et al., 1987) and the member feels uniquely capable (Huguet et al., 1999).

4. *Hold members accountable.* Provide each member with specific and easily identifiable tasks and set aside time for the group to assess each member's contribution to the overall project (Gammage et al., 2001). Face-to-face peer appraisal that focuses on development of each group member's abilities, not on criticizing weak effort, diminishes social loafing (Druskat & Wolff, 1999).

5. *Enhance group cohesiveness.* Members of weakly cohesive groups are more prone to social loafing than members of highly cohesive groups (Karau & Hart, 1998). See the steps for enhancing cohesiveness discussed earlier in this chapter.

6. *Confront the loafer.* If the steps above are insufficient, either the leader of the group, a designated member, or the group as a whole should approach the loafer and ask why the lethargic attitude exists. Encourage stronger participation, reaffirm the importance of the loafer's contribution to the team effort, and solicit suggestions regarding how the group might help the person become a contributor. Do not name-call or personally attack the loafer.

7. *Consult a higher power* (not to be confused with divine intervention, although that would be impressive). When all of the above steps fail, consult a supervisor, teacher, or someone with greater authority than the group members and ask for advice. The authority figure may need to discuss the problem with the loafer.

8. *Boot out the loafer.* This is a last resort. Do not begin with this step, as many groups would prefer to do. You may not have this option available, however.

9. *Sidestep the loafer.* Reconfigure individual responsibilities and tasks so even if the loafer contributes nothing to the group effort, the group can still maneuver around the loafer and produce a high-quality result.

Social loafing from some group members can produce an opposite reaction from other group members called **social compensation**—an increased motivation to work harder on a group task to counterbalance the lackluster performance of others. Several studies show that when group members expect listless effort from others in the group, they display greater motivation to work harder and exhibit higher than expected productivity compared to when they work alone (Williams & Karau, 1991; Williams & Sommer, 1997). **Social compensation is especially likely when a high-ability group member senses that his or her maximum effort is required for the group to be successful on a meaningful task because other group members have less ability to perform effectively** (Hart et al., 2001). If poor performance from low-ability group members is perceived to be caused by external forces (bad luck, life stresses) then compensation is likely. If, however, the poor performance is attributed to internal causes (laziness), then compensation is unlikely. **Compensation is especially unlikely when high-ability group members are suspected of loafing.** Few wish to play the sucker and cover for the able but unwilling sluggards in the group (Hart et al., 2001).

When Groups Outperform Individuals: Three Heads Are Better Than One

Groups will usually outperform individuals when certain conditions exist (Forsyth, 1990; Pavitt & Curtis, 1994). First, **when the task requires a wide range and variety of information and skills, groups tend to be superior to any individual.** One study found that the group scored significantly higher than its highest scoring member (Stasson & Bradshaw, 1995). It did this by *pooling knowledge.* When the highest-scoring member didn't know the answer to a question, another member typically knew the answer to that specific question. Thus, the group as a whole benefited because members had nonoverlapping knowledge. As humorist Will Rogers once said, "Everybody is ignorant, just on different subjects." A key to successful group performance is putting together a team composed of members who do not share ignorance, but instead pool nonoverlapping areas of knowledge (Stasson & Bradshaw, 1995).

Dr. Don Wukasch spent 19 years as part of a high-performance cardiac surgery team. He cites an instance of effective team performance that resulted from pooling nonoverlapping knowledge (Larson & LaFasto, 1989). When he performed surgery at the Texas Heart Institute, a hurricane hit during one procedure and the power was knocked out. The heart–lung machine quit, leaving about a minute or two before the patient would start to die. Wukasch didn't know how to restore the heart–lung machine, but functioning as a cohesive, well-trained unit, team members began hand-cranking the machine and surgery continued within 15 seconds.

Besides pooling knowledge, another reason groups outperform individuals when the task is comprehensive is the *group remembering* phenomenon or collective recall of information. Quantitatively, the research on group remembering has consistently shown that groups are superior to individuals (even compared to the best individual) in recall of information (N. Clark & Stephenson, 1989).

Why is group remembering significant? Juries more often than not arrive at verdicts on the basis of recall of the evidence and pertinent information reflecting guilt or innocence. In one study, individual jurors averaged only a 60% accuracy rate on recall of specific evidence and less than 30% on questions pertaining to the judge's instructions to the jury. As a group, however, the jury scored 90% accuracy on evidentiary material and 80% accuracy on the judge's instructions (Hastie et al., 1983). "The group memory advantage over the typical or even the exceptional individual is one of the major determinants of the superiority of the jury as a legal decision mechanism" (Hastie et al., 1983). Not surprisingly, larger-sized (12-member) juries have superior recall of evidence compared to smaller-sized (6-member) juries (Hastie et al., 1983).

Group remembering can be a significant benefit for a group such as personnel-interviewing panels that often must sift through huge amounts of information and listen to hours of oral responses to questions from numerous candidates for a job. Group remembering is also a significant advantage for student study groups preparing for an exam.

Second, **groups generally outperform individuals when both the group and any individual compared are without expertise on the task.** Here *synergy* is at work. As D. W. Johnson and R. T. Johnson (1987) remark in somewhat overstated fashion, "None of us is as smart as all of us" (p. 131). In a recent study, even though no individual group member knew the correct answer on a test question, the group as a whole selected the correct answer in 28% of the cases. Individual members working alone, however, selected the correct answer only 4% of the time (Stasson & Bradshaw, 1995). Watson and his colleagues (1991) found that the longer group members work together, the greater is this result. They also found that long-term groups typically scored significantly higher than even their best member.

Third, **groups will usually outperform an individual when both the group and the individual have expertise and the task is an especially large and complex one.** The ability of a group to divide labor, to *share the load*, will normally result in a better decision than any overburdened individual could manage. Legal cases such as the Microsoft antitrust suit in 1999 require armies of attorneys. In cases such as these, a single attorney would be easily overwhelmed by workload and by information overload without extensive assistance from other attorneys. Shaffner (1999) provides the arithmetic logic for sharing the load. If one person had all the knowledge and skills to single-handedly build a Boeing 777, it would take about *250 years* to deliver one plane. The logic of working in groups is indisputable when the task is large and complex.

A group of experts is especially effective when members are highly motivated and they are trained to work as a team. One study found that expert groups outperform their best member 97% of the time (Michaelson et al., 1989). *Teamwork* allows a group to coordinate efforts and to work at optimum effectiveness.

Fourth, **even when comparing a group of reasonably bright and informed non-experts to an individual with special expertise, group decisions are sometimes superior.** One of the reasons for this superiority is that when groups are functioning effectively, members perform an *error correction* function for the group (Hastie et al., 1983). Assumptions are challenged and alternatives are offered that an individual might overlook. In addition, the collective energy and chemistry of the group may produce a synergistic result.

When Individuals Outperform Groups: No Magic in Groups Although groups frequently outperform individuals, this is not always the case. Under certain conditions, individuals outperform groups. Simply gathering individuals into a group won't magically produce effective decision making and problem solving. There are five conditions supported by research in which individuals outperform groups.

First, **groups composed of uninformed laypersons will not usually outperform someone with special expertise, such as a doctor or lawyer, on issues of medicine and law.** There is certainly no advantage to be gained from *pooling ignorance*. As already noted, however, even in uninformed groups, synergy sometimes compensates for lack of knowledge. *Negative synergy*, nevertheless, is more likely when group members are uninformed.

Second, **individuals outperform groups when groups establish norms of mediocrity.** Some groups are composed of members who are satisfied with relatively low productivity. If norms of mediocrity prevail in a group, performance will be sluggish or worse (Stogdill, 1972). Even individual members who may wish to perform at a higher level will become discouraged because of *insufficient motivation to excel*. Since the group rewards middling performance, why bother trying harder than the rest?

Third, **when groups become too large, individuals outperform groups.** Again, the rule of thumb is to select the smallest-sized group capable of performing the task effectively. Quality performance is usually enhanced in moderately sized groups (i.e., 7 to 10 members). Much larger than this, however, and *problems of coordination and*

GROUP VERSUS INDIVIDUAL PERFORMANCE

GROUP SUPERIOR TO INDIVIDUAL

Conditions	Reason(s)
Broad-range task	Pool knowledge, group remembering
Neither have expertise	Synergy
Experts, complex task	Share the load, teamwork
Individual expert, informed group	Error correction, synergy

INDIVIDUAL SUPERIOR TO GROUP

Conditions	Reason(s)
Individual expert, uninformed group	Pooling ignorance, negative synergy
Groups establish mediocrity norms	Insufficient motivation to excel
Group becomes too large	Difficulty coordinating, social loafing
Simple task	Minimal resources required
Time is a critical factor	Groups too slow

efficiency increase. Just assembling a dozen members can be daunting when schedules have to be coordinated. Social loafing also becomes a bigger problem in large groups (J. M. Jackson & Williams, 1985).

Fourth, **when the task is a simple one, groups are not superior to individuals.** There is no special advantage in having a group work on a remedial task. Minimal resources are required. If any individual can likely do the task, why involve a group?

Finally, **when time is a critical factor, groups usually perform less effectively than individuals.** In emergency situations or in circumstances where speed and efficiency are paramount, individuals can often perform better than groups, especially large groups. The reason is simple. Groups tend to be abominably slow, and larger groups usually take longer to make decisions than smaller groups (Davis et al., 1997). There are exceptions, however, such as disaster teams and emergency surgical teams trained to perform under pressure and time constraints.

Most groups, though, are not trained to operate swiftly and efficiently under pressure. As previously noted, small groups are usually faster than larger groups, but even small groups can lag behind a single individual in the performance of a task.

Groups outperform individuals in a variety of conditions. There is no magic, however, in assembling groups to perform tasks. There are conditions in which groups perform abysmally.

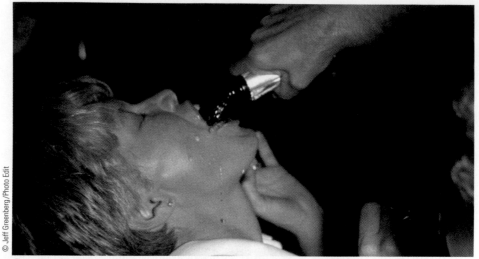

Groups often promote risk-taking such as binge drinking by college students.

Risk-Taking and Polarization: From Gambling to Guarded Researchers of small group decision making used to believe that group members inevitably influence each other to take greater collective risks than members' initial preferences. This was called the *risky shift phenomenon*, often seen when teenagers goad each other to engage in goofy and dangerous group actions, for example. Teens in Rio de Janeiro, Brazil, exhibit this risky shift when they "surf" as a group on the tops of high-speed trains, standing with arms outstretched. Even though 150 teens, on average, die each year and another 400 are injured when they fall off the trains or they hit the 3,000-volt electric train cables, the teens continue to take the risk at the prompting of peer group members (Arnett, 1995). I already discussed the power of groups to encourage high-risk binge drinking by college students. The frequency of talking about drinking within groups is a particularly important influencing factor (Dorsey et al., 1999). Terrorists concoct riskier, bolder, fanatical acts of violence when they discuss their schemes in a group (McCauley & Segal, 1987). After hundreds of studies, however, **there is ample evidence that groups sometimes have a conservative shift rather than a risky shift** (J. Levine & Moreland, 1990). Thus, group decisions tend to polarize.

Group polarization is the group tendency to make a decision after discussion that is more extreme, either riskier or more cautious, than the initial preferences of group members. (Group polarization does not mean that disagreement among group members becomes more pronounced.) This "move to the fringe," as D. G. Myers and Bishop (1970) termed it, can be seen on the Internet (Spears et al., 1990). Clay Shirky (1995), author of *Voices of the Net*, explains:

The greatest loss in public discourse on the Net is the loss of moderate voices. In many public political forums, it is almost impossible to develop and refine ideas of real political complexity because there is a spate of constant challenges from the extremes. For instance, people who want to reform welfare have a difficult time talking without being attacked by those wanting to abolish it altogether.

Factors that produce group polarization "are present in abundance on the Internet, so we should hardly be surprised when we run into discussion groups whose regular members firmly hold some weird or extreme viewpoints" (Wallace, 1999, p. 80). Many of these extreme viewpoints encourage high-risk, even reckless political positions (e.g., use of nuclear weapons in the Middle East).

What influences the direction of the polarization? **Groups tend to polarize decision making if there is a clear majority leaning one way (risk) or the other (caution).** If most members of a group lean slightly toward risk-taking initially, the group will become more prone to take even greater risks than any individual member might have initially preferred, and if most members of a group lean slightly toward playing it safe, the group will likely become even more cautious than it was initially. It is unlikely that a group will polarize when group members are about evenly split between risk-taking and playing it safe. This is where compromise, or depolarization, may result.

Research also indicates that group decisions will likely shift toward risk-taking when groups are large, when members do not know each other well, and when members are knowledgeable and well-informed about the problem. Groups will likely shift toward more cautious decision making when the decision is steeped in uncertainty, when the results could be severe, and when the probability of successful risk-taking is questionable (BarNir, 1998). The direction of the group polarization also appears strongly influenced by the preference of the group's informal leader (Pescosolido, 2001). Culture also plays a role. For instance, U.S. groups are more likely to polarize in the direction of risk, whereas Chinese groups are more likely to polarize in the direction of caution (Hong, 1978). Risk could produce disharmony, especially if it turns out badly.

There are two primary explanations for group polarization (BarNir, 1998). **The first explanation is social comparison** (normative influence). The assumption here is that an individual uses the group norm regarding riskiness or caution as a point of reference. The individual is inclined to shift after group discussion, to conform more closely to the perceived expectations of the group in this regard. The individual member compares his or her position on risk or caution to that of the group as a whole. If most group members initially tend toward riskiness, cautious members are inclined to move in the direction of the majority. If most members initially favor caution, all members feel pushed to be cautious.

> ▷ ●● SECOND LOOK
>
> ## COMPETENT COMMUNICATION AND GROUP DEVELOPMENT
>
> **FORMING PERIODIC PHASE**
>
> Express positive attitudes and feelings
>
> Appear friendly, open, and interested
>
> **STORMING PERIODIC PHASE**
>
> Tolerate, even encourage, disagreement and deviance
>
> Keep a civil tongue
>
> Be an active listener
>
> **NORMING PERIODIC PHASE**
>
> Adapt communication to the norms of the group
>
> Encourage change when norms are excessively rigid
>
> Encourage change when norms are too elastic
>
> **PERFORMING PERIODIC PHASE**
>
> Focus on the task
>
> Encourage participation from group members (in most instances)

A second explanation for the group polarization effect is **persuasive argumentation** (informational influence). Individuals in a group will move toward either greater risk or caution when exposed to arguments and information that were not available to members when they made their initial decision. In general, the greater the number of arguments advanced during discussion that support the initial majority group opinion, the more cogent, reasonable, and persuasive they seem to be; and the more original or nonredundant the arguments are, the greater will be the group polarization (M. Smith, 1982). As these arguments get repeated during discussions, they validate the risk-taking or caution predominant in the group (Brauer et al., 1995). Naturally, if the majority is predisposed toward risk-taking (or caution), the number of arguments advanced will usually favor that predisposition.

The performance phase of group development is a complex process. I have merely laid the groundwork for more detailed discussion of group performance in later chapters. Nevertheless, some general advice regarding communication competence can be offered. A competent communicator does the following to enhance group performance:

1. *Focus on the task.* Because task and social dimensions of groups are interconnected, focusing on the task to the detriment of social relationships among

members obviously makes little sense. Nevertheless, when there is work to be done, the primary focus is on the accomplishment of the task. Cohesiveness can be built when the pressure to perform has lessened. Task accomplishment also increases cohesiveness.

2. *Encourage participation from group members.* The group needs to utilize its resources fully, which means that even social loafers may have much to contribute. A note of caution here: Encouraging member participation should not be a blanket rule. Some group members should not be encouraged to participate because they disrupt the group's decision-making process (more on this in Chapter 8).

Newcomers and Group Development

The interconnectedness of all components of a system makes the entry of even a single new member into a group a highly significant event (Anderson et al., 1999). As groups develop, relationships among members stabilize and the roles and norms in the group become more complex. "The entry of a newcomer into the group can threaten this development by forcing members to alter their relationships with one another" (Moreland & Levine, 1987, p. 156).

NATURE OF THE GROUP: THE CHALLENGE OF ACCEPTANCE

Several characteristics of a group directly affect the acceptance of a newcomer (Moreland & Levine, 1987). First, **the level of group development has a direct bearing on newcomer acceptance.** Several research and development groups in a large corporation were studied for 4 months (Katz, 1982). Members of those groups that had been in existence for a relatively short time communicated more with newcomers and were more open to their ideas than were members of older groups. A newcomer in a younger group is less disruptive because he or she enters early on in the group development process. Entering a long-standing group, however, where development has progressed far beyond the initial stages, can be a far greater shock to the system and requires greater adaptation by the members. The newcomer seems more like an outsider in older groups than in younger ones.

Second, **the level of group performance affects the acceptance of newcomers.** When the system is functioning well, group members may not want to take a chance on altering a successful formula. Accepting a newcomer may pose a big risk. When a group is performing poorly, however, there is a strong impetus for change. The arrival of a newcomer may be perceived as a welcome addition. The newcomer might turn the group around.

Third, **the number of members affects acceptance of a newcomer into a group.** Those groups that have too few members to perform necessary tasks well usually are eager to accept newcomers. Newcomers mean less work for each member and potentially greater success for the group. Groups that have too many members to function efficiently, however, will probably view a newcomer as an additional burden.

Finally, **the degree of turnover in a group also affects acceptance of newcomers.** Groups accustomed to frequent entry and exit of members will accept newcomers more readily than groups unaccustomed to turnover.

Newcomer Strategies: Gaining Acceptance

There are several strategies newcomers can employ to improve their chances of gaining acceptance from a group (Moreland & Levine, 1987).

1. *Conduct a thorough reconnaissance of the group.* Most newcomers do a poor job of scouting out a group to determine whether they and the group are a good match (Wanous, 1980). Newcomers should exploit all available sources of information about the group to form a reasonably accurate assessment of the group they contemplate joining.

2. *Play the role of newcomer.* Seek the advice of longtime members, avoid disagreements with old-timers, and talk less than they do. Listen, to show respect. This obviously is not a permanent role. As you become more accepted by the group, your communication can move away from the newcomer role pattern.

3. *Seek mentors within the group.* Mentors are old-timers who develop a close personal relationship with the newcomer and assist the newcomer's entry into the group. The mentoring process can increase the newcomer's understanding of the group and enhance his or her level of group satisfaction (Allen et al., 1999; Seibert, 1999).

4. *Collaborate with other newcomers.* When more than one newcomer enters a group, they stand to gain from banding together. Newcomers can lend emotional support and encouragement to each other. They can provide useful information about the group. They can act as a friendly face, making the group climate more inviting.

In summary, all groups have a task dimension and a social dimension. The output of the task dimension is productivity. The output of the social dimension is cohesiveness. Productivity can affect cohesiveness and vice versa.

Group development encompasses four periodic phases: forming, storming, norming, and performing. These periodic phases do not occur in rigid sequence. They frequently overlap, and groups may jump around between phases depending on the circumstances and situations groups face. Some groups never progress beyond the forming and initial storming phases. These are groups that dissolve because they do not work.

Member Diversity and Group Development

GROUPS USUALLY BENEFIT significantly from diverse membership (P. L. McLeod et al., 1996, p. 251). Heterogeneous (member dissimilarity) groups are more likely to have members with diverse skills, perspectives, backgrounds, and experiences who can provide a wider array of problem-solving and decision-making resources than are likely to be found in homogeneous (member similarity) groups (V. E. Barker et al., 2000; Haslett & Ruebush, 1999).

One study showed that gender diversity in small groups enhanced the team performance even on male-oriented tasks (Rogelberg & Rumery, 1996). Another study found that groups whose membership included Asian, African, Latino, and Anglo Americans had superior performance to groups that included only Anglos (P. L. McLeod et al., 1996). Groups with a mix of males, females, and ethnicities also counteract biases more effectively than more homogeneous groups (Marcus-Newhall et al., 1993).

There is no magic, however, from merely adding traditionally excluded members to decision-making and problem-solving groups. Adding a single ethnic minority or woman to a group can easily appear to be tokenism. Tokens are often the targets of prejudice and sexism (Fiske, 1993). They can be easily ignored, harassed, or silenced.

In situations where group composition can be considered during the forming phase (e.g., task force or ad hoc groups), a maximum effort should be made to have a diverse membership with women and ethnic minorities fairly represented. The **Twenty Percent Rule** is an important minimum standard to achieve in this regard. Researchers have observed that discrimination against minorities and women drops substantially when no less than 20% of a group, and no fewer than two members, are ethnic minorities and/or women (Pettigrew & Martin, 1987).

Diverse group membership presents challenges. The storming phase can be more prolonged and intense. Groups with diverse composition can have greater difficulty agreeing on decisions and solutions to problems. Cohesiveness and group satisfaction can also be more difficult to achieve, especially in the initial phases of the group (V. E. Barker et al., 2000). Competent communication is the key to meeting these challenges of diversity effectively.

Questions for Thought

1. Why does the Twenty Percent Rule work to diminish discrimination against minorities and women?
2. How important do you think it is to have a diverse group membership? Is there any connection to group synergy? Explain.

Finally, the entry of newcomers into a group can be a disturbing event. Competent communicators learn about the nature of the group to which they seek membership, and they learn the strategies that will assist their acceptance into the group. Women and ethnic minorities, who are often in the newcomer role, add diversity to a group, which presents challenges but usually benefits group decisions. ● ●

Questions for Critical Thinkers

1. When is it appropriate to be a nonconformist in a small group?
2. Are there ever times when the task is so important that concern for the social dimension of the group must be ignored?
3. Should group members make an effort to integrate newcomers into the group, or is it primarily the task of the newcomer to adapt to the group?

InfoTrac College Edition

Log onto InfoTrac College Edition.

1. Type "hazing" in the search window. Choose an article to read. SUGGESTIONS: (a) Article A75087111 by Paul Ruffins entitled "Spring ushers in a bloody hazing season for Black frats"; (b) Article A68642658 in *Contemporary Pediatrics* entitled "The high cost of hazing."
2. Type "cliques" in the search window. Choose an article to critique. SUGGESTION: Article A87407268 in *Internet Wire* entitled "Medzilla.com probes into cliques in the workplace."
3. Type "social loafing" in the search window. Choose an article to read. SUGGESTIONS: (a) Article A72300370 in *Research Quarterly for Exercise and Sport* entitled "A closer look at the social loafing phenomenon: Investigating the individual effort of females as members of gender-specific groups"; (b) Article A55715820 by Naoki Kugihara entitled "Gender and social loafing in Japan."
4. Type "ostracism" in the search window. Choose an article to critique. SUGGESTION: Article A19601485 by Kipling D. Williams and Kristin L. Sommer entitled "Social ostracism by coworkers: Does rejection lead to loafing or compensation?"
5. Type "conformity" in the search window. Choose an article to read. SUGGESTION: Article A80163118 by Kathiann Kowalski entitled "What's your group ID? How far would you go to fit in with the group?"

Video Case Studies

*My Cousin Vinny (1992). Comedy; R; ****

If you don't laugh repeatedly while watching this movie, then you should have your funny bone checked by a specialist. Vinny is an inexperienced Brooklyn lawyer asked to defend his cousin on charges of murder in a backwater town in Alabama. Analyze this movie in terms of norms and conformity. Which norms are explicit and which are implicit? Is the stuttering defense lawyer a nonconformist?

*Bulworth (1998). Comedy; R; ***1/2*

Warren Beatty is hilarious as a lackluster U.S. Senator who revives his failing re-election campaign by speaking his mind—without editing anything. Which norms does Bulworth violate and with what effects?

*Lord of the Flies (1963). Drama; NR; ****

There is a 1989 remake of William Goldman's grim allegory of schoolboys stranded on a deserted island, but it is a pale, lifeless effort compared to the splendid original film. Analyze in detail all four phases of group development.

*The Four Seasons (1981); Comedy/Drama; PG-13; ***1/2*

A longtime (older) group of close, successful, middle-aged friends whose group membership had not changed in years (no turnover) is thoroughly disrupted when one member marries a young woman after divorcing his wife. Analyze the effects this unwelcome newcomer has on the group's dynamics. What newcomer strategies, if any, are attempted to gain acceptance? Were any mistakes made in attempting to gain acceptance?

4 Developing the Group Climate

I DEO IS "THE LARGEST and most influential product design firm in the world" (Myerson, 2001, p. 11). The company's 350 designers in six cities (Palo Alto, San Francisco, Chicago, Boston, London, and Munich) work on about 500 projects each year (B. Stone, 2003). IDEO has won more design awards than any competing design firm (Nussbaum, 2004). In the 1990s, IDEO designed, among other things, the Palm V handheld organizer, AT&T's answering machines and telephones, Polaroid's I-Zone pocket camera, Nike sunglasses, the insta-cholesterol test and single-dose insulin pen, virtual reality headgear, and the animatronic whale for the movie *Free Willy*. More recently, IDEO has turned to designing consumer services for some of the largest and most respected companies and institutions in the world. IDEO has worked with Mayo Clinic, Kaiser Permanente, Intel, Hewlett-Packard, NASA, Samsung, AT&T Wireless Services, Amtrak, Vodaphone, Nestle, Lufthansa, and the BBC, among others (Nussbaum, 2004).

What IDEO has accomplished, however, is not nearly as impressive as how the firm has accomplished it. David Kelley, the founder and driving force behind IDEO, is the most unique corporate executive you're likely to find (Kelley & Littman, 2001). Kelley has established a corporate climate that is the antithesis of most companies and small businesses. Kelley wanted three things when he established IDEO: to work with friends, to have no bosses in charge of employees' lives, and to eliminate jerks from the workplace (O'Brien, 1995).

Kelley organizes weekly company bike rides, hosts birthday celebrations for workers according to their zodiac signs, and often conducts Monday morning meetings seated on the floor of a room devoid of furniture. IDEO teams go to baseball games, movies, take field trips (e.g., George Lucas's Industrial Light and Magic at Skywalker Ranch), or sail around San Francisco Bay to recharge team members' creative energy. They often engage in such activities during other businesses' regular working hours.

Bob Sutton, a Stanford professor of organizational behavior, spent 15 months studying IDEO to understand the secret of its success. His conclusion: "The secret is simple but complex. It's about people who aren't focusing on office politics" (O'Brien, 1995, p. 25). At IDEO, developing and maintaining a positive group climate of fun, excitement, and support that is free of negative infighting is essential.

A **group climate** is the emotional atmosphere, the enveloping tone that is created by the way we communicate in groups. A communication climate permeates all groups and affects every aspect of a group's social and task dimensions. A **positive climate** exists when individuals perceive that they are valued, supported, and treated well by the group. A **negative climate** exists when group members do not feel valued, supported, and respected, when trust is minimal, and when members perceive that they are not treated well.

The purpose of this chapter is to identify and explain why a positive group climate is far more likely to develop when cooperative communication patterns are emphasized and competitive communication patterns are de-emphasized. There are two objectives related to this purpose:

1. to discuss the effects of competitive and cooperative communication patterns on group climate and group effectiveness, and
2. to explore ways to construct cooperation in small groups.

Competition and Cooperation

This section compares competition and cooperation in small groups. The effects of competition and cooperation on small group climate and goal attainment are presented.

▶ **Focus Questions**

1. Is competition ever constructive?
2. What is the relationship between communication competence and competition/cooperation?
3. Does competition increase motivation to succeed?
4. Does competition improve achievement and performance?

DEFINITIONS: CONCEPTUAL CLARITY

Although seemingly straightforward, the terms competition, cooperation, and individual achievement aren't always used in a conceptually clear manner. To avoid any confusion, these three terms are defined, and the term *hypercompetitiveness* is introduced. The relationship of these concepts to group communication is explored as this chapter unfolds.

Competition: Winners Take All Alfie Kohn (1992) defines **competition** as a mutually exclusive goal attainment (MEGA) process. When transactions in groups are competitive, individual success is achieved at the expense of other group members. **Competition, by definition, necessitates the failure of the many for the success of the few.** When the city of San Francisco solicited applications for 50 new firefighters, more than 10,000 individuals applied. That's 50 winners and more than 9,900 losers. Pick any contest and the disproportionate number of losers compared to winners is usually enormous.

Cooperation: Winners All Distinctly unlike competition, **cooperation** is a mutually inclusive goal attainment (MIGA) process. Individual success is tied directly to the success of other group members. **Group members work together, not against each other, when attempting to achieve a common goal.** The phenomenally successful Mars rover called Sojourner, which explored the surface of Mars in 1997, served as the model for future equally successful rovers. The Sojourner project was a cooperative team effort under the direction of Donna Shirley (1997). Sojourner's challenge was to take pictures, measure the chemistry of Martian rocks, and test the difficulty of maneuvering the rover on Martian soil. Sojourner, which looked like a stripped-down microwave oven on six wheels, was built at a cost of $25 million, a mere pittance for an interplanetary project. Sojourner had to weigh less than 22 pounds, survive 150-degrees-below-zero temperatures, and operate at a peak power of 16 watts. Expected to operate for only 1 week and travel no more than 10 meters from its mother spacecraft, Sojourner lasted 3 months and explored 100 meters across the surface of Mars at a top speed of 0.0037 miles per hour. The extraordinary success of the project was cause for jubilation from the entire team. Every team member had the exact same goal—to successfully explore Mars with the rover they built from scratch (sometimes using parts from local hardware stores to keep within their meager budget). The team members succeeded or failed as a unit in attaining their goal. Team members helped each other on every part of the project; to do otherwise might have sabotaged the success of the entire mission.

Individual Achievement: Going It Alone Independently accomplishing a goal previously unrealized, such as performing more push-ups than ever before or earning a higher grade on a calculus exam than at any other time in your academic life, is neither competition nor cooperation. It is **individual achievement**—the attainment of a personal goal without having to defeat another person. It is, however, often mistakenly referred to as "competing with oneself." When Mariah Nelson (1998) asked 1,030 girls and women from ages 11 to 49 to indicate with whom they compete generally, 75% responded "with myself; my own standards and goals." **For conceptual clarity it is important that we understand the difference between competition and individual achievement.** If you "compete with yourself," you will be both the victor and the vanquished—a conceptual contradiction. As Kohn (1992) notes, competition is not a solitary undertaking. Claiming that we compete with ourselves is like saying we arm-wrestled with ourselves. Arm wrestling, and all competition, is an interactive phenomenon necessitating at least one other party.

Hypercompetitiveness: Winning Is Everything In a study of 198 of the world's top athletes, more than half of the participants said that they would take a drug that would improve their chances of winning every competition for a 5-year period. Here's the stunner—these same top athletes would take the performance-enhancing drug even if they knew that it would *kill them* at the end of the 5 years ("Superhuman Heroes," 1998). The excessive emphasis on defeating others to achieve one's goals is called **hypercompetitiveness.** Psychologist Elliot Aronson (1999) claims, "We manifest a staggering cultural obsession with victory" (p. 263). Nathan Miller bitingly asserts that "conversation in the United States is a competitive exercise in which the first person to draw a breath is declared the listener" (cited in Bolton, 1979, p. 4).

Competition in the United States is everywhere. A high school athlete has only a 1 in 300 chance of receiving a "full-ride" scholarship to college. Nevertheless, parents increasingly sign up their kids when they are pre-adolescents for expensive private lessons and enroll them in club programs and "traveling teams" that supplement traditional athletic experiences such as Little League (Emmons, 2005). In the elusive drive to win a future scholarship to college, children are being put at risk for overuse injuries and emotional and psychological abuse from hypercompetitive coaches. As Lazenby Blaser, Commissioner of the Central Coast Section of California high school athletics notes, "It's almost like prostituting your children for the family benefit of getting a scholarship. How could volleyball or soccer be so important that you put your kid in a situation like that?" (quoted in Emmons, 2005, p. 13A).

Our economic, judicial, and political systems are also based on intense competition. U.S. universities are "intensely individualistic and highly competitive. Student is pitted against student through the grading system, and faculty member against faculty member for promotion and other academic favors" (P. Smith, 1990, p. 13). According to one report, academic competition will continue to intensify (Bronner, 1999, p. 13A).

The competitive obsession in the United States is graphically illustrated by a now-famous incident that occurred in Lakewood, California. On March 19, 1993, police arrested eight members of a high school boys' clique called the "Spur Posse" (named after the San Antonio Spurs professional basketball team). The boys, ages 15 to 19, were charged with 20 counts of various sex crimes involving girls from ages 10 to 16. The boys readily admitted that one of the main activities of this group was to have sex with as many girls as possible (Seligman & Murr, 1993).

The boys, many of them top athletes at their high school, coolly admitted to investigators that they kept count of the young girls with whom they had sex. Billy Shehan boasted 66 conquests, the most of any Posse member ("Who's Keeping Score?" 1999). Apparently, this was more of a contest about "scoring" than simply having sex. As sociologist Donna Eder of Indiana University explains, "They take the competitive sense and move it into the realm of sexuality" (Gelman & Rogers, 1993).

Members of the Spur Posse argue with a female antagonist on a talk show.

Contests in the United States can be about almost anything because competition "is the common denominator of American life" (Kohn, 1992, p. 1). (See Focus on Gender: "Gender and Hypercompetitiveness.")

CONSTRUCTIVE COMPETITION: TEMPERING THE NEED TO WIN

It is hypercompetitiveness, not competitiveness itself, that poses the greatest challenge to establishing a positive group climate of trust, openness, directness, supportiveness, and accomplishment. Arguing that all competition is bad and that our goal should be to replace every instance of competition with cooperation is unrealistic and pointless. There will be numerous times in groups where, despite Herculean efforts to cooperate, competition prevails. In some cases a cooperative alternative may not exist. How does a hiring committee, for example, transform the competition among hundreds of candidates into a cooperative endeavor when there is only a single position? In such cases, the competent communicator has to have the flexibility of skills to adapt to an adversarial, competitive situation. As we will see when conflict management is discussed in Chapter 10, sometimes a competitive communication style is required to manage a conflict effectively.

Aside from the inevitability of competition in some circumstances, competition can be constructive. **Constructive competition** occurs when competition produces a positive, enjoyable experience and generates increased efforts to achieve without

Gender and Hypercompetitiveness

COMPETITION IS EVERYWHERE in the United States, but is it predominantly a male fascination? After all, Tannen (1990) argues that men view conversations from a status (competitive) perspective but women view them from a connection (cooperative) perspective. This greater concern with connection may be the primary reason that women express significantly greater discomfort with direct competition than do males (Benenson et al., 2002). Research shows that men are more overtly competitive than women (Benenson et al., 2001), engaging in more use of commands, boasts, and threats and exhibiting more egotistical behavior (Goodwin, 1990; Leaper, 1991). Men also engage in competitive interference—actively trying to prevent an opponent from winning—far more than women (Roy & Benenson, 2002). Pat Heim (1992), in her book *Hardball for Women,* however, encourages women to use more competitive interference to get ahead in the business world of cutthroat competition. She advises, "Drop comments about his [a male coworker's] incompetence, point out his past cost overruns to your superiors, or even conveniently 'lose' his files and sabotage his progress—in short, pull out all the stops to undermine his winning the project" (p. 29). Resisting such questionably ethical advice may prove difficult for women in a hypercompetitive climate in which generous salaries, promotions, and perks are given typically to the hypercompetitive.

Some of the gender difference in competitive communication may be attributable to group size (Deal, 2000). Boys and men tend to operate in larger groups than do girls and women, and larger groups tolerate higher degrees of competitive behavior than smaller groups (Benenson et al., 2000).

Mona Harrington (1995) studied female attorneys. She claims that female lawyers reject the combative approach to settling disputes typical of male lawyers. Female lawyers prefer finding common ground, not trying to conquer adversaries. Nelson (1998) isn't "terribly

▶

jeopardizing positive interpersonal relationships and personal well-being (Tjosvold et al., 2003).

Necessary Conditions: A Trinity Under certain conditions, competition can be constructive and won't create a negative group climate (D. W. Johnson, 2003). These conditions are as follows:

1. *When winning is relatively unimportant.* The less group members emphasize winning as the primary goal of competition and instead focus more on having fun

concerned that women will follow in men's footsteps" (p. 24) and adopt what she calls the "Conqueror's way," the win-at-all-costs approach typical of male culture in America. Nevertheless, she admits "the Conqueror's way demands our attention, complicating and influencing any female or feminist form of competition that we might imagine" (p. 25).

Women—although not as competitive as men overall—are becoming more competitive as they enter the workforce in larger numbers (Kohn, 1992). A study of conflict management practices in the workplace found that women are no less competitive than men when conflicts arise (Gayle, 1991). In some instances, women who have advanced in their professions exhibit the "Queen Bee Syndrome" (Cooper,

1997; Mathison, 1987). They climb up the competitive ladder of success and then, instead of assisting other women in doing likewise, they protect their position as top woman in the company. They do this by making it tough for other talented women, who are seen as possible rivals, to advance. Consequently, women, especially those who support traditional gender roles, "continue to be an important obstacle in keeping other women from being successful in leadership positions" (Cooper, 1997, p. 483). In business, sports, entertainment, medicine, law—virtually all facets of our society—women increasingly are pressured to emulate the previously male preoccupation with competition (Kohn, 1992).

Questions for Thought

1. Do you believe that women have become increasingly competitive to succeed in a hypercompetitive society? Explain.
2. How should you deal with the Conqueror mentality in a workplace, for example, when you would rather be more cooperative?
3. Is there any advantage to adopting the Conqueror mentality at work? Is it ethical?

and developing skills while competing, the more positive will be the group climate. A study of kids involved in Little League revealed that the more winning is emphasized, the higher is the dropout rate. Hypercompetitive managers who made winning the central goal had a team dropout rate *five times greater* than teams whose manager emphasized having fun and developing skills, not winning ("Put Enjoyment Ahead," 1994). There was no difference in the win–loss records of the two comparison groups. Legendary college basketball coach, John Wooden, validates the importance of de-emphasizing winning. "Many people are surprised to learn that in 27 years at UCLA, I never once talked about winning" (quoted in

Aguayo, 1990, p. 99). Wooden instead emphasized that every team member learn offensive and defensive skills and give his best effort. The results of Wooden's coaching philosophy are, to this day, jaw-dropping: 10 national championships in his last 12 years at UCLA, including an 88-game winning streak—still the record for major college basketball.

2. *When opponents are equally matched, allowing all participants a reasonable chance to win.* Professional athletes such as Michael Jordan, Serena Williams, and Lance Armstrong will sing the praises of competition. Why wouldn't they? Their phenomenal ability to win against the very best athletes in the world has propelled them to superstardom and staggering wealth. Clearly, competition is often rewarding for those who have a reasonable shot at winning. Even those individuals who are not the best but are a tier below the superstars, with great effort and perhaps some luck, can become winners at least occasionally. They will likely find competition fun and enjoyable, challenging, motivating, and personally gratifying. But what about the vast majority of people who have no special talents; who are average or worse? If the driving force of competition is winning and attaining the rewards that go with victory, why would those who know that they will never reap such rewards be motivated by competition to excel? In fact, why wouldn't the prospect of being a persistent "loser" demoralize and deject competitors? More than 41 million youths ages 18 and younger participate in organized sports programs in the United States, but 70% of these kids quit by age 13 because the pressure to win is too great and most don't believe that they have a reasonable chance of winning (Emmons, 2005). In the workplace, employees who feel unable to compete effectively want to quit their jobs (Tjosvold et al., 2003). As sports psychologist Terry Orlick (1978) observes, "For many children competitive sports operate as a failure factory which not only effectively eliminates the 'bad ones' but also turns off many of the 'good ones' " (p. 129).

3. *When there are clear, specific rules that ensure fairness.* When there are clear rules enforced without bias, competition can be a constructive enterprise. When there are no rules, or rules are enforced selectively or haphazardly, competition induces strong dissatisfaction with remaining a member of a group (Tjosvold et al., 2003) and it promotes cheating. David Callahan (2004), in his book *The Cheating Culture*, concludes, "Cheating thrives where unfairness reigns" (p. 263). Callahan documents widespread cheating in America. Cheating proliferates because, in a pervasive atmosphere of hypercompetitiveness, rules of fair play are either nonexistent or unenforced. The steroid scandal in professional baseball is a prime example. Until Congressional hearings in 2005, little effort was made to stem the tide of rampant steroid use in the major leagues. As a result, those players who may have wanted to "stay clean" were tempted to use steroids to prevent losing the competitive edge against those who were cheating with

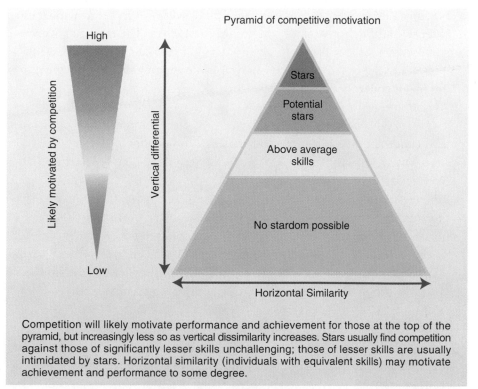

FIGURE 4.1   Pyramid of competition.

performance-enhancing drugs (Callahan, 2004). From the steroid scandal in professional baseball to rampant cheating by students trying to "get ahead," the "everybody's doing it" mantra encourages unethical competition.

As I begin to address the specific effects of competition compared to cooperation, please understand that **all three of the above conditions must be satisfied for constructive competition to occur.** These three conditions form a single unit. Remove one condition and constructive competition erodes. Apply rules unfairly, for example, and watch mildly competitive teams transform into hypercompetitive monsters. Hypercompetitive teams may even perceive unfairness where none objectively exists. Even closely matched teams engaged in a hypercompetitive contest can produce some very ugly consequences, as we have all observed so often in professional sporting events. Also, the less these three conditions for constructive competition are met, the more likely that competition will turn negative. Being "a little bit fair" or a little less intensely competitive might reduce the negative effects, but it won't likely eliminate them and replace them with constructive outcomes.

AP/Wide World Photos

Esther Kim and Kay Poe, longtime close friends, were to face each other for the final spot on the U.S. Olympic tae kwon do team. Poe's knee, however, was injured in her semifinal bout and she was prepared to forfeit her final match. Kim, however, forfeited. "It wasn't fair for me to go in there having two legs and her having only one." Competition sometimes produces a selfless act when winning isn't everything.

Competition and Communication Competence: Can Me Be We? If cooperation is We-oriented (working together) and competition is Me-oriented (working against others for one's own sake), how can competitive patterns of interaction be anything but incompetent communication? First, **communication competence is a matter of degree.** Drinking a small amount of alcohol does not make you an alcoholic and it may be beneficial in some instances, if kept to a minimum. Likewise, a small amount of competitiveness in groups does no harm and may be beneficial to the group. Second, **although competent communication requires a We-orientation (rather than a Me-orientation), this does not exclude any consideration of individual needs.** Orientation implies primary, not exclusive, focus. The emphasis matters, not the mere presence of occasional competitive, individualistic communication patterns. Third, **many activities combine both competition and cooperation.** *Intergroup* (between groups) competition usually requires a great deal of *intragroup* (within a group) cooperation.

INTRAGROUP COMPETITION AND COOPERATION: CHALLENGING ORTHODOXY

The pervasiveness of competition in American society and the vehemence with which it is defended make competition difficult to challenge. Bruce Ogilvie, a professor emeritus at San Jose State University and a pioneer in sports psychology, states, "We have to be careful in our country about ever attacking winning. It's a deeply embedded ethic in our culture" (quoted in Kutner, 1994, p. D2). Nevertheless, a sober, analytical review of the research comparing the effects of competition and cooperation is warranted, if for no other reason than to base common beliefs on credible evidence, not mere anecdotal experiences. More than 750 research studies have been conducted on the relative merits and demerits of competition and cooperation (D. W. Johnson, 2003). This section discusses intragroup effects derived from this voluminous research. The following section addresses intergroup effects.

Group Productivity: Achievement and Performance on Tasks Reviews of hundreds of studies clearly show that cooperation, not competition, produces higher levels of group achievement and performance on a wide variety of tasks (D. W. Johnson, 2003). For example, cooperative, not competitive, learning clearly leads to higher academic achievement (D. W. Johnson & R. T. Johnson, 1987, 1998). As David Johnson concludes, "There's almost nothing that American education has seen with this level of empirical support" (Kohn, 1987, p. 54). One study determined that when competitive groups were compared to cooperative groups within an organization, overall the cooperative groups vastly outperformed the competitive groups. Even the *worst* cooperative groups that were relatively weak on task accomplishment, on average, outperformed the *best* competitive groups (Van Oostrum & Rabbie, 1995). **The cooperative advantage is especially significant when compared to the disadvantages of competition that is hypercompetitive, between unequal opponents, and conducted unfairly** (Stanne et al., 1999).

There are two primary reasons why cooperation promotes and competition dampens achievement and performance for most groups and individuals (Kohn, 1992). First, **attempting to achieve excellence and trying to beat others are different goals.** A series of studies conducted at a business school at Cambridge University makes the point. Teams composed of members with high IQ scores performed worse than teams whose members had more ordinary IQ scores. (The groups did not compete against each other, but were merely compared on the basis of results.)

Why did the high-IQ groups perform relatively poorly? High-IQ members spent a great deal of time in hypercompetitive debate, attempting to outshine each other. Moderate-IQ members worked as a team, uninterested in competing with each other for intellectual star status (Belbin, 1996). Trying to beat other group members diverts attention from achieving group excellence.

Second, **resources are used more efficiently in a cooperative climate.** A cooperative climate promotes the full utilization of information by a group, whereas a competitive climate typically promotes information hoarding (D. W. Johnson et al., 1986; Stanne et al., 1999). When group members work interdependently toward a common goal, not competitively to advance individual goals, there is likely to be less duplication of effort, better utilization of members' skills, and greater pooling of information and knowledge. Synergy is more likely to occur in a cooperative climate.

Group Cohesiveness: Social Relationships among Group Members Closely associated with group achievement and performance is group cohesiveness. When group members feel liked, valued, supported, and accepted, cohesiveness is strong. When group members feel disliked, unvalued, unsupported, and rejected, cohesiveness suffers. Does competition enhance intragroup cohesiveness? A review of more than 180 studies concluded that cooperative communication promoted significantly greater liking, support, and acceptance of group members than did competitive communication (D. W. Johnson, 2003).

Jules Henry (1963) noted that "a competitive culture endures by tearing people down." Although many adolescents quit sports because they fear failure and they can't handle the pressure of intense competition, many others never try out because they wish to avoid embarrassment and the ridicule of team members. Remember those agonizing moments in childhood when you engaged in the ritual of choosing up sides for basketball, soccer, or some other competitive game? If you were considered a star by your schoolmates, your inclusion on the team was assured. Your main concern was the prestige and enhanced self-esteem that accompanies being chosen first, second, or third. If you were viewed as inept at sports by schoolmates, however, then your main concern was whether you would suffer the humiliation of being taken last in the playground draft.

In a competitive environment, the most skillful are valued. The less skillful just make defeat more probable and thereby become a burden on the team. Most people quit rather than absorb the torment of being called a loser. "We reward winners and are disdainful of losers" (Aronson, 1999, p. 263).

INTERGROUP COMPETITION AND COOPERATION: THEM VERSUS US

In one of my group communication classes, students were assigned a symposium project. When we discovered that two of the four term groups had chosen the same topic, hypercompetitiveness erupted. One of the two groups immediately negotiated with me to present its symposium first, thereby hoping to steal the thunder of the other group. When members of the competitor group overheard the negotiations, they screamed foul. Bitter recriminations flew between the antagonists. I stepped in to calm tempers. I instituted a random drawing to designate the order of presentations. Despite my assurance that both groups could work on the same topic and that grades would not be determined on any comparison between groups, the competitors seemed unsatisfied.

Outside of class the antagonism continued. Members of the two competing groups verbally accosted each other during lunch in the cafeteria. When class resumed, both groups could be heard muttering unflattering comments about their adversaries. Information from researching was jealously guarded by each group. On her own initiative, one member asked to speak to the rival group, but her rivals rudely rebuffed her.

Neither group needed to compete, yet compete they did. By pooling resources and emphasizing different aspects of the topic, they could have improved both of their final presentations. Instead, the two groups became instantly rigid and systemically hostile, each demanding that the other group choose a different topic. The result? Both groups gave mediocre symposium presentations.

A huge body of research shows conclusively that intergroup interactions are generally far more competitive than interactions between individuals (Wildschut et al., 2003). Plato in his *Republic* has Polemarchus stating that "justice consists of helping one's friends and harming one's enemies." This is an ancient statement of what is now referred to as the **norm of group interest**—a collective prescription that group members should pursue maximum group outcomes (winning at all costs), even if this means acting hypercompetitively against other groups when members may privately not wish to do so (Wildschut et al., 2002). We want to help our group succeed, even if we may disagree with the ultimate goal of defeating another group and preventing its success. Just in the last decade of the twentieth century, this intergroup hypercompetitive hostility claimed the lives of 30 million people worldwide (McGuire, 1998).

The norm of group interest can produce some astoundingly bizarre hypercompetitive behavior between groups and individuals "fighting" for their team's victory. A Little League organization in Albuquerque, New Mexico, canceled the baseball season for 500 kids because of hostility and fights among parents, coaches, and league officials brought about by intergroup hypercompetitiveness. A coach in Whitehall, North Carolina, slashed the throat of a rival coach, spattering blood on one of the Little Leaguers. A teen umpire was shot at by an assistant coach in East St. Louis, Illinois, over a perceived bad call (Corcoran, 1993). So widespread is the aggressive behavior of parents at youth team sporting events that Fred Engh, president of the National Alliance of Youth Sports, has begun the Parents Association of Youth Sports to teach parents sportsmanship (Dreyfuss, 1999).

Competition and Culture

THE PERVASIVENESS of competition in the United States can easily trick us into believing that humans are competitive by nature. But where is the evidence that humans must compete because nature makes it inescapable? Recent brain research suggests that humans are neurologically wired for cooperation, not competition (cited in Angier, 2002). Even the depiction of life in the animal world as "survival of the fittest" and "red in tooth and claw," to use Tennyson's metaphorical description, vastly overstates the competitive aspects of life on earth. Anne Fausto-Sterling (1993) observes that "research in the past two decades shows that cooperation among species plays at least as big a role as violent struggle" (p. 24). Zoologist Frans de Waal notes, "Aiding others at a cost or risk to oneself is widespread in the animal world" (Boyd, 1996). Cooperation, according to this new school of thought, has survival value. Animals that help each other find food and ward off predators do better than those that go it alone (Boyd, 1996).

Comparing cultures reveals that "it is the norms of the culture that determine its competitiveness" (Kohn, 1992, p. 39), not human nature. Anthropologist Margaret Mead (1961) claimed that "it is the way the structure of the society is built up that determines whether individual members shall cooperate or shall compete with one another" (p. 481).

Consider the typical case of an elementary student who experiences difficulty discerning the correct answer to a math problem. The teacher urges the student to "think harder," applying further pressure to the intimidated youngster, who desperately hopes for a flash of brilliance. Meanwhile, fellow classmates are frantically waving their hands, certain in their own minds that they have deduced the right answer. Finally, giving up on the perplexed child, the teacher recognizes another student who excitedly shouts the correct answer. One child's misery is another child's triumph. Henry (1963) summarizes this commonplace competitive situation in U.S. classrooms this way: "So often somebody's success has been bought at the cost of our failure. To a Zuni, Hopi, or Dakota Indian, [besting another student] would seem cruel beyond belief, for competition, the wringing of success from somebody else's failure, is a form of torture" (p. 35).

Chuck Otterman's experience coaching football to students at Arizona's Hopi High School illustrates the normative nature of competitiveness. Football, with its emphasis on hitting opponents, psyching up for the game, and total commitment to victory, contradicts almost nine centuries of Hopi culture and religion.

Located on a reservation, Hopi High hardly embraced football. As Otterman explains, "They aren't used to our win-at-all-costs, beat-the-other-man mentality. Their understanding of life, of what it means to be a good Hopi, goes against what it takes to be a good football player" (Garrity, 1989, p. 11). Hopi football players did not initially understand the game. Hopi fans didn't know what to do at games, so Otterman had to be both coach and cheerleader, frequently urging the slim crowds to stand up and shout their support for the team.

In the second year of the program, the team posted a respectable 6–4 win–loss record, thanks to an excellent quarterback and sure-handed wide receivers. Nevertheless, their quarterback, Jarrett Huma, was uncomfortable with his impressive record-setting personal statistics. Huma and his teammates felt more comfortable when his proficiency at quarterback fell off the next season. Otterman observed that individual success made them uneasy.

After three seasons of bringing football to a community that was skeptical from the outset, Otterman resigned, citing lack of community support for the program. Otterman explained, "These people [were] just waiting to say, 'Football is bad, we don't want it.' And maybe they're right. I really don't know. I don't think the Hopis knew what they were getting into" (Garrity, 1989, p. 16).

There is abundant evidence demonstrating that American hypercompetitiveness flows primarily from an individualist cultural value system, not a biological imperative (Chatman & Barsade, 1995). Collectivist cultures tend to be far less competitive than the United States (Cox et al., 1991). Two separate studies comparing American groups (highly individualist) with Vietnamese groups (highly collectivist) found that Americans were competitive but the Vietnamese exhibited an "extraordinarily high rate" of cooperation, even when faced with competitive strategies from others. The authors of these studies concluded: "The difference between the extremely individualist and extremely collectivist cultures was very large and consistent with cultural norms" (Parks & Vu, 1994, p. 712). Cultural norms heavily influence the degree of competitiveness in a society.

Questions for Thought

1. In your judgment, was it appropriate to introduce football to the Hopis? Explain.
2. Is it possible for a cocultural group such as the Hopi to remain mostly cooperative when the predominant culture is largely competitive?
3. Have you had experience with other cultures in which cooperation is emphasized?

Despite the intergroup hostility, doesn't wanting to defeat another group increase cohesiveness within your group? This is true to an extent. There are "weak indications" that intergroup competition generates internal group cohesion. This is primarily true, however, when your group has to pull together to face a common foe. In the long run, however, **cohesiveness is enhanced primarily for winning teams.** Losing teams typically fall apart and members look for someone to blame (Van Oostrum & Rabbie, 1995). Competition is simply more enjoyable for winners than it is for losers (Tauer & Harackiewicz, 2004).

Even if intergroup competition stimulates internal group cohesion, however, this method is a questionable way to achieve such a result. The group will have to manufacture enemies to defeat in order to maintain cohesion within the group. Cohesion, then, is artificially induced. It doesn't flow naturally from group interaction. Once the foe has been bested, the reason for cohesion is removed. A cooperative group climate, on the other hand, enhances the social relationships within the group, thereby increasing cohesiveness and group productivity as a by-product (Rabbie, 1993).

Communication and Group Climate

Urgent pleas and pious pronouncements ("Let's all just get along") rarely produce cooperation in groups, even if our intentions are noble. Learning cooperative communication skills, however, is critical to the establishment of a positive group climate (D. W. Johnson, 2003).

▶ **Focus Questions**

1. Can both negative and positive evaluation of others produce defensiveness?
2. Is controlling communication always unavoidable?
3. What's the difference between a shift response and a support response?

DEFENSIVE AND SUPPORTIVE COMMUNICATION: SHAPING GROUP CLIMATE

Jack Gibb (1961), in an 8-year study of groups, identified specific communication patterns that both increase and lessen **defensiveness**—a reaction to a perceived attack on our self-concept and self-esteem. Defensive communication patterns invite hypercompetitiveness. Supportive communication patterns invite cooperation. As each of these communication patterns is discussed, see if you recognize any of them in your own experience with groups (take the self-assessment test in Box 4.1).

Evaluation versus Description A friend of mine was in his townhouse when the 6.9-magnitude Loma Prieta earthquake hit Santa Cruz, California, in October 1989.

BOX 4.1 REACTIONS TO DEFENSIVE AND SUPPORTIVE COMMUNICATION

Project yourself into each situation below and imagine how you would react. Choose a number for each situation that reflects how much you would like or dislike the statements presented.

1. You live with two roommates in an apartment. You forgot to clean your dishes twice this week. One of your roommates says to you, "Do your dishes. I'm tired of cleaning up your mess."

   STRONGLY 5 4 3 2 1 STRONGLY
   DISLIKE   LIKE

2. You're working with your team on a group project. One member says to the group, "I'm feeling very concerned that we will not finish our project in time. We're about halfway and we only have 2 days before our presentation. What do the rest of you think?"

   STRONGLY 5 4 3 2 1 STRONGLY
   DISLIKE   LIKE

3. You are a member of a softball team. Your coach says to you in front of the team, "You blew the game last week. Are you prepared to do better this game?"

   STRONGLY 5 4 3 2 1 STRONGLY
   DISLIKE   LIKE

4. At work, you tripped and badly bruised your shoulder. Your boss says to you, "I heard that you injured yourself yesterday. Do you need time off? That must really hurt. Can I do anything to make you more comfortable while you work in your office?"

   STRONGLY 5 4 3 2 1 STRONGLY
   DISLIKE   LIKE

5. Your support group meets once a week to share experiences and solve personal problems. The group facilitator announces to the group, "We haven't got time to hear from (your name). We have more important things to consider."

   STRONGLY 5 4 3 2 1 STRONGLY
   DISLIKE   LIKE

6. During a group problem-solving session, one member says to the group, "I have a suggestion that might solve our problem. Perhaps this will move us forward."

   STRONGLY 5 4 3 2 1 STRONGLY
   DISLIKE   LIKE

7. You are a member of the Student Senate. During discussion on a controversial campus problem, the Senate president says to the group, "We're obviously divided on this issue. Because I'm the president of this body, I'll have to make the final decision."

   STRONGLY 5 4 3 2 1 STRONGLY
   DISLIKE   LIKE

8. During a Dorm Council meeting, one member says to the Council, "I know we all have strong feelings on this issue, but let's put our heads together and see if we can find a solution everyone can support. Does anyone have ideas they wish to share with the group?"

   STRONGLY 5 4 3 2 1 STRONGLY
   DISLIKE   LIKE

9. During a heated group discussion with fellow classmates, one group member says, "I know I'm right and there isn't any way any of you will convince me that I'm wrong."

STRONGLY 5 4 3 2 1 STRONGLY
DISLIKE   LIKE

10. Your class project group approaches your teacher and proposes an idea that your teacher initially dislikes. She says to your group, "I can see that you really like this idea, but it doesn't satisfy the requirements of the project. I suggest that you keep brainstorming."

STRONGLY 5 4 3 2 1 STRONGLY
DISLIKE   LIKE

11. You're a member of a hiring panel. During a break from an interviewing session, one member of the panel takes you aside and says, "Look, I want you to support my candidate. We've been friends a long time. This is important to me. Whadaya say? Can I count on you to back me up?"

STRONGLY 5 4 3 2 1 STRONGLY
DISLIKE   LIKE

12. You've been asked to work on a committee to solve the parking problem on campus. The chair addresses the committee, "It is my hope that this committee can come to a consensus on solutions to this parking problem. I'll conduct our meetings, but I only have one vote, the same as everyone else."

STRONGLY 5 4 3 2 1 STRONGLY
DISLIKE   LIKE

1, 3, 5, 7, 9, and 11 = **defensive communication** (control, evaluation, indifference, superiority, certainty, and manipulation—in that order); 2, 4, 6, 8, 10, and 12 = **supportive communication** (description, empathy, provisionalism, problem orientation, assertiveness, and equality—in that order). Find your average score for each set (divide by six both the sum of the odd-numbered items and the sum of the even-numbered items). Which do you like best (*lower average score*)—defensive or supportive communication?

Objects flew across the rooms, kitchen cabinets emptied onto the counters and floor, and glass shattered throughout his home. When the 15 seconds of rocking and rolling to Mother Nature's syncopation subsided, a momentary quiet ensued. Then from the back room came the timid, frightened little voice of his 5-year-old daughter: "Daddy, it wasn't my fault." We are quick to evaluate each other in American society, especially negatively, and we are ready to defend ourselves even when no evaluation is offered.

Negative evaluations include criticism, contempt, and blame. Positive evaluations include praise, recognition, and flattery. Negative evaluations produce defensiveness (Robbins et al., 2000). A study of 108 managers and white-collar workers found that criticism produced more conflict in the workplace than mistrust, personality clashes, pay, or power struggles (Baron, 1990). In another study, harsh criticism demoralized participants, reduced their work effort, and led to refusals to work with criticizers on future tasks (Baron, 1988).

Praise, on the other hand, is usually welcome. A survey of 150 executives from Fortune 1,000 firms by Robert Half International found that scant praise and limited recognition were the main reasons employees left their companies. Robert Half, who conducted the research, notes, "Praising accomplishments provides psychological rewards that are critical to satisfaction" ("Praise the Employees," 1994). A Gallup study of more than 80,000 managers likewise concluded: "Praise and recognition are essential building blocks of a great workplace" (Buckingham & Coffman, 2002b). Nevertheless, even praise can induce defensiveness, especially when one group member receives praise and others don't, or when we suspect an ulterior motive prompts the positive evaluation.

Besides giving praise and recognition, description can substitute for negative evaluations and neutralize defensiveness. **Description** is a first-person report of how an individual feels, what the individual perceives to be true, and what behaviors have been observed in a specific context. There are three primary steps necessary to become more descriptive. They are

1. *Use first-person-singular language* (Narcisco & Burkett, 1975). First-person singular uses I-statements, not you- or we-statements, at the beginning of a sentence.

   Typically, first-person-singular statements begin with an identification of the speaker's feeling, followed by a description of behavior linked to the feeling. "I feel excluded and isolated when my contributions receive no response from the group" is an example of a first-person-singular descriptive statement. Such an I-statement focuses the attention on the person speaking.

   A you-statement, however, places the focus on someone who is an object of attack. "You have excluded me from the group and you make me feel isolated" is a statement that accuses and blames. Finger-pointing invites defensiveness.

2. *Make your descriptions specific, not vague.* "I feel weird when you act inappropriately around my boss," is an inexact description. "Weird" and "inappropriately" require specific elaboration. Get to the point. "I feel awkward and embarrassed when you tell my boss jokes that ridicule gays and women" is much more specific.

3. *Eliminate editorial comments from descriptive statements.* This is perhaps the most challenging step. Some I-statements are undisguised personal assaults. "I feel ashamed when you act like a social retard in front of my colleagues" uses the I-statement form without the supportive intent or phrasing. Even an I-statement that may appear to be a specific description devoid of judgment sometimes inadvertently travels into evaluative territory. "I get irritated when you waste the time of this committee by commenting on trivial side issues" loads the statement with provocative phrasing. "Waste time" and "trivial" retain the evaluative and

attack elements likely to induce defensive responses. Simply jettison the loaded language.

Textbook-perfect, first-person-singular, specific, editorial-free statements, of course, induce no supportive climate if the tone of voice used is sarcastic or condescending, eye contact is threatening, facial expressions and body language are intimidating, and gestures are abusive. We must be willing and able to place the focus on our own feelings and spotlight the specific behaviors we find objectionable without sending mixed messages composed of verbal descriptions and nonverbal, negative evaluations.

Control versus Problem Orientation English poet Samuel Butler once said, "He who agrees against his will, is of the same opinion still." **Issuing orders and demanding obedience, especially when no input was sought from group members that were told what to do, is controlling communication.** Jack Brehm (1972) developed a theory of psychological reactance to explain our resistance to efforts aimed at controlling our behavior. Simply put, **psychological reactance** means the more someone tries to control us by telling us what to do, the more we are inclined to resist such efforts, or even to do the opposite. The following bit of wisdom captures this well: "There are three ways to make sure something gets done—do it yourself; hire someone to do it; *forbid* your kids to do it" (Landers, 1995). The more intensely parents admonish their kids not to smoke, ingest drugs, or get various portions of their anatomies pierced, the more likely their children are to do these behaviors so they can restore their sense of personal freedom (Dowsd et al., 1988).

Tell someone they can't do something and, typically, it is what they want to do most. A 15-year study of "radical groups," involving more than a thousand subjects, concluded that the coercive practice of "deprogramming" individuals to give up their cult membership "can drive young people back into their group, or into a pattern of cult-hopping, for years" (S. Levine, 1984, p. 27).

We help prevent a defensive climate from emerging when we collaborate on a problem and seek solutions cooperatively. The orientation is on the problem and how best to solve it, not on how best to control those who have less power. All controlling communication can't be eliminated (parents want to protect their children from foolish or dangerous behavior), but it can be kept to a minimum (LaFasto & Larson, 2001). Group members that are not acting responsibly (late with reports from laziness) may have to be told to change their behavior by the group leader or the group as a whole. Generally, however, the focus should be on problem solving, and personality conflicts and power struggles should fade into the background.

A study of decision making at 356 U.S. companies discovered that 58% of strategic plans were rejected when executives overseeing the plans attempted to impose

Psychological reactance can occur even when we care little about that which is prohibited.

their ideas on colleagues. When executives asked instead for problem-solving ideas from colleagues, however, 96% of the plans were approved (McNutt, 1997). Ownership of a solution to a problem comes not from mandating it ("This is what I've decided and you must do it"), but from collaborating as a group (parents and child together) and brainstorming possible solutions.

Wanting to be less controlling and more oriented toward problem solving is not the complete answer. The competent communicator must know how to problem-solve, have the requisite skills, and be committed to finding solutions. More will be said about these in later chapters.

Manipulation versus Assertiveness The experience of buying a new car is a trial for me. I loathe the initial fake friendliness from the salesperson. I recoil when the salesperson starts in with the transparent compliments (e.g., "You look like a smart guy" or "You strike me as the kind of guy who can spot a steal when you see one"). I retreat (usually out of the showroom entirely) when the auto hucksters try to double-team me, one on each side, with their transparent, stereophonic sales pitch.

Most people resent and resist being manipulated. If you are like most people, simply knowing that someone is attempting to influence you for his or her own benefit is repellent. I experienced my own private purgatory when I sold encyclopedias door to door for a brief time one summer following graduation from college. Working out of Denver, Colorado, I diligently knocked on doors of strangers, most of whom were not exactly thrilled by my presence on their doorsteps. After suffering many rude comments and slammed doors, the first person to invite me in was a young, friendly woman who had no idea I hoped to sell her encyclopedias. I was trained to camouflage my real purpose to avoid immediate rejection (rarely successful). Upon entering her home, I noticed the woman's inebriated husband and his snarling German Shepherd. "If you're selling something," the unpleasant husband snapped at me, "you'll be dealing with my dog." I concocted a quick excuse and exited. I found refuge in the house of an older Czechoslovakian couple. I was served tea and cookies while I engaged in friendly conversation about "the old country" for almost 3 hours. I gave up trying to sell encyclopedias for the evening, having recognized how intensely people in my sales territory resented being disturbed by a stranger attempting to sell them something. To this day, I wonder if that sweet couple ever remembered the young man who came to visit them for no apparent reason. I quickly retired from the encyclopedia business.

A study of 6,000 team members in 600 organizations found that playing politics, an especially cutthroat version of manipulative communication, destroys social relationships and team effectiveness (LaFasto & Larson, 2001). **Hidden agendas**—personal goals of group members that are not revealed openly and that can interfere with group accomplishment—can create a defensive atmosphere. When you suspect that a team member is complimenting your performance merely to gain an ally against other members in a dispute, this hidden agenda will likely ignite defensiveness.

Assertiveness is the alternative to manipulation. Assertiveness is honest, open, and direct, but not aggressive, communication. It is the opposite of game playing and strategic manipulation. An assertive message says, "This is how I feel and this is what I need." A much more extensive discussion of assertiveness appears in Chapter 9.

Indifference versus Empathy We like being acknowledged when we are present in a group. We dislike being treated like a piece of the furniture, sitting alone in a corner. Indifference to group members, or what Gibb (1961) calls neutrality, makes us defensive. Making little or no effort to listen to what a member of your group has to say exhibits indifference and treats the communicator as a nonperson. Failure to acknowledge another person's communication effort either verbally or nonverbally is called an **impervious response** (Sieberg & Larson, 1971). Such indifference is disconfirming.

You counter indifference with empathy. Howell (1982) defines **empathy** as "thinking and feeling what you perceive another to be thinking and feeling" (p. 108). Empathy is built on concern for others. It requires that we try to see from the perspective of the other person, perceiving the needs, desires, and feelings of a group member because that is what we would want others to do for us. "How would you like it if I treated you the way you treat me?" is a plea for empathy from others.

Rosenfeld (1983) determined that creating a supportive climate in the college classroom was a key determinant of whether classes would be liked by students. In classes liked by students, instructors show interest in the problems students face, they exhibit a perception of subject matter as students see it, and they make students feel understood. Showing that we understand and relate does make a difference.

Superiority versus Equality Communicating superiority sends the message that one is me-deep in self-importance. It can be a tremendous turnoff for most people. The Rosenfeld (1983) study on defensiveness in the college classroom found that the behavior of instructors in classes that are disliked by students is characterized as predominantly superior. One of the key factors characterizing classes that were liked was "My teacher treats us as equals with him/her." Whatever the differences in our abilities, talents, intellect, and the like, treating people with respect and politeness—as equals on a personal level—encourages harmony and productivity. Treating people like they are IRS agents at the awards ceremony for the state lottery winner will invite enmity and retaliation.

Equality does not mean we all have the same abilities. Equality from the standpoint of group climate means that we give everyone an equal opportunity to succeed. We accord all group members respect unless they earn our disrespect. We do not make people feel stupid. Despite variability in talent, ability, achievements, money, and so forth, we do not make issues of these differences in the group. We do not sabotage the efforts of one person in the group by demeaning that member as inferior. Task accomplishment is thwarted by diminishing the self-esteem of any member. The diminishment of even one member may send a system-wide message to all members—you could be the next target. *Be on guard.*

Certainty versus Provisionalism There are very few things in this world that are certain—death, taxes, and that your clothes dryer will eat your socks are a few that come to mind. Communicating certainty to group members, however, is asking for trouble. I listened to students in my class argue with one of their group members who insisted that crystals really do have healing powers and that only pigheadedness

> **●● SECOND LOOK**

DEFENSIVE VERSUS SUPPORTIVE COMMUNICATION PATTERNS

DEFENSIVE	SUPPORTIVE
1. Evaluation	1. Description
2. Control	2. Problem orientation
3. Manipulation	3. Assertiveness
4. Indifference	4. Empathy
5. Superiority	5. Equality
6. Certainty	6. Provisionalism

kept the group from accepting the truth of what he was adamantly asserting. This individual would entertain no contrary point of view, so certain was he of the unalterable correctness of his belief, nor would he accede to requests from members for hard evidence of crystals' healing power. He was certain he was right and anyone who couldn't accept this truth must be stupid. This was dogmatism in action.

Dogmatism is the belief in the self-evident truth of one's opinion. The dogma, or declaration of truth, warrants no debate in the mind of the dogmatist. A dogmatic individual exhibits closed-mindedness and rigid thinking. Alternative ideas are not seriously considered. Interestingly, the word dogma spelled backward is *am-god*. Dogmatists act godlike in the certitude of their own point of view. These self-appointed deities can easily inflame the tempers of group members. Some people derive pleasure from trying to prove the dogmatist wrong. Competitive contests fought over assertions of truth by dogmatists and their antagonists can degenerate into adolescent bickering.

Leathers (1970) conducted a study in which typical dogmatic statements were introduced into group discussions ("You are wrong, dead wrong!"). Subjects responded with increased tension (e.g., rubbing hands together nervously and squirming in their seats). These statements also elicited opinionated statements from group members. A climate of inflexibility was produced and trust among group members deteriorated.

Certainty is also reflected in terms such as *never, always, must, impossible, can't,* and *won't.* These terms shut down group discussion and leave no room for alternatives.

Provisionalism counters certainty. **Provisionalism** means you qualify statements, avoiding absolutes. Provisionalism is reflected in the use of qualifying terms such as *possibly, probably, perhaps, occasionally, maybe, might,* and *sometimes.* This is the language of precision, not fence-straddling. Problems are approached as interesting questions to be investigated and discussed, not defensive power struggles regarding who is right or wrong.

Reciprocal Patterns: Like Begets Like Once a group climate develops, it can set in motion a reciprocal pattern—tit for tat. One such famous tit-for-tat exchange occurred between Lady Astor, the first female member of the British Parliament, and Winston Churchill. Exasperated by Churchill's opposition to several of the causes she espoused, Lady Astor acerbically remarked, "Winston, if I were married to you, I'd put poison in your coffee." Churchill replied, "And if you were my wife, I'd drink it" (Fadiman, 1985, p. 122). Verbal attack begets verbal attack.

One study found that supportive/confirming communication patterns by one party during a conflict elicited similar responses from the other party (Burggraf & Sillars, 1987). The same held true for defensive/disconfirming communication patterns (Sundell, 1972).

The challenge in any group experience is to maintain the positive reciprocal pattern of support and to break the cycle of the negative reciprocal pattern of defensiveness. A positive reciprocal pattern of support and cooperation must emerge from the communication transactions among group members. Group leaders may play an important role in this process by setting a cooperative tone for the group. The responsibility for establishing a positive group climate, however, rests on all group members.

COMPETITIVE AND NONCOMPETITIVE LISTENING: SHIFTING AND SUPPORTING

A report from the U.S. Department of Labor (1991) reveals that the average worker spends about 55% of time on the job listening to others. Another study found that college students devote more than half of their communicating time to listening (L. Barker et al., 1981). Despite the obvious importance of listening well in groups, evidence shows that for the most part we don't listen very well. One report (cited in R. Adler & Towne, 1999) discovered that only 12% of college students were actively listening to a class lecture and another 20% were mildly attentive. The remaining students were pursuing erotic thoughts (20%), reminiscing (20%), or worrying, daydreaming, or thinking about lunch or religion (8%). **Active listening is focused listening.** We make a conscious effort to focus our attention on the speaker and his or her message. Too often when sitting in groups we do not make the effort to listen actively. We allow our minds to wander.

Competent listening, however, goes far beyond actively listening to other group members. **How we listen is also extremely important.** In this section I will briefly discuss competitive and noncompetitive listening.

Shift Response versus Support Response: Focusing on Me or Thee Listening can become a competitive event. When we vie for attention during a group discussion, our listening becomes competitive. Conversation becomes a contest. An attention-*getting* initiative by a listener, called the **shift response,** is a key competitive listening strategy. Here the listener attempts to shift the focus of attention from others to oneself by changing the topic of discussion. The shift response is Me-oriented. The **support response,** in contrast, is an attention-*giving,* cooperative effort by the listener to focus attention on the other person, not on oneself (Derber 1979; Vangelisti et al., 1990). Consider the following example:

> Maria: I'm feeling very frustrated by our group's lack of progress on our project.
> Michael: I was more frustrated by Jerry's snotty attitude during yesterday's meeting. (*Shift response*)

Notice how Michael does not respond to Maria's frustration. Instead, he shifts the focus to his own frustration about another issue in the group. Now compare this shift response with a support response, as follows:

> Maria: I'm feeling very frustrated by our group's lack of progress on our project.
> Michael: I hear you. What do you think we should do about it? (*Support response*)

Here, the response from the listener keeps the focus on the speaker and encourages Maria to explore the topic she initiated.

A shift response can easily provoke shift responses from other group members in a hypercompetitive battle for attention, such as in the following example:

> Beth: I don't think our project fulfills the requirements of the class assignment. I'm worried that we will get a bad grade.
> Greg: The assignment is too difficult. I don't understand what we are supposed to do. (*Shift response*)
> Carla: The project isn't too difficult. It is really interesting and fun. I'm looking forward to the next project, aren't you? (*Shift response*)
> Beth: But what about our report on this current project? I still don't think we've fulfilled the assignment. (*Shift response* to refocus attention on initial topic)
> Greg: You worry too much. I need help on my speech. What's the main point I need to make first? (*Shift response*)

Although the shift response may be appropriate in some instances where individuals drift from the main topic of conversation and need to be refocused, **competent communicators emphasize support responses and use shift responses infrequently.** *Background acknowledgment* ("really," "uh-huh," "yup"), a *supportive assertion* ("That's super," "Nicely done") and a *supportive question* ("How do you think we should proceed?") are the types of supportive responses that encourage cooperative discussion, not competitive struggles for attention.

Competitive Interrupting: Seizing the Floor Competitive interrupting is closely related to the shift response. It differs, however, in one key way. **Listeners who use the shift response usually observe the "one speaker at a time" rule of conversation. Competitive interrupters do not.**

Interrupting becomes competitive when the listener attempts to seize the floor from the speaker and dominate the conversation. Not all interrupting, of course, is competitive. Sometimes group members interrupt to express support ("I agree with Joe") or enthusiasm ("Great idea"), seek clarification ("I'm confused. Could you explain that again before we move on?"), warn of danger ("Look out. You're falling over backwards"), or cut short a "talkaholic's" nonstop monologue that prevents other group members from participating (James & Clarke, 1993).

Competitive interrupting is Me-oriented. The focus is on individual needs, not group needs. Competitive interrupting creates antagonism, rivalry, hostility, and in some cases withdrawal from group discussion by frustrated members. Group members often mirror the interrupting patterns of others. If one member interrupts to seize the floor, another member will likely interrupt to seize it back. If members rarely interrupt, and when they do, primarily offer support, however, others will likely follow suit and keep the conversation supportive and cooperative.

Ambushing: Preparing Rebuttals When we are ready to pounce on a point made by a speaker, we are listening with a bias. The bias is to attack the speaker verbally, not try to understand the speaker's point of view. This is called **ambushing.** Ambushing is clearly competitive listening. Ambushers aim to defeat a speaker in a verbal jousting match. Preparing a rebuttal while a speaker is still explaining his or her point shows little interest in comprehending a message. In competitive debates, message distortion is a common problem. The focus is on winning the argument, not discerning a message accurately.

Should we ever debate ideas? Debating ideas is a useful and important process in a democratic society. Ambushing, however, puts the caboose in front of the train engine. Defeating an opponent becomes the driving force for ambushers, not clarity of messages. During group discussion, we need to understand messages clearly and accurately *before* evaluating them. Otherwise, we may be evaluating and refuting ideas that were never advanced by any group member.

Probing and paraphrasing can short-circuit ambushing. **Probing** means seeking additional information from a speaker by asking questions. Probing includes clarifying questions ("Can you give me an example of an important goal for the group?"), exploratory questions ("Can you think of any other approach to this problem?"), and encouraging questions ("Who can blame us for making a good effort to try a new approach?").

Paraphrasing "is a concise response to the speaker which states the essence of the other's content in the listener's words" (Bolton, 1979, p. 51). Paraphrasing should be concise and precise. For example:

Gabriela: I'm so sick and tired of working and working on this report and we have so little to show for it. If we'd started earlier, we would be done by now.
Frank: You seem frustrated and unhappy with the group's effort.
Gabriela: I am frustrated, but I'm not unhappy with our group. We've all worked hard. None of us could arrange our schedules to begin any sooner on this.

Paraphrasing can reveal misunderstanding. Ambushing merely assumes a message is understood without checking. Noncompetitive listening is a useful communication skill.

In summary, there is perhaps no greater challenge nor more important task in a group than establishing a positive, cooperative climate. A negative, competitive climate will bode ill for your group. Defensive climates promote conflict and disharmony in groups. Supportive climates do not free groups entirely from conflict, but such an atmosphere enhances the likelihood of constructive solutions to conflict in groups. ● ●

Questions for Critical Thinkers

1. Why do you think supervisors faced with poor employee performance use predominantly controlling, not problem-solving, strategies?
2. Are there instances when you should act as a model of cooperative behavior even though other group members will take advantage of you?
3. Is hypercompetitive communication ever ethical?

InfoTrac College Edition

Log onto InfoTrac College Edition.

1. Type "competition" in the search window. Choose an article to critique. SUGGESTION: Article A89427543 by Joyce F. Benenson et al. entitled "Greater discomfort as a proximate cause of sex differences in competition."

2. Type "competition and gender" in the search window. Choose an article to read. SUGGESTION: Article A61892279 by Stefanie Gilbert and J. Kevin Thompson entitled "Winning or losing against an opposite-sex peer on a gender-based competitive task."

Video Case Studies

Who's Afraid of Virginia Woolf? (1966). Drama; R; *****

Engrossing, but lengthy film depicting George and Martha, a troubled couple, "entertaining" another couple in the wee hours of the morning. This film is loaded with examples of defensive communication. Identify as many examples as you can find.

Playing by Heart (1998). Romantic Comedy; R; ****

This is a wonderful, romantic comedy about peoples' lives intersecting, sometimes poignantly. Look for defensive and supportive communication patterns.

Remember the Titans (2000). Drama; PG; ****1/2

Feel-good true story of a black football coach who has to deal with racism in a newly integrated high school in Virginia. Examine this film for both intragroup and intergroup competition. Do the results of competition depicted in the movie parallel the research in this chapter? Is the competition constructive?

5 Roles and Leadership in Groups

I N A STUDY OF A SURGICAL TEAM at St. Joseph's Hospital in Ann Arbor, Michigan, the distinction between the role of doctor and nurse was evident. During a coronary bypass operation, the two surgeons (both males) began swapping stories about the Detroit Tigers while loud rock music played in the background. Two nurses (both women) assisting with the operation began a quiet discussion of their own, only to be reprimanded by the head surgeon, who bellowed, "Come on, people; let's keep it down in here!" (Denison & Sutton, 1990, p. 301). Nurses did not have the same leeway to talk, laugh, and joke with each other as surgeons did. Surgeons, by necessity, were in charge of the operation. Surgeons were in the leader role and nurses were in the follower role, expected to do the bidding of the surgeons without question. Surgical teams have clearly defined roles. Nurses, nevertheless, complained bitterly that the doctors were unnecessarily oppressive in exercising their superior power (that is, they used defensive communication patterns of control and superiority). Nurses described being treated like slaves, and often were expected to perform demeaning tasks when ordered by surgeons to do so.

In the drama of life we play many roles. A group **role** is the pattern of expected behavior associated with parts that we play in groups. Individuals act out their roles in transactions with group members. What might have begun as a casual or unnoticed pattern of behavior may quickly develop into an expectation. For example, when you tell a few jokes during the initial meeting of your group, you may be assuming the role of tension reliever without even noticing. Other group members may come to expect you to interject humor into tense situations.

Roles are not static entities. When the composition of your group changes, when phases of development change, when the group climate shifts either toward or away from a cooperative/supportive one, or when you move from one group to another, you have to adapt to these changes in the system. The required behaviors for your role may change as a consequence, or the roles members play may change.

The principal purpose of this chapter is to discuss group roles, with special focus on the prime group role of leader. There are five objectives relevant to this purpose:

1. to explain the significance of roles in groups,
2. to identify the different types of group roles,

3. to discuss the role emergence process,
4. to explore how members gain and retain group leadership, and
5. to discuss how to be an effective leader in groups.

Group Roles

Norms and roles form the basic structure of a group. Structure is the systematic interrelation of all parts to the whole. Structure provides form and shape for a group. Norms are *broad* rules that designate appropriate behavior for *all* group members while roles stipulate *specific* behaviors that are expected for *individual* group members. A norm for a group might be that every member works hard on all tasks. Roles, however, specify different task behaviors for a vice president, a middle manager, and an office worker. In this section, the effects of roles on behavior, types of roles, role emergence, and role fixation are explored.

▶ **Focus Questions**

1. Are there some group roles that the competent communicator should avoid?
2. When two roles conflict, which role is likely to prevail?

INFLUENCE OF ROLES: NOT JUST PLAYING GAMES

The expectations attached to roles can have a marked influence on group members' perceptions (see Closer Look: "The Stanford Prison Study"). This influence was demonstrated in a study in which pairs of students performed the roles of questioner and contestant in a college bowl type of quiz game (L. Ross et al., 1977). Questioners were instructed to think of 10 difficult questions for which they knew the answers. They then were to ask contestants these questions. Both students and the audience knew that the roles of questioner and contestant were randomly assigned. Yet, both the audience and the contestants thought that those students playing the questioner role were smarter than those students playing the contestant role. Questioners, of course, looked more impressive asking difficult questions for which they already knew the answers, while contestants looked less impressive trying to answer the questions and sometimes making mistakes. Despite the obvious advantage given to the questioners and despite the fact that students playing both roles were equally intelligent, the predominant perception was markedly influenced by the role each student played.

Role Reversal: When Students Become Teachers The effects of roles on perceptions can be seen in a dramatic way by doing a **role reversal,** which is stepping into a role distinctly different from or opposite of a role we usually play.

THE STANFORD PRISON STUDY

IT HAPPENED ONE SUNDAY MORNING. Police officers, with vehicle sirens screeching, swept through the college town and arrested 10 male college students. Charged with a felony, the students were searched, handcuffed, and taken to police headquarters for booking. Then they were blindfolded and transported to the Stanford County Prison, located in the basement of the Stanford University Psychology department building. Upon arrival they were stripped naked, issued a smock-type uniform with an ID number across the front and back, and forced to wear a cap made out of nylon to simulate a shaved head. Each prisoner received towels, soap, a toothbrush, and bed linen. Jail cells were sparsely furnished—cots and bucket toilets. Personal belongings were prohibited.

The 10 inmates were guarded by 11 other college students. These guards carried clubs, handcuffs, and whistles. They dressed in khaki uniforms and wore reflecting sunglasses to make eye contact difficult. They remained nameless.

Guards established a set of rules that the prisoners were to follow without hesitation or resistance. The rules were rigid: no talking during meals, rest periods, or after lights were out. Head counts were taken at 2:30 a.m. Troublemakers faced loss of "privileges." At first, these privileges included opportunities to read, write, or talk to other inmates. Later, privileges were defined as eating, sleeping, and washing.

The inmates revolted against the repressive conditions. Some barricaded the doors of their cells with cots. Some engaged in hunger strikes. Several tore off their ID numbers. The guards became increasingly abusive and authoritarian in response to the revolt. They used a fire extinguisher to quash the rebellion. Punishment for disobedience included cleaning toilets with bare hands, doing push-ups, and spending time in solitary confinement (a closet). Head counts were used as a means of harassment. Head counts took 10 minutes or less on the first day. By the fifth day, the head counts lasted several hours as the guards vilified prisoners, who were standing at attention the entire time, for minor infractions of the rules.

Within a short time some of the prisoners began to act depressed, dependent, and disturbed by their incarceration. Several prisoners experienced severe stomach cramps. One prisoner wept uncontrollably. He flew into fits of rage and experienced disorganized thinking and bouts of severe depression. Three other inmates developed similar symptoms. Another inmate developed a psychosomatic rash over his entire body when his "parole" was denied.

The chief form of communication initiated by the guards to the prisoners consisted mostly of commands, insults, verbal and physical abuse, degrading references, and threats. The principal form of communication used by the prisoners when interacting with the guards consisted mostly of resistance and ridicule in the beginning, but became more compliant later (e.g., answering questions and giving information).

Stanford psychologist Phillip Zimbardo (1992), who conducted this mock prison study, terminated the experiment after only 6 days. The study was originally planned for a 2-week period, but he decided that the roles had become real. As Zimbardo (1992) concluded: "In guard roles, college students who had been pacifists and 'nice guys' behaved aggressively—sometimes even sadistically. As prisoners, psychologically stable students soon behaved pathologically, passively resigning themselves to their unexpected fate of learned helplessness" (p. 576).

Zimbardo had taken 21 healthy, well-adjusted male students who exhibited no signs of emotional instability or aberrant behavior when given extensive personality tests and clinical interviews prior to the experiment, and he had transformed them into pathological guards and compliant prisoners. The guard and prisoner roles were randomly assigned by the flip of a coin, so pathological behavior cannot be explained by looking for character flaws in the men acting as guards. Clearly, the young men in this controversial field study became the product of their designated roles.

The parallels of the Stanford prison study to the shocking abuse by American soldiers of Iraqi prisoners at Abu Ghurayb prison near Baghdad in 2004 are stunning. In both the real and the experimental prison, guards stripped prisoners naked, forced them to wear bags over their heads, chained prisoners together, and finally forced prisoners to endure sadistic sexual degradation and humiliation. Guards said to one group of prisoners, "Bend over; you're female camels." Guards said to another group of prisoners, "You're male camels; hump them" (quoted in Reddy, 2004). This was just one of the many examples of verbal abuse heaped upon prisoners, not by guards at Abu Ghurayb, but by college students playing the role of guards in the Stanford prison study. In both instances, the guards were ordinary individuals placed in extraordinarily bad situations, and they acted brutally.

As Zimbardo notes, although students are unlikely ever to play the roles of prisoner or guard in real life, this study is analogous to more commonplace role status differences. Whenever the power accorded certain roles establishes unequal power distribution, the potential for abuse is real. Teacher–student, doctor–patient, supervisor–employee, and parent–child relationships are just a few examples of role status differences that can potentially lead to verbal, even physical mistreatment.

Questions for Thought

1. Considering the effects this experiment had upon its subjects, do you have any ethical concerns about conducting similar studies?

▶

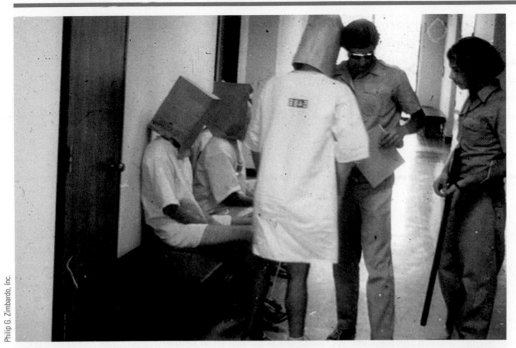

Philip G. Zimbardo, Inc.

Getty Images

The Stanford prison study and Abu Ghurayb show chillingly similar results.

▶

2. Can you think of roles outside of a prison environment that exert similar influence and power over individuals' lives as exhibited in this experiment?

3. Would you have preferred to be a prisoner or a guard? Why?

4. As a guard, would you have treated the prisoners abusively? Are you uncertain of how you would have behaved? Explain.

5. As a prisoner, would you have been docile or rebellious? Are you uncertain of how you would behave in the prisoner role? Explain.

A study (Geis et al., 1984) on the impact of **role status**—the relative importance, prestige, or power accorded a particular role—showed the power of role reversal. When viewers saw television commercials depicting a man in a high-status, important person role (his wishes, needs, and preferences were the central concern of the commercial) and a woman in the relatively low-status, helpmate role (her wishes, needs, and preferences were never addressed or acknowledged), they described the man as a "rational, independent, dominant, ambitious leader." The woman, by contrast, was described as an "emotional, dependent, submissive, contented follower." A markedly different result from these stereotypic depictions of male–female interactions occurred when the roles were exactly reversed. When the woman in the commercial performed the high-status role and the man acted out the low-status role, viewers described the woman as a "rational, independent, dominant, ambitious leader" and the man as an "emotional, dependent, submissive, contented follower."

Role Conflict: Torn between Two Roles The effects of roles can be seen in another way. When we find ourselves playing roles in different groups that contradict each other, we experience **role conflict.** Usually we are forced to make a choice between the two. For instance, when a disastrous fire in Texas City, Texas, endangered the entire city, police officers were faced with a serious role conflict. Should they continue to protect the citizens of the city in their role as police officers, or should they consider their role as parents and spouses to be more important? They couldn't do both. In every case except one they chose their family role over their professional role. The exception was a man who knew his family was safe in another city (Killian, 1952). Undoubtedly, the 2004 tsunami in Indonesia, triggered by a 9.3-magnitude undersea earthquake that lasted almost 3 hours and created a huge ripple effect globally that killed 280,000 people, presented many individuals with a similar role conflict during the immediate aftermath of the disaster. Hurricane Katrina in 2005 did likewise. Which role, the personal (spouse, parent) or the professional (doctor, rescue worker), would you choose if faced with such a dilemma?

Similarly, students who have children are often faced with conflict between their student role and their parent role. Do you take the final exam or do you stay home with your sick child? Women with careers and families are increasingly concerned with this perceived role conflict. When a woman is in an important business meeting in which colleagues depend on her input and she receives a phone call from her child's school, what does she do? Let me note that the same role conflict could also exist for a man, but women are still typically cast as the primary caregiver except in single-parent situations. The perception that family demands will intrude upon a woman's work world more than on a man's can impede women's advancement in organizations (Haslett et al., 1992).

An extensive review of 42 studies on role conflict (C. Fisher & Gitelson, 1983) showed significant effects. When individuals felt role conflict within organizations, they exhibited an increased tendency to leave an organization. They also showed decreases in commitment to the organization, involvement in the job, satisfaction with the job, and participation in decision making.

Some roles have a greater impact on us than others. **The role that has the greatest importance and most potent effect on us is usually the one we choose when we have to decide between conflicting roles.** The expectations associated with group roles and the perception of the value, prestige, influence, status, or stigma attached to each role by both the group and the individual can strongly affect us.

TYPES OF ROLES: FORMAL AND INFORMAL

It is not possible to enumerate all the roles a person can play in groups. **In the broadest sense, roles are categorized as formal and informal.** A **formal role** is a position assigned by an organization or specifically designated by the group leader. Titles such as president, chair, and secretary usually accompany formal roles. Especially within larger organizations, a set of expected behaviors to fulfill the role is explicitly spelled out. A job description used to hire an individual to fill a specific position is an example. Formal roles exist within the structure of the group, team, or organization. They are designated; they do not emerge naturally from communication transactions. Formal roles are often independent from any person filling the role.

In smaller groups, the roles are mostly informal. An **informal role** emerges from the group transactions, and **it emphasizes functions, not positions.** A group member may fulfill leadership functions, that is, perform as a leader, without any formal designation. No single, informal role is found in all or even most groups, with the probable exception of leader.

Table 5.1   SAMPLE OF INFORMAL ROLES IN GROUPS

Task Roles

1. *Initiator-Contributor:* Offers lots of ideas and suggestions; proposes solutions and new directions.
2. *Information Seeker:* Requests clarification; solicits evidence; asks for suggestions and ideas from others.
3. *Opinion Seeker:* Requests viewpoints from others; looks for agreement and disagreement.
4. *Information Giver:* Acts as a resource person for group; provides relevant and significant information based on research, expertise, or personal experience.
5. *Clarifier-Elaborator:* Explains, expands, extends the ideas of others; provides examples and alternatives.
6. *Coordinator:* Draws together ideas of others; shows relationships between facts and ideas; promotes teamwork and cooperation.
7. *Secretary-Recorder:* Serves group memory function; takes minutes of meetings; keeps group's records and history.
8. *Facilitator:* Keeps group on track; guides discussion; reminds group of goal; regulates group activities.
9. *Devil's Advocate:* Challenges prevailing point of view for the sake of argument to test and critically evaluate the strength of ideas, solutions, or decisions.

Maintenance Roles

1. *Supporter-Encourager:* Bolsters the spirits and goodwill of the group; provides warmth, praise, and acceptance of others; includes reticent members in discussion.

Actual duties and specific behaviors expected from a group member playing an informal role are implicitly defined by communication transactions among members. The group does not tell an individual explicitly how to be a good leader, but members do indicate degrees of approval or disapproval when an individual assumes the role. Informal role playing is improvisational, not scripted.

Informal roles are typically classified into three types: task, maintenance, and self-centered (Benne & Sheats, 1948; Mudrack & Farrell, 1995). **Task roles** move the group toward the attainment of its goals. **The central communicative function of task roles is to extract the maximum productivity from the group.** **Maintenance roles** focus on the social dimension of the group. **The central communicative function of maintenance roles is to gain and maintain the cohesiveness of the group.** Self-centered or **disruptive roles** serve individual needs or goals (Me-oriented)

Table 5.1 CONTINUED

2. *Harmonizer-Tension Reliever:* Maintains the peace; reduces tension through humor and by reconciling differences between members.
3. *Gatekeeper-Expediter:* Controls channels of communication and flow of information; encourages evenness of participation; promotes open discussion.
4. *Feeling Expresser:* Monitors feelings and moods of the group; suggests discussion breaks when mood turns ugly or when energy levels flag.

Self-Centered or Disruptive Roles

1. *Stagehog:* Seeks recognition and attention by monopolizing conversation; prevents others from expressing their opinions fully; wants the spotlight.
2. *Isolate:* Deserts the group; withdraws from participation; acts indifferent, aloof, uninvolved; resists efforts to be included in group decision making.
3. *Clown:* Engages in horseplay; thrives on practical jokes and comic routines; diverts members' attention away from serious discussion of ideas and issues; steps beyond the boundaries of mere tension reliever.
4. *Blocker:* Thwarts progress of group; does not cooperate; opposes much of what group attempts to accomplish; incessantly reintroduces dead issues; makes negative remarks to members.
5. *Fighter-Controller:* Tries to dominate group; competes with members; abuses those who disagree; picks quarrels with members; interrupts to interject own opinions into discussion.
6. *Zealot:* Tries to convert members to a pet cause or idea; delivers sermons to group on state of the world; exhibits fanaticism.
7. *Cynic:* Displays sour outlook; engages in faultfinding; focuses on negatives; predicts failure.

while impeding attainment of group goals. Individuals who play these roles often warrant the tag "difficult group member." **The central communicative function of self-centered, disruptive roles is to focus attention on the individual.** This focus on the individual can diminish group productivity and cohesiveness. Competent communicators avoid these roles. Table 5.1 provides samples of task, maintenance, and disruptive roles with corresponding communication behaviors.

Playing roles is a fluid process. During a single committee meeting, an individual may play several roles. A group member may even adopt a disruptive role following an unsuccessful attempt to play a maintenance role such as tension reliever or encourager. Individuals in a system are so interconnected that what one group member does can influence significantly the roles other group members play.

ROLE EMERGENCE: SPRINGING TO LIFE

In large groups and organizations, roles are largely determined by their formal structure. Even within this formal structure, however, role emergence occurs. Functional roles operate in smaller group meetings within the organization or in factional subunits of large groups.

Role emergence, however, is a relevant concern primarily to small, informal, leaderless groups without a history. These groups could be ad hoc project groups set up within formal organizations (e.g., self-managed work teams), classroom discussion groups formed for the purpose of completing a class project, or a jury in a criminal trial. The roles each member will play have not been designated in advance but emerge from the transactions conducted among group members. How roles emerge in zero-history groups has been studied extensively at the University of Minnesota (Bormann, 1990).

Group Endorsement: Accepting a Bid Individuals initially make a bid to play a role. They may bid for a role because they have special skills that suit the role, or they may succumb to gender role stereotyping. **Group endorsement** of the bid to play a specific role must occur before a person gets to play that role. In a competitive culture, high-status roles are generally perceived to be those that are task oriented. Accomplishing tasks brings victories, tangible accomplishments, and recognition. The roles of facilitator, initiator-contributor, information giver, and devil's advocate are high-status roles because individuals are perceived as doers—they accomplish important tasks for the group's success.

Despite their critical importance to group success, **maintenance roles are often viewed as lower status in a competitive culture such as the United States.** Those who play maintenance roles are viewed as the helpers, not the doers. Helpers typically receive less status than doers in our society (e.g., surgeons are viewed as the doers and nurses are seen as the surgeon's helpers). Women have been socialized to play primarily the lower-status maintenance roles. As Wood (1997) notes, "Women remain disproportionately represented in service sectors and human relations divisions of companies, while men are moved into executive positions. Women are still asked to take care of social activities on the job, but men in equivalent positions are seldom expected to do this" (p. 63). Thus, group roles such as supporter-encourager, harmonizer–tension reliever, feeling expresser, and secretary-recorder (a task role that is lower status and helping in nature) are roles traditionally played more by women than men (Wood, 1997). When women are underrepresented in groups, it is particularly difficult to break through the stereotyping and receive the endorsement of the group to play nonstereotypic, higher-status roles or to enhance the perceived status of maintenance roles.

The endorsement process proceeds by trial and error. A group member tries out a role, perhaps initiator-contributor, for example. If the group does not reinforce the effort (e.g., by ignoring the contributions), then the member will try another role, hoping to get an endorsement. An individual who persists in an effort to play a specific role in the face of group resistance may be characterized as inflexible and uncooperative.

Role Specialization: Settling into One's Role Once a role for a member has been endorsed by the group, **role specialization**—when an individual member settles into his or her primary role—occurs. If the group wants you to be an information giver, then that will be your principal function. This specialization doesn't preclude you from assuming other roles, however. Role specialization does not grant a monopoly to a single member. There may be more than one harmonizer in the group, although there is likely to be only one member with the primary responsibility. Too much effort to operate in what is perceived to be another member's primary role territory can invite negative feedback from the group.

ROLE FIXATION: STUCK PLAYING ONE PART

In the movie *The Great Santini,* Robert Duvall plays a Marine Corps pilot. He is a rather odd character because he interacts with members of his family as if they were military recruits at boot camp. He orders his children to stand at attention early every morning while he inspects them. The children are required to address their father as "Sir" in a snappy voice. Duvall expects absolute obedience from his kids as he would from his subordinates in the military. He is aggressive and savagely competitive with his son. Duvall's character is fixated in a single role. Despite the inappropriateness of this role acted out in a family context, despite the disruption it causes his wife and children, Duvall's character seems incapable of playing any role other than that of officer in the military.

Competent communication requires the ability and the willingness to adapt communication behavior to changing situations. Some individuals, however, get locked into the mindset that they must play a certain role and there are no good substitutes. Leader, information giver, feeling expresser, and tension reliever are among the most likely candidates for **role fixation**—the acting out of a specific role and that role alone no matter what the situation might require (Postman, 1976).

Professional comedians sometimes don't know when to be serious in social gatherings. They are always "on." Lawyers who cross-examine their spouses as they do hostile witnesses on the stand at a criminal trial may find their role fixation is a ticket to a court of a decidedly civil sort.

Role fixation in decision-making groups can occur when an individual moves from one group to another, or it can happen within a single group. If you were a gatekeeper in your last group, you may insist on performing the same role in your new group. There may be another member, however, who can play the role better. If you insist on competing for the role instead of adapting to the new group by assuming another role, you will be a source of conflict and disruption. If the other member is truly better in the role than you are, then the resources of the group will not be utilized to their fullest if you continue to fight for the role.

Sometimes the group insists on role fixation to its own detriment. The reluctance of men to accept women in high-status roles, for instance, can lead to role fixation against a woman's wishes. Expecting women to play feeling expresser in all or most groups erects overly restrictive boundaries within the system and uses group resources inefficiently. Women should have the opportunity to play roles that require more than nurturing (e.g., supporter-encourager) or low involvement (e.g., secretary-recorder).

You can demonstrate appropriate and effective communication in terms of group roles as follows:

1. *Demonstrate flexibility.* Playing a variety of maintenance and task roles adapts to the needs of the group. Fighting for roles perceived to be more prestigious and desirable may leave vital group needs unattended.
2. *Avoid disruptive roles.* Show commitment to group effectiveness, not self-centeredness at the expense of group success.
3. *Be experimental.* Try different roles in different groups. Don't get locked into playing the same role in all groups. You'll become role fixated.

Leadership

Scholars, philosophers, social scientists, even novelists have exhibited an intense interest in leadership. "Authors have offered up over nine thousand different systems, languages, principles, and paradigms to help explain the mysteries of management and leadership" (Buckingham & Coffman, 1999, p. 53). One communication scholar estimates that nearly 8,000 studies have been published on group leadership (Pavitt, 1999).

Why do people want to be leaders? There are numerous reasons, but the most obvious ones are *status* that comes from running the show, *respect* from group members for doing a good job of guiding the group, and *power* accorded leaders that allows them to influence others and produce change.

Wanting to be a leader, however, isn't the same as becoming a leader and being an effective one. In this section leadership is defined, how to gain and retain leadership is discussed, and several perspectives on what constitutes effective group leadership are explored.

▶ **Focus Questions**

1. How is the process for retaining the leader role different from the process for emerging as group leader?

2. Are women and ethnic minorities equally capable leaders as white males? Does your experience parallel the research results on this question?

3. After considering all the perspectives on leadership, what is the central overriding point that can be made about leadership in small groups?

DEFINITION OF LEADERSHIP: AN EVOLVING CONSENSUS

As far back as 1949, there were at least 130 different definitions of leader and leadership (M. Bass, 1960). Despite the numerous definitions, there is an evolving consensus on what leadership is and is not.

Leadership and Influence: A Two-Way Process **There seems to be agreement that leadership is a social influence process** (M. Hackman & Johnson, 2004; Rost, 1991). This influence can come from status, authority, personality, interpersonal and group communication skills, and a host of other factors. "Credibility is the foundation for successful influence . . ." (M. Hackman & Johnson, 2004, p. 154). The ancient Greeks called it ethos, defined by Aristotle as good will, good character, and good sense. More recently, communication scholars have defined **credibility** as a composite of competence (knowledge, skills), trustworthiness (honesty, consistency, character), and dynamism (confidence, assertiveness). "We want to believe in our leaders. We want to have faith and confidence in them as people. We want to believe that their word can be trusted, that they have the knowledge and skill to lead . . ." (Kouzes & Posner, 2003, p. 22).

The social influence, however, occurs with the consent of the governed. Leaders influence followers, but followers also influence leaders by making demands on them, requiring them to meet members' expectations, and evaluating their performance in light of these expectations (Nye, 2002).

Leadership and Followership: It Takes Two to Tango **The leader and follower roles either exist together or they exist not at all.** A leader must have someone to lead and followers must have someone to follow. Behavior labeled as leadership in the absence of followers "is no more leadership than the behavior of small boys marching in front of a parade, who continue to strut along Main Street after the procession has turned down a side street toward the fairgrounds" (Burns, 1978, p. 427).

Negative connotations associated with the term *follower,* such as passive, pliable, sheep-like, even unintelligent, have inclined some scholars to use terms such as constituents, participants, stakeholders, or collaborators instead. All of these substitute terms have connotative problems as well (Rost, 1991). The central point is that leaders and followers are like ballroom dance partners. One leads and the other follows, but they influence each other, and they must work in tandem to be effective. **There are no special guidelines for being an effective follower that diverge from what makes an effective team member (see Chapter 6) and a competent communicator in small groups.**

Leader versus Manager: Interpersonal versus Positional Influence There are two primary differences between a leader and a manager (M. Hackman & Johnson, 2004; Rost, 1991). First, **a leader does not ordinarily operate from positional authority; a manager does.** Anyone in a group can exhibit leadership even without being designated the leader. Only a manager is permitted to manage. Thus, managers are formally assigned the position of authority even though they may exercise little influence with their "subordinates." A leader exercises interpersonal influence (leader–follower relationship), but a manager exercises positional influence (supervisor–subordinate relationship). "Persons who can require others to do their bidding because of power are not leaders" (Hogan et al., 1994). This means that as a student you won't exercise managerial authority, but you can become a leader on your project team, during discussion sessions, or in study groups through your communication with group members.

Second, **managers typically maintain the status quo. They don't try to change it but they do try to manage it efficiently. Leaders work to change the status quo.** Managers implement "the vision and strategy provided by leaders" (House & Aditya, 1997, p. 445). They do this by working with budgets, by organizing tasks, and by carrying out directives from and plans devised by leaders. "There are many institutions that are very well managed and very poorly led. They may excel in the ability to handle all the routine inputs every day, yet they may never ask whether the routine should be preserved at all" (Bennis, 1976, p. 154).

Leadership implies change. "People expect leaders to bring change about, to get things done, to make things happen, to inspire, to motivate" (Husband, 1992, p. 494). Some have called this **transformational leadership,** and they have distinguished it from transactional leadership (B. M. Bass, 1990; Burns, 1978). **Transactional leadership** is described in terms that are similar to what I've described as management, not leadership. I agree with Rost (1991) and his postindustrial model of leadership, however, when he claims, "Leadership, properly defined, is about transformation, all kinds of transformations" (p. 126). Change, small and large, brought about through the leadership process is inherently transforming. Influencing group members through persuasion (not coercion) transforms them from what they were to what they become.

This doesn't mean that every leader must be **charismatic**—loosely defined as exhibiting a constellation of personal attributes that group members find highly attractive and strongly influential. Leaders perceived to be highly transformational, however, are sometimes referred to as **charismatic leaders** (T. A. Judge & Piccolo, 2004). Hackman and Johnson (2004) label them the "superstars of leadership" (Gandhi, Martin Luther King, Mother Teresa, or Pope John Paul II, for example). Charismatic leaders are visionary, decisive, inspirational, and self-sacrificing (House & Javidan, 2004). They have a significant impact on group members' lives and they provoke fierce loyalty, commitment, and devotion from followers. A strong identification with the leader develops, and the followers' goals, self-esteem, and values become entangled with the charismatic leader–follower relationship (Fiedler & House, 1988). Bennis and Nanus (1985), however, studied 90 top American leaders and concluded that hardly any were charismatic. In fact, "charisma is (probably) the result of effective leadership, not the other way around" (Bennis & Nanus, 1985).

These distinctions do not exclude managers from being leaders, anymore than being a leader excludes you from being a manager. One person can be both (House & Aditya, 1997). Some even argue that being both a strong leader and a manager is the ideal (Kotter, 1990). **The point is not to denigrate managers in order to exalt leaders. The two can overlap, and often do.** Leaders who inspire and motivate followers to strive for wholly unreachable goals, who can't organize a plan of action, or who quickly lose focus on one challenge when a new challenge emerges will have very limited effectiveness because they lack management skills. Conversely, a manager may be interested in more than merely maintaining the status quo. When a manager seeks change, motivates and inspires followers, and creates direction for the group, however, he or she is acting as a leader, not a manager.

Leadership and Communication: Duct-Taped Together **Leadership is fundamentally a communication process** exercised within the group (Barge & Hirokawa, 1989). As Hackman and Johnson (2004) proclaim, "Extraordinary leadership is the product of extraordinary communication" (p. 98). Competent communication is a necessary precondition for a high-quality leader–follower relationship to develop (Flauto, 1999). Those leaders rated as the most skillful communicators are deemed the most effective leaders (Riggio et al., 2003). The leader sets the emotional tone for the group. Leaders who fail typically do so because they exhibit insensitivity toward group members, are brutally critical, and are too demanding (Goleman, 1998). Consider the president of a large organization whose open contempt for his employees was reflected in his oft-stated motto: "Bring 'em in and burn 'em out." He seemed to enjoy bullying and abusing his workers. A junior staff member, for instance, announced that it was her birthday and offered a piece of cake to fellow workers, including the president. The president's response was to complain loudly to a nearby manager, "Can't you get your staff to work?" Then, to the junior staffer, he looked at her derisively and said, "And you sure don't need the calories in that cake" (Goleman et al., 2002, p. 194). Would you want to work for such a jerk?

Emotional outbursts, or what Birgitta Wistrand, CEO of a Swedish company, calls *"emotional incontinence,"* also create a ripple effect that spreads fear, mistrust, and anger in all directions. This is not a climate conducive to effective leadership and group performance. As the old maxim goes, "A fish rots from the head down." Effective leaders create a supportive, cooperative group environment (Goleman, 1998). As Kouzes and Posner (1987) put it, there is "a simple one-word test to detect whether someone is on the road to becoming a leader. That word is *we*" (p. 162).

Leadership, then, is an influence process between leader and followers, directed toward change that reflects mutual purposes of group members; it is largely accomplished through competent communication (M. Hackman & Johnson, 2004; Rost, 1991). Conceptualizing what constitutes leadership, however, is a far cry from knowing how to exercise leadership in a group. How leaders emerge and the ways to retain leadership in groups are discussed next.

GAINING AND RETAINING LEADERSHIP: GETTING THERE IS JUST THE START

Some zero-history groups never do settle on who will lead and who will follow. In a study of 16 such groups that worked for as long as 12 weeks, almost a third of the groups never had a leader emerge (Geier, 1967). These leaderless groups were uniformly unsuccessful at their tasks and were also socially unsuccessful. Strife predominated. Time was wasted and members became frustrated. Cohesiveness suffered and members began skipping meetings rather than suffer more disharmony. In contrast, groups that have leaders emerge and that develop stable roles for their members are usually successful (De Souza & Kline, 1995). The emergence of leaders, therefore, is a significant event in the life of a group.

How Not to Become a Leader: Thou Shalt Not It is often easier to determine what you shouldn't do if you wish to become a leader than what you should. We know that corruption or sex scandals, for instance, can send the media into a feeding frenzy and can torpedo a promising political career, but the absence of such scandals won't capture any headlines. Having a spotless character may just brand you as dull in some people's minds. Lack of negatives does not necessarily equal leadership potential.

There are important negatives to avoid, however, if you hope to have a chance to become group leader. The competent communicator who wishes to emerge as group leader should heed the following dictums (Bormann, 1990; B. A. Fisher & Ellis, 1990; Geier, 1967):

1. *Thou shalt not show up late for or miss important meetings.* Groups choose individuals who are committed, not members who exhibit insensitivity to the group. As an anonymous wit once observed, "Absence makes the heart grow fonder—of someone else."

2. *Thou shalt not be uninformed about a problem commanding the group's attention.* Knowledgeable members have a greater chance of emerging as leaders. The clueless need not apply.

3. *Thou shalt not manifest apathy and lack of interest by sluggish participation in group discussions.* Group members are not impressed by "vigor mortis." Indifference provokes defensiveness. Participation is a sign of commitment to the group, and commitment to the group and its goals is part of the leadership process (De Souza & Kline, 1995).

4. *Thou shalt not attempt to dominate conversation during discussion.* Learning when to shut up is a useful skill.

5. *Thou shalt not listen poorly* (Bechler & Johnson, 1995). Leadership is not a monologue; it's a dialogue. As someone once said, a monologue is "the egotist's version of a scintillating conversation." Dialogue means leaders and followers listen carefully to each other.

6. *Thou shalt not be rigid and inflexible when expressing viewpoints.* A hardened position is plaque on the cortex. It decays the mind and contracts the brain.

7. *Thou shalt not bully group members.* Browbeating members to do your bidding will gain few admirers. There may be no way to avoid issuing orders in some situations (e.g., in the military), but watch out for psychological reactance. Bullies get banished to the playground.

8. *Thou shalt not use offensive and abusive language.* Blue language produces red faces. This will surely alienate many, if not most, group members, except in rare instances such as locker room talk within some sports teams.

Some of these counterproductive communication patterns are more likely than others to prevent an individual from becoming a group leader (Geier, 1967). The three most relevant, in order of importance, are: being uninformed, not participating, and being rigid and inflexible.

General Pattern of Leader Emergence: Process of Elimination The extensive research conducted at the University of Minnesota under the direction of Ernest Bormann (1990) discovered a pattern of leader emergence in small zero-history groups. In general, a group selects a leader by a process of elimination in which potential candidates are systematically removed from consideration until only one person remains to be leader. We may be quite clear on what we don't want in a leader but not as sure about what we do want. This narrowing of the candidate field makes good sense. As we eliminate candidates, complexity is reduced. The breadth of possibilities is narrowed, while the depth of understanding of each candidate's qualifications for the role is increased.

There are two phases to the process-of-elimination explanation of leader emergence. During the first phase, roughly half of the members are eliminated from consideration. The criteria for elimination are crude and impressionistic. **Negative communication patterns—the "thou shalt nots"—weigh heavily. Quiet members are among the first eliminated.** Nonparticipation will leave the impression of indifference and noncommitment. There was not a single instance in the Minnesota studies of a quiet member who became a leader.

Conversely, talkativeness also influences the leadership emergence process. **Those who talk the most are perceived initially as potential leader material** (Riggio et al., 2003). The group will quickly eliminate a group member from consideration, however, if he or she blathers or makes pronouncements on subjects without making a great deal of sense. Such individuals are reminiscent of William Gibbs McAddo's characterization of President Warren G. Harding as "an army of pompous phrases moving over the landscape in search of an idea." Windbags gain no favor.

The members who express strong, unqualified assertions are also eliminated. These individuals are perceived to be too extreme and too inflexible in their points of view to make effective leaders. The attitude of certitude will provoke defensiveness from group members. **The uninformed, unintelligent, or unskilled are next in line for elimination.** Groups look for task-competent individuals who are committed to the group goals to emerge as leaders (De Souza & Klein, 1995). Inept members distract the group from goal attainment.

In the second phase, about half the group still actively contend for the leader role. This part of the process can become quite competitive. Frustrations and irritations can mount. **Of these remaining contenders, those who are bossy or dictatorial and those whose communication style is irritating or disturbing to group members are eliminated.**

So who emerges as leader if more than one member survives the elimination rounds? There are several possibilities. First, if the group feels threatened by some external or internal crisis (e.g., the inability to choose a topic for a symposium presentation, or if members with expertise fall sick or leave the group), **the group often turns to the member who provides a solution to the crisis and he or she becomes the leader.** Second, **those members perceived to be effective listeners can make a strong bid to be chosen leader** (S. Johnson & Bechler, 1998). Third, members who remain active contenders for the leader role often acquire lieutenants. A lieutenant is an advocate for one of the contenders. He or she boosts the chances of the contender becoming the group leader. **If only one of the members gains the support of a lieutenant, then this person will likely become the leader.** If two members each gain a lieutenant, then the process of leader emergence can be drawn out, or can even end in stalemate.

The general tendency is for groups to accept as leader the person who provides the optimum blend of task efficiency and sensitivity to social considerations. This tendency, of course, does not translate into a tidy formula or precise recipe. Some groups prefer a leader who concentrates more on task accomplishment and less on the social dimension of the group. Other groups prefer the opposite.

Ultimately, if you want to become the leader of a group you should take the following steps (Bormann, 1990):

1. Manifest conformity to the group's norms, values, and goals.
2. Display proper motivation to lead.
3. Avoid the "thou shalt nots" previously identified.

Deviants, dissenters, and disrupters will be eliminated early as potential leaders. Women and ethnic minorities may also have greater difficulty emerging as leaders (see Focus on Gender/Ethnicity: "Gender and Ethnic Bias in Leader Emergence"). Groups prefer leaders who will assist them in the attainment of their goals, who will defend the group vigorously against threats, and who will remain loyal to the group. Since most group members think of a leader as the single individual who does most of the work, anyone hoping to be leader must also demonstrate a willingness to work hard for the group (Hollander, 1978).

Retaining the Leader Role: Hanging onto Power The process for retaining the leader role is not the same as the process for emerging as the group leader. An individual could conform to group norms, display a strong motivation to lead the group, and avoid the "thou shalt nots" and still not retain the role of leader, as many political leaders have learned. A leader is sometimes deposed if his or her performance is felt by members to be unsatisfactory. **There are three primary qualifications for retaining leadership** (Wood et al., 1986):

1. You must demonstrate your competence as leader.
2. You must accept accountability for your actions.
3. You must satisfy group members' expectations.

Retaining the role of leader can be a tricky business. Groups can be fickle. Carly Fiorina was named CEO of Hewlett-Packard (HP) in 1999, one of only a handful of women leading a Fortune 500 company. Expectations were high that Fiorina, a charismatic and articulate leader in her previous positions, would reverse the gradual downward slide the company had been experiencing in recent years. Her signature decision was the controversial purchase of Compaq Computer in 2002. "Fiorina was a controversial figure at HP, partly because of the abrasive manner in which the takeover of Compaq was fought in 2001 and 2002" (Oates & Cullen, 2005). In February 2005 Fiorina was forced to resign her position. She failed to meet expectations and to demonstrate her leadership competence in a cutthroat business.

Gender and Ethnic Bias in Leader Emergence

THE PROBLEM OF GENDER AND ETHNIC bias complicates the pattern of leader emergence. The research on gender bias is far more voluminous than it is on ethnic discrimination.

Studies of gender bias in the workplace, where emerging leaders live their daily lives and engage in small group communication, provide mixed results. The issue of a **glass ceiling,** an invisible barrier of subtle discrimination that excludes women from top jobs in corporate and professional America, is apparent. Only 9 women were CEOs of the 500 largest companies in the United States in 2005, and only 19 were CEOs of Fortune 1,000 companies ("Women CEOs," 2005). Women held only 20% of senior management positions in medium-sized U.S. companies in 2004 ("Harper's Index," 2004). A mere 2.7% of the top-income earners are women. Even when women climb to the highest leadership levels in corporate America, the pay disparity between male and female executives is significant. Female senior executives earn, on average, only 67 cents for every dollar that male senior executives are paid (Armas, 2000). Although the number of women in the United States Congress has steadily increased in recent years, currently only 80 members of Congress are women (15%).

That's the bad news. **The encouraging news is that women are poised to make huge strides.** Economic consultant Nuala Beck argues that women are well positioned to advance in the new information-based economy driven by the microchip. She claims that the Fortune 500 companies, and women's place in their hierarchy, are largely irrelevant— mere relics of the manufacturing economy that is dwarfed by the knowledge-based industries. The ratio of female-to-male information workers (engineers, technicians, scientists, professionals, and senior managers) is almost one to one (Collingwood, 1997). The new economy is based primarily on the knowledge and skills of the workers instead of seniority, and women are poised to take advantage of this trend.

Consider the evidence. Almost half (49%) of all managerial and professional positions in the United States are held by women (White, 2002). According to the American Association of University Women (2005), 56% of all college students in the United States are women, and 58% of all graduate students are women. In schools of law, business, and medicine, 47% of the enrollees are women. Women earn more than 60% of biology undergraduate degrees and nearly half of all mathematics degrees conferred, although they lag in engineering (21%) and computer science (28%). In 2002, 57% of all bachelor's degrees went to women (Goodman, 2002). Women earn slightly more than half of all doctorates granted to U.S. citizens (Hoffer et al., 2003). In the 1960s, only a handful of women were full-time college professors. Four decades later, 36% of full-time college professors are women and half of all full-time professors at 2-year colleges are

▶

women (R. Wilson, 2001). According to the Center for American Women and Politics at Rutgers University (2005), three decades ago only 4% of state legislators were women. In 2005, 23% of state legislators and 26% of statewide executive officials were women. Despite historic disparities in pay (women still average 81 cents for every dollar earned by men [Robison, 2002] even when comparable education and experience are considered), a third of wives in the United States out-earn their spouses (Avila, 2001).

Nevertheless, women still have difficulty becoming leaders despite convincing evidence that women and men are equally capable (Eagly & Karau, 2002). Addressing the perceived issue of deficiency in female leadership effectiveness, Margaret Thatcher once remarked, "I was always asked how it felt to be a woman prime minister. I would reply: 'I don't know: I've never experienced the alternative'" (Thatcher, 1993, p. 18). A study conducted by the Hagberg Consulting Group and reported on NBC Nightly News on August 10, 1999, revealed that women scored better than men on 41 of 47 team skills. Richard Hagberg, head of the consulting firm, concludes that women have "a much more team oriented style" of leadership appropriate for today's workplace. Nevertheless, in a variety of group settings, men are typically favored over women when leaders are selected and evaluated, even when no differences in actual leadership behavior occur (Eagly & Karau, 2002; Forsyth et al., 1997). Even when women do emerge as leaders, they suffer penalties for their success. They are less liked and more personally disparaged than equivalently successful men. These penalties can negatively affect the careers of female leaders both in advancement and in recommendations for pay increases (Heilman et al., 2004).

This is a good news–bad news record, but, overall, the outlook for women in leadership positions is optimistic. The outlook for ethnic minorities in leadership positions is less optimistic. African Americans occupy barely 7% of senior management positions in the federal government, and Latino Americans occupy a mere 3% of such positions. The private sector hires even fewer ethnic minorities for senior management positions (Kampeas, 2001). Only three African American males were CEOs of Fortune 500 companies in 2002 ("Rethinking Black Leadership," 2002). African American and white American males earn about the same in lower status jobs, but as jobs become more prestigious (doctors, lawyers, managers), black males earn as little as 72 cents for every dollar earned by white males in the same occupations (Tran, 2001). Asian Americans, despite their phenomenal success in technical and scientific fields, are less likely than African Americans to ascend to positions of leadership in those fields (J. Tang, 1997).

Female ethnic minorities tend to have the toughest time emerging as leaders because they face a double bias (Morrison & Von Glinow, 1990). Only 1.6% of corporate officers in Fortune 500 companies in 2002 were female ethnic minorities (Files, 2002). There were no ethnic minority female CEOs in these companies. African American women

▶

earn 66% of the average white male wage, and Latina American women earn a mere 55% (Burk, 2005).

Despite these figures, there is some encouraging news. One-fifth of black American adults are in management or professional jobs compared to 31% for whites ("Moving Forward," 1999). According to the Center for American Women and Politics (2005), 25% of all women in the U.S. Congress are women of color. Almost 40% of Asian American women have 4-year college degrees compared to 26% of all males in the United States. Almost 19% of all doctorates granted to U.S. citizens go to ethnic minority candidates (Hoffer et al., 2003).

How do we combat gender–ethnicity bias in emergent leadership in groups? First, the **Twenty Percent Rule** again comes into play. When women and minorities find themselves flying solo in groups, the chance that they'll land in a leadership position is remote. **As the number of women and ethnic minorities increases in a group to as much as twenty percent of the membership, however, the likelihood that a woman or a minority will emerge as leader also increases because bias decreases** (Shimanoff & Jenkins, 1996). When women and ethnic minorities are no longer perceived as tokens, but instead form a substantial portion of group membership and increasingly occupy top leadership positions, then competence will be judged less on gender and ethnic bias and more on actual performance (Karakowsky & Siegel, 1999).

Second, **if group members are allowed to mingle, interact, and work on a project**

Corky Trewin, UW Athletic Communications

A mere 3 of 117 major college football teams are coached by African Americans as of 2005. Tyrone Willingham at the University of Washington is one of the three head coaches.

before determining a leader, the decision is more likely to be made on the basis of individual performance rather than gender (or ethnicity, if we extrapolate the research findings). Small groups that met for 6 to 15 weeks on a project were as likely to name a woman as their leader as they were a man (Goktepe & Schneier, 1989). Allowing women and minorities to display their strengths increases their chances of emerging as group leaders.

Third, **engaging in task-relevant communication behavior is a key to emerging as leader of a small, task-oriented group** (Hawkins, 1995). Task-relevant com-

▶

munication includes initiation and discussion of analysis of the group problem, establishment of decision criteria, generation of possible solutions to problems, evaluation of possible solutions, and establishment of group operating procedures. Task-oriented female group members are as likely to emerge as leaders of small task groups as are task-oriented male group members (Hawkins, 1995). This finding is bolstered by a May 10, 2002, Gallup poll (Moore, 2002) showing that the rate at which both males and females prefer or accept female bosses is the highest that it has ever been (males are actually slightly more accepting than females—70% to 66%).

Fourth, **if women and minorities are among the first to speak in the group and they speak fairly frequently, their chances of emerging as leaders increase** (Shimanoff & Jenkins, 1996). Speaking early and often without dominating discussion is perceived as assertive. Speaking early is more important for women and minorities than it is for men.

Finally, **women and ethnic minorities can advance their chances of becoming leaders in small groups by honing their communication skills and abilities.** Developing competence in communication by using skills appropriately and effectively can go a long way toward combating gender and ethnic leadership bias (M. Hackman & Johnson, 2004).

Questions for Thought

1. Should group members encourage women and minorities to speak early and often by inviting their participation?
2. Do you feel that the glass ceiling will shatter soon, as the number of women and minorities in the middle ranks of leadership swells? What might prevent this from happening?
3. What responsibilities do white males have regarding the issue of leadership bias?

Her vision clashed with that of stockholders and employees, thousands of whom were forced out of HP in painful cost-cutting measures. As a *San Jose Mercury News* editorial summed it up, "In the corporate world, change must be a catalyst for results, and at HP, it wasn't. And so Fiorina was asked to leave" ("Out of 'Internet Time,'" 2005, p. 6B).

> ►●● SECOND LOOK
>
> ## PATTERN OF LEADER EMERGENCE
>
> ### GENERAL PATTERN
> ### (PROCESS OF ELIMINATION)
>
> Phase One
>
>   Quiet members eliminated
>
>   Members who express strong, unqualified assertions eliminated
>
>   Uninformed, unintelligent, and/or unskilled eliminated
>
> Phase Two, part one
>
>   Bossy, dictatorial members eliminated
>
>   Members with irritating or disturbing communication style eliminated
>
> Phase Two, part two
>
>   Member who provides solution in time of crisis considered
>
>   Member who exhibits effective listening skills considered
>
>   Member who acquires a lieutenant considered
>
>   If more than one member acquires lieutenant—possible stalemate
>
> ### HOW TO BECOME A LEADER
>
>   Manifest conformity to group norms, values, and goals
>
>   Display proper motivation to lead
>
>   Avoid the "thou shalt nots"
>
> ### MODIFYING FACTORS OF LEADER EMERGENCE
>
>   Gender bias
>
>   Ethnic bias

Group expectations of a leader may shift as circumstances alter. Members' confidence in and loyalty to their leader may be shaky. A leader must demonstrate competence and satisfy group expectations on a continuing basis or member loyalty may disappear quickly. Last year's success may not compensate adequately for this year's failure, as Fiorina and many athletic coaches have learned.

PERSPECTIVES ON EFFECTIVE LEADERSHIP: AN EVOLVING VIEW

Scholarly perspectives on leadership have changed greatly over the three-quarters of a century since the first serious research was conducted on this central group role. In this section, the primary perspectives that have generated considerable interest are discussed.

© Lynn Goldsmith

Amy Henry was expected to win the leadership competition on *The Apprentice* television show because of her "leadership traits." She didn't win. Donald Trump, however, made note of how "beautiful" she is.

Traits Perspective: The Born Leader View This is the "leaders are born not made" perspective. The earliest studies on leadership set out to discover a universal set of traits applicable to all those who become leaders. A huge number of traits were studied. We know, for instance, that height, weight, and physical attractiveness have a bearing on social influence. Tall individuals usually have greater influence with others than do shorter individuals. In the last 27 U.S. presidential elections, the taller candidate won 22 of the elections. Very heavy or skinny people have less influence than more "ideal weight" types (Hickson & Stacks, 1989). Good-looking individuals can influence a group.

So why don't all tall, fit, and physically attractive individuals become leaders instead of short, dumpy, plain-looking individuals? How did much taller John Kerry lose to George W. Bush in 2004? How did diminutive Barbara Boxer and Barbara Mikulski become U.S. senators? And what are we to make of Microsoft's CEO, Bill Gates, who is a walking advertisement for *Revenge of the Nerds*?

Leader emergence and leadership effectiveness, however, are not identical. The characteristics necessary even to be considered for the leader role in a small group (e.g., being talkative, confident, motivated, knowledgeable, punctual, adaptable, and a good listener) don't assure effective leadership.

Will any single trait likely make a person an effective leader? Clearly not (M. Hackman & Johnson, 2004). A trait such as intelligence could be neutralized by unfriendliness, ethical indifference, laziness, arrogance, insensitivity, or a host of other characteristics. What combination of traits might make a leader effective? Fiedler and House (1988) claim that "effective leaders tend to have a high need to influence others, to achieve, and they tend to be bright, competent, and socially adept, rather than stupid, incompetent, and social disasters" (p. 87). Stogdill (1948), however, reviewed 124 studies on the relationship between traits and leadership and concluded that no universal set of traits assures leader emergence or leader effectiveness. The lists of leadership traits among this vast number of studies reviewed were often inconsistent, even contradictory. Stogdill (1974) reviewed an additional 163 trait studies on leadership conducted between 1949 and 1970. He again concluded that traits alone could not explain leadership effectiveness.

Consider, for example, the analysis of a *USA Today* expert panel assembled to explain why Amy Henry, the front-runner candidate on Donald Trump's "reality" television show *The Apprentice*, appeared to have a lock on winning the show's ultimate prize in its first season (she didn't, as you may remember). Consisting of CEOs, entrepreneurs, and management experts, each panel member offered a separate and distinct list of leadership traits that Amy Henry supposedly exhibited. Panel member Joe Moglia listed spiritual soundness, dedication, courage, and love. Jay Sidhu offered clear vision and human skills. Stephen Covey said character and moral authority were her critical traits. Deborrah Himsel claimed she had humility, strength, and was a team player. Jeffrey Sonnenfeld suggested being upbeat, intelligent, and confident were her strong traits. Alfred Edmond offered sense of humor and keeping cool under pressure. Necole Merritt claimed that she had "the heart to serve." David Moore asserted that Amy was a strong leader because she had "an engaging personal style" and "a really neat haircut" (D. Jones, 2004, p. 4B).

Perhaps intelligence, social and verbal skills, integrity, sense of humor, extroversion, likability, confidence, or some other set of characteristics accounts for effective leadership in groups. These and other traits seem appropriate, even essential, for a leader to possess. **These traits, however, may be *necessary yet not sufficient for an individual to be an effective group leader.*** Certain basic traits move an individual into the leadership arena. They may be the irreducible minimum qualifications to become a leader, but to retain the role of leader and ultimately to perform effectively in this role, other factors play a more important part. A 25-year study by the Gallup Organization of 80,000 leaders found that the greatest leaders in the world don't share a common set of characteristics (Buckingham & Coffman, 1999).

The principal problem with the trait approach to effective leadership is the assumption that leadership resides in the person, not in transactions conducted within the group context (Northouse, 1997). As Hollander (1985) notes, "Leadership is a process and not a person" (p. 487). No one set of leadership traits will fit every situation and group. Why do individuals become leaders in some groups, but not in others, if an individual possesses the requisite leadership traits? Why doesn't every intelligent, outgoing person become a leader? Probably for the same reason that every tall person doesn't become a star basketball player. There's more to it than just traits. Leaders are not born; they are developed (Ruvolo et al., 2004).

Styles Perspective: One Style Doesn't Fit All Unsatisfied with the trait approach to leadership, Kurt Lewin and his associates developed a new approach based on three leadership styles: autocratic, democratic, and laissez-faire (Lewin et al., 1939). Autocratic style exerts control over group members. The autocratic leader is highly directive. This leadership style does not encourage member participation. Douglas McGregor (1960) describes autocratic leadership as a "my way or the highway" approach: do what I say or hit the road. Autocratic leaders are not concerned about making friends or getting invited to parties. The autocratic style (usually referred to more neutrally as the **directive style**) puts most of the emphasis on the task, with little concern for the social dimension of the group (high task, low social).

The democratic style encourages participation and responsibility from group members. Democratic leaders work to improve the skills and abilities of group members (Gastil, 1994). Followers have a say in what the group decides. The democratic style (usually referred to more neutrally as the **participative style**) puts a balanced emphasis on both the task and social dimensions of the group (high task, high social).

The laissez-faire style is a do-nothing approach. This style provides no direction, and no regard is accorded the social transactions in the group (low task, low social). **Laissez-faire amounts to a sit-on-your-derriere style.** It doesn't try to influence anyone, so it is by definition non-leadership. Thus, it has been dropped from serious consideration in most of the research.

The extensive research comparing autocratic-directive and democratic-participative leadership styles shows mixed results (Northouse, 1997). Both directive and participative styles can be productive, and although the participative style fosters more member satisfaction than does the directive style (Van Oostrum & Rabbie, 1995), the difference is neither large nor uniform (Gastil, 1994). Participative leadership seems to work best when it springs naturally from the group itself. Not all small groups, however, want or expect their leaders to adopt the participative leadership style. Some cultures prefer the "paternal authoritative" (benevolently directive) style to the participative style (Brislin, 1993). In such cultures, the participative style may not work as well as the directive style.

Gender also plays a role in the leadership style-effectiveness equation. Male and female leaders are evaluated by group members as equally competent when the democratic-participative style is used (Eagly et al., 1992). When the autocratic-directive style is used, however, group members evaluate women as substantially less competent leaders than men. Apparently, group expectations influence judgments of leader competence. Female leaders are expected to adopt the participative leadership style, which complements the desire for connection, but groups are unaccustomed to seeing women use the directive style, which places more emphasis on independence and power than on connection (Tannen, 1990). Men clearly have more flexibility in choice of leadership style. With time, this stereotype that locks women into a single style of leadership should virtually vanish as women challenge the expectation.

One weakness of the participative/directive leadership style duality is that these styles are viewed as extreme opposites. Individuals operate as either participative or directive leaders, but not both. **Realistically, though, a combination of participative and directive leadership styles is required in small groups.** In organized sports, the autocratic leadership style is preferred by some athletes but not by others, and among high school wrestlers, autocratic is preferred toward the end of the season but not at the beginning (Turman, 2003). Also, consider a "temp worker" who is new on a job. Should this person be consulted on how the job should be accomplished when he or she doesn't even have a good idea what the job entails? Should teachers consult their students before determining course content when the students know little or nothing about the subject? Should military commanders seek the advice of their troops before launching an offensive? "All those in favor of attacking the heavily armed enemy signal by saying aye; those opposed, nay. Okay, the nays have it. We'll stay put and live another day." Group members can't always meaningfully participate in decision making.

No one style of leadership will be suitable for all situations anymore than one set of leadership traits will mesh with every situation. This realization has led researchers to explore yet another approach to leadership—the situational or contingency perspective.

Situational (Contingency) Perspective: Matching Styles with Circumstances

This is the "it depends" approach to leadership. Since no one style of leadership is appropriate for all situations, effective leadership is contingent upon matching styles with situations. Those leaders whose style fits well with their situation exhibit strong confidence and perform at a high level (Chemers, 2000).

There are two principal situational models of leadership effectiveness. The first is Fred Fiedler's (1967) contingency model. Fiedler's model, however, does not offer guidance on how to become a more effective leader once you're in a group. In this sense it has rather limited application for our purposes, so I will spare you an explanation of his complicated model.

A more flexible and useful situational model of leadership effectiveness has been offered by Hersey and Blanchard (1996). Although their model is targeted at organizations, it applies well to groups large and small, especially ones with long life cycles. **Hersey and Blanchard have combined three variables in their situational model:**

1. The amount of guidance and direction (*task emphasis*) a leader provides
2. The amount of relationship support (*socio-emotional emphasis*) a leader provides
3. The *readiness level* in performing a specific task, function, or objective that followers demonstrate

There are four leadership styles in the Hersey and Blanchard model that flow from the first two variables. The **Telling Style** (high task, low relationship emphasis) is directive. A leader using this style provides specific instructions regarding a task and closely supervises the performance of followers but places minimal focus on developing social relationships with followers. The **Selling Style** (high task, high relationship) is also directive. A leader using this style explains and clarifies decisions but also tries to convince followers to accept directives. The **Participating Style** (low task, high relationship) is nondirective. A leader using this style encourages shared decision making with special emphasis on developing relationships in the group. The **Delegating Style** (low task, low relationship) is nondirective. A leader using this style allows the group to be self-directed. Responsibility for decision making and implementation of decisions rests with the group. **The key to leadership effectiveness is matching the appropriate style to the group environment.**

Fisher (1986) criticizes the situational approach to leadership by contending that no leader could consider all possible situational variables to know which style to use. Hersey and Blanchard agree with the thrust of Fisher's criticism. They contend, however, that there is no need to consider all or even most variables. The relationship between the leader and followers is the prime consideration because if group members decide not to follow the leader, then all other situational variables (nature of the task, time involved, expectations, etc.) are irrelevant.

The primary situational variable that the leader must consider when adapting leadership styles to the specific group is the readiness level of followers. Hersey and Blanchard (1988) define **readiness** as "how ready a person is to perform a particular task" (p. 175). They identify two principal components of readiness: ability and willingness. "Ability is the knowledge, experience, and skill that an individual or group brings to a particular task or activity" (p. 175). They define willingness as "the extent to which an individual or group has the confidence, commitment, and motivation to accomplish a specific task" (p. 175). This all sounds remarkably like communication competence.

Decisions are leader directed at lower levels of readiness; decisions are follower directed at higher levels of readiness. **As readiness levels increase, effective leader-**

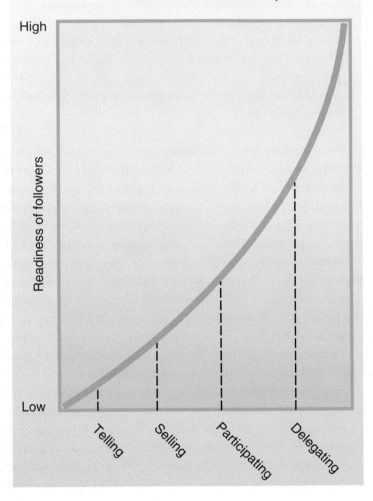

FIGURE 5.1
The Telling (S1), Selling (S2), Participating (S3), and Delegating (S4)
leadership styles related to follower
readiness.

ship requires reduced guidance and direction from the leader and less socio-
emotional support for followers. These relationships are depicted in Figure 5.1.

Followers, for whatever reasons (e.g., divorce, midlife crisis, lack of challenges),
may regress in their readiness levels, losing motivation or slipping in their skill
performance. In such cases, the leader moves backward through the styles curve
(i.e., from delegating to participating or even to telling), adapting to the change in
circumstances.

Is situational leadership effective? A study at Xerox Corporation (Gumpert & Hambleton, 1979) revealed that highly effective managers knew more about and used situational leadership more frequently than less-effective managers. When situational leadership was applied according to the Hersey and Blanchard model, subordinate job performance was higher than when it was not. Hersey and Blanchard (1988) cite additional studies in educational settings (e.g., classrooms, college boards of trustees) where situational leadership has proven to be highly effective.

Functional Perspective: Leadership Responsibilities The functional perspective views leadership in terms of certain functions, or responsibilities, that must be performed for the group to be successful. Typically, these functions fall into two categories: task requirements and social or maintenance needs.

The functional perspective can be divided into two schools of thought. William Schutz dubbed the first as the **leader-as-completer** viewpoint. Leaders are thought to perform those essential functions within a group that other members have failed to perform. Typically, the list of possible functions falls into the standard task and social (maintenance) responsibilities. The list of task and maintenance roles previously identified indicates functions essential to a group (e.g., giving information, coordinating, facilitating, gatekeeping, and relieving tension). Leader, then, is seen as an adaptive role. Leadership is demonstrated when any member steps in and assumes whatever role in the group is required at a particular time that has not been filled by any other member (e.g., researching an issue on the group task or making a list of group members' phone numbers).

A second school of thought, the **vital functions** viewpoint, sees leaders performing key responsibilities different in kind and/or degree from other members. Fisher and Ellis (1990) offer a list of such functions:

Group Procedural Responsibilities

1. *Plan an agenda.* Group meetings proceed more smoothly when the leader has constructed a list of topics for discussion and decision making.
2. *Handle routine "housekeeping" details.* These include taking roll, calling the meeting to order, making important announcements, modifying the agenda before discussion proceeds, and so forth.
3. *Prepare for the next meeting.* Announce the time, place, and date of the next meeting. Plan ahead by making certain that the meeting room is appropriate in size and physical conditions.

Task Responsibilities

1. *Initiate a structure.* The leader identifies issues to be discussed, proposes procedures for such discussion, guides the discussion, focuses members on the agenda, and may suggest possible solutions to problems.
2. *Seek information.* More so than other members, the leader requests facts, asks for clarification of points that are unclear, and asks questions.
3. *Give information.* Leaders are the most prepared group members. They research the important issues in advance. They can inform other group members when there are gaps in their knowledge.
4. *Offer informed opinions.* Leaders give opinions based on evidence and sound reasoning. So as not to stifle discussion, these opinions will usually be offered after other group members have had their say.
5. *Clarify, summarize, and elaborate.* The leader provides closure for the group. Points agreed to and points still disputed are identified.

Social Responsibilities

1. *Facilitate involvement and communication.* Leaders encourage participation from all members. Keeping meetings lively and fast-paced can prevent the nonparticipation that results from boredom.
2. *Harmonize.* The leader is responsible for establishing a supportive climate. This may mean confronting members who are disrupting meetings or creating competitiveness. Humor helps to relieve tension and improve the group climate.
3. *Express feelings.* A leader expresses feelings when appropriate and promotes a supportive environment in which others can express their feelings.

Of the two functional viewpoints, the leader-as-completer seems to have the greater merit. A large-scale investigation of the question "Which communicative functions do leaders perform more frequently or more characteristically than nonleaders?" revealed no unique functions associated with the leader role (Drecksel, 1984). **The set of leader responsibilities listed above is essential for the effective functioning of a small group,** but Fisher (1986) also observes that "there is no particular reason to believe that leaders should or do contribute more of those functions than other members" (p. 212). During the 9/11 terrorist attacks in 2001, many ordinary people exhibited extraordinary leadership. Office workers carried injured coworkers down daunting flights of stairs. Heroes emerged to rescue strangers because everyone, not just designated leaders (managers; fire battalion chiefs), felt responsible for the lives of fellow citizens and coworkers. They completed what was needed.

From the leader-as-completer functional perspective, leadership is a shared responsibility not a specific individual's responsibility. This perspective truly embraces the view that leadership is a process, not a person. No one person can provide a group with everything that it needs to be successful. A designated leader has a few procedural duties such as conducting an efficient meeting and guiding group discussion. All the members, however, especially in informal small groups, have the responsibility for leadership. This is especially true of teams (Pearce & Sims, 2002; see also the next chapter). If the group strays off task, any member can and should refocus the group. If a minority point of view has been ignored, any member can and should encourage the group to listen and give a fair hearing to a differing viewpoint. If conflict is smoldering beneath the surface of group discussion, any member can and should confront this.

With so many perspectives and viewpoints, what do we really know about leadership in groups? The central, overriding point to make about leadership is that effective leaders adapt to changing situations. Leaders have to function within a system, and change is unavoidable in any system. The "one leadership style fits all" approach is doomed to fail much of the time. Leadership and communication competence are inextricably bound (see Closer Look: "'Chainsaw Al' and the Ethics of Leadership"). No specific set of traits, particular style, situational readiness, or set of functions will produce effective leadership without the knowledge, skills, sensitivity, commitment, and ethics of all group members participating in the leadership process together.

Culture and Leadership: Are Leadership Theories Universal? "Almost all of the prevailing theories of leadership, and about 98% of the empirical evidence at hand, are rather distinctly American in character" (House & Aditya, 1997, p. 409). Can we apply the leadership theories discussed in this chapter universally across cultures? At this point we simply don't know. "It is likely that there are both some leader behaviors that are universally accepted and effective, and some for which acceptance and effectiveness is culture-specific, but little is known about such behaviors and their culture-specificity or universality at present" (House & Aditya, 1997, p. 455).

Nevertheless, research does suggest that differences across cultures regarding leadership do exist. Even though in the United States the importance of leadership is widely taken for granted, other cultures do not necessarily share this view. A huge research project called GLOBE, conducted by a collaborative group of 170 scholars worldwide, studied 62 cultures and 17,300 managers in 951 organizations. It revealed that the status and influence accorded leaders varies widely among cultures (House, 2004). Americans, Arabs, Asians, British, Eastern Europeans, French, Germans, Latin Americans, and Russians tend to idealize strong leaders, erecting

CLOSER LOOK

"CHAINSAW AL" AND THE ETHICS OF LEADERSHIP

HE'S BEEN CALLED "the most cold-blooded businessman around . . . brutal, heartless, and arrogant" (Plotz, 1997, pp. 1, 3). He's been nicknamed "Rambo in Pinstripes," "The Shredder," and "Chainsaw Al" for his savage "downsizing" tactics when he is called in to "save" a company. He wrote a self-promoting book entitled *Mean Business*.

Albert Dunlap is a notorious corporate turnaround specialist, a hired gun who is given the position of CEO in a company. He uses this position to "turn around" the company by eliminating thousands of employees' jobs, increasing stock values, and selling off the remaining shell of a business. Dunlap slashed 18,000 jobs when he was CEO of Scott Paper Company. He cut more than 6,000 jobs when he took over the helm at Sunbeam. In the bargain, he received a 3-year, $70 million contract with Sunbeam. He bragged, "You can't overpay a great executive . . . Don't you think I'm a bargain?" (Byrne, 1999, p. 185).

"Nothing that is valued by less steely businessmen—loyalty to workers, responsibility to the community, relationships with suppliers, generosity in corporate philanthropy—matters to Dunlap" (Plotz, 1997, p. 2). In his book, Dunlap offers this glib advice to those who lose their jobs and livelihood to his slash-and-burn tactics: "Those whose jobs will be eliminated in a restructuring should still consider the outcome philosophically, and have enough confidence in themselves to know they will have opportunities somewhere else. A company is not your high school or college alma mater. Don't get emotional about it" (Dunlap, 1997, p. 272). "Don't get emotional," he tells workers who must find a way to pay their mortgages and support their families after abruptly losing their jobs in a tight job market—this flippant advice coming from a multimillionaire. As former Labor Secretary Rob-

Andrew Itkoff

Al Dunlap reveled in his Rambo-like tactics. His leadership ethics can be seriously questioned.

▶

ert Reich remarked when he heard that Dunlap planned to cut thousands of employees at Sunbeam, "There is no excuse for treating employees as if they are disposable pieces of equipment" (Byrne, 1999, p. 68).

Dunlap's leadership style consisted of intimidation and fear (Byrne, 1999). As Richard Boynton, president of the household products division of Sunbeam Corporation, put it, "It was like a dog barking at you for hours. He just yelled, ranted, and raved. He was condescending, belligerent, and disrespectful" (Byrne, 1999, p. 5).

Ironically, Dunlap himself was fired as CEO of Sunbeam in June 1998. His trademark downsizing strategy faltered. The company's board of directors lost faith in Dunlap's leadership. Those employees who remained at Sunbeam after the downsizing reportedly cheered when they heard that he had been fired.

Al Dunlap's leadership ethics certainly can be questioned. Dunlap exhibited disrespect toward workers. He told workers that if they wanted a friend, "get a dog." He created a defensive work climate that squelched personal choice. Dunlap came into an organization ready to wield the downsizing axe, and those most affected by his "burn the walls to heat the house" (Fenton, 2005) tactics were given little consideration and say in the matter. Instead of responsibility he showed "the worse kind of corporate irresponsibility" (Fenton, 2005). Even his honesty became an issue. In 2002, Dunlap paid $500,000 to settle charges by the Securities and Exchange Commission that he defrauded investors by inflating sales at Sunbeam. He also paid $15 million to settle a class-action shareholder lawsuit that was based on similar charges (Roland & Mathewson, 2002). Dunlap has been barred from working as an executive at a public company. His attorney, Frank Razzano, remarked that following the settlements Dunlap could now "pursue his retirement" (Roland & Mathewson, 2002).

Questions for Thought

1. Should we always view Dunlap's approach to business as deplorable?
2. Why is getting rid of fear a desirable goal for groups?

statues and naming streets and buildings after those thought to be extraordinary. German-speaking parts of Switzerland, the Netherlands, and Scandinavia, however, are generally skeptical of strong leaders and fear their abuse of power. In these countries, public commemoration of leaders is sparse. Leadership characterized as elitist, self-centered, and egotistical is perceived to be slightly effective in Albania, Taiwan, Egypt, Iran, and Kuwait. All other countries in the GLOBE study, however, especially Northern European countries, had a very negative opinion of such leadership.

The participative leadership style, typically accepted or even preferred in Western individualist cultures, is questionably effective in collectivist Eastern cultures (Dorfman, 2004). Directive leadership is strongly favored more in Middle Eastern cultures (Scandura et al., 1999). Listening carefully is also more preferred in the United States than it is in Asian cultures such as China (A. Jones et al., 1990). This could have implications for leader emergence because being a good listener correlates with assuming a leader role in groups, at least in the United States, as previously noted.

There do seem to be some universals in the cross-cultural research on leadership. The GLOBE study revealed strong endorsement by all cultures examined of such leadership attributes as being trustworthy and honest; having foresight and planning ahead; being positive, encouraging, dynamic, motivating, communicative, and informed; and being a team builder. Conversely, being individualistic, status conscious, and a risk taker were viewed as enhancing outstanding leadership in some cultures but impeding outstanding leadership in other cultures (Dorfman et al., 2004). Again, agreement on a certain set of traits perceived by individuals as constituting effective leadership (sometimes referred to as *implicit leadership theory*) is a far cry from actually demonstrating that someone who possesses this set of attributes will prove to be an outstanding or even credible leader in actual practice. In any case, we still have much to learn about effective leadership and cultures.

In summary, there are many roles to play in small groups. Competent communicators learn to play a variety of roles. Leaders emerge in a process of elimination. There are different requirements, however, for gaining the leader role and retaining it once the role has been secured. The key to effective leadership is the ability to adapt to changing situations and to exhibit communication competence in the process.

I've discussed how groups develop and how to create a cooperative and supportive climate during that development, and I've explained the roles we play during the life of a group and how to function effectively in those roles. In the next chapter, how all these processes combine in the more specialized environment of team building and teamwork is discussed. ● ●

Questions for Critical Thinkers

1. Have you experienced role fixation? Have you observed it in others?
2. Do Adolf Hitler, Joseph Stalin, Jim Jones, David Koresh, Charles Manson, and Marshall Applewhite qualify as leaders? Why?
3. Can a transformational leader be effective and still unethical?

$\overset{\bullet}{i}$ InfoTrac College Edition

Log onto InfoTrac College Edition.

1. Type "leadership" in the search window. Choose an article to read. SUGGESTION: Article A80158365 by Walter O. Einstein and John H. Humphreys entitled "Transforming leadership: Matching diagnostics to leader behaviors."

2. Type "empowering leadership" in the search window. Choose an article to critique. SUGGESTION: Article A93920202 by Ramona M. Wis entitled "The conductor as servant-leader."

Video Case Studies

Dave (1993). Comedy; PG; ****

Kevin Kline plays a dual role as the president of the United States who suffers a stroke, and as a look-alike character who runs a temp-work agency and is surreptitiously induced to play president for the stricken chief executive. Apply the traits, styles, situational, and functional leadership perspectives.

The American President (1995). Comedy-Drama; PG; *****

Michael Douglas plays the president of the United States as a noble character. Analyze his leadership as an influence process. What style of leadership does he exhibit? Does his leadership seem more managerial/transactional or charismatic?

Erin Brockovich (2000). Drama; R; ****1/2

This is Julia Roberts's Oscar-winning performance as the title character who stumbles into a leadership role. Examine this movie for leader emergence. Does the Roberts character follow the typical leader emergence pattern?

Twelve Angry Men (1957; 1997). Drama; PG-13; *****

Either version of this taut drama that depicts a jury locked in animated argument because one juror votes "not guilty" in a capital murder case is wonderful entertainment. Which informal roles—task, maintenance, and disruptive—do each of the characters play? Are there any formal roles depicted?

6 Developing Effective Teams

A. HOW TEAMS DIFFER FROM GROUPS

1. Level of Cooperation: The Working Together Imperative

2. Diversity of Skills: Looking for Complementarity

3. Group Identity: Operating as a Unit

4. Time and Resources: Commitment to the Team

B. TEAM MEMBERS

1. Team Slayers: Members' Bad Attitudes

   a. *Egocentrism: Me-Deep in Omnipotence*

   b. *Cynicism: Can't-Do Attitude*

   c. *Team Member Removal: Purging the Rotten Egg*

2. Team Builders: Choosing and Developing Team Members

   a. *Experience and Problem-Solving Abilities: Core Competencies*

   b. *Cultural Diversity: Members with Different Perspectives*

   c. *Communication Training: Developing Members' Competence*

C. BUILDING TEAMWORK

1. Developing Team Goals: The Four C's

   a. *Clear Goals: Everyone on the Same Page*

   b. *Cooperative Goals: Interdependent Challenges*

   c. *Challenging Goals: Denting the Universe*

CLOSER LOOK: THE U.S. WOMEN'S OLYMPIC BASKETBALL TEAM

   d. *Commitment to Goals: A Passion to Succeed*

2. Developing a Team Identity: Unifying Members

   a. *Symbolic Convergence: Developing Fantasy Themes*

   b. *Solidarity Symbols: Unifying with Uniforms*

   c. *Team Talk: The Language of We*

3. Designating Clear, Appropriate Roles: Room for One Quarterback

   a. *Appropriate Roles for Team Members: Choosing Wisely*

   b. *Formal Role Designations: Spreading Responsibility*

I N DECEMBER 2001, the Joint Commission on Accreditation of Healthcare Organizations issued its second alert in 3 years on surgical mistakes in U.S. hospitals (Altman, 2001). An alarming number of "wrong-site surgeries," in which surgeons operated on the wrong arm, leg, eye, kidney, or other body part, removed the wrong kidney, and sometimes even operated on the wrong patient, triggered the commission's alert. In one case, two surgeons at the Long Island College Hospital in Brooklyn operated on the wrong side of a patient's brain. An additional commission concern involved surgical instruments that were inadvertently left inside patients. The commission's focus on preventing such surgical errors centered on improving surgical teamwork.

On September 4, 2004, the De La Salle high school football team lost 39–20 to Bellevue high school in Washington. Why is this noteworthy? This was De La Salle's first loss in nearly *13 years*. Located in Concord, California, this all-boys Catholic high school of about a thousand students that sends 98% of its graduates to college saw the most remarkable win streak in U.S. organized sports history finally come to an end. De La Salle's 151-game win streak dwarfs the college record 88-game win streak of UCLA's basketball team during the John Wooden era of the 1970s. Paralleling Wooden's philosophy, however, De La Salle coach Bob Ladouceur never mentioned winning during the entire streak (Gomez, 2003).

What distinguishes successful from unsuccessful teams? Although there are certainly differences between surgical teams and football teams, **the key to all successful teams resides in the communication competence of members** (LaFasto & Larson, 2001). The wide variety of teams—from sports, legal, classroom project, and creative design, to mountain climbing, surgical, computer programming, and script-writing teams—makes team effectiveness a challenge. **The primary purpose of this chapter is to explore how to build and sustain a wide variety of effective teams.** Toward this end there are four chapter objectives:

1. to describe what is likely to make effective team members,
2. to discuss ways to develop competent team relationships,
3. to explain what structures and functions should be established to build and sustain effective teams, and
4. to identify what constitutes effective team leadership.

The need for effective teams increases as our society and world become evermore complex. This is what Maxwell (2001) calls the Law of Mount Everest: "As the challenge escalates, the need for teamwork elevates" (p. 52). This is especially true in "high-pressure workplaces, such as nuclear plants, aircraft cockpits, or the military [in which] teamwork is essential to survival" (Appleby & Davis, 2001, p. B2).

The wisdom of teams, however, is sometimes a tough sell in an individualistic culture such as the United States, where individual performance is extolled and personal ego is celebrated (Acuff, 1997). The wisdom of teams, nevertheless, is an underlying theme of this chapter and it will be explored further in subsequent chapters on decision making and problem solving.

How Teams Differ from Groups

All teams are groups but not all groups are teams. Teams are specialized groups. There are four principal characteristics that distinguish small groups from teams that are discussed in this section.

LEVEL OF COOPERATION: THE WORKING TOGETHER IMPERATIVE

Teams typically manifest a higher level of cooperation than standard groups. Members of standard groups may actually oppose each other, not work together on a common goal. In 1998, the House Judiciary Committee sent four articles of impeachment against President Bill Clinton to the full House of Representatives for a vote. Committee members voted along party lines—every Republican voted for impeachment and every Democrat voted against. This committee clearly was not a team. The common goal of the committee was to decide whether Bill Clinton should be impeached, but members did not work cooperatively to accomplish a common mission. Democrats uniformly rejected what they perceived to be the mission of Republicans—to weaken the Democratic Party by bringing down the president. Committee members acted as adversaries, not team members.

The essence of all teams is collaborative interdependence (Guzzo & Dickson, 1996; D. W. Johnson & R. T. Johnson, 2003; Swezey & Salas, 1992). Team members generally must work together or they will be unsuccessful in achieving their goals. When you think of the "world's best teams" you probably consider football, baseball, basketball, or soccer teams. One of the best sports teams ever, however, was the eight-member U.S. Postal Service cycling team. Seven of the team members sacrificed their bodies and egos to escort Lance Armstrong across the finish line of the annual Tour de France, cycling's most prestigious race, six times in a row. No solo rider could tackle the grueling 3-week, 2,200-mile race. Teammates run inter-

Getty Images

Lance Armstrong (left) and the U.S. Postal Service team at the Tour de France illustrating teamwork in action. Dubbed the "Tour de Lance," Armstrong won a seventh time in 2005 with the Discover team.

ference for the team's lead rider, protecting Armstrong from disastrous accidents, shielding him from wind resistance, providing food and water for him, chasing down breakaway riders, and setting a gut-wrenching pace in various stages of the race to exhaust competing cyclists (Jenkins, 2003). Armstrong's success is their success. Wearing the yellow jersey, the symbol of leading in the previous day's stage of the race, Armstrong once remarked, "I figure I only deserve the zipper. The rest of it, each sleeve, the front, the back, belongs to the guys" (quoted in Jenkins, 2003, p. 3D).

When members work mostly for themselves, attempting to advance individual agendas (scoring more points than other teammates), the essence of a team is missing. Unlike the U.S. Postal Service cycling team, the 2004 U.S. men's Olympic basketball team was a huge disappointment (some would say embarrassment). Composed of NBA players such as Tim Duncan and Allen Iverson, American players displayed individual prowess at times, but little actual teamwork (Killion, 2004). Dismantled 92–73 in a preliminary round game by Puerto Rico, a team with just one NBA player, the United States went on to lose three games (equal to the total number of losses in all previous Olympics). Coach Larry Brown remarked after the loss to Puerto Rico, "We have to become a team in a short period of time. Throw your egos out the window" (quoted by Killion, 2004, p. 3D). Beginning to play more like a team in the medal bracket, the U.S. won the bronze medal, much better than another group of NBA players who couldn't do better than sixth place for the United States in the 2002 World Games. When you don't work together, regardless of individual skill levels, you're a team in name only.

DIVERSITY OF SKILLS: LOOKING FOR COMPLEMENTARITY

Teams usually consist of members with more diverse skills than those found in standard groups. In standard small groups, membership is usually a potluck. You may have lots of desserts but few main dishes. Project groups in my classes have often been stymied because no member has sufficient technical skills to permit the group to choose some of the project options. New members of the Student Senate are not typically chosen for how well they might blend with and complement other senate members.

A team requires complementary, not identical, skills. When ABC's *Nightline* with Ted Koppel challenged the IDEO design firm to redesign the common grocery store shopping cart to "see innovation happen," a diverse team of individuals was assembled for the 5-day challenge captured on camera. Engineers and industrial designers collaborated and brainstormed with team members whose backgrounds included psychology, architecture, business administration, linguistics, and biology. Peter Skillman led the team because he "had proved an able facilitator under fire, great at leading brainstorms and bringing disparate teams together" (Kelley & Littman, 2001, p. 9).

GROUP IDENTITY: OPERATING AS A UNIT

Teams typically have a stronger group identity than standard groups. In a standard small group, there are only superficial indicators of identity. I serve on the bookstore committee on my campus, whose purpose has been to explore ways to reduce the costs of textbooks for students. No one would recognize from mere appearances what group is meeting. Members certainly don't wear uniforms, brandish a team tattoo, or exhibit anything that might identify the group to the casual observer. Members would have to tell outsiders what group this is and what is our primary purpose. A small group may not even have a specific name. Teams, however, are almost always easily identified by those who aren't members. Team names are important and often the subject of intense debate when the team first forms. Team members have a sense of cohesiveness and oneness that exceeds the typical, standard, small group.

TIME AND RESOURCES: COMMITMENT TO THE TEAM

Most small groups that we join require a limited time commitment and few resources to function. A hiring committee normally requires a few meetings. Once the decision has been made the committee disbands. Little or no money is necessary to sustain the panel. Teams, however, often require substantial resources and long-term time commitments. Sports teams play for a season and return the next year. Some members may change but the team remains intact. Team members may devote huge time allotments to perfecting skills to help the team succeed. Teams in organizations may require substantial financial resources, even if the team was formed to work on a specific project, such as the Mars rover team at NASA.

Small groups can become teams, however, when they assume the four characteristics of teams. With these characteristics in mind, I define a **team** as a small number of people with complementary skills who act as an interdependent unit, are equally committed to a common mission, subscribe to a cooperative approach to accomplish that mission, and hold themselves accountable for team performance (Katzenbach & Smith, 1993).

Given this definition, obviously not all small groups can become teams. Boards of directors, student and faculty senates, class discussion groups, task forces, and standing committees are not usually teams because members may simply represent diverse factions at odds with each other. Such groups often lack cohesiveness and cooperation, and group members are usually chosen for reasons other than complementary skills that they bring to the group. Members are expected to attend periodic meetings in which discussion occurs and an occasional vote is taken, but members do not have to work together to accomplish the group's primary goals.

Similarly, not every group dubbed a team truly qualifies. Those small groups that only half-heartedly exhibit the several criteria included in the above definition are more **pseudo-teams** than actual teams. Pseudo-teams give the appearance of being teams and of engaging in teamwork without exhibiting the substance of teams. This doesn't mean that every team that fails to meet its goals is a pseudo-team. When small groups truly incorporate all the elements of the definition of teams, yet fail, they are still teams, just relatively ineffective ones for whatever reasons. Sometimes the challenge is simply too great for any team to be successful.

Teams embody a central theme of this text—that cooperation in groups has distinct advantages that should be pursued. Although most material presented in other chapters applies to teams, the analysis and advice is sometimes too general to be practical enough to make teams successful. This chapter offers more specific detail to respond to the unique differences between teams and small groups.

Finally, all groups cannot be teams, but small groups usually benefit from acting more team-like. Ways that you build teams and induce teamwork are now addressed.

Team Members

Team members are the raw materials of any successful team. **Assembling the optimum combination of individuals is the starting point for team building.** "Among the top predictors of a team's effectiveness are the qualities of the individuals who make up the team: the skills and competencies they possess, the attitudes they display, the behaviors they engage in" (LaFasto & Larson, 2001, pp. 2–3). Notice that personality traits were not specifically included on this list. **There is no solid evidence that any specific personality trait such as conscientiousness, extroversion, agreeableness, and so forth likely contributes significantly to team success** (Kichuk & Wiesner, 1998).   ◆

▶ Focus Questions

1. What is the ideal team member?
2. Why is the attitude of team members at least as important as their aptitude for decision making and problem solving?
3. Should ineffective team members ever be removed from the group?

TEAM SLAYERS: MEMBERS' BAD ATTITUDES

For teams to be effective, attitude is at least as important as aptitude. A member's natural ability and potential can't compensate for a bad attitude. "Good attitudes . . . do not guarantee a team's success, but bad attitudes guarantee its failure" (Maxwell, 2001, p. 106).

Egocentrism: Me-Deep in Omnipotence Those who communicate egocentrically reveal the "me-first" attitude that promotes team friction and weakens team cohesiveness. Egocentrics may even ridicule the fundamental underpinnings of teamwork, namely cooperation. As one T-shirt trumpeted, "My idea of a team is a whole lot of people doing what I tell them to do." Contrast this egocentrism with soccer superstar Mia Hamm's (1999) "there's no me in Mia" We-orientation:

> Soccer is not an individual sport. I don't score all the goals, and the ones I do score are usually the product of a team effort. I don't keep the ball out of the back of the net on the other end of the field. I don't plan our game tactics. I don't wash our training gear (okay, sometimes I do), and I don't make our airline reservations. I am a member of a team, and I rely on the team. I defer to it and sacrifice for it, because the team, not the individual, is the ultimate champion. (pp. 5–6)

Egocentrism can be a significant problem. A 1999 Institute of Medicine report estimated that hospital errors produce 98,000 deaths and a million injuries each year. One of the problems that contributes to this startling situation is physicians "steeped in a culture of quiet heroism and taught to exude a confident omnipotence" ("Medical Mistakes," 2003, 4C). Dr. Dennis O'Leary, president of the Joint Commission on Accreditation of Healthcare Organizations, which issued the wrong-site surgery alert, comments: "Right now, we're dealing with the problem of retraining surgeons who were taught to believe they were the center of the universe, and they're not" (Altman, 2001). O'Leary notes that about 40% of orthopedic surgeons refuse to mark the site of an operation because they are convinced that they could never make a serious site error. Instead of doctors acting godlike, they need to set aside their egos and become team members. As one physician observed in the study of high-performance surgical teams, "The surgeon needs to be willing to allow himself [herself] to become a partner (with the rest of the team) so he can accept input" ("Teamwork," 2002, p. 5). Bloated egos can destroy teams. They can foster defensiveness and perpetuate errors from egocentric control freaks who desire to protect their image more than correct their mistakes.

Team members with a We-orientation have a very different effect on a team than egocentric team members. We-oriented team members typically are more inclined than egocentric members to improve their own performance and to enhance other members' performance (Driskell & Salas, 1992).

Cynicism: Can't-Do Attitude Teams are systems, so even a single member can demoralize an entire team. **The attitude that most destroys teamwork and team effectiveness is cynicism.** H. L. Mencken described a cynic as someone who "smells flowers [and] looks around for a coffin." **Cynics** focus on the negative, predicting failure and looking for someone or something to criticize, sapping the energy from the team with their negativity. "Cynicism, like a disease, constantly spreads, seeking new receptive hosts. The attitude and the behavior associated with it are contagious" (LaFasto & Larson, 2001, p. 23).

Experience and talent are not contagious, but attitude is. **What you want in a team member is an optimistic, can-do attitude, not a cynical can't-do attitude.** An optimistic attitude nourishes a team's spirit, braces it for coming challenges, and encourages aspirations to rise and motivation to increase.

Team Member Removal: Purging the Rotten Egg Because even a single member can destroy a team, the "weakest link" in the chain may have to be removed if it prevents the team from being effective (Maxwell, 2001). This action, however, should never be taken casually. Removal should be a last resort after efforts to correct problem behavior have been undertaken (see Chapter 2).

The principal candidates for expulsion from a team should be those who persistently display incompetent communication, especially if they show no interest in improving, and those with egocentric and cynical attitudes that disrupt team relationships. Even knowledgeable and highly skilled team members who exhibit cynicism may need to be removed. Team members with only average skills and knowledge but who have optimistic, contagious attitudes are far more valuable. Bad attitudes are poison for a team. Those with skills and knowledge deficits can be trained to become more effective team members. Those with poisonous attitudes must either make an attitude adjustment or be expelled before they irreparably ruin the team.

TEAM BUILDERS: CHOOSING AND DEVELOPING TEAM MEMBERS

Unlike standard groups, teams aren't usually stuck with potluck when member composition is the focus. There are usually choices to be made. Who should become a team member depends on what each potential member has to offer the team.

Experience and Problem-Solving Abilities: Core Competencies "Experience and problem-solving ability are the core competencies that move a team toward its objective" (LaFasto & Larson, 2001, p. 7). We look for experienced members when forming teams. No one wants a cardiac surgeon performing his or her first operation. Who wants to fly with an inexperienced pilot, copilot, or navigator handling the plane? You don't want to mountain climb with a bunch of inexperienced team members. In each case you may forfeit your life. Experience counts because with experience comes knowledge and from knowledge comes problem-solving ability. Experienced group members "have been here before." Those who have limited experience may compensate by demonstrating a strong problem-solving aptitude.

Although the problem-solving potential of technical experience is necessary for team effectiveness, other elements are also required. In a study of high-performing and low-performing surgical teams, it was found that high-performing teams had handpicked their team members. Members were chosen not on the basis of surgical experience, because all members had such experience, but on the basis of prior experience working together as a team and the demonstrated ability of each member to work well in a group. Low-performing teams picked members mostly on the basis of availability. As one nurse commented about her hospital's method of choosing surgical group members, "We don't have any real teams here. It's just who gets assigned on any given day" ("Teamwork," 2002, p. 5).

Cultural Diversity: Members with Different Perspectives Increasingly, teams are composed of members from diverse cultures. This is especially true of virtual teams. With member diversity comes a rich array of different, complementary skills and knowledge with the potential for great decision-making and problem-solving creativity (see Chapter 2 discussion).

Nevertheless, culturally diverse team membership poses significant challenges (N. Adler, 2002; Ivancevich & Matteson, 2002). Americans, for instance, take pride in decisive decision making. In Japan and China, however, speed is not a high priority. Decision making is a lengthy process of chewing over all possible options before choosing (N. Adler, 2001).

There are several guidelines to managing membership diversity in teams (N. Adler, 2002).

1. Accept diversity as an advantage, not a disadvantage, for the team. With greater challenge can come greater rewards.
2. Choose team members for their complementary skills and knowledge but also for their similarity of attitude. Regardless of cultural background, there is no place for egocentrism or cynicism on teams.
3. Choose a superordinate, transcending goal to bridge differences (more on this in the section on team goals).
4. Be respectful of all team members and avoid cultural bias. The American way of doing things is not always the best way. Be experimental and try different approaches.
5. Keep communication open. Solicit feedback on the decision-making process so that if problems arise, they can be addressed immediately.

Communication Training: Developing Members' Competence Team members often lack necessary communication competence. A study (LaFasto & Larson, 2001) of diverse teams from sports, law, law enforcement, science, education, healthcare, computing, transportation, and telecommunications, among others, asked the question: "If you could discuss one issue in an open way, involving the team in the discussion, what would that issue be?" Overwhelmingly, team members responded, "the team's communication." Team communication is critical to its effectiveness, and high-performing team members typically exhibit superior communication skills (Curtis et al., 1988).

Training, however, must be an integral part of the team equation for success. A college course can provide useful communication training for student team members, but workplace training is often of dubious quality and efficacy (Goleman, 1998). Often these training programs consist of little more than a weekend "dog and pony show" by an outside consultant followed by "happy sheets" that indicate participants' degree of liking for the training. Liking, however, does not equal learning, and popularity ratings favor slick, cleverly packaged training programs that provide fun and entertainment but are as worthwhile as a sugar donut to a diabetic. Training programs that teach team members specific communication knowledge and skills relevant to the team's task (crews flying an airplane; design teams solving problems) are effective in enhancing teamwork and team effectiveness (Stout et al., 1997).

Building Teamwork

Does teamwork improve team performance? The evidence clearly shows that it does (see Stout et al., 1997, for a review). Building teamwork, however, is a complicated process that unfolds over time. In this section, key aspects of building teamwork are discussed.

▶ **Focus Questions**

1. What kinds of goals work best to build a team?
2. How is a team identity developed?
3. Should team roles be chosen by team members?

DEVELOPING TEAM GOALS: THE FOUR C'S

Setting specific goals is an important step in the team-building process. "As Outward Bound and other team-building programs illustrate, specific objectives have a leveling effect conducive to team behavior. When a small group of people challenge themselves to get over a wall . . . their respective titles, perks, and other stripes fade into the background" (Katzenbach & Smith, 1993, p. 114). Everyone becomes a team member, not a member of a power structure. Team goals should be *clear, cooperative,* and *challenging,* and team members should be *committed* to team goals.

Clear Goals: Everyone on the Same Page LaFasto and Larson's (2001) study of 600 teams and 6,000 team members found that "With amazing consistency, team members acknowledge the unease that comes with trying to achieve an ambiguous goal" (p. 74). In one study, all teams were effective that had clear, identifiable goals that members thoroughly grasped (Larson & LaFasto, 1989). Ambiguous goals, such as "do our best" or "make improvements," offer no clear direction. "Complete the study of parking problems on campus by the end of the term," "raise $350,000 in donations within 2 years for a campus child care center," or "institute a textbook loan program on campus by the start of spring term" are clear, specific goals. For a group to become an effective team, clearly stated and understood goals are essential (Hoegl & Parboteeah, 2003). This means that terms such as "parking problems," "campus child care center," and "textbook loan program" have to be defined clearly at the very start of a team's effort. Definitional discussions should identify what is and is not included in the team's charge. The **charge** is the task of the team, such as to gather information, to analyze a problem and make recommendations, to make decisions and implement them, or to tackle a specific project from inception to completion. A team can determine that a goal has been clearly articulated when all members can identify how they will know when the charge has been accomplished.

For example, is an oral or written report required? Does the team report to a higher authority with its results? Are there statistical measures that indicate completion ($350,000 is raised for the child care center)?

In some cases the goals will be specified by the organization within which teams operate. In other instances, the team will decide what goals they wish to pursue through discussion. In either case, the number of goals should be limited to what can reasonably be accomplished within the specified time period. Romig (1996) found one departmental team in an organization that pursued 60 goals in a single year. None of its goals were achieved, and the team actually threatened the future of the entire organization by losing huge sums of money as it flailed aimlessly in all directions. **A few clear goals that each team member can recite from memory are preferable to goals that are too numerous for members to recall.**

Cooperative Goals: Interdependent Challenges   Cooperative goals require interdependent effort from all team members. It is in every member's self-interest to promote the team goal and help each other achieve team success. Members share information, offer advice, share rewards, and apply their abilities to make every team member optimally effective. **Research clearly shows that cooperative goals enhance team performance** (Tjosvold & Yu, 2004).

Superordinate goals, a specific kind of cooperative goal that overrides differences that members may have because it supersedes less important competitive goals, is particularly effective for developing teamwork (Sherif, 1966; Sherif et al., 1988). When a group faces a common predicament that jeopardizes its very existence, for example, survival becomes the superordinate goal that can galvanize members to pull together in common cause.

The story of Fred Beasley, a fullback for the San Francisco 49ers, illustrates a superordinate goal in action. Fred's father died when he was 12 years old, leaving a wife and nine children to survive on a paltry Social Security income. The superordinate family goal following the loss of Fred's dad was to keep the family intact. No other goal was as important. Achieving this goal was accomplished by sharing labor and resources interdependently. Alma Beasley, Fred's mom, got jobs cleaning houses. All nine kids found odd jobs. Whatever income was earned from these jobs was pooled to cover family, not individual, needs. Four boys slept in the same room. Dresser drawers were divided among the kids. Household chores were everybody's responsibility. Alma Beasley explains how the family remained together through difficult times: "It was tough on all of us. . . . I just did the best I could. I think we all pulled together" (C. Judge, 1998, p. D8).

Sometimes groups choose a cooperative goal of simply doing the best they can for all members of the team. The first women's team to be invited to climb Mount

© Stephanie Maze/CORBIS

Collaborative interdependence is the essence of
teams, and challenging
goals encourage motivation
to succeed.

Kongur in China didn't set as its target getting one team member on top of the
mountain. Instead, the team chose a cooperative goal to get as many team members
as high up the mountain as possible (Larson & LaFasto, 1989). With a cooperative
goal, success is determined by everyone pulling together to produce the best results
for every member—no winners or losers.

Challenging Goals: Denting the Universe Accomplishing the mundane motivates no one. Teams need challenging goals to spark members' best efforts. **Members need to feel that they are embarking on a shared mission, with a common
vision of how to translate the dream into a team achievement.** The team that built
the first successful Macintosh computer had this elevated sense of purpose. Randy

CLOSER LOOK

THE U.S. WOMEN'S OLYMPIC BASKETBALL TEAM

A WILDLY CHEERING CROWD of 32,987 in Atlanta was on its feet as the final seconds ticked down. The U.S. women's basketball team had convincingly defeated its long-time nemesis, Brazil, to earn the gold medal in the 1996 Olympics. The final score was 111–87. The U.S. total was the most points ever scored by a women's basketball team in the Olympics, and remains the record to this day. Brazil, a powerful team, had humbled the U.S. women's team in the 1991 Pan American games, the 1992 Olympics, and again in the 1994 world championships. The bronze medal earned by the U.S. team in the 1992 Olympics at Barcelona was its worst showing ever since women's basketball became an Olympic event in 1976.

Under the able coaching of Tara VanDerveer, the success of the women's basketball team was primarily the result of embracing a clear, cooperative, challenging goal; putting aside individual egos and adopting a We-orientation; and exhibiting total commitment to accomplishing the team's mission (VanDerveer & Ryan, 1997). Sportswriter Ann Killion (1996) attributed the U.S. women's success to "setting [their] sights on a goal and working for it, [and] sacrificing one's self for the team" (p. D1). Tara VanDerveer explained her team's success this way: "There's a stereotype that women can't work together. What makes this special is that people had a team agenda. They weren't individuals. This team put the gold medal as its mission" (Killion, 1996, p. D3).

▶

Wigginton, a team member, remembers: "We believed we were on a mission from God" (Bennis & Biederman, 1997, p. 83). Steve Jobs, the team leader and coinventor of the first Apple computer, promised team members that they were going to develop a computer that would "put a dent in the universe" (p. 80). The De La Salle football team was on a 13-year mission to perpetuate its record win streak.

Changing the world or setting records, of course, doesn't have to be the team's dream. More down-to-earth visions can easily motivate team members. "Lowering the cost of textbooks by 25%," "doubling the number of effective tutoring programs on campus," or "making the campus safer by replacing old lighting systems with brighter, energy-efficient systems" can be challenging goals for campus teams. My own experience testifies to what students can accomplish when they form teams whose members share a vision of what could be. One of the teams formed in my group discussion class was instrumental in identifying student safety concerns due

All team members made significant sacrifices. They took a year out of their lives, traveling more than 100,000 miles during the year prior to the Olympic games to play international powerhouse teams such as China and Russia. Players participated in long and intensive physical training. Team members engaged in a team-building experiment in Colorado Springs. Players and coaches walked on parallel cables 30 feet above ground as the cables gradually split wider apart, forcing everyone to rely on each other to prevent falling. As a result of this commitment to excellence and team building, the women's team won all 52 of its preparation games, then swept through the eight Olympic games to post a perfect 60–0 record (unparalleled by any other international basketball team), culminating in the gold medal. In the process, they brought national attention to women's basketball and set the stage for the institution of a women's professional basketball league soon after (VanDerveer & Ryan, 1997).

Questions for Thought

1. Can the approach taken by VanDerveer to build a successful basketball team be emulated by other team leaders not associated with sports?
2. How would you try to duplicate the women's basketball team success if you didn't have the luxury of spending a year building a team whose members could commit themselves totally to this single enterprise for that period?

to poor lighting on campus. The team's effort provoked an audit of all campus lighting by a consulting group and fostered a 50% improvement in the lighting of all campus parking lots, walkways, and buildings, with the added bonus of a huge energy savings for the college. Your team may not put a dent in the universe, but it may chip away at a serious local problem.

Commitment to Goals: A Passion to Succeed In a massive study of 1.4 million workers in 66 countries for the Gallup Organization, one key finding was that "trusting that one's coworkers share a commitment to quality is a key to great team performance" (Buckingham & Coffman, 2002). Commitment is a key element of communication competence. It is also essential to team success. "Without it, groups perform as individuals; with it, they become a powerful unit of collective performance" (Katzenbach & Smith, 1993, p. 112).

A primary reason for the unparalleled success of the De La Salle football team was the commitment of its players. Erik Sandie, a senior lineman on the 2002 championship team, noted, "You better be ready to commit four years of your life to this program, or you're in the wrong school. That's why we're so good" (Emmons, 2002, p. 14A). De La Salle players demonstrated synergy in action. Though the team each year is usually not bigger or even more talented than other high school teams, team members' commitment to being the best team perpetuated the win streak. Mike Otterstedt, the school's director of guidance, observed, "Everyone thinks we feed the football players raw meat, but if you were to see them walking between classes, you wouldn't be able to pick them out from the other students" (Emmons, 2002, p. 14A). The starting offensive line usually averages about 6 feet, 220 pounds, which is ordinary by today's standards. The old-fashioned veer offense was employed by coach Bob Ladouceur, partly to counteract bigger opponents. A committed group of individuals all embracing a common mission and a shared vision of success can perform wonders.

One key way to create commitment is to have team members share in setting goals for the team (Romig, 1996). **Although not always possible, whenever participatory goal setting can be instituted it is advisable to do so.** We all respond better to goals that we have had a hand in creating than to those that are foisted upon us by others.

DEVELOPING A TEAM IDENTITY: UNIFYING MEMBERS

A group becomes a team when it establishes its own identity, both to team members and to outsiders. Team identity is an important part of team building. There is no single way to create a team identity; there are a number of possibilities. Certainly, establishing a mission is a key element. Strategies for developing a team identity are developing fantasy themes, creating solidarity symbols, and using team talk.

Symbolic Convergence: Developing Fantasy Themes Ernest Bormann (1986) developed what he termed **symbolic convergence theory.** Moving beyond an analysis of the individual, Bormann focused on how people communicating with each other develop and share stories that create a "convergence," a group identity that is larger and more coherent than the isolated experiences of individual group members. These stories, or fantasies, create a shared meaning for group members. Bormann defines fantasies without the negative connotation of "delusions" or "flights from reality." **Fantasies,** he says, are the dramatic stories that provide a shared interpretation of events that bind group members and offer them a shared identity. These fantasies will have heroes and villains, a plot, conflict—anything a well-told story would have.

In my own Communication Studies department, composed of between 9 and 12 members over the years, a common **fantasy theme**—a consistent thread that runs through the stories told by departmental members—is the challenge to survive and thrive among many much larger departments with far greater clout. I periodically tell the story of my early days at Cabrillo College when our department was under attack from some members of the administration. I relate the drama over the battle for full-time replacements of two retiring instructors, how this battle got me kicked out of the president's office, and how I waged our departmental campaign before the College Board, the Faculty Senate, and the Faculty Union. Each new member of the department gets to hear a retelling of this story, embellished somewhat over the years. The story serves to create our team identity as a small but determined, even formidable, department.

More recently, after exhibiting substantial growth in student demand, I have offered the fantasy theme of empire building. Initially seen as a dubious undertaking, the theme has more recently gained adherents. It permits departmental members to imagine a time when our department will be regarded as a major player on campus. The fantasy theme serves as a motivation to team members to strive for goals that are not merely ordinary, but rather, extraordinary. Department members share a common experience, and fantasies provide a shared interpretation of these events. Each member of our department can relate additional stories that play on the fantasy theme, creating **fantasy chains**—a string of connected stories that amplify the theme. In this way, a team creates its own identity.

Solidarity Symbols: Unifying with Uniforms Another way to develop team identity is by creating "solidarity symbols" (Kelley & Littman, 2001). A team name or logo can be a solidarity symbol. The presidential campaign team headed by James Carville that guided Bill Clinton to victory in the 1992 election was dubbed the War Room team. A uniform or style of dress can also serve as a solidarity symbol. The Green Berets uniform or the jeans and T-shirt attire often found at IDEO are examples. In fact, T-shirts with individualized inscriptions or sayings—humorous, profound, or just plain whimsical—help establish the loose team climate characteristic of design teams. In other instances an entire team may wear T-shirts with the same inscription, such as a computer-programming team that wore T-shirts inscribed: "Talk Nerdy to Me."

Team Talk: The Language of We Team talk is another strategy for creating a team identity and cohesiveness. "A shared language bonds a team together and serves as a visible sign of membership" (Bolman & Deal, 1992, p. 40). One software team refers to unproductive discussions as *ratholes;* team members spending too much time agreeing with each other are said to be *piling on* (K. Fisher, 2000, p. 300). The U.S. Postal Service cycling team refers to riding strong as *no chain,* calls riding for yourself and not the team *dead man's rules,* and describes a team rider who seems to pedal effortlessly up mountain roads as *fingers in the nose.*

A team uniform, in this case a simple T-shirt, acts as a solidarity symbol that helps establish team identity.

Teams establish an identity, a oneness, when they speak in terms of "we" and "our" and "us," not "he/her/they" (Donnellon, 1996). Team talk emphasizes interdependence and avoids terminology that emphasizes individuality. The language of individual blame and criticism is avoided. Effective teams speak of collective blame for failure and give collective praise for success. This is the language of team accountability.

Team accountability means that the team, rather than individual members, assumes responsibility for success and failure. Team accountability cannot be coerced; it flows naturally from collaborative interdependence that accrues from a shared mission. In the first round of the 2003 NFL playoffs, the New York Giants mounted a seemingly insurmountable 38–14 lead by late in the third quarter. The San Francisco 49ers, however, came storming back from apparent defeat and took the lead 39–38 with 1 minute remaining in the game. The Giants, in a last-gasp effort to salvage a win, drove to the 49ers' 27-yard line and with 6 seconds remaining attempted a game-winning field goal. Trey Junkin, the Giants' long snapper, made an erratic snap and the holder, Matt Allen, couldn't set the ball in time for the kicker so he tried to pass downfield for a touchdown. The pass fell incomplete. Junkin, in bitter disappointment, tried assuming the entire blame for the Giants' collapse, "*I* cost this team a chance to go to the Super Bowl. This is the best team in the NFC, and *I* screwed it up" (Emmons, 2003, p. 7D). Despite the crushing defeat and controversy that ensued over a missed pass interference call by referees on the final play that would have resulted in another field goal chance for the Giants (prompting David Letterman to quip that this "denied the Giants another opportunity to blow the game"), players nevertheless assumed responsibility for the loss as a team. Refusing to blame a single team member, many Giants players insisted it was a team collapse that allowed the 49ers to make the second greatest comeback in playoff history. As Matt Allen explained, "I know he's [Junkin is] upset. It's awful for somebody to bear all that weight. But he shouldn't feel all the weight. *We* did give up 25 points in the second half" (Emmons, 2003, p. 7D).

Team failure is *our* failure. Team accountability isn't the wistful logic of a feel-good philosophy. The Giants lost because of a *team* meltdown. The blown field goal was merely the last in a series of mistakes by many team members. Foolish penalties, a dropped pass in the end zone, an offense that transmogrified from fearsome scoring machine into impotent ineptitude, and repeated defensive breakdowns throughout the final 20 minutes of the game sealed the Giants' defeat.

Team success is also a matter of collective responsibility, and team talk should reflect this. Rafael Aguayo (1990) teaches team accountability for success, not individual glory, when he coaches a Little League soccer team. Following each game, he asks his players, "Who scored that first goal?" Typically at first, only the player who kicked the ball into the net raises a hand. "No!" Aguayo cries. "*We* all scored that goal. Every person on a team is responsible for scoring a goal." Then he repeats the question, "Now, who scored that goal?" All team members learn to raise their hands. In 4 years of coaching Little League soccer, Aguayo's teams lost only a single game.

Language that exhibits power differences also should be avoided. "Think about the difference between 'the boss holds me accountable' and 'we hold ourselves accountable'" (Katzenbach & Smith, 1993, p. 116). "Powerful" and "powerless" language is discussed in detail in Chapter 9.

DESIGNATING CLEAR, APPROPRIATE ROLES: ROOM FOR ONE QUARTERBACK

Unlike most informal small groups in which roles emerge from the transactions of members, teams usually require a formal designation of roles. A football team can't function effectively if individual team members decide which roles they plan to play. You might end up with 15 quarterbacks and no cornerbacks. Remember that formal roles identify a position (goalie, defensive end, project leader, chief surgeon), and a description of the expected behavior is explicitly spelled out (orally or in writing by a coach, supervisor, or team leader).

Appropriate Roles for Team Members: Choosing Wisely **A team must have every group function covered by a qualified member playing a specific role so there is little or no duplication of effort.** A surgical team has clearly designated roles for each member. Nurses aren't supposed to step in and begin performing heart surgery. Every function is critical to the success of the team. If only some roles are played but others are ignored, several important team functions will be sacrificed, sometimes with disastrous results.

In a huge Gallup study of 80,000 managers and 1 million employees (Buckingham & Coffman, 1999), one manager named Michael who runs a highly successful restaurant in the Pacific Northwest was singled out. He was asked to tell about his best restaurant team ever. He told of his waitstaff of four individuals: Brad, Gary, Emma, and Susan. According to Michael's description, Brad was a professional waiter who ascribed to being the best waiter in town. He could anticipate what customers wanted—more water or coffee, a dessert menu—without needing to be asked. Gary always smiled and was cheerful. Everyone liked him, especially the customers. He had an optimistic attitude. Emma was the unspoken team builder. She regularly assembled the team and alerted the crew members to potential problems. Finally, there was Susan, who was the greeter. She was lively, energetic, and pleasant. She kept track of customers at lunch who typically needed quick service to return to work. She was attentive. "These four were the backbone of my best team ever. I didn't really need to interfere.

They ran the show themselves . . . For a good three years they were the restaurant" (Buckingham & Coffman, p. 14). Michael noted that each team member had his or her clearly defined role. "Brad is a great waiter, but he would be a terrible manager . . . He respects the customers. He is less respectful of some of the new employees" (p. 16). Qualities that made Susan a great greeter wouldn't necessarily translate into being an efficient waitperson. Emma worked well with her team members, but she had a quiet personality not particularly suitable for a greeter. Gary would have been a weak team builder. Michael actually fired him, twice, but hired him back. His joking around went too far and he had to be reined in before he created team friction. Finding the appropriate roles for each team member can be a big challenge. It is vital, however, that each member plays the role suited to his or her abilities. Finding the appropriate team member for each vital role permits full utilization of the team's resources.

Formal Role Designations: Spreading Responsibility When Phil Jackson (1995) became coach of the Chicago Bulls, the team had never won an NBA championship despite Michael Jordan's prodigious personal scoring statistics the previous five seasons. To implement his vision of "the selfless ideal of teamwork," Jackson had to get Jordan to give up the ball more often and take fewer shots. In a meeting with Jordan, Jackson observed, "You've got to share the spotlight with your teammates because if you don't, they won't grow" (p. 101). Hesitant at first, Jordan became convinced when Jackson explained that having his teammates become spectators watching Jordan work his magic allowed opponents to key on Jordan, often double- or even triple-teaming him. "You can't beat a good defensive team with one man. It's got to be a team effort," Jackson noted. What Jackson hoped to create was a team in which every player truly had a vital role to perform. "My idea was to use 10 players regularly and give others enough playing time so that they could blend in effortlessly with everybody else when they were on the floor" (p. 99). Jackson also named center Bill Cartwright cocaptain, to make the team "less Jordan-centric." Jackson's approach paid off, with three successive NBA championships for the Chicago Bulls from 1991 to 1993 and again from 1995 to 1997.

Jackson's coaching philosophy and success utilizing his entire team's resources show that team members' roles usually must be explicitly designated. It is unlikely that Jordan would have chosen to reduce his role of star player and "go-to guy" without

© ATC Productions,/CORBIS

Teams usually require a formal designation of roles. Imagine this surgical team functioning effectively with every member vying for the chief surgeon role.

Jackson's prodding. Cartwright would also not have played the cocaptain role without the coach's designation.

The original reason that a person is asked to join a team may make role designation automatic. It is not unusual, however, to find that the roles originally contemplated for team members don't work well and must be changed to make the team more effective. **One of the responsibilities of a team leader is to make determinations regarding role designations.**

STRUCTURING TEAM EMPOWERMENT: ENHANCING MEMBERS' CAPABILITIES

"Highly empowered teams are more effective than less empowered teams" (Jordan et al., 2002). A key element of team building is structuring team empowerment.

Definition of Empowerment: Four Dimensions The concept of **empowerment** is the process of enhancing the capabilities and influence of individuals and groups. **There are four dimensions of empowerment: potency, meaningfulness, autonomy, and impact** (Kirkman & Rosen, 1999). **Group potency** is the "shared belief among team members that they can be effective as a team" (Jordan et al., 2002, p. 125). There is a strong relationship between group potency and team performance. Those teams whose members are confident that their team can perform effectively, not just on a single task but across many different tasks, typically perform effectively, whereas teams with low group potency do not perform as well (Jordan et al., 2002). Feeling empowered to perform effectively as a team can contribute significantly to team success.

Meaningfulness is a team's perception that its tasks are important, valuable, and worthwhile (Kirkman & Rosen, 1999). Team members collectively influence this perception of meaningfulness by their communication. Cynicism expressed by some team members can create a "why bother" attitude throughout the team. Optimism expressed by team members can have the reverse effect, convincing members that the team's task is important and worth performing well.

Autonomy is "the degree to which team members experience substantial freedom, independence, and discretion in their work" (Kirkman & Rosen, 1999, p. 59). Ironically, high levels of team autonomy manifested by relatively unfettered power to make choices may decrease the autonomy of individual team members. Team autonomy means that important decision making is a shared undertaking by all members. Thus, individual team members' responsibilities and choice making are diffused. Because of interdependence, no single team member entirely runs the show. Nevertheless, **autonomy doesn't mean that teams have no supervision or guidance.** Teams with a great deal of member autonomy and with limited supervision (facilitation, coordination) are far more effective than teams with virtually unlimited autonomy (Romig, 1996). IDEO has substantial member autonomy but some supervision by David Kelley and team leaders.

Impact is the degree of significance given by those outside of the team, typically the team's organization, to the work produced by the team (Kirkman & Rosen, 1999). Impact is often manifested by change outside of the team. If a team makes proposals for change in an organization but those proposals are mostly ignored and little change occurs, impact would be low.

Hierarchical Organizations: The Enemy of Empowerment Traditionally, organizations have been hierarchical, meaning that members of the organization are rank ordered in a kind of pyramid of power: CEOs, presidents, and vice-presidents are at the top of the pyramid, upper management is next, followed by middle and lower management, and finally spreading out at the base with the common worker. Top-down decision making is the rule, with those at the top of the power pyramid issuing edicts to managers, who in turn tell the worker bees what to do. Employees at the bottom of the pyramid mostly check their brains at the door because they won't be asked to participate in decision making and problem solving. Their role is merely the "heavy lifting."

Hierarchy in traditional organizations is the enemy of empowerment (Kelley & Littman, 2001). Although some degree of hierarchy provides necessary structure for organizations, flattening traditional, rigid hierarchy somewhat is desirable. Empowerment flattens the organizational hierarchy by sharing power. The organizational system becomes more open with information and communication flowing in all directions, with few gatekeepers obstructing the flow, and with decision making across the organizational spectrum encouraged.

Quality Circles: Lame First Attempt Motivated by the economic success of Japan in the early 1980s and its successful experience with teams, coupled with anemic economic growth in America, organizations in the United States began attempts to flatten the hierarchy. Initial attempts involved the establishment of **quality circles**— teams composed of workers who volunteered to work on a similar task and attempted to solve a particular problem. Quality circles proved to be a half-hearted attempt to empower workers. Typically, these teams had little autonomy to make final decisions and implement the team's wisdom. Mostly, recommendations were offered that could be, and often were, easily ignored by the higher-ups in the organization. Change (impact) rarely occurred so the meaningfulness of participation in quality circles became an issue for team members. By the mid-1980s, quality circles had failed in more than 60% of the organizations that tried them because teams

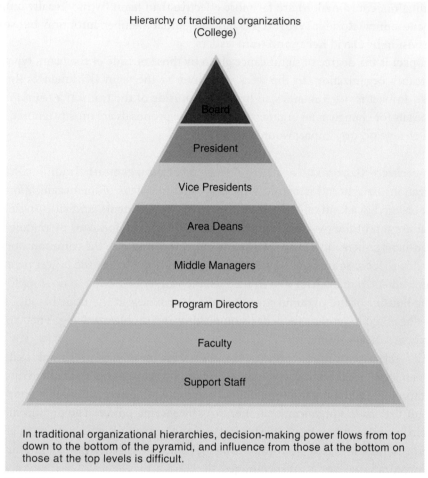

Hierarchy of traditional organizations
(College)

Board

President

Vice Presidents

Area Deans

Middle Managers

Program Directors

Faculty

Support Staff

In traditional organizational hierarchies, decision-making power flows from top down to the bottom of the pyramid, and influence from those at the bottom on those at the top levels is difficult.

FIGURE 6.1
Hierarchy in traditional organizations with its rigid rules and roles makes empowerment challenging.

lacked real autonomy, and the entire effort too often seemed like a meaningless charade (Hollander & Offerman, 1990; Marks, 1986). Many organizations abandoned quality circles as a failed experiment within a year of initiating them (Dubrin et al., 1989).

Self-Managing Work Teams: The IDEO Model Self-regulating teams that complete an entire task are called **self-managing work teams.** This type of team emerged as a more effective alternative to quality circles. Self-managing work teams embrace empowerment (see Closer Look: "IDEO and Team Empowerment"). After sufficient training and education, team members share responsibility for planning, organizing, setting goals, making decisions, and solving problems (Teubner, 2000). They have a great deal of autonomy because they are self-managed, and since they control a great deal of their own decision making and problem solving, team results seem meaningful to members and have impact on organizations. As self-managing teams manifest success, group potency increases, further reinforcing members' desire to continue with the team.

Impediments to Team Empowerment: No Buy In There are four primary impediments to team empowerment (Hollander & Offerman, 1990). First, **organizations can sabotage their own teams.** David Kelley's careful structuring of IDEO to foster team empowerment illustrates how important it is that the larger organization doesn't work at cross-purposes with teams working within the organization (LaFasto & Larson, 2001). Teams functioning within organizations are subsystems operating within a larger system. Their interconnectedness requires that every part of the organizational structure embrace empowerment for teams to be successful (Harris & Beyerlein, 2003). IDEO's corporate culture embraces and nurtures empowerment and teamwork. When organizations establish teams but fail to provide sufficient structural support for team empowerment, the organization is merely paying lip service to the concept of empowering teams. Not all organizations, of course, are as dependent on teams as IDEO is, nor should they be. In some organizations, **ad hoc teams**—teams that are assembled to solve an immediate problem, then dissolved once the solution has been implemented—are sufficient. Self-managing teams may be too time consuming and irrelevant for simple tasks more easily and efficiently tackled by one or two knowledgeable individuals.

Second, **not everyone embraces empowered teams.** Those accustomed to receiving and following directives from supervisors may not adapt well to new responsibilities and autonomy (Thoms et al., 2002). Some individuals' attitudes may be antagonistic to empowered teams. If so, they are unlikely to become effective, self-managing team members. This can be true of individuals assigned to teams to act as project leaders. If team leaders are held responsible for team failure when team decisions may contradict the leader's preference, it is not difficult to understand the reluctance of the leader to embrace self-managing teams.

Third, **when participation in decision making is a sham,** empowerment is thwarted. Collaborative effort will disintegrate if group members feel that their participation merely rubber-stamps decisions already made by others with more power. If the team is not trusted to make careful, deliberative decisions, and if the team's choices are not respected, then participative decision making will quickly be perceived as a deceptive game that only creates the illusion of choice.

A review of 47 studies revealed that meaningful participation in decision making increases worker productivity and job satisfaction (K. Miller & Monge, 1986).

CLOSER LOOK

IDEO AND TEAM EMPOWERMENT

IDEO, A DESIGN FIRM discussed briefly in Chapter 4, is a prime example of the empowered team approach. In fact, IDEO is considered so effective at team empowerment that for the last several years it has served as a consultant for diverse organizations from all over the world (Kelley & Littman, 2001). "IDEO has been on a mission not just to serve business, but to reform it" (Myerson, 2001, p. 8). This effort has been dubbed IDEO University.

IDEO has a flattened hierarchy characterized by few titles and no time clocks or specified vacation schedules. Employees are free to transfer to overseas offices in London or Tokyo or to transcontinental offices in Chicago or New York, as long as someone from those offices agrees to swap jobs. A team of designers, not "the boss," chooses new team members. At IDEO, employees are treated as equals who set their own schedules (typically 50- to 60-hour workweeks) while meeting demanding standards and strict deadlines. Designers can pick project teams and even occasionally specific projects to tackle. "Its flat multi-disciplinary 'hot team' structure is democratic, engages the client directly in the work, and reflects the idea that 'big ideas come from small teams'" (Myerson, 2001, p. 30).

The pyramid structure and the star system are replaced with team empowerment. Status at IDEO is based on talent, not seniority (Kelley & Littman, 2001). As one designer puts it, "The only way to enhance your reputation in the organization is by earning the respect of your peers" (Myerson, 2001, p. 31). Each of IDEO's six studios, with between 25 and 30 designers apiece, has maximum autonomy to shape its work environment. Each studio reflects the personality of the design team residing in the space provided. One studio team hung a $4,000 DC3 airplane wing from the ceiling to create a "cool space."

▶

When participative decision making fails, it typically fails because participation was minimal, only some individuals were allowed to participate, the decisions teams were allowed to make were relatively inconsequential, or the team's choices were essentially ignored by upper management (Kohn, 1993).

Finally, **when rewards are distributed based on individual effort or ability, not team success,** empowerment is impeded. There are essentially three ways rewards can be distributed in a group: winner-take-all, equitable distribution (proportional), and equal distribution. An equal distribution of rewards to all team members gives the best results for team success; the competitive winner-take-all system gives the

"Hierarchy is the enemy of cool space" (Kelley & Littman, 2001, p. 136). As founder David Kelley explains, "The general principle with work environments at IDEO is to try stuff and then ask forgiveness, rather than ask for permission first" (Myerson, 2001, p. 30). Traditional organizations assign office space and create a pecking order for the high-status "corner office with a window." Rules forbidding personal items such as family photos, wall posters, and the like are rigidly enforced. Office square footage traditionally is a status symbol in hierarchical organizations. IDEO's director of business development, David Haygood, tells the story of one of his previous employers who assigned workers to dismal, tiny cubicles if they were "grade 19" or lower, while workers given a grade 20 or above got hard-walled offices with an actual door. When reorganization occurred, grade 20 employees engaged in a competitive squabble to seize the offices with the most square footage. When Haygood moved to another company, he had the false ceiling of his office ripped out and overhead fixtures spray-painted black. His office was purposely the worst in the building. When some of his employees complained to him about their inferior offices, Haygood offered to switch with them (Kelley & Littman, 2001). He got no takers. David Kelley's office at IDEO is remarkably similar to the offices of his designers.

Questions for Thought

1. Do you think the IDEO empowered team approach would work in every organization? What might prevent it from translating well to some organizations?
2. Internationally renowned business consultant Tom Peters has stated that IDEO is the only organization among the hundreds that he has studied that he found appealing if he were looking for employment. Would an IDEO-type organization appeal to you? Explain. Would you have any reservations about working in an organization structured like IDEO?

poorest results (Deutsch, 1985; Kirkman & Shapiro, 2000). Equal distribution of rewards provides potential motivation for all group members. It also enhances mutual self-esteem and respect, team loyalty, and congenial personal relationships within the group (Deutsch, 1979). A merit system of rewards (winner-take-all) is intrinsically competitive. Designating only some team members as meritorious implicitly brands other members as deficient and unworthy of rewards for team success. Almost all of the 3,000 studies conducted on merit pay show either no positive results or serious disadvantages, such as divisiveness and demoralization (Charnofsky et al., 1998).

▶●● SECOND LOOK

TYPICAL CHARACTERISTICS OF EMPOWERED TEAMS

1. Teams set their own goals and rules.
2. Team members often set their own work schedules.
3. Teams usually design their own work space.
4. Work space is divided relatively equally among members.
5. Members devise and embrace rules for appropriate member behavior.
6. Teams as a whole are accountable for team performance.
7. Teams determine their membership and remove members who are deemed ineffective or disruptive.
8. Team members are trained to operate collaboratively and supportively.
9. Decision making is typically democratic, and leadership is participative.
10. Team members don't ask for permission from the team leader to take risks or make changes, but negotiate with the team and strive for consensus.

There are also serious drawbacks to equitable reward distribution—proportional reward based on individual effort and influence. "The quest for individual rewards often leads to a great deal of tension when benefits are to be distributed. People disagree if they do not receive as much as expected" (Brislin, 1993, p. 53).

Establishing Individual Accountability: Minimum Standards

Team accountability diffuses the blame for failure and spreads the praise for success. Team building, however, also requires **individual accountability, which establishes a minimum standard of effort and performance for each team member to share the fruits of team success.** Team effort is not truly cooperative if some members are slackers who let others do all the work. You must have a mechanism for individual accountability to discourage social loafing (D. W. Johnson & R. T. Johnson, 1987).

Individual accountability standards should not be set so high that they assure failure. Opportunities for social loafers to redeem themselves should be available. **The focus should be on raising all team members above the minimum standards— way above if possible—not on looking for ways to designate failures** (Druskat & Wolff, 1999). Minimum standards agreed to in advance by the group might include the following: no more than two missed meetings, no more than two tardies or early exits from meetings, work turned in to the group on time, and work of satisfactory quality as determined by peer appraisal.

Individual accountability is not the same as rank ordering of group members' performances or distributing rewards based on merit. **Individual accountability merely establishes a floor below which no one should drop, not a ceiling that only a very few can reach.** A plan to deal with social loafing was discussed in Chapter 3. Implement it.

Competent Team Leadership

Teams require leadership even if they are self-managing. Remember that leadership is not a person but a process. A team may have a designated leader (coach, manager, project director), but leadership in teams is a shared responsibility. It is not what some have termed "mushroom management," that is, put the team in the dark, feed it manure, and watch it grow (Bolman & Deal, 1992). Teams don't require management from a supervisor, and they don't need to be left leaderless. They do need guidance and facilitation to ensure that goals are being met. In this section, communication strategies that produce competent team leadership are explored.

▶ **Focus Questions**

1. Which style of leadership, directive or participative, is usually most effective with teams? In all situations?
2. How does fear diminish teamwork and team effectiveness?
3. What are supportive rules and how should they be established in a team?

FOSTER PARTICIPATIVE LEADERSHIP: NURTURING EMPOWERMENT

Team leaders don't act like bosses or supervisors if they hope to be effective. Team leaders are teachers and facilitators—skill builders. They are open to input from team members. The head coach of a football team may make many final decisions, but participative leadership requires consultation with assistant coaches in devising game plans, utilizing personnel effectively, and dealing with the inevitable problems that emerge during the course of a season. Coaches for offensive, defensive, and special teams encourage input from players so that difficulties arising during the game can be discovered, analyzed effectively, and solved before it's too late. As a teacher, a coach/team leader is "the guide on the side, not the sage on the stage." One person cannot be expected to know everything, so participative leadership encourages the sharing of knowledge and wisdom. Encouraging skill building, delegating meaningful responsibility, and sharing decision making and problem solving empowers members (Hollander & Offerman, 1990). Maximum utilization of team resources requires all members, not just the leader, to think for themselves. That's how group potency is fostered. Remember, coaches can't think for the players when they're out on the field playing the game.

As explained in Chapter 5, **a situation (such as military combat) may require directive leadership, but the general leadership pattern for most teams should be participative** (Pearce & Sims, 2002). A cardiac surgery team typically operates under directive leadership during the operation when swift, coordinated action by the entire team is essential, but participative leadership is appropriate when the surgical team considers new operating procedures, ways to improve coordination, and strategies to improve the team's communication. You want to involve team members in decision making and problem solving. Directive leadership typically operates from fear—fear of making a mistake, of looking foolish, and of being criticized. Operating from fear "prevents people from thinking" (Aguayo, 1990, p. 184). A team leader wants to drive away fear. One study by the Positive Employee Practices Institute found that 70% of employees see a problem at work but won't tell anyone because they are afraid to tell management (cited in Romig, 1996). At IDEO, there is a saying, "Fail often to succeed sooner." Those who fear failure can be paralyzed into a play-it-safe stasis. "Failure is the flip side of risk taking, and if you don't risk, odds are you won't succeed" (Kelley & Littman, 2001, p. 232). Team leaders should seek to kill the fear that closes a system and kills thinking, input, innovation, and success.

INSIST ON A COOPERATIVE CLIMATE: JERKS NEED NOT APPLY

An effective team leader is a competent communicator capable of using supportive communication and avoiding defensive communication patterns with team members. Effective team leaders create a climate in which making a mistake is an expected part of learning. When mistakes are made, members are encouraged to learn from the errors. They aren't criticized, ridiculed, or made to feel stupid, especially in front of other team members. Berating members for making mistakes instills fear of failure.

Effective team leaders also suppress their egos to encourage a cooperative climate (Chemers, 2000). Egos create defensiveness and competitiveness. In 1984, Millard Fuller, founder of Habitat for Humanity, approached former president Jimmy Carter in hopes of getting his help. When Carter expressed an interest to work with Habitat, Fuller drew up a list of 15 possible roles the former president of the United States could play. Fuller expected Carter to agree to one or two roles, and almost everything on the list was a high-profile, prestige activity (speaking through the media, raising money, making a video). Carter agreed to all 15 roles, including working on a building crew. Beyond working on a crew for one day, as Fuller envisioned for him, Carter put together his own work crew, traveled by bus to Brooklyn, New York, worked vigorously every day for a week on building a Habitat house, and slept in a local church with the rest of his crew. Jimmy Carter has assembled a building crew and served in similar fashion every year since (Maxwell, 2001).

Imagine the result if Carter had demanded special treatment, played prima donna and swung a hammer on a building site only when cameras were rolling, and slept in expensive hotels while crew members slept uncomfortably in a church. Imagine the grumbling and disenchantment such egotism would have engendered. Who would have wanted to work with him, follow his lead, and be inspired by his example? Instead, Carter didn't expect special treatment, even though he was once the most powerful leader in the world. He completely suppressed any ego needs and became just one of the crew. He led by example, and in the process he gave Habitat a massive boost in visibility and participation.

Finally, **effective team leaders work with team members to develop supportive rules.** Please note: This does not mean that the leader concocts a set of rules and then imposes the rules on the team. It also does not mean that organizational policy rules ("always wear a suit to work" or "file an absence report immediately upon your return to work following an illness") should be followed without question. Supportive rules refer to communication behaviors that empower teams, not to policy rules in organizations.

Supportive rules should emerge from team discussion during the initial meeting of the team. "When the team members set the rules, they follow them" (Romig, 1996, p. 161). All rules should help create a supportive environment and avoid a defensive climate. Some possible rules that the team could embrace might be "no personal attacks," "listen fully and patiently to team members before responding," "treat every member equally," "never bad-mouth a team member behind his or her back," and "always show up on time for meetings." Team members should agree to the rules, they should be posted, and there should be between 5 and 15 rules. Fewer rules likely means something has been left out; more than 15 makes it too difficult for team members to remember the rules (Romig, 1996).

STRUCTURE DECISION MAKING AND PROBLEM SOLVING: USING A PLAN

Decision making and problem solving without a systematic structured procedure will usually waste huge amounts of time in aimless and unfocused discussion while producing negligible results. Effective teams typically have a systematic, structured procedure for decision making and problem solving; ineffective teams typically do not (LaFasto & Larson, 2001). The point to note here is that team leaders play an important role in assuring that systematic procedures are established for the team. This usually involves keeping the team focused on using the Standard Agenda, consensus decision making, and brainstorming procedures. A detailed discussion of these systematic procedures is presented in Chapter 8, not here, because they require substantial explanation and they apply to a much broader spectrum of small groups than just teams.

Teams have a higher level of cooperation, team members have more diverse skills, there is a stronger group identity in teams, and teams usually require greater allocation of time and resources than what is found in most conventional small groups. Developing effective teams begins with assembling effective team members. The best team members eschew egotism and cynicism, are experienced and have strong problem-solving abilities, are optimistic, and have received communication training. You build teamwork by developing team goals and team identity, designating clear and appropriate roles for each member, structuring empowerment into the fabric of the team, and having competent leadership. Competent team leadership is a shared process. Team leaders should foster participative leadership, insist on a cooperative team climate, and make sure that team members are guided by a systematic decision-making and problem-solving process. The next two chapters discuss defective and effective decision making and problem solving, also vital considerations for teams as well as small groups in general. ● ●

Questions for Critical Thinkers

1. Can you think of any teams that don't require clear, challenging goals, a team identity, and designated roles?
2. Can a team identity be established that doesn't conform to the team leader's preference?
3. How much say do you think a team member should have when roles are designated? Should this be the exclusive choice of the team leader?

InfoTrac College Edition

Log onto InfoTrac College Edition.
1. Type "teamwork" in the keywords search window. Choose an article to read.
2. Type "team building" in the keywords search window. Choose an article to read and analyze.

Video Case Studies

*The War Room (1993). Documentary; PG; ****

This documentary about Bill Clinton's 1992 presidential campaign received an Oscar nomination for best documentary. Analyze the film for team building and teamwork.

*Gung Ho (1985). Comedy/Drama; PG-13; ****

An automobile plant in a small town is rescued by Japanese ownership and an imported management team. Analyze this for teamwork and team building in the context of cultural differences. How does individualism and collectivism relate to problems of team building?

7 Group Discussion: Defective Group Decision Making and Problem Solving

I RVING JANIS (1982) relates the story of a tragedy that occurred years ago in the mining town of Pitcher, Oklahoma. The local mining engineer warned the inhabitants that due to an error, the town was in danger of imminent cave-in from undermining. Residents were advised to evacuate immediately. The warnings went unheeded. At a meeting of the local Lion's Club, leading citizens of the town joked about the doom-and-gloom forecast. One club member evoked raucous laughter from the membership when he entered the meeting wearing a parachute on his back in mock preparation for the predicted disaster. Within a few days, several of the club members and their families died when parts of the town caved in, swallowing some of those who spoofed the warnings.

Why would people ignore the threat? We read and hear stories every year of similar collective misjudgments and disasters. How do scandals such as Watergate, the Iran-Contra affair, and Whitewater ever occur in the first place? On a more local level, how do clear glass windows in a men's restroom at my college get installed to replace opaque windows, when the new windows leave men who stand at the urinals plainly visible to passersby? What gives rise to poor decision making in groups? How can group fiascos be averted? These are some of the questions that will be addressed in this chapter.

The terms *decision making* and *problem solving* are sometimes used synonymously. The terms are interconnected but not identical. A decision requires a choice between two or more alternatives. Groups make decisions in the process of finding solutions to problems (e.g., where to meet, what process to use in making choices, what is the best solution to the problem, how to implement the solution). Problem solving necessitates decision making, but not all decision making involves a problem to be solved.

The principal purpose of this chapter is to explore sources of defective group decision making and problem solving. There are four chapter objectives:

1. to analyze the adverse effects of excessive or insufficient information quantity on group decision making and problem solving,
2. to explain the role of mindsets in defective decision making/problem solving,

3. to explore the contribution of collective inferential error to defective decision making/problem solving, and

4. to describe and analyze groupthink as an ineffective group decision-making process.

Put succinctly, **this chapter explores ways in which small groups manifest defective critical thinking, a major cause of bad decision making and problem solving. Critical thinking** requires group members to analyze and evaluate ideas and information in order to reach sound judgments and conclusions. Critical thinking, therefore, is central to any discussion of small group decision making and problem solving.

One note of caution, however. Russian author Fyodor Dostoyevsky once remarked that "everything seems stupid when it fails." Determining degrees of decision-making and problem-solving effectiveness simply on the basis of outcomes would be misleading and inaccurate. Although suggestive, bad outcomes do not automatically signal defective decision making and problem solving because bad luck, sabotage, poor implementation by those outside the group, or misinformation may have caused the undesirable result.

Information Overload: Too Much of a Good Thing

Information is the raw material of group decision making and problem solving. With the advent of rapidly proliferating electronic technologies, information overload has become *the* problem of the new century. **Information overload** occurs when the rate of information flow into a system and/or the complexity of that information exceed the system's processing capacity (Farace et al., 1977). This section will examine the scope and consequences of information overload and ways decision-making and problem-solving groups can cope with it.

▶ **Focus Questions**

1. What problems are created by information overload?
2. What means do groups have of coping with information overload?

SCOPE OF THE PROBLEM: THE INFORMATION AVALANCHE

Jeff Davidson (1996) puts the problem succinctly, "This generation is more besieged by information than any that preceded it, and perhaps more so than all previous generations combined" (p. 495). One study generates staggering statistics to quantify the scope of information overload (Lyman & Varian, 2003). Almost *18 exabytes* of new information are communicated through electronic channels (telephone, radio, TV, and the Internet) annually, and the volume is increasing. An exabyte is a billion gigabytes. The 18 exabytes of new information flooding the world's electronic channels amount to 133,000 new Libraries of Congress (the largest library in the world). New information generated each year amounts to a stack of books more than 100 feet high for every person on earth. There are about 31 billion e-mails sent daily, and this is expected to double before the end of the decade. Instant messaging accounts for 5 billion messages per day. The storage of new information in books, on film, and on magnetic and optical disks is increasing at a rate of more than 30% a year. Clearly, information overload will not diminish in importance but will likely increase in years to come.

CONSEQUENCES: THE DOWNSIDE OF INFORMATION

Information overload is not inconsequential. There are four main consequences of information overload relevant to group decision making and problem solving.

Impairs Critical Thinking: Separating Wheat from Chaff Information overload *impairs critical thinking* (Shenk, 1997). A glut of information makes it very difficult to distinguish useless from useful information. Critical thinking and effective decision making are hampered because group members have trouble digging through the garbage heap of useless information to discover the treasured nugget. Consider a riddle that illustrates this point (Halpern, 1984):

> Suppose you are a bus driver. On the first stop you pick up six men and two women. At the second stop two men leave and one woman boards the bus. At the third stop one man leaves and two women enter the bus. At the fourth stop three men get on and three women get off. At the fifth stop two men get off, three men get on, one woman gets off, and two women get on. What is the bus driver's name? (p. 201)

Don't reread the riddle! Have you figured it out? The answer, of course, is *your* name since the riddle begins, "Suppose *you* are a bus driver." All the information about the passengers is irrelevant and merely diverts your attention from the obvious and correct answer.

Students working on group projects recognize the problem of information overload and its disruptive quality. When surrounded by a Mount Everest–size pile of books and articles or a stack of printouts from the Internet related to a group project, you lose sight of the larger picture. How does all this information fit together into a coherent package? Simply sorting through the gigaheaps of information on a subject leaves little time for group members to examine the information critically.

Indecisiveness: Conclusion Irresolution Information overload promotes indecisiveness (Shenk, 1997). Paradoxically, the technologies that have ushered in the Information Age speed up almost everything enormously, but a group's ability to make decisions is slowed (see Closer Look: "Technology and the Bias of Speed"). "The psychological reaction to such an overabundance of information . . . is to simply avoid coming to conclusions" (Shenk, 1997, p. 93). We become overly concerned that some new, instantly available fact or statistic that would invalidate a group decision will be overlooked, making the group appear foolish.

Information Bulimia: Binging and Purging Information overload encourages "information bulimia" (Wurman, 1989). **Information bulimia** is a binge-and-purge cycle of information processing. For example, students cram facts into their heads, regurgitate them for a test or group presentation, then quickly purge them from their minds forever (sound vaguely familiar?). We become so focused on the quantity of information that we hardly notice if the quality is substandard. Little information is retained. No meaningful decisions have been made in the process; no vital answers to problems have been discovered.

Group Attention Deficit Disorder: Difficulty Concentrating Information overload produces a kind of group attention deficit disorder (ADD). People with ADD, a brain syndrome, find that it is extraordinarily difficult to concentrate on any one thing for more than a fleeting moment. Similarly (though not literally), the megamountains of information competing for group members' attention makes focusing on any one idea, concept, or problem extremely difficult. Add to this what Shenk (1997) calls our "electronic leashes"—cell phones, pagers, faxes—that either distract our attention or make us wary that an interruption is imminent, and you can appreciate the problem. When cell phones and pagers go off during group meetings, classes, and the like everyone is distracted and attention is diverted from decision making and problem solving.

COPING WITH INFORMATION OVERLOAD: WRESTLING THE BEAST

Coping with information overload can't be accomplished by turning back the clock. Brian Lamb, C-SPAN's founder and chairman, explains:

> You can't stop the process. It's the American way. Which part of the library or the Internet do you want to shut down? Let me tell you something: If we can't survive all the information that we're going to develop, then we're in real trouble. No one is going to stop writing books. No one is going to stop creating information. (quoted in Shenk, 1997, p. 22)

You can cope with information overload in several ways.

TECHNOLOGY AND THE BIAS OF SPEED

❝MUCH TIME IS LOST by slow moving passengers who make no effort to hurry," claimed the president of Otis in a 1953 sales pitch for automated elevators. "They know the attendant will wait for them. . . . But the impersonal operatorless elevator starts closing the door after permitting you a reasonable time to enter or leave." He noted, "People soon learn to move promptly" (Gleick, 1999, p. 29).

Our technology makes "faster" possible, even necessary. As soon as faster becomes possible, it becomes our expectation. We perceive a "need for speed" whether or not it is required. Thus, computer printers of a dozen years ago seem painfully slow by today's standard, even though they were viewed as almost miraculously swift in their day. Waiting even a few seconds to log on to our computers produces agitation for many users. When the push-button phone was invented, the rotary dial seemed interminably slow by comparison, but now we have a speed-dial button. Some telephone-answering machines have quick-playback buttons. The speed of the message when played back can be increased by 25%. Federal Express ushered in overnight mail service. Suddenly, regular mail service seemed annoyingly slow. The advent of e-mail initiated speed-of-light transmission of messages. Now regular mail service is "snail mail." Everything compared to e-mail seems like the pace of a slug on tranquilizers. "Faster is better" has become the modern maxim.

Faster, however, may seem better because we supposedly "save time," yet all these technologies that accelerate the pace of our lives don't actually provide most of us with free time to make careful, deliberate decisions. We now have to "multitask" to keep pace (Gleick, 1999). Harvard economist Juliet Schor explains, "Technology reduces the

▶

Screening Information: Separating the Useful from the Useless Screening information much like you do phone calls by simply choosing to ignore much of the information is one effective method of coping with information overload. If you find 100 e-mail messages waiting for your attention when you return from a vacation, how do you cope? One way is to use a software program that automatically screens e-mail messages from designated senders. E-mails from virtual group members may be given highest priority. E-mails advertising rental housing may be deleted. A more low-tech screening method is merely to delete unread messages based on the title and author of the message.

amount of time it takes to do any one task, but also leads to the expansion of tasks people are expected to do. . . . It's what happens to people when they get computers and faxes and cellular telephones and all of the new technologies that are coming out today" (Shenk, 1997, p. 56). Where once a group might be given a month to finish a report, it now might be expected to finish a professional-looking report in only a few days. Little time is available to reflect, think, analyze, evaluate, or decide. We can become paralyzed into indecisiveness or forced to make rash decisions by the unrelenting pressure to act swiftly.

Group discussion can seem interminably long in a fast-track society. Allowing every group member to express his or her point of view seems like "wasted time." The pressure is to act, not deliberate. We become impatient with searching for creative solutions to complex problems. We feel a need to move quickly to the next problem, not linger on an "old" one. Crises and emergencies proliferate because everything becomes "last minute." "This is the Information Age, which does not always mean information in our brains. We sometimes feel that it means information whistling by our ears at light speed, too fast to be absorbed" (Gleick, 1999, p. 87). Technology is rapidly eliminating the pauses in our lives, and group decision making is probably not the better for it.

Questions for Thought

1. Have you experienced the difficulties associated with group decision making when faster is perceived to be better? How do you cope with it?
2. Should we try to slow the pace? How could this be done?
3. Is ever-increasing pace an inevitable product of technology?

Shutting Off Technology: Hitting the Off Switch A closely related method to screening is shutting off the technology. Information overload is largely a problem of too much openness in a system. Access to information needs to be closed off some. Cell phones are a primary source of information transmission. A standard rule for most group meetings should be that all cell phones and pagers will be shut off to prevent interruptions. Computers can also be turned off, although this may require some individual discipline. Don't check e-mails and messages until group meetings have ended.

Specializing: Knowing More and More about Less and Less When you specialize you can manage to know a lot about a little. Some specialization is undoubtedly

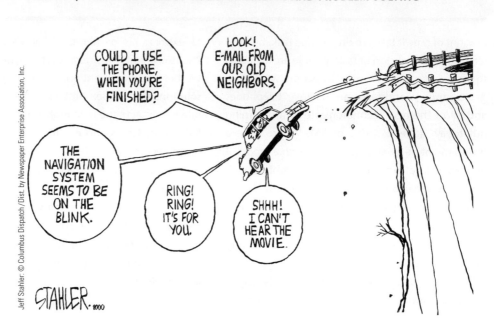

Too much information can produce group attention deficit disorder.

necessary to cope with information overload. No individual or group can possibly manage information sufficiently so that experts on vital subjects will never be required. Increasing specialization within groups, however, will probably not improve decision making, and may worsen it. When a group's knowledge is limited in scope, it becomes more dependent on experts, more vulnerable to their characterizations and perceptions of reality, and more prone to let the experts do the thinking for the group. If group members know little or nothing about the law, for instance, they may be forced to trust the advice of a lawyer counseling the group on some legal issue.

Becoming Selective: On a Need-to-Know Basis Another method of coping with information overload is selectivity (Klapp, 1978). Since group members can't attend to all information bombarding them, they should choose selectively on the basis of group priorities and goals. Setting group priorities helps members select which information requires their urgent attention and which can be delayed or ignored entirely. Setting priorities distinguishes what we *need* to know from what there *is* to know. Selecting the specific information that is required avoids burial by the information dump truck.

Limiting the Search: When Enough Is Enough The search for information must stop at some point to allow time to reflect and evaluate information. There is a time for searching and a time for thinking and deciding. Setting deadlines for group decisions is critical. Deadlines force a group to bring a search for information to a

▶●● SECOND LOOK

COPING WITH INFORMATION OVERLOAD

Screening Information—limit exposure to information

Shutting Off Technology—turn off cell phones, pagers, and so on

Specializing—know a lot about a little

Becoming Selective—attend to information that relates directly to group goals and priorities

Limiting the Search—set time for searching and time for deciding

Narrowing the Search—use credible databases; find patterns

halt. This means, however, that the search for information should begin early, instead of being postponed until the last minute. Otherwise, with time constraints, the search for relevant information may be far too limited to be effective.

Narrowing the Search: Databases and Patterns Searching the Internet by merely typing a topic into the keyword search window will likely prove to be unproductive. For example, typing "information overload" into the Google search window produces more than *5 million websites*. The search clearly has to be narrowed. One way to do this is to access high-quality databases. Many academic disciplines provide their own specialized databases that provide credible information, not general information from sources both credible and not so credible.

Pattern recognition is another means of narrowing the search. Discerning patterns is a group's best defense against information overload. "Once a pattern is perceived, 90% of information becomes irrelevant" (Klapp, 1978, p. 13). Football teams preparing for a game against an opponent could not possibly perform effectively without a specific game plan (pattern). Only a small number of plays are chosen. The players are instructed by the coaches to concentrate on a few key strategies: establish the running game, contain the opponent's quarterback, double-team the wide receivers. No player can concentrate on more than a few crucial strategies. The plan simplifies the team's approach to the game. It establishes recognizable patterns for players.

Information Underload: Poor Sharing

Although information overload is a far more prevalent and significant problem, information underload can also present problems for groups. **Information underload** refers to an insufficient amount of information (inadequate input) available to a group for decision-making purposes.

The 1986 *Challenger* space shuttle disaster that blew up an entire shuttle crew moments after takeoff was partly a result of information underload (Kruglanski, 1986). The compartmentalized deliberation and small group discussion process at NASA prevented vital information concerning potential sources of an accident from being communicated to the responsible decision makers. This conclusion was supported by the Report of the President's Commission on the Space Shuttle *Challenger* Disaster (1986).

As tragic as the loss of the *Challenger* crew was, however, this flaw in group decision making could have been infinitely more serious if the faulty O-rings that caused the accident had failed on the very next shuttle flight scheduled, instead of during the *Challenger* flight. According to Berkeley professor Dr. John Gofman, codiscoverer of Uranium 233, if the O-rings had failed one flight later you could have "kissed Florida good-bye" (cited in Clanton, 1988). The next shuttle flight after the *Challenger* was scheduled to carry 47 pounds of plutonium 238. According to Dr. Helen Caldicott in her book *Nuclear Madness: What You Can Do,* 1 ounce of plutonium 238 could induce lung cancer in every person on earth. Effective group decision making is serious business.

The problem of unshared information in small groups is serious. Many studies show that unshared information in groups leads to poor-quality decision making (Propp, 1997; Schittekatte & Van Hiel, 1996; Stasser et al., 2000). The problem of unshared information may even lead to disaster. A study (H. Foushee & Manos, 1981) of cockpit crews flying large commercial planes revealed that crews who shared little information did not perform as well as crews who shared a greater quantity of information. Seventy percent of all civil aviation accidents and near-misses during a 5-year period reported by the NASA Safety Reporting System were caused by either improper transmission of information from one crew member to another or by failure to transmit vital information at all (Burrows, 1982). Fewer errors related to mishandling of the engines, hydraulic systems, fuel systems, misreading instruments, and failing to use ice protection were found when sufficient information was communicated to all crew members.

Information underload is usually a problem of too much closedness in a system. The general solution to this problem is greater openness in the lines of communication. All members of the group must have access to the relevant information in order to make quality decisions. Finding the balance between too little and too much information, however, requires critical thinking skills. The competent communicator must acquire sufficient knowledge to recognize within a specific context what information is directly relevant to the task and what is irrelevant or marginal. Increasing the quantity of irrelevant or minimally useful information will confuse rather than assist the group in making effective decisions and solving problems.

Mindsets: Critical Thinking Frozen Solid

Perceptual **mindsets** are psychological and cognitive predispositions to see the world in a particular way. They interfere with effective group decision making and problem solving. Cognitively, we are prepared to receive only certain messages and ignore others. We are conditioned to view the world narrowly.

Try this demonstration of a mindset on your unsuspecting friends. Have them spell the word *shop* out loud. Now ask them to respond immediately to the question, "What do you do when you come to a green light?" The vast majority will unthinkingly reply "stop." Why? Because spelling the word *shop* narrows our focus to rhyming words even though the correct answer does not rhyme. Our minds are set to view the world in a particular way even if this is inappropriate.

You may be surprised by the power of mindsets. Follow the "shop–stop" demonstration with this version of the same illustration: Spell *joke* out loud. "What do you call the white of an egg?" Most people will be victimized a second time by answering "yolk."

▶ **Focus Questions**

1. Why does confirmation bias lead to defective decision making/problem solving?
2. Why is dichotomous (either–or) thinking usually false?

CONFIRMATION BIAS: ONE-SIDED INFORMATION SEARCHES

Confirmation bias is our strong tendency to seek information that confirms our beliefs and attitudes and to ignore information that contradicts our currently held beliefs and attitudes. A 2004 Pew Research Center study showed that 77% of listeners who tuned in to conservative radio talk-show host Rush Limbaugh are conservative, 16% are moderate, and only 7% are liberal (cited in Thomma, 2004). We listen to those who will likely tell us what confirms our current beliefs and more rarely listen to those who might challenge those beliefs.

The Problem: Poor Decisions and Solutions   Confirmation bias is a prime example of a mindset that can produce defective decision making and problem solving. Nickerson (1998) observes, "If one were to attempt to identify a single problematic aspect of human reasoning that deserves attention above all others, confirmation bias would have to be among the candidates for consideration" (p. 175).

Contemplate this real example of confirmation bias. A man sued the phone company for several million dollars when he was seriously injured by an automobile that crashed into the phone booth he was occupying. The insurance industry has cited this as an obvious example of a frivolous lawsuit. Obviously, the injured man sued the "deep pocket," the party with the megabucks, not the party truly responsible for the injury, namely, the driver of the car. If you already hold a strong opinion that Americans suffer from lawsuit mania, then you probably would seek no additional or contradictory information regarding this case. Why look any further when your predisposition is confirmed? You give up the investigation before you have a chance to discover contradictory information that would challenge your confirmation bias.

The facts, however, paint a more complex picture. The phone company had been notified on many occasions that the particular phone booth in question had a defective door. The door stuck regularly and trapped occupants in the booth. Even in normal circumstances this could pose a danger and obviously a considerable inconvenience to occupants. In the case in question, an automobile spun out of control and headed for the phone booth. The man tried desperately to escape from the phone booth but was unable to do so because the door jammed. The automobile crashed into the booth and permanently crippled the man. The victim won the suit because of negligence on the part of the phone company.

The predisposition many people have that Americans are lawsuit happy acts as a filter for the facts in the case just described. Because our bias is to search for information that supports our points of view, once we think we've had a confirmation, there is little motivation to search any further. Our minds slam shut on the subject.

Confirmation bias is alive and well in small groups (Nickerson, 1998; Schittekatte & Van Hiel, 1996). The consequences of confirmation bias to group decision making and problem solving are serious. Looking for the potential weaknesses and disconfirming evidence regarding decisions and solutions is a significant element of effective, group decision making and problem solving (Orlitzky & Hirokawa, 2001). Assessing positive qualities or consequences is not nearly as important. Thus, groups that resist confirmation bias and actively search for possible flaws in decisions and solutions usually make better choices than groups that don't.

In one study, three-member groups evaluated résumés of three candidates who applied for a marketing manager position. The positive and negative attributes of the candidates were skewed so that one candidate best met the criteria for the job. Each member of a group was given a different part of the information on the résumés, so information (positive and negative) had to be shared to get a complete picture of each candidate. Confirmation bias was common. Positive information about a candidate that each subject initially favored was readily shared and discussed with group members; negative information was not. Negative information, however, was shared about disfavored candidates but positive information was not. Although groups meeting face to face exhibited confirmation bias, online groups reviewing the résumés were more than twice as likely to engage in confirmation bias. Almost none of the groups chose the best candidate for the position (Hightower & Sayeed, 1995).

So what happens when disconfirming information is unavoidable and seems indisputable? Groups may still engage in **rationalization of disconfirmation**. Group members invent superficial, even glib alternative explanations for information that contradicts a belief. The Heaven's Gate group exhibited rationalization of disconfirmation. Members purchased a high-powered telescope so a clearer view of the Hale-Bopp comet and the spaceship they steadfastly believed was traveling in its wake—a spacecraft that was to transport Heaven's Gaters to a new cosmic life—could be discerned. The telescope was returned, however, and the owner of the store was politely asked for a refund. When the owner asked what was wrong with the telescope, he was informed, "We found the comet, but we can't find anything following it" (quoted in Aronson, 1999, p. 3). The Heaven's Gaters thought the telescope must be defective, not the original belief of a spaceship trailing the comet.

The perpetuation of unwarranted beliefs is the result of confirmation bias and its ally, rationalization of disconfirmation (Nickerson, 1998). False beliefs that pollute the decision-making and problem-solving group process won't be corrected when we aren't open to information that questions our beliefs.

Combating Confirmation Bias: A Plan The competent communicator combats the problem of confirmation bias by taking the following steps:

1. *Seek disconfirming information and evidence.* Since most group members will be predisposed to seek confirming evidence, someone will have to perform an error-correction function for the group. Consider it your personal responsibility to find the disconfirming information and share it. If, after a concerted effort, you find little disconfirming evidence of note, then your decision or solution has an excellent chance of turning out well.

2. *Vigorously present disconfirming evidence to the group.* Be persistent. Members will usually ignore information that disconfirms a strongly held belief unless you assert yourself. Messengers with bad news aren't always killed. Sometimes they're received as heroes when they prevent the group from making an embarrassing error.

3. *Play devil's advocate.* The term *devil's advocate* originated many centuries ago with the Roman Catholic Church (Forsyth, 1990). Investigations of claims of sainthood were viewed by the church as so important that a formal position called devil's advocate was instituted for the express purpose of challenging the qualifications of candidates. Play devil's advocate. Develop the habit of asking yourself and others the question, "So what's another side of the issue?" Challenge the assumptions and claims of those defending a decision or solution in your group. Do it in the spirit of problem orientation (supportive communication pattern), not as an effort to force your will on the group (defensiveness triggered

by psychological reactance). Clearly indicate your intentions so there will be no misunderstanding of your motives or intent. Anyone may play devil's advocate in a group. If groups establish a norm of devil's advocacy, the responsibility won't fall on only one member's shoulders.

4. *Gather allies to help challenge confirmation bias.* Women and ethnic minorities especially profit from developing support with those members of a group who are respected and open-minded.

FALSE DICHOTOMIES: EITHER-OR THINKING

A **false dichotomy** is the tendency to view the world in terms of only two opposing possibilities when other possibilities are available, and to describe this dichotomy in the language of extremes. Describing objects, events, and people in such extreme

"C'mon, c'mon—it's either one or the other."

Most dichotomies are false.

polarities as moral–immoral, good–bad, rich–poor, corrupt–honest, intelligent–stupid locks us into a mindset of narrow vision. Most objects, events, and people are more accurately described in shades of gray, not black or white (pregnancy being a rare exception since it is difficult to be "sort of pregnant").

For instance, when does success turn into failure? When does a small group become a large group, and vice versa? Dichotomous descriptions of events and objects are usually false because most of reality consists of more-to-less, not either–or.

False dichotomies contribute to defective group decision making and problem solving. When group members are predisposed to see problems and solutions only in extremes, the vast middle ground goes largely unexplored. City councils, faced with reduced revenues during a recession, see only layoffs and reductions in public services when they think dichotomously (i.e., tax revenues up—fund services and jobs; tax revenues down—cut services and jobs). They may fail to explore other avenues for raising revenues besides taxes.

Dichotomous thinking can lead to a friends–enemies duality when controversy brews. Group members may then shrink from making hard decisions or be provoked into making decisions from less-than-pure motives. Even the decision to make a decision can be a product of dichotomous thinking. Groups locked into the mindset that a decision has to be made may never consider a third alternative besides voting for or against some proposal. Postponing the decision until adequate study of the problem can take place and potential solutions can emerge may be a more viable option.

The competent communicator combats the problem of false dichotomies in small groups as follows:

1. *Be suspicious of absolutes.* When group members argue only two extreme possibilities (e.g., a solution is either all good or all bad), look for a third or even fourth possibility.
2. *Employ the language of provisionalism.* When engaged in group discussion, speak in terms of degrees (i.e., to what extent an argument is true). You'll be using terms such as *sometimes, rarely, occasionally, mostly, usually, unlikely,* and *moderately,* not *always, never,* or *impossible.*

Collective Inferential Error: Uncritical Thinking

Two American women—a matronly grandmother and her attractive granddaughter—are seated in a railroad compartment with a Romanian officer and a Nazi officer during World War II. As the train passes through a dark tunnel, the sound of a loud kiss and an audible slap shatters the silence. As the train emerges from the tunnel, no words are spoken but a noticeable welt forming on the face of the Nazi officer is observed by all. The grandmother muses to herself, "What a fine grand-daughter I have raised. I have no need to worry. She can take care of herself." The granddaughter thinks to herself, "Grandmother packs a powerful wallop for a woman of her years. She sure has spunk." The Nazi officer, none too pleased by the course of events, ruminates to himself, "This Romanian is clever. He steals a kiss and gets me slapped in the process." The Romanian officer chuckles to himself, "Not a bad ploy. I kissed my hand and slapped a Nazi."

This story illustrates the problem of inferential error. **Inferences** are conclusions about the unknown based on what is known. They are guesses varying by degrees from educated to uneducated (depending on the quantity and quality of information on which the inferences are based). We draw inferences from previous experiences, factual data, and predispositions. The facts of the story are that the sounds of a kiss followed by a slap are heard by all members of the group. Based on what is known, the three individuals who do not know for sure what happened all draw distinctly different and erroneous inferences.

Making inferences is not a problem in itself. The human thinking process is inferential. Our minds "go beyond the information given" (Nisbett & Ross, 1980). We could not function on a daily basis without making inferences. You can't know for certain that the grocery store is open. It may have burned down or closed due to a power outage. You draw the conclusion that it is open on the basis of what is known. If the store has always been open 24 hours, 7 days a week, then you infer it will be open now, which is a relatively safe inference. The principal problem with inferences is that we too often assume our inferences are mere descriptions of fact, even when they rest on insufficient or faulty information. This can pose serious problems for group decision making. If we don't exercise our critical thinking abilities by closely examining important inferences central to decision making in groups, bad decisions are highly likely to result.

▶ **Focus Questions**

1. What are the primary, general sources of collective, inferential errors?
2. Should we avoid making inferences?
3. Why are most correlations noncausal?

PREVALENCE OF THE PROBLEM: IT'S A GROUP THING

The centrality of inferences to decision making and problem solving in groups is made apparent by Gouran (1982b) when he explains:

In virtually every phase of discussion, inferences come into play. Whether you are assessing facts, testing opinions, examining the merits of competing arguments, or exploring which of several alternatives best satisfies a set of decisional criteria, you will have occasion to draw inferences suggested by the information you are examining. How well you reason, therefore, can have as much to do with the effectiveness of a decision-making discussion as any other factor that enters the process. (pp. 96–97)

Individuals are inclined to make inferential errors (see Self-Assessment Test: "The Uncritical Inference Test"). The problem can be magnified in groups. Gouran calls this collective inferential error. President Bush and his group of advisors made a serious, collective, inferential error when, based on limited and ultimately faulty information, they drew the conclusion that Iraq under Saddam Hussein had developed weapons of mass destruction. This erroneous inference served as the primary justification for invading Iraq in 2003. When no weapons of mass destruction were found in Iraq, world opinion and relations with most U.S. allies turned embarrassingly sour.

Studies have established the prevalence of inferential errors in groups (Gouran, 1981, 1982, 1983). As many as half of a group's discussion statements may be inferences. Groups often accept these inferences uncritically. One study (Gouran, 1983) examined student group discussions in which 80 inferences were made regarding questions of policy. Only one inference was challenged. The rest were reinforced or extended, or new inferences were added. Why is this significant? Because ineffective decision-making groups that arrived at faulty decisions displayed more inferential errors in their discussions than did effective groups (Hirokawa & Pace, 1983).

GENERAL SOURCES OF INFERENTIAL ERRORS: QUALITY AND QUANTITY

Inferences that rely on a quality information base in plentiful supply are educated guesses—not always correct, but nevertheless probable. Inferences that are drawn from a limited, faulty information base, however, are uneducated guesses—likely to produce inferential errors (Gouran, 1986). The two general sources of inferential errors, then, are a faulty information base and a seriously limited information base.

Faulty Information Base: The Problem of Misinformation   Inferences drawn from faulty information are common. Consider an example from a study of ineffective decision making in small groups (Hirokawa, 1987). The group task was to choose 10 items from a list of 30 salvageable articles most crucial to surviving 5 days in a remote wilderness area of Canada in the middle of winter following a plane crash. In one group, the following discussion took place:

B: I think we should go with the wine next. . . . That would be helpful for survival, I would think.

C: How so?

BOX 7.1 THE UNCRITICAL INFERENCE TEST

SELF-ASSESSMENT TEST

Individuals are prone to make inferential errors (Nisbett & Ross, 1980). See if you have such a tendency. Read the following story. For each statement about the story, circle "T" if it can be determined without a doubt from the information provided in the story that the statement is completely true, "F" if the statement directly contradicts information in the story, and "?" if you cannot determine from the information provided in the story whether the statement is either true or false. Read the story *once*.

Dr. Chris Cross, who works at St. Luke's Hospital, hurried into room #314 where Yoshi Yamamoto was lying in bed. Pat Sinclair, a registered nurse, was busy fluffing bed pillows when Dr. Cross entered. Dr. Cross said to the nurse in charge, "This bed should have been straightened out long ago." A look of anger came across Nurse Sinclair's face. Dr. Cross promptly turned around and hurried out the door.

1. Chris Cross is a medical doctor who works at St. Luke's Hospital. **T F ?**

2. Dr. Cross is a man in a hurry. **T F ?**

3. Yoshi Yamamoto, who is Japanese, was lying in bed. **T F ?**

4. Pat Sinclair was in room #314 when Dr. Cross entered and found her fluffing bed pillows. **T F ?**

5. Dr. Cross was irritated with Nurse Sinclair because the bed was not straightened out. **T F ?**

6. Yoshi Yamamoto is a patient at St. Luke's Hospital. **T F ?**

7. Nurse Sinclair's face reddened because Dr. Cross was stern with her. **T F ?**

8. When Dr. Cross entered he became the third person in room #314. **T F ?**

9. This story takes place at St. Luke's Hospital. **T F ?**

10. This story concerns a series of events in which only three persons are referred to: Dr. Cross, Nurse Sinclair, and Yoshi Yamamoto. **T F ?**

B: Well, uh, first, it can help to keep us warm—we established that as one of our needs . . . plus, you know, like wine can be used for medicinal purposes.

A: I don't understand.

B: What? About wine keeping us warm? Medicinal value?

A: Yeah.

B: Well, OK, wine . . . have you ever drunk wine, you have, haven't you? It warms you up, right? That's because of the alcohol in it, but also, that alcohol, that's how it can be used for medicinal purposes. Say if someone got cut, we could wash it with it, cleanse it, keep it from getting infected.

C: Plus, also, if we need to, I guess we could also use it to help us get a fire going. Like if the twigs and sticks were wet, and wouldn't burn, we could pour some wine over them and light it.

I created this version of what Haney (1967) originally devised and called "The Uncritical Inference Test." **"?"** is the correct answer for all of the statements. Without exception, these statements are based on guesses regarding what is likely but not verifiably true from the information provided. The reasons these statements are uncertain are as follows:

1. Chris Cross is a doctor of some sort but not necessarily a medical doctor (Dr. Cross may be a Ph.D., chiropractor, dentist, etc.).

2. Dr. Cross is not necessarily a man.

3. Yoshi Yamamoto has a Japanese name, but isn't necessarily Japanese (married name, assumed name, adoptive name).

4. Pat Sinclair may be a *male*, not a "her."

5. This requires an inference that Dr. Cross is irritated and that Nurse Sinclair and "the nurse in charge" are one and the same person, which cannot be ascertained from the information provided.

6. Yoshi Yamamoto may be an orderly taking a break or a visitor resting, not a patient.

7. This requires an inference that a "look of anger" automatically produces a "reddened face." Again, Nurse Sinclair may be male.

8. There may have been four people in room #314 if Nurse Sinclair and the nurse in charge are not the same person.

9. Dr. Cross works at St. Luke's. Nowhere does it say this story occurred there.

10. Again, four people may be in the story: Dr. Cross, Nurse Sinclair, the nurse in charge, and Yoshi Yamamoto.

If we don't even recognize that we've made an inference, then we're not likely to notice when the inference is a bad one. If individually you do poorly on recognizing and critically evaluating inferences, imagine the quality of decision making in a group when most or all of the members are inclined to make inferential errors.

A: Like lighter, or what, yeah, charcoal-lighting fluid?
B: Yeah, right, same idea. So, see, the wine has several uses. . . .
C: Yeah, let's go with the wine. (pp. 17–18)

There are several bad inferences in this example because the information used to draw the inferences is faulty. The feeling of warmth from drinking alcohol does not mean the body is heated by drinking wine. Alcohol dilates the blood vessels in the skin, which in turn chills the blood when a person is exposed to very cold weather. An intoxicated person is more likely to get hypothermia. The low level of alcohol in wine also makes it ineffective as a disinfectant, and have you ever tried to ignite wine? There isn't a high enough level of alcohol in wine to act as a fire starter.

Dan Coyro/Santa Cruz Sentinel

Look at the college basketball coach pictured above. How did you decide which individual was the coach? Did you assume that the male is the coach? If so, you made an inaccurate inference. Laura Mitchell, at the time of this photo, was the coach of the University of California at Santa Cruz women's basketball team.

Limited Information Base: Information Insufficiency Inferential error resulting from severely limited information is equally problematic for a group. There have been several documented near-collisions in the sky because pilots made faulty inferences (H. Foushee & Manos, 1981). In one case a critical alarm went off in the cockpit of a plane. Shortly thereafter, the alarm went silent, leading the captain to infer that it was probably a false warning. After landing, however, the pilot learned that the flight engineer had pulled the circuit breaker for the alarm system, that it was not a false warning, and that the alarm could have been potentially serious.

Upon questioning, the flight engineer revealed that he had asked the captain if he wanted the alarm turned off. When the captain made no reply, the flight engineer wrongly inferred that he was complying with the captain's wishes by switching off the alarm. The engineer based his inference on the extremely limited information that the captain did not specifically tell him to keep the alarm operational and check for the source of the problem. The captain inferred that the alarm was a false one simply because it stopped. That's very limited information on which to draw such a significant inference.

CLOSER LOOK

THE BLANDINA CHIAPPONI CASE

A DRAMATIC EXAMPLE of inferential error made international headlines in 1989 (Brecher, 1989). A woman named Blandina Isabella Chiapponi said she had been raped by a man named Steven Lamar Lord, an unsavory character, in a Denny's parking lot in Fort Lauderdale, Florida, at 3:00 a.m. The case went to trial and the jury acquitted the defendant after 2 hours of deliberations. One of the jurors, Ray Diamond, gave the verdict worldwide attention when he explained after the trial that the jury all felt she was asking for it, the way she dressed (Brecher, 1989, p. B1). Blandina Chiapponi was wearing a lace miniskirt, tank top, white high heels, and no underwear on the night in question.

Within days, the 22-year-old woman was an international celebrity. On both Oprah Winfrey's and Larry King's talk shows, she claimed, "I was kidnapped, I was beaten, I was almost murdered before being raped three times. My life has been ruined, not only by the brute who raped me, but by a jury who decided I was to blame because of what I was wearing" (p. B1). The media had a field day. The *London Daily Mail* described her as "an innocent, convent-educated girl from a close-knit Catholic family who are standing by her" (p. B1). Blandina Chiapponi, so went the story, had been victimized twice—once by her brutal rapist and again by the jury. A "Take Back the Night" march on the county courthouse made her case a central issue. On the basis of her version of the incident and the one

inflammatory comment of a juror (who later "explained" that he simply meant that Chiapponi was a prostitute whose form of dress purposely advertised her desire to sell sex), most people seemed to think that the jury had performed a terrible injustice.

On closer inspection, the following inconsistencies and errors in Blandina Chiapponi's story created a reasonable doubt in the minds of jurors:

1. She said she was with friends the night of the incident, but she couldn't remember their names.

2. She asserted that she was going into Denny's for something to eat, yet she had no money or any place to keep money on her person.

3. She changed her story on the witness stand regarding where the rape allegedly took place.

4. She told the investigating officer that she was wearing underpants, then admitted during the trial that she wasn't.

5. She claimed she worked at a modeling and talent agency, which was false; she actually worked at a massage parlor thought by police to be a front for prostitution.

6. After charging rape, she later refused to cooperate with the prosecution and was arrested for ignoring subpoenas—she resisted arrest.

7. She claimed she had inherited a substantial amount of money, which was never proven.

▶

8. She asserted, "I was hit over the head and cut up and left for dead," but although there was evidence of sexual intercourse, there was no evidence of physical violence except for a small finger wound that looked like a paper cut.

9. She claimed she had a close-knit family who staunchly stood behind her—this also proved to be untrue.

In fact, the jury did not decide its verdict on the basis of what this woman wore (Brecher, 1989). In their discussions, despite the later misleading remark by Ray Diamond, the jurors agreed that what she wore and how she lived her life were irrelevant to the verdict. The case ultimately was decided on whose story the jury believed—Chiapponi's or Lord's (he claimed she was a prostitute looking for money and cocaine). The fact that she was shown to be a liar of no small proportions left the jury with a reasonable doubt. Elinor Brecher (1989) summarizes:

What mattered to the jury was this: Blandina Chiapponi had clearly misrepresented herself under oath, not once but several times. Although it pained them, in a case where the physical evidence was inconclusive, the jury had no choice but to look to the victim's credibility in order to remove that last shred of reasonable doubt, as the law demands. They looked but they still doubted. (p. B1)

Blandina Chiapponi may have been raped. It's not likely the truth will ever be ascertained. The inference that the jury had failed in its duty and had perpetrated an abomination, however, cannot be drawn validly from the facts. The jury in the Blandina Chiapponi case was an effective decision-making group because individuals in the group performed an error-correction function and overcame the serious temptation to make inferential errors. The attire worn by Blandina Chiapponi and the fact that Steven Lamar Lord was an unsavory

▶

Group members are prone to make inferences based on extremely limited or faulty information without even realizing that they've made a guess, and not identified a fact. If no group member challenges the validity of inferences made during discussion, if members just assume as fact that alcohol makes you warm because you get a warm feeling from it, or that silence means consent, then groups may stack one faulty inference upon another. This makes a poor basis for high-quality group decision making.

Specific Sources of Inferential Errors

There are several specific sources of inferential errors that can adversely affect group decision making. I will discuss three of the most prevalent.

Vividness: The Grim, Grisly, and Graphic The graphic, outrageous, shocking, controversial, dramatic event draws our attention and sticks in our minds. This is

character who may have looked capable of rape did not sway the jury to make faulty inferences. They drew conclusions from the facts available, not from assumptions concerning what could have happened or how they might have wanted the verdict to come out.

The public, in general, and the media, in particular, were guilty of collective inferential error, of jumping to a conclusion unsupported by the facts available. Based on the slimmest information—one inflammatory statement by Ray Diamond—the inference was drawn that this jury had perpetrated an outrageous injustice. Later, this faulty inference was bolstered by Blandina Chiapponi's one-sided

and erroneous presentation of the "facts." It is understandable that Ray Diamond's comment would incite an angry response from the public. His was an example of communication incompetence. He made an insensitive, completely inappropriate remark. Yet, why assume he spoke for the entire jury of 12 members? Why not interview jury members before declaring in the media that an outrageous injustice had been perpetrated? Check your facts before leaping to conclusions. Since faulty inferential leaps are more likely when the issues are emotionally charged, as was the case in the Chiapponi trial, scrutinizing inferences is all the more important when the issues are combustible.

Questions for Thought

1. Do you agree that the jury in this case was an effective decision-making group? Explain.
2. Can you think of instances when you have jumped to conclusions, very much like the public reaction to Ray Diamond's incendiary statement?

called the **vividness effect.** Producer Gary David Goldberg captured the essence of the vividness effect when he pointedly observed, "Left to their own devices, the networks would televise live executions. Except Fox—they'd televise live naked executions" ("TV or not TV," 1993, 5E).

We tend to overvalue a shocking example and undervalue statistical information that shows patterns and trends. Barry Glasner (1999), in his book *The Culture of Fear*, identifies numerous examples of the vividness effect in action. He notes, "Producers of TV newsmagazines routinely let emotional accounts trump objective information. In 1994 medical authorities attempted to cut short the brouhaha over flesh-eating bacteria by publicizing the fact that an American is 55 times more likely to be struck by lightning than die of the suddenly celebrated microbe. Yet TV journalists brushed this aside with . . . stomach-turning videos of disfigured patients" (p. xxii).

On March 21, 2005, Jeff Weise, a student at Red Lake High School on an American Indian reservation in Bemidji, Minnesota, went on a shooting rampage. He ultimately

AP/Wide World Photos

The vividness of the Columbine High School massacre provoked SWAT team drills in schools around the United States.

killed five students, a security guard, a teacher, and himself at the school. He also killed his grandparents at their home. Reminiscent of the infamous shootings at Columbine High School in Littleton, Colorado, by Eric Harris and Dylan Klebold on April 20, 1999, that left 12 students and one teacher dead and 23 others injured, these examples of vivid carnage become international news. They also have the power to create collective inferential error. A *Newsweek* poll of 757 randomly selected adults conducted 2 days after the Columbine school massacre revealed that 63% of the adults thought a shooting incident similar to Columbine was very or somewhat likely at their children's school ("Anatomy of a Massacre," 1999). School boards around the country deliberated proposals to protect students from such violence. SWAT teams performed drills in several high schools. Yet among the 20,000 secondary schools in the United States, only six similar incidents occurred in the 5 years prior to Columbine—six too many, but hardly an epidemic of random violence worthy of national hand-wringing and breast-beating about our violent youth (Glassman, 1998). Including the Columbine shootings, there were 32 students and three teachers shot and killed in elementary and secondary schools between 1997 and 2001 (Lott, 2001). These involved gang conflicts, robberies, and accidents as well as Columbine-type events. During the same period, 53 students died while playing football for their school team (Lott, 2001). Among the

52 *million* public school students in the United States, fewer than 4,000 are expelled annually for bringing weapons of any kind to school (Ramirez, 1999). Only 10% of public schools each year report even *one* serious violent crime (J. Adler & Springen, 1999). Vigilance is appropriate, but vivid media coverage can distort our perceptions; precipitate overreactions, even panic; and foster faulty group inferences that grossly exaggerate the problem.

The power of the vivid example to shape and distort group decision making is real. The potency of the vividness effect is so real that Stanovich (1992) concludes that it "threatens to undermine the usefulness of any knowledge generated by any of the behavioral sciences" (p. 141). Be immediately wary of any claim that rests on the veneer of the vivid example.

Unrepresentativeness: Distorting the Facts When we make a judgment, we assess the resemblance or accuracy of an object or event presumed to belong to a general category. Is a specific example representative of a general category? If the answer is yes, then the inference drawn from the representative example is on solid footing. If the example is unrepresentative, however, inferences drawn from it are likely to be erroneous. If the example is both unrepresentative and vivid, then the potential for inferential error is magnified.

Ray Diamond did not speak for the Chiapponi jury (see Closer Look: "The Blandina Chiapponi Case"), yet the public and the mass media assumed that he represented all 12 members. If you said to yourself as I related the details of the Chiapponi case that you wished I hadn't chosen this example to illustrate collective inferential error because the issues are sensitive and some might erroneously assume that Chiapponi's conduct was typical of rape victims, then you have manifested an appreciation for the potential dangers of unrepresentativeness. Those who would assert from the Chiapponi case that rape victims frequently lie in such trials and therefore testimony from such victims is highly unreliable make a huge inference based on a single, unusual instance. This inference has as much validity as asserting that because your second cousin is a pathological liar, most of your family must be too. Blandina Chiapponi hardly qualifies as a representative complainant in a rape trial.

One study (Quattrone & Jones, 1980) illustrates inferential error among college students resulting from unrepresentativeness. College students indicated their belief that if one member of a group made a particular decision, then all members of the group would make the same decision. This was especially true if the students were observing the decisions of students from other colleges. In other words, we stereotype an entire group on the basis of a single individual who may or may not be representative of the group as a whole.

Correlation Inferred as Causation: Covariation A third specific source of inferential error is correlation. A **correlation** is a consistent relationship between two or more variables. There are two kinds of correlations: positive and negative. A positive correlation occurs when X increases and Y also increases (e.g., as you grow older your ears grow larger—nature's practical joke on the elderly; as you increase in height your weight also increases). A negative correlation occurs when X increases and Y decreases (e.g., as adults increase in age their capacity to run long distances decreases; as cars increase in age they decrease in value).

Most correlations are not perfect; a perfect correlation has no exceptions. Not everyone who grows taller increases in weight, especially if a teenager aggressively diets to slim down as he or she grows. Not every automobile loses value as it ages, especially if it is an antique classic car.

The main problem with correlations is the strong inclination people have for inferring causation (X causes Y) from a correlation. A large research team collected data in Taiwan to determine which variables best predicted use of contraceptive methods for birth control (Li, 1975). Of all the variables, use of birth control was most strongly correlated with the number of electric appliances (i.e., toasters, ovens, blenders, etc.) found in the home. Birth control usage increased as the number of electric appliances increased (GE doesn't bring good things to life?). So does it make sense to you that a free microwave oven or electric blender for every teenager in high school would decrease teen pregnancy rates? I'm confident that you can see the absurdity of such a suggestion.

The birth control–electric appliances correlation is an obvious case where a correlation, even though a very strong one, is not a causation. The number of electric appliances more than likely is a reflection of socioeconomic status and education levels, which undoubtedly have more to do with the rates of birth control usage than do the number of electric irons and toasters found in the home.

▶●● SECOND LOOK

SOURCE OF INFERENTIAL ERRORS

General Sources of Inferential Errors

  Seriously limited information base (insufficient quantity of information)

  Faulty information base (poor-quality information)

Specific Sources of Inferential Errors

  Vividness

  Unrepresentativeness

  Correlation

Stephen Jay Gould (1981) explains that "the vast majority of correlations in our world are, without doubt, noncausal" (p. 242). The fact that most correlations are noncausal, however, does not prevent most people from making the inferential error of correlation mistaken for causation. As Gould states, "The invalid assumption that correlation implies cause is probably among the two or three most serious and common errors of human reasoning" (p. 242).

I have witnessed the correlation as causation inferential error in my own classes. Consider the following discussion that took place in a small group in one of my classes:

J: I think we should choose capital punishment for our topic. I just did a paper on it. We can show that capital punishment works. In a lot of states that have it, murder rates have decreased.

A: Yeah, did you ever see that video where they show executions? Really gross. You know most criminals would think twice about killing someone if they realized they'd fry in the electric chair.

B: Well, I heard that when they execute a guy, the murder rate goes up right after. I don't think capital punishment is a very effective solution to murder.

In this brief conversation, group members managed to allege the truth of an asserted causation based only on a correlation, affirm the validity of the inferential error with a little common-sense reasoning, then refute the effectiveness of capital punishment by introducing yet another correlation assumed to be a causation. Correlations are not causations.

Error Correction: Practicing Critical Thinking

For the error-correction function of group discussion to kick in, competent communicators must recognize the sources of inferential errors just discussed. Assertively focusing the group's attention on sources of inferential error can help prevent faulty decision making from occurring. In other words, group members must put their critical thinking abilities into practice if effective decision making is to take place. Group discussion promotes higher-quality decision making when the following conditions occur:

1. The validity of inferences is carefully examined.
2. Inferences are grounded in valid and plentiful information.
3. At least one member of the group exerts influence to guide the group toward higher-quality decisions (Hirokawa & Pace, 1983).

Notice the last point. A single individual can prevent or minimize inferential error in group decision making because one person can affect the entire system. Communication competence can be contagious. Collective inferential error, the manifestation of defective critical thinking by a group, is the product of the communicative efforts of individual members. Note that "an individual can prevent the occurrence of errors by influencing the group to accept correct information and conclusions" (Hirokawa & Scheerhorn, 1986, p. 78). Learning how to evaluate information to prevent inferential error will be discussed in the next chapter. If one person can create problems for a group, one person can also help a group perform effectively.

Groupthink: Critical Thinking in Suspended Animation

What are we to make of the monumental blunder at Pearl Harbor? How could this country have been caught so flat-footed that infamous morning of December 7, 1941? There were ample warnings that Japan was preparing for a massive military operation. On November 27, 1941, Admiral Stark in Washington, D.C., sent Pearl Harbor a "war warning" predicting an attack from the Japanese somewhere "within the next few days" (Janis, 1982, p. 75). Since Pearl Harbor was not specifically cited as a likely target for the Japanese attack, however, the warning was discounted. No special

DPA / Landov

A Titanic instance of groupthink. Captain Edward Smith sailed the doomed oceanliner full-speed into an iceberg despite four warning messages. "God himself could not sink this ship," he proclaimed before the Titanic was launched on its maiden voyage.

reconnaissance was ordered to provide a sufficient alert that Japanese aircraft carriers were steaming toward Pearl Harbor. Two army privates spotted large, unidentified aircraft on a radar screen heading toward Pearl Harbor an hour before the actual attack. They reported this to the Army's radar center. Again, the information was discounted. Patrols encountered hostile submarines in advance of the bombings. No action was taken.

As Vice Admiral William S. Pye testified after the disaster, with even 10 minutes' warning, the Japanese airplanes could have been shot down before inflicting much damage on our vulnerable fleet. Incredibly, no alert was even sounded until the bombs were actually exploding. Eight battleships, three cruisers, and four other ships were sunk or damaged. More than 2,000 men were killed and at least as many were wounded or missing. Pearl Harbor was our worst military disaster. How could it have happened?

▶ **Focus Questions**

1. What causes groupthink?
2. Do groups have to display all the symptoms of groupthink to exhibit poor-quality decisions that accompany full-blown groupthink?

GENERAL CONDITIONS: EXCESSIVE COHESIVENESS AND CONCURRENCE SEEKING

Sociologist Irving Janis (1982), who has extensively analyzed decision-making debacles, argues that Pearl Harbor, the Bay of Pigs fiasco, Watergate, the escalation of the Vietnam War, and other blunders of recent U.S. history sprang from a defective decision-making process he calls groupthink. Studies of small group decision making also support the deleterious consequences of groupthink (Turner et al., 1992). Janis defines **groupthink** as "a mode of thinking that people engage in when they are deeply involved in a cohesive in-group, when the members' strivings for unanimity override their motivation to realistically appraise alternative courses of action" (p. 9).

Cohesiveness and its companion, concurrence-seeking, are the two general conditions necessary for groupthink to occur. Janis does not argue that all groups that are cohesive and seek agreement among its members exhibit groupthink. These are necessary but not sufficient conditions for groupthink to occur (Mullen et al., 1994). Obviously, a noncohesive group can spend most of its time and energy on social upheaval, diverted from task accomplishment. Also, cohesiveness in a group can be a very positive factor (Miranda, 1994).

Groupthink is rooted in *excessive* cohesiveness and a resulting pressure to present a united front to those outside of the group. The more cohesive a group is, the greater is the danger of groupthink. This is especially true as the size of the group increases (Mullen et al., 1994). Critical thinking and effective decision making are sacrificed when members are *overly concerned* with reaching agreement, avoiding conflict, and preserving friendly relations in the group. A study (cited in Cole, 1989) of 275 members of high-level management teams at 26 major U.S. companies by Robert Lefton and V. R. Buzzotta of Psychological Associates, Inc., found that 19% of the team members carried on business by "not making waves" and another 9% revealed that their teams preferred getting along instead of getting things done.

No group member has to squash dissent openly. The concurrence-seeking norm is so firmly established in the group system that critical faculties are often paralyzed seemingly without notice. Frequently, members fail to see issues that should be challenged, positions that should be questioned, and alternatives that should be explored. Even if they do recognize such problems, they choose to go along in order to get along.

Groupthink is not the cause of every decision-making fiasco. Information overload or underload, mindsets, collective inferential error, and sometimes the plain stupidity of decision makers may be primarily responsible for blunders. As Janis (1982) argues, however, groupthink often is a contributing cause and sometimes it is a primary cause. In this next section, some of the evidence that supports the Janis groupthink explanation for abominably bad group decision making is summarized.

IDENTIFICATION OF GROUPTHINK: MAIN SYMPTOMS

How do you recognize groupthink? Janis lists eight specific symptoms of groupthink, which he then divides into three types. The eight symptoms are discussed within the context of these three types.

Overestimation of the Group's Power and Morality: Arrogance   Repeatedly, the main decision makers associated with the Pearl Harbor debacle communicated a sense of invulnerability. Pearl Harbor was thought to be impregnable, much as the French Maginot Line was thought to be an impenetrable defense until the Germans in World War II proved that to be a laughable notion. The U.S. command in Pearl Harbor ridiculed the idea of a Japanese attack. Torpedo planes were discounted because U.S. torpedoes required a water depth of at least 60 feet to function and Pearl Harbor had a 30-foot depth. Little consideration was given to the possibility that the Japanese had developed a torpedo capable of striking a target in shallow water. The *illusion of invulnerability* exhibited by the fleet command at Pearl Harbor exploded with nightmarish rapidity.

The illusion of invulnerability is a common precursor to major accidents. Edward J. Smith, captain of the *Titanic*, said, "I cannot imagine any condition which would cause a ship to founder. . . . Modern shipbuilding has gone beyond that" (Bennett, 1961, p. 144). The owners of this ill-fated luxury liner were so certain that the *Titanic* was invulnerable to sinking that they equipped the ship with an insufficient supply of lifeboats. More than 1,500 people died. A year prior to the meltdown at the Chernobyl nuclear power plant, a deputy minister of the Soviet power industry declared that engineers were certain no serious accident would occur for at least 100,000 years (Rampton & Stauber, 2001). The disaster at Three Mile Island nuclear power plant in Pennsylvania exhibited this same illusion of invulnerability. "The people in charge of Three Mile Island had bought into the myth that such an accident could never happen. When it did, they were as clueless and helpless as the rest of us" (Cass, 2001, p. 3C).

In addition to an inflated sense of power, groups sometimes overestimate their morality. The U.S. sense of higher moral purpose contributed to the Bay of Pigs invasion. The purpose, after all, was to upend a communist dictator and free the Cubans. The Iran-Contra affair was partially the result of an excess of moral righteousness. The Reagan administration was trying to secure the release of the hostages. Sometimes you have to engage in unsavory dealings (so went the logic), such as trading arms for the hostages, when your purpose is righteous. This *unquestioned belief in the inherent morality of the group* is symptomatic of groupthink.

Closed-Mindedness: Clinging to Assumptions Closed-mindedness is manifested by *rationalizations* that discount warnings or negative information that might cause the group to rethink its basic assumptions. On February 1, 2003, the space shuttle Columbia disintegrated on its return to Earth, the victim of damage from a chunk of foam that knocked a hole in the shuttle's wing on takeoff. NASA knew that previous shuttle flights had been hit by foam debris, but shuttle engineers' weak efforts to sound a warning about possible catastrophic consequences from the debris went unheeded by NASA officials (Oberg, 2003; Wald & Schwartz, 2003). The operating assumption was that foam debris did not pose a serious problem to the safety of the shuttle mission.

Another aspect of closed-mindedness leading to groupthink is *negative stereotyped views of the enemy* as weak, stupid, puny, or evil. This characterization helps justify the recklessness of the group. The Japanese were characterized as a "midget nation" by the command at Pearl Harbor. Lyndon Johnson reputedly characterized the North Vietnamese during the Vietnam War in this racist fashion: "Without air power, we'd be at the mercy of every yellow dwarf with a pocket knife" (Lewallen, 1972, p. 37). President Kennedy's advisors considered Castro and his military force to be a joke. The real joke was the invasion plan that sent 1,400 Cuban exiles up against Castro's military force of 200,000. Simple arithmetic should have shot down that idea.

Pressures toward Uniformity: Presenting a United Front The last type of symptom of groupthink is the pressure to maintain uniformity of opinion and behavior among group members. Sometimes this pressure is indirect and in other cases it is very direct. An indirect form is manifested when group members engage in *self-censorship*, assuming an apparent consensus exists in the group. The importance of doubts and counterarguments is minimized as a result of the perceived uniformity of opinion. Silence is considered assent, which can lead to what some have called "pluralistic ignorance." Other group members have their doubts, but everyone assumes agreement exists and no one wants to rock the boat, so no one questions or raises an objection. Thus, an *illusion of unanimity* is fostered.

The film adaptation of Tom Wolfe's bestseller *The Bonfire of the Vanities* was a $50-million box-office bomb. Many people involved in making the movie, starring Tom Hanks and Melanie Griffith, had doubts about the casting choices and changes in the storyline, but they never voiced these doubts to the director, Brian De Palma (Stern, 1992). Apparently, De Palma also had some reservations, but because no dissent was voiced, he convinced himself that he had made the correct decisions. The illusion of unanimity led to a disastrous motion picture.

To maintain the uniformity of the group, *direct pressure on deviants* is applied. David Stockman became the center of a cyclone when he was quoted in an *Atlantic Monthly* article by Bill Greider characterizing the tax cut portion of Reaganomics—the Reagan administration's policy of minimalist government—as a Trojan horse: a most unflattering metaphor. Here was President Reagan's budget director seeming to expose the fantasy of achieving a balanced budget, vigorous economic growth, and minimal inflation in part by lowering taxes. The winds of controversy swirled around the White House following the Stockman admission.

Reagan's group of advisors was furious with Stockman for his apparent treason. The president's chief of staff, Jim Baker, called Stockman into his office and coldly issued the following directive:

> My friend, he started, I want you to listen up good. Your ass is in a sling. All of the rest of them want you . . . canned right now. Immediately. This afternoon. If it weren't for me, he continued, you'd be a goner already. But I got you one last chance to save yourself. So you're going to do it precisely and exactly like I tell you. Otherwise you're finished around here. . . . You're going to have lunch with the president. The menu is humble pie. . . . When you go through the Oval Office door, I want to see that sorry ass of yours dragging on the carpet. (Stockman, 1986, p. 5)

Stockman was thrashed back into line with the group. Intellectually, he was convinced that a tax cut was economic folly. To remain a member of Reagan's inner circle, however, Stockman was coerced into an act of public humiliation—a confession of his supposed rhetorical excesses.

Finally, uniformity is maintained by information control. *Self-appointed mind-guards* protect the group from adverse information that might contradict shared illusions. The system closes off to negative influences, protecting uniformity. Once John Kennedy had decided to proceed with the ill-fated Bay of Pigs invasion, his brother Robert dissuaded anyone from disturbing the president with any misgivings about the mission.

Dissent of group members is often suppressed or ignored. One study (Laughlin & Adamopoulos, 1980) found that in almost 75% of the cases, the one person in a six-member group who knew the correct answer to a problem was unable to convince the group because the group suppressed the divergent point of view.

A group does not have to display all the symptoms to experience the poor-quality decisions that accompany full-blown groupthink. As Janis (1982) explains, "Even when some symptoms are absent, the others may be so pronounced that we can expect all the unfortunate consequences of groupthink" (p. 175). He argues that "the more frequently a group displays the symptoms, the worse will be the quality of its decisions, on the average" (p. 175). Nevertheless, the higher the number of symptoms, the worse the group's performance is likely to be (Herek et al., 1987).

PREVENTING GROUPTHINK: PROMOTING VIGILANCE

To prevent groupthink, groups must become vigilant decision makers. Vigilant decision making requires that several steps be taken (Janis, 1982; Wood et al., 1986). First, and most obvious, **members must recognize the problem of groupthink as it begins to manifest itself.** Knowledge is required of the competent communicator. If even a single member recognizes groupthink developing and points this out energetically to the group, the problem can be avoided.

Second, **the group must minimize status differences.** High-status members exert a disproportionate influence on lower-status group members. High-status leaders who use strongly directive leadership styles are particularly problematic (Street, 1997). The resulting communication pattern is one of deference to the more powerful person (Milgram, 1974). Such deference can produce ludicrous, even disastrous, consequences.

Michael Cohen and Neil Davis (1981), Temple University pharmacy professors and authors of *Medication Errors: Causes and Prevention,* argue that the accuracy of a doctor's prescription is rarely questioned, even when a prescribed treatment makes no sense. Nurses, for example, are used to being told what to do by doctors (directive leadership). They cite one comical instance of blind deference to high-status authority. A physician ordered application of eardrops to a patient's right ear to treat an infection. The physician abbreviated the prescribed treatment to read, "Place in R ear." The duty nurse read the prescription and promptly administered the eardrops where they presumably would do the most good to "cure" the patient's "rectal earache." Neither the nurse nor the patient questioned the doctor's rather unconventional treatment.

On a more serious level, airline industry officials have become alarmed at what has been dubbed "Captainitis" (M. Foushee, 1984). The status and decision-making authority of the flight captain make it difficult for crew members to correct obvious errors that could lead to a plane crash. A study by a major airline showed that passengers have something extra to worry about besides wind shear, metal fatigue, and baggage being sent mistakenly to the Falkland Islands. In the experiment, crews were subjected to flight simulations under conditions of severe weather and poor visibility. Unknown to the crew members, the captains feigned incapacitation, making serious errors that would lead to certain disaster. Airline officials were stunned to learn that 25% of the flights would have crashed because no crew member took corrective action to override the captain's faulty judgment. Weick (1990) claims that this contributed to the Tenerife air disaster in 1977, the worst commercial aviation accident in history.

Thus, status differences in groups can encourage groupthink, especially when these status differences are magnified by a directive style of leadership (Mullen, 1994). Of particular concern is the form of directive leadership manifested when the leader promotes one idea initially instead of seeking many ideas from members (Flippen, 1999). John Kennedy, anxious not to commit another blunder like the Bay of Pigs, instituted several new procedures for top-level decision making. One of these procedures was leaderless group discussions. On occasion, primarily during the initial stages of discussion where alternatives were being generated, Kennedy would absent himself from the proceedings. Robert Kennedy, the president's brother and close advisor, commented, "I felt there was less true give and take with the president in the room. There was the danger that by indicating his own view and leanings, he would cause others just to fall in line" (Janis, 1982, p. 142).

The group leader, as high-status member, has the primary responsibility to minimize the influence of status differences. The leader could withhold his or her point of view from the group until everyone has had an opportunity to express an opinion. As management training consultant Michael Woodruff, speaking of potential employee disagreement with a supervisor, explains, "If I present an idea as something that I am excited about, then my staff has to go against me. But if I present it neutrally, they will be more likely to speak out if they think it is wrong. Staffers will seldom criticize what the boss has endorsed" (Stern, 1992, p. 104). The high-status group member could also indicate ambivalence on an issue, thereby encouraging the open expression of a variety of viewpoints.

Seeking information that challenges an emerging concurrence is a third way to prevent groupthink. Assessing the negative consequences of choices is a mark of an effective decision-making group (Hirokawa, 1985). Closely related to this, **developing a norm in the group that legitimizes disagreement during discussion sessions** is a final way to prevent groupthink. Minority dissent stimulates divergent thought in groups and acts to prevent groupthink (DeDreu & West, 2001). This disagreement norm may have to be structured into the group process. Groupthink is more likely to occur when there is no structured method in place for evaluating alternative ideas during group discussion (Street, 1997).

There are several ways to accomplish these last two ways of preventing groupthink. First, assign one or two group members or a subgroup to play **devil's advocate**. The primary group presents its proposals and arguments and the devil's advocates critique it. This process can proceed through several rounds of proposals and critiques until the group, including devil's advocates, is satisfied that the best decision has been made. It is a very effective method of overcoming the excessive concurrence-seeking characteristic of groupthink (Stasser & Titus, 1987).

Second, institute a **dialectical inquiry** (Sims, 1992). This procedure is very similar to devil's advocacy, except that in dialectical inquiry a subgroup develops a counterproposal and defends it side by side with the group's initial proposal. Thus, a debate takes place on two differing proposals. One or the other may be chosen by the group, both may be rejected in favor of further exploration and inquiry before a final

> ●● **SECOND LOOK**

GROUPTHINK

PRIMARY SYMPTOMS

Overestimation of Group's Power and Morality

  Illusion of invulnerability

  Unquestioned belief in the inherent morality of the group

Closed-Mindedness

  Rationalizations

  Negative stereotyped views of the enemy

Pressures toward Uniformity

  Self-censorship of contradictory opinion

  Illusion of unanimity

  Direct pressure applied to deviants

  Self-appointed mindguards

PREVENTING GROUPTHINK

  Recognize groupthink when it first begins

  Minimize status differences

  Seek information that challenges emerging concurrence

  Develop norm that legitimizes disagreement

decision is made, or a compromise between the two proposals may be hammered out. Both devil's advocacy and dialectical inquiry are effective antidotes to groupthink, but dialectical inquiry may be slightly more effective (Pavitt & Curtis, 1994).

Third, assign a group member to play the **reminder role** (Schultz et al., 1995). This is a formally designated role. The reminder raises questions in a nonaggressive manner regarding collective inferential error, confirmation bias, false dichotomies, and any of the myriad symptoms of groupthink that may arise. The reminder role is an effective method of combating groupthink tendencies (Schultz et al., 1995). Groupthink can be a primary source of poor decision making in groups (Hensley & Griffin, 1986; Herek et al., 1987; Leana, 1985; Moorhead & Montanari, 1986). Recognizing the symptoms of groupthink and taking steps to prevent it from occurring play an important role in any effort to improve the quality of group decisions.

In summary, group members must exercise their critical thinking abilities. The quality of decision making and problem solving in groups is significantly affected by problems of information quantity, mindsets, inferential errors, and groupthink. If groups learn to cope with information overload and underload, recognize and counteract mindsets, avoid or correct collective inferential errors, and avoid groupthink, then decision making and problem solving will be of higher quality.

Questions for Critical Thinkers

1. Why is information overload such a problem when we have laborsaving technologies such as desktop computers to process huge quantities of data?
2. Why are collective inferential errors more likely when issues are emotionally charged?
3. If cohesiveness is a positive small group attribute, why can it lead to groupthink?

InfoTrac College Edition

Log onto InfoTrac College Edition.

1. Type "information overload" in the keywords search window. Choose an article to read. SUGGESTIONS: (a) Article A94124243, by Martin Herman, entitled "Have a problem with information overload now? Just wait a while"; (b) Article A91086031, by Fogarty and Bahls, entitled "Information overload: Feel the pressure?"
2. Type "groupthink" in the search window. Choose an article. SUGGESTIONS: (a) Article A19018113, by Christopher Neck, entitled "Letterman or Leno: A groupthink analysis of successive decisions made by the National Broadcasting Company"; (b) Article A19336054, by Thomas Horton, entitled "Groupthink in the boardroom: Clarence Darrow said, 'To think is to differ.'"

Video Case Studies

*Thirteen Days (2000). Drama; PG-13; ***1/2*

Semi-accurate depiction of the harrowing 13 days of the Cuban Missile Crisis. The Kennedy administration avoided the groupthink mistakes that it made during the Bay of Pigs fiasco. Examine what prevented groupthink during the Cuban Missile Crisis.

*Tora! Tora! Tora! (1970). Drama; G; ****

Still the best dramatic depiction of the Japanese attack on Pearl Harbor, providing both sides' perspectives on the worst naval disaster in the United States. Examine events leading up to the attack from the standpoint of groupthink.

8 Group Discussion: Effective Decision Making and Problem Solving

c. *Relevance: Looking for Logical Connections*

d. *Representativeness: Reflecting the Facts*

CLOSER LOOK: THE INTERNET: RESOURCE FOR INFORMATION AND MISINFORMATION

e. *Sufficiency: When Enough Really Is Enough*

E. CREATIVE PROBLEM SOLVING

1. General Overview

2. Specific Creative Techniques

a. *Brainstorming and Nominal Group Techniques: Generating Lots of Ideas*

b. *Framing/Reframing: It's All in the Wording*

c. *Integrative Problem Solving: Satisfying Everyone*

THERE ARE APPROXIMATELY 14,000 students that attend Cabrillo College in Santa Cruz county, California, every semester. It is a huge challenge to streamline the registration process to accommodate this many students each term. In 2005, Cabrillo's new president came to the Faculty Senate, among other campus bodies, and presented his proposal for a "one-stop" registration process. It was his initial assessment, following a few months of "walking the campus," that the registration process was too diffuse, requiring students, many new to the campus, to visit several buildings to complete registration. His suggestion was to consolidate in one building all processes related to registration. He suggested the cafeteria might be appropriate. There was an immediate and vociferous uproar from students, faculty, and staff. When quizzed on the cost of such consolidation, the initial estimate was $500,000. Many student services would have to be relocated, creating significant disruption. The campus was in the middle of a $200-million facelift. Adding yet another renovation project seemed unnecessary to many on campus.

At the Faculty Senate meeting on the president's proposal, he was repeatedly challenged to show that a real problem existed. Construction plans had already been approved for consolidating all on-campus registration procedures to a single location by 2009, and 98% of students registered by phone or online anyway. Few students needed to come onto campus to register. The president backed away from his cafeteria renovation idea, but steadfastly clung to the vision of a hastened one-stop, on-campus registration. He offered the administration building as an alternative location for consolidation at a cost assessment of $50,000. This meant that human resources and financial services would have to be relocated at great inconvenience to all involved. Again, members of both the faculty and student senates challenged the president to show an actual, significant problem that necessitated immediate action. No data were provided, but the president pressed on with his idea and the administration building became the *temporary* home for all registration processes until the 2009 planned consolidation.

This was a solution in search of a problem. There is little doubt that had the president established a campus committee to investigate the need for such a project, the conclusion would have been to wait until the planned 2009 consolidation. It would have saved significant money and avoided unnecessary, substantial disruption on campus.

The primary purpose of this chapter is to explore the process of effective group decision making/problem solving. The Cabrillo College one-stop project is testament to the importance of implementing effective procedures for group decision making and problem solving. Toward this end there are five chapter objectives:

1. to explain procedures for conducting productive group discussions that will result in effective decisions and solutions to problems,
2. to explore ways to encourage productive participation from group members,
3. to describe ways to conduct effective decision-making group meetings,
4. to discuss ways to gather and evaluate information necessary for effective decision making and problem solving, and
5. to explain several techniques of creative group problem solving.

Discussion Procedures

In this section, guidelines and procedures for conducting effective group discussion will be presented. Special emphasis will be given to the Standard Agenda.

PHASES AND FUNCTIONS: GENERAL CONSIDERATIONS

All decision-making and problem-solving groups exhibit recognizable phases. They follow certain paths to decisions and solutions. The importance of using a systematic approach during group discussion cannot be underestimated.

▶ **Focus Questions**

1. How does Standard Agenda relate to the functional perspective on effective group discussion procedures?
2. What constitutes a true consensus?
3. What are the advantages and disadvantages of various decision-making rules?

Multiple Sequence Model: Phases of Decision Making The most widely accepted phasic model of group decision making is Poole's (1983) multiple sequence model of decision emergence. The **multiple sequence model** pictures groups moving along three activity tracks: task, relational, and topic. Groups do not necessarily proceed along these three tracks at the same rate or according to the same pattern. Some groups may devote a significant amount of time to the relational (social) activities of groups before proceeding to a task discussion; other groups may start right in on the task.

Groups take three principal paths in reaching decisions (Poole & Roth, 1989a, 1989b). The first path is called the *unitary sequence.* Groups on the unitary sequence path proceed in the same step-by-step fashion toward a decision. The second path is called *complex cyclic*. These groups engage in repeated cycles of focusing on the problem, then the solution, and back again to the problem, and so forth. Finally, the third principal path to decision making is *solution oriented*. Here the group launches into discussion of solutions with little focus on an analysis of the problem. Groups most often choose the complex cyclic path, less often the solution-oriented path, and infrequently the unitary sequence path.

Poole's multiple sequence model of decision development emphasizes that group discussion does not necessarily proceed along a single predictable path. There are several ways that decisions occur in groups.

Functional Perspective: Being Systematic **Discussions that follow some systematic procedure tend to be more productive and result in better decisions than relatively unstructured discussions** (LaFasto & Larson, 2001). The drawbacks to unstructured group discussion include: aimless deliberations that are time-consuming and inefficient; premature focus on solutions (the solution-oriented path); inclination to accept the first plausible solution, which may not be the best option; discussion tangents and topic-hopping; domination by the most vociferous group member; and failure to address group conflict (Hirokawa, 1985; Sunwolf & Seibold, 1999).

There is no single, systematic discussion procedure that guarantees effective decision making and problem solving. "What happens at each stage and how well necessary functions are executed are the real determinants of success" (Gouran, 1982, p. 30). Rigidly following a set of prescribed steps, such as the unitary sequence path, can stifle natural discussion and seem robotic. **Steps in any systematic discussion procedure should be looked at as guidelines, not commandments.** Some allowance should be made for cycling back to steps previously addressed as group members discuss problems and solutions. The complex cyclic path to decision making does this.

Variations in the quality of decisions by groups can be accounted for by the relative ability of members to perform systematically five critical decision-making functions (Orlitzky & Hirokawa, 2001). These five functions are problem analysis, establishment of evaluation criteria, generation of alternative solutions, evaluation of positive consequences of solutions, and evaluation of negative consequences of solutions. This functional perspective is reflected in the Standard Agenda discussion procedures.

THE STANDARD AGENDA: STRUCTURING GROUP DISCUSSION

John Dewey (1910) described a process of rational problem solving and decision making that he called reflective thinking. The Standard Agenda is a direct outgrowth of Dewey's reflective-thinking process. It is a highly effective, structured method for decision making and problem solving in groups. The Standard Agenda places the emphasis on the problem initially to counteract premature consideration of solutions, an emphasis that was missing from the Cabrillo College one-stop proposal. The Standard Agenda has six steps. This section explains the procedure using smoking on the Cabrillo College campus as the problem. Note that, unlike the one-stop proposal, this was a problem handled effectively through systematic group discussion.

Problem Identification: What's the Question? **The problem should be formulated into an open-ended question identifying what type of problem the group must consider.** Questions may be phrased as fact, value, or policy. The choice will identify the nature of the problem. A **question of fact** asks whether something is true and to what extent. Objective evidence can be used to determine an answer to the question. "Are there dangers to nonsmokers from secondhand smoke, and, if so, what are these dangers?" is a question of fact. A **question of value** asks for an evaluation of the desirability of an object, idea, event, or person. "Does permitting smoking on campus raise any quality-of-life concerns?" is a question of value. Objective evidence does not lead to any clear answers on questions of values. Quality of life, for example, can't be determined scientifically or statistically. It is a perception based on subjective views of the world. Smokers might find the smell of smoke pleasant, even stimulating, whereas nonsmokers may find it grossly unpleasant. A **question of policy** asks whether a specific course of action should be undertaken to solve a problem. "What changes, if any, should be made regarding the smoking policy on campus?" is a policy question.

Once the problem is phrased as a question of fact, value, or policy, any am-biguous terms should be defined. "Quality of life" would require some further description (i.e., no strong odors, freedom from pollutants that might trigger respiratory difficulties, etc.). "Smoking policy on campus" would need to be explained so the group knows exactly what policy is currently in place.

Problem Analysis: Causes and Effects **The group researches and gathers information on the problem defined, tries to determine how serious the problem is, what harm or effect the problem produces, and what causes the problem.** Smoking on campus has been a contentious issue at Cabrillo College for many years. Non-smoking students complained repeatedly to their student senators about the problem. Research revealed that originally, students and faculty were allowed to smoke anywhere on campus, including in class. Eventually, smoking was banned in all classrooms but permitted everywhere else.

In an open hearing instituted by the Student Senate to gather information and help determine the extent of the problem, tempers flared. One student, defending the "rights of smokers," told nonsmokers to "quit school if you don't like our smoking." A student defending nonsmokers' rights vehemently retorted, "Polluters have no rights." Another nonsmoker facetiously suggested "public floggings as a penalty for smoking." The conclusion of the Student Senate, after much debate, was that the smoking policy was too permissive and this was causing numerous hazards and significant unpleasantness for students. The policy needed to be changed. One note of caution here: **Although analyzing the problem is important and should be undertaken before exploring potential solutions,** *analysis paralysis,* **or bogging down by analyzing the problem too much, can also thwart effective decision making.** It prevents a group from ever getting on with business and making a decision.

Solution Criteria: Setting Standards **Criteria** are standards by which decisions and solutions to problems can be evaluated. In the summer of 1998, the American Film Institute released its list of 100 Best American Movies. *Citizen Kane* topped the list. For most college students of today, this must seem a perplexing choice. *Citizen Kane,* released in 1941, is a black-and-white film, has no real body count, the action is plodding by today's frenetic standards, and the special effects probably seem goofy compared to the blockbuster movies of today. Without knowing the criteria used by the Film Institute to judge the quality of movies, it is very difficult to understand many of the choices that made the 100 Best list and the rankings. Knowing that "influence on future American filmmaking" is a primary criterion helps you understand better why *Citizen Kane* ranked as the top all-time American film. If "entertainment value" were a prime criterion, however, the top choice may not have faired so well. Even if you knew the criteria used, you may still disagree with the decisions made, but at least you would have a basis for discussion. Criteria help us determine whether our decisions make sense and are likely to be effective.

The group should establish criteria for evaluating solutions before solutions are suggested. Not all criteria, however, are created equal. The group must consider the relevance and appropriateness of each criterion. For example, *U.S. News & World Report* magazine produces an annual list of "America's Best Colleges and Universities." Amy Graham, a data researcher who oversaw the list for 2 years and then resigned from the magazine, claims that the criteria used to rank colleges place too much emphasis on a school's reputation and wealth with "scant attention to measures of learning or good educational practices." She continues, "That's like measuring the quality of a restaurant by calculating how much it paid for silverware and food; not completely useless, but pretty far from ideal" (Kuczynski, 2001).

Some relevant and appropriate criteria on the smoking question devised by an ad hoc campus committee to explore the smoking problem included: protect the health of nonsmokers, be simple to understand and enforce, avoid alienating either group (smokers or nonsmokers), cost less than $5,000, and maintain a comfortable environment. **The criteria should be ranked in order of priority.** The committee prioritized the criteria on the smoking policy in the order just listed.

Solution Suggestions: Generating Alternatives **The group brainstorms possible solutions without evaluating any suggestions until the best alternatives are likely to have emerged.** (See the "Creative Problem Solving" section at the end of this chapter for proper brainstorming technique.) At IDEO, brainstorming sessions may last up to an hour, with a hundred ideas generated (Kelley & Littman, 2001). Some possibilities on the smoking issue that emerged from the committee deliberations included making a total ban on smoking across the campus, designating certain locations outside for smoking, building outside shelters in designated locations around the campus to protect smokers from weather, permitting smoking only in automobiles, and allowing smoking only in parking lots both in cars and outside.

Once a list of ideas has been generated, **the group should clarify any ambiguous or confusing ideas. Ideas that overlap should be consolidated into a single idea.**

Solution Evaluation and Selection: Deciding by Criteria The story of a military briefing officer asked to devise a method for raising enemy submarines off the ocean floor illustrates the importance of this step. The briefing officer's solution? Heat the ocean to the boiling point. When bewildered Pentagon officials asked him how this could be done he replied, "I don't know. I decided on the solution; you work out the details." The devil is in the details. **Explore both the merits and demerits (avoid confirmation bias) of suggested solutions.** Devil's advocacy and dialectical inquiry (see Chapter 7) are useful techniques for accomplishing this aspect of the Standard Agenda.

Consider each solution in terms of the criteria established earlier. For instance, protecting the health of faculty, staff, and students was a prime concern of those addressing the smoking policy. Of all the solution suggestions, a total ban on smoking met this criterion best. It didn't avoid alienating smokers on campus, however. Concern was raised that a total ban might alienate student smokers to such an extent that significant enrollment declines would result, costing a great loss of money to the college. Smoking in designated areas seemed to be a promising solution, and was tried on a temporary basis, but smokers had difficulty determining where the designated smoking areas were on campus despite posted maps indicating them. This solution proved to be too complicated and difficult to enforce. Complaints also arose that there weren't shelters in all designated areas so smokers were exposed to some nasty weather. This violated the "maintain a comfortable environment" criterion. Building shelters for smokers to address this complaint proved to be too costly, far exceeding the criterion that set a $5,000 limit on expenses. Relegating smokers to their automobiles proved to be impractical because this would ban smoking for those who chose mass transit or bicycled to campus. Finally, the suggestion that smoking be relegated to parking lots protected the health of nonsmokers; was a simple, easily understood policy; cost less than $5,000 (some concrete ashtrays were distributed in all parking lots at minimal expense); and mostly avoided alienating smokers because smoking was still permitted, though restricted, on campus. Only the maintaining-a-comfortable-environment criterion was not met satisfactorily because smokers were still not sheltered from the elements unless they smoked in their cars.

There are three decision-making methods that are used to make solution choices: majority rule, minority rule, or consensus. A thorough discussion of the merits and demerits of each method appears in the next section of this chapter. The ad hoc campus committee used consensus (unanimity rule); the faculty and student senates and the Board of Trustees used majority rule. Permitting smoking only in parking lots was the eventual policy adopted by the Board of Trustees with support from the faculty and student senates. It made Cabrillo College one of the very first colleges in the nation to restrict smoking to this extent.

Solution Implementation: Follow-through A common failing of decision-making groups is that once they arrive at a decision there is no follow-through. Making the decision is one thing; implementing it is another. **Force field analysis,** suggested by the work of Kurt Lewin (1947), is one method for planning implementation of a group solution or decision. Using force field analysis, groups brainstorm a list of *driving forces*—those that encourage change—and *restraining forces*—those that resist change. Driving forces that encourage implementation of the new smoking policy at Cabrillo College include multiple complaints from students, stated concerns about the health risks to nonsmokers, and a fear that nonsmokers would stop enrolling at the college.

Restraining forces working against implementation of the new smoking policy mostly involve a more general resistance to change itself. Social philosopher Eric Hoffer titled one of his books *The Ordeal of Change.* Change does not come easily to most of us.

There are five ways to reduce resistance to change and consequent restraining forces impeding solution implementation (Tubbs, 1984). They are:

1. As noted previously, **people are more likely to accept change when they have had a part in the planning and decision making.** Imposing change produces psychological reactance and therefore increases resistance to change.
2. **Changes are more likely to be accepted if they do not threaten group members.** The larger concern on the smoking issue was whether students would drop out of Cabrillo College because the policy was too permissive, even though some

concern was expressed that the more restrictive policy would threaten enrollment declines among smokers.

3. **Changes are more likely to be accepted when the need for change affects individuals directly.** The great majority of students at Cabrillo College are nonsmokers directly affected by a permissive smoking policy.

4. **There will be less resistance to change when the change is open to revision and modification.** The smoking policy revision was presented as a temporary fix, subject to revision if necessary.

5. **The three factors (degree, rate, and desirability) affecting a group's ability to adapt to change in a system should be considered.** The smoking policy at Cabrillo College addressed excessive degree of change by not banning smoking entirely, addressed too rapid a rate of change by phasing in the policy (designated areas were tried first), and addressed desirability by conducting open hearings on the issue.

A helpful decision-making method that stipulates systematically how to implement small group decisions once resistance to change has been addressed is called **PERT** (Program Evaluation Review Technique). The steps in the PERT method are:

1. **Determine what the final step should look like** (e.g., restricting smoking to parking lots only).

2. **Specify any events that must occur before the final goal is realized** (e.g., obtaining the Board of Trustees' endorsement).

3. **Put the events in chronological order** (e.g., the committee must secure the support of the student and faculty senates, then the college president, before going to the board for endorsement).

4. **If necessary, construct a diagram of the process to trace the progress of implementation** (useful only if there are numerous steps).

5. **Generate a list of activities, resources, and materials that are required between events** (e.g., hold a strategy session before making presentations to the student and faculty senates, and again before seeking the president's endorsement).

6. **Develop a time line for implementation.** Estimate how long each step will take.

7. **Match the total time estimate for implementation of the solution with any deadlines** (e.g., end of school year approaching). Modify your plan of action, as needed (e.g., take any appointment time available with the president that will move along the process).

8. **Specify which group members will have which responsibilities.**

CLOSER LOOK

MURPHY'S LAW

IN OCTOBER 1999, the $125-million Mars Climate Orbiter flew too deep into the Martian atmosphere and disintegrated. A simple math error was responsible for navigating the spacecraft into a disastrously low orbit. Navigators failed to convert calculations from feet and inches (used by the contractor Lockheed Martin) into meters and millimeters (used by NASA). "That is so dumb," stated John Logsdon, director of George Washington University's space-policy institute. "There seems to have emerged over the past couple of years a systematic problem in the space community of insufficient attention to detail" (Hotz, 1999, p. 1A).

The Japanese government and nuclear experts were slow to respond to the nuclear accident in Tokaimura, Japan, that occurred just hours prior to the Mars Orbiter mishap. Taisuke Sasanuma, a graduate of the John F. Kennedy School of Government, relates a conversation he had with a Kennedy School classmate who works for Japan's Science and Technology Agency that oversees nuclear power plants in Japan, "When I asked about safety training, he told me it was totally meaningless and a waste of time to discuss it. 'It is obvious that Japanese power plant systems are safe,' he told me. 'We never had a problem, so why think about it?'" (Zielenziger & Lubman, 1999, p. 20A). An unidentified chief executive of Tokyo Electric Power added this, "If you assume that one [an accident] might

happen, that will only make people scared. So we try not to generate people's fear. Accidents can't happen" (p. 20A).

Murphy's Law states that anything that can go wrong likely will go wrong—somewhere, sometime. **A common mistake made by groups is failure to plan for Murphy's Law to minimize the chance of error or mishap.** Human error or simply bad luck must be considered. The more complex the system, the more likely serious errors can and will occur. Failure to plan for errors or unusual occurrences can be catastrophic. Imagine if Boeing built airplanes that could fly only if all engines worked perfectly. Would you want to travel on such a plane?

The enormously successful Mars rover *Sojourner*, mentioned previously, was extensively tested prior to its launch. David Gruel, an engineer assigned the task of creating any conceivable problems *Sojourner* might encounter, tested the rover in a "sandbox" that simulated the surface of Mars. The *Sojourner* team needed to know in advance whether the rover could meet any difficulty it might face. Gruel and his team took into account Murphy's Law. *Sojourner* passed every test in the sandbox and was a huge success on Mars (Shirley, 1997).

During the solution evaluation and selection phase of discussion, groups should

AP / Wide World Photos

Team members anticipate Murphy's Law by preparing the Mars rover *Sojourner* for a test in the sandbox simulation of the Mars surface.

address possible mishaps and mistakes. Backup plans and emergency procedures should be developed. By doing so, likelihood of success, while not guaranteed, is certainly markedly improved. At worst, the consequences of actual mishaps are minimized.

Questions for Thought

1. Can you provide examples of group decision-making errors that could have been avoided or minimized had the group accounted for Murphy's Law?
2. Is planning for what might go wrong with a decision or plan the group wants to implement always a good idea?

GROUP DECISION-MAKING RULES: MAJORITY, MINORITY, UNANIMITY

As stated earlier, rules help groups achieve their goals. They foster stability and reduce variability in a system. Majority, minority, and unanimity are the three primary decision-making rules. Any of these decision-making rules can be applied to the Standard Agenda format.

Majority Rule: Tyrannical or Practical No one should be surprised that majority rule is a popular method of decision making in the United States because the U.S. democratic political system relies on it. Majority rule in groups, however, is not exactly the same as majority rule in our political system. Minorities are protected by

THE FAR SIDE® BY GARY LARSON

"Okay, Williams, we'll just vote. ... How many here say the heart has four chambers?"

Majority rule isn't always advisable. Sometimes minority rule of one—the chief surgeon—proves to be a better alternative.

Majority rule can produce bigoted, ludicrous decision making.

the Bill of Rights. Congress is guided by the realization that legislation must not violate constitutional guarantees of individual liberties. Most small groups provide no similar protection for minorities. The quality of the group's decision is a particularly troublesome problem with majority rule. Majorities can sometimes take ludicrous, even dangerous positions. Mob rule is a manifestation of the tyranny of the majority. Racism, sexism, and other bigotry in the United States have been the products of majority rule.

Studies comparing juries using the unanimous decision rule and majority rule (Oregon requires a 10–2 majority and Louisiana a 9–3 split for felony convictions) found several deficiencies in majority rule applicable to most small groups (Abramson, 1994; Hastie et al., 1983). First, **deliberations are significantly shorter and less conscientious.** Deliberations typically end once a requisite majority is reached. Consequently, less error correction takes place, sometimes resulting in faulty decisions. Second, **minority factions participate less frequently and are less influential,** thereby underutilizing the group's resources. Third, **jurors' overall satisfaction with the group is lower.** Minorities feel that their point of view is ignored and the style of deliberation is typically more combative, forceful, and bullying.

Despite the disadvantages of majority rule, there are some advantages. **When issues are not very important, when decisions must be made relatively quickly, and** when commitment of all members to the final decision is unimportant, majority rule can be useful. Majority rule is efficient and provides quick closure on relatively unimportant issues. As groups become larger, majority rule may be necessary for democratic decision making to take place because consensus becomes increasingly difficult the larger the group becomes.

Minority Rule: Several Types Majorities don't always make the decisions. **Minority rule as a group decision-making method occurs in several forms.** First, the *group designates one of its members as an expert* to make the decision. This method relieves group members from devoting time and energy to solving problems. Decision by designated expert, however, is mostly ineffective. Trying to determine who is the clear expert in the group is often difficult, even impossible. Lack of group input also fails to capitalize on synergy.

Second, a *designated authority* (usually from outside the immediate group) makes the decision for the group, either after hearing discussion from group members or without their consultation. Decision by designated authority is popular in business organizations because it reinforces hierarchical power structures and it is efficient. The Cabrillo College one-stop proposal was instituted primarily by the president, despite opposition from student and faculty senates. Sometimes the group acts in an advisory capacity to the designated authority and sometimes not. Since the group has no ultimate authority, however, this method of decision making has drawbacks. The quality of the designated authority's decision will depend a great deal on how good a listener he or she is. If the group discussion is merely a formality, then none of the benefits of collective deliberations will accrue. Since power is unevenly distributed, group members are likely to vie competitively for attention and seek to impress the authority (D. W. Johnson & R. T. Johnson, 1988). Members will be tempted to report to the authority what he or she wants to hear, not what should be said. If the authority encourages genuine disagreement and in no way penalizes members for their honesty, however, he or she can benefit enormously from a dialectical clash of ideas.

Third, in some instances, *executive committees* must be delegated responsibility for making certain decisions because the workload for the group as a whole is overwhelming or the time constraints are prohibitive. The challenge here is to persuade the group to get behind the decision.

Finally, minority rule can take the form of a *forceful faction* making a decision for the group by dominating less forceful members. On rare occasions this may be advisable when the minority faction consists of the most informed, committed members. Too often, however, dominant group members who flex their muscles focus on personal gain more than on what's good for the group (Murnighan, 1978).

Unanimity Rule: Consensus The unanimity rule governs some groups. Juries are the most obvious example. Persuading all members of a group to agree on anything can be daunting. Group consensus is based on the unanimity rule. **Consensus** is "a state of mutual agreement among members of a group where all legitimate concerns of individuals have been addressed to the satisfaction of the group" (Saint & Lawson, 1997). Not all unanimous decisions can be considered a true consensus.

True consensus requires agreement, commitment, and satisfaction (De-Stephen & Hirokawa, 1988). All members must agree with the group's final decision, but consensus does not require adoption of every member's personal preference. **Consensus usually requires some give-and-take.** If all members can agree on an acceptable alternative, even if this alternative is not each member's first choice, then you have come close to achieving a true consensus. Once unanimous agreement has been reached, members must be willing to defend the decision to outsiders. This shows commitment. Finally, we rarely commit to a group decision when we have little part in formulating it. True consensus requires the opportunity to influence group discussion and choice. Thus, group members must feel satisfied with the decision-making process. Satisfaction is not derived from bullying members into conformity. Satisfaction comes from a cooperative group climate and reasonable opportunities for all members to participate meaningfully in the decision making.

Groups that use a consensus approach tend to produce better decisions than groups using other decision rules because full discussion of issues is required, every group member must be convinced that the decision is a good one, and minority members are heard. Members feel more confident about the correctness of their decisions with consensus, and they are more satisfied with the group as a whole (Abramson, 1994; C. Miller, 1989). Group consensus decision making is especially effective when group members have extensive experience using this method (W. Watson et al., 1991).

Nevertheless, there are two principal limitations to consensus decision making. First, **achieving unanimous agreement from group members is very difficult, especially when the issues are emotionally charged and time for decision making is limited** (see Focus on Culture: "Japan's Nuclear Emergency and Consensus Decision Making"). Discussions can become contentious and time-consuming. Members who resist siding with the majority lengthen the deliberations and increase the frustration level among those looking for a quick decision. Second, **consensus is increasingly unlikely as groups grow larger.** Groups of 15 or 20 will find it nearly impossible to achieve a consensus on much of anything. Seeking a consensus, however, even if one is never quite achieved, can produce most of the benefits of true consensus.

Several guidelines can help a group achieve a consensus (J. Hall & Watson, 1970; Saint & Lawson, 1997).

Japan's Nuclear Emergency and Consensus Decision Making

SEPTEMBER 30, 1999, saw Japan's worst-ever nuclear accident. A processing plant at Tokaimura, 75 miles northeast of Tokyo, released radiation levels that were 20,000 times the normal rate (R. Watson et al., 1999). Three workers were severely injured and 69 other people, mostly workers, were exposed to significant doses of radiation ("Uranium crew," 1999). Potentially catastrophic effects were avoided only because the amount of fissionable material was small and radioactive particles were not released into the air, only radioactive isotopes with a short half-life (Efron, 1999).

What was particularly noteworthy and alarming, however, was the incredibly slow response by nuclear officials and the government to the emergency. Prime Minister Keizo Obuchi wasn't informed about the emergency until an hour and a half after it occurred. Even then, an emergency crisis management team wasn't established for nearly 11 hours (Zielenziger & Lubman, 1999). Citizens living in close proximity to the plant were making calls from pay phones, shopping in a nearby convenience store, or standing in the radioactive drizzle, ignorant of the danger.

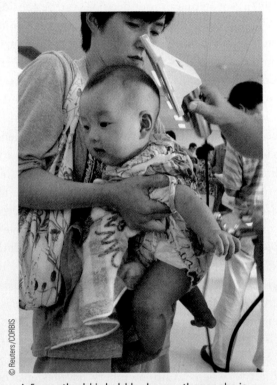

© Reuters/CORBIS

A 5-month-old is held by her mother as she is checked for radiation following the September 1999 nuclear accident in Tokaimura, Japan. Slow decision making from government officials exposed Japanese citizens to a potentially serious health hazard.

1. *Follow the Standard Agenda.* Structured group discussion, not aimless conversation, improves the chances of achieving consensus.
2. *Establish a cooperative group climate.* Supportive patterns of communication encourage consensus; defensive patterns discourage consensus.

Why was the response so slow? This is not the first emergency that Japanese officials have been slow to address. "Be it a massive earthquake in Kobe, the surprise launch of a missile by North Korea over Japan's airspace, the breakup of a Russian oil tanker on Japan's northwest coast, or Thursday's nuclear accident, Japanese have grown weary, not to mention wary, of a government unable to respond crisply and decisively to national crises" (Zielenziger & Lubman, 1999, p. 20A). Takao Toshikawa, a political commentator in Japan, notes, "We have a habit of being not very decisive on serious issues involving security, a crisis or even diplomacy" (Zielenziger & Lubman, 1999, p. 20A).

One suggested reason for the slow response is "the cultural preference for the slow process of making decisions by consensus, rather than valuing decisive leadership" (Zielenziger & Lubman, 1999, p. 20A). This highlights an important limitation of consensus decision making. In times of crisis where quick, decisive action must be taken to avert catastrophe, deciding by group consensus is inappropriate. Lives can be lost while groups discuss, debate, and strive for unanimity. Steven Vogel, a political scientist and specialist on Japan at the University of California–Berkeley, explains that consensus decision making works well for Japan when long-term policy is devised, but it works poorly in a crisis situation. "When a policy decision is made, everyone is on board and implementation tends to be more effective because all sides know about it and are in agreement," says Vogel. "In that sense, the Japanese system is highly efficient. But when you have a crisis, the same decision procedures that work well for more routine long-term policy changes become totally ineffective" (Lubman, 1999, p. 21A).

Questions for Thought

1. Can you think of any crisis situation where consensus decision making might be appropriate and effective?
2. Has the U.S. government ever been slow to respond to a crisis situation? If so, what was the reason for the slow response since the United States generally favors majority rule?

3. *Identify the pluses and minuses of potential decisions under consideration.* Write these positives and negatives on a chalkboard, large tablet, or transparency so all group members can easily see them. (Avoid confirmation bias.)

4. *Discuss all concerns of group members and attempt to resolve every one.* Try to find alternatives that will satisfy members' concerns. (Avoid groupthink.)

5. *Avoid adversarial, win–lose arguments.* Don't stubbornly argue for a position to achieve a personal victory. Seek ways to break a stalemate. (Avoid "enemy–friend" competitive false dichotomy.)

6. *Request a "stand aside."* A **stand aside** means a team member continues to have reservations about the group decision but, when confronted, does not wish to block the group choice. (Avoid the blocker role.)

7. *Avoid conflict-suppressing techniques such as coin flipping and swapping* ("I'll support your position this time if you support mine next time"). The primary objective is to make a high-quality decision, not avoid conflict. Seek differences of opinion. Conflict-suppressing techniques also will not usually produce commitment to the group decision. (Resist groupthink.)

▶ ●● SECOND LOOK

GROUP DECISION-MAKING RULES

RULES	PROS	CONS
Majority Rule		
	Quick	Minorities vulnerable to tyranny of majority
	Efficient	Quality of decision questionable
		Usually alienates minority
	Expedient in large groups	Underutilization of resources
Minority Rule		
Designated Expert	Saves time	Expertise hard to determine
		No group input
Designated Authority	Clear	Members vie for attention
	Efficient	Members vie to impress authority
Executive Committee	Divides labor	Weak commitment to decision
Forceful Faction	Faction may be informed/committed	Likely Me not We oriented
Unanimity Rule (Consensus)		
	Quality decisions	Time-consuming
	Commitment	Difficult
	Satisfaction	Tension-producing

8. *If consensus is impossible despite these guidelines, seek a supermajority (a minimum two-thirds agreement).* A supermajority at least captures the spirit of consensus by requiring substantial, if not total, agreement.

Participation

The Standard Agenda and decision-making rules used by groups are likely to be effective only if group members are active, effective participants in the process. As important as participation of group members is to group synergy, all participation is not created equal. No one wants to encourage participation from members who are obnoxious or bent on sharing misinformation. Nevertheless, low participation from group members, especially those who are merely shy or reticent to contribute for a variety of reasons, can severely impact group effectiveness. In this section, the challenge of cultural diversity and rates of participation is discussed. Ways to encourage low-participators to become more actively engaged in group discussions are also offered.

▶ **Focus Questions**

1. Should nonminority Americans value silence as much as some ethnic minorities do?
2. Should Americans de-emphasize speaking ability?
3. Should you expect ethnic minority group members to become more assertive and outspoken participators in small groups, even though this is not highly valued in their communities?

CULTURAL DIVERSITY AND PARTICIPATION: IS SILENCE GOLDEN?

One of the significant challenges facing teachers in an increasingly multicultural educational environment is how to increase the participation level in class of some ethnic minority students. Japanese students, for example, initiate and maintain fewer conversations and are less apt to talk in class discussions than are other students (Ishii et al., 1984). This reticence to participate verbally in class carries over to small group situations. Contributions to group decision making by ethnic minorities are consistently lower than those by nonminorities (Kirchmeyer, 1993). In 76% of the small groups in one study (Kirchmeyer & Cohen, 1992), the member who contributed the least was Asian.

Why is there this difference in verbal participation in small group decision making? First, **the value of verbal participation in decision making is perceived differently from culture to culture.** As already noted, silent individuals are not seriously considered for the role of leader in American culture. Speaking is highly valued in the United States. Talking in an individualist culture is a way of showing one's uniqueness

(Samovar & Porter, 2004). In collectivist cultures and subcultures, by contrast, speaking is not highly prized. Students from collectivist cultural traditions typically see speaking too much in class as a sign of conceit and superficiality (Samovar & Porter, 2004). Among the Japanese, Vietnamese, Cambodians, and Chinese, emphasis is given to minimal vocal participation. The Chinese have a proverb that states "Those who know do not speak; those who speak do not know" (Lewis, 1996). Inagaki (1985) surveyed 3,600 Japanese regarding their attitude toward speaking. He found that 82% agreed with the saying "Out of the mouth comes all evil" (p. 6). For the Japanese, "silence is considered a virtue as well as a sign of respectability and trustworthiness" (McDaniel, 1993, p. 19). In business negotiations, Japanese, Chinese, and Koreans are more at ease with long pauses and silences than are Americans. As Andersen (1985) explains, "Cultures reflecting Buddhist tradition hold that knowledge, truth, and wisdom come to those whose quiet silence allows the spirit to enter" (p. 162). Many Native Americans equate silence with a great person (Samovar & Porter, 2004). Johannesen (1974) claims that the Native American "derives from silence the cornerstone of character, the virtues of self-control, courage, patience, and dignity" (p. 27).

Second, **a relative disadvantage in ability to communicate effectively in groups limits verbal participation of ethnic minorities.** Minorities report considerably less facility for communicating with others in a college setting (Kirchmeyer, 1993). Not only are ethnic minorities at a distinct disadvantage if English is their second language, but they are at a disadvantage during group discussions dominated by members who are more aggressive and less concerned about other group members (Kirchmeyer, 1993).

Third, **lackluster participation from ethnic minorities in decision making may result from weak commitment to the group.** Weak commitment may result from group members' failure to indicate that participation from minorities is valued, or cultural differences with members of the dominant culture may make minorities feel less like they belong in the group (Kirchmeyer & Cohen, 1992).

If tapping the resources of cultural diversity is an important group goal, and this would seem to be significant given the synergistic potential inherent in diversity (P. L. McLeod et al., 1996), then finding ways to boost the verbal participation rates of ethnic minorities in an American culture that values speech is a worthy undertaking. The methods outlined in the next section for encouraging constructive participation from low-contributors in general apply well to ethnic minorities.

INCREASING CONSTRUCTIVE PARTICIPATION: JUMP-STARTING LOW-PARTICIPATORS

There are several steps that can be taken to promote constructive participation from group members. First, **encourage contributions from low-participators.** This is especially important for involving those ethnic minorities whose cultural values discourage assertiveness (S. Tang & Kirkbride, 1986). Solicit input from reticent members by asking open-ended questions of the group (e.g., "What does everyone think?"). When low-participators offer contributions, indicate that their participation is valued by actively listening to what that person has to say, and perhaps thank them for their contribution.

Second, **make issues and problems for discussion relevant to the interests of low-participators.** When groups work on interesting, involving, or challenging tasks, member contributions increase (Forsyth, 1990).

Third, **give low-participators responsibility for certain tasks.** When individuals are designated as responsible for certain important tasks, they are less likely to sit back and wait for someone else to assume the responsibility. If low-participators believe that their efforts have an impact on the group's final decision or product, they are less likely to remain uninvolved (Kerr & Bruun, 1983).

Fourth, **establish a cooperative group climate.** This is particularly important for ethnic minorities from collectivist cultures, who are likely to feel more comfortable and committed in such an atmosphere.

Fifth, **encourage devil's advocacy and dialectical inquiry.** These two methods of combating groupthink also encourage constructive participation from all group members. With their emphasis on stimulating a variety of ideas and opinions, fully sharing information, openly addressing differences of opinion, and carefully evaluating alternatives, devil's advocacy and dialectical inquiry substantially increase the participation of ethnic minorities (Kirchmeyer & Cohen, 1992).

Conducting Effective Meetings

Humorist Dave Barry (1991), comparing meetings to funerals, seems to prefer funerals. He claims, "The major difference is that most funerals have a definite purpose. Also, nothing is ever really buried in a meeting" (p. 311). Then there's Mitchell's Law: "Any simple problem can be made insoluble if enough meetings are held to discuss it." This section discusses ways to master the meeting monster. Despite bad press, meetings are an indispensable part of group decision making and problem solving.

GROUP MEETINGS: THE GOOD, THE BAD, AND THE UGLY

Meetings can actually save time and increase productivity of groups. Cecilia Sharpe, who was managing an audit team of six accountants at the time, decided to calculate the effects of eliminating the team's weekly meeting with the understanding that group members would maintain direct communication with each other to coordinate their efforts (Shaffner, 1999). When a proposal to revise work schedules for her auditing team emerged, she discovered that this one decision in the absence of a weekly meeting resulted in a net loss of 18 person-hours in productivity. There were 102 disruptions of team members with phone calls to discuss the proposal, compared to only seven disruptions of any kind during team meetings. The decision was 2 days late and no team member was happy with the final decision. Meetings permit face-to-face participation on issues of mutual concern where each member's ideas and arguments can be heard and evaluated simultaneously by all group members. This saves time spent contacting each member separately for input.

Business consultant Mitchell Nash (Dressler, 1995) lists **six common complaints associated with group meetings:** there is an unclear purpose for the meeting, participants are unprepared, key individuals are absent or late, discussion drifts into irrelevant conversation on unrelated topics, some participants dominate the conversation and stifle discussion, and decisions made at meetings are not implemented. Effectively addressing these complaints can make meetings highly productive time-savers.

CHAIR'S RESPONSIBILITIES: CONTROLLING THE MEETING MONSTER

Whoever chairs a small group meeting has specific responsibilities. Using parliamentary procedure, however, isn't necessarily one of them. Parliamentary procedure is a set of hundreds of rules for conducting meetings (see *Robert's Rules of Order* at www.robertsrules.com). **Parliamentary procedure, however, is appropriate for large, formal groups (the U.S. Senate) and even a few smaller groups with formal responsibilities (boards of directors), but for most small groups the rules are too rigid and artificial.** They can stifle productive discussion and squash the creative process. Imagine saying "point of order" or "call the question" when meeting with a project team that is trying to generate creative ideas on a task. Saying "I rise to a point of privilege" or "I move to table the motion" among a small group of close colleagues or friends would likely trigger consternation from group members, if not guffaws or good-natured teasing. Using an abbreviated version of parliamentary procedure such as skipping the technical terminology but making clearly stated and concise motions, adopting formal votes, and requiring recognition from the chair before speaking is advisable for some small groups meetings, especially when the issues discussed are controversial.

As the chair, there are several ways that you can structure meetings to make them efficient and effective decision-making arenas.

1. ***Don't call a meeting unless there is no good alternative.*** Don't hold a meeting if disseminating information, meeting because you are scheduled to do so every Tuesday afternoon, using the meeting as an opportunity to recruit help in researching a topic, or hoping to try out new ideas on colleagues is your only justification. If these objectives can be accomplished without meeting in a

group, then don't meet. One of life's little pleasures is the surprise notification, "Meeting has been canceled." Hold a meeting if an immediate response is required, group participation is essential, participants are prepared to discuss relevant issues, and key players can be present.

2. *Contact every participant.* Indicate in a memo or e-mail what the specific purpose of the meeting is ("to make our final decision on the smoking policy"); where, when, and how long it will be held; and what materials, if any, each participant should bring to the meeting.

3. *Prepare a clear agenda and distribute it to all participants 3 days or more in advance of the meeting.* Absence of an agenda is a primary cause of failed meetings (Drew, 1994). The agenda should list the topics of discussion (see Box 8.1). If reading materials must accompany the agenda, make certain that they are concise and essential to the discussion. Avoid information overload.

4. *Move the agenda forward.* Provide accurate information on all issues, clarify complex issues, correct misconceptions, and especially keep the discussion on track and on point. Aimless discussions suck the life out of meetings and cause participants to feel a little like hostages in a hijacking—captive listeners forced to endure tedious, brain-killing chatter. Do not allow any participant to be a stagehog and dominate the discussion. "Let's hear from other members" and "Does anyone have a different point of view" are ways of limiting talkaholics from dominating discussion.

5. *Designate a specific time allotment for every discussion item.* A timekeeper should be assigned at the start of each meeting. When the time on a discussion item has elapsed, the group may decide to extend the time allotment or move to the next item. Time limits establish a crisp pace for the meeting. Keep meetings as short as possible and you'll garner accolades from grateful members.

6. *Reserve a few minutes at the end of the meeting to determine whether the objectives of the meeting were accomplished.* If further work and discussion are deemed necessary, schedule discussion of unfinished business for the next meeting. If the group has made decisions, implementation of those decisions must be monitored. This is usually the chair's responsibility, but all participants have some responsibility for this.

7. *Distribute the minutes of the meeting as soon as possible.* Someone attending the meeting should be delegated the responsibility for taking notes and turning them into meeting minutes. The minutes should indicate what was discussed, who said what, what action was taken, and what remains to be deliberated and decided. Minutes record the gist of a meeting. Don't attempt to provide a transcript of meeting proceedings. Also, do not include confidential information, and keep language neutral and unbiased.

Box 8.1   SAMPLE AGENDAS FOR GROUP MEETINGS

AGENDA FOR A BUSINESS MEETING
(*Meeting of the student senate*)

Date

Boardroom

2:00–3:30 p.m.

Purpose: Biweekly meeting

   I. Call meeting to order

  II. Approval of the minutes of last meeting (5 minutes)

 III. Additions to the agenda (2 minutes)

 IV. Committee reports
    A. Student fee committee (5 minutes)
    B. Student activity committee (5 minutes)
    C. Student union committee (5 minutes)

  V. Officers' reports
    A. Treasurer's report (5 minutes)
    B. President's report (10 minutes)

 VI. Old business
    A. Textbook prices (10 minutes)
    B. Campus parking problems (10 minutes)
    C. Pub on campus (5 minutes)

 VII. New business
    A. Computer access on campus (5 minutes)
    B. Safety on campus (20 minutes)

VIII. Building agenda for next meeting (5 minutes)

 IX. Adjournment

AGENDA FOR A DISCUSSION MEETING
(*Curriculum task force*)

Date

Boardroom

3:00–5:00 p.m.

Purpose: To improve the curriculum change and approval process

   I. How does the current curriculum process work?

  II. What are the primary problems with the present curriculum process?

 III. What causes the problems?

 IV. What criteria determine an ideal curriculum process?

  V. What are some possible improvements in the curriculum process?

 VI. Which suggested improvements are the most promising? Why?

 VII. Are there any drawbacks to these suggested improvements?

VIII. What needs to occur to implement the most promising suggested improvements?

Critical Thinking and Effective Decision Making

Group members must exercise their critical reasoning abilities at every stage of the Standard Agenda to maximize the probabilities of effective decisions (Hirokawa, 1992). Consequently, how you go about gathering information and the critical eye you focus on information gathered should be primary concerns.

GATHERING INFORMATION: ACCUMULATING INPUT

The output of groups is likely to be no better than the input available to its members. Faulty or insufficient information easily produces collective inferential error. **Information gathering is used in all six steps of the Standard Agenda and should be a focused effort by all group members.** The group should divide the labor. Some members may concentrate on certain issues (problem causes and effects), while other members research different ones (potential solutions).

For the most up-to-date information, use the Internet. Learning to use the proper search engines and focusing your search take time to master. Consult your librarian for assistance if necessary. Briefly, an Internet search usually begins with a **search engine,** a tool that computer-generates indexes of web pages that match keywords typed in a search window. Some of the most popular ones are: AltaVista (http://www.altavista.com); Google (http://www.google.com); HotBot (http://www.hotbot.com); Excite (http://www.excite.com); and Lycos (http://www.lycos.cs.cmu.edu).

Metasearch engines send your keyword request to several search engines at once. Some popular metasearch engines are: MetaCrawler (www.metacrawler.com); Dogpile (http://www.dogpile.com); and ProFusion (http://www.profusion.com).

A **virtual library** is a search tool that combines Internet technology and standard library techniques for cataloging and evaluating information. Virtual libraries are usually associated with colleges, universities, or organizations with strong reputations in information dissemination. Some of the most popular virtual libraries are: Internet Public Library (http://www.lii.org) and WWW Virtual Library (http://www.vlib.org).

To limit information overload, it is critical to narrow your search so that you don't access half-a-million websites on a topic. The quickest way to learn how to do this is to locate the "Help," "Frequently Asked Questions," or "Search Tips" button on the Internet search tool's home page. When you click on one of these buttons, instructions will appear on-screen identifying how to use the search engine, directory, or virtual library effectively.

Despite the popularity and utility of the Internet, the library is still a useful place to search for information. Libraries have access to many electronic databases such as the general-purpose InfoTrac (available to you with this text) and education-related ERIC. Libraries also have numerous standard references. There are numerous periodical indexes such as *Readers' Guide to Periodical Literature,* the *Public Affairs Information Service* (journal articles and government documents), *Hispanic American Periodicals Index* (Hispanic American interests), *Index to Black Periodicals* (African American issues), and *Women's Resources International* (women's issues). Excellent guides to professional and scholarly articles include *Psychological Abstracts, Sociological Abstracts,* and *International Index: Guide to Periodical Literature in the Social Sciences and Humanities.*

Good sources of statistical information on a wide range of topics include the *Statistical Abstract of the United States, Facts on File, Information Please Almanac, Vital Statistics of the United States, World Almanac, Monthly Labor Review, Report of the President's Council of Economic Advisors,* and the *FBI Uniform Crime Report.* For government-related information consult the *Monthly Catalog of United States Government Publications, The Congressional Index, Congressional Quarterly Weekly Report,* and *The Congressional Record.* For information of general interest, consult encyclopedias such as *Encyclopedia Britannica, World Book Encyclopedia,* and *Collier's Encyclopedia* as well as newspaper indexes such as *New York Times Index* and an index to your local newspaper. There are also online versions of most of these resources.

Searching for information can be a tedious process. Remaining focused by following the suggestions I've offered will reduce the tedium and increase group efficiency.

EVALUATING INFORMATION: APPLYING CRITERIA

Knowing where to find appropriate information is helpful, but group members must also know how to evaluate information. All information is not created equal. There are five criteria for evaluating information.

Credibility: Is It Believable? Is the information believable and reliable? When the source of your information is biased (gains something by taking certain positions), credibility is low. The Quaker Oats Company sponsored studies that reported reduction in cholesterol from eating oat bran contained in its cereals. The reduction was a paltry 3%, meaning that you would have to eat almost nothing but oatmeal to gain even a marginal health benefit. Authorities quoted outside of their field of expertise are also not credible. Iben Browning predicted a major earthquake for December 3 and 4, 1990, along the New Madrid Fault located in the Midwest. Schools in several states were dismissed during these 2 days as a result of his prediction. Was Browning a credible expert on earthquakes? He had a doctorate in physiology and a bachelor's degree in physics and math. He was the chief scientist for Summa Medical Corp. He studied climatology in his spare time. Earthquake experts around the country repudiated Browning's predictions. He was not a credible source since earthquake predictions were not in his field of expertise. (As you undoubtedly know, his predictions were wrong.)

Dr. Edgar Suter (1994), national chair of the Doctors for Integrity in Policy Research, Inc., wrote in an article published in the prestigious *Journal of the American Medical Association* that "between 25 and 75 lives may be saved by a gun for every life lost to a gun." There were 648,046 gun deaths in the United States in the final two decades of the twentieth century (Sugarmann, 2001). If Suter's estimation of lives saved by gun ownership is credible, this means that as many as 48,603,450 Americans would have died in the same 20-year period if guns had been inaccessible to Americans to protect themselves (648,046 × 75). This amounts to one-sixth of the entire U.S. population and almost *50 times more fatalities* than the total American combat deaths in all the wars in U.S. history. One can only wonder why Great Britain, with its almost universal ban on guns, had only a few thousand homicides during the same time period (Sugarmann, 2001). Other arguments and evidence can be used to oppose gun control, but Suter's statistics are not credible despite his credentials.

Let me also note here that the Internet itself is not a credible source (see Closer Look: "The Internet: Resource for Information and Misinformation"). The Internet is merely a vehicle for finding information. Quoting the Internet as your source is tantamount to quoting the radio.

Currency: Is It Up-to-Date? Information should be as up-to-date as possible. What used to be taken as fact may be called into question with new information. Only a few years ago cholesterol levels below 300 were thought to pose no significant risk of heart disease. Now, the current advice calls for cholesterol levels below 200, and a 150 level is preferred to keep heart disease risk low. Currency is especially important when an event or situation is volatile and likely to change rapidly. Quoting last month's or even last week's stock prices could leave you a pauper if you act on such outdated information. Interest rates on home mortgages change daily. You must have current rates before you decide to lock in a fixed-rate mortgage on a house you're purchasing.

Relevance: Looking for Logical Connections Information should actually support claims made. Claiming that the public education system in the United States is the world's best because America spends more money in total than any other nation is irrelevant. Total spending doesn't necessarily equate with educational excellence, especially if the money is largely wasted or spent on the wrong priorities.

Representativeness: Reflecting the Facts A single example or statistic may or may not accurately reflect what is true in a particular instance. If a vivid example (e.g., a testimonial from a victim of black lung disease on the health risks of mining coal) illustrates the truth of a claim already supported by solid scientific evidence, then it is representative and provides dramatic impact to the claim. If, however, a claim rests solely on a few testimonials or even many examples, then a real question of representativeness exists. Examples to support a claim may be selectively chosen (confirmation bias), so they may not reflect what is true generally.

There are two principal guidelines for determining whether statistics are representative. **First, the sample size (in polls, surveys, and studies) must be adequate.** This can be determined most easily by the margin of error, which is the degree of sampling error accounted for by imperfections in selecting a sample. As the margin of error increases, the representativeness of the statistic decreases. If the margin of error reaches

C L O S E R   L O O K

THE INTERNET: RESOURCE FOR INFORMATION AND MISINFORMATION

THE INTERNET IS A RICH RESOURCE of information, but it is also a resource for rumor, gossip, urban legends, and hoaxes. Author Kurt Vonnegut's commencement address to graduates at MIT was printed on the Internet in its entirety. Vonnegut advised graduates to "wear sunscreen. If I could offer you only one tip for the future, sunscreen would be it." He also counseled graduates to "floss," to "get plenty of calcium," and to "be kind to your knees." Vonnegut never gave a commencement address at MIT. The address was a hoax (Harmon, 2001).

After the terrorist attacks on the World Trade Center towers, the Internet spawned misinformation faster than New York City's emergency management officials could keep track (Filkins, 2001). A police officer surfed a wave of collapsing rubble for 82 stories and survived, Arab schoolchildren in Jersey City informed their classmates of the impending terrorist attack, and the CIA knew about the attacks and could have prevented them were just some examples of misinformation spread on the Internet at the speed of light. (You can check the validity of Internet rumors and stories at www.snopes.com; see also urbanlegends.about.com.)

Singer Mariah Carey was victimized twice by bogus Internet hoaxes. In 1996, this quote was attributed to her: "When I watch TV and see those poor, starving kids all over the world, I can't help but cry. I mean, I'd love to be skinny like that, but not with all those flies and death and stuff." In 1999, an Internet story circulated that Carey made this comment on the death of King Hussein of Jordan: "I'm inconsolable at the present time. I was a very good friend of Jordan. He was probably the greatest basketball player this country has ever seen" ("Mariah 'Quote' Spreads," 1999). Tennis star Serena Williams was similarly victimized in December 2004. In a supposed interview she says, "If you are a successful black female you only have two choices: date outside of your race or date other successful black females." She continues, "Black men over the years have become less and less of value to black women both rich and poor." She suggests loving black men "like a poor homeless dog." Williams never made any of these statements. The interview was a hoax that continues to circulate on the Internet ("Serena Williams Interview," 2005).

Be extremely cautious about information found on the Internet. Apply the criteria of credibility, currency, relevance, representativeness, and sufficiency. You can do this by following a few simple steps.

▶

First, **consider the source.** If no author for the information is provided on the website, be highly skeptical of its validity. If a name is provided but no credentials are offered, again be highly skeptical unless the information can be validated from another source that is reputable (e.g., a national news agency).

Second, attempt to **determine whether the source is biased.** Websites that use a hard sell to promote their ideas, therapies, and products are probably offering misinformation. Search for websites that appear to have no vested interest, no products to sell, and no ideas or conspiracies to peddle. The website address can provide hints; if it contains a *.gov* or a *.edu,* this means that the site is sponsored and maintained by a governmental or educational institution with a reputation to protect. Sites with *.com* or *.org* in their address are commercial ventures, or they are sponsored by reputable and sometimes not so reputable organizations. Their credibility varies widely.

Third, **determine the currency of the information.** Many websites are not regularly updated. You may be accessing a site whose information is 5 to 10 years old. Look for a date when the site was last updated (often at the end of the document). Look for recency of information in the document to approximate the date of the original authorship.

Fourth, **assess the accuracy of information on the site.** Try to verify the accuracy of any information and statistics by comparing them to reputable sources. Do the facts and statistics offered on the site contradict information from reputable sources? For example, population and census statistics can be checked at the U.S. Census Bureau site (http://www.census.gov). Health and medical information can be checked at (http://www .healthcentral.com), the American Medical Association site (http://www.ama-assn.org/consumer .htm), the Centers for Disease Control site (http:// www.cdc.gov), or the health fraud site (http:// www.quackwatch.com). News events can be checked at reputable news agencies' sites (http:// www.nytimes.com or http://www.abcnews.com or http://www.cnn.com).

Questions for Thought

1. A quotation with amusing grammatical errors is attributed to President George W. Bush. How would you determine whether the quotation is a hoax or the real thing?

2. A list of a dozen "actual comments" written on students' report cards by teachers in the New York City public schools is circulated on the Internet (a colleague e-mailed me the list). The list includes statements such as, "I would not allow this student to breed," "Your son is depriving a village somewhere of an idiot," and "If this student were any more stupid, he'd have to be watered twice a week." Is this list a hoax? How would you determine whether it is a hoax?

more than plus or minus 3%, the representativeness of the statistic becomes questionable. A study ("Pre-employment," 1990) of 103 California companies testing job applicants for drug use revealed that 17.8% of the applicants tested positive. The margin of error, however, was 7.8%. Thus, the results are questionable since the true level of drug use among the job applicants may have been 25.6% (17.8% *plus* 7.8% margin of error) or 10% (17.8% *minus* 7.8% margin of error). The drug use problem may be substantially overstated or understated by the 17.8% statistic.

A second guideline for assuring representative statistics is that the sample must be randomly selected, not self-selected. A random sample is a part of the population drawn in such a manner that every member of the entire population has an equal chance of being selected. A self-selected sample is one in which the most committed, aroused, or otherwise atypical parts of the population studied are more likely to participate. For example, in January 2004, the American Family Association (AFA) posted an online survey asking its constituents about their position on gay marriage (Terdiman, 2004). The AFA supports a constitutional amendment banning gay marriage. It expected overwhelming support from its conservative constituency, so much so that it planned to send the results to members of Congress. Gay activist groups, however, got wind of the poll, forwarded the survey to its supporters and subverted the intended biased leaning of the results. Within weeks of the survey's release online, 60% of self-selected respondents said that they *favored* outright legalization of gay marriage and another 8% favored a civil union with full benefits. A CNN poll of randomly selected respondents, however, conducted about the same time as the AFA survey found that 64% opposed gay marriage (Espo, 2004). The AFA abandoned its intention of using the results of its poll to bolster its case against gay marriage.

Sufficiency: When Enough Really Is Enough When do you have enough information to support your claims? There is no magic formula for sufficiency. Determinations of sufficiency are judgment calls. Nevertheless, there are some guidelines for making such a determination.

First, **what type of claim are you making?** Causal relations require more evidence than a single study. In January 2000, results of a study showed that men with significant hair loss on the crown of their heads had a higher risk of heart attack than men with hair loss on the front of their heads. One study is insufficient to establish a causal relationship, so no conclusion can be drawn from this study. Claiming that violence depicted on television "may contribute" to antisocial behavior, however, requires less stringent criteria for sufficiency since only a weak connection is claimed.

Second, **extraordinary claims require extraordinary proof** (Abell, 1981). When a claim contradicts a considerable body of research and knowledge, extraordinary proof must accompany such a claim. A claim that Earth has been visited by extraterrestrials requires much more evidence than a few alleged sightings. Claims of cancer cures must be rigorously tested. The claims are extraordinary, so they require more than ordinary, commonplace evidence. Ordinary claims, however, such as "flu viruses pose a serious health hazard to the elderly" can be demonstrated sufficiently with one authoritative statistic from the Centers for Disease Control. (See Appendix B for additional relevant material on critically examining information and claims.)

Creative Problem Solving

Years ago, a prisoner escaped from a penitentiary in the western United States. He was recaptured after a few weeks. On his return, prison officials grilled him. "How did you cut through the bars?" they demanded. Finally, he confessed. He said he had taken bits of twine from the machine shop, dipped them in glue, then in emery. He smuggled these makeshift "hacksaws" back to his cell. For 3 months he laboriously sawed through the 1-inch-thick steel bars. Prison officials accepted his story, locked him up, and kept him far away from the machine shop. Is that the end of the story? Not quite. Three and one-half years later, he escaped again by cutting through the cell bars. He was never recaptured, but how he escaped became a legend in the underworld. It seems that his original story was a phony. He hadn't fashioned a hacksaw from any materials in the machine shop. Instead, he had used woolen strings from his socks, moistened them with spit, and rubbed them in abrasive dirt from the floor of his cell, then painstakingly sawed through the cell bars (Rossman, 1931). The prisoner had fashioned a creative solution to a challenging problem. Creative problem solving is the focus of this section.

▶ **Focus Questions**

1. How do imagination and knowledge relate to creative problem solving?
2. What makes the brainstorming technique an effective, creative, problem-solving tool?
3. What is integrative problem solving and reframing?

GENERAL OVERVIEW

The story of the prisoner's resourceful escape highlights several important points about creativity and problem solving. First, **to borrow Thomas Edison's comment on genius, creativity is more perspiration than inspiration.** We have to work to find creative solutions to problems. This means devoting time and energy to the task, not hoping for imaginative ideas to fall from the sky and clunk us on the head.

Second, **creativity is spurred by challenges.** As the old adage says, "Necessity is the mother of invention." We are creative in response to some felt need, to some problem that requires a solution. The bigger the challenge, the more complex the problem, the greater is the need for creativity.

Third, **creativity flourishes in cooperative, not competitive environments.** In a competitive atmosphere, thinking "may be used to plan, strategize, and coerce rather than to problem solve and collaborate" (Carnevale & Probst, 1998, p. 1308).

Fourth, **creativity requires sound ideas, not just imaginative ones.** As Vincent Ruggiero (1988) puts it, creative ideas must be more than uncommon; they "must be uncommonly good" (p. 77). Creative solutions are original, but they also must work.

I once heard a radio commentator read recipes submitted by children for preparing a Thanksgiving turkey. One child wrote: "Put 10 pounds of butter on the turkey and 5 pounds of salt. Cook it for 20 minutes." M-m-m-m-m good! Some culinary concoctions just don't work. The recipes are imaginative, but repulsive, like spaghetti and liver sauce or a tofu and oyster milkshake. Creative problem solving and decision making require both imagination and knowledge. Children create foolish things because they don't know any better. Competent communicators create solutions that are workable and effective.

Fifth, **creativity requires many ideas.** Although sheer quantity doesn't guarantee great solutions, the fewer the ideas the less probable is the discovery of at least one good idea—that flower among all the thistles. In the pharmaceutical industry it can take as many as 5,000 ideas before a good one emerges (Lamb et al., 2004).

Finally, **creativity requires breaking mindsets and thinking "outside the box."** Unless we try adopting different ways of approaching problems, we'll remain stuck in place.

Specific Creative Techniques

As I have emphasized already, group decision making and problem solving are usually more effective when systematic procedures are followed. Systematic procedures apply to group creativity as well (Firestein, 1990). Haphazard, unfocused efforts to induce creativity are often not as productive as more focused efforts.

Brainstorming and Nominal Group Techniques: Generating Lots of Ideas

At IDEO, faced with the problem of an electric car that is so quiet that it would likely cause accidents, a product design team brainstorms solutions to the problem. "How about tire treads that play music?" one team member offers. "How about a little Eric Clapton?" another chimes in, and the ideas begin to fly (O'Brien, 1995).

Alex Osborn introduced the brainstorming technique in 1939. **Brainstorming** is a creative problem-solving technique that promotes plentiful, even zany, ideas in an atmosphere free from criticism and with enthusiastic participation from all

"Never, ever, think outside the box."

Sometimes the answer is in the box when creativity is not welcomed.

group members. Rational approaches to decision making and problem solving run the danger of becoming methodical, stale, and unimaginative. Brainstorming can regenerate a group by opening up a stuffy, plodding, and inhibited group process.

There are several guidelines for using this technique (Kelley & Littman, 2001; Nussbaum, 2004):

1. *Encourage wild ideas.* At IDEO this is a motto that appears in large print on the walls of each brainstorming room. If edicts such as "it must be practical" or "it can't cost too much" are stated before brainstorming occurs, the group will go silent. Worry about the practical stuff after ideas have been generated in rapid-fire brainstorming sessions. What appears to be a dumb idea initially can provoke a really good solution to a problem. Bolton (1979) cites the example of a brainstorming session by managers of a major airport who were generating ideas

regarding ways to remove snow from the runways. One participant offered the idea that snow could be removed by putting a giant frog on the control tower. The frog could push the snow aside with its enormous tongue. This zany idea provoked a practical solution—a revolving cannon that shoots a jet airstream. Even if zany ideas never trigger effective solutions to problems, they at least encourage a freewheeling, fun climate conducive to creativity.

2. *Don't evaluate ideas while brainstorming.* Critiques will inhibit contributions from group members. Group members need to be self-monitoring. Idea slayers, such as "You can't be serious," "That will never work," and "It's completely impractical," should be squelched by members. Even a positive evaluation, such as "Great idea," is out of order because group members will quickly interpret absence of positive evaluation as a negative assessment of their ideas.

3. *Don't clarify or seek clarification of an idea.* This will slow down the process. Clarification can come later after a list of ideas has been generated.

4. *Do not engage in task-irrelevant discussion.* Idea generation is significantly diminished when conversation is permitted during brainstorming sessions (Dugosh et al., 2000). With conversation often comes irrelevant chatter. A brainstorming facilitator should invoke this rule whenever talking interrupts idea generation.

5. *Stay focused on the topic.* You want all suggestions to be related to the topic. Wild ideas that are not on topic are not helpful.

6. *Expand on the ideas of other group members.* Halpern (1984) cites the example of a food manufacturer seeking better ways to bag potato chips. Corporate executives were asked to identify the best packaging solution they had ever seen. One brainstormer said that bagging leaves wet was the best method. Dry leaves crumble and use up more air space. Wet leaves pack more easily and require fewer bags. Expanding on this idea, the manufacturer tried packing potato chips wet. When the potato chips dried they became tasteless crumbs. Nevertheless, from this initial failure sprang the popular potato chips in a can, in which a potato mixture is cooked in chip-shaped molds and then stacked in the can. From a bad idea came a good one.

7. *Record all ideas without reference to who contributed the idea.* Do not censor any ideas, no matter how silly they may seem, as long as they are focused on the problem.

8. *Encourage participation from all group members.* The maximum number of ideas requires the maximum effort from every group member.

Brainstorming normally is instituted during the solutions suggestion step of the Standard Agenda. Determining the quality of the ideas generated from brainstorming comes during the solution evaluation and selection step. Ideas are evaluated in terms of solution criteria established earlier in the Standard Agenda process.

A second creative problem-solving method is **nominal group technique** (Delbecq et al., 1975). Individuals work by themselves generating lists of ideas on a problem, then convene in a group where they merely record the ideas generated (usually on a chart or blackboard for all to see). Interaction occurs only to clarify ideas, not to discuss their merits and demerits. Individuals then select their five favorite ideas, write them on a card, and rank them from most to least favorite. The rankings are averaged and the ideas with the highest averages are the ones selected by the group.

Some research has shown nominal group technique generates more and better ideas than brainstorming (Paulus et al., 1993; Valacich et al., 1994). Mongeau (1993), however, argues that "although considerable research has been performed on brainstorming, little of this research is a valid test of Osborn's ideas" (p. 22). Results have been derived from student groups that: have no history together and no future, have no training and experience using the brainstorming technique (aside from a brief explanation of the rules), are provided no opportunity to research the task prior to brainstorming, are given little time to think about the task, and are given tasks often unrelated to students' interests; also, groups never actually make choices regarding which ideas are best (Kramer et al., 1997).

One study of brainstorming at IDEO (Sutton & Hargadon, 1996) also found that **idea generation isn't the only value of brainstorming.** Regular brainstorming can reinforce an organizational culture, impress clients, provide opportunities for skill improvement, attract skilled employees to an organization, and improve employee retention. "Brainstorming is the idea engine of IDEO's culture" (Kelley & Littman, 2001). Designers at IDEO refer to brainstorming sessions as "vacations" and note that "brainstorms are a nice change of pace" from other work performed. One designer offered, "Brainstorms are one of the rewards of working here" (Sutton & Hargadon, 1996, p. 701).

Brainstorming, if done properly, can be highly effective (Kelley & Littman, 2001). Osborn actually suggested that **the proper brainstorming format should involve first an individual, then a group, followed by an individual brainstorming session.** Members should be provided with a well-defined problem a few days in advance of the group brainstorming session so members can research it and think of solutions to contribute. Then members meet as a group to share their ideas and generate new ones. After the group session, individuals are given a few days to contemplate further ideas on their own. In addition, members should not be strangers and they should belong to a long-standing (not a zero-history) group. They should also receive training and experience in how to use the brainstorming technique. Research shows that training and experience in brainstorming vastly improve idea generation (Firestein, 1990); use of a trained facilitator also improves brainstorming results (Kramer et al., 2001). In addition, having a trained facilitator encourage brainstormers to focus on the ideas of others during brainstorming, not simply attend to their own ideas, improves idea generation beyond that of the nominal group

Scott Adams, creator of the comic strip *Dilbert,* enlisted IDEO to brainstorm "Dilbert's Ultimate Cubicle" pictured here. Technological features include devices that alert employees to an approaching boss and rid the office cubicle of unwanted guests.

technique (Dugosh et al., 2000). This piggybacking process is stimulated by hearing ideas from other brainstormers and building on those ideas.

Electronic brainstorming occurs when group members sit at computer terminals and brainstorm ideas using a computer-based, file-sharing procedure (e.g., Group Decision Support System). This offers an additional method for improving idea generation and creativity. Group members type their contributions, then send the file to a shared pool. Ideas are added and shared with group members. This can be done anonymously if group members fear a critique. Electronic brainstorming has sometimes outperformed nominal groups in idea generation (Dugosh et al., 2000; Valacich et al., 1994), but most studies show that for small groups, electronic brainstorming is not the most effective method for brainstorming (Barki & Pinsonneault, 2001).

Framing/Reframing: It's All In the Wording Consider the following problem offered by psychologists Tversky and Kahneman (1981):

Imagine that the government is preparing for an outbreak of a rare disease that is expected to kill 600 people. Two programs are available. If Program A is adopted, then 200 people will be saved. If Program B is adopted, then there is a one-third chance that 600 people will be saved, and a two-thirds chance that nobody will be saved. Which program should be adopted?

When the problem is framed in this way, the vast majority of subjects prefer Program A to Program B. People want to avoid the risk that nobody will be saved. Now consider this statement of the problem:

Imagine that the government is preparing for an outbreak of a rare disease that is expected to kill 600 people. Two programs are available. If Program X is adopted, then 400 people will die. If Program Y is adopted, then there is a one-third chance that nobody will die, and a two-thirds chance that 600 people will die.

When the problem is framed in this way, the vast majority of subjects choose Program Y over X. Subjects want to avoid the certainty that 400 people will die. Yet, Programs A and X have identical outcomes, as do B and Y. So why did one group predominantly choose Program A while the other group predominantly chose Program Y? The wording of the problem is identical and the outcomes are identical, yet the predominate choices are opposite. The reason for the difference lies in how the problem is **framed**—the way in which language shapes our perception of choices.

When MBA students and managers were informed that a particular corporate strategy had a 70% chance of success, most favored it. When it was framed as a 30% chance of failure, however, the majority opposed the strategy (Wolkomir & Wolkomir, 1990). When people were presented with two options for treating lung cancer, 84% chose the surgery option when it was framed in terms of living, while 56% chose the surgery option when it was presented in terms of dying (McNeil et al., 1982).

Our frame of reference can lock us into a mindset, making solutions to problems difficult if not impossible to discover. This mental gridlock can block the free flow of creative ideas. Postman (1976) provides an example. You have the number VI. By the addition of a single line, make it into a seven. The answer is simple: VII. Now consider this problem: You have the number IX. By the addition of a single line, make it into a six. The answer is not so obvious because of your frame of reference, which identifies the number as a Roman numeral and all lines as straight. Not until you break away from this frame of reference by reframing the problem—by no longer assuming that the answer must be in terms of a Roman numeral and that all lines are straight—will you solve the problem. Have you found the answer? How about **SIX**?

Frames determine whether people notice problems, how they understand and remember problems, and how they evaluate and act on them (Fairhurst & Sarr, 1996). **Reframing** is the creative process of breaking a mindset by describing the problem from a different frame of reference. For example, a service station proprietor put an out-of-order sign on a soda machine. Customers paid no attention to the sign, lost their money, then complained to the station owner. Frustrated and annoyed, the owner changed the sign to read "$5.00" for a soda. No one made the mistake of putting money in the faulty soda pop dispenser. The problem was reframed. Instead of wondering how to get customers to realize that the machine was on the fritz, the owner changed the frame of reference to one that would make customers not want to put money in the dispenser. Learning to reframe problems can be a highly useful skill for the competent communicator, and it is an essential part of effective leadership in groups (Fairhurst & Sarr, 1996).

When groups become stumped by narrow or rigid frames of reference, interjecting certain open-ended questions can help reframe the problem and the search for solutions. My personal favorite is "What if . . .?" The group asks, "What if we don't accept this cutback in resources as inevitable?" "What if employees really want to produce quality work but find the work environment tedious?" "What if we tried working together instead of against each other?" Additional reframing questions include: "Why are these the only options?" "What happens if we reject the proposal?" "How could this be turned into a win–win situation for everyone?"

One of the advantages of reframing is that once a different frame of reference is presented, the mindset often is broken permanently. For instance, what is the correct answer to the following problem?

Radar is to level as pup is to:

a. Mitten
b. Madam
c. Bird
d. Pope

Stuck? If so, then the likely reason is your frame of reference. When faced with questions framed as analogies, we are inclined to look for strictly logical connections. Try looking for a nonlogical relationship. What if you reframed the problem as a search for a common construction of the words? Does this help? The correct response is b. All four words are palindromes—words that read the same forward and backward. Now that you know the frame of reference, you're not likely to be stumped in the future by such an analogy on a standardized test. Likewise, once your group has met a challenge in the past by reframing the problem, it has the experience and know-how to meet similar challenges when they present themselves.

Integrative Problem Solving: Satisfying Everyone Decision making often involves conflicts of interest. Groups, or factions within groups, perceive each other as desiring mutually exclusive goals. Thus, they compete, entering into a power struggle hoping that the other side will capitulate. **Integrative problem solving,** on the other hand, is a creative approach to conflicts of interest; it searches for solutions that benefit everyone. Two forms of integrative problem solving are expanding the pie and bridging (Pruitt & Rubin, 1986).

Expanding the pie refers to increasing the resources as a solution to a problem. When faced with scarce resources, groups often become competitive and experience serious strife, warring over who gets the biggest or best piece of the limited pie. Groups, however, sometimes accept the inevitability of scarce resources—what Bazerman and Neale (1983) call the "bias of the fixed pie"—without fully exploring options that might expand the resources. School districts in California, faced with ever-present lean budgets, could issue a collective sigh and proceed to cut programs and teachers. Instead, many districts have found creative ways to increase resources beyond what the state legislature provides. Some districts have established private foundations, raising as much as $435,000 each year in community donations. These foundations throw $125-a-plate dinners, organize black-tie auctions, stage celebrity tennis and golf tournaments, and do car washes. One district foundation purchased a 10-acre vacant school site, developed it, and sold it for a $4-million profit (Le, 1995). These efforts to expand the resource pie save teachers' jobs and maintain important educational programs.

Bridging is the second type of integrative solution to conflicts. Bridging offers a new option devised to satisfy all parties on important issues. Bridging was used to solve a conflict of interest over where to eat dinner involving a couple, a friend of the couple's, and the friend's two teenage children. All three adults wished to eat dinner at a moderately priced restaurant specializing in fresh-fish entrees served with wine. The teenagers wanted burgers, fries, and colas. After a fair amount of wrangling, the pouting and whining began—from the teenagers, not the adults. Frustrated, the mother of the teenagers declared, "I think we'll just take off and eat at home. This isn't working out." A suggestion was made by one of the other adults: "Why don't we send the kids over to that burger joint up the street and have them bring back their meal? We can ask the restaurant if they mind having food brought in by the kids, and, if not, the adults will order dinners with all the trimmings." The restaurant cooperated and both the adults and the teenagers enjoyed their meals.

Competent communicators vigorously explore possible integrative solutions to conflicts of interest. To do this successfully, they should take the following steps (Pruitt & Rubin, 1986):

1. *Conflicting parties should formulate a clear statement of issues and goals.* If all are to benefit from the integrative solution, what the parties want to accomplish must be apparent. Rausch and his colleagues (1974) discovered that 66% of the conflicts they examined were successfully resolved when the issues were clearly stated; only 18% of the conflicts were effectively resolved when the issues remained vague or unstipulated.

2. *Parties in conflict must determine whether a real conflict of interest exists.* Family members argue over whether to get a dog or not. The two kids say they want a dog very much; the father and mother say they do not. On the surface this looks like a standard conflict of interest. Yet when the issue is discussed, what becomes clear is that the mother doesn't want to take care of the dog and the father dislikes barking. When asked whether a cat would serve as an adequate substitute, the kids enthusiastically agree since they really just want a pet. No conflict really exists since the parents actually like cats, which are low maintenance and mostly quiet, and the kids get their pet.

> ●● ● SECOND LOOK
>
> ### THE EFFECTIVE PROBLEM-SOLVING PROCESS
>
> | STANDARD AGENDA | TECHNIQUES |
> | --- | --- |
> | Problem identification | Form questions of fact, value, or policy |
> | | Define ambiguous terms |
> | | Use framing/reframing |
> | Problem analysis | Explore causes of problem (gather info) |
> | | Explore effects (significance) of problem |
> | | Avoid analysis paralysis |
> | Solution criteria | Establish criteria |
> | | Prioritize criteria |
> | Solution suggestions | Brainstorm solutions |
> | | Clarify ambiguous or confusing ideas |
> | | Consolidate overlapping ideas |
> | | Use integrative problem solving |
> | Solution evaluation/selection | Explore merits/demerits of solutions |
> | | Use devil's advocacy |
> | | Use dialectical inquiry |
> | | Consider solutions in terms of criteria |
> | | Use majority or minority rule, or consensus |
> | Solution implementation | Use force field analysis |
> | | Use PERT |
>
> NOTE: Although the consensus technique is used most directly during the solution criteria and solution evaluation/selection steps of the Standard Agenda, consensus rules may operate throughout the problem-solving process. Majority or minority rule may also be inserted at various steps if appropriate conditions exist.

3. *The parties in disagreement should stick to their goals but remain flexible regarding the means of attaining them.* Both expanding the pie and bridging allow conflicting parties to find flexible, creative means of attaining goals without compromising those goals.

4. *If stalemated, concede on low-priority issues or discard low-priority interests.* The prime goals remain intact. The focus continues to be a solution that satisfies the goals of both parties. You give on minor issues that are relatively unimportant to you but are perhaps more important to the other party.

In summary, there is no dichotomy between rational and creative decision making and problem solving. The two can be complementary paths to effective decisions in groups. The discussion process, however, should be systematic, not haphazard. Consideration of the problem should come before deliberations on solutions. Standard Agenda is the most common and useful set of procedures for rational decision making. Consensus, when applicable, is an effective process for guiding members toward rational decisions. Brainstorming and nominal group technique, framing/reframing, and integrative problem solving all provide systematic techniques for the discovery of creative solutions to problems.

In the next two chapters, I will discuss the interconnected concepts of power and conflict. These concepts have already been addressed superficially in earlier chapters. Those brief references, however, were merely the preliminaries. Power and conflict are integral parts of the small group process that are inescapable in any human system. ● ●

Questions for Critical Thinkers

1. Why is majority rule so popular when consensus decision making, by comparison, is more advantageous?

2. Since a true consensus requires agreement, commitment, and satisfaction of group members, do you think groups are likely to achieve a true consensus, or is this mostly an ideal?

3. What are some drawbacks to the Standard Agenda approach to decision making? Explain your answer.

InfoTrac College Edition

Log onto InfoTrac College Edition.

1. Type "brainstorming" in the search window. Choose an article to critique. SUGGESTIONS: (a) Article A90384792, by Robert Barker, entitled "The art of brainstorming";

(b) Article A77385076, by Joy Colwell, entitled "Beyond brainstorming: How managers can cultivate creativity and creative problem-solving skills in employees"; and (c) Article A89648627, by Jeffrey Fleishman et al., entitled "Brainstorming questions: Asking questions is 'such a supremely human endeavor.' "

2. Type "consensus decision making" in the search window. Choose an article to critique. SUGGESTIONS: (a) Article A90357306, by Michael Polanyi, entitled "Communicative action in practice: Future search and the pursuit of an open, critical and non-coercive large-group process," and (b) Article A15237678, by Jeffrey Hornsby et al., entitled "The impact of decision-making methodology on job evaluation outcomes: A look at three consensus approaches."

Video Case Studies

*Apollo 13 (1995). PG; ****

This dramatization of the nearly disastrous Apollo 13 space mission to the moon illustrates creative problem solving. What creative problem-solving techniques are exhibited?

*O Brother Where Art Thou? (2000). PG-13; ****

Three convicts escape from a Depression-era chain gang. Their problem-solving knowledge and skills are severely deficient. Contrast the problem-solving mistakes of this small group of convicts with advice provided in this chapter on effective problem solving.

Power in Groups:
A Central Dynamic

"Power tends to corrupt, and absolute power corrupts absolutely," Lord Acton reputedly observed. This is a popular view. We are used to thinking of power as illegitimate or unpleasant, unless, perhaps, we are the person accorded the power. Then, as former Secretary of the Navy John Lehman once quipped, "Power corrupts. Absolute power is kind of neat."

The terms *power politics, seizure of power, power struggles, power brokers, power hungry, power mad, power play, high powered,* and *overpowered* reflect just some of the negative views most of us associate with this central element of human interaction. Being relatively powerlessness, however, is not a virtue. Perceptions of powerlessness can induce indifference toward group tasks, diminish task performance, foster member passivity and withdrawal, destroy group cohesiveness, strain personal relationships with group members, erode group members' self-esteem, and trigger destructive group conflict (Keltner et al., 2003; B. Lee, 1997).

Bennis and Nanus (1985) claim that power is "the quality without which leaders cannot lead" (p. 15), and it is a common notion to think of power as a force that only leaders exercise and followers wish they had. Nevertheless, power is not the exclusive prerogative of group leaders. Every group member exercises power in some capacity. Power is inherent in all small group transactions. **Power is unavoidable when we communicate in groups.** It is central to group decision making and problem solving, managing conflict, and evoking change. No group can achieve its goals without exercising some power. As Wilmot and Hocker (2001) explain, "One does not have the option of not using power. We only have options about whether to use power destructively or productively" (p. 104). **The primary purpose of this chapter is to explain how you can use power productively and constructively in the small group arena.** The following are three chapter objectives:

1. to define power, distinguishing its three types,
2. to identify various indicators of power and power resources, and
3. to address ways that power imbalances produce negative consequences in groups and how these imbalances can be addressed.

Power Defined

▶ **Focus Questions**

1. What does it mean to say that power is group-centered?
2. What are the primary forms of power?

Power *is the ability to influence the attainment of goals sought by yourself or others.* This is a general definition. Let me explain more specifically what power is and conversely what it is not.

THE NATURE OF POWER: NO ONE IS POWERLESS

First and foremost, **power is group-centered.** The power that you wield is dependent on the relationships you have with group members. Leaders, for instance, require the support of followers to remain in power. As president of the United States, Richard Nixon wielded immense power. The Watergate scandal, however, soured his relationship with the American public like a quart of milk in a desert sun. He was forced to resign his office in disgrace. Power did not reside in the persona of Richard Nixon. The American people granted him power. Conversely, Bill Clinton weathered the storm of impeachment in 1999 principally because 70% of the adult population in the United States approved of the job he was doing as president, even though his personal behavior with Monica Lewinsky may have disgusted them.

We often speak of powerful or powerless individuals as if the power distribution were all one way or the other. Is a child in a supermarket completely powerless against his or her parents when candy is the target? Have you ever witnessed a child whining, begging, and throwing a fit until exasperated parents capitulate and shove the candy into the child's grasping hands to silence the obnoxious din? The powerful–powerless dichotomy is not an accurate assessment of power distribution. **No group member is completely powerless.** The interconnectedness of components in a system means that all group members have some influence, even if it is to resist or to defy the group. What one member does or does not do influences other members.

If all group members have some degree of power, then a more accurate description of power distribution in a group should be phrased in terms of *degrees* of power. The relevant question then becomes "How much power does Person A exert relative to other members in that group?" rather than the false dichotomy "Is Person A powerful or powerless?"

FORMS OF POWER: COMPETITION AND COOPERATION REVISITED

There are three forms of power (Hollander & Offermann, 1990). **Dominance** or *power over* others flows from a hierarchical structure or from differences in status among group members. Dominance is competitive. My gain in power is your loss.

A second form of power is called **prevention** or *power from* the efforts of others to influence (e.g., we resist or defy leader dominance). When someone tries to dominate us, psychological reactance occurs. We try to prevent the dominance. This also is a competitive form of power. Here you're striving not to lose to dominators.

A third form of power is **empowerment**—enhancing the capabilities and influence of individuals and groups. Empowerment is *power to* accomplish your own goals or help others achieve theirs through processes of group potency, meaningfulness, autonomy, and impact, as discussed in Chapter 6. Empowerment is cooperative, not competitive. The group as a whole profits from all of its members gaining the ability to succeed together. For example, group members who improve their speaking skills for a class presentation benefit the entire group. One of the positive aspects of the situational leadership model discussed in Chapter 5 is the emphasis on empowerment rather than dominance. The leader role is not geared toward ordering underlings around and keeping followers in their place. Instead, **an effective leader actively seeks to increase the readiness levels of followers, thereby empowering them to accomplish tasks without the leader watching their every move.**

The three forms of power are substantially different from one another. Those who try to dominate see power as finite, as an *active* effort to advance personal goals at the expense of others. The power pie is only so large and cannot be expanded. Power, therefore, is seen as a struggle between the haves and have-nots. Those who try to prevent domination by fighting back see power as *reactive*. Power is seen in competitive win–lose terms by those who try to dominate and by those who try to prevent the domination. Those group members who try to empower see the power pie as expandable (see Figure 9.1). Resources can be acquired and shared. Integrative problem solving discussed in Chapter 8 is a practical example. Empowerment is *proactive*, meaning each group member takes positive action to assist himself or herself and others to attain goals cooperatively.

Those who harbor a negative concept of power are usually responding to dominance and its companion form—prevention. This may partly explain why women, historically dominated by men, are more inclined than men toward empowerment (Maroda, 2004). I would be naive to argue, however, that we can replace dominance with empowerment in all cases. Dominance will assuredly remain as the primary form of power in a competitive society. What can be hoped for is that empowerment will gain a wider audience and become more broadly applied.

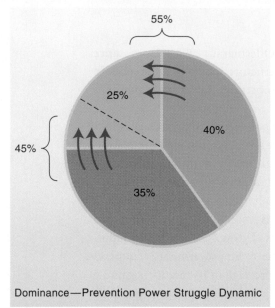

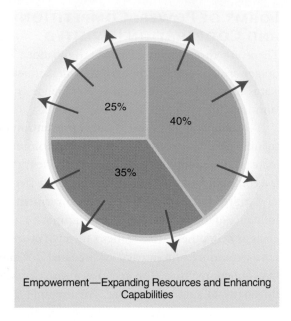

Dominance—Prevention Power Struggle Dynamic

Empowerment—Expanding Resources and Enhancing Capabilities

FIGURE 9.1
Dominance-prevention power struggles are based on seeing the power pie as a fixed, zero-sum contest.
Empowerment is based on seeing the power pie as expandable.
From *In the Company of Others,* Second Edition, by J. Dan Rothwell. © 2004 McGraw-Hill Companies, Inc.
Reprinted with permission of The McGraw-Hill Companies.

●●● SECOND LOOK

FORMS OF POWER

TYPE	DEFINITION	DESCRIPTION
Dominance	Power over	Active
Prevention	Power from	Reactive
Empowerment	Power to	Proactive

Indicators of Power

Power indicators are the ways in which relative degrees of power are communicated in groups. If you can spot power indicators, then you will see the presence of power dynamics and appreciate the importance of power in small groups. There are three main categories of power indicators: general, verbal, and nonverbal.

▶ Focus Questions

1. "Those who define others exercise control." What does this mean?
2. In what ways do male and female communication patterns differ in regard to verbal dominance?
3. What are the effects of "powerless" verbal and nonverbal communication patterns?

GENERAL INDICATORS: LABELING, FOLLOWING, AND OPPOSING

There are several general indicators of power in groups. First, **those who define others exercise control.** Ordinarily we define people by attaching a label to them. Teachers define students (e.g., smart; slow learner), physicians define patients (hypochondriac; unhealthy), psychiatrists define clients (schizophrenic), parents define children (sweet; incorrigible), and bosses define employees (good worker; loafer).

Whose decisions are followed is a second general indicator of power in a group. The individual with the position of authority in a group (chair, president) may not be the group member exercising the most power. Another group member respected more by the members may actually be calling the shots.

Who opposes significant change is a third general indicator of power. Those who have been accorded power by the group are usually uncomfortable with change that goes much beyond a little fine-tuning. Substantial change may risk altering the power relationships. The disaffected, who are also relatively powerless, clamor for substantial change as a general rule.

VERBAL INDICATORS: POWERLESS AND POWERFUL SPEECH

Power is reflected in the way we speak. The speech of a subordinate is often flooded with self-doubt, hesitancy, approval seeking, overqualification, and self-disparagement (Mulac & Bradac, 1995). Examples of speech patterns perceived to be relatively powerless include:

Hedges: "*Perhaps* the best way to proceed is . . ." "I'm a *little* concerned that this *might* cause problems."

Hesitations: "*Well, um,* the important thing to remember is *ah* . . ." "*Gosh, ah,* shouldn't we, *ah,* delay the decision?"

Tag Questions: "The meeting will be at noon, *okay?*" "This point seems redundant, *doesn't it?*"

Disclaimers: "This is *probably not very important,* because I *haven't thought it out much,* and you *probably already considered* it, and *you know best* anyway, but . . ."

Excessive Politeness: "I'm *extremely sorry* to barge in like this, *sir,* but . . ."

Powerless speech suggests uncertainty, indecisiveness, lack of confidence, vacillation, and deference to authority. Speech patterns perceived to be relatively powerful are generally direct, fluent, declarative, commanding, and prone to interrupting or overlapping other group members' speech (Pearson et al., 1991).

In general, group members who use more powerful language patterns are perceived to be more credible, attractive, and persuasive than those using less powerful language. These perceptions are particularly strong for computer-mediated

FOCUS ON GENDER/CULTURE

Powerful Language Differences

THERE ARE GENDER DIFFERENCES in verbal indicators of power. Men are typically more verbally dominant. Thus, they are more verbose, more given to long-winded verbal presentations, and more talkative in mixed-sex groups than are women (James & Drakich, 1993). Men are also more verbally aggressive than women (Nicotera & Rancer, 1994; Stewart et al., 1996), meaning they are more inclined to verbally attack the self-concepts of others.

Men are also more argumentative than women (Stewart et al., 1996), meaning men are more likely to advocate controversial positions during group discussions or to challenge the positions on issues taken by other group members. Women are inclined to view verbal aggressiveness and argumentativeness as strategies of dominance and control—a hostile, combative act (Nicotera & Rancer, 1994). Since men are more likely to seek status and women are more likely to seek connection in conversations (Tannen, 1990),

these gender differences in verbal indicators of power are not surprising.

Tavris (1992) argues, however, that the use of relatively powerless speech by women can be used to influence men. One study (Carli, 1990) supports this interpretation. Women were more inclined to use powerless speech patterns when conversing with men, but not with other women. Tag questions, hesitations, and the like seem to reassure men that women are not attempting to enhance their status. Thus, women pose no threat to male status in groups, so men are more likely to listen to non-threatening women. Does the strategy work? Apparently it does, because, paradoxically, women are more influential with men when using powerless speech. Other women, however, view powerless speech as annoying when it is used to influence them.

The issue of powerless versus powerful speech has interesting cultural complexities. The Japanese, for example, and most Asian cultures view our version of powerful speech as

groups (transactions conducted by e-mail or computer conferencing) primarily because language patterns become more influential in the absence of nonverbal cues (Adkins & Brashers, 1995). The consequences of using powerful or powerless speech can be seen from a study of student impressions of teachers (Haleta, 1996). Teachers created a positive impression by using powerful language that made them seem significantly more dynamic, credible, organized, professional, knowledgeable, and of higher status than teachers using powerless language. It is critical that teachers es-

immature because it indicates insensitivity to others and is likely to make agreement more difficult (Wetzel, 1988). In Malagasy society (Madagascar) "women have lower status than men but they use our stereotypical 'powerful' language; they do the confronting and reprimanding and in so doing . . . their constant violation of societal norms is seen as confirmation of their inferiority" (Smith-Hefner, 1988, p. 536). In Western societies, verbal obscenity and swearing are perceived as powerful language—an aggressive flouting of societal norms. Neither Japanese men nor women, however, use such language except in rare instances (De Klerk, 1991). In Malagasy and the Bhojpuri community in northeast India, "women are more abusive than men, and this . . . increases as we go down in the caste hierarchy" (Misra, 1980, p. 177).

When cultures clash over issues of significance, these different views of powerful and powerless speech can pose serious problems. When negotiating teams from Japan and the United States meet, misunderstandings easily arise (Hellweg et al., 1994). The language of Japanese negotiators is rife with indirect language viewed as powerless to American negotiators unfamiliar with cultural differences in perception. Japanese negotiators use such expressions as *I think, perhaps, probably,* and *maybe* with great frequency. They will also expect no interruptions while they speak. Americans negotiate in blunt terms, interrupt, and view indirect and qualifying language as signs of weakness and lack of resolve. Misunderstandings of this nature make negotiations difficult and decision making troublesome.

Questions for Thought

1. If the powerless speech used by some women influences men, doesn't that make the language powerful, not powerless?

2. Do you think there is a relationship between powerful–powerless speech patterns in a culture and the individualism–collectivism focus of the culture? Explain.

tablish a positive impression in the classroom. "Negative impressions may impede the learning process and contribute to a negative or hostile classroom climate. Conversely, a positive climate based on positive impressions may influence students' behavior to the extent that learning is enhanced" (p. 27).

Besides powerful language, **verbal dominance** is also indicated by competitive interrupting, contradicting, berating, and sheer quantity of speech. Monopolizing a conversation in these ways has obvious power implications. Those who dominate conversations during group meetings are able to get their point presented to members. Those who can't sandwich a word into the conversation are unable to articulate their point of view. More importantly, as previously discussed, those who talk the most are more likely to be perceived as leaders in groups.

Powerful speech is not always appropriate (see Focus on Gender/Culture: "Powerful Language Differences"). Abusive and obscene language may be perceived in our culture as powerful speech, but it can offend group members and can destroy the cohesiveness of the group. Sometimes deferential language is a sign of respect and not merely powerless speech. Even tag questions can sometimes be used powerfully. If the leader of a small group says, "You'll see that this is done, won't you?" this may be issued more as a directive than a request. Then the tag question is authoritative, not weak.

Nonverbal Indicators: Silent Power

There are many nonverbal indicators of power. Let me provide just a sample of the more important ones.

Space is the prerogative of the powerful. Dorothy Parker once noted, "He and I had an office so tiny that an inch smaller and it would have been adultery" (Fitzhenry, 1993, p. 296). The powerful get the best offices with the most space (Durand, 1977). Parents get the master bedroom while children get stacked vertically in bunk beds in a smaller bedroom. The prime parking spaces are reserved for the higher-status individuals. Lower-status individuals get to park in the next time zone, as students experience on college campuses across the nation. Allocation usually follows a pecking order. Private space is the prerogative of the powerful. Those individuals who are regarded as powerful may violate the space of those less powerful, but not vice versa. You must be granted access to the chambers of the privileged.

Posture and gestural communication are also markedly different for superordinates and subordinates. Generally, the powerful exhibit more relaxed, casual posture and gestures (Pavitt & Curtis, 1994). Subordinates can be directed to "sit up straight" or told to "stop slouching" by superordinates. Parents, for example, can tell children how to stand, sit, and move their bodies, but children do not have the same prerogative.

Touch clearly indicates power relationships in groups (Henley, 1995). Superordinates touch subordinates far more frequently than vice versa. The less powerful often feel required to yield to the touch of their superiors even when the touching triggers a gag reflex. Laws prohibiting sexual harassment have been established in the United States to protect the less powerful from the tactile abuse (among other inappropriate acts) of the more powerful. These statutes recognize that uneven power distribution plays a primary role in most cases of sexual harassment.

Space communicates power and influence.

Eye contact is yet another nonverbal indicator of relative degrees of power (Henley, 1995). Staring is done more freely by the powerful. The less powerful must monitor their eye contact more carefully. If a superordinate is speaking to a group of subordinates during a meeting, eye contact connotes active listening and deference to authority. Superordinates, however, may feel no obligation to exhibit interest or attentiveness to subordinates by maintaining eye contact. Lowering your eyes and looking down also indicates submissiveness.

Finally, **nonverbal symbols of power include a wide variety of objects and tangible materials:** large desks, plush carpets, office windows, leather chairs, master keys, company cars, computers, and the list could go on and on.

One study involving a personal injury lawsuit compared relatively powerful and powerless nonverbal communication (M. Lee & Ofshe, 1981). When a speaker exhibited powerful nonverbal communication while *arguing for a reduction* in the damage award, subjects reduced the award by an average of $4,273. When the speaker exhibited powerless nonverbal behaviors, however, subjects *increased* the award an average of $2,843.

Much more could be added here regarding nonverbal indicators of power, but the point has been made. You can discern the relative distribution of power in a group by observing both verbal and nonverbal indicators and noticing a few general communication patterns.

Power Resources

When transacting power in groups, members utilize power resources. A **power resource** is "anything that enables individuals to move toward their own goals or interfere with another's actions" (Folger et al., 1993, p. 100). There are five primary

▶ ● ● **SECOND LOOK**

INDICATORS OF POWER

GENERAL INDICATORS

Who defines whom

Whose decisions are followed

Who opposes significant change

NONVERBAL INDICATORS

Space

Posture and gestural communication

Touch

Eye contact

Objects and tangible materials

VERBAL INDICATORS

Powerless/powerful language

Verbal dominance

power resources relevant to group situations: information, expertise, punishments and rewards, personal qualities, and legitimate authority. These resources closely parallel French and Raven's (1959) classic types of power in groups.

▶ **Focus Questions**

1. Information is power, but is all information power?

2. For expertise to serve as a power resource, must the expert always avoid errors?

3. What are the primary drawbacks of punishment and rewards as power resources?

4. How does authority become legitimate?

INFORMATION: RESTRICTED OR SCARCE

Unquestionably, information is power. In an age of information, how could it be otherwise? Not all information, however, serves as a source of power. **Information assumes value or usefulness when it is perceived to be unavailable.** If information is readily available to everyone, it has no power potential. Consultants can charge thousands of dollars to groups and organizations because they have information not readily available to members of the group. Who would bother to hire a consultant if that individual merely reiterated what everyone in the group already knew?

Information becomes unavailable primarily from *restrictions* and *scarcity* (Brock, 1968). In this era of information overload, restricted or scarce information is the exception, not the rule. Thus, when information is restricted or scarce, whatever is available seems terribly important.

For example, a young woman in my small group communication class told her project group that she could get a highly technical, information-rich report on the subject chosen for the class project. The information from this report, so she claimed, was unavailable anywhere else, but she could get the report from her father, who had access to it. Her group members were thrilled. Her prestige and influence in the group immediately soared. Unfortunately, she never produced the report, and 2 weeks after she offered to obtain the report, she dropped the class. Unavailable information has power potential, but only if it's not too scarce, so you can actually produce it.

The competent communicator can capitalize on information as a power resource as follows:

1. *Provide useful but scarce or restricted information to the group.* Careful, diligent research often produces valuable information relevant to the group task. If this information is unknown to other group members, it then assumes a power potential by increasing your prestige and influence in group decision making.
2. *Be certain information is accurate.* Sharing misinformation could earn you the enmity of group members. Misinformation could easily lead to collective inferential error, a prime cause of faulty decision making.

Expertise: Knowing and Showing

Information and expertise are closely related, but not identical. A group member can possess critical information without being an expert. You can download a hard drive full of data for your group, but if you don't know how to decipher the data, you need someone who does (an expert). **Experts** not only have valuable and useful information for a group, but they also understand the information and know how to use it to help the group. An expert can give knowledgeable advice (Franz & Larson, 2002).

The twin problems of information overload and rapid change mean that no individual or group could ever hope to function effectively without requiring the services of experts at some point. What academic department is not dependent on the expert who saves faculty members from exploding blood vessels in their brains by solving hyper-stressful computer problems? What board of directors has never needed the advice of an attorney? Even our families require plumbers, financial advisors, roofers, exterminators, counselors, mechanics, and experts who repair our broken appliances and broken hearts.

For expertise to function as a power resource, a minimum of two conditions must be met. First, **the group must be convinced that the person has the requisite skills, abilities, knowledge, and background to function as a real expert.** Experts must demonstrate a mastery of relevant information and exhibit skill using it. When judging a group member's expertise, men and women are not viewed through the same lens. Men more than women are encouraged by groups to contribute their expertise, partly because group members, both males and females, don't initially think

© John Neubauer/Photo Edit

We have a love–hate relationship with experts, requiring their help but often resenting their power. Lawyers are among our favorite experts to deride (e.g., How can you tell the difference between a dead lawyer and a dead snake in the road? There are skid marks in front of the snake).

of women as experts (Propp, 1995). As a result, male experts are more influential than female experts (Littlepage & Mueller, 1997). Group members, however, are more likely to accept females as experts when women talk frequently and knowledgeably (Littlepage & Mueller, 1997). Once the group accepts the expertise of an individual of either sex, members are strongly influenced by the expert to accept recommendations that even contradict members' initial points of view (Foschi et al., 1985).

Second, **the person who has been accorded status as an expert must demonstrate trustworthiness.** Power is not derived from expertise if the group suspects that the expert will lie for personal gain or self-protection. People the world over are more influenced by experts who stand to gain nothing personally than they are by experts who would gain substantially by lying or offering poor advice (McGuinnies & Ward, 1980).

There are some interesting intercultural differences related to power and expertise. Although expertise is an important consideration for Americans in choosing individuals for negotiating teams, status is more important than expertise to the French, British, Chinese, Japanese, and Saudi Arabians (Hellweg et al., 1994). How expertise is perceived also varies from culture to culture. In the United States, an individual with exceptional expertise in one field might be perceived as irrelevant when the group discusses issues unrelated to that person's specialization. In Africa, however, opinion leaders are respected and valued as experts over a broader range of topics for which they have no special technical knowledge (Dodd, 1995). Expertise is in the eye of the beholder.

Assuming that a group member has special knowledge, skills, or abilities useful to the group, he or she could capitalize on the power potential of expertise as follows:

1. *Maintain skills, abilities, and knowledge currency.* You're only an expert for as long as the group perceives you as such. Let your knowledge grow out-of-date or your skills and abilities diminish and the group will quickly see you as yesteryear's expert—a relic.

2. *Demonstrate trustworthiness and credibility.* You should exhibit a We-not-Me orientation. Your expertise should be used to benefit the group, not merely bring personal advantages to yourself. Even when a group hires an expert from outside, the group expects that the lawyer, accountant, consultant, or whoever will show commitment to helping the group gain its goals, not simply make a buck for himself or herself.

3. *Be certain of your facts before advising the group.* Bad advice is like misinformation. The results can be disastrous for the group. Advice should be based on the best available information. An occasional error may not tarnish your credibility as an expert. Relatively frequent or serious errors will.

4. *Don't assume an air of superiority.* Putting on an air of superiority will trigger defensiveness among group members. Remember that an egotist is someone who "thinks no one can hold a candle to him, although a lot of people would like to" (Perret, 1994).

REWARDS AND PUNISHMENTS: CARROTS AND STICKS

Parceling out rewards or meting out punishment can be an important source of power. Salaries, bonuses, work schedules, perks, hirings, and firings are typical job-related rewards and punishments. Money, privacy, car keys, and grounding are a few of the rewards and punishments found in family situations. Social approval or disapproval, performance awards, suspension, and expulsion are a few of the rewards and punishments available to educators when dealing with students.

Punishment is a source of power if it can be and likely will be exercised. If employees are protected from termination by civil service regulations or tenure, threatening to fire them is laughable. Threats of punishment, however, seem to be more effective when we perceive that the chances of punishment are highly probable (Wooton, 1993).

There are serious drawbacks to using punishment to influence group members, however (Kassin, 1998; Uba & Huang, 1999). First, punishment indicates what you *should not do* but it doesn't indicate what you *should do*. Firing a worker doesn't teach that person how to perform better in the future. Second, targets of punishment can become angry and hostile toward their perceived tormenters. If the punishment is perceived to be unfair or excessive, a backlash can easily occur from other group members. Third, punishment can produce a negative ripple effect throughout the group. If the punishment doesn't achieve the desired effect, other group members may be encouraged to engage in similar deviance. Issues of fairness and just cause may surface and escalate into ugly conflicts, spreading tension and creating a competitive group climate. The sign found in workplaces stating that "The beatings will continue until morale improves" expresses ironically the difficulty of using punishment to produce positive results in groups.

Rewards, viewed as the opposite of punishment, seem as though they would produce only positive results for groups. Everyone likes to be rewarded, so surely this is a powerful resource for influencing group members. A reward can be an effective power resource. Rewards, however, should be used carefully.

Consider the story of an old man who was besieged daily by a group of 10-year-old boys hurling insults at him as they passed his house on their way home from school. One day, after enduring the boys' abusive remarks about how stupid, bald, and ugly he was, he decided on a plan to deal with the little troublemakers. On the following day, he approached the boys and told them that anyone who came the next day and shouted insults at him would receive a dollar. Dumbfounded, the boys left and returned the next afternoon to scream epithets at the old man. He gave each boy a dollar. He then told them that he would pay each boy 50 cents if they returned the next day and repeated their rude behavior. They returned, shouted insults, and were paid. The old man then said that he would pay them only a dime if they returned the next day and repeated their ugly behavior. At this point, the boys said, "Forget it. It isn't worth it." They never returned.

This story illustrates how **an extrinsic reward can diminish intrinsic motivation to behave in certain ways.** An **extrinsic reward** motivates us to behave or perform by offering us an external inducement such as money, grades, praise, recognition, or prestige. An **intrinsic reward** is enjoying what one does for its own sake (Kohn, 1993). An intrinsic reward motivates us to continue doing what brings us pleasure. The boys initially were intrinsically motivated by perverse pleasure in tormenting the old man. When paid to continue the torment, it became more like a job. Once the pay became minimal, the job seemed pointless and they quit. "Work sucks, but I need the bucks" is a bumper sticker that expresses the common effect an extrinsic reward such as money can have on our interest in and enjoyment of work.

Work teams are likely to perform well when members are intrinsically motivated by commitment to a shared goal, a desire to "change the world," or a keen interest in the task. Teams that are held together only by the extrinsic rewards of money, recognition, or prestige are not as likely to be effective. As a survey of 500 professionals found, "95% agreed that pay and benefits were not the main motivation in their decision whether or not to stay with a job. The key issue was the ability to develop trusting relationships with upper management" (Shilling, 2000). The intrinsic reward derived from good relationships and a trusting group climate outweighs the extrinsic reward of money and benefits.

Does use of extrinsic rewards always produce negative results, as some have argued (Kohn, 1993)? The answer is no. Verbal praise (extrinsic reward), as long as it is not offered as an obvious manipulative strategy to control group members' behavior, can actually *increase* intrinsic motivation (Carton, 1996; Eisenberger & Cameron, 1996). Also, it depends on how recipients perceive the extrinsic reward. If they perceive it as a treat, it can increase intrinsic motivation to perform, but if they perceive it as pressure to perform and be creative, it can decrease their intrinsic interest and motivation to perform (Eisenberger & Armeli, 1997).

Competent communicators use punishment and rewards carefully. Here are some guidelines:

1. *Punishment should be a last resort.* Punishment as a power resource must be exercised with caution and discretion. Because it can produce serious negative consequences, it should be employed rarely and then only when efforts to change group members' behavior by noncoercive means have failed.
2. *Punishment should be appropriate to the act.* Anemic punishment for seriously flawed, irresponsible performance or severe punishment for relatively inconsequential error is out of proportion to the act. In the former instance, group members will likely ridicule the ineffectual action, and in the latter instance, group members will likely rebel against the severity of the sanction.
3. *Punishment should be swift and certain.* The more disconnected punishment becomes from an objectionable act because of delays or uncertainty that punishment will occur, the more ineffectual it becomes. Idle threats are pointless. Inconsistent punishment will foster inconsistent compliance from members.
4. *Be generous with praise that is warranted.* Praise recognizes accomplishment, nurtures a positive group climate, and can increase intrinsic motivation unless it is obviously manipulative.
5. *Determine what rewards group members value before offering any.* A $1,000 bonus may motivate a poor person, but Bill Gates would likely view it as pocket change. Extrinsic rewards diminish intrinsic motivation when group members are already interested in and committed to the task. They do not diminish

intrinsic motivation, however, when group members are not initially interested in a task or they feel inadequate (Uba & Huang, 1999). Thus, money, awards, recognition, and the like may be effective extrinsic rewards in circumstances where group members aren't initially motivated intrinsically to accomplish a task effectively if group members value the rewards.

6. *Administer both punishments and rewards equitably and fairly.* Perceived favoritism in receiving rewards creates a competitive group climate.

PERSONAL QUALITIES: A POWERFUL PRESENCE

We all know individuals who exert some influence over us, not because of any of the previous power resources already discussed, but because of attractive personal qualities they seem to possess in abundance. We are more likely to be influenced by those individuals whom we find attractive than by those we don't.

Communication researchers have known for some time that physical attractiveness, expertise and mastery of certain persuasive and communication skills, dynamism, trustworthiness, reliability, similarity of values and outlook, and identification with the group all contribute to an individual's ability to influence others. Some or all of these qualities contribute to charisma. Some people have a great deal of charisma, and others have less charisma than driftwood.

Any group member can be charismatic. Charisma, however, is not determined objectively. Groups decide what is attractive and what is not. Mention charisma and historically John Kennedy becomes the political standard for comparison. When John and Jacqueline Kennedy visited Paris in 1962 as president and first lady, however, they made a lasting impression, but Jacqueline more than John. Jacqueline, with her combination of beauty, poise, grace, and ability to speak French, charmed President Charles de Gaulle and the people of France. She stole the spotlight from her normally charismatic husband who, as president, characteristically commanded center stage. Jacqueline's impact on the French was so complete that when the couple departed, John Kennedy held a press conference (a rare moment when he became the center of attention). In typical witty fashion and recognizing the irony of his wife upstaging the president of the United States, he began, "I do not think it is altogether inappropriate to introduce myself to this audience. I am the man who accompanied Jacqueline Kennedy to Paris, and I have enjoyed it" (Fadiman, 1985, p. 328). Jacqueline Kennedy exercised little tangible power, but she displayed a powerful presence because of her personal qualities.

Learning to be charismatic is difficult, perhaps fruitless for some. Nevertheless, charismatic leaders typically exhibit extraordinary communication skills (M. Hackman & Johnson, 2004). Developing communication competence certainly can improve one's charismatic potential.

AFP/Getty Images

Who has the charisma, Bill Gates or professional wrestler/"actor" Dwayne "The Rock" Johnson? On what do you base your answer?

LEGITIMATE AUTHORITY: YOU WILL OBEY

We all play roles, but some of us exercise greater influence in groups because of our acknowledged position or title. Power can be derived from the shared belief that some individuals have a legitimate right to influence us and direct our behavior by virtue of the roles that they play. Society grants parents legitimate authority. In addition to other power resources they have at their disposal, parents are supposed to be accorded respect and deference simply because they are parents. We believe parents have the right to discipline their children and to expect obedience. Similarly, teachers and supervisors at work occupy an authority position considered legitimate by most groups.

Obedience to legitimate authority is intricately woven into the fabric of our society. We learn about the virtues of obedience to authority figures in school, at work, in church, in courtrooms, and in military barracks. The result is a mental set lasered into our brains: OBEY LEGITIMATE AUTHORITY (see Closer Look: "The Milgram Studies").

To have power potential, authority must be viewed as legitimate. We are not inclined to comply with directives from those individuals acting authoritatively but who are not deemed legitimate. Group members must grant legitimacy before authority will have any weight. One study (Read, 1974) revealed that how the leader becomes an authority figure could be a decisive issue. Leaders who usurp authority are not granted legitimacy by the group. Thus, they have less influence than

CLOSER LOOK

THE MILGRAM STUDIES

AN AMAZING SERIES of studies conducted by Stanley Milgram (1974) in the 1960s lends substantial support to the fear that as a society we have thoroughly absorbed the lesson of obedience to legitimate authority. The basic design of the obedience to authority studies by Milgram consisted of a naive subject who acted as "teacher" and a confederate who acted as "student." The naive subjects were told that the purpose of the experiment was to determine the effects of punishment on memory. Punishment consisted of electric shocks. The electric shocks were administered to the student for every wrong answer on a word association test. Shocks began at 15 volts and increased by 15-volt increments up to a maximum of 450 volts for each wrong answer from the victim. The experimenter directed the subjects to administer the increasingly intense shocks for every wrong answer even when the subjects objected. The experimenter served as legitimate authority in each of Milgram's experiments.

Almost two-thirds of the subjects progressed to 450 volts and delivered the maximum shock until they were instructed to stop by the experimenter. Subjects continued to administer the shocks even when they could hear the victim's screams of pain and agony. (The victim's anguish was cleverly faked: no electric shocks were actually delivered, but all except an insignificant few of the subjects perceived the punishment to be real.)

In one of the experiments, the victim complained of a heart condition exacerbated by the shocks. Nevertheless, 26 of the 40 subjects administered the maximum shocks at the direction of the experimenter. In all, Milgram conducted 18 variations of the obedience to authority study. More than 1,000 subjects from a wide range of ages and walks of life participated. Others replicated his experiments in America and abroad with similar results (A. G. Miller, 1986).

One of the more dramatic replications was conducted by Sheridan and King (1972). In this experiment, the victim was a cute, fluffy puppy dog, not a human confederate. Although the victim in Milgram's studies appeared to be, but was never actually, shocked, Sheridan and King had the subjects actually shock the helpless puppy.

Despite the disbelief commonly expressed by my students that anyone would continue to shock an adorable, helpless puppy held captive in a box whose floor was an electrified grid from which there was no escape, the results of the experiment contradict conventional wisdom. **Three-quarters of the subjects,** *all college students,* **were obedient to the end** (54% of the men and 100% of the women). At the behest of the experimenter, they delivered the maximum-intensity shock to the cute puppy dog whose pain they could witness directly. They complained, some female subjects even wept, but they obeyed.

In a more recent replication, subjects were ordered to disturb and make nervous an applicant taking a test for an important job (Meeus & Raaijmakers, 1986). Obeying the authority's order to be

▶

Patricia Doyle/Getty Images

Would you administer 450-volt shocks to this cute puppy? In one experiment 100% of the women and 54% of the men did just that to a puppy.

disruptive caused the applicant to fail the test and remain unemployed. More than 90% of the subjects obeyed the orders, although they considered their actions unfair and troubling. Subjects obeyed not because they were evil or sadistic, but because they couldn't defy legitimate authority.

During a 23-year period, the 18 obedience studies by Milgram and 15 replications in a half-dozen countries have revealed a remarkably consistent pattern (Blass, 2000). Levels of obedience appear unaffected by time period (1960s, 1970s, or 1980s), place, or "contemporary" attitudes toward legitimate authority. There is little reason to believe that today levels of obedience to legitimate authority would be lower than in previous decades (Blass, 2000).

Group members, however, do not have to be the pawns of legitimate authority. In fact, if group members are vigilant and challenge authorities when unethical or destructive decisions are ordered, they can withstand the authority's power. One study (Gamson et al., 1982) found that when group members discussed their misgivings about what a legitimate authority told them to do, most defied the authority figure. One advantage of groups is that there is strength in numbers. Group discussion, however, is a critical factor in defiance. Group members must share concerns about what authorities tell them to do, so individual members realize that they are not alone in their dissension.

Questions for Thought

1. Are the Milgram studies and their replications ethical research? Explain by using the five standards of ethical communication discussed in Chapter 1.
2. Do you think you would have refused to obey the experimenter in these studies? If yes, explain what makes you different from the majority of subjects.
3. Would the results of the Milgram studies have been the same if a woman had been the authority figure? If a woman had been the victim? If a child had been the victim?
4. In Sheridan and King's (puppy dog as victim) replication of the Milgram studies, 100% of the female subjects but 54% of the male subjects obeyed. Why the difference in results? Do you think women are more inclined to obey legitimate authority?

appointed or elected group leaders. Groups whose leaders have a weak basis of legitimacy (e.g., randomly appointed leaders) exhibit inferior performance compared to groups whose leaders have a strong basis of legitimacy (e.g., leaders appointed for their competence or elected by the membership) (Hollander, 1985).

The sad, sorry lot of inexperienced substitute teachers illustrates the problem of authority without legitimacy. Teachers are authority figures in a school environment, but substitute teachers must struggle to establish legitimacy in students' eyes. They must combat the strong impression that as a substitute, they are not "real teachers."

Although the results from the Milgram studies (see Closer Look) and subsequent replications by other researchers are disturbing, defiance of all authority is as empty-headed as consistent compliance. What kind of society would you live in if few people obeyed police, teachers, parents, judges, bosses, or physicians? There are solid reasons why you should obey legitimate authorities in most circumstances. **The answer to the excessive influence of legitimate authority rests with your ability to discriminate between appropriate and inappropriate use of authority, not the exercise of indiscriminate rebellion against all authority.**

Those who aspire to be competent communicators while capitalizing on legitimate authority as a power resource can try the following:

1. *Become an authority figure.* There are two principal sources of authority: appointed (designated) leader and emergent leader (Forsyth, 1990). Becoming either grants you authority. Emergent leader has already been discussed in Chapter 5. Appointed leader occurs because you gain favor of a powerful person, earn the right to be appointed (e.g., by seniority), or are the only group member willing to accept the appointment.

2. *Gain legitimacy.* Legitimacy comes from conforming to accepted principles, rules, and standards of the group. Authority that is imposed on the group (leader appointed from outside the group) usually has problems of legitimacy because the group resents nonparticipation in making the appointment. Authority that springs from the group (e.g., being voted by membership to represent the group in bargaining talks or earning it by demonstrating competence) has a solid base of legitimacy.

3. *Encourage participative decision making.* Keeping in mind the qualifiers attached to participative decision making discussed in the preceding chapter if you are in a position of authority, encouraging participative decision making can help maintain the legitimacy of your authority by retaining the goodwill of group members.

4. *Act ethically.* The abuses of legitimate authority are the product of unethical practices. Honesty, respect, fairness, choice, and responsibility should guide legitimate authorities whenever they use their power in groups.

► ●● SECOND LOOK

COMPETENT COMMUNICATOR'S GUIDE TO POWER RESOURCES

POWER RESOURCE	COMMUNICATION GUIDELINES
Information Power	Provide group scarce but useful information
	Be certain information is accurate
Expertise	Maintain knowledge currency
	Demonstrate trustworthiness and credibility
	Be certain of your facts before advising
	Don't assume air of superiority
Rewards/Punishments	Punishments should be a last resort
	Punishment should be appropriate to the act
	Punishment should be swift and certain
	Be generous with praise that is warranted
	Determine what rewards group members value before offering any
	Administer both punishment and reward equitably and fairly
Personal Qualities	Groups specify qualities that are preferred
Legitimate Authority	Become an authority figure
	Gain legitimacy
	Encourage participative decision making
	Act ethically

In summary, power resources are not properties of individuals. A person does not possess power, but is granted power by the group through transactions with members. As such, the group must endorse the resource for it to be influential (Folger et al., 1993). Group endorsement usually depends on whether the resource meets a need of the group. Will the group find this resource valuable and significant? Will it assist the group in attaining an important goal?

Effects of Power Imbalances

When power is inequitably distributed in a group and dominance becomes the focus, systemwide power struggles often ensue (Wilmot & Hocker, 2001). With these power struggles come aggression and contempt.

▶ **Focus Questions**

1. How are power imbalances and violence related?

2. "Dominance breeds conflict." What does this mean?

PHYSICAL VIOLENCE AND AGGRESSION: WAGING POWER STRUGGLES

Significant power disparities often foster violent or aggressive transactions. Gelles and Straus (1988) in their extensive study of family violence conclude: "The greater the inequality, the more one person makes all the decisions and has all the power, the greater the risk of violence. Power, power confrontations, and perceived threats to domination, in fact, are underlying issues in almost all acts of family violence" (p. 82). In families and marriages in which the husband insists on being the dominant decision maker, breakup of the marriage and family or persistent unhappiness experienced by all parties is *four times more likely* than in families in which the husband shares power (Gottman & Silver, 1999).

Violence easily spills beyond the husband–wife relationship and becomes a systemwide problem. The anger and frustration a victim of violence feels often becomes displaced when the victim attacks innocent, less powerful targets. "It is not unusual to find a pattern of violence in a home where the husband hits his wife, the wife in turn uses violence toward her children, the older children use violence on the younger children, and the youngest child takes out his or her frustration on the family pet. . . . At each level the most powerful person is seeking to control the next least powerful person" (Gelles & Straus, 1988, p. 35).

When people exercise power over us, destructive conflict often results. In the workplace, nasty conflicts are a serious problem. The United States has the highest rate of homicide in the workplace of any industrialized nation, averaging more than 1,000 homicides each year ("Survey," 1998). Many of these homicides are the direct result of firings or attempted firings of workers by supervisors or teams. According to a report by the U.S. Justice Department, almost 2 million people each year are victims of violence on the job (Lardner, 1998). Too often we "settle" our power struggles at work with aggression. "Workplace bullying" is also an increasing problem. **Workplace bullying** "is a persistent form of badgering, abuse, and 'hammering away' at targets" who have less power than their bullies (Lutgen-Sandvik et al., 2005). In the United States, almost a third of workers studied have experienced workplace bullying (Lutgen-Sandvik, 2005). Although a troublesome problem in the United States, workplace bullying is even worse in other countries. An International Labor Organization survey conducted in 1998 in 32 countries found that workplace bullying is one of the fastest-growing areas of workplace aggression in these countries ("Survey," 1998). In Britain, 58% of the workers surveyed reported being victims of workplace bullying. In Japan, the problem is so bad that a "bullying hotline" has been established to assist harassed workers ("Survey," 1998). Dominance breeds conflict.

VERBAL AND NONVERBAL CONTEMPT: INSULTING OTHERS

Power struggles in families and groups do not always end in physical violence. In fact, a more likely initial consequence of power imbalance in groups is verbal and nonverbal expressions of contempt. Coaches of teams, for example, may simply tear apart the self-esteem and self-worth of players. Team leaders in the workplace may berate less powerful team members.

Contempt is the verbal or nonverbal expression of insult that emotionally abuses others. It is a potent form of verbal aggression. Contempt is not merely criticism (Gottman, 1994). It is more destructive than criticism because it seeks to humiliate, even destroy, whoever is targeted. Name-calling ("stupid," "fool," "idiot," "incompetent"), cursing, hostile humor (jokes that hurt and ridicule others), vicious sarcasm, and insulting body language (rolling your eyes, curling your upper lip in a sneer, shaking your head side-to-side while laughing snidely) are types of contempt.

Power imbalances easily create a climate that encourages physical, verbal, and nonverbal aggression (see Focus on Culture: "Power Distance and Cultural Differences" for a different twist). Both aggressors and victims engage in such negative behavior in a dominance–prevention power struggle. A more equitable sharing of power is a primary preventive of such competitive ugliness in groups.

Addressing Power Imbalances

Transacting power in groups can involve any of five general responses. These responses are Compliance, Alliance, Resistance, Defiance, and Significance (**C-A-R-D-S**). **The last four alternatives are the ways less powerful members attempt to balance the power in groups.** In this section the pros and cons of each alternative for balancing power are addressed.

▷ **Focus Questions**

1. How are obedience and conformity similar to and different from each other?
2. What are the disadvantages of forming alliances?
3. Since resistance strategies rely on deceit and mixed messages, should competent communicators always avoid them?
4. Why are defiant members a threat to the group?
5. In what ways do aggressiveness and assertiveness differ?

Power Distance and Cultural Differences

IN THE UNITED STATES, power imbalances are often the catalyst for aggressive behavior. The responses to power imbalances in some cultures, however, are strikingly different from our own. Cultures vary in their attitudes concerning the appropriateness of power imbalances. Hofstede (2001) terms these variations the power distance dimension (herein referred to simply as PD).

Countries that are culturally classified as low-PD (relatively weak emphasis on maintaining power differences), such as the United States, Sweden, Denmark, Israel, and Austria, are guided by norms and institutional regulations that minimize power distinctions among group members and between groups. Challenging authority (not easy in any culture, as the Milgram studies demonstrate), flattening organizational hierarchies, and using power legitimately are subscribed to by low-PD cultures. Low-PD cultures do not advocate eliminating power disparities entirely, and in a country such as the United States, power differences obviously exist. The emphasis on maintaining hierarchical boundaries between the relatively powerful and the powerless, however, are de-emphasized in low-PD cultures. Workers in low-PD cultures may disagree with their supervisors; in fact, disagreement may be encouraged by bosses. Even socializing outside of the work environment and communication on a first-name basis between workers and bosses is not unusual (Brislin, 1993).

Countries culturally classified as high-PD (relatively strong emphasis on maintaining power differences), such as the Philippines, Mexico, India, Singapore, and Hong Kong, are guided by norms and institutional regulations that accept, even cultivate, power distinctions. The actions of authorities are rarely challenged, the powerful are thought to have a legitimate right to use their power, and organizational and social hierarchies are encouraged (Lustig & Koester, 2003). Workers normally do not feel comfortable disagreeing with their bosses, and friendships and socializing between the two groups are rare.

The reactions by members to power imbalances in small groups are likely to reflect where a culture falls on the power distance dimension. One study (M. Bond et al., 1985) compared people's reactions to insults in a high-PD (Hong Kong) and a low-PD (United States) culture. Subjects from Hong Kong were less upset than those from the United States when they were insulted, as long as the initiator of the insult was a high-status person. As Brislin (1993) explains, "When people accept status distinctions as normal, they accept the fact that the powerful are different than the less powerful. The powerful can engage in behaviors that the less powerful cannot, in this case insult people and have the insult accepted as part of their rights" (p. 225).

Differences in power distance do not mean that high-PD cultures never experience conflict

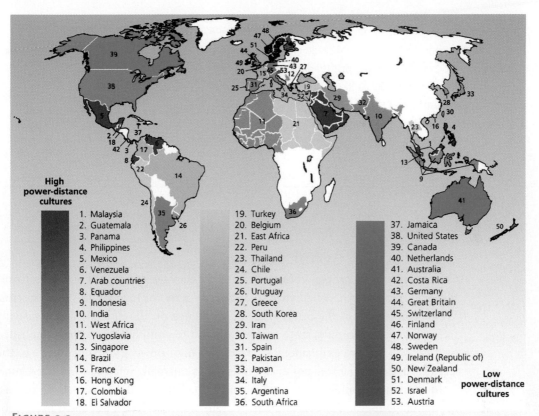

FIGURE 9.2
From *In the Company of Others,* Second Edition, by J. Dan Rothwell. © 2004 McGraw-Hill Companies, Inc. Reprinted with permission of The McGraw-Hill Companies.

High power-distance cultures

1. Malaysia
2. Guatemala
3. Panama
4. Philippines
5. Mexico
6. Venezuela
7. Arab countries
8. Equador
9. Indonesia
10. India
11. West Africa
12. Yugoslavia
13. Singapore
14. Brazil
15. France
16. Hong Kong
17. Colombia
18. El Salvador

19. Turkey
20. Belgium
21. East Africa
22. Peru
23. Thailand
24. Chile
25. Portugal
26. Uruguay
27. Greece
28. South Korea
29. Iran
30. Taiwan
31. Spain
32. Pakistan
33. Japan
34. Italy
35. Argentina
36. South Africa

37. Jamaica
38. United States
39. Canada
40. Netherlands
41. Australia
42. Costa Rica
43. Germany
44. Great Britain
45. Switzerland
46. Finland
47. Norway
48. Sweden
49. Ireland (Republic of)
50. New Zealand
51. Denmark
52. Israel
53. Austria

Low power-distance cultures

and aggression in small groups emanating from power imbalances. Members of low-PD cultures, however, are more likely to respond with frustration, outrage, and hostility to power imbalances than are members of high-PD cultures because low-PD cultures value power balance even though the experience of everyday life in such cultures may reflect a somewhat different reality. In a low-PD culture, the struggle to achieve the ideal of balanced power in small groups is more compelling and the denial of power is likely to be perceived as more unjust, even intolerable, than in a high-PD culture where power balance is not viewed from the same vantage point.

Questions for Thought

1. Is it merely ethnocentric bias ("My culture is better than your culture") that Americans typically regard power balance as preferable to power imbalance?

2. Which leadership style would likely be preferred in high-PD cultures, directive or participative? How about low-PD cultures? Explain.

3. If you were an exchange student in a high-PD culture, would you have difficulty adjusting to the "Don't challenge your teachers" norm in the high-PD culture?

COMPLIANCE: GROUP POWER

Compliance is the process of consenting to the dictates and desires of others. **Compliance involves both obedience to authority and conformity to group norms.** When compliance is the result of group influence on the individual, it is usually referred to as conformity, since we are expected to comply with norms established by the group. When compliance is the result of a high-power group member (e.g., the leader) influencing lower-power members, it is normally referred to as obedience.

In one study, conformity is pitted against obedience to determine which is most influential (Milgram, 1974). Two confederates administered a test and a naive subject administered punishment (increasing levels of electric shock) for incorrect answers. At the 150-volt shock level, one of the confederates refused to continue taking part in the experiment. At 210 volts, the second confederate bailed out of the experiment. With two defectors for support, 90% of the naive subjects refused to comply with the experimenter's command to increase the shocks all the way to 450 volts. Most of the 40 naive subjects, 60%, stopped at 210 volts or less. Yet in a comparison study where the naive subject faced the experimenter alone, only 35% refused to comply with the experimenter's command and refusal never occurred before 300 volts. **Conformity to group norms can sometimes prove to be a more powerful tendency than obeying authority.** The defectors created a group norm that opposed shocking a victim against his will. Most subjects complied with the norm instead of following the authority figure's insistent directives. This punctuates the power of groups to withstand the unethical or wrong-headed directives of a powerful group leader or member. There is strength in numbers. Garnering allies to defy the orders of a group leader can be an effective strategy.

ALLIANCE: COALITION FORMATION

Alliances are associations in the form of subgroups entered into for mutual benefit or a common objective. Groups normally splinter into subgroups when there is a disagreement concerning how best to achieve a group goal. In most circumstances, alliances in groups are temporary. They are expedient unions between two or more group members primarily to increase the influence of specific individuals in matters of mutual importance. These temporary alliances are called **coalitions.**

Power is central to coalition formation (Grusky et al., 1995). Group members form coalitions to increase their power and thus control decisions made in the group when group members don't agree on issues of significance to the group.

Coalitions must be negotiated among group members. Sometimes we form coalitions based more on interpersonal attraction or revulsion for members than we do on more objective determinations of personal rewards, attitudinal similarity, or power potential. Incompetent communication can dampen enthusiasm for the development of any alliance. Skillful, competent communication, however, can enhance the probabilities that a coalition will form even in unlikely circumstances.

Because coalitions can change the distribution of power in a group, coalition formation is typically adversarial, competitive, and contentious. Coalitions are formed not simply to advance the goals of the allied members (e.g., choosing the preferred topic or option for a group project), but also to prevent the attainment of noncoalition members' goals (e.g., choosing an objectionable topic or option for a group topic). Consequently, powerful members often move to stymie formation of coalitions among weaker members. This can be accomplished by forming their own coalitions with weaker parties or by confusing issues and arousing discontent in the ranks of the weak, thus splintering potential allies.

Coalitions may be useful in the political realm and sometimes coalitions help less powerful group members influence group decisions and prevent unethical or disastrous decisions ordered by the group leader, but they can pose problems for groups. In families, parental coalitions may be necessary to present a united front when a dispute with children occurs. Parent–child coalitions (e.g., father–son vs. mother–daughter), however, can disrupt the family system (Rosenthal, 1997). Asking children to choose sides in a dispute between parents can risk eroding family solidarity and may threaten the survival of the family system.

Coalitions can also produce intragroup competition between rival coalitions that encourages risky, poorly conceived decisions (Myers & Brashers, 1999). The overall effectiveness of a group might also be diminished by coalitions because communication between the factions often becomes limited and external threats or problems impacting the group are ignored (Myers & Brashers, 1999). Coalitions generally suffer the disadvantages associated with competition by creating a dominance–prevention transaction between group members.

RESISTANCE: DRAGGING YOUR FEET

Resistance is normally the choice of the less powerful. **Resistance** is a covert form of communicating noncompliance, and it is often duplicitous and manipulative. Resisters are subtle saboteurs. When faced with a dominant individual (supervisor, parent, or group leader), it is often safer to employ indirect means of noncompliance than direct confrontation or open defiance. Nevertheless, even high-power individuals on occasion will use resistance strategies. If undercurrents of dissatisfaction are apparent, openly defying the wishes of group members may provoke outright rebellion.

Resistance is the prevention form of power (power from). Done craftily, resistance can be difficult to identify unequivocally for those who are its targets because the sabotage is ambiguous, often communicating a seemingly sincere effort to comply. The target is often left mostly convinced that resistance is taking place, but is unable to make this apparent to the group due to the mixed messages being sent.

In this section I will discuss specific communication strategies of resistance, or what Bach and Goldberg (1974) term "passive aggression." I have combined their list of strategies with my own.

Strategic Stupidity: Smart Members Acting Dense Your group is working on an important class presentation. Each member has been assigned a topic area to research. At one of your meetings, an inventory is taken regarding information collected up to this point on relevant topic areas. When asked for a status report, one of the members of your group whines, "I couldn't find anything on world hunger." Are you faced with a drooling dolt or is this person covertly resisting active involvement in the group project? Bet your money on the latter. When group members do not want to expend energy on a project, especially if the project was not of their choosing, they may feel hesitant to complain directly to the group about their dissension. If they have been outvoted in the group when the proposal for the project was decided, they may resent having little influence on the group decision. They may feign stupidity to penalize the group and to exercise influence, at least in a negative way. When the success of the group presentation depends on all members pulling a load, even one resistant member can create systemwide problems.

Strategic stupidity can effectively thwart compliance attempts by more powerful group members because in most instances the strategy is part of a recurring pattern. If used only once, it becomes an isolated incident. If used repeatedly, as is often the case, strategic stupidity can frustrate the dominant party to the point of capitulation. If group members must spoon-feed their strategically stupid member on where to look on the Internet or in the library for information on world hunger, they may decide in exasperation that this takes too much effort and end up doing the research themselves.

Strategic stupidity works exceedingly well when the low-power person claims stupidity, is forced to attempt the task anyway, then purposely performs the task ineptly. Doing a half-baked job of a simple task can frustrate even the most patient person. If criticized for doing a poor job, the low-power person can always retort, "How was I supposed to know?" or "I told you I didn't know how to do it." The pathetic performance becomes proof that the stupidity was "real." To expect any better performance in the absence of careful and persistent tutelage would be an injustice.

Loss of Motor Function: Attack of the Clumsies This resistance strategy is an effective companion to strategic stupidity. Here the low-power person doesn't pretend to be stupid. The resister just acts incredibly clumsy, often resulting in costly damage. There is a mixed message here. The nonverbal behavior displays resistance, but the verbal statement that often accompanies it feigns a genuine attempt to comply.

I still remember an incident that happened to me years ago when as a college student I worked summers at a can factory. I was a worker in quality control. In a less-than-admirable effort to avoid the horrid press department, I kept ducking out of sight at the start of the morning shift to avoid the supervisor, who had a habit of selecting some poor college student employee to replace a worker who had quit the press department. The press department was where can lids were stamped out and sent through a machine, coated, and packed in boxes or paper sleeves stacked onto wood pallets.

One day the supervisor spotted me and sent me to the press department to replace someone who had quit. I went reluctantly. The job I was given pitted me against a machine that pumped out can lids in rapid fashion. I had to stack the lids without spilling them onto the floor. I purposely adopted the loss of motor function strategy to get out of the job. By the end of my shift, I had spilled thousands of lids onto the factory floor, shut the machine down four times, incensed the machinist who had to spend 20 minutes starting up the machine each time it was shut down, and forced my supervisor to call in two workers to clean up my mess. I was making the system adapt to my act of sabotage. All the while I insisted in bellicose tones to my upset supervisor that I was trying hard but that the job was impossible to do. The next day I returned to my previous job (half-expecting to be fired), hid out, watched my supervisor pick another college student to take my press job, and I spent the rest of the summer free from press department duties. I even received a promotion a month later. Ironically, I ended up in the press department the next summer and, with a change of attitude, managed to master the job with little difficulty.

It is the apparent effort exerted that makes this strategy so effective. In my can factory incident I had sweat rolling down my face. I seemed to be making every effort possible to keep up with the diabolical machine. I just couldn't quite stay with it. If the high-power person alleges deliberate sabotage, the low-power person can always become incensed, even incredulous that anyone would even suggest such a thing. It's an awkward position for a high-power person. How does one conclusively prove willfulness? You don't want to look like you're beating up on a less-powerful group member. If you make an accusation of willfulness but fail to convince the group, then you may lose power by diminishing your credibility (personal qualities as a power base).

The Misunderstanding Mirage: Feigning Confusion This is the "I thought you meant" or the "I could have sworn you said" strategy. The resistance is "expressed behind a cloak of great sincerity" (Bach & Goldberg, 1974, p. 110).

I have observed numerous instances of this strategy in my group communication classes. Typically, a student will deliberately miss an important meeting with his or her group and then claim, "Oh, I thought we were going to meet on Thursday. Sorry. I just got confused." I have lost count of the number of times students have used this strategy to excuse their late assignments. "You said it was due Friday, not today, didn't you?" they'll say hopefully. If I respond, "No, your paper is due today," my resistant student often replies, "Well, I thought you said Friday, so can I turn my assignment in then without a penalty?" The implied message attached to this ploy is clear: "Since this is a simple misunderstanding, penalizing me for a late assignment would be unfair."

Again, the high-power person is placed in a seemingly awkward position. The teacher may lose some power (legitimate authority) if the class sees his or her behavior as capricious, unfair, or lacking compassion ("Everyone makes mistakes").

High-power persons sometimes use this strategy of misunderstanding to avoid felt obligations. Teachers may purposely miss appointments with students or committee meetings on campus because they'd prefer to leave town before the rush-hour traffic. Pretending to have misunderstood when the meeting was scheduled relieves them of having to confront directly their own irresponsibility.

Selective Amnesia: Forgetting the Distasteful Sometimes we get a brain cramp and forget things, but have you ever noticed that certain people are very forgetful, especially about those things that they find distasteful? This temporary amnesia is highly selective when used as a resistance strategy. We rarely forget what is important to us, or what we like doing.

The message is again mixed. You manifest no outright signs of noncompliance. You outwardly agree to perform the distasteful task. Appointments, promises, and agreements just slip your mind. If your group insists that you assume a larger share of unpleasant tasks, you can always agree, then forget to do them.

A more sophisticated version of this strategy, however, is truly selective. Take an errand such as purchasing office supplies for your department. Remember to buy all the items except one or two important ones. Hey, you did pretty well, didn't you? So you forgot cartridges for the laser printers and now the entire office staff is affected. No one's perfect. If your selective amnesia proves to be a recurring problem, that errand gig may shift to someone else.

Tactical Tardiness: Not So Grand an Entrance When you really don't want to go to a meeting, a class, a lecture, or whatever, you can show your contempt by arriving late. If you don't arrive too late, you can still claim that you attended the event, so you're protected from punishment for being absent. Showing up late irritates, frustrates, and even humiliates those who take the meeting seriously. Tactical tardiness is intended to produce these very feelings in those requiring attendance.

Tactical tardiness asserts power in disguised form. The group is faced with a dilemma. The group may wait for your arrival, but this holds the entire group hostage until you appear. Members' plans for the day may be trashed by the delay. The other alternative is to commence without you. This also may prove to be problematic, however. If you offer reasonable-sounding excuses for your late arrival, the group will feel bound to clue you in on what has already transpired, thereby halting progress until you have been informed.

All instances of tardiness are not necessarily tactical. Occasionally, getting to meetings on time is not possible through no fault of our own. **Tactical tardiness is a recurrent pattern of resistance, not a rare occurrence.**

Tactical tardiness is not the sole province of the less powerful. High-power persons may also use this strategy to reinforce their dominance. Self-important celebrities with egos swelled like puffer fish often arrive late to functions. They hope to underscore their perceived superiority over worshipful fans by making them wait.

Purposeful Procrastination: Intentional Delaying Tactic Most people put off doing that which they dislike. There is nothing purposeful about this. There is no strategy involved. Procrastinators just tend to be hedonistic: they pursue pleasure and avoid pain. Procrastination, or what someone once called the "hardening of the oughteries," can become a resistance strategy when it is purposefully aimed at a target.

Purposeful procrastinators pretend that they will pursue a task "soon." While promising imminent results, they deliberately refuse to commit to a specific time or date for task accomplishment. **Trying to pin down a purposeful procrastinator is like taking a knife and stabbing Jell-O to a wall—it won't stick.** They'll make vague promises. When you become exasperated by the ambiguity and noncommittal attitude, the purposeful procrastinator will try to make you the problem. "Relax! You'll stroke out if you're not careful. I said I'd get to it, didn't I?" The implication is clear. You're impatient and unreasonable. The job will get done—not without delay

> ●● SECOND LOOK

RESISTANCE STRATEGIES

Strategic Stupidity—smart people acting dumb on purpose; feigned stupidity

Loss of Motor Function—sudden attack of the clumsies

The Misunderstanding Mirage—illusory mistakes

Selective Amnesia—no fear of Alzheimer's; forgetting only the distasteful

Tactical Tardiness—late for reasons within your control

Purposeful Procrastination—promising to do that which you have no intention of doing anytime soon, if ever

after delay, however. If the task doesn't get accomplished, it is because "something came up unexpectedly." If you express irritation at the delays, you're a nag.

Resistance strategies are generally viewed as negative and unproductive (Bach & Goldberg, 1974). This is true in an ideal sense. Resistance strategies are underhanded, deceitful, and rest on mixed messages. Resistance strategies are not the type of skills a competent communicator needs to learn. Nevertheless, I am not willing to rule them out unequivocally. Low-power members may have no better tools to resist dominant group members. Hoping that treatment by dominant group members will improve by itself is too passive. Hope is not a strategy. The essence of the problem, however, doesn't lie in the resistance strategies. **The dominance form of power creates a competitive group atmosphere in which resistance strategies are nurtured and encouraged.**

From the standpoint of competent communication, however, my emphasis must be on how to deal effectively with resistance, since the resistance may not always be noble. **There are three principal ways for the competent communicator to deal with resistance strategies in groups:**

1. *Confront the strategy directly.* Identify the communication pattern and ferret out the hidden hostility. Once this has been accomplished, efforts must be made to discover alternatives to dominance–submissiveness power patterns. Care should be taken to use the descriptive pattern of communication discussed in Chapter 4.

2. *Thwart the enabling process.* We become enablers when we allow ourselves to become ensnared in the resister's net of duplicity. When we continue to wait for the chronically late, we encourage tactical tardiness. If we perform the tasks for those who use loss of motor function to resist, we reward their behavior and

guarantee that the behavior will persist. Group members thwart the enabling process by refusing to be a party to the resistance. If a staff member "forgets" an item at the supplies store, guess who gets to make a return visit? If you hear the old refrain, "I can't be expected to remember everything," tell him or her to make a list. If the person is repeatedly late for committee meetings, refuse to interrupt the meeting to fill him or her in on what was missed and encourage the person to come on time. Continued tardiness may necessitate expulsion from the group.

3. *Give clear directions regarding specific tasks.* You want no possibility that confusion or misunderstanding can be used to excuse the poor behavior. Have the group members repeat the directions if resistance is suspected.

Again, the appropriate focus should not be on how to combat resistance, but instead on why the resistance occurs in the first place. If the main cause of resistance resides in the dominance form of power, then the focus of attention should be on how to reduce the power imbalance, or at least its perception.

Defiance: Digging in Your Heels

Defiance stands in bold contrast to resistance. **Defiance** is an overt form of communicating noncompliance. It is unmitigated, audacious rebellion against attempts to induce compliance. Defiance, like resistance, is a prevention form of power, but unlike resistance there is no ambiguity or subtlety. No one is left guessing whether an individual supports a specific norm or goal of the group.

When individuals exhibit behaviors that do not conform to group norms, they are called nonconformists or deviants. When this nonconformity is a purposeful, conscious, overtly rebellious act against the wishes of a group leader or the group itself, it becomes defiance. Group members typically turn to defiance when they perceive little or no chance of enhancing their power position through formation of an alliance, resistance strategies seem either inappropriate or ineffective, or they feel like exhibiting independence from group conformity.

Threat of Contagion: Spreading Dissension Defiance can be contagious. In the Asch (1952) study, previously discussed, an interesting wrinkle was added. When one of the confederates deviated from the group judgment regarding the correct length of a line, naive subjects' conformity dropped precipitously to a mere 8%. A single deviant encourages independent decision making, even outright rebellion. In another study, even when the deviant was wearing glasses with "Coke bottle" lenses and the task required visual discrimination, the influence of the deviant was so strong that the support of an obviously visually impaired person was sufficient to induce naive subjects to defy the collective misperception of the group (V. Allen & Levine, 1971).

AP/Wide World Photos

A courageous, unarmed man stops tanks during the Tiananmen Square upheaval in China in 1989. An imbalance of power, starkly evident here, often leads to conflict and defiance. To this day, no one has identified this man publicly or indicated what happened to him.

The concern that defiance from even one member could spread throughout the group like a cold virus in a daycare center motivates groups to act quickly to squash it. In Chapter 3, the four strategies to quell nonconformity—reason, seduction, coercion, and ostracism—were discussed. These strategies are what usually await defiant group members. A defiant individual can threaten the power of a group to command compliance from its members.

Variable Group Reaction: Discriminative Defiance All defiance is not created equal. Some instances of noncompliance will produce nary a ripple of concern in the group. Other instances will be perceived as intolerable. Whether a group takes steps to crush noncompliance, adopts a calculated indifference to the defiance, or explores ways to adapt to the challenge posed by the deviant depends in large part on three factors.

First, **some norms are not as important to a group as others, so the reaction to defiance will vary.** For a basketball team, curfews and eating meals together before a game may be considered terribly important, but socializing with team members outside of the basketball environment may be perceived as relatively unimportant.

Second, **the degree of deviation from the norm also affects whether a group discourages noncompliance and, if so, to what extent.** A group may have a norm requiring punctuality. If a member is a few minutes late to a meeting, this deviance is usually ignored. If a member arrives two-thirds of the way through a meeting, however, group members may view this as outright defiance and quite intolerable.

Third, **the deviation from the norm has to be a matter of obvious defiance, not inadvertent noncompliance.** Showing up for a new job dressed inappropriately is rarely an act of defiance. Normally, this show of nonconformity will be interpreted as a clueless blunder, not an act of rebellion. Not all nonconformity is defiance. Deviance must be overt, conscious, and clearly intended to flout group norms to prevent domination by more powerful group members before it becomes defiance. The group reaction to inadvertent deviance will likely be mild compared to unmistakable defiance. We smile indulgently when a small child bangs on the bathroom door and inquires, "Whatdya doin' in there?"

Defiant Member's Influence: Alone against the Group Given the tremendous pressure to conform exerted on those who defy, how do we explain the individual who converts the group to his or her way of thinking, as dramatized in the movie *Twelve Angry Men*? Admittedly not a frequent occurrence (Meyers & Brashers, 1999), defiance from members does influence groups (Pennington & Hastie, 1990), more often when the minority viewpoint comes from more than one group member (R. D. Clark, 2001). For example, a minority view on a jury rarely converts a majority from a guilty to an innocent verdict, but it often convinces the majority of jurors to change their minds on the severity of guilt (from first-degree murder to second-degree murder or manslaughter). Presenting high-quality arguments and effectively refuting majority arguments are primary ways to accomplish such modification of verdicts (Meyers & Brasher, 1999).

If the group cannot reject you (e.g., a jury or an elected official), then the deviant's best chance of converting the group is to remain unalterably and confidently defiant throughout discussions—in other words, defy without cracking (Gebhardt & Meyers, 1995). If, however, the group has the power to exclude the deviant from the group or the deliberations, then the deviant stands a better chance if he or she remains uncompromisingly defiant until the group seems about fed up. At this point, the deviant should indicate a willingness to make some degree of compromise (Wolf, 1979). The group is more likely to modify its position if it sees the deviant as coming around and being more reasonable. Remaining intransigent when the group can reject you is a losing battle. Your consistent defiance will be taken as legitimate justification for your ostracism.

Remaining unalterably defiant will win you no friends. Unwavering deviants are seen as less reasonable, fair, warm, cooperative, liked, admired, and perceptive than other group members (Moscovici & Mugny, 1983). This is not surprising since the deviant creates secondary tension in the group. Although the consistent deviant is not viewed as competent by the group, deviants are perceived to be confident and self-assured, independent, active, and even original.

Consistency may increase the influence of defiant members in groups, especially when there is some ambiguity and indecision among majority members, but it does not necessarily improve group decision making (Gebhardt & Meyers, 1995). Flexibility is a key to communication competence in groups. Intransigence aimed at winning over the group will likely produce rigidity from the majority of group members. When both the defiant individual and the group members remain rigidly consistent, the majority prevails (Gebhardt & Meyers, 1995).

SIGNIFICANCE: SELF-EMPOWERMENT

When group members grow tired of being dominated by more powerful individuals, they can do more than merely resist or defy demands for compliance. Less powerful members can enhance their relative influence or they can balance the power in the group more evenly by increasing their value to the group. Becoming more significant to the group can occur in two primary ways: by developing assertiveness and by increasing personal power resources.

Assertiveness: Neither Doormat nor Foot Wiper The terms *assertive* and *aggressive* are often used synonymously, even in scholarly circles (see especially Infante et al., 1997). Distinguishing assertiveness and aggressiveness conceptually does seem important. This is especially true in light of how psychologist David Myers (2003) defines **aggression**—"any physical or verbal behavior intended to hurt or destroy" (p. 719). If assertiveness is associated with aggression, then ethically I could not encourage anyone to learn and use such incompetent communication.

Adler (1977) defines **assertiveness** as the "ability to communicate the full range of your thoughts and emotions with confidence and skill" (p. 6). Assertiveness falls in between the extremes of passivity and aggressiveness and is distinctly different from either. Aggressiveness puts one's own needs first; you wipe your shoes on other people. Passivity underemphasizes one's needs (Lulofs, 1994); you're a doormat in a world of muddy shoes. Assertiveness takes into account both your needs and the needs of others.

Assertiveness is perceived by many people to be merely communicating the full range of thoughts and emotions—period. The ability and skill part of the definition is overlooked. So group members sound like arrogant little Nazis in the process of telling the group what they think or feel. Assertiveness is not a "looking out for number one" competitive communication strategy. To be assertive is to be sensitive to others while also looking out and standing up for yourself. You can stand up for yourself without trampling others in the process. Defining assertiveness in terms of empowerment makes this point obvious.

Assertiveness is not a strategy of resistance. As previously explained, resistance tactics are acts of passive aggression. On the surface you seem to be compliant (passive), but under the surface you're sabotaging (aggression). I have not included assertiveness in the section on defiance because it is a primarily empowering form of communication. **We most often use assertive communication not to defy the group, but instead to assure that our individual needs, rights, and responsibilities or that of other group members are not submerged or ignored by the group.** When a formerly passive member is assertive, the group may view this as a highly constructive change, wholly consistent with the norms of the group, and worthy of encouragement, not ostracism.

There are distinct advantages to learning assertiveness. Self-assertion makes you a more significant person in a group. Your potential influence in group decision making will be enhanced. Passive members become isolates and are easily ignored by the group. Assertive members make their presence felt and express their ideas and feelings to the group for consideration. This increases the group's resources and helps promote group synergy.

Assertiveness may also prove to be lifesaving. Following an airline crash in 1978, the National Transportation and Safety Board recommended that training for cockpit crews include assertiveness, implying that the lack of assertiveness was a causal factor in the crash (M. Foushee, 1984). In another incident, a jet slid off the runway because of excessive speed. Although the captain was apparently unaware of the excessive speed, the first officer knew but could only manage a sheepish comment about a possible tailwind.

Considering previous evidence on compliance rates already cited, it isn't surprising that research shows that **assertiveness is conspicuous by its absence** (Moriarity, 1975). In one study, small groups composed of four members met to decide which 12 individuals from a list of 30 were best able to survive on a deserted island. During discussion, a male group member (actually a confederate of the experimenters) utters three sexist remarks ("We definitely need to keep the women in shape"; "One of the women can cook"; "I think we need more women on the island to keep the men satisfied"). Imagine yourself in this situation. Would you speak up and protest, or endure the sexist remarks passively? When a comparative group of college students were asked this, only 5% said that they would keep quiet and 48% said that they would be assertive and speak up. When female participants were put to the test, however, 55% said nothing and only 16% spoke out against the sexism. The rest mostly asked questions or joked nervously (Swim & Hyers, 1999).

Recently, a group of students in my small group communication class did a field study as a "Candid Camera" project. Three group members formed a line in front of two side-by-side ATMs. Neither cash machine was in use and no "Out of Order" sign was posted. Within minutes a long line of people wanting to use the ATM formed behind my students. Some individuals seemed agitated at having to wait in line without anyone using the cash machine, but most never said a word. Several people waited 10 to 15 minutes before giving up and leaving in disgust. One woman did ask my students at the head of the line, "Is there something wrong with the ATM?" My students replied, "I don't know." The woman inquired further, "Why are you standing in line?" My students responded again, "I don't know." Did this inspire the woman to move out of line and use the ATM? No it didn't. She rejoined the line, waited a few more minutes, then left. No one used the ATM the entire time my students stood in line.

The competent communicator, however, cannot assume that assertiveness is always appropriate. Cultural differences, for example, must be taken into account (Den Hartog, 2004). Assertiveness is not valued in many Asian cultures (Samovar & Porter, 2001). Standing up for yourself and speaking your mind are seen as disruptive and provocative acts likely to create disharmony.

One study (Schmidt & Kipnis, 1987) also discovered that you could be overly persistent in asserting yourself. Excessive assertiveness can result in less favorable evaluations from supervisors, lower salaries, greater job tension, and greater personal stress than a less vigorous assertion of one's needs and desires.

These results show that **assertiveness is not preferable to passivity or aggressiveness in every circumstance.** The advantages and disadvantages must be weighed within each context. As a general rule, however, assertiveness is empowering, especially in American culture, and more advantageous with far fewer and less severe disadvantages than aggressiveness or passivity.

So how do you become more assertive? Bower and Bower (1976) provide a useful framework for learning assertiveness. They call it DESC Scripting. The D is for describe, E is for express, S is for specify, and C is for consequences.

Describe: This first step was discussed at length in Chapter 4. Review first-person-singular language of description.

Express: Here you express how you think and feel about the offending behavior. Again, this is not a verbal assault on the offender. All an attack will do is precipitate defensiveness and counterattack. Instead, you formulate a statement from your perspective (e.g., "I believe," "I feel," "I disagree"). The express step is not an opportunity for finger-pointing and accusation (e.g., "You made me feel . . ."). This step requires a statement of personal reaction from you to the offensive behavior from another group member.

Specify: This step identifies the behavior you would like to see substituted for the bothersome behavior. Once more, the request needs to be concrete and spelled out, not vague or merely suggestive. "I think it is only fair that I receive sole credit for this proposal, and in the future I expect to receive credit for my ideas" is better than "I want you to stop plagiarizing my ideas immediately."

Consequences: The consequences of changing behavior or continuing the same behavior patterns should be articulated to the offending party. The emphasis, if possible, should be on rewards, not punishments. "I like working here and expect to continue as long as I'm treated fairly" is better than "If you continue to steal my ideas I'll be forced to quit." The DESC guidelines for assertiveness will prove to be nothing more than an idealized fantasy cooked up by academic types unless "powerless" language and anemic, nonverbal behavior are eliminated from the process. Expressing your thoughts and feelings must be accomplished with confidence and skill. This requires direct eye contact, not looks cast downward or side-to-side. Posture should be erect, not slouched in a cowering whipped-puppy stance. Tone of voice should be modulated so aggression or passivity doesn't emerge. Tag questions, hedges, hesitations, disclaimers, and overly polite references should be minimized or eliminated if possible. If you are interrupted, calmly indicate, "I'm not finished with my thought."

Everything I've suggested regarding how to be assertive requires practice. To become a competent communicator you must be willing to expend some energy honing your skills. You will find that assertiveness is far easier in some circumstances than in others. Assertiveness is an important, empowering communication skill.

Increasing Personal Power Resources: Mentoring and Networking Since the group confers power on the individual, a person can enhance his or her power by increasing personal resources valued by the group. There are a number of avenues available for personal power enhancement.

Husbands who assume a greater portion of the domestic chores may increase their value in the family. Children whose parents are unemployed or underemployed can exercise greater power if they find a part-time job to supplement family income. Learning certain skills valued by the group can enhance your power position. If you master the skills required to use computers and no one in your group is computer proficient, then your power increases when the group requires such technical expertise.

Finally, the mentoring and networking processes can enhance personal power resources. **Mentors** are knowledgeable individuals who have achieved some success in their profession or jobs and who assist individuals trying to get started in a line of work. Mentors can provide information to the newcomer that prevents mistakes by trial and error. Mentoring seems to have been especially useful for women in their rise to upper echelons of organizations (Noe, 1988). One study showed that women

BOX 9.1 ASSERTIVENESS SELF-ASSESSMENT QUESTIONNAIRE

Fill out the following Assertiveness Self-Assessment Questionnaire. Be as honest as you can. This is not an assessment of your "ideal self." This should be your "real self." For each situation indicate how likely you would be to take the action indicated by using the following scale:

5 = Very likely
4 = Likely
3 = Maybe
2 = Unlikely
1 = Very unlikely

_____ 1. You have been invited to a party but you don't know anyone except the friend who invited you, who is not present when you enter the room. You see dozens of strangers. You walk up to a group of people and introduce yourself and begin a conversation.

_____ 2. There is a definite undercurrent of tension and conflict in your group. You are feeling that tension as your group begins discussing their project for class. You stop the discussion, indicate that there is unresolved conflict in the group, and request that the group address this issue.

_____ 3. You strongly disagree with your group's choice for a symposium project. Nevertheless, you say nothing and go along with the majority decision.

_____ 4. During class your instructor makes a point that angers you greatly. You raise your hand, are recognized by the instructor, and you vehemently challenge your instructor's position, raising your voice to almost a shout.

_____ 5. You're sitting in the back of the class. Two students sitting beside you engage in an audible conversation that is distracting. You can't concentrate on the instructor's lecture. You lean over and calmly ask them to stop talking so you can listen to your instructor.

_____ 6. At a family holiday dinner gathering, your uncle makes a blatantly racist remark, then tells a sexist joke. You sit silently.

_____ 7. While on vacation you sign up to receive a group lesson in a new sport (jet skiing, rock climbing, snow skiing). After the instructor has explained the basics, everyone in the group appears to understand perfectly. You, however, are unclear about a couple of instructions. You raise your hand and ask the instructor to repeat the instructions and explain them more fully.

_____ 8. Three individuals representing a religious group knock on your door. When you answer they begin to proselytize, trying to sell you on their religious point of view. You stand there waiting patiently for them to finish, wishing they would go away.

_____ 9. A small group of teenagers talks loudly during a movie you attend at a local theater. You become increasingly annoyed but say nothing to them.

_____ 10. You live in a dorm room with two roommates. Next door loud music is playing, making it impossible for you to study. Your roommates seem not to care but you are becoming increasingly annoyed by the noise. You walk next door, pound on the door, and, when the door is opened you demand that the music be turned way down immediately.

_____ 11. A member of your group couldn't afford to buy the textbook for the class. He asks you if he can borrow your book for "a couple of days." You agree. He has had the book for more than a week and shows no sign of returning it to you. You wait for him to return the book or explain why he hasn't mentioned it.

_____ 12. At work, you are a member of a project team. Every member of the team makes considerably more money than you do, yet your jobs are equivalent. You believe that you deserve a hefty raise. You make an appointment with your boss to ask for a substantial raise.

_____ 13. You receive an e-mail from a team member that has a condescending tone. It angers you that this team member, whom you view as a bit of a screw-up, lectures you on the "right way" to approach your part of the group task. You write back a sarcastic, biting reply.

_____ 14. The coach of your sports team berates players at a team meeting for "lackluster play" and "lackadaisical attitudes." The coach is shouting and abusive. You believe the criticism is mostly unfair and doesn't apply to most of the players. You

remain silent, wishing he/she would wind down.

_____ 15. A group member pulls you aside and begins accusing you of "unethical behavior." She is shouting at you, her face is flush red and she is wildly gesturing. People are noticing. You shout back at her.

_____ 16. The family that lives next door has a dog that barks all hours of the night. It is disturbing to you and your family members. You meet one of the dog owners during a walk through the neighborhood. You stop, begin to talk, and you calmly bring up the barking dog problem.

_____ 17. You are taking an exam. You notice several students cheating on the exam. You're upset because this gives these students an undeserved advantage and may lower your own grade because the instructor grades on a curve. The instructor doesn't notice the cheating. You report the cheating to the instructor after class.

_____ 18. During a group discussion, your point of view clashes with that of another group member. You want very much to convince the group that your viewpoint should be accepted. You interrupt when the member who disagrees with you tries to voice her opinion, you keep talking when she tries to disagree with a point you make, and you insist that she is wrong and you are right.

_____ 19. At work, a member of your project team "steals" your idea and takes credit for work you have done. You angrily denounce him in front of the entire team and insist that he own up to his deception.

_____ 20. One of your team members has extremely bad breath. This is a common problem when you meet. His bad breath bothers you a great deal. Nevertheless, you say nothing and try sitting as far away from him as possible during meetings.

_____ 21. You are waiting in line to be served at a local store. Just as you are about to be waited on, a group of three individuals steps in front of you. You demand that they step aside, insisting that you were in line ahead of them.

SCORING DIRECTIONS: Total your scores for numbers 4, 10, 13, 15, 18, 19, and 21 (aggressiveness). Now total your scores for numbers 1, 2, 5, 7, 12, 16, and 17 (assertiveness). Finally, total your scores for numbers 3, 6, 8, 9, 11, 14, and 20 (passivity). Enter these raw totals in the appropriate blanks.

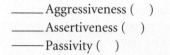

_____ Aggressiveness (   )

_____ Assertiveness (   )

―――― Passivity (   )

Now average each raw score by dividing it by seven (e.g., 21 on aggressiveness divided by 7 = 3.0 average). Put averages in parentheses above.

NOTE: Generally speaking, you want to average between 4.0 and 5.0 on assertiveness, and average 2.0 or less on aggressiveness and passivity. This reflects the general desirability of assertiveness and the general undesirability of aggressiveness and passivity. A low score on a specific assertiveness scenario or a high score on a specific aggressiveness or passivity scenario may also mean a need for improvement in these particular situations. Please note, however, that the appropriateness of assertiveness, aggressiveness, and passivity is situational. Assertiveness, although generally a desirable skill, is not always appropriate, especially if harm may come to you by being assertive. Conversely, aggressiveness, although generally an undesirable communication pattern, is not always inappropriate. Likewise, occasionally the appropriate choice is passivity.

who have mentors move up the corporate ladder much faster than women without mentors. Women also receive promotions more quickly when they are helped by mentors (Kleiman, 1991). Mentors are essential for women trying to advance to the highest levels of corporate leadership (M. Hackman & Johnson, 2004).

Networking is a form of group empowerment. Individuals with similar backgrounds, skills, and goals come together on a fairly regular basis and share information that will assist members in pursuing goals. Networks also provide emotional support for members, especially in women's networks (Stewart et al., 1996).

In summary, power is a central dynamic in all groups. Power is the ability to influence the attainment of goals sought by yourself and others. Power is not a property of any individual. Power is the product of transactions between group

> ●● SECOND LOOK

SIGNIFICANCE (EMPOWERMENT)

ASSERTIVENESS

Describe the behavior that is troublesome.

Express how you think and feel about the offending behavior.

Specify behavior preferred as a substitute for bothersome behavior.

Consequences of changing behavior or continuing without change should be articulated.

INCREASING PERSONAL POWER RESOURCES

Personal improvement

Learn valued skills

Mentoring and networking

members. Information, expertise, rewards and punishments, personal qualities, and legitimate authority are primary resources of power. Groups must endorse these resources before they have power potential. The influence that you wield cannot be determined precisely. Nevertheless, you can approximate the distribution of power in groups by observing certain general patterns of communication, plus verbal and nonverbal indicators.

An imbalance of power in groups promotes conflict and power struggles and in some instances can lead to violence. The five ways we transact power in groups, especially when power is unequally distributed, are compliance, alliance, resistance, defiance, and significance. Compliance primarily aims to bring the less powerful in line with the dictates of the more powerful and to discourage deviance, which can be contagious. Alliance, resistance, defiance, and significance are all means used by members to balance the power more equitably in small groups. ● ●

Questions for Critical Thinkers

1. Information is power. Can misinformation also serve as a power resource?

2. If punishment has significant drawbacks, why is it typically used more frequently than rewards by those in power positions?

3. Have you ever used resistance strategies? Did they work? Were they used against dominant individuals?

4. Can you think of instances in your own experience in which assertiveness was inappropriate?

InfoTrac College Edition

Log onto InfoTrac College Edition.

1. Type "Milgram's studies" in the search window. Choose an article and write a brief essay on it, focusing on agreements and disagreements with the original Milgram obedience studies. SUGGESTION: Article A79981455, by Mike Cardwell, entitled "Obedience to authority: The legacy of Milgram's research."

2. Type "self-help groups" in the search window. Choose an article and critique it. SUGGESTION: Article A87375586, by Scott Wituk et al., entitled "Factors contributing to the survival of self-help groups."

Video Case Studies

Crimson Tide (1995). Drama; R; ****1/2

Taut undersea drama that pits the captain of a nuclear submarine (Gene Hackman) against a new executive officer (Denzel Washington). The Washington character must decide whether to obey his superior officer and launch a nuclear "retaliation" against Russian rebels, risking total nuclear war, or to assume command of the submarine by force. All members of the crew must decide where their allegiance and duty lie. Relate this dramatic decision to the Milgram obedience studies and issues of compliance in groups. Consider the ethics of such a decision and how it was implemented.

Lord of the Rings: Fellowship of the Ring (2001). Fantasy/Drama; PG-13; *****

Terrific screen adaptation of the first in a trilogy of the J. R. R. Tolkien fantasy epics. Analyze characters for their power resources. Are there any resistance or defiance strategies evident? Consider the corrupting effects of power.

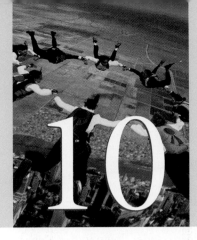

10 Conflict Management in Groups

ONCE UPON A TIME there was a quiet little condominium complex composed of 18 units beside a meandering creek in a forest setting. The residents enjoyed seeing the deer wander down in the evening from their habitat above the complex. Wildlife was abundant. A climate of tranquility enveloped this special place.

Then one day, bulldozers and earthmovers of every variety rumbled in unannounced. Peace and quiet were abruptly replaced by ear-splitting noise, incessant vibration from the heavy equipment thundering back and forth across the once-emerald terrain. Families residing in Village Haven were understandably shaken by the realization that 32 additional units were about to be squeezed onto every speck of available space a mere 30 feet across from the original 18 residences.

The situation did not improve once construction of the condos began. Residents were awakened regularly at 6:30 a.m. on weekdays and sometimes on weekends to the sounds of hammering, sawing, and shouting from workers. Cars previously parked along the curb of the one-way road into and out of the complex had to be moved to a small paved area in the center of the development where bulldozers and forklifts whizzed by, showering the autos with dirt and debris. Tires were regularly punctured by nails strewn across the road by careless workers. Huge trucks and construction equipment frequently blocked the single-lane road into and out of the complex, stranding residents in their cars, sometimes for 10 to 15 minutes. Residents occasionally found pathways to their homes dangerous to traverse.

At one point, a signed message from the developer and contractor was taped to the doors of the condos. Residents were instructed to remove their cars from the street so "demolition and reconstruction" could take place. Residents were now ordered to park their cars on a street overlooking the complex about two blocks up a very steep, poorly lighted hill. During the demolition, two residents had stereos stolen out of their cars while parked on this street. The homeowners as a group were not happy!

The inhabitants of Village Haven, working under the auspices of the complex's Homeowners Association, considered legal action, but ran into numerous technical and political roadblocks. The developer and the contractor were asked to begin construction at 8 a.m. instead of 6:30 a.m. Residents were informed that early starts were "the nature of construction" and couldn't be changed. When representatives of the association raised objections to the edict requiring removal of all cars to the street above, they were told that this was an unavoidable inconvenience. Several residents got into shouting matches with the developer and the contractor.

Vandalism started to crop up here and there. The professionally painted sign at the entrance to the complex that read "Village Haven Forest Townhomes" was painted over to read "Village of the Damned." Another sign that read "Welcome to Village Haven" was changed to read "Welcome to Hell." Windows freshly installed in new units were sporadically smashed. Security patrols were increased to thwart the vandals, with little apparent success.

A few days after the message ordering the removal of all cars from paved areas was attached to residents' doors, a tongue-in-cheek message appeared on everyone's doorstep. Attributed to the contractor and developer (real author unknown), but obviously intended as an underground satirical jibe at these two individuals, the message was addressed to Village Haven residents and purported to answer complaints from homeowners. The bogus message was signed under the names of the contractor and developer, with the appellation "The Village Idiots" added.

Frustrated and weary, residents began listing their units for sale, but few potential buyers were interested once they saw the 50 units crammed onto the once beautiful and serene acreage. The project was finally completed; some of the original residents left, but the animosities lingered.

The principal purpose of this chapter is to show you constructive ways to manage a group conflict such as the Village Haven fracas. In previous chapters, several sources of conflict and their corresponding antidotes were discussed at length. Briefly, these include:

Sources	Solutions
Competitive group climate	Structure cooperative group climate
Defensive communication patterns	Structure supportive communication
Self-centered disruptive roles	Adopt strategies for dealing with difficult group members
Imbalance of power	Balance power among group members
Conflicts of interest	Use integrative problem solving

Building on this foundation of previous discussion, **there are three chapter objectives:**

1. to define conflict, identifying the difference between its constructive and destructive form,
2. to explain the pros and cons of five communication styles of conflict management, and
3. to discuss how to transact conflict effectively in small groups.

Definition of Conflict

The Village Haven case study (based on a real situation) provides us with a means of explaining the general definition of conflict in a group context. In this section, destructive conflict and constructive conflict are also differentiated.

GENERAL DEFINITION: INTERCONNECTEDNESS, INCOMPATIBILITY, AND INTERFERENCE

In general, **conflict** is the expressed struggle of interconnected parties who perceive incompatible goals and interference from each other in attaining those goals (Donohue & Kolt, 1992; Wilmot & Hocker, 2001). You can see all of the elements of this definition in the Village Haven battle.

First, conflict is an *expressed struggle* between parties. If the homeowners of Village Haven had merely sat and stewed over perceived outrages, then no conflict would have existed because the developer and contractor wouldn't have known there was a problem. Often the expression of a struggle is manifested in shouting matches, such as those that occurred between the residents of Village Haven and the developer and contractor. Sometimes it is expressed more indirectly, such as the exchange of written messages placed on residents' doorsteps. Occasionally, the expression is of a nonverbal nature. Vandalism and the reaction to it (beefed up security) are examples from the Village Haven conflict.

Second, conflict occurs between *interconnected parties* in a group system. This means that for a conflict to exist, the behavior of one or more parties must produce consequences for the other party or parties. The invasion of the bulldozers significantly affected the residents of Village Haven. Likewise, the developer and contractor could not completely ignore residents' angry reactions.

Third, conflict involves *perceived incompatible goals.* The residents of Village Haven would have preferred an 18-unit instead of a 50-unit complex. The developer and contractor couldn't make any money that way. The goal of the builders to erect 32 additional units collided squarely with the desire of the residents for a quiet, natural, uncrowded setting.

Finally, conflict involves *interference from each other* in attaining desired goals. Unless one party attempts to block the attainment of another party's goal, there is no conflict. You and I may express a disagreement, be interconnected parties, and we may even perceive our goals to be incompatible, yet conflict may not exist even then. You may, in an act of pure selflessness, assist me in the attainment of my goal at the expense of attaining your own goal. There must be an attempt to interfere with another's goal attainment for conflict to exist.

In Village Haven, interference abounded. Builders interfered with residents' tranquility and convenience and transformed the environment from a desirable, low-density development to an undesirable, high-density development. Residents interfered with builders in the form of verbal abuse and vandalism (again assuming the culprits were residents).

DESTRUCTIVE AND CONSTRUCTIVE CONFLICT: IT'S ALL IN THE COMMUNICATION

Most conflict probably seems destructive, given how poorly conflict is typically managed in groups, and a high level of conflict can be counterproductive for groups because it can interfere with task accomplishment. Low levels or the absence of conflict, however, can lead to complacency and groupthink (Jehn, 1995). **Moderate amounts of conflict can be a constructive force in groups if the conflict is managed competently.** Conflict can instigate positive changes that foster individual and group growth, it can promote creative problem solving, it can encourage power balancing, and conflict can even enhance group cohesiveness (Nicotera, 1995). Conflict can also prevent groupthink (Jehn, 1995).

So what distinguishes destructive from constructive conflict? **The principal difference is how competent the communication is when transacting the conflict** (Olson, 2002). **Destructive conflict** is characterized by dominating, escalating, retaliating, competing, defensive, and inflexible communication patterns (Lulofs, 1994; Wilmot & Hocker, 2001). When conflicts spiral out of control they push conflict to unmanageable levels. Participants lose sight of their initial goals and focus on hurting their adversary.

The Village Haven conflict was essentially a destructive conflict. Escalation, vandalism, threats, shouting, inflexibility on both sides, and expressions of contempt and ridicule occurred. Neither side seemed able to work together to find a mutually satisfactory solution to the conflict.

Recognizing destructive conflict while it is occurring may not always be easy. When it becomes obvious to you that *"Gee, I'm getting stupid,"* you're engaged in destructive conflict (Donohue & Kolt, 1992). When you see yourself engaging in petty, even infantile, tactics to win an argument, you're getting stupid. Becoming physically and verbally aggressive moves the conflict into destructive territory. This doesn't mean that you can never raise your voice, express frustration, or disagree with other group members. **Conflict can remain constructive even when discussion becomes somewhat contentious.** When conflict becomes more emotional than reasonable, however, when you can't think straight because you are too consumed by anger, then conflict has become destructive (Gottman, 1994).

Constructive conflict is characterized by communication that is We oriented, de-escalating, cooperative, supportive, and flexible (Lulofs, 1994; Wilmot & Hocker, 2001). It is competent communication in action. The principal focus is on trying to achieve a solution between struggling parties that is mutually satisfactory to everyone.

Getty Images

Destructive conflict is characterized by "getting stupid" with adversaries in a dispute. This often involves shouting, finger-pointing, and even physical violence.

Even if no mutually satisfactory solution is achieved at the time, the communication process that characterizes constructive conflict allows conflicting parties to maintain cordial relationships while agreeing to disagree. This makes the ultimate emergence of a creative solution that is mutually satisfactory to conflicting parties more likely.

Styles of Conflict Management

Communication is central to conflict in groups. Our communication can signal that conflict exists, it can create conflict, and it can be the means for managing conflict constructively or destructively (Wilmot & Hocker, 2001). Consequently, communication styles have been the center of much research and discussion. A **communication style of conflict management** is an orientation toward conflict. Styles exhibit predispositions or tendencies regarding the way conflict is managed in groups. Individual group members may exhibit a specific style or an entire group may adopt a normative preference for a certain style of conflict management (Kuhn & Poole, 2000). There are five communication styles of conflict management (Blake & Mouton, 1964; Kilmann & Thomas, 1977). I will explain each of the five styles and add some modifications of the original theoretical descriptions.

Let me offer one quick clarification. I have chosen the term conflict "management" instead of "resolution" in most instances because it is more appropriate for a systems perspective. Resolution suggests settling conflict by ending it, as if that is always desirable. **Since conflict can be an essential catalyst for growth in a system, increasing conflict may be required to evoke change** (D. W. Johnson & R. T. Johnson, 2000). Civil rights demonstrators purposely provoked conflict to challenge racist laws in the South. Women who file sexual harassment lawsuits provoke conflict to end an evil. "Managing conflict" implies no end to the struggle. Although some conflict episodes end within a group and are therefore resolved, conflict overall in a system is a continuous phenomenon that waxes and wanes. Management of conflict also implies no judgment on the goodness or badness of struggles in general.

▶ **Focus Questions**

1. How do communication styles of conflict management differ on task and social dimensions of small groups?
2. Should group members always use the collaborating style and avoid the competing (power-forcing) style?

COLLABORATING: PROBLEM SOLVING

The most complex and potentially productive communication style of conflict management is collaborating, or what some refer to as problem solving. The **collaborating** style is a win–win, cooperative approach to conflict. It attempts to satisfy all parties. **Someone employing this style has a high concern for both task and social relationships in groups.** The collaborating style recognizes the interconnection between the task and social components of groups and deals directly with both requirements. **A collaborating style has three key components: confrontation, integration, and smoothing.**

Confrontation: Addressing the Problem The overt recognition that conflict exists in a group and the direct effort to manage it effectively is called **confrontation.** Although the news media are fond of using the term *confrontation* in a negative sense, as in "There was a violent confrontation between protesters and police," this is not the meaning relevant to this discussion. Confrontation as a conflict-management technique incorporates all the elements already discussed at length regarding assertiveness (describe, express, specify, and identify consequences) and supportive communication patterns (description, problem orientation, etc.). The purpose of confrontation is to manage conflict in a productive way for all parties involved.

Not all issues are worth confronting. Members who confront even trivial differences of opinion or can't let a momentary flash of pique go unattended can be like telemarketers at the dinner hour—beyond annoying. Groups have to decide which issues and concerns are priorities and which are tangential. You can overuse confrontation and make yourself a nuisance.

Integration: Seeking Joint Gains A collaborative technique that devises creative solutions that are mutually satisfactory for all parties in conflict is called **integration.** Since integrative solutions to problems were discussed in Chapter 8, they will not be repeated here. Integration as a collaborative technique, however, has not been given the attention that it deserves. Negotiators in organizations are typically better at maximizing their own gains (competitive) than they are at maximizing joint gains (integrative) (Brett et al., 1990). Also, negotiators tend to reach agreement on the first satisfactory proposal that comes along rather than looking for a better solution (Pruitt, 1981). Training through lecture, reading, and exercises, however, can vastly improve integrative skills of group members (Neale et al., 1988). Programs that provide extensive training for students on how to negotiate integrative agreements have proved to be highly effective (D. W. Johnson & R. T. Johnson, 2000).

Smoothing: Calming Troubled Waters The act of calming the agitated feelings of group members during a conflict episode is called **smoothing.** When tempers ignite and anger morphs into screaming and shedding of tears, no collaboration is possible. Turbulent emotions need to be smoothed. A simple "I'm sorry" is a useful smoothing response. "Let's all calm down. Attacking each other won't help us find a solution everyone can accept" is another example of smoothing. Calming the emotional storm opens the way to confronting conflict and brainstorming integrative solutions.

Since collaborating is such an effective communication style for solving conflicts of interest, why isn't it always used in these situations? There are several reasons. First, **collaborating usually requires a significant investment of time and effort along with greater-than-ordinary communication skills.** Even if you are willing to employ the collaborating techniques of confrontation, integration, and smoothing, collaborating requires mutually agreeable parties. I have witnessed several instances in which an integrative solution was devised, but the group rejected it because the members disliked the person who originated the proposal. Second, **collaboration is built on trust.** If parties are suspicious of each other and worry that one will betray the other by not honoring agreements, then even an integrative solution may be rejected. Third, **parties in a conflict sometimes do not share the same emotional investment in finding an agreeable solution for all involved.** Hypercompetitive group members want a clear "victory," not a mutually satisfactory solution that benefits all parties.

ACCOMMODATING: YIELDING

The **accommodating** style yields to the concerns and desires of others. **Someone using this style shows a high concern for social relationships but low concern for task accomplishment.** This style may camouflage deep divisions among group members to maintain the appearance of harmony. If the task can be accomplished without social disruption, fine. If accomplishing the task threatens to jeopardize the harmonious relationships within the group, however, a person using this style will opt for appeasing members, even though this may sacrifice productivity. Generally, group members with less power are expected to accommodate more often and to a greater degree than more powerful members (Lulofs, 1994).

Although we tend to view accommodating in a negative light, as appeasement with all its negative connotations, this style can be quite positive. A group that has experienced protracted strife may rejoice when one side accommodates, even on an issue of only minor importance. **Yielding on issues of incidental concern to your group but of major concern to other parties while holding firm on issues of importance to your group usually achieves mutually advantageous outcomes** (Lax & Sebenius, 1986; Mannix et al., 1989).

COMPROMISING: HALVING THE LOAF

When **compromising,** we give up something to get something. Some have referred to this as a lose–lose style of conflict management because neither party is ever fully satisfied with the solution. Compromising is choosing a middle ground. **Someone using this style shows a moderate concern for both task and social relationships in groups.** The emphasis is on workable but not necessarily optimal solutions.

Compromise evokes ambivalence—both negative and positive reactions. We speak disparagingly of those who would "compromise their integrity." On some issues, usually moral or ethical conflicts such as abortion or capital punishment, compromise is thought to be intolerable. Yet despite this negative view of compromise, negotiations of labor-management contracts and political agreements are expected, even encouraged, to end in compromise. Members of task forces, ad hoc groups, and committees of many shapes and sizes often seek a compromise as an admirable goal.

Half a loaf is better than starvation—not in all circumstances, but certainly in some. **When an integrative solution cannot be achieved, when a temporary settlement is the only feasible alternative, or when the issues involved are not considered critical to the group, compromise can be useful.**

AVOIDING: WITHDRAWING

Avoiding is a communicating style of withdrawing from potentially contentious and unpleasant struggles. Groups typically change the subject under discussion soon after a period of disagreement among members (Gouran & Baird, 1972). *Flights from fights* may seem constructive at the time because they circumvent unpleasantness. In the long run, however, facing problems proves to be more effective than running from them. **Someone using the avoiding conflict style shows little concern for both task and social relationships in groups.** Avoiders shrink from conflict, even fear it. By avoiding conflict they hope it will disappear. Group tasks are sacrificed to a preoccupation with dodging trouble. Social relationships within the group have scant possibility of improving when the conflict distorts the behavior of those doing the avoiding.

Avoiding, nevertheless, is sometimes appropriate. If you are a low-power person in a group and the consequences of confrontation are potentially hazardous to you, avoiding might be a reasonable strategy until other alternatives present themselves. Standing up to a bully may work out well in movies, but confronting antisocial types (workplace bullies) who look like they eat raw meat for breakfast and might eat you for lunch may not be a very bright choice. Staying out of a bully's way, although perhaps ego-deflating, may be the best *temporary option* in a bad situation.

If the advantages of confrontation do not outweigh the disadvantages, avoiding the conflict might be a desirable course of action. In some cases, tempers need to cool. Avoiding contentious issues for a time may prove to be constructive. When passions run high, reason usually trails far behind. We often make foolish, irrational choices when we are highly stressed.

In most cases, however, avoiding rather than confronting is highly counterproductive. From their research on family violence, Gelles and Straus (1988) suggest *confronting the very first incident of even minor violence,* not avoiding the issue while waiting to see if it happens again. They conclude: "Delaying until the violence escalates to a frequency or severity that would generally be considered abusive is too late. A firm, emphatic, and rational approach appears to be the most effective personal strategy a woman can use to prevent future violence" (p. 159).

COMPETING: POWER-FORCING

When we approach conflict as a win–lose contest, we are competing. The competing style is exhibited in a variety of ways that are likely to produce destructive conflict: threats, criticism, contempt, hostile remarks and jokes, sarcasm, ridicule, intimidation, faultfinding and blaming, and denials of responsibility (Wilmot & Hocker, 2001). The competing style is aggressive, not assertive. It is not confrontation as previously defined; it is an attack. The competing or power-forcing style flows from the dominance perspective on power. **Competing** and forcing your will on others is a win–lose style. **Someone using a competing or forcing style shows high concern for task but low concern for relationships in groups.** Task comes first. If accomplishing the group task requires a few wounded egos, that is thought to be the unavoidable price of productivity. Someone using the competing/forcing style sees task accomplishment as a means of furthering personal more than group goals (Me-Not-We orientation). Making friends and developing a positive social climate are secondary and expendable.

One notable aspect of the competing style is the tendency to ascribe blame when groups don't function perfectly. Blame "produces disagreement, denial, and little

▶●● SECOND LOOK

COMMUNICATION STYLES OF CONFLICT MANAGEMENT

STYLE	TASK–SOCIAL DIMENSION
Collaborating (Problem Solving)	High task, high social
Accommodating (Yielding)	Low task, high social
Compromising	Moderate task, moderate social
Avoiding (Withdrawing)	Low task, low social
Competing (Power-forcing)	High task, low social

learning. It evokes fears of punishment . . . Nobody wants to be blamed, especially unfairly, so our energy goes into defending ourselves" (D. Stone et al., 1999, pp. 11–12). Blame is about looking backward to judge a group member. "You blew it" is blame aimed at assigning responsibility, not on solving the problem.

As with all other styles, however, the competing style also has its constructive side. If a troublemaker in the group shows no signs of ending disruptions and the seriousness of the situation is clear, then forcing out this difficult member may be the correct choice. Eliminating a troublemaker can revitalize the remaining members and allow progress on the task to proceed unimpeded.

All five styles of conflict management show different emphases on task and social dimensions of groups. Nevertheless, someone using the competing style may, in some circumstances, manifest genuine concern for social climate. Low concern doesn't mean no concern. An accommodator, on occasion, may regard the task accomplishment as vital. All of these styles represent tendencies, not unalterably fixed ways of managing conflict in every situation.

COMPARING STYLES: LIKELIHOOD OF SUCCESS

As a general rule, research clearly favors some conflict styles over others, even though more than one style may need to be used, perhaps by a single group member, over the course of a conflict (see Closer Look: "KILL Radio Conflict Case Study"). Collaborating is the most constructive and effective style of conflict management (Carver & Vondra, 1994; Kuhn & Poole, 2000; Tutzauer & Roloff, 1988; Van de Vliert et al., 1999). Impressive field research on a program called Peacemakers, involving students from kindergarten to ninth grade, supports the efficacy of the collaborative method of conflict management. The Peacemaker program specializes in training students in schools throughout North America, Europe, Asia, Central and South America, the Middle East, and Africa to use the collaborative method of conflict management. A review of 17 studies on the Peacemaker program shows that trained students almost always used the method in actual conflict incidents both at school and at home. As a result, student conflicts referred to teachers for resolution were reduced by 80% and referrals to the school principal were reduced to *zero*. Conflicts between students became less severe and destructive (D. W. Johnson & R. T. Johnson, 2000).

Overall, the collaborating style in a variety of contexts produces the best decisions and greatest satisfaction from parties in conflict (Gayle-Hackett, 1989; Kuhn & Poole, 2000; Tutzauer & Roloff, 1988). The competing/forcing style is least effective for reasons already discussed concerning the disadvantages of competition and the drawbacks of the dominating form of power (Isenhart & Spangle, 2000; Kuhn & Poole, 2000; Van de Vliert et al., 1999). Collaborating encourages constructive conflict. Competing tends to promote destructive conflict.

Despite the clear benefits of the collaborating style, the disadvantages of the competing style, and mixed results for the other three styles, **typically we use the least effective styles when attempting to manage conflict in groups.** Students who were not trained to use collaboration in the Peacemakers experiments *never* used integrative negotiations, rarely used accommodation, and most often chose the competing or avoiding styles. Consequently, they left many conflicts unresolved, and they experienced mostly negative outcomes (D. W. Johnson & R. T. Johnson, 2000). One study compared collaboration and power-forcing styles in 52 conflict cases in the workplace. Forcing was used twice as often as collaboration, yet in about half the situations in which forcing was used the outcomes were bad, whereas in all instances in which integrative problem solving was used the outcomes were good (Phillips & Cheston, 1979). In another study, a scant 5% of first-line supervisors, middle managers, and top managers and administrators admitted to actually using the collaborating style in specific conflict situations; 41% selected competing and 26% chose avoiding styles (Gayle, 1991). Both male and female supervisors and managers, according to this study, typically select the least effective styles of conflict management.

Even if the style with the greatest likelihood of success is chosen, when and how it is used must also be figured into the equation. Confrontation used as a collaborative tactic can be highly effective, but it is not effective when used in a hit-and-run fashion (D. W. Johnson & R. T. Johnson, 1987a). Confronting contentious issues 5 minutes before the group is due to adjourn or just before you leave for a luncheon date provides no time for another person to respond constructively. **Hit-and-run confrontations** look like guerrilla tactics, not attempts to communicate competently and work out disputes. Likewise, when to use power-forcing is an important concern. **Power-forcing is a style of last resort, except in times of emergencies in which quick, decisive action must be taken and discussion has no place.** If all other approaches to managing conflict produce little result, then competing may be a necessary means of managing the dispute. Power-forcing typically produces psychological reactance. If you try to force, are met with resistance, then attempt to collaborate or accommodate, you may find that this sequence of styles suffers from poor timing. Trying to collaborate after unsuccessfully forcing will be seen as the disingenuous act of a person whose bluff and bluster were challenged. On the other hand, temporarily withdrawing after a protracted feud has stalemated might allow heads to clear and passions to cool. Sometimes we just need a break from the struggle, a chance to think calmly and dispassionately.

Situational Factors

Although some conflict styles have a higher probability of effectiveness than do others, the choice of styles always operates within a context. To understand how to transact conflict effectively in a small group context, certain situational factors should be considered, such as the type of conflict and cultural views of conflict-management communication styles.

▶ **Focus Questions**

1. How do group members short-circuit conflict spirals?
2. Why is principled negotiation superior to other negotiating strategies?

TYPES OF CONFLICT: TASK, RELATIONSHIP, AND VALUE

There are several types of conflicts, and we shouldn't attempt to handle them all exactly the same. Communication styles of conflict management have to be adapted to the different types of conflict to be appropriate and effective.

Task Conflict: Routine or Nonroutine Whether conflicts regarding group tasks are beneficial or detrimental depends largely on the type of task, routine or nonroutine, performed by the group. A **routine task** is one in which the group performs processes and procedures that have little variability and little likelihood of change. A **nonroutine task** is one that requires problem solving, has few set procedures, and has a high level of uncertainty. **Conflicts about routine tasks often have a negative effect on group performance, while conflicts about nonroutine tasks often have a positive effect** (Jehn, 1995). Conflicts regarding routine tasks easily deteriorate into gripe sessions with little opportunity for resolution. As one participant in Jehn's (1995) study noted: "We seem to fight about these things (routine tasks) and they typically can't be changed because that's the way the job has to be done. So the arguments just seem to get in the way of the work" (p. 272). Conflicts about nonroutine tasks, however, promote "critical evaluation of problems and decision options, a process crucial to the performance of nonroutine tasks" (p. 275). These positive results, of course, are predicated on group members choosing a collaborative (problem-solving) style rather than a competing style.

Relationship Conflict: It's Personal Conflicts are not always about task accomplishment. Some of the most frustrating and volatile conflicts are provoked by personality clashes and outright dislike between group members. Participants in the Jehn (1995) study expressed strong frustration with relationship conflicts of this ilk. One person offered, "Trina and I don't get along. We never will get along. We dislike each other and that's all there is to it" (p. 271). Another participant said, "Personality conflicts, personality conflicts. I can't handle it" (p. 271). Although these relationship conflicts usually produce dissatisfaction for group members, they do not necessarily result in low task productivity. Typically, individuals try to avoid each other when personality clashes and outright dislike emerge (Jehn, 1995). They may even redesign their workspace or job to avoid such conflicts.

In actual practice, we do make style choices in terms of our relationships with other parties. Managers typically are accommodating with superiors and compromising with peers (Rahim, 1985). The reality of power imbalances sometimes makes choosing accommodation a matter of self-preservation. Lower-power group members may want to collaborate. Dominating, high-power group members, however, may see little need to collaborate since they can impose their will on other group members. Granted, power-forcing may be an unwise choice for the powerful parties in the long run, but it may be an unavoidable reality you have to face if you're the lower-power person in a conflict.

If a relationship is one of trust and cooperation, regardless of the power disparities, then collaborating has real potential. In one study (Tjosvold, 1986), high-power supervisors in cooperative environments actually used their power to assist subordinates in solving problems. This was not so true in environments characterized by a competitive or individualistic climate. If a relationship is one of mistrust and suspicion, then collaborating will be difficult. Power-forcing is the style of choice among supervisors dealing with subordinates they do not trust (Riccillo & Trenholm, 1983).

In relationships poisoned by mistrust, a collaborative attempt by one party may be seen as a ploy to gain some unforeseen advantage. Accommodating by one party, even as a gesture to change the negative dynamics of the parties in conflict, may be viewed as weakness and a sign that capitulation is likely to occur after a period of waiting.

Interconnectedness of Task and Relationship Conflict: A Critical Concern
Recognizing the interconnectedness of task and relationship dimensions of

groups can be critical when conflict arises (see Closer Look: "KILL Radio Conflict Case Study"). A conflict initially about task accomplishment can easily morph into mostly a relationship conflict, especially if task accomplishment is frustrated (Jehn, 1995). At a college where I was employed, the faculty union and management engaged in bitter negotiations for 2 years. Resources were tight. The union's opening position called for a salary increase of 4% the first year of the new contract and 5% the next. Management countered with opening offers of 0% and 1% salary increases, respectively. Management apparently hoped to send a message to the union that tough bargaining was ahead. The message that was received was quite different. Faculty members felt unvalued and were incensed by what they perceived to be an insulting and contemptible initial offer.

Management miscalculated. A tense, combative climate permeated the bargaining. Even though management eventually accepted the initial salary increase the union proposed, which should have been viewed as a task achievement by the union, a residue of hard feelings remained for years. The dollars and cents proved to be less important than the attitude management communicated to the faculty. If you damage the relationship between disputing parties, even concessions or an integrative solution may not wash away the stains of ill feelings. The conflict may take on a different dimension of a more personal nature.

The following year, management shifted to a collaborative style of bargaining after receiving training from a federal dispute mediator, made a reasonable opening offer, and negotiations were completed in record time without the bitter recriminations. Both the task and the relationship conflict were addressed effectively during negotiations.

Values Conflict: Deeply Felt Struggles The most difficult disputes to manage are values conflicts (Borisoff & Victor, 1989). **Values** are the most deeply felt views of what is deemed good, worthwhile, or ethically right. We may clash over beliefs and still walk away friends, especially if the ideas do not touch much on values. **Beliefs** are what we think is true or probable. "Republicans favor big business" or "Democrats are beholden to labor" are beliefs that don't ordinarily degenerate into fistfights or verbal assaults. When disputes about beliefs spill over into value clashes, however, especially when the values are held passionately, then you have a conflict of a different ilk. Battles over abortion, pornography, creationism versus evolution, flag burning, hate speech, and the like are fundamentally about values such as freedom, right to privacy, and equality. Such conflicts do not lend themselves much to compromise (would you compromise your values?). When dichotomous battle lines are drawn— friends versus enemies, saviors versus sinners—power-forcing is often the style required for conflict management. The courts have had to settle these issues by declaring what is permissible, even essential, and what is prohibited.

CLOSER LOOK

KILL RADIO CONFLICT CASE STUDY

THE SITUATION (based on a real event): Open warfare has been raging for almost a year at public radio station K-I-L-L (slogan: "Live radio that'll knock you dead"). The station operates from facilities on the campus of Bayview Community College in Tsunami, California. KILL radio has 1,000 watts of power, enough to reach into the local Tsunami community (population 42,000).

The program director quit after a feud with the general manager (GM). The GM resigned soon after. His reasons for leaving, stated in his letter of resignation, were as follows:

1. The volunteer staff (community members who were not students) inappropriately editorialized while reading news on the air and presented only one side on controversial issues; both are violations of Federal Communications Commission (FCC) regulations for public radio stations.
2. The volunteers were "insubordinate" when they refused to obey his directives concerning substitution of other programs for previously scheduled regular shows.
3. The volunteers threatened him with bodily injury when he ordered them either to implement his directives or terminate their association with the station.

The volunteer staff countered these allegations with its own accusations: the GM showed them little respect and treated them abusively; they were overworked and underappreciated; and the GM never sought their input on programming and scheduling concerns.

The volunteers issued the following demands:

1. Programming should not be determined by one person, but by a consensus of the staff.
2. Program substitution should be made only when prior notice (at least 2 weeks in advance) has been given so staff members will not prepare material destined to be preempted at the last minute.
3. Volunteers should run the station since they do the lion's share of the work and are the only ones with the necessary technical expertise.

The college supports the station with $85,000 annually, but is seriously considering a drastic cut in the station's budget due to the persistent conflict and because students are not actively involved in the station. The administration wants the station to be a learning laboratory for students interested in pursuing careers in broadcasting.

The volunteer staff has threatened to quit en masse unless their demands are met. The school's board of trustees is getting twitchy because of all the commotion; the faculty in the department of mass communication are in a dither about the conflict because it is disruptive. The local community highly values the station and is upset by the dispute. The college administration named the

▶

chair of the mass communication department at Bayview College as the new general manager and temporary program director of the station.

Before reading further, analyze this dispute. How would you manage this conflict if you were the new GM? Which conflict styles would you employ? When? How?

The Analysis: The KILL radio dispute is a power struggle. Competing/forcing has become the primary style of managing the conflict. The previous GM threatened the staff with termination and the staff threatened the GM with bodily injury. So far, the power-forcing style has produced two resignations, the threat of a mass exodus by the staff, several demands from the staff, and a reservoir of ill feeling and disruption. If you, as the new GM, were to continue in this vein by terminating the volunteer staff, you might ignite a conflict spiral. Disgruntled volunteers might vandalize the station in retaliation, and relations between the college and the community would be strained further. The station would have to shut down until qualified staff could be found to replace those individuals terminated. In such an atmosphere, the board and administration just might decide to close the station permanently and cut their losses.

Since the staff has not been actively consulted in the past regarding programming (at least that's the allegation, and perception is the reality you must confront), the climate is one of control, not problem orientation. The staff feels disconfirmed and defensive. The perception exists among them that the previous GM treated them as expendable technicians, not talented employees worthy of respect. A task conflict spilled over into a relationship conflict.

This situation cries out for collaboration. The first step is confrontation. The new GM should immediately meet with the volunteers, probably individually first, to gather information from their perspective. Staff members feel unappreciated and undervalued. Supportive, confirming statements concerning the essential role volunteers play in the functioning of the station should be made to all involved. Smoothing statements (e.g., "We're starting fresh. I want us to work together") should be delivered to the staff. You're seeking a cooperative working relationship with the volunteers.

In keeping with the desire for cooperation, an appeal to the superordinate goal of keeping the station on the air should be delivered. The new GM must impress on the staff that violations of FCC regulations could result in the revocation of the station's operating license. This is not a matter of personal preference but of law. The GM could further state, "Unless we handle our differences constructively, the college may shut down the station. None of us wants this to happen." There should be no threats about firing anyone. The tone and climate should be positive and focused on the central cooperative goal all can agree to, namely, maintaining the station.

Although final say on the programming issue is the GM's responsibility, input from the staff should be sought actively and given serious consideration. After all, the staff has to make the programming work on the air. That's difficult to accomplish if you'd like to play rhythm and blues but are ordered to play country and western. The staff could conduct a survey of the community (this is a public radio station) to determine the programming preferences of the station's audience. The GM could then make programming decisions based on data from the survey and not on personal tastes of a single

▶

individual or the (possibly narrow) preferences of the staff. One or two experimental programs could be tried as a compromise if community preferences do not match staff preferences in programming. Some compromise may be possible on program substitution (perhaps 1 week prior notice, not 2 weeks as demanded).

Integrating the radio station into the college curriculum should be a fairly simple process. Involving students in the actual operation of the station, perhaps as supervised interns earning class credit, would satisfy a primary concern of the administration and board. This would also expand the resources of the station by training additional individuals to help staff members who already feel overworked.

Finally, the demand that the volunteers run the station would have to be denied. More than likely, however, this demand was made without any expectation that it would be accepted. Avoid this issue unless a staff member raises it. Power-forcing would be required if this issue came to a showdown. Handling other issues effectively may reduce this issue to irrelevance. If disruptions or violations of FCC regulations recur, then those responsible should be terminated.

The key to the management of this conflict by a competent communicator is the flexible use of several conflict styles. No single style alone could effectively manage this complex dispute. The overriding conflict style, however, is collaboration. You begin by confronting central concerns of disputing parties, not competing/forcing. You find integrative solutions where possible. Termination (power-forcing) is a last resort, not a first choice. You compromise only when a better solution cannot be found. You smooth hurt feelings because a supportive environment is essential to the management of conflict. You avoid emotional issues that seem tangential to the real sources of the conflict and are likely to provoke a power struggle.

None of these styles of conflict management, of course, will work unless you think through each step before you take it *(act, don't just react)*. The competent communicator must have knowledge of different conflict styles, the skill to use all the styles, a sensitivity for the requirements of the specific situation and the likely outcomes of each choice made, and a commitment to resolving the dispute as equitably as possible. Complex conflicts require sufficient time to be resolved. This means patience.

Questions for Thought

1. Before you read the analysis of this case study, what action would you have proposed to resolve the conflict? In what ways were your proposals different from the ones suggested in the analysis?
2. Do you disagree with any suggestions provided in the analysis? Explain.

Values conflicts are especially difficult to manage when members of different cultures clash over divergent worldviews. Rubenstein (1975) presented a hypothetical situation to Arabs and Americans. Suppose that a small boat is occupied

Is the contentious issue of the implied importance of "Bushisms" essentially a conflict of belief or value? Does it amuse you, make you mildly irritated, or really upset you?

by a man and his wife, mother, and child when it capsizes. The man is the only occupant who can swim. He can save only one of the three nonswimmers. Which person should he save? All of the Arabs asked by Rubenstein would save the mother because a wife and child can be replaced, but not a mother. Sixty of 100 American college freshmen, however, would save the wife and 40 would save the child. Saving the mother while sacrificing the wife and child was thought to be laughable. Who has the greatest value among the three is a cultural conundrum. Intercultural values conflicts are probably the most difficult to manage.

CULTURE AND CONFLICT: STYLISTIC DIFFERENCES

Individualist and collectivist cultures exhibit a specific difference in communication patterns. Individualist cultures such as the United States and most Western European countries typically employ what Hall (1981) calls low-context communication while collectivist countries such as most Latin American and Asian countries use a high-context communication (Griffin, 1994). **Low-context communication** has a message-*content* orientation and **high-context communication** has a message-

context orientation. "In low-context communication, the listener knows very little and must be told practically everything. In high-context communication, the listener is already 'contexted' and does not need to be given much background information" (E. Hall & M. Hall, 1987, p. 183).

The primary difference between the two is exhibited in verbal expression. Low-context communication is verbally precise, direct, literal, and explicit. A legal contract is an example of low-context communication. Instructions given to computers and e-mail addresses are also examples of low-context communication. Computer instructions must be exact for the computer to function as you desire and e-mail addresses must have every space, number, period, and letter typed exactly.

High-context communication is indirect, imprecise, and implicit. For example, an indirect verbal expression, such as "I'll think about it," may be a face-saving means of saying no in Japan, or it may be assumed that no verbal expression is required to state what should be obvious from the nonverbal context. You are expected to "read between the lines" by recognizing hints and knowing the cultural context and unspoken rules, rituals, and norms. During the Tiananmen Square protest in China in the summer of 1989, there was much confusion concerning who was in control of the government and what position would be taken regarding political and economic reform in the country. Rumors abounded that Chinese leader Deng Xiaoping was dead and civil war was imminent. No statement was released by the government to clarify the situation, as would certainly occur in a low-context culture such as the United States under similar circumstances. Instead, Chinese Premier Li Peng, a hard-line conservative, appeared on Chinese national television. He made no effort to clarify the situation verbally, but he wore a "Chairman Mao uniform" instead of the more usual Western business suit. Viewers could easily interpret what this meant within the context of Chinese culture and history. Li Peng's clothing was a throwback to the uniform commonly worn by Chinese citizens during the conservative, hard-line era of Mao Tse Tung. Li Peng was signaling that he was in charge and a conservative position on political and economic reform prevailed in the government (Muir, 1992).

Individualist, low-context cultures favor direct competitive or compromising styles of conflict management (Cupach & Canary, 1997). Communication during conflict is explicit and direct, sometimes "brutally honest" (Holtgraves, 1997). Americans are inclined to become impatient when members of collectivist cultures "beat around the bush." Allowing a conflict to go unresolved makes most Americans uncomfortable, even agitated. Collectivist, high-context cultures favor avoiding or accommodating styles of conflict management (Chen & Starosta, 1998). Assertive confrontation is considered rude and offensive. It is too direct, explicit, and unsettling. The Chinese culture, for example, considers "harmony as the universal path which we all should pursue" (Chen & Starosta, 1997, p. 6). This philosophy translates into avoiding conflicts that might stir up trouble and disharmony. Conflicts handled ineptly might bring shame on the individual and the entire group. Thus, while Americans tend to focus immediately on task conflicts, Chinese tend to focus on relationship conflicts and avoid task conflicts until the relationships among all disputing parties have had time to build (Jehn & Weldon, 1997). To Americans this may look like stalling to gain advantage.

Conflicts with individuals from other cultures (outgroups), however, are often handled differently in collectivist cultures than are conflicts within the culture (ingroup). Although not the initial choice, competing is not an uncommon way to approach conflict with outsiders, especially if the interests of the opposing parties are highly incompatible. Vicious quarrels, even physical fights, are not uncommon in such circumstances (Chen & Starosta, 1998; Yu, 1997).

Managing intercultural conflicts where expectations on the appropriateness of different communication styles differ is challenging. Remaining flexible by employing a style that is well suited to cultural expectations is a key to effective conflict management in such situations.

Negotiating Strategies

Negotiation is "a process by which a joint decision is made by two or more parties" (Pruitt, 1981, p. 1). **Negotiating strategies are the ways we transact these joint decisions when conflicts arise.** In this section, commonly used strategies of negotiating conflict are discussed.

TIT FOR TAT: DO UNTO OTHERS

The tit-for-tat strategy begins with an act of cooperating, and if the other party or parties in the negotiation follow suit and cooperate, you continue to do the same (you reciprocate). If, however, the other party competes after your initial cooperative offer, then you switch to competing (again you reciprocate).

Those who tout tit for tat (Axelrod, 1984) can make a case for the utility of the strategy when cooperation does occur. Tit for tat will maintain cooperation once it has been initiated because you reciprocate an act of cooperation, thereby encouraging further cooperation from the other party. Tit for tat has been shown to be moderately effective in producing cooperation in some circumstances, particularly when participants are perceived to be firm but fair (Sheldon, 1999). In real situations, however, this strategy runs the risk of provoking **conflict spirals**—the escalating cycle of negative communication that produces destructive conflict. With tit for tat, "once a feud gets started, it can continue indefinitely" (Axelrod, 1984, p. 138). If someone tries to cheat, blackmail, or exploit you in a dispute, should you reciprocate in kind? If another party has a snit fit, should you likewise throw a temper tantrum? If your antagonist demands outrageous concessions from you, should you mindlessly match the demands? Does any of this sound to you like competent communication? As Fisher and Brown (1988) explain, "If you are acting in ways that injure your own competence, there is no reason for me to do the same. Two heads are better than one, but one is better than none" (p. 202). Tit for tat predisposes us to stoop to whatever level the other party is willing to sink. Although a common negotiating strategy, it is not recommended.

REFORMED SINNER: SPREADING REDEMPTION

A second strategy of negotiating is called reformed sinner (Pruitt & Kimmel, 1977). Someone using the **reformed sinner strategy** initially competes or acts tough, then cooperates and relaxes demands. The inducement to cooperate is the demonstrated willingness to compete if necessary. Unlike tit for tat, you try to break a conflict spiral by making the first move toward cooperation.

A rather interesting version of the reformed sinner strategy is Osgood's (1959; 1966) GRIT proposal. **GRIT** stands for **G**raduated and **R**eciprocated **I**nitiatives in **T**ension reduction. Originally offered as a means to de-escalate the international arms race, the strategy has been employed in less-global conflicts.

GRIT tries to break conflict spirals and impasses by initiating a cycle of de-escalation, thus moving from destructive to constructive conflict. This strategy uses the following sequence of steps (see Folger et al., 1993, for greater detail):

1. Issue a *sincere public statement* expressing a desire to de-escalate the conflict.
2. *Specify the concession* to be made, clarifying what, when, and how the action will be undertaken.
3. Follow through and *complete the concession,* but do not make this contingent on reciprocation by the other parties.
4. *Encourage, but do not demand, reciprocation* from the other parties.
5. *Make no high-risk concessions* that leave you vulnerable or in an indefensible position. Don't give away the store.

Someone using this method of promoting cooperation in a competitive conflict situation should consider following the first concession with another concession if no progress is made after a time. Here lies the main weakness of the GRIT strategy—it appears to reward obstinate behavior from the other party (Brett et al., 1998). Thus, don't pile concession onto concession with nothing offered in return. This strategy may take patience and persistence. Offering a minor concession and then withdrawing it when no immediate reciprocation is forthcoming from the other party is not a true GRIT.

POSITIONAL BARGAINING: HARD AND SOFT NEGOTIATING

In positional bargaining, parties take positions on contested issues, then they haggle back and forth until concessions are made and an agreement is reached. There are two styles of positional bargaining: hard and soft. *Hard bargainers* (sometimes called tough bargainers) see negotiation as a contest of wills. Hard bargaining is the "negotiate from strength" approach to conflicts of interest heard so often in foreign affairs deliberations. The focus is on conveying strength and resilience so the other party or parties will yield.

Hard bargaining is a competing/forcing strategy. Hard bargainers can be abusive or sarcastic in an attempt to gain an advantage over the other party. When both sides adopt a hard bargaining style, the battle is joined. Both sides attempt to cut the best deal for themselves (Me-Not-We orientation), instead of finding the most equitable and constructive solution to the conflicts of interest. Opening positions typically are extreme and unreasonable. The more hard bargainers publicly defend these positions, the more hardened the positions tend to become. Egos become identified with positions (task conflict transforms into relationship conflict as well). Concessions easily take on the appearance of "selling out." **Walking out on the negotiations in a huff, refusing to budge even on trivial issues, and issuing ultimatums are commonplace tactics in hard positional bargaining.** "Getting stupid" is a common hard bargaining tactic.

Consider this example of hard positional bargaining among housemates:

A: I want to have a party here at the house on Saturday.

B: Hey, that's a great idea.

C: Sorry, no can do. I have to study for my law exam and I sure can't do that with a couple of dozen of your belching, retching friends cranking the music to a decibel level equivalent to a jet airplane taking off. I'd have to lug a truckload of books and notes to the library or anywhere else I might choose to study.

A: Who appointed you king? This is our house too. Since when do you dictate what can and can't happen around here?

C: Since I pay a third of the rent and am not about to sacrifice my standing in law school so you can get drunk with your brain-dead friends and act like imbeciles. I'm vetoing your little beer bash.

B: I don't even know why we're bothering to ask for your permission to hold this party. There's no way you can stop us anyway. I say we just go ahead and do it. If you don't like it, sue us, Perry Mason.

A: Yeah! Get used to the idea because we're going to have this party and there isn't anything you can do about it.

C: On the contrary, there is a great deal I can do about it. Suing you is actually an option that appeals to me. I could sue you for damages, especially if I do poorly on the exam. I could also argue in small claims court that you violated a verbal contract not to have parties without the consent of all housemates—I have witnesses affirming that you both agreed to such an arrangement. So don't start issuing ultimatums unless you want this party to cost a lot more than the price of beer.

And on and on the silliness escalates, a contest of wills complete with recriminations, threats, name-calling, and anger.

Hard bargaining doesn't have to mean ruthless bargaining and obstinacy, even though it often degenerates into such behavior. A person can achieve positive results by acting tough (Chertkoff & Esser, 1976). Eventually, though, there has to be some give-and-take for a stalemate to be avoided if all parties assume a hard bargaining strategy. The key to making this a constructive conflict strategy is to appear tough but fair.

The main difficulty with this strategy is how tough should you be without seeming pigheaded? **As with any competitive strategy, when hard bargainers face off against each other, their moves and countermoves can easily produce an impasse. Hard bargainers lower the odds of reaching an agreement** (Pavitt & Curtis, 1994). The 2005 National Hockey League strike and impasse that wiped out a season was a hard bargaining fiasco.

Soft bargainers, recognizing the high costs of hard bargaining on relationships with people they may have to interact with once the negotiations are concluded, yield to pressure. To soft bargainers, making an agreement and remaining friends is more important than winning a victory. The major drawback to soft bargaining is that the accommodator may give away too much to maintain harmonious relationships during negotiations.

PRINCIPLED NEGOTIATION: INTEREST-BASED BARGAINING

Fisher and Ury (1981) offer a third choice besides hard and soft positional bargaining—**principled negotiation,** or interest-based bargaining. Principled negotiation embodies the essential elements of competent communication.

The Four Principles: Appropriate Rules All negotiations are conducted according to rules. Principled negotiation changes the rules from competitive (hard bargaining) to cooperative. The four basic elements to this approach with corresponding principles for each element are:

People: Separate the people from the problem.
Interests: Focus on interests, not positions.

Options: Generate a variety of possibilities before deciding what to do.
Criteria: Insist that the result be based on some objective standards.

(R. Fisher & Ury, 1981, p. 11)

Separating the people from the problem reaffirms the importance of supportive climates (e.g., description, problem orientation, equality, or provisionalism) and the inappropriateness of defensive communication patterns (e.g., evaluation, control, superiority, or certainty) during negotiations. Principled negotiation also focuses on task conflicts and strives to diminish relationship conflicts during negotiations.

When Frank Lorenzo became president of Eastern Airlines in 1986, relations between management and labor immediately became tense and personal, and after a year of fruitless negotiations, Eastern's machinists and pilots went on strike. The machinist union targeted Lorenzo as the issue in negotiations, painting him as an unscrupulous takeover artist. The Airline Pilots Association characterized Lorenzo as a Machiavellian sleazeball whose middle name was Greed. Lorenzo fired back, calling the pilots' role in the strike "suicidal" and akin to the Jonestown tragedy. Eastern filed for bankruptcy, and thousands lost their jobs because the parties in conflict could not separate the people from the problem.

Negotiating interests first, not arguing positions, is critical. Positions differ from interests. For instance, a group in my class working on a symposium presentation got into a dispute over topic choice. Two members wanted the group to choose "The Greenhouse Effect." Two other members pushed for "Capital Punishment." The three remaining group members advocated "Animal Rights." Bickering broke out as each faction chose a hard bargaining approach. Nobody was willing to budge. The focus of the bargaining became the weaknesses of each topic advocated by one faction or the other. Put-downs, snide comments, and abusive remarks were flung back and forth.

When instructed to explore their interests, not the positions of each faction, the group found a mutually satisfactory solution. The capital punishment faction had already done a great deal of research on the topic for other classes. Their primary interest was time management since they had families who wanted them home. They wanted to "double dip" by using research for two classes instead of just one. The greenhouse effect faction turned out to have a similar interest. They had done some research on environmental issues. The animal rights faction simply wanted to do a presentation that dealt with an issue of values, not some "dry, scientific report of facts and figures on the environment."

Once the interests of each faction were identified and discussed, the greenhouse effect faction realized that the capital punishment faction had already done most of the necessary research for the entire group presentation. This was far more extensive than the research already completed by those urging the environmental topic. The animal rights group agreed that capital punishment was an issue of values as well as "facts and figures," so they settled on capital punishment as the group topic.

Positions are the concrete things one party wants. **Interests** are the intangible motivations—needs, desires, concerns, fears, aspirations—that lead a party in the conflict to take a position (Ury, 1993). The struggle over which topic best fulfills the assignment is a position, but time management is the interest behind the position in the example above. Interest answers the question why a party takes a position. Focusing on interests instead of positions underlines the importance of structuring cooperation into the deliberations. Positional bargaining structures negotiations as a win–lose game. Negotiating interests structures cooperation into the deliberations because the focus is on the problem and a mutually satisfactory solution, not on the position or the people advocating the position. Focusing on interests, not on positions, is the basis of integrative conflict management.

Generating a variety of options is another aspect of principled negotiation. This involves brainstorming, as already explained in my discussion of problem solving. Integration by expanding the pie or bridging may be discovered in a brainstorming session. The nominal group technique may also prove to be useful here.

Finally, principled negotiation rests on *establishing objective standards* (criteria) for weighing the merits and demerits of any proposal. In the conflict over topic choice just discussed, one primary objective standard that was agreed to was "the least number of hours doing research in the library." An objective standard for "fairness" might be that both parties share equally all risks and financial costs.

Remaining Unconditionally Constructive: Sound Judgment The principled negotiation approach to conflicts of interest must include two additional elements: remaining unconditionally constructive (R. Fisher & Brown, 1988) and developing a **BATNA** (**B**est **A**lternative **T**o a **N**egotiated **A**greement) (R. Fisher & Ury, 1981).

Being unconditionally constructive means you make choices and take only those actions that benefit both you and the other parties in the dispute, regardless of whether the other parties reciprocate. **Remaining unconditionally constructive during negotiations short-circuits conflict spirals.** If they become abusive, you remain civil. If they purposely misunderstand or confuse issues, you clarify. If they try to bully, you neither yield nor bully back. You try to persuade them on the merits of your proposal. If they try to deceive you, neither trust nor deceive them. You remain trustworthy throughout the negotiations. If they do not listen carefully, you nevertheless listen to them carefully and empathically. This is not a guide to earning your way into heaven. This is a realistic, eyes-wide-open guide to *effective* negotiations. You remain unconditionally constructive because it serves your own best interests to do so (Brett et al., 1998).

A story told (Fadiman, 1985) about Gautama Buddha, an Indian prince who lived in the sixth century B.C. and whose teachings formed the basis of Buddhism, exemplifies the unconditionally constructive attitude necessary for principled negotiations. A man interrupted Buddha's preaching with a torrent of abuse. Buddha waited for the man to finish. He then asked his detractor, "If a man offered a gift to another but the gift was declined, to whom would the gift belong?" The man responded, "To the one who offered it." "Then," said Buddha, "I decline to accept your abuse and request you to keep it for yourself" (p. 84). Reciprocating abuse with abuse only sidetracks negotiations onto unproductive avenues of mutual disparagement. Abuse needs to be short-circuited, not encouraged.

What do you do if the other parties insist on hard bargaining, not principled negotiations? You remain unconditionally constructive. If one of your interests is fairness, ask the other parties to explain how their position is fair. Don't assert that the other side offers an unfair proposal. Asking the hard bargainers to justify their position translates positions (e.g., no parties on weekends) into interests (e.g., peace and quiet in order to study). Personal attacks, threats, and bullying tactics can be handled by confronting them openly and immediately. For example, "Threats are not constructive. They won't work. I negotiate only on merit. Can we return to the substantive issues?" Research shows that labeling the hard bargaining tactic as ineffective and refusing to reciprocate bad bargaining behavior effectively refocuses the negotiations on interest-based issues and prevents conflict spirals (Brett et al., 1998). If necessary, short-circuit the hard bargainers' game plan by forthrightly asking for the rules of the game. For instance, "Before we go any further, I need to know what rules we are following during this bargaining. Does everyone here want to achieve a fair settlement in the quickest amount of time, or are we going to play the hard bargaining game where blind stubbornness wins out?" Make them convince you that their intentions are honorable. In the process they may convince themselves that hard bargaining isn't appropriate. You want to bring hard bargainers to their senses, not to their knees (Ury, 1993).

The BATNA: Best Alternative To a Negotiated Agreement   You also need to develop a BATNA as a standard against which any proposal can be measured. Your BATNA tells you what is the best you can do if negotiations fail to produce an agreement. Most importantly, your BATNA keeps you from accepting an agreement worse than what you could have done without negotiations.

For instance, if you have ever visited towns on the Mexican side of the border with the United States, you have undoubtedly engaged in street negotiations with local merchants on items such as handcrafted rugs, sunglasses, pottery, and other items. Not having a BATNA before entering into negotiations with merchants can lead you to overpay for merchandise. If you have no idea how much comparable items would cost in the United States, then you are likely to make a charitable contribution to the Mexican economy when negotiating with a savvy merchant on what you think is a hot deal. Your BATNA in this instance is a comparable item that sells at a slightly higher price in the United States, a similar item of better quality for more money, or a similar item of lesser quality for less money. You know when you've negotiated a real value if you have such a BATNA. Information is power. A BATNA can save you from making a serious mistake (R. Fisher & Ury, 1981).

Anger Management

Conflict in most situations produces anger. Workplace anger, for example, has become widespread and a national concern (Glomb, 2002; Marino, 2000). Although it is not always harmful to dispute resolution in groups, anger can easily trigger a tit-for-tat response of retaliatory anger from others that disrupts constructive negotiations (Friedman et al., 2004). The most commonly reported communication behaviors associated with workplace anger include: yelling, swearing, hurling insults, using sarcasm, criticizing, giving dirty looks, making angry gestures, throwing things, and physical assault (Glomb, 2002). Thus, managing anger is an important aspect of constructive conflict management in groups.

CONSTRUCTIVE AND DESTRUCTIVE ANGER: INTENSITY AND DURATION

There are numerous ways group members express anger. One study (Domagalski, 1998) reported that women more commonly than men use avoiding, crying, and holding back tears as expressions of anger. Men are more likely than women to express anger outwardly toward others rather than to camouflage or hold in the anger. "Domineering, uncivil behavior by others" is the most common trigger of anger in work situations.

The **difference between constructive and destructive anger depends on two conditions: the intensity and the duration of the anger expression** (R. Adler & Towne, 1999). The *intensity* of anger can vary from mild irritation to outright rage. The more intense the anger, the more likely it is that outcomes will be negative (Glomb, 2002). Mild to moderate expressions of anger can signal problems that must be addressed in groups. In such circumstances the anger can be constructive. Rage, however, is destructive. It is the antithesis of competent communication because the group member expressing the rage is out of control. In the workplace, rage is not appropriate because it "shows you've lost control—not to mention that it's tough to be articulate if you're having a conniption" (Black, 1990, p. 88). Temper

Bruce Ayres/Getty Images

Hard bargaining often leads to destructive anger.

tantrums, ranting, and screaming fits make you look like a lunatic because you're "getting stupid." When used as a power-forcing strategy during conflict, it will likely provoke counter rage.

The *duration,* or how long the anger lasts, also determines whether anger is constructive or destructive. The length of an anger episode can vary from momentary to prolonged. Quick flashes of anger may hardly cause group members to notice. Even intense anger, if brief, can underline that you are very upset without causing irreparable damage. Prolonged expressions of anger, even if mild, however, can cause group members to tune out and ignore you. Highly intense anger that is long-lasting is a combustible combination. Venting our anger, despite popular notions to the contrary, merely rehearses our anger and can *increase it* (Tavris, 1989). "Blowing off steam" awakens our anger. It doesn't put it to bed. As Rage Against the Machine guitarist Tom Morella noted after Zack de la Rocha quit the band in November 2000 citing the group's poor decision-making process, "We have spent so much time raging against one another that we have often left raging against the machine by the side of the road" ("Perspective," 2000, p. 23).

MANAGING YOUR OWN ANGER: TAKING CONTROL

There are several steps you can take to diffuse your own anger when you sense that it is approaching the destructive stage of intensity and duration.

1. *Reframe self-talk.* Thoughts trigger anger. If you think a group member intentionally sabotaged your work, you feel righteously angry, even vengeful. If you believe that no sabotage was intended and that there was merely a misunderstanding, then anger usually doesn't ignite. As a first step in managing your own anger, try assuming group members did not intend to harm you. View harm as accidental or simply the result of clumsiness unless there is clear evidence to the contrary. Reframing the way we think about events can deflate our anger before it escalates (Baron, 1990).

2. *Listen nondefensively.* When group members criticize, blame, or ridicule you, refuse to be defensive. Reframe the criticism or blame as a challenge or problem, not an opportunity for retaliation. Counter defensive communication from others with supportive communication.

3. *Deliberately calm yourself.* Exercise discipline and refuse to vent your anger. When you sense anger boiling to the surface, deliberately slow your breathing. Count to 10 before responding to collect yourself. A cooling-off period may be necessary. Typically, it takes about 20 minutes to recover from a surge of adrenaline that accompanies anger. This cooling-off period can work effectively to calm your anger (Goleman, 1995).

4. *Find distractions.* Don't rehearse your anger by constantly revisiting past injustices or slights instigated by fellow group members. Distract yourself when old wounds resurface. Read a newspaper, watch television, play with the dog, or take a walk with someone and discuss subjects unrelated to the anger-inducing subject.

Don't attempt to employ all four of these steps at once. Pick one and work on making it an automatic response when your anger wells up. Then try a second step and so on.

MANAGING THE ANGER OF OTHERS: COMMUNICATION JUJITSU

Managing conflict constructively means defusing and de-escalating the anger of other group members so you can confront issues without eruptions of verbal or physical aggression. It is usually best to address a group member's anger first before dealing with the substance of the dispute that triggers the anger (Donohue & Kolt, 1992). Try these suggestions for defusing the anger of others:

1. *Be asymmetrical.* When a group member is expressing anger, especially if it turns to rage, it is critical that you not strike back in kind. Be asymmetrical, which means do the opposite. Counter rage with absolute calm. Stay composed. Hostage negotiators are trained to defuse highly volatile individuals by remaining

absolutely calm throughout the interaction. Imagine the outcome if hostage negotiators flew into a rage while talking to hostage takers. Use smoothing techniques to quiet the enraged group member.

2. *Validate the other person.* Validation is a form of the smoothing technique of collaborating. Let the person know that his or her point of view and anger have some validity, even though you may not agree. You can validate another person in several ways. First, you can take responsibility for the other person's anger. "I made you angry, didn't I?" acknowledges your role in provoking anger. Second, you can apologize. "I'm sorry. You have a right to be angry" can be a very powerful validation of the other person. Apologies, of course, should be offered only when truly warranted. Third, actively listening and acknowledging what the other person has said can also be very validating. "I know it upsets you when I don't come to meetings on time" makes the other person feel heard, even if conflict remains.

3. *Probe.* Seek information from an angry group member so you can understand his or her anger (McKay et al., 1989). When you ask a question of an angry group member, it forces the person to shift from emotional outburst to rational response. Simply asking, "Can we sit down and discuss this calmly so I can understand your point of view?" can momentarily defuse a group member's anger.

4. *Distract.* Shifting the focus of attention when a person is really out of control can sometimes short-circuit rage. A humorous quip, an odd question, a request for help, or pointing to an unrelated event can break a rage cycle.

5. *Assume a problem orientation.* This is supportive communication. This step should occur once you have calmed the angry group member by using previous steps. Approach the anger display as a problem to be solved, not a reason to retaliate. The question "What would you like to see occur?" invites problem solving.

6. *Refuse to be abused.* Even if you are wrong, feel guilty, or deserve another person's anger, do not permit yourself to be verbally battered (McKay et al., 1989). Verbal aggression is unproductive no matter who is at fault in a conflict. "I cannot discuss this with you if you insist on being abusive. I can see you're upset, but verbally assaulting me won't lead to a solution" sets a ground rule on how anger can be expressed.

7. *Disengage.* This is the final step when all else fails to defuse a group member's anger. This step is especially important if the person continues to be enraged and abusive despite your best, most constructive efforts to calm the emotional storm. Firmly state, "This meeting is over. I'm leaving. We'll discuss this another time."

Keeping track of all seven steps to quell the anger of group members, particularly when faced with an enraged person, is too much to expect. **Concentrate on one or**

two steps until they become almost a reflex reaction, a habit. Being asymmetrical is the crucial first step, with validation a close second. The remaining steps can gradually become part of your anger-defusing skill package.

Anger is a common companion of group conflict. The constructive management of conflict can occur only when anger is kept under control. This does not mean squelching anger. A group member can feel angry for good reasons. Anger acts as a signal that changes need to occur. Anger should not be used as a weapon, however, to abuse others. We want to learn ways to cope with and express anger constructively, not be devoured by it.

In summary, conflict is a reality of group life. Although most people would prefer that conflict didn't exist, there are both positive and negative aspects to conflict. Constructive management of conflict can turn conflict into a positive experience for the group. The five primary communication styles of conflict management— collaborating, accommodating, compromising, avoiding, and competing—all have pros and cons depending on the situation. Nevertheless, collaborating has a higher probability of producing constructive outcomes than does competing. Negotiation is a universal process used to manage conflicts of interests. Principled negotiation is the most productive means of resolving conflicts of interests. ◦ ●

Questions for Critical Thinkers

1. If competition has so many disadvantages, why would the competing/forcing style ever be appropriate for a competent communicator?
2. If principled negotiating is so effective, why isn't it used more often?

InfoTrac College Edition

Log onto InfoTrac College Edition.

1. Type "collaboration" in the search window. Choose an article and write an essay on it comparing its conclusions to material in this text. SUGGESTION: Article A15312597, by Stephen Anderson, entitled "Unions/management create collaborative culture."
2. Type "conflict" in the search window. Choose an article to critique. SUGGESTION: Article 30863749, by Granger Macy and Joan Neal, entitled "The impact of conflict-generating techniques on student reactions and decision quality."

Video Case Studies

*The War of the Roses (1989). Black Comedy; R; *****

This is a very dark comedy depicting all the ways not to manage conflict. Analyze this film for destructive conflict and communication styles of conflict management. Which styles are predominately used by the main characters?

*What's Cooking? (2000). Comedy/Drama; PG-13; ***1/2*

This is a portrayal of four separate families (African American, Vietnamese, Mexican American, and Jewish) trying to celebrate Thanksgiving. Identify the communication styles of conflict management used by the characters. Are conflicts mostly task, relationship, or a combination of both? How does culture affect conflict management? In what ways is anger managed? Are these ways effective?

11 Technology and Virtual Groups

T HE COMPUTER REVOLUTION was slow to incorporate small groups and teams (Majchrzak et al., 2004). The early mainframe computers were behemoths that facilitated companywide operations but were largely unavailable to the average worker in an organization. The advent of the personal computer in the 1970s and 1980s facilitated individual productivity. It wasn't until the 1990s when the Internet and the World Wide Web were readily available, however, that virtual groups became a staple of most organizations. In 1995, a mere 16 million people worldwide used the Internet (Bazeley, 2005). A billion people worldwide were Internet users 10 years later (Internet Usage Statistics, 2005). Although rudimentary versions of virtual groups already existed prior to the Internet revolution (e.g., teleconferences), the stratospheric rise in Internet access accelerated the widespread growth of virtual groups.

A **virtual group** is a small group whose members rarely interact face to face, and who mostly communicate by means of electronic technologies (Lipnack & Stamps, 1997). Virtual groups have three primary characteristics that make them different from conventional groups (K. Fisher, 2000): their members are spread across multiple locations and often across multiple time zones; group members often have more diverse backgrounds incorporating members from different cultures speaking multiple languages and harboring varied organizational allegiances; and membership tends to be less stable. In short, virtual groups are members "working together apart" (K. Fisher, 2000).

Although researchers and scholars often make no clear distinction between a virtual group and a virtual team (see Godar & Ferris, 2004; Rad & Levin, 2003), the two are not identical. They have electronic technologies and remote communication in common, but they differ in the same ways that standard face-to-face groups and teams differ: level of cooperation, diversity of skills, group identity, and commitment of members (see Chapter 6). An online class discussion group, for example, is a virtual group but not a virtual team. Electronic technologies make remote communication possible, so class members may never see fellow students face to face. Participants, however, join the virtual discussion to express points of view and share perceptions. A high level of cooperation is not required to participate, members aren't chosen because of diversity of skills, little effort is made to establish a group identity (students are merely fulfilling a course requirement), and commitment to the discussion may be lackluster and sporadic.

The primary purpose of this chapter is to explore the vast potential of and the new challenges posed by virtual groups. This chapter focuses on the broader topic of virtual groups, not the narrower virtual teams, although virtual teams qualify as a type of virtual group. The suggestions offered for making virtual groups effective apply well to virtual teams, especially if previous advice on making teams effective is employed. There are three chapter objectives relevant to the primary purpose:

1. to describe the many ways technology integrates with small group communication,
2. to discuss the advantages and disadvantages of virtual groups, and
3. to offer suggestions regarding how to develop and maintain effective virtual groups.

Let me offer one cautionary note before addressing these objectives. Despite considerable research that compares virtual groups to face-to-face groups, significant gaps in our knowledge about virtual groups remain. Our experience with virtual groups is barely beyond its infancy. Nevertheless, that should not prevent sharing what is known and offering tentative advice based on the available research.

Technological Group Options

Multiple electronic communication technologies make virtual groups possible. A **technology** is a tool to accomplish some purpose. A communication technology is a tool to achieve a communication purpose. Electronic communication technologies that make virtual groups possible include the Internet, e-mail, fax, phones, video, and voice mail. Any of these technologies, singly or in combinations, create a variety of virtual group opportunities discussed in this section.

TEXT-MESSAGING: TYPING GONE HIGH-TECH

There are several text-based options for virtual groups. E-mail has become so popular and so taken for granted as part of most of our daily lives that it's difficult to remember when this technological marvel was not readily available. E-mail is a principal method of communicating in organizations, both within an organization (intranet) and between organizations (Internet) (Barnes, 2003).

In its most fundamental form, e-mail can be used for communicating in virtual groups by typing a message and sending it to group members. They in turn can respond to your message, add additional information and opinions, and include the ever-popular attachments to the message. The ease with which attached information can be sent to any and all group members is potentially a benefit and a drawback simultaneously. The benefit is that a large amount of information is available to the group with minimal effort required, but e-mail attachments can easily produce information overload and can create unreasonable expectations regarding how much information each group member can digest in a short time.

Text-only messaging is not relegated to computer-based e-mail. Text-messaging with cell phones has become a worldwide phenomenon. Approximately 3 billion text messages are sent each day worldwide, with almost 40% originating from Asia (Ha, 2005). Although not yet a popular tool for virtual groups, the potential to communicate with team members who are dispersed across the globe is real. Electronic bulletin boards and newsgroups in which posted messages are available to group members and everyone's responses are available to be read is yet another option in the text-only toolbox for virtual groups. These are popular options for online college classes.

Text-only interactive meetings are facilitated by hardware and software options called Group Decision Support Systems (GDSS). The simplest version permits participants to register votes electronically on issues discussed during meetings. This allows for anonymity. Another version of GDSS is for electronic brainstorming, previously discussed in Chapter 8. There are chat rooms that permit group member interaction through text-messages. Even more elaborate (and expensive) systems can be used that add audio and video to computer e-mail messaging for virtual group work, taking the technology beyond text-only. More sophisticated hardware and software options will surely be developed.

AUDIOCONFERENCES: VOICE-ONLY TECHNOLOGY

In-person meetings are what most of us are accustomed to, but as our globe becomes more village-like with the ever-expanding reach of electronic technology, and organizations increasingly conduct business internationally, meeting face to face is often a poor choice. There are several electronic alternatives to the standard in-person format. One of the simplest is the teleconference, commonly referred to as the conference call. This version of a virtual group allows several individuals to conduct a joint meeting over the telephone, or in some instances by a computer-based voice link. Teleconferences are easy to set up. Most business and many residential phone services provide conference call capability. Remember that a teleconference is not simply a phone conversation. Its primary purpose for virtual groups is to conduct meetings. Most of the guidelines for conducting efficient and effective meetings already discussed in Chapter 8 apply to teleconferences. **The conference call should be necessary, focused, organized, and short.**

VIDEOCONFERENCES: SIGHT AND SOUND

Videoconferences are more technologically sophisticated than teleconferences. Meetings are conducted via closed-circuit or satellite-linked television. The videoconference, similar to the teleconference, is a useful option when participants cannot meet easily in person. Videoconferences provide nonverbal cues such as facial

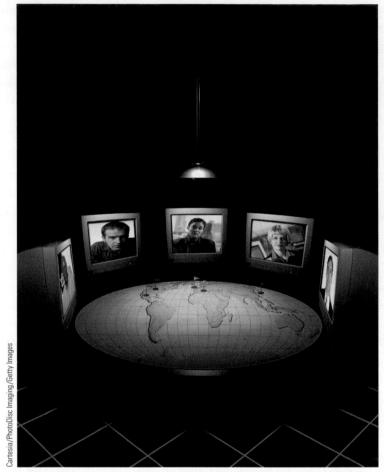

Cartesia/PhotoDisc Imaging/Getty Images

Videoconferencing is one way technology has created the "death of distance" advantage of virtual groups.

expressions, gestures, posture, and eye contact unavailable in teleconferencing. Body language cues help participants assess messages more accurately and they are instrumental in defining relationships between participants (Thompson & Coovert, 2003).

The technology has become so sophisticated that virtual team members meeting by videoconferencing across several time zones begin to feel that they are all in the same room. Members will offer each other sandwiches or snacks, forgetting they're thousands of miles apart (Lipnack & Stamps, 1997). The technology necessary to produce such an effect, however, is more complicated and expensive than what is required for a teleconference. Adding the visual element to a virtual meeting can require a studio equipped with pricey cameras, lighting, and a crew. Less expensive digital cameras connected to personal computers is one alternative to the more elaborate videoconference production, but the quality of the video images remains an issue. Pictures often are too small (a cell phone videoconferencing option is available, but the image is hardly bigger than a postage stamp), and images can be fuzzy. Technological improvements may rectify these problems soon. **Videoconferences, as with any meeting, should be necessary, focused, organized, and short.**

Benefits and Challenges of Virtual Groups

Virtual groups present a mixed batch of advantages and disadvantages. In this section, several important pros and cons of virtual groups are addressed with the repeated notation that further research will likely modify some of what we "know" about virtual groups.

TIME AND SPACE: THE DEATH OF DISTANCE

Time and space can be transcended by electronic technologies. Cairncross (1997) coined the phrase "the death of distance" to emphasize, in somewhat overstated fashion, that virtual groups are not restricted by distances separating group members. Group members can communicate with each other at the speed of light over vast distances, even continents. Finding one central meeting place available at a specific time is not an issue for virtual groups. Members can connect at home, at their office, even in airport terminals, or restroom stalls—a survey by Wirthlin Worldwide showed that 39% of respondents would converse on a cell phone while answering nature's call (cited in Carpenter, 2000). As wireless technology becomes evermore sophisticated and readily available, few limitations on where and when a group member can join discussions and meetings will exist.

Being able to communicate over vast distances, however, removes group members from physical proximity to each other. **Communication competence becomes a significant challenge.** What works well in face-to-face communication may not work well in virtual group communication. Sarcasm, gentle teasing, or harmless joking may be taken as hurtful or insulting in the absence of a glint in the eyes of the sender, a smile, a clarifying gesture, or a subtle facial expression. The absence of nonverbal cues that we all depend on for helping determine meaning of messages is a substantial limitation of text-only and voice-only virtual groups.

DECISION MAKING: QUALITY OF THE OUTPUT

Valacich and Schwenk (1995) state, "There are no compelling theoretical or empirical reasons for predicting differences in decision quality" (p. 161) when comparing face-to-face and virtual groups. This may be true in general when comparing

Don Wright — Palm Beach Post

The death of distance and the ability to "meet" with virtual group members almost anywhere isn't always an advantage, especially for outsiders.

face-to-face communication to all types of virtual groups lumped together. There are exceptions, however. Virtual groups working under time pressure, for example, do not perform as well as face-to-face groups in the same condition (Thompson & Coovert, 2003). Text-only electronic technology may slow down decision making if delays occur because group members haven't checked their e-mail or don't respond immediately, for whatever reason. Presumably, videoconferencing would not produce such delays or consequent frustration from group members pressured to decide, unless technological glitches occur that force delays or require cancellation of the virtual conference. **One study of 64 virtual groups revealed no significant differences in decision quality when comparing text-only and audio-only technologies, but the addition of video to the audio-only group produced a significant improvement in decision quality** (Baker, 2002).

The more time-consuming it is for virtual groups to make decisions, the less satisfied members are with final decisions (Thompson & Coovert, 2003). Frustration and annoyance with learning elaborate new technologies, sometimes referred to as "mechanical friction," may impair the decision-making process, at least until all members feel confident using the technology (Poole et al., 1993). Mechanical friction may invite human friction—abrasiveness in social relationships—as group members struggle with the frustrations of trying to manage technologies that aren't always user-friendly.

SOCIAL RELATIONSHIPS: DEVELOPING PERSONAL CONNECTIONS

Group decision quality can also be significantly affected by social relationships among members (interconnectedness of task and social dimensions). This is no less important in virtual groups than in face-to-face ones. Virtual groups pose unique challenges in this respect. How do you identify with team members whom you have never met personally or ever seen?

Virtual groups seem to require more time than face-to-face groups to develop positive social relationships and cohesiveness (Griffith & Neale, 1999). Virtual group members tend to rate each other unfavorably early in the development process, but after several weeks of interacting, ratings of members on trust, receptivity, sociability, informality, and relaxation become more positive (Walther & Burgoon, 1992).

One potential benefit of text-only and audio-only group communication is that social bonds between group members can be based on more substantive features such as the quality of conversation, values and beliefs similarities, and apparent friendliness of members, instead of more superficial physical appearance (McKenna & Green, 2002). Physical features are not readily available in text-only or audio-only group interactions (although members' photographs can be scanned onto websites and e-mail locations). This advantage, however, is more speculative than tested, and to what extent this appearance deficit might be an advantage of virtual groups is not known.

POWER DISTANCE: PROMINENCE OF STATUS CUES

Power differences may be less prominent in virtual groups. Rank is less obvious when e-mailing group members than it is when communicating face to face. This status equalization effect, however, is probably more prominent in text-only group discussion than it is in audioconferences or especially videoconferences.

There are two types of status characteristics that are hidden from text-only communication: (1) physical characteristics such as ethnicity, gender, and age, and (2) communication cues such as rapid speaking rate, fluency of speech (few pauses or disfluencies such as "Ums" and "Ahs"), emphatic tone of voice, strong eye contact when speaking, and head of the table seating location (Driskell et al., 2003). E-mail-only communication among group members screens these status markers that are immediately available in face-to-face communication. Audioconferencing screens out some of these status markers, although age, gender, ethnicity, and even physical attributes can often be discerned from voice-only communication (Krauss et al., 2002). It should be noted, however, that this status equalization effect might be only temporary—experienced during the initial development of a virtual group. More mature groups typically develop status markers even when relegated to text-only communication, such as waiting a long time to respond to messages from less-powerful group members, answering questions with curt responses, and using "powerful" language (Rocheleau, 2002). Conversely, grammatical errors and misspellings, especially if they occur often and in numerous messages, may taint a group member as poorly educated, careless, and unconcerned about credibility with other group members (all status diminishing). **This is why it is important to proofread text messages before sending them.**

CONFLICT: CONSTRUCTIVE AND DESTRUCTIVE

As discussed in Chapter 10, not all conflict is counterproductive for groups. Conflict that is competently managed can promote important, positive changes. Face-to-face groups engage in significantly more constructive conflict management than virtual groups. Virtual groups are more likely to move in the direction of destructive conflict than are face-to-face groups (Zornoza et al., 2002). Overall, face-to-face is a more suitable medium for constructive conflict management than technological alternatives (Zornoza et al., 2002).

Transactions among virtual group members are more likely to become incendiary than in face-to-face groups, especially in text-only formats (Driskell et al., 2003). "Emotional incontinence"—incompetent outbursts of anger called "flaming"—is more likely (Locke, 1998). The absence of normal constraints on incivility and insults found in face-to-face transactions (such as implicit norms discouraging nasty public displays of rage), coupled with the ease and swiftness of text-only communication, encourage more negative interactions. As Brin (1998) explains:

> Electronic conversations seem especially prone to misinterpretation, suddenly and rapidly escalating hostility between participants, or else triggering episodes of sulking silence. When flame wars erupt, normally docile people can behave like mental patients. . . . Typing furiously, they send impulsive text messages blurting out the first vituperation that comes to mind, abandoning the editing process of common courtesy that civilization took millennia to acquire. (p. 166)

Communication filters that operate in face-to-face communication to short-circuit emotional incontinence are less apparent when communicating electronically. Nonverbal indicators of disapproval, such as a glance, a frown, or an eye roll, are missing from text-only and audio-only group interactions. What you wouldn't say to a member's face you might say in an e-mail. Research shows that members of virtual groups are more inclined to offer negative, even extreme evaluations, disapproval, and censure of other members (Walther, 1997). Software has even been developed that automatically warns e-mailers about potential flames. One such version displays an ice cube icon as a group member composes an e-mail, indicating that no flame has been detected. The instant that the e-mailer slips into flame territory, however, a chili pepper icon appears on screen. An extremely incendiary message receives three chilies with the warning, "Your message is the sort of thing that might get your keyboard washed out with soap" (Weber, 2000).

Misunderstandings can be a big problem for virtual teams because perceived slights, insults, or a negative tone in e-mails may not be quickly cleared up. Members may have to stew over a perceived insult for a day, even a week, if an e-mail response is not accessed right away. **Differences that emerge from virtual group membership that may represent several diverse cultures can also lead to misunderstandings and perceived insults.** Establishing group norms can be difficult in virtual groups when cultural differences create clashes about approaches to addressing conflicts, directness of communication, and respect for high-power group members. Cultural differences are often challenging to address in face-to-face groups, but they can be doubly so when text-only or sometimes even audio-only communication is available. The ambiguity of language discussed in Chapter 1 is not easily recognized or clarified when the communication media limit nonverbal contextual cues that help with understanding messages.

Virtual groups, however, don't always have greater difficulty with conflict than face-to-face groups. One study showed that virtual groups have less tendency to transform task conflicts into relationship conflicts than face-to-face groups when conflict is escalated by a member using personal attacks, trivialization of issues, and disagreements about policies (Dorado et al., 2002). Text-only communication in particular tends to focus members on the task and less on personality clashes and interpersonal hostilities. It may also be appropriate when face-to-face communication among members has a history of being awkward or intimidating (Markus, 1994).

Sometimes we can be more honest and assertive in an e-mail than in person. Words can also be more carefully chosen, and messages can be edited for tone more judiciously than a group member may be able to do when feeling angry and communicating face to face. How often have you replayed a hostile conversation in your mind and wished you hadn't made certain statements or had cushioned negative comments? In some instances, setting aside an angry e-mail response to a perceived insult or slight by another group member and deciding, upon reflection, to delete it entirely, is a wise choice. **E-mail allows you to edit intemperate messages, but** only if you resist firing a flame in the heat of the moment by adopting a standard practice of never responding heatedly to an e-mail until you have had time to reflect, simmer down, and edit offensive remarks.

MEMBER PARTICIPATION: MOTIVATION TO PERFORM

Motivating group members to participate actively and constructively is one of the common complaints about group work and a frequent reason for grouphate. Virtual groups can enhance participation in some instances and diminish it in others.

Social Anxiety: Reticence to Participate Text-only group discussions encourage low-status members to participate in discussions and to stand their ground more firmly on controversial or contentious issues (Sproull & Kiesler, 1991). In-person discussions can be intimidating, especially if some participants are dominating and aggressive when expressing their points of view. Typing responses on a computer keyboard can embolden reticent group members to be assertive. In one study of social anxiety that compared face-to-face communication to Internet chat room interactions, highly anxious individuals (shy, reticent to communicate) reported feeling extremely uncomfortable in the face-to-face condition; during chat room, text-only communication, however, highly anxious individuals reported feeling almost as comfortable as nonanxious individuals in the face-to-face condition (Green & McKenna, 2002). In addition, these same anxious individuals were perceived by other group members to be confident, likable, and outgoing—exactly the opposite perception group members reported when anxious individuals engaged in face-to-face communication. **There is even some evidence that after 2 years of active participation in chat room group discussions, socially anxious individuals experience diminished social anxiety in face-to-face interactions** (McKenna & Green, 2002). These results suggest that text-only group communication can encourage greater constructive participation from reticent members, thereby potentially enriching the discussions and producing greater overall satisfaction with the group experience, with the added potential bonus of diminished social anxiety in face-to-face interactions.

Videoconferencing, however, may be *more* intimidating for reticent group members. The surest way to discourage reticent group members from participating is to conduct meetings electronically when members feel intimidated by the hardware and unskilled in the use of software alternatives. Appearing on camera may increase anxiety for reticent members. The mere presence of a camera can cause some individuals to freeze or appear unnatural in their movements, speaking rate, tone of voice, and overall appearance. Gaining experience and skill with videoconferencing will likely diminish such anxiety.

Social Loafing: Virtually Unproductive Social loafing can be a maddening problem for face-to-face groups because all parts in a system are interconnected.

Although little research has been conducted on social loafing in virtual groups, the potential for this to be an even more serious problem than in face-to-face groups is real (Driskell et al., 2003). My wife, Marcy, has taken almost a dozen on-line university courses relevant to her employment as a computer program analyst at Cabrillo College. In every instance, she has expressed enormous frustration with social loafers—virtual group members whose lackluster motivation leaves the bulk of group projects to members who are more motivated to excel.

The nature of virtual groups makes addressing this problem particularly difficult (see Chapter 3 for a detailed discussion of methods to address social loafing). Developing cohesiveness, one method of reducing social loafing, is challenging because strangers are often thrown together in online classes and told by an instructor to magically become a team. Holding members accountable, another method to combat social loafing, is especially challenging because face-to-face appraisal of members' efforts and production is an effective deterrent to social loafing (Druskat & Wolff, 1999). Unless virtual group members meet in-person from time to time, however, this option is not available when conducted by e-mail or audioconferences, and delivering a negative appraisal of a virtual group member in a videoconference will likely seem awkward at best. Confronting the loafer about lackluster participation is one promising approach in face-to-face groups, but text-only formats can easily be ignored by loafers when their lackluster effort is addressed directly. Marcy and other online group members confronted loafers on several occasions, and almost every time the response was prolonged silence from the loafers. They simply ignored the direct concerns of more motivated members. In a couple of instances, loafers were contacted by phone and asked why the lethargic performance occurred, and they were encouraged to participate in the group project more enthusiastically. This approach worked well in some instances, especially in one instance in which sporadic participation was actually the result of a family crisis. It didn't work in every case, however.

In one especially troublesome example of loafing faced by one of Marcy's online groups, the course instructor was contacted (a higher power was consulted) and asked to intervene, which she did. The loafer dropped the course. No loafer was ever officially booted out of any of Marcy's online course groups for loafing (obviously not an option for students participating in online courses). Ultimately, the most flagrant cases of loafing required motivated members to sidestep the loafer. They engaged in social compensation (discussed in Chapter 3), bailing out the group by doing far more than their share of the work, so that the group didn't perform poorly. Social compensation is clearly not a perfect solution to social loafing. It places an undue burden on the most motivated members.

The ideal solution to social loafing is to choose virtual group members who find the group task challenging and interesting, and who all seem motivated to excel. This is often the result when virtual teams are formed within organizations. Those most interested in the task and members whose skills are complementary (overlapping but not redundant) are chosen to become part of a team. Nevertheless, because group membership for online courses is usually haphazard (little opportunity is provided to choose members knowledgeably in a virtual environment), social loafing is likely to be a serious problem in most online classes that require group work. Social compensation is frequently the best alternative unless the course instructor takes a very active role in monitoring group participation.

CONVERSATIONAL DOCUMENTATION: TRANSACTIONAL TRANSCRIPTS

Reconstructing group conversations is easier and the message fidelity can be better than what is usual in face-to-face group communication when using text-only, computer-mediated communication. When group members communicate by e-mail, there is a transcript of conversations that can be accessed by all team members at any time. Arguments concerning what one member actually said can be settled by consulting previous e-mailed messages for the exact wording. It's untenable for a group member to insist that he or she said one thing when the e-mail transcript clearly indicates a different message.

This potential advantage of an e-mail transcript, however, could also be a disadvantage in some circumstances. Proving a member wrong by consulting the e-mail record may provoke contentious communication within the group. Settling

---

> ●● SECOND LOOK

POTENTIAL ADVANTAGES AND DISADVANTAGES OF VIRTUAL GROUPS

ADVANTAGES	DISADVANTAGES
Distance not a problem—members connected across many time zones	Learning unfamiliar, complicated technologies
Cost savings on travel, lodging, food	Decision quality jeopardized under time pressure
Initial status equalization	Difficulty developing positive social relations among group members
Greater assertiveness from reticent members	Greater likelihood of destructive conflict
Decreased social anxiety (text-only and audio-only media)	Cultural misunderstandings difficult to address
Settling arguments by consulting text transcripts (e-mail)	Increased social anxiety (videoconferencing—camera-shy)
	Embarrassment from private e-mails becoming public transcripts

an issue may stir up hostile, defensive communication patterns. Rocheleau (2002) also points out that e-mail communication can pose potential problems for groups because of its transcript availability. Teams operating in organizations could experience a loss of cohesiveness if members forward e-mails to team leaders or outside supervisors, which attempt to present a member in a negative light. "Ratting" on a team member may bring issues of social loafing or disruption to everyone's attention, but constructively addressing such issues only by e-mail is enormously difficult. Therapy groups conducted by e-mail also raise legal issues of confidentiality. Inappropriate jokes, comments, and gossip e-mailed to group members have a way of leaking beyond the group and igniting legal concerns about sexual harassment (creating a hostile group environment) and bias. **A good rule to follow is don't type anything in an e-mail to any group member that would cause you shame or embarrassment, or necessitate an apology if it were read by individuals other than those who were sent the message.** Private e-mails can become public revelations.

Virtual Group Effectiveness

Virtual groups experience the same challenges and have the same capacity for success as face-to-face groups (Tullar & Kaiser, 2000). Making virtual groups effective is often more difficult, however, than producing successful face-to-face groups. "Misunderstandings are more likely to arise and more things are likely to go wrong" (Lipnack & Stamps, 1997, p. xxi). Integrating different technologies into the group process complicates both the task and social dimensions of virtual groups. In this section, general factors influencing virtual group success are discussed, and specific suggestions for virtual group effectiveness are offered.

GENERAL FACTORS: GETTING SET FOR SUCCESS

There are three general factors that need to be considered as fundamental underpinnings of potential success in virtual groups. They are temporality, media richness, and media synchronicity.

Temporality: Long-Term versus Short-Term Virtual Groups Most research studies on virtual groups use ad hoc groups of strangers (usually college students) that meet for short periods of time, then disband. Relatively few studies have been conducted on virtual groups whose members have worked together extensively in a computer-mediated, communication environment. This fact requires caution when interpreting research that compares virtual groups to face-to-face groups (Driskell et al., 2003). Groups that gain experience in the virtual world likely have fewer difficulties than those unfamiliar with new technologies. Even a technology as simple as the teleconference can pose initial difficulties when group members are unfamiliar with each other. Identifying who is speaking when you haven't matched the voices with the group members can be quite perplexing. When group members have a shared history developed in long-term transactions, virtual group effectiveness improves (Alge et al., 2003). When virtual group members work together long enough to receive training in media use, effectiveness also improves (Lurey & Raisinghani, 2001). Finally, when time together permits the development of personal relationships in a virtual environment, effectiveness improves (Pauleen & Young, 2001). Along this line, e-mail messages may pose fewer problems of misinterpretation and confusion when exchanged between virtual group members who know each other well (Mennecke et al., 2000). Virtual group members may have opportunities to meet in person, talk on the phone, and see each other in videoconferences when working together long-term. Combining several media can provide a richer group environment.

Media Richness: The Lean and Meaty Theory   Daft and Lengel's (1986) media richness theory (MRT) posits that communication media vary along a continuum of **richness**—the information-carrying capacity of each form of communication. Determinations of richness are based on the inherent capacity of each medium to show nonverbal cues, provide rapid feedback, present personality traits, and permit language variety. **Media richness varies from high to low as you move, in order, from face-to-face transactions, to video, to audio, and finally to text-only communication** (Zornoza et al., 2002). Communication media with high richness are presumed to be personal and warm, and communication media with low richness ("lean") are impersonal (detached) and cold (factual) (Rasters et al., 2002). MRT predicts that lean media, such as text-only varieties, are most effective for group discussions of simple, unambiguous topics and tasks (for example, text-only brainstorming that involves transmission of specific ideas but is hindered by "richer" emotional, personal responses that might interfere with task accomplishment). Rich media (especially face-to-face communication), however, are predicted to be most effective for complex, uncertain topics and tasks, such as conflicts of interest that require information about attitudes, feelings, expectations, commitment to resolving disagreements, and so forth (Zornoza et al., 2002).

MRT has some intuitive appeal. Virtual group members may view e-mail as a godsend when quick transmission of factual information to all members simultaneously is advantageous, but they may feel constrained by text-only communication when cultural misunderstandings emerge. In fact, there appears to be a strong need to enrich virtual group technology when it seems too lean. Emoticons (such as ☺ for happy; ☹ for very sad or frowning; and =:O for screaming in fright with hair standing on end) and abbreviations (such as LOL for laughing out loud; POS for parents over shoulder change subject; ROTFL for rolling on the floor laughing; and

<Y> for yawning and <G> for grinning) have been created to provide more enriched feedback when nonverbal cues are unavailable.

Despite the intuitive appeal of MRT, research supporting it has been mixed (Strab & Karahanna, 1998). The theory is well supported when applied to traditional media (face-to-face communication, letters, and memos), but when newer electronic media are considered, such as e-mail and videoconferencing, the research results are inconsistent (Dennis & Kinney, 1998). Many researchers argue, however, that MRT has not been appropriately tested because media choices by virtual groups and members' perceptions of those choices have received emphasis, but actual virtual group performance related to these choices has received comparatively little attention (Rasters et al., 2002).

Although MRT isn't an overarching theory of effective media use in virtual groups, it is one explanatory piece of the virtual group puzzle. MRT draws attention to the richness of face-to-face communication and to the challenges posed by leaner technological media. E-mail, for instance, is often a poor choice for addressing complex conflicts and issues. Its constricted richness, however, makes resolving complex relational conflicts difficult but certainly not impossible.

Media Synchronicity: Extending MRT Media synchronicity theory (MST) extends media richness theory by providing a dynamic, time-changing quality to the richness of each communication medium (Dennis & Valacich, 1999). MST suggests that no communication medium can be designated "richest" or "leanest" based on an inherent, unchangeable information transmission capacity. Instead, **the richest media are those that best meet the communication needs of the group.** Sometimes this means using synchronous media and other times asynchronous media. **Synchronous media** are those that permit simultaneous, same-time interactions among group members, modeled after face-to-face meetings. Teleconferences, videoconferences, and chat rooms are examples of synchronous media. **Asynchronous media** are those that permit anytime/anyplace communication among group members without interruption. Messages are posted and read at the convenience of other group members. Standard e-mail, bulletin boards, and text-messaging are examples.

Media synchronicity theory is appealing and potentially insightful, but little research has been conducted on it. Nevertheless, it offers some help in making media choices for virtual groups. For example, one study of computer-mediated Alcoholics Anonymous (AA) meetings found that "Asynchronous AA groups, in some ways, appear to be the prototypical supportive environment" (VanLear et al., 2005). Asynchronous AA meetings were characterized by highly personal communication, and they were more supportive (exhibited more frequent empathic responses) and less defensive (fewer negative evaluations) than synchronous AA meetings. Asynchronous support groups permit delayed, thoughtful responses, so hair-trigger criticisms may be squelched before they are ever sent (this is probably true more for support groups, given their empathic purpose, than work groups). Individuals too shy to share intensely private revelations during in-person AA meetings are more inclined to share in virtual groups, especially asynchronous bulletin boards. Consider one such bulletin board exchange between a newcomer just joining the virtual group and old-timer AA members (VanLear et al., 2005):

> **BB:** I've gone 12 days [sober]. . . . I'm realizing my incredible shyness is gonna get me drunk. I went to a mtg [meeting] to meet ppl [people] but I left; didn't talk to anyone. . . . I wish I could force myself not to be shy . . . thanks for letting me share.
>
> **DD:** Glad you're here BB. KCB [Keep coming back].
>
> **EE:** Thanks BB, I'm shy too. I learned to ask open-ended questions. (p. 23)

BB wasn't able to share her personal revelation about shyness during face-to-face AA meetings, but she shared this almost effortlessly in her new virtual asynchronous group. The impersonal nature of text-only, asynchronous media can permit the communication of highly personal revelations by blunting the awkwardness of face-to-face public disclosure of private information. Text-only asynchronous media may make embarrassing or uncomfortable disclosures less awkward by removing the intimidating and immediate presence of some who might stare or others whose eyes might glaze over from apparent lack of interest.

SPECIFIC SUGGESTIONS: TENTATIVE ADVICE

The virtual group experience is still relatively new. In fact, most of you probably have had little, if any, experience with electronic brainstorming, videoconferences, or even group conference calls, although you'll likely take an online course that requires group projects, if you haven't already.

Any suggestions offered to meet the unique challenge of integrating technologies into the group process are necessarily tentative until much more is learned about virtual groups. Nevertheless, some suggestions can be made that will likely prove helpful should you have an opportunity to participate in a virtual group.

Choosing Media: Richness and Synchronicity Because the use of electronic media is the principal distinction between virtual groups and standard, face-to-face groups, choosing media wisely is a key consideration. Groups that choose communication media haphazardly are likely to regret their casual decision. Of course, media choice may be out of your hands. Students doing group projects for online courses are usually told by the instructor to use certain media to accomplish the task (usually what is affordable).

Enriching the virtual group environment is especially important during the initial stages of group development (Thompson & Coovert, 2003). Most virtual teams, recognizing the importance of an enriched media environment during initial group development, tend to rely heavily on face-to-face communication to build cohesiveness (Kerber & Buono, 2004). In-person contact and socializing builds trust and improves group success (Creighton & Adams, 1998; Furst et al., 2004). In organizations, this usually involves travel. **The in-person, meet-and-greet process is highly recommended, if possible, during group formation.** Online courses often have an initial face-to-face meeting at the beginning of the course, and some (such as public-speaking classes) usually have several interspersed throughout the term. If face-to-face meetings are not feasible, teleconferences or videoconferences are suitable compromises for enriching the online group environment. **As virtual groups mature in development, media richness is not as critical because members learn to function effectively based on member familiarity and acquired knowledge** (McGrath & Hollingshead, 1994).

As indicated previously, sometimes virtual groups are more effective using synchronous media and other times asynchronous, depending on the communication needs of the group. Real-world support for this is provided by a study of 54 highly successful teams whose members represented 26 companies from a wide variety of industries and cultures spread across many time zones (Majchrzak et al., 2004). Detailed reports and interviews from leaders and members of these successful teams noted that when projects require complementary competencies and diverse perspectives and the tasks can be performed using electronic technologies, virtual groups are a better choice than face-to-face groups.

Teams generally had a negative view of asynchronous e-mail and synchronous videoconferences, but they had a positive view of synchronous teleconferences and asynchronous, text-only postings. E-mailing in one-to-one exchanges inevitably caused other members to feel left out of the conversational loop, eroding trust and producing dysfunctional behavior (instant messaging apparently wasn't available). To rectify this, some teams copied all members on every e-mail message. This produced information overload. Members resorted to deleting e-mails without reading them. This produced confusion. Dissatisfaction with videoconferencing mostly involved poor quality video production. Those who used desktop videoconferencing were frustrated by the fuzzy picture quality. Returning to the videoconferencing facility at work after normal business hours, especially when working with members located in vastly different time zones, was also an unwelcome inconvenience. Teleconferences, however, were easy to conduct (often from home), and they

CLOSER LOOK

COMCORP CASE STUDY

FOR A YEAR-AND-A-HALF, Kerber and Buono (2004) studied the launch and development of a virtual team in the corporate training and development section of a company they refer to as Com-Corp. ComCorp is a $3-billion company with about 8,000 employees. The team was composed of 11 members spread across many time zones and four countries (United States, England, Ireland, and Australia). A teleconference, for example, would begin at 1:00 p.m. for some members, 9:00 p.m. for others, and 6:00 a.m. for still other members. The challenge facing this newly developed team was to design training and development solutions that would work well for a large global company experiencing a significant restructuring.

Fostering strong social relations among team members was a challenge for the ComCorp team. The team leader (not identified by name) immediately recognized the need for a rich communication environment. His immediate goal was "to establish, develop, and sustain lavish information flow among all team members, despite their geographic distance and virtual presence" (Kerber & Buono, 2004, p. 12). This was accomplished by using a combination of synchronous (such as, teleconferences, one-on-one phone calls, and in-person meetings between members who were able) and asynchronous communication media (such as e-mail, fax, and voice-mail messages). The team leader established a routine to solidify group cohesiveness and build social relationships among members. This routine consisted of exchanging photographs during the forming stage and later to update personal events in members' lives that help cement social bonds; conducting weekly group teleconferences; having person-to-person phone meetings between the leader and each member every 2 weeks; engaging in "icebreaker" exercises during teleconferences (such as each member describing his or her most embarrassing experience);

▶

functioned well to discuss disagreements. Text-only postings worked well to prepare members for teleconferences. **Successful teams adapted technology to meet their communication needs** (see Closer Look: "ComCorp Case Study").

Conducting Virtual Meetings: Special Challenges The specific steps for conducting productive group meetings discussed in Chapter 8 all apply well to virtual groups. Review these steps before your first virtual meeting.

There are several additional concerns that you should address as the group leader or meeting chair. First, choose the appropriate technology for the meeting.

and encouraging social conversation during a designated part of the teleconferences. The leader remained accessible to all members.

Team performance was also monitored routinely. Teleconference agendas routinely consisted of open discussions that reviewed the team purpose and relevant results attained by the group at that point, possible modification of objectives, recognition of breaking issues, brainstorming possibilities for achievement, making decisions in a collaborative process, and implementing decisions by assigning members to the implementation process (in other words, the Standard Agenda was mostly followed). Ongoing evaluations of team progress on training projects were conducted during teleconferences. Quarterly reports were issued on team accomplishments. Team members were supported through coaching, frequent feedback, recognition of accomplishments, and an emphasis on

personal development. This approach has the effect of reducing social loafing and increasing commitment to the team's challenging goals.

Team leaders must work harder to sustain strong member satisfaction in virtual groups than in face-to-face groups (Hoyt & Blascovich, 2003). Group members reported strong satisfaction with the virtual group experience and the overall team leader and group performance. As one member explained, "Our team leader did an excellent job of leading while respecting the wealth of expertise and experience in the team. We did not feel stifled . . . We really worked well as a team, particularly when [the team leader] had us continually focus on our major priorities and strategies" (p. 11). A variety of measures indicated that the Com-Corp virtual group was highly successful, due in no small part to the team leader's attention to media richness and synchronicity.

Questions for Thought

1. Is the success of this virtual team the result of unique circumstances or can the results be generalized to all virtual groups?
2. Would videoconferencing have improved the group cohesiveness?

Sophisticated technologies are just complicated toys if they are not matched properly with the purposes and objectives of the group. If videoconferencing equipment is old and of poor quality, a teleconference may be a better choice. Trial and error will eventually indicate what works best for the group given group goals and restrictions on equipment and facilities. Second, limit the size of the group. It is more difficult to recognize when a group has grown too large for an effective meeting to take place when there are no rooms to get stuffy and no seating capacity concerns. Keep the group size as small as possible so the technology does not complicate the discussion process. Third, plan for scheduling difficulties. If your virtual group is composed of members spread across multiple time zones, don't schedule a meeting at 6 p.m. San Francisco time, for example. Members living in London would have to meet at 2 a.m. Fourth, check all technological equipment before each meeting to be sure that everything is in top working order. Technological glitches can disrupt the flow of a meeting, even destroy it. Have someone available at short notice who can correct technological problems during a virtual meeting. Fifth, make certain each group member is well versed in the technology used to conduct the meeting. Remind members that sensitive microphones may pick up whispers between members during videoconferences. This could cause embarrassment or create cross talk that interferes with the fidelity of message transmission. Virtual meetings, at first, may seem stilted and difficult to manage, but with practice the technology can almost seem to disappear.

This concludes my discussion of communication competence in small groups. One of the central points that I hope has come through loudly and clearly is that one person can make an enormous difference in the quality of the group experience. What you individually do or don't do may be the difference between a successful and a less-than-successful group. Competent communication begins with you. The We-orientation is the core of group effectiveness. Don't look to others to make groups work. Take the knowledge you've garnered from this textbook and the skills that you will develop as you put this knowledge into practice and focus them on improving the group experience. ● ●

Questions for Critical Thinkers

1. As technology continues to improve, is it likely that virtual groups will ever seem exactly like face-to-face groups?
2. As technology becomes more sophisticated, and complicated, which challenges presented by virtual teams might become more problematic? Will any become less so?

ℹ️ InfoTrac College Edition

Log onto InfoTrac College Edition.
1. Type "virtual groups" in the keywords search window. Choose an article to read. SUGGESTIONS: Article A126315479, by Kenneth Kerber and Anthony Buono, entitled "Leadership challenges in global virtual teams: Lessons from the field."
2. Type "computer mediated communication" in the keywords search window. Choose an article. SUGGESTION: Article A131163250, by C. Arthur VanLear and others, entitled "AA online: the enactment of supportive computer mediated communication."

Video Case Studies

Citing movies, even recent ones, that involve virtual groups can seem quickly outdated, even quaint because technology changes so rapidly. Nevertheless, there are movies that can be analyzed and applied to chapter material despite "old" technology.

*Sneakers (1992). Drama; PG-13; ****; Mission Impossible (1996). Drama/Action; PG-13; ****

Consider both of these movies. Are there examples of virtual groups? Identify synchronous and asynchronous communication media. How does either affect communication?

Group Oral Presentations

Groups sometimes have public-speaking responsibilities. In some cases the group has been formed to present information orally before an audience of interested people. To assist those with little or no training or experience in public speaking, I am including this brief appendix, which covers some of the basics of oral presentation. I discuss types of group oral presentations, speech anxiety, attention strategies, organization, and use of visual aids.

Typical Types of Group Oral Presentations

There are three main types of oral group presentations. They are panel discussions, symposiums, and forums.

PANEL DISCUSSIONS: FREE EXCHANGE OF IDEAS

Panel discussions assemble a small group of participants, usually experts, to engage in a free exchange of information and ideas on a specific issue or problem before an audience. Purposes of a panel discussion include solving a difficult problem, informing an audience on an issue or topic of interest, or stimulating audience members to think about the pros and cons of a controversial issue.

Panel discussions require a moderator. The moderator usually organizes the group presentation by soliciting panel members who represent different points of view on the topic or issue. Panel members should be informed in advance of the topic to be discussed and major issues that should be addressed by panelists. **The moderator should follow several steps to make the panel discussion successful.**

1. Suitable physical arrangements for the panel discussion should be organized in advance. Usually, the number of panelists should be no fewer than three and no more than seven. Panelists should be seated at a long table in front of the audience, normally on a stage overlooking audience members. When group discussions involve more than four or five participants, seating panelists at two tables formed in a slight V-shape to the audience helps panelists address each other during discussions without closing off the audience. Name cards placed on the table in front of each speaker will help the audience become familiar with each panelist. If the room where the panel discussion takes place is relatively large, a microphone at the table should be available for each speaker. If panelists request

a VCR/DVD and monitor, computer hook-up, easel, chalkboard, or other means of presenting visual aids, provide these and place them in a location where access to them is easy and will not block the audience's view.

2. The moderator usually begins by welcoming the audience, providing a brief background on the topic or issue to be discussed, and introducing each panel member, citing specific background and qualifications of each speaker.

3. Panelists should be encouraged to bring notes, but discouraged from reading a prepared manuscript.

4. Begin the discussion with a question posed to the panel (e.g., What is the extent of the problem of binge drinking on college campuses?). The opening question can be posed to the entire panel, or a specific panelist can be asked to begin the discussion. The moderator identifies who has the floor during the discussion.

5. The moderator acts as a discussion guide. If a panelist has been left out of the discussion, the moderator may direct a question to him or her. If a panelist begins to dominate discussion, the moderator should step in and request participation from other panelists. Controversy should be encouraged, but polite conversation should be the norm. It is the responsibility of the moderator to keep the conversation civil. If it begins to turn ugly, the moderator should remind panelists to disagree without being disagreeable. Move the discussion along so that all major issues are discussed in the allotted time (usually about 45 minutes to an hour).

6. The moderator closes discussion by summarizing main points made by panelists and identifying new issues raised during the discussion to be further explored.

SYMPOSIUM: STRUCTURED GROUP PRESENTATIONS

A **symposium** is a relatively structured group presentation to an audience. It is composed of several individuals who present uninterrupted speeches with contrasting points of view on a central topic. A symposium is similar to a panel discussion except that speakers do not engage in a discussion with each other. They present relatively short speeches (usually 4–6 minutes apiece) addressing the pros and cons of a controversial issue or problem. Often an open forum with the audience occurs once all speeches have been presented. The primary purpose of a symposium is to enlighten an audience on a controversial issue or to inform audience members on a subject of interest.

A symposium also benefits from having a moderator. **The moderator should follow a few important steps to ensure a successful symposium.**

1. Physical arrangements made for a panel discussion, just discussed, should also be used for a symposium.

2. To avoid redundancy, speakers should be chosen who represent different points of view.

3. The moderator should provide a brief background on the subject, introduce the speakers, and identify the speakers' order of presentation.

FORUM DISCUSSION: AUDIENCE PARTICIPATION

A **forum discussion** allows members of an audience listening to a public speech, panel discussion, symposium, or debate to participate in a discussion of ideas presented. The primary purpose of a forum is to engage the audience in the discussion of issues raised. The moderator's role is critical to the success of a forum discussion. **Some suggestions for the moderator who directs the forum include:**

1. Announce to the audience that an open forum will occur after a panel discussion or symposium has concluded. Audience members can prepare questions or short remarks as they listen to speakers.
2. Rules for forum participation should be clearly articulated before any discussion occurs. Rules may include: raise your hand to be recognized or stand in a line where a microphone has been placed and wait your turn; keep remarks and questions very brief (about 30 seconds); only one follow-up question for each person.
3. Set a time limit for the forum (usually about 30 minutes). Indicate when there is time for only one or two more questions. Accept questions until the deadline has been reached, then conclude the forum by thanking the audience for its participation.
4. Encourage diverse points of view from the audience. A pro and con line might be established. The moderator could move back and forth, recognizing audience members on both sides so a balanced series of questions and comments will be presented.
5. If a question cannot be heard by all members of the audience, the moderator should repeat the question. If a question is confusing, the moderator may ask for a restatement or try to paraphrase the question so panelists or forum speakers can answer.

Speech Anxiety

Virtually everyone experiences some anxiety about having to make a public presentation. In one survey, 85% of the respondents reported that speech anxiety (also referred to by some as stage fright or performance anxiety) was a major and serious fear in their lives (Motley, 1995). With any four individuals, odds are that two will feel at least an occasional butterfly in the stomach before giving a speech. The third person will suffer nervousness that can be bothersome, but not incapacitating.

The fourth person will be so anxiety-ridden that he or she will avoid classes that require oral presentations, skip meetings, refuse job promotions, or even change jobs or occupations to escape public speaking.

Even college instructors experience speech anxiety. In one study, 87% of psychology instructors confessed that they had experienced speech anxiety associated with some aspect of teaching (Gardner & Leak, 1994). Sixty-five percent of these same subjects rated their most extreme case of speech anxiety between "definitely unpleasant" and "severe or extreme." You're not alone if you are anxious about having to make an oral presentation in your class.

You can "cure" speech anxiety with heavy doses of tranquilizers, but, aside from the physiological dangers associated with them (they're potentially addictive), they will make you appear witless in front of an audience because they deaden mental acuity. So if you're concerned about appearing lobotomized in front of groups, avoid drugs used as a cure for anxiety.

Speech anxiety, however, is not necessarily a demon to be exorcised. **The degree of anxiety, not the anxiety itself, requires attention.** A moderate amount of anxiety can enhance performance and energize a speaker. You can present a more dynamic, forceful presentation when energized than when you feel so comfortable that you become almost listless and unchallenged by the speaking experience.

When the intensity of your fear about speaking in front of people gets out of control, however, it then becomes debilitative and detracts from your performance. Intense anxiety can be cause for real concern if ignored. It will congest your thought pathways, thereby clogging your free flow of ideas. In such a condition, every speaker's nightmare—going blank—will likely occur. Also, a terror-stricken speaker feels an urge to escape. Consequently, a 7-minute speech is compressed into 3 minutes by a staccato, hyper-speed delivery. The quicker the speech presentation, the quicker the escape.

The causes of speech anxiety are complex and varied. Space does not permit a thorough discussion of these causes. **Generally speaking, the causes of speech anxiety are self-defeating thoughts and situational factors.**

Self-defeating thoughts include negative thoughts that predict failure, desire for complete approval from an audience, and an awareness that audience members will evaluate your speaking performance. *Negative thoughts* about your speaking performance can wildly exaggerate potential problems and thus stoke the furnace of anxiety. Those harboring negative thoughts predict not just momentary lapses of memory, but a complete meltdown of mental functions ("I know I'll forget my entire speech and I'll just stand there like a idiot"). Minor problems of organization are magnified into graphic episodes of total incoherence and nonstop babbling. Perfectionists also anguish over every flaw in their speech and overgeneralize the significance of even minor defects. A flawless public-speaking performance is a desirable goal but why beat up on yourself when it doesn't happen? Perfectionists make self-defeating statements to themselves such as "I'm such a fool. I mispronounced the name of one of the experts I quoted"; "I must have said 'Um' at least a dozen times. I sounded like a moron"; and "My knees were shaking. The audience must have thought I was afflicted with a disorder of my nervous system." Ironically, the imperfections so glaringly noticeable to perfectionists usually go unnoticed by most people in the audience. Even the most talented and experienced public speakers make occasional errors in otherwise riveting performances.

Another self-defeating thought that triggers speech anxiety is the *desire for complete approval* from your audience, especially from those whose opinion we value. It is irrational thinking, however, to accept nothing less than complete approval from an audience. You cannot please everyone, especially if you take a stand on a controversial issue. When you set standards for success at unreachable heights, you are bound to take a tumble.

The fact that *an audience evaluates you* every time you give a speech, even if no one is formally grading your performance, will usually trigger some anxiety. Human beings are social creatures who dislike, even fear, disapproval from others. Even if you aren't seeking complete approval or adulation from your listeners, you would be a rare individual if you were completely immune to the judgments of others hearing you speak. Public speaking becomes doubly intense when formal grades are given for each speech performance.

There are many situational causes of speech anxiety. Two prominent ones are novel situations and conspicuousness. *Novel situations*— ones that are new to you— create uncertainty, and uncertainty can easily make you tense. For most students, public speaking is a novel situation. Few students have given many speeches in their lifetime, and some have never given a formal public address. Fortunately, as you gain experience speaking in front of audiences, the novelty wears off and your anxiety will diminish.

The *conspicuousness* of the public-speaking situation increases most people's anxiety. Most students tell me that speaking to one or two persons is usually not very difficult, but speaking in front of an entire class or an auditorium filled with a thousand people really makes them want to toss their lunch. Here the interaction of conspicuousness and approval can be easily seen. Standing alone before a few people and possibly failing is not nearly as big a deal as possibly failing in front of a huge crowd. In the former situation, your potential failure would likely remain an isolated event, but in the latter situation the entire school might be in on your humiliation— so goes the logic.

So how do you manage your speech anxiety, given the variety of causes that induce it? Numerous individuals have suggested to me that picturing your audience nude, or clothed only in underwear or in diapers, can be helpful (assuming you can stifle your laughter when the image pops into your mind). Breathing deeply is also a favorite tidbit of wisdom offered by many as a quick-fix coping strategy for stage fright. These remedies have some merit, especially if they work for you. None of them, however, offers a reliable solution to speech anxiety. There are many more effective methods.

First, there is no substitute for *adequate preparation.* Conducting proper research on your speech topic, organizing your speech clearly and carefully, and practicing it several times are all essential if you hope to manage your anxiety effectively. Adequate preparation also must include physiological preparation, such as ensuring proper nutrition just prior to the speech event. Ignoring your physiological preparation for a speech may cancel out the benefits of other methods used to manage your speech anxiety. Consequently, do not deliver a speech on an empty stomach, but also do not fill your stomach with empty calories. You need high-quality fuel such as complex carbohydrates to sustain you while you're speaking. Simple sugars (doughnuts, Twinkies), caffeine (coffee, colas, chocolate), and nicotine (cigarettes) should be avoided or ingested in very small quantities. Adequate preparation will reduce uncertainty and the fear of failure.

Second, *gain perspective* on your speech situation. Consider the difference between rational and irrational speech anxiety. A colleague of mine, Darrell Beck, worked out a simple formula for determining the difference between the two. **The severity of the feared occurrence times the probability of the feared occurrence** provides a rough approximation of how much anxiety is rational and when you have crossed the line into irrational anxiety. Severity is approximated by imagining what would happen to you if your worst fears came true—you bombed the speech. Would you leave the state? Would you drop out of school? Probably not, since even dreadful speaking performances do not warrant such drastic steps. You might consider dropping the class, but even this is unlikely since fellow students are very understanding when a classmate delivers a poor speech. So even a poor speech does not rationally warrant joining the monastic life or making any significant life changes. The probability that your worst nightmare will come true and you will give a horrible speech, however, is extremely unlikely if you have adequately prepared. Thus, working yourself into a lather over an impending speech lacks proper perspective if you follow the advice given here.

Third, *refocus your attention* on your message and your audience and away from yourself (Motley, 1995). You cannot concentrate on two things at the same time. If you dwell on your nervousness, you will be distracted from presenting your message effectively. Focus on presenting your message clearly and enthusiastically. View the speaking experience as a challenge to keep your audience interested, maybe even an opportunity to change their minds on an issue.

Fourth, *make coping statements* to yourself as you give your speech, especially when you momentarily stumble. When inexperienced speakers make mistakes during a speech, they tend to make negative statements to themselves. You forget a point, momentarily lose your train of thought, or stammer. Immediately, the tendency is for you to say to yourself "I knew I would mess up this speech" or "I told everybody I couldn't give a decent speech." Instead, try making coping statements while you're delivering the speech. When problems arise say "I can do better" or "I'm getting to the good part of my speech." Talk to yourself during your speech in positive ways to counteract self-talk that defeats you. When parts of your speech go well, compliment yourself on a job well done (to yourself, of course, not out loud). This sustains and energizes you as you proceed through the speech.

Gaining and Maintaining Attention

Audience interest doesn't just happen magically. Interest is garnered by carefully planning and utilizing strategies of attention. Although gaining and maintaining attention throughout your speech is an important goal for any speaker, attention strategies should enhance a speech, not detract from it. A disorganized speech gains attention but in a negative way. Frequent verbal and vocal fillers such as "you know," "um," and "ah" draw attention to inarticulateness.

Some attributes of stimuli, by their very nature, attract attention. Consider just a few of these attributes and how they can become attention strategies.

First, *intensity* is a concentrated stimulus that draws attention. Intensity is an extreme degree of emotion, thought, or activity. Relating a story of a woman fleeing for her life from a stalker can be intense, especially for those who fear such an occurrence. Don't be too graphic when describing emotionally charged events, however, or you may offend and alienate your audience.

There are several basic stylistic techniques that promote intensity and rivet an audience's attention. Direct, penetrating eye contact is a useful technique. How does a daydreamer continue to ignore you when you are zeroing in on the daydreamer? **The lack of eye contact so typical of manuscript speeches, in which every word of your speech is written on the paper in front of you, underlines the importance of not reading a speech to an audience because you break connection with your listeners.** Direct eye contact is an attention builder, but lack of eye contact is an attention destroyer.

Variation in vocal volume is a second technique for provoking intensity. A raised voice can be quite intense. It punctuates portions of your speech much as an exclamation point punctuates a written sentence. The use of a raised voice, however, can be a rather shattering experience for an audience. Incessant, unrelenting, bombastic delivery of a message irritates and alienates an audience. Punctuate with a raised voice only those points that are especially significant and deserve closer attention.

Silence can also be intense. A pregnant pause—silence held a bit longer than usual if you were merely taking a breath—interjects drama into your speech and spotlights significant points.

A second stimulus attribute that induces attention is called *the startling.* You try to stun, surprise, and shake up your audience. A startling statement, fact, or statistic can do this quite effectively. Startling statements such as, "AIDS clearly has the potential to decimate the human population"; "Calories can kill you"; and "You may be living next door to a terrorist" can make an audience sit up and take notice. That it costs more to feed and house a criminal in prison than it does to send him or her to the most expensive university in the country is a startling fact. Of course, you do not want to startle your audience if you can't support your claims with evidence.

Every startling stimulus does not produce constructive attention from an audience. Speakers can startle and offend at the same time. A few examples from my own experience and those of my colleagues make this point. One student (during a speech on food poisoning) gained attention by vomiting scrambled eggs into his handkerchief, raising serious doubts about the speaker's good taste. Another student punched himself so hard in the face that he momentarily staggered himself (the speech was on violence in America). Yet another student fired a pistol at his audience (blanks only). After classmates dusted themselves off, they showed no inclination to listen to the rest of his speech on gun control.

All of these examples have one thing in common: the speakers startled their audience but lost credibility in the process. Tasteless jokes, ethnic slurs, and offensive language will also startle an audience and gain attention, but at a substantial cost to the speaker. The general rule applies—**attention strategies should enhance the effectiveness of your speech, not detract from it.**

Making a problem or issue appear *vital* to an audience is a third attention strategy. There are two principal ways to do this. First, the problem must be made vital not in some abstract or general sense, but in a specific, immediate, and meaningful sense. An audience's primary question when told that a problem exists is "How does it affect me?" The problem becomes vital and therefore meaningful when listeners can see how the consequences of inaction directly affect their interests and well-being. "One out of every 10 women in this audience will contract breast cancer and a similar number of men listening to me will contract prostate cancer. Those of you who escape the disease will likely know one or more friends or relatives who will die from these forms of cancer" is an example of how to personalize a problem and make it seem vital to an audience. Be careful, however, not to overstate your case by depicting relatively trivial concerns as vital. For an issue to be accepted as vital, it must have the ring of truth. Credible evidence must substantiate your claim that the problem is vital.

Using *novelty* is a fourth attention strategy. Audiences are naturally drawn to the new and different. Unusual examples, clever quotations, and uncommon stories attract attention because they are new and different. Beginning your speech with a novel introduction is especially important. Do not begin by telling the audience what your topic is. That is very unoriginal and boring. Create interest in your topic with a novel opening—an unusual news event, story, or human interest example related to your subject. For instance, notice how the following introduction grabs attention by using novelty:

Acting as his own attorney, an Oklahoma City robbery suspect became agitated when a witness identified him in court as the guilty party. I should have blown your head off, he screamed, adding on quick reflection, if I'd been the one that was there. The verdict? Guilty. Lesson to be learned? Acting as your own attorney is a foolish idea.

Novelty can be a very effective attention strategy, especially for the introduction to your speech, but also throughout your presentation.

Finally, using *humor* is a superior attention strategy if used adroitly. You should be able to incorporate humorous anecdotes, quotations, and personal stories throughout your speech. **There are several important guidelines, however, for using humor effectively as an attention strategy.** First, don't force humor. If you aren't a particularly funny person and have never told a joke without omitting crucial details or flubbing the punch line, then don't try to be a comedian in front of your audience. Humorous quotations, funny stories, and amusing occurrences can be used without setting them up as jokes. Simply offer them as illustrations of key points, and, if the audience members are amused, they will laugh.

Second, use only relevant humor. Unrelated stories and jokes may be suitable for a comic whose principal purpose is to make an audience laugh, but a formal speech requires you to make important points. Your use of humor needs to make a relevant contribution to the advancement of the speech's purpose.

Third, use good taste. Coarse vulgarities, obscenities, and sick jokes invite anger and hostility. Humor that rests on stereotypes and put-downs may alienate vast sections of your audience. Sexist, racist, and homophobic jokes that denigrate groups exhibit bad taste and poor judgment.

Fourth, don't overuse humor. Don't become enamored with your own wittiness. Telling joke after joke or telling one amusing story after another will likely produce laughter, but the audience will also be dissatisfied if you substitute humor for substance.

Humor can be risky but very satisfying when it works. Using humor is probably the most effective attention strategy when used appropriately and skillfully.

Organizing and Outlining

Presenting a well-organized speech is critical to your success as a speaker. This section, by necessity, will be a cursory treatment of organization and outlining.

Perhaps the easiest way of developing the organization of your speech is to think of your speech as an inverted pyramid. The base of your upside-down pyramid represents the most general part of your speech, namely, the topic. Moving down toward the tip of the pyramid, you fill in the purpose statement, then the main points that flow from the purpose statement, then elaborate on each main point with subpoints and sub-subpoints, and so forth. You begin with the abstract and work toward the concrete and specific.

Let's say that your group has chosen for its symposium topic the problem of violence in America. First, your group must divide this general topic into manageable subtopics so each group member will have about a 4- to 6-minute speech. Subtopics might include violence on television, violence in the movies, guns and violence, gang violence, social and economic causes of violence, and potential solutions to violence (which could be divided even further into specific proposals such as "three strikes and you're out," outlawing handguns, prison reform, and social programs). Each group member would then be given his or her subtopic.

Once you have your subtopic for the symposium, each group member must construct a specific purpose statement. A **purpose statement** is a concise, precise, declarative statement phrased in simple, clear language that provides both the general purpose (to inform or to persuade) and the specific purpose (exactly what you want the audience to understand, believe, feel, or do).

TOPIC: Guns and violence
PURPOSE STATEMENT: To inform you that handgun violence is a serious problem in America.

Your purpose statement becomes the blueprint for your entire speech. **You determine your main points from your purpose statement.**

MAIN POINT I: Death from handguns is a serious problem.
MAIN POINT II: Serious injury from handguns also poses a serious problem for America.

Each main point is then divided into subpoints, sub-subpoints, and so on.

MAIN POINT I: Death from handguns is a serious problem.
    SUBPOINT A: There are more than 16,000 murders from handguns every year in America; Japan has fewer than 100.

SUBPOINT B: More than 1,400 American youths between the ages of 10 and 19 commit suicide with a handgun each year.

Each subpoint is then broken down further with more detail, examples, and supporting evidence.

SUBPOINT A: There are more than 16,000 murders from handguns every year in America; Japan has fewer than 100.
>   SUB-SUBPOINT 1: Teenage homicide from handguns has almost doubled in the last decade to more than 5,000 annually.
>   SUB-SUBPOINT 2: The teenage handgun death rate now exceeds the mortality rate for young people from all natural causes combined.
>   SUB-SUBPOINT 3: Three times more American young men are killed by handguns every 100 hours than were killed during the 100-hour Persian Gulf War.
>   SUB-SUBPOINT 4: Provide examples of teenagers gunned down in street violence.

SUBPOINT B: More than 1,400 American youths between the ages of 10 and 19 commit suicide with a handgun each year.
>   SUB-SUBPOINT 1: Nearly two-thirds of suicides are from handguns.
>   SUB-SUBPOINT 2: Handguns put at risk large numbers of young people who consider suicide.
>>   SUB-SUB-SUBPOINT a: More than one in four high school students seriously contemplate suicide.
>>   SUB-SUB-SUBPOINT b: Sixteen percent of high schoolers make a specific plan to commit suicide, and half of these actually try to kill themselves.
>>   SUB-SUB-SUBPOINT c: Ready availability of handguns makes teen suicide more likely.
>>   SUB-SUB-SUBPOINT d: Tell the story of 14-year-old Paul Hoffman.

The resulting outline for your first main point would look as follows:

PURPOSE STATEMENT: To inform you that handgun violence is a serious problem in America.

I. Death from handguns is a serious problem.
>   A. **There are more than 16,000 murders from handguns every year in America; Japan has fewer than 100.**

    1. Teenage homicide from handguns has almost doubled in the last decade to more than 5,000 annually.

    2. The teenage handgun death rate now exceeds the mortality rate for young people from all natural causes combined.

    3. Three times more American young men are killed by handguns in 100 hours than were killed during the 100-hour Persian Gulf War.

    4. Provide examples of specific teenagers gunned down in street violence.

B. More than 1,400 American youths between the ages of 10 and 19 commit suicide with a handgun each year.

    1. Nearly two-thirds of suicides are from handguns.

    2. Handguns put at risk large numbers of young people who consider suicide.

        a. More than one in four high school students seriously contemplate suicide.

        b. Sixteen percent of high schoolers make a specific plan to commit suicide, and half of these actually try to kill themselves.

        c. Ready availability of handguns makes teen suicide more likely.

        d. Tell the story of 14-year-old Paul Hoffman.

    You follow the same procedure for outlining your second main point. *(For examples of complete outlines see those preceding each chapter in this text.)* Note that every subpoint must relate specifically to the main point and likewise every subsubpoint must relate specifically to the subpoint above it.

    The form used in the sample outline follows a standard set of symbols composed of Roman numerals, capital letters, and Arabic numbers. Indent all subdivisions of a more general point. This will help you follow the development of your points as you speak. **Every point that is subdivided has at least two subpoints.**

    Preparing the body of your speech is your most difficult and primary organizational task. The introduction, however, creates the all-important first impression with an audience. **Your introduction should satisfy the following objectives, usually in this order:**

1. Gain the attention of the audience.

2. Provide your purpose statement.

3. Relate the topic and purpose statement to the needs and interests of the audience (answering the question "Why should the audience care about your topic and purpose?").

4. Preview the main points of your speech (state them exactly as they appear in your outline).

The conclusion of your speech should strive to accomplish two objectives:

1. Wrap up the speech with a brief summary of your main points.
2. End the speech with an effective attention strategy that brings closure to the speech.

Once you have prepared your speech outline composed of your introduction, body, and conclusion, practice your speech several times. Speaking from an outline instead of a written manuscript is called the *extemporaneous style* of speaking (extemp for short). When you have prepared your full-sentence outline as already explained, **you may want to condense full sentences into terse words or phrases for your actual speaking outline.** Under pressure of performing before an audience, it is usually easier to speak extemporaneously when you do not have to read whole sentences. Glancing at a few words or a phrase to remind you of a point allows you to maintain strong eye contact with your listeners without losing your train of thought.

Finally, as you present your speech, **signpost your primary points. Signposts** indicate exactly where you are in your speech so the audience can follow along easily. Restating your main points as you get to each one is an example of signposting. If you had "three causes of gun violence in America" you would signpost each one as you addressed them in turn, such as "the first cause of gun violence is poverty"; "the second cause of gun violence is the ready availability of guns"; and "the third cause of gun violence is the breakdown of the criminal justice system." In this way, signposting underscores your important points as you present your speech.

Using Visual Aids

Visual aids can add interest, clarify complex material, make points memorable, and enhance the credibility of the speaker. There are many types of visual aids and with the advent of computer graphics and technologies still being developed, the possibilities are almost limitless. For inexperienced speakers, however, it is best to keep visual aids simple. Photographs, diagrams, charts, graphs, physical models, video clips, and slides are the standard types of visual aids.

Poorly designed and clumsily used visual aids will detract from your speech. **The following guidelines will assist you in preparing and displaying visual aids effectively:**

1. *Keep visual aids simple.* Visual aids that work well in books, magazines, or newspapers rarely work well in a speech. In printed material a visual aid can be studied carefully. A complicated visual aid used in a speech will distract audience

members from listening to the speaker while they try to figure out the complex graph, chart, or diagram.

2. *Visual aids should be large enough to be seen easily.* The general rule of thumb here is that a person in the back of the room should be able to see the visual aid easily.

3. *Visual aids should be neat and attractive.* Sloppy, hastily constructed visual aids are worse than no visual aids at all.

4. *Display the visual aid where it can be seen easily by all members of the audience.* Audience members should not have to stand up or elongate their necks to see the visual aid.

5. *Practice with the visual aids.* Remember Murphy's Law: whatever can go wrong likely will go wrong. Make certain that any equipment used is in proper working order. Do not attempt to use electronic technology without practicing with it first.

6. *Talk to the audience, not the visual aid.* Don't turn your back on your audience while explaining your visual aid. Stand facing your audience, point the toes of your feet straight ahead, and imagine that your feet have been nailed to the floor. Stand beside the visual aid when referring to it and use your finger or a pointer to guide the audience.

7. *Keep the visual aid out of sight when it is not in use.* Audience members may be distracted by the visual aid when you are talking about an unrelated point. I once had a symposium group, whose topic was surfing, play a surfing movie during all members' speeches. Not surprisingly, the audience was far more attentive to the wave riders than the speakers.

8. *Do not circulate a visual aid among the audience members.* Passing around pictures or other visual aids while you're still speaking will distract listeners.

Critical Thinking Revisited: Arguments and Fallacies

Chapters 7 and 8 have already delved substantially into the process of critical thinking in small group decision making and problem solving. Group members must be able to recognize and deal effectively with problems of information overload and underload, confirmation bias, false dichotomies, collective inferential error, and groupthink. In addition, critical thinking is involved in every step of the Standard Agenda, especially when information is gathered and evaluated, criteria for decision making are developed and applied, and final decisions are made by the group.

This bonus appendix is included because in classrooms in some parts of the country, heavier emphasis is placed on reasoning and use of evidence in the small group context than is true of other parts of the country. This appendix is divided into two segments: the structure of arguments and types of fallacies.

The Structure of Arguments

An argument or "train of reasoning" is composed of several constituent parts (Toulmin et al., 1979). These parts are: the **claim**—that which is asserted and remains to be proven; **data**—the grounds (support/evidence) for the claim, such as statistical evidence, expert testimony, documents, objects, exhibits, conclusions from test results, verifiable facts, and conclusions previously established; **warrant**—the reasoning used to link the data to the claim, usually assumed (implied), not stated directly; **backing**—additional evidence and reasoning used to support the inference made in the warrant; **reservations**—exceptions or rebuttals that diminish the force of the claim; and **qualifier**—degree of truth of the claim (such as, highly probable, plausible, possible, and so forth).

Consider the following example of all six parts of an argument:

Claim: Jim Davis should be given antibiotics.
Data: Davis suffered severe cuts and injuries on his arms and legs in an auto accident.
Warrant: There is a risk of infection in such injuries.

Backing: Hospital reports and numerous studies indicate that risk of infection is serious and that antibiotics can prevent infection from occurring.

Reservations: Overuse of antibiotics can produce superbugs. Antibiotics should be used only when absolutely necessary, or they will eventually be useless to fight disease.

Qualifier: "Probably." This is a strong claim based on solid evidence and reasoning.

Fallacies

Understanding fallacies will help you determine the validity of your claim, the strength of your data, and the solidity of your warrant and backing. The list of fallacies below is not exhaustive. I have chosen only those specific fallacies that seem to occur frequently and that students are likely to encounter almost daily. I am dividing this list of fallacies into three types: **material fallacies**—errors in the process of using supporting materials as proof; **logical fallacies**—errors in the process of reasoning; and **psychological fallacies**—claims that rest on emotional appeal rather than logic and evidence.

MATERIAL FALLACIES: MISUSE OF STATISTICS

There are two primary material fallacies: misuse of statistics and misuse of authority. Misuse of statistics fallacies are numerous. I cover five common ones.

Manufactured or Questionable Statistic: Making Them Up This fallacy consists of statistics that have been fabricated, or statistics whose validity is highly questionable because there is no reasonable method for compiling such statistics, or that which is quantified is too trivial to warrant the time, effort, and resources necessary to compile accurate statistics. Every year the claim is made during the Academy Awards that the presentation of Oscars is viewed by 1 billion people worldwide. Considering that about 44 million viewers in the United States watch it, according to Nielsen ratings surveys, and that the Academy Awards is of greater interest to Americans than to other countries because most movies nominated for Oscars are American made, and further considering that the program is aired in English which is not the language of most other countries, the 1 billion viewers claim is almost certainly a preposterously inflated statistic of pure fabrication (Radosh, 2005).

Irrelevant Statistic: Does Not Apply These are statistics that do not directly prove the implied or stated claim yet they are offered as evidence supporting the claim. For example, "The United States spends a trillion dollars a year on healthcare, more than any other nation. Clearly, our healthcare system is the world's best." The amount of money spent doesn't prove money was spent wisely, efficiently, or effectively.

Sample Size Inadequate or Unspecified: Not Nearly Enough This fallacy occurs when the sample size is very small, resulting in a margin of error in excess of plus or minus 3%, or when you are left guessing what the sample size might have been. For example, "Eighty percent of those surveyed support the cable TV legislation." How many were surveyed? Ten people, eight of whom favored the legislation?

Self-Selected Sample: Not Exactly Random Call-in polls by local television stations, and surveys or questionnaires printed in magazines asking readers to respond, are examples. Those who are angry or have a vested interest in the outcome are most likely to participate.

Dated Statistics: Lack of Currency Statistics should be as up-to-date as possible, especially if the event, phenomenon, or situation is volatile and likely to change quickly (such as, number of unemployed, long-term interest rates on mortgages, murder rates in various cities, and international monetary exchange rates). Some phenomena change very slowly, if at all, over time (such as, percentage of U.S. population who call themselves Catholics, Protestants, and other denominations). They require less attention to recency of statistics. "According to the Department of Housing and Urban Development in a 2000 report to Congress, the median price of a new home in the United States is $120,000" is a statistic that hardly qualifies as current in today's volatile housing market.

MATERIAL FALLACIES: MISUSE OF AUTHORITY

Testimony of experts and authorities is useful as supporting material for claims because experts draw on a larger data and knowledge base than do nonexperts. Experts are not always correct, but they are more reliable than someone who is uninformed or only marginally knowledgeable, especially about a highly technical subject.

Incomplete Citation: Reference Is Neither Specific nor Complete Minimum requirements for a complete citation include the qualifications of the authority (if not obvious), place of publication, and date of reference. For example, "The President's Commission on Mental Health, in its January report of this year entitled "Mental Health, Mental Illness," concludes, "The biggest stigma in America is the mental illness label." "Research indicates" (unless offered by an expert interpreting the latest results in his or her field), "studies show," and the like are incomplete citations.

Biased Source: Ax Grinders Special-interest groups or individuals who stand to gain money, prestige, power, or influence simply by taking a certain position on an issue, or crusaders for a cause are all biased even though they may have expertise. Quoting R. J. Reynolds Tobacco Company on the safety of cigarette smoking is an example.

Authority Quoted Out of His/Her Field: Expertise Is Not Generic Quote experts in their area of specialization. "Professor of Biology, Dr. Ernhard Bousterhaus, claims that electric cars are impractical and will remain so for at least the next 50 years" is quoting an expert in one field that has little to do with the claim regarding electric cars.

LOGICAL FALLACIES: REASONING GONE AWRY

Reasoning is the basis of warrants for arguments. Sometimes our logic is faulty.

Hasty Generalization: Overgeneralizing Drawing conclusions (generalizations) from too few or atypical examples is called a hasty generalization. Testimonials exalting cancer cures, faith healings, and so on are generalizations based on too few and probably atypical experiences of individuals. Audience members at a talk show generalizing on the basis of their individual experiences is another example.

False Analogy: Bogus Comparison A false analogy occurs when two items, events, or phenomena with superficial similarities are viewed as identical, even when a significant point or points of difference exist between the two things compared. "In Turkey, farmers grow poppies (source of heroin) as a cash crop. In the United States, farmers grow corn and soybeans for cash crops. Why outlaw poppies when we don't outlaw corn and soybeans?" This is a false analogy because the poppy crop is not a critical food source capable of feeding the hungry of the world, but corn and soybeans are. Also, poppies are grown as a source of drugs. Although corn can be made into alcohol, that is not its primary purpose.

Correlation Mistaken for Causation: Covariation Fallacy When two phenomena vary at the same time, a causal linkage is often incorrectly asserted. "I ate a lot of chocolate this week and now my face has acne. I guess I'll have to stop eating chocolate so I can get rid of these blasted pimples." This is an example of correlation incorrectly asserted as causation.

Single Cause: Complexity Oversimplified Attributing only one cause to a complex phenomenon with many causes is a single-cause fallacy. "Poor communication is the reason for the alarming increase in the divorce rate" is an example. Poor communication is probably a cause of some divorces, but not necessarily the most important or the only cause.

PSYCHOLOGICAL FALLACIES: EMOTION DISGUISED AS LOGIC

Pretending that an emotional attack is logical steps into fallacious territory. Consider two primary examples: ad hominem and ad populum.

Ad Hominem: Personal Attack Attacking the messenger to divert attention away from the message is an ad hominem fallacy. Not all attacks on a person's credibility, character, and qualifications, however, are fallacious. If character or credibility is the real issue, then it is relevant argumentation (for example, attacking Bill Clinton's integrity during the impeachment proceedings was not a fallacious personal attack). "Why are you always on my back for not studying? Last semester *your* GPA fell nearly a full point" is an ad hominem fallacy.

Ad Populum: Popular Opinion A claim based on popular opinion rather than reasoning and evidence is an ad populum fallacy. "Go ahead and smoke marijuana. More than a third of all college students do" is an example.

Glossary

A glossary of terms does not substitute for clear understanding of the concepts represented. You can memorize a definition without knowing what it means. Clear understanding requires a context for the terms. By reading the following terms in the context of this book, you will see the interconnections between and among the terms. All terms included in the glossary appear in **boldfaced** type in the body of the text (see the index for location).

Accommodating Style of conflict management that yields to the concerns and desires of others.

Activities groups Groups that engage in specific activities such as chess teams and sports teams.

Ad hoc teams Teams that are assembled to solve an immediate problem, then are dissolved once the solution has been implemented.

Adaptability The adjustment of group boundaries in response to changing conditions.

Aggregation A collection of individuals who do not interact with each other or influence each other to achieve common goals.

Aggression Any physical or verbal behavior intended to hurt or destroy.

Alliances Associations in the form of subgroups entered into for mutual benefit or a common objective.

Ambushing Biased listening in which the listener focuses on attacking a speaker's points instead of striving to comprehend them.

Analysis paralysis Bogging down decision making by analyzing a problem too extensively.

Appropriateness Complying with rules and their accompanying expectations.

Argot Private vocabulary peculiar to a specific group.

Artistic groups Groups that form to perform artistic endeavors such as choirs, bands, and quilting circles.

Assertiveness The ability to communicate the full range of your thoughts and emotions with confidence and skill.

Asynchronous media Those forms of communicating that permit anytime/anyplace interaction among group members without interruption.

Autonomy (and empowerment) The degree to which team members experience substantial freedom, independence, and discretion in their work.

Avoiding Style of conflict management in which a group member withdraws from potentially contentious and unpleasant struggles.

Backing Additional evidence and reasoning used to support the inference made in the warrant.

BATNA (Best Alternative To a Negotiated Agreement) A fallback position if a negotiated settlement fails to occur.

Beliefs What we think is true or probable.

Boundary control Regulation that determines the amount of access a group has to input and thus influence from outsiders in a system.

Brainstorming A creative problem-solving technique that promotes plentiful, even zany, ideas in an atmosphere free from criticism and encourages enthusiastic participation from all group members.

Bridging An integrative problem-solving technique that offers a new option devised to satisfy all parties on important conflicting issues.

Bypassing When we assume that everyone has the same meaning for a word and fail to check for any differences.

Charge The task of a team, such as to gather information, to analyze a problem and make recommendations, to make decisions and implement them, or to tackle a specific project from inception to completion.

Charisma A constellation of personal attributes that people find highly attractive in an individual and strongly influential.

Charismatic leaders All leaders are transformational to some degree, but charismatic leaders are thought to be *highly* transformational.

Chunking A process of recoding information into larger, more meaningful patterns.

Claim That which is asserted and remains to be proven.

Cliques Small, narrowly focused subgroups that create a competitive atmosphere.

Coalitions Temporary alliances.

Cohesiveness The degree to which members feel a part of a group, wish to stay in the group, and are committed to each other and to the group's work.

Collaborating Style of conflict management that recognizes the interconnection between the task and social components of groups and deals directly with both requirements; win–win cooperative approach to conflict management.

Collective Effort Model It suggests that group members are strongly motivated to perform well in a group if they are convinced that their individual effort will likely help in attaining valued results.

Commitment The conscious decision to invest time, energy, thought, and feeling to improve oneself or one's relationships with others.

Communication A transactional process of sharing meaning with others.

Communication climate The emotional atmosphere, the enveloping tone that is created by the way we communicate in groups.

Communication competence Communicating effectively and appropriately in a given context.

Communication style of conflict management An orientation toward conflict; predisposition or tendency regarding the way conflict is managed in groups.

Competing (power/forcing) Win–lose style of conflict management that attempts to force one's will on another group member.

Competition A mutually exclusive goal attainment process.

Compliance The process of consenting to the dictates and desires of others.

Compromising Style of conflict management that gives up something to get something.

Confirmation bias A strong tendency to seek information that confirms our beliefs and attitudes and to ignore information that contradicts our currently held beliefs and attitudes.

Conflict The expressed struggle of interconnected parties who perceive incompatible goals and interference from each other in attaining those goals.

Conflict spirals The escalating cycle of negative communication that produces destructive conflict.

Conformity The adherence to group norms by group members.

Confrontation A collaborative component of conflict management characterized by the overt recognition that conflict exists in a group and the direct effort to manage it effectively.

Consensus A state of mutual agreement among members of a group in which all legitimate concerns of individuals have been addressed to the satisfaction of the group.

Constructive conflict Conflict that is characterized by communication that is We-oriented, cooperative, de-escalating, supportive, and flexible.

Contempt The verbal or nonverbal expression of insult that emotionally abuses others.

Content dimension (of messages) The information transmitted.

Context An environment in which meaning emerges, consisting of who communicates to whom, why the communicator does it, and where, when, and how it is done.

Cooperation A mutually inclusive goal attainment process.

Correlation A consistent relationship between two or more variables.

Credibility A composite of competence (knowledge, skills), trustworthiness (honesty, consistency, character), and dynamism (confidence, assertiveness).

Critical thinking Analyzing and evaluating ideas and information to reach sound judgments and conclusions.

Cult A group that forms around a person who claims he or she has a special mission or knowledge, which will be shared with those who turn over most of their decision making to that self-appointed leader.

Cyberostracism A remote form of ostracism that occurs in virtual groups.

Cynics They focus on the negative, predicting failure and looking for someone or something to criticize, sapping the energy from a team with their negativity.

Data The grounds (support/evidence) for the claim, such as statistical evidence, expert testimony, documents, objects, exhibits, conclusions from test results, verifiable facts, and conclusions previously established as credible.

Defensiveness A reaction to a perceived attack on our self-concept and self-esteem.

Defiance An overt form of communicating noncompliance; unmitigated, audacious rebellion against attempts to induce compliance.

Delegating style (of situational leadership) Nondirective leadership that has low task, low relationship emphasis; lets other group members shoulder the burdens once confidence in their readiness has been deemed.

Description A first-person report of how an individual feels, what the individual perceives to be true, and what behaviors have been observed in a specific context.

Destructive conflict Conflict that is characterized by domination, escalation, retaliation, competition, defensiveness, and inflexible communication patterns.

Devil's advocate A group role, sometimes assigned to a specific member, that requires the individual "for the sake of argument" to critique and question ideas and proposals that emerge during group discussion.

Dialectical inquiry A subgroup develops a counterproposal and defends it side by side with the group's initial proposal.

Directive style (of leadership) Leadership behavior that puts most of the emphasis on the group task with little concern for the social relationships among members.

Disruptive roles Informal group roles that serve individual needs or goals while impeding attainment of group goals.

Dogmatism The belief in the self-evident truth of one's opinion.

Dominance A form of power in which individuals attempt to gain power over others.

Dyad Academic term for a two-person transaction.

Dynamic equilibrium A range in which systems can manage change effectively to promote growth and success without pushing the system to disaster.

Effectiveness How well we have progressed toward the achievement of goals.

Electronic brainstorming Occurs when group members sit at computer terminals and brainstorm ideas using a computer-based, file-sharing procedure.

Emoticons Typed icons or combinations of punctuation marks meant to indicate emotional tone; a substitute for nonverbal communication in written text messages.

Empathy Thinking and feeling what you perceive another to be thinking and feeling.

Empowerment The process of enhancing the capabilities and influence of individuals and groups.

Entropy A measure of a system's movement toward disorganization and eventual termination.

Equifinality Groups with similar or identical goals may accomplish these goals in highly diverse ways.

Ethics A set of standards for judging the moral correctness of our behavior.

Expanding the pie An integrative problem-solving technique in which creative means of increasing resources as a solution to a problem are generated.

Expert A person who not only has valuable and useful information for a group but also understands the information and knows how to use it to help the group.

Explicit norms Rules in groups that expressly identify acceptable behavior.

Extrinsic reward An external inducement such as money, grades, praise, recognition, or prestige that motivates us to behave or perform.

False dichotomy The tendency to view the world in terms of only two opposing possibilities when other possibilities are available, and to describe this dichotomy in the language of extremes.

Fantasies Prime element of symbolic convergence theory; dramatic stories that provide a shared interpretation of events that bind group members and offer them a shared identity.

Fantasy chain A string of connected stories that amplify fantasy; a fantasy theme.

Fantasy theme A consistent thread that runs through the stories that create a shared group identity.

Force field analysis A process for group implementation of decisions by anticipating the driving forces (those that encourage change) and restraining forces (those that resist change).

Formal role A position assigned by an organization or specifically designated by the group leader.

Forum discussion Permits members of an audience listening to a public speech, panel discussion, symposium, or debate to participate in a discussion of ideas presented.

Frame The way in which language shapes our perception of choices.

Glass ceiling An invisible barrier of subtle discrimination that excludes women and minorities from top jobs in corporate and professional America.

GRIT (Graduated and Reciprocated Initiatives in Tension reduction) A technique of de-escalating cycles of conflict.

Group A human communication system composed of three or more individuals interacting for the achievement of some common goal(s), who influence and are influenced by each other.

Group climate The emotional atmosphere, the enveloping tone that is created by the way we communicate in groups.

Group endorsement The acceptance by the group of a member's bid to play a specific role.

Group polarization The group tendency to make a decision after discussion that is more extreme, either riskier or more cautious, than the initial preferences of group members.

Group potency (and empowerment) The shared belief among team members that they can be effective as a team.

Grouphate The hostility people harbor from having to work in groups.

Groupspeak The jargon of a cult used to mystify outsiders.

Groupthink A mode of thinking that people engage in when they are deeply involved in a cohesive in-group, and members' strivings for unanimity override their motivation to realistically appraise alternative courses of action.

Hazing Any humiliating or dangerous activity expected of individuals to join a group, regardless of their willingness to participate in the activity.

Hidden agendas Personal goals of group members that are not revealed openly and that can interfere with group accomplishments.

High-context communication style Cultural tendency to emphasize the cultural context of a message when determining meaning.

Hindsight bias The tendency to overestimate our prior knowledge once we have been told the correct answers.

Hit-and-run confrontations Confronting contentious issues but leaving just enough time to make your point and not enough time for other group members to respond adequately.

Hypercompetitiveness An excessive emphasis on defeating others to achieve one's goals.

Impact (and empowerment) The degree of significance that is given by those outside of the team, typically the team's organization, to the work produced by the team.

Impervious response Failure to acknowledge another person's communication effort either verbally or nonverbally.

Implicit norms Rules in groups that are indirectly indicated by uniformities in the behavior and expressed attitudes of members.

Individual accountability An established minimum standard of effort and performance for each team member to share the fruits of team success.

Individual achievement The attainment of a personal goal without having to defeat another person.

Individualism–collectivism dimension (of cultures) The degree to which cultural values emphasize either the individual or the group as paramount.

Inferences Conclusions about the unknown based on what is known.

Informal role A role that emerges in a group from the group transactions; it emphasizes functions, not positions.

Information bulimia A binge-and-purge cycle of information processing.

Information overload The rate of information flow into a system and/or the complexity of that information exceeds the system's processing capacity; excessive input.

Information underload An insufficient amount of information (inadequate input) available to a group for decision-making purposes.

Input Resources that come from outside a system, such as energy (sunlight, electricity), information (Internet, books), and people (a new group member).

Integrative problem solving Creative approach to conflicts of interest that searches for solutions to problems that benefit everyone.

Interdependence When all group members work together to achieve a desirable goal.

Interests The intangible motivations such as needs, desires, concerns, fears, and aspirations that lead a party in a conflict to take a position.

Interpersonal communication Communication between two people.

Intrinsic reward Enjoying what one does for its own sake; an inner motivation to continue doing what brings us pleasure.

Knowledge Learning the rules for and understanding what is required to be appropriate and effective in one's communication.

Language A structured system of symbols for sharing meaning.

Leader as completer (functional leadership viewpoint) Leaders are thought to perform those essential functions within a group that other members have failed to perform.

Leadership An influence process between leader and followers directed toward change that reflects mutual purposes of group members and is largely achieved through competent communication.

Learning groups Groups that enhance members' knowledge such as college seminar groups and class study groups.

Linguistic barriers (for group boundary control) The use of private vocabulary, or argot, peculiar to a specific group to create an in-group/out-group division.

Logical fallacies Errors in the process of reasoning.

Low-context communication style Cultural tendency to emphasize the explicit content of a message when determining meaning.

Maintenance roles Informal group roles that focus on social relationships among group members.

Material fallacies Errors in the process of using supporting materials as proof.

Meaningfulness (and empowerment) A team's perception that its tasks are important, valuable, and worthwhile.

Media richness The information carrying capacity of each form of communication.

Mentors Knowledgeable individuals who have achieved some success in their profession or jobs and who assist individuals trying to get started in a line of work.

Metasearch engines An Internet tool that sends a keyword request to several search engines at once.

Mindsets Psychological and cognitive predispositions to see the world in a particular way, such as biases, preconceptions, and assumptions, that interfere with effective group decision making and problem solving.

Mixed message Positive verbal and negative nonverbal communication, or vice versa; contradictory verbal and nonverbal communication.

Multiple sequence model (of group decision emergence) Groups move along three activity tracks—task, relational, and topic—and take three principal paths to reaching decisions—unitary sequence, complex cyclic, and solution orientation.

Murphy's Law Anything that can go wrong likely will go wrong, somewhere, sometime.

Negative climate Group members do not feel valued, supported, and respected; trust is minimal; and members perceive that they are not treated well.

Negative reciprocation A form of retaliation for perceived wrongs from group members.

Negative synergy Group members working together produce a worse result than expected based on perceived individual skills and abilities of members.

Negotiation A process by which a joint decision is made by two or more parties.

Neighborhood groups Groups that provide a sense of community such as homeowners associations and PTAs.

Network A structured pattern of information flow and personal contact.

Networking A form of group empowerment in which individuals with similar backgrounds, skills, and goals come together on a fairly regular basis and share information that will assist members in pursuing goals.

Nominal group technique Individuals work by themselves generating lists of ideas on a problem, then convene in a group where they merely record the ideas generated and interaction occurs only to clarify ideas. Rankings of each member's five favorite ideas are averaged with the highest average ideas selected by the group.

Nonroutine task Work to be accomplished that requires problem solving, has few set procedures, and has a high level of uncertainty.

Nonverbal communication Sharing meaning with others without using words.

Norm of group interest A collective prescription that group members should pursue maximum group outcomes (winning at all costs), even if this means acting hypercompetitively against other groups when members may privately not wish to do so.

Norms Rules that regulate behavior in groups.

Openness Degree of continuous interchange with the environment outside of a system.

Output The continual results of the group's throughput (the transformation of input), such as decisions made, solutions created, and projects completed.

Panel discussion A small group of participants who engage in an exchange of information and ideas on a specific issue or problem before an audience.

Paraphrasing A concise response to a speaker which states the essence of the speaker's content in the listener's own words.

Participant–observer A self-monitoring process whereby you assume a detached view of yourself communicating in groups.

Participating style (of situational leadership) Nondirective leadership that has low task, high relationship emphasis.

Participative style (of leadership) Leadership behavior that puts a balanced emphasis on both task and social dimensions of the group.

Pattern recognition A means of coping with information overload; one way to narrow the search for information by noticing patterns that indicate relevant from irrelevant information.

PERT (Program Evaluation Review Technique) A systematic process for group implementation of decisions.

Physical barriers (of group boundary control) Includes walls, locked doors, an inconvenient location in a building, and partitions and cubicles in offices to restrict input.

Positions Concrete things that one party wants in a negotiation.

Positive climate Group members perceive that they are valued, supported, and treated well.

Power The ability to influence the attainment of goals sought by yourself or others.

Power distance dimension (of cultures) Degree to which different cultures vary in their attitudes concerning the appropriateness of power imbalances.

Power resource Anything that enables individuals to move toward their own goals or to interfere with another's actions.

Prevention A form of power in which group members resist or defy attempts to dominate them by other group members.

Primary groups Groups that provide a sense of belonging and affection such as family and friends.

Primary tension The initial jitters and uneasiness felt by individuals when they first join a group.

Principled negotiation Interest-based bargaining process that uses a collaborative approach to negotiating conflicts of interest, focusing on merits of arguments, not on hard bargaining strategies.

Probing Seeking additional information from a speaker by asking questions.

Productivity The result of the efficient and effective accomplishment of a group task.

Project groups Groups that work on specific tasks such as self-managing work teams and task forces.

Provisionalism Qualifying statements and avoiding absolute claims.

Pseudo-teams Small groups that only half-heartedly exhibit the several criteria that constitute a true team. They give the appearance of being teams and of engaging in team-

work without exhibiting the substance of teams.

Psychological barriers (for group boundary control) Anything that makes an individual feel that he or she is not a true member of a group.

Psychological fallacies Claims that rest on emotional appeal rather than logic and evidence.

Psychological reactance The more someone tries to control us by telling us what to do, the more we are inclined to resist such efforts, even to do the opposite.

Public speaking Communication in a formal setting between a clearly identified speaker and an audience of listeners.

Qualifier Degree of truth of the claim (such as, highly probable, plausible, possible, and so forth).

Quality circles Teams composed of workers who volunteer to work on a similar task and attempt to solve a particular problem.

Question of fact Asks whether something is true and to what extent.

Question of policy Asks whether a specific course of action should be undertaken to solve a problem.

Question of value Asks for an evaluation of the desirability of an object, idea, event, or person.

Rationalization of disconfirmation Inventing superficial, glib alternative explanations for information that contradicts beliefs.

Readiness How ready a person is to perform a particular task; determined by ability and willingness of the person.

Reformed sinner strategy Negotiating strategy in which one party initially competes or acts tough, then cooperates and relaxes demands.

Reframing A creative process of breaking a

mindset by placing the problem in a different frame of reference.

Relationship dimension (of messages) How messages define or redefine the relationship between group members.

Reminder role A formally designated role in which the individual assigned the role raises questions in a nonaggressive manner regarding collective inferential error, confirmation bias, false dichotomies, and any of the myriad symptoms of groupthink that may arise during group discussions.

Reservations Exceptions or rebuttals that diminish the force of the claim.

Resistance A covert form of communicating noncompliance, often duplicitous and manipulative.

Ripple effect A chain reaction that begins in one part of a system and spreads across an entire system.

Role A pattern of expected behavior associated with parts that members play in groups.

Role conflict When group members play roles in different groups that contradict each other.

Role fixation The acting out of a specific role, and only that role, no matter what the situation might require.

Role reversal Stepping into a role distinctly different from or opposite of a role one usually plays.

Role specialization When an individual group member settles into his or her primary role.

Role status The relative importance, prestige, or power accorded a particular role.

Routine task Work to be accomplished in which the group performs processes and procedures that have little variability and little likelihood of change.

Rule Prescription that indicates what you should or shouldn't do in specific contexts.

Search engine An Internet tool that computer-generates indexes of web pages that match, or link with, keywords typed in a search window.

Secondary tension The stress and strain that occurs within a group when disagreements and conflicts emerge and decisions must be made.

Self-help groups Groups that provide social support.

Self-managing work teams Self-regulating teams that complete an entire task.

Selling style (of situational leadership) Directive leadership that is high task, high relationship in emphasis.

Sensitivity Receptive accuracy whereby you can detect, decode, and comprehend signals sent in groups.

Service groups Groups that provide social service to others such as fraternities and sororities and Rotary and Lions clubs.

Shift response An attention-getting initiative by listeners in which the listeners attempt to shift the focus of attention from others to themselves by changing the topic of discussion.

Signposts A speech organizational technique that indicates exactly where you are in your speech so the audience can follow along easily.

Skill (in communicating) The successful performance of a communication behavior and the ability to repeat such a behavior.

Smoothing Collaborative component of conflict management characterized by acting to calm agitated feelings during a conflict episode.

Social compensation A group member's increased motivation to work harder on a group task to counterbalance the lackluster performance of other members.

Social dimension (of groups) The relationships that form among members in a group and their impact on the group as a whole.

Social groups Groups that provide social connections and whose goal is to help others.

Social loafing The tendency of a group member to exert less effort on a task when working in a group than when working individually.

Stand aside A team member continues to have reservations about the group decision but, when confronted, does not wish to block the group choice.

Structure The systematic interrelation of all parts to the whole, providing form and shape.

Style shift A flexible adaptation of one's communication to the changes in a system.

Superordinate goals A specific kind of cooperative goal that overrides differences that members may have because the goal supersedes less important competitive goals.

Support groups Groups that provide social support to address life problems.

Support response An attention-giving process in which listeners focus their attention on another group member, not on themselves, during discussion.

Symbolic convergence theory Focuses on how group members communicating with each other develop and share stories (fantasies) to create a convergence or group identity that is larger and more coherent than the isolated experiences of individual group members.

Symbols Representations of referents (whatever the symbol refers to).

Symposium A relatively structured group presentation to an audience composed of several individuals who present uninterrupted speeches with contrasting points of view on a central topic.

Synchronous media Those forms of communicating that permit simultaneous, same-time interactions among group members modeled after face-to-face meetings.

Synergy Group performance from joint action of members exceeds expectations based on perceived abilities and skills of individual group members.

System A set of interconnected parts working together to form a whole in the context of a changing environment.

Task dimension (of groups) The work to be performed by a group.

Task roles Informal group roles that move the group toward attainment of its goals.

Team A small number of people with complementary skills who act as an interdependent unit, are equally committed to a common mission, subscribe to a cooperative approach to accomplish that mission, and hold themselves accountable for team performance.

Team accountability The team, rather than individual members, assumes responsibility for success and failure.

Technology A tool to accomplish some purpose.

Telling style (of situational leadership) Directive leadership that is high task, low relationship in emphasis.

Throughput The process of transforming input into output to keep a system functioning.

Transaction A process in which each person communicating is both a sender and a receiver simultaneously, not merely a sender or receiver, and all parties influence each other.

Transactional leadership Leadership often associated with management that typically strives to maintain the status quo efficiently.

Transformational leadership Leadership often associated with changing the status quo; frequently linked to charisma.

Twenty percent rule The minimum standard to combat gender and ethnic bias in groups;

when no less than 20% of group members are composed of women and minorities, discrimination against these groups drops substantially.

Values The most deeply felt views of what is deemed good, worthwhile, or ethically right.

Verbal dominance A verbal form of dominance characterized by competitive interrupting, contradicting, berating, and high quantity of speech.

Virtual group A small group whose members rarely interact face-to-face, and who mostly communicate by means of electronic technologies.

Virtual library A search tool that combines Internet technology and standard library techniques for cataloging and evaluating information.

Vital functions (functional leadership viewpoint) Sees leaders performing a list of vital group functions different in kind and/or degree from other members.

Vividness effect A graphic, outrageous, shocking, controversial, dramatic event draws our attention and sticks in our minds, prompting us to overvalue such events and undervalue statistical information that shows patterns and trends that often contradict the sensational event.

Warrant The reasoning used to link the data to the claim, usually assumed, not stated directly.

Workplace bullying A persistent form of badgering, abuse, and "hammering away" at targets who have less power than their bullies.

References

Abell, G. (1981). Astrology. In G. Abell & B. Singer (Eds.), *Science and the paranormal.* New York: Charles Scribner's Sons.

Aboud, F. E., & Mendelson, M. J. (1998). Determinants of friendship selection and quality: Developmental perspectives. In N. Burkowski (Ed.), *The company they keep: Friendship in childhood and adolescence.* New York: Cambridge University Press.

Abramson, J. (1994). *We, the jury.* New York: Basic Books.

Acuff, F. L. (1997). *How to negotiate anything with anyone anywhere around the world.* New York: American Management Association.

Adkins, M., & Brashers, D. E. (1995). The power of language in computer-mediated groups. *Management Communication Quarterly, 8,* 289–322.

Adler, J., & Springen, K. (1999, May 3). How to fight back. *Newsweek,* 36–38.

Adler, N. J. (2001). *From Boston to Beijing: Managing with a world view.* Cincinnati, OH: South-Western.

Adler, N. J. (2002). *International dimensions of organizational behavior.* Cincinnati, OH: South-Western.

Adler, R. (1977). *Confidence in communication: A guide to assertive and social skills.* New York: Holt, Rinehart & Winston.

Adler, R., & Towne, N. (1999). *Looking out, looking in.* New York: Holt, Rinehart & Winston.

Aguayo, R. (1990). *Dr. Deming: The American who taught the Japanese about quality.* New York: Simon & Schuster.

Alexander, N. (1989, September 17). How to stop wasting time at meetings. *San Jose Mercury News,* p. 1PC.

Alge, B. J., Wietfhoff, C., & Klien, H. J. (2003). When does medium matter? Knowledge-building experiences and opportunities in decision-making teams. *Organizational Behavior and Human Decision Processes, 91,* 26–37.

Allen, T. D., McManus, S. E., & Russell, J. E. A. (1999). Newcomer socialization and stress: Formal peer relationships as a source of support. *Journal of Vocational Behavior, 54,* 453–470.

Allen, V., & Levine, J. (1971). Social support and conformity: The role of independent assessment of reality. *Journal of Experimental Social Psychology, 7,* 48–58.

Altman, L. K. (2001, December 11). The wrong foot, and other tales of surgical error. *The New York Times.* Retrieved May 5, 2003, from http://www.nytimes.com/2001/12/11/health/policy/11DOCS.html

American Association of University Women (2005). Five frequently asked questions about university and college women. Retrieved February 7, 2005, from http://www.aauw.org/research/statedata/faq.cfm

Amparano, J. (1997, January 23). Taking good care of workers pays off. *The Arizona Republic,* pp. E1, E3.

Anatomy of a massacre. (1999, May 3). *Newsweek,* 25–31.

Andersen, J. (1985). Educational assumptions highlighted from a cross-cultural comparison. In L. Samovar & R. Porter (Eds.), *Intercultural communication: A reader.* Belmont, CA: Wadsworth.

Andersen, J. (1988). Communication competency in the small group. In R. Cathcart & L. Samovar (Eds.), *Small group communication: A reader.* Dubuque, IA: Wm. C. Brown & Company.

Andersen, P. (1999). *Nonverbal communication: Forms and functions.* Mountain View, CA: Mayfield.

Anderson, C. M., Riddle, B. L., & Martin, M. M. (1999). Socialization processes in groups. In L. R. Frey, D. S. Gouran, & M. S. Poole (Eds.), *The handbook of group communication theory and research.* Thousand Oaks, CA: Sage.

Angier, N. (2002, July 23). Why we're so nice: We're wired to cooperate. *The New York Times.*

Retrieved March 12, 2003, from http://www
.nytimes.com/2002/07/23/health/psychology/
23COOP.html?8vd_&pagewanted_print&posi
tion_bottom

Appleby, J., & Davis, R. (2001, March 1). Teamwork used to be a money saver, now it's a lifesaver. *USA Today,* pp. 1B–2B.

Argyle, M., & Henderson, M. (1985). The rules of relationships. In S. Duck & D. Perlman (Eds.), *Understanding personal relationships: An interdisciplinary approach.* London: Sage.

Armas, G. C. (2000, April 24). Women cracking the glass ceiling. *Santa Cruz Sentinel,* pp. A1, A14.

Arnett, J. (1995). The young and the reckless: Adolescent reckless behavior. *Current Directions in Psychological Science, 4,* 67–71.

Aronson, E. (1999). *The social animal.* New York: Worth.

Arrow, H., & Crosson, S. (2003). Musical chairs: Membership dynamics in self-organized group formation. *Small Group Research, 34,* 523–556.

Asch, S. E. (1955). Opinions and social pressure. *Scientific American, 19,* 31–35.

Avila, J. (2001, August 3). Women bringing home the bacon. MSNBC. Retrieved May 17, 2003, from http://www.msnbc.com/news/609357.asp#BODY

Axelrod, R. (1984). *The evolution of cooperation.* New York: Basic Books.

Bach, G., & Goldberg, H. (1974). *Creative aggression.* New York: Avon.

Baker, G. (2002). The effects of synchronous collaborative technologies on decision making: A study of virtual teams. *Information Resources Management Journal, 15,* 79–93.

Barge, J., & Hirokawa, R. (1989). Toward a communication competency model of group leadership. *Small Group Behavior, 20,* 167–189.

Barker, L., Edwards, C., Davis, K., & Holly, F. (1981). An investigation of proportional time spent in various communication activities by college students. *Journal of Applied Communication Research, 8,* 101–109.

Barker, V. E., Abrams, J. R., Tiyaamornwong, V., Seibold, D. R., Duggan, A., Park, H. S., & Sebastian, M. (2000). New contexts for relational communication in groups. *Small Group Research, 31,* 470–503.

Barki, H., & Pinsonneault, A. (2001). Small group brainstorming and idea quality: Is electronic brainstorming the most effective approach? *Small Group Research, 32,* 158–205.

Barnes, S. B. (2003). *Computer-mediated communication.* New York: Allyn & Bacon.

BarNir, A. (1998). Can group- and issue-related factors predict choice shift? *Small Group Research, 29,* 308–338.

Baron, R. (1988). Negative effects of destructive criticism: Impact on conflict self-efficacy and task performance. *Journal of Applied Psychology, 73,* 199–207.

Baron, R. (1990). Countering the effects of destructive criticism: The relative efficacy of four interventions. *Journal of Applied Psychology, 75,* 235–243.

Baron, R. S., Vandello, J. A., & Brunsman, B. (1996). The forgotten variable in conformity research: Impact of task importance on social influence. *Journal of Personality and Social Psychology, 71,* 915–927.

Barry, D. (1991). *Dave Barry's guide to life.* New York: Wings Books.

Bass, B. M. (1990). *Bass & Stogdill's handbook of leadership.* New York: Free Press.

Bass, M. (1960). *Leadership, psychology and organizational behavior.* Westport, CT: Greenwood Press.

Baumeister, R. F., & Leary, M. R. (1995). The need to belong: Desire for interpersonal attachments as a fundamental human motivation. *Psychological Bulletin, 117,* 497–529.

Bazeley, M. (2005, August 7). Brave new Web. *San Jose Mercury News,* pp. 1A, 26A.

Bazerman, M., & Neale, M. (1983). Heuristics in negotiation: Limitations to dispute resolution effectiveness. In M. Bazerman & R. Lewicki (Eds.), *Negotiating in organizations.* Beverly Hills, CA: Sage.

Bechler, C., & Johnson, S. (1995). Leadership and listening: A study of member perceptions. *Small Group Research, 26,* 77–85.

Belbin, R. (1996). *Team roles at work.* London: Butterworth-Heinemann.

Bell, M. (1974). The effects of substantive and affective conflict in problem-solving discussions. *Speech Monographs, 41,* 19–23.

Benenson, J. F., Gordon, A. J., & Roy, R. (2000). Children's evaluative appraisals of competition in tetrads versus dyads. *Small Group Research, 31,* 635–652.

Benenson, J. F., Nicolson, C., Waite, A., Roy, R., & Simpson, A. (2001). The influence of group size on children's competitive behavior. *Child Development, 72,* 921–934.

Benenson, J. F., Roy, R., Waite, A., Goldbaum, S., Linders, L., & Simpson, A. (2002). Greater discomfort as a proximate cause of sex differences in competition. *Merrill-Palmer Quarterly, 48,* 225–248.

Benne, K., & Sheats, P. (1948). Functional roles of group members. *Journal of Social Issues, 4,* 41–49.

Bennett, G. (1961). *By human error: Disaster of a century.* London: Seeley Service.

Bennis, W. (1976). *The unconscious conspiracy: Why leaders can't lead.* New York: AMACOM.

Bennis, W., & Biederman, P. (1997). *Organizing genius: The secrets of creative collaboration.* New York: Addison-Wesley.

Bennis, W., & Nanus, B. (1985). *Leaders: The strategies for taking charge.* New York: Harper & Row.

Berg, D. (1967). A descriptive analysis of the distribution and duration of themes discussed by task-oriented small groups. *Speech Monographs, 34,* 172–175.

Bernieri, F. J. (2001). Toward a taxonomy of interpersonal sensitivity. In J. A. Hall & F. J. Bernieri (Eds.), *Interpersonal sensitivity: Theory and measurement.* Mahwah, NJ: Lawrence Erlbaum.

Berscheid, E., & Reis, H. T. (1998). Attraction and close relationships. In D. T. Gilbert, S. T. Fiske, & G. Lindzey (Eds.), *The handbook of social psychology* (Vol. 2). New York: McGraw-Hill.

Bettinghaus, E., & Cody, M. (1987). *Persuasive communication.* New York: Holt, Rinehart & Winston.

Black, K. (1990, March). Can getting mad get the job done? *Working Woman,* 86–90.

Blake, R., & Mouton, J. (1964). *The managerial grid.* Houston: Gulf Publishing.

Blass, T. (2000). *Obedience to authority: Current perspectives on the Milgram paradigm.* Mahwah, NJ: Lawrence Erlbaum.

Blumner, R. (1999, August 15). "Voyeur" case bears watching. *San Jose Mercury News,* p. 3C.

Bok, S. (1978). *Lying: Moral choice in public and private life.* New York: Random House.

Bolman, L. G., & Deal, T. E. (1992). What makes a team work? *Organizational Dynamics, 21,* 34–44.

Bolton, R. (1979). *People skills: How to assert yourself, listen to others and resolve conflicts.* New York: Simon & Schuster.

Bond, M., Wang, K., Leung, K., & Giacalone, R. (1985). How are responses to verbal insults related to cultural collectivism and power distances? *Journal of Cross-cultural Psychology, 16,* 111–127.

Bond, R., & Smith, P. B. (1996). Culture and conformity: A meta-analysis of studies using Asch's line judgment task. *Psychological Bulletin, 119,* 111–137.

Bordewich, F. (1995, February). The country that works perfectly. *Reader's Digest,* pp. 101–106.

Borisoff, D., & Victor, D. (1989). *Conflict management: A communication skills approach.* Englewood Cliffs, NJ: Prentice-Hall.

Bormann, E. G. (1986). Symbolic convergence theory and group decision making. In R. Y. Hirokawa & M. S. Poole (Eds.), *Communication and group decision making.* Beverly Hills, CA: Sage.

Bormann, E. G. (1990). *Small group communication: Theory and practice.* New York: Harper & Row.

Bormann, E. G., & Bormann, N. (1988). *Effective small group communication.* Edina, MN: Burgess Publishing.

Bostrom, R. (1970). Patterns of communicative interaction in small groups. *Speech Monographs, 37,* 257–263.

Bower, S., & Bower, G. (1976). *Asserting yourself.* Reading, MA: Addison-Wesley.

Boyd, R. (1996, June 9). Survival of the most cooperative? New insights into Darwin's theory. *San Jose Mercury News,* p. 1C.

Brannigan, M. (1997, May 30). Why Delta Air Lines decided it was time for CEO to take off. *The Wall Street Journal,* pp. A1, A8.

Brauer, M., Judd, C. M., & Gliner, M. D. (1995). The effects of repeated expressions on attitude polarization during group discussion. *Journal of Personality and Social Psychology, 68,* 1014–1029.

Brecher, E. (1989, December 15). Furor over Florida rape case clouds disturbing facts. *The Seattle Times,* p. B1.

Brehm, J. (1972). *Responses to loss of freedom: A the-*

ory of psychological resistance. Morristown, NJ: General Learning Press.

Brett, J. (1990). Designing systems for resolving disputes in organizations. *American Psychologist, 45,* 162–170.

Brett, J. M., Shapiro, D. L., & Lytle, A. L. (1998). Breaking the bonds of reciprocity in negotiations. *Academy of Management Journal, 41,* 410–425.

Brin, D. (1998). *The transparent society: Will technology force us to choose between privacy and freedom?* Reading, MA: Addison-Wesley.

Brislin, R. (1993). *Understanding culture's influence on behavior.* Fort Worth, TX: Harcourt Brace Jovanovich.

Brock, T. (1968). Implications of commodity theory for value change. In A. Greenwald, T. Brock, & T. Ostrom (Eds.), *Psychological foundations of attitudes.* New York: Academic Press.

Bronner, E. (1999, June 13). Colleges are getting more competitive, students find. *San Jose Mercury News,* p. 13A.

Brownell, J. (1990). Perceptions of listening behavior: A management study. *Journal of Business Communication, 27,* 401–416.

Bruess, C. J., & Pearson, J. C. (1996). Gendered patterns in family communication. In J. Wood (Ed.), *Gendered relationships.* Newbury Park, CA: Sage.

Buckingham, M., & Coffman, C. (1999). *First, break all the rules: What the world's greatest managers do differently.* New York: Simon & Schuster.

Buckingham, M., & Coffman, C. W. (2002a, Spring). Item 9: Doing quality work. *Gallup Management Journal.* Retrieved January 12, 2003, from http://www.gallupjournal.com/q12Center/articles/19990517.asp

Buckingham, M., & Coffman, C. W. (2002b, Spring). Recognition or praise. *Gallup Management Journal.* Retrieved January 12, 2003, from http://www.gallupjournal.com/q12Center/articles/19990412.asp

Burggraf, C., & Sillars, A. (1987). A critical examination of sex differences in marital communication. *Communication Monographs, 54,* 276–294.

Burk, M. (2005, April 6). 40 years after Pay Equity Act, women still earn less than men. *San Jose Mercury News,* p. 9B.

Burns, J. (1978). *Leadership.* New York: Harper & Row.

Burrows, W. (1982, November). *Psychology Today,* 43.

Buzaglo, G., & Wheelan, S. (1999). Facilitating work team effectiveness: Case studies from Central America. *Small Group Research, 30,* 108–129.

Byrne, J. (1999). *Chainsaw: The notorious career of Al Dunlap in the era of profit-at-any-price.* New York: HarperBusiness.

Cairncross, F. (1997). *The death of distance: The trendspotter's guide to new communications.* Boston: Harvard Business School Press.

Caldicott, H. (1994). *Nuclear madness: What you can do.* New York: W. W. Norton.

Callahan, D. (2004). *The cheating culture: Why more Americans are doing wrong to get ahead.* New York: Harcourt.

Canary, D. J., & Hause, K. S. (1993). Is there any reason to research sex differences in communication? *Communication Quarterly, 41,* 129–144.

Carletta, J., Garrod, S., & Fraser-Krauss, H. (1998). Placement of authority and communication patterns in workplace groups: The consequences for innovation. *Small Group Research, 29,* 531–559.

Carli, L. (1990). Gender, language, and influence. *Journal of Personality and Social Psychology, 59,* 941–951.

Carnevale, P., & Probst, T. (1998). Social values and social conflict in creative problem solving. *Journal of Personality and Social Psychology, 74,* 1300–1309.

Carpenter, D. (2000, August 2). Americans' new hang-up: Cell phone rudeness. *Santa Cruz Sentinel,* p. D5.

Carreon, C. (2005, March 1). Internet sites caught up in gangs' wars of words. *San Jose Mercury News,* pp. 1A, 9A.

Carron, A., & Spink, K. (1995). The group size-cohesion relationship in minimal groups. *Small Group Research, 26,* 86–105.

Carter, S., & West, M. (1998). Reflexivity, effectiveness, and mental health in BBC-TV production teams. *Small Group Research, 29,* 583–601.

Carton, J. (1996). The differential effects of tangible rewards and praise on intrinsic motivation: A comparison of cognitive evaluation theory and operant theory. *Behavior Analyst, 19,* 237–255.

Carver, T. B., & Vondra, A. A. (1994, May–June). Alternative dispute resolution: Why it doesn't work and why it does. *Harvard Business Review,* pp. 120–130.

Center for American Women and Politics (2005, April). Women in elected office 2005. Retrieved May 23, 2005, from http://www.cawp.rutgers .edu/Facts/Officeholders/cawpfs.html

Charnofsky, H., Cherny, R., DuFault, D., Kegley, J., & Whitney, D. (1998, December 16). Final report of Merit Pay Task Force, CSU Academic Senate. Retrieved March 3, 2005, from http://www .academicsenate.cc.ca.us

Chatman, J., & Barsade, S. (1995). Personality, organizational culture, and cooperation: Evidence from a business simulation. *Administrative Science Quarterly, 40,* 423–443.

Cheating at work blamed on squeeze of job pressures. (1997, April 5). *San Jose Mercury News,* pp. 1C, 10C.

Chemers, M. M. (2000). Leadership research and theory: A functional integration. *Group Dynamics: Theory, Research, and Practice, 4,* 27–43.

Chen, G., & Starosta, W. (1997). Chinese conflict management and resolution. Overview and implications. *Intercultural Communication Studies, 7,* 1–16.

Chen, G., & Starosta, W. (1998). *Foundations of intercultural communication.* Boston: Allyn & Bacon.

Chertkoff, J., & Esser, J. (1976). A review of experiments in explicit bargaining. *Journal of Experimental Social Psychology, 12,* 464–486.

Chin, P. (2000, January 24). The buddy system. *People,* 98–105.

Christensen, D., et al. (1980). Sensitivity to nonverbal cues as a function of social competence. *Journal of Nonverbal Behavior, 4,* 145–156.

Cialdini, R. (1993). *Influence: The new psychology of modern persuasion.* Glenview, IL: Scott, Foresman.

Clanton, J. (1988). The Challenger disaster that didn't happen. In L. Schnoor (Ed.), *Winning orations.* Northfield, MN: Interstate Oratorical Association.

Clark, N., & Stephenson, G. (1989). Group remembering. In P. Paulus (Ed.), *Psychology of group influence.* Hillsdale, NJ: Lawrence Erlbaum.

Clark, R. D. (2001). Effects of majority defection and multiple minority sources on minority influence.

Group Dynamics: Theory, Research, and Practice, 5, 57–62.

Clemetson, L. (1999, June 7). Trying to close the achievement gap. *Newsweek,* 36–37.

Coates, J. (1993). *Women, men, and language.* New York: Longman.

Cohen, M., & Davis, N. (1981). *Medication errors: Causes and prevention.* Philadelphia: G. F. Stickley.

Cole, D. (1989, May). Meetings that make sense. *Psychology Today,* 14–15.

Collingwood, H. (1997, January). Forget the Fortune 500: For big bucks, think smaller and smarter. *Working Woman,* 24–25.

Conboy, W. (1976). *Working together: Communication in a healthy organization.* Columbus, OH: Charles Merrill.

Conquergood, D. (1994). Homeboys and hoods: Gang communication and cultural space. In L. Frey (Ed.), *Group communication in context: Studies of natural groups.* Hillsdale, NJ: Lawrence Erlbaum.

Conrad, C. (1990). *Strategic organizational communication: An integrated perspective.* New York: Holt, Rinehart & Winston.

Conway, F., & Siegelman, J. (1995). *Snapping: America's epidemic of sudden personality change.* New York: Stillpoint Press.

Cookson, P., & Persell, C. (1983, March). The price of privilege. *Psychology Today,* 31–35.

Cooper, V. (1997). Homophily or the Queen Bee Syndrome: Female evaluation of female leadership. *Small Group Research, 28,* 483–499.

Corcoran, K. (1993, May 30). Society's violence mirrored on ball field. *San Jose Mercury News,* pp. 1A, 10A.

Cose, E. (1999, June 7). The good news about black America. *Newsweek,* 29–32.

Costanzo, M. (1992). Training students to decode verbal and nonverbal cues: Effects on confidence and performance. *Journal of Educational Psychology, 84,* 308–313.

Cotterell, N., Eisenberger, R., & Speicher, H. (1992). Inhibiting effects of reciprocation wariness on interpersonal relationships. *Journal of Personality and Social Psychology, 62,* 658–668.

Cox, T., Lobel, S., & McLeod, P. (1991). Effects of ethnic groups' cultural differences on cooperative and competitive behavior on a group task. *Academy of Management Journal, 34,* 827–847.

Creighton, J. L., & Adams, W. R. (1998). The cyber meeting's about to begin. *Management Review, 87,* 29–31.

Crystal, D. (1997). *English as a global language.* Cambridge, UK: Cambridge University Press.

Cult compound grew on rules, isolation. (1993, March 3). *San Jose Mercury News,* p. 8A.

Cupach, W. R., & Canary, D. J. (1997). *Competence in interpersonal conflict.* Prospect Heights, IL: Waveland Press.

Curtis, B., Krasner, H., & Iscoe, N. (1988). A field study of the software design process for large systems. *Communications of the ACM, 31,* 1268–1287.

Daft, R. L., & Lengel, R. H. (1986). Organizational informational requirements, media richness, and structural design. *Management Science, 32,* 554–571.

Davidson, J. (1996). The shortcomings of the information age. *Vital Speeches,* 495–503.

Davis, J. H., Au, W. T., Hulbert, L., Chen, X., & Zarnoth, P. (1997). Effects of group size and procedural influence on consensual judgments of quantity: The example of damage awards and mock civil juries. *Journal of Personality and Social Psychology, 73,* 703–718.

Deal, J. J. (2000). Gender differences in the intentional use of information in competitive negotiations. *Small Group Research, 31,* 702–723.

De Cremer, D., & Leonardelli, G. J. (2003). *Group Dynamics: Theory, Research, and Practice, 7,* 168–174.

De Dreu, C. K. W., & West, M. A. (2001). Minority dissent and team innovation: The importance of participation in decision making. *Journal of Applied Psychology, 86,* 1191–1201.

De Klerk, V. (1991). Expletives: Men only? *Communication Monographs, 58,* 156–169.

Delbecq, A., et al. (1975). *Group techniques for program planning.* Glenview, IL: Scott, Foresman.

Den Hartog, D. N. (2004). Assertiveness. In R. J. House, P. J. Hanges, M. Javidan, P. W. Dorfman, & V. Gupta (Eds.), *Culture, leadership, and organizations: The GLOBE study of 62 societies.* Thousand Oaks, CA: Sage.

Denison, D., & Sutton, R. (1990). Operating room nurses. In J. Hackman (Ed.), *Groups that work (and those that don't).* San Francisco: Jossey-Bass.

Dennis, A. R., & Kinney, S. T. (1998). Testing media richness theory in the new media: The effects of cues, feedback and task equivocality. *Information Systems Research, 9,* 256–274.

Dennis, A. R., & Valacich, J. S. (1999). *Rethinking media richness: Towards a theory of media synchronicity.* In Proceedings of the 32nd Hawaii International Conference on System Sciences, Maui, Hawaii.

Derber, C. (1979). *The pursuit of attention: Power and individualism in everyday life.* New York: Oxford University Press.

Derber, C. (1996). *The wilding of America: How greed and violence are eroding our nation's character.* New York: St. Martin's Press.

De Souza, G., & Kline, H. (1995). Emergent leadership in the group goal-setting process. *Small Group Research, 26,* 475–496.

DeStephen, R., & Hirokawa, R. (1988). Small group consensus: Stability of group support of the decision, task process, and group relationships. *Small Group Behavior, 19,* 227–239.

Deutsch, M. (1979). Education and distributive justice: Some reflections on grading systems. *American Psychologist, 34,* 391–401.

Deutsch, M. (1985). *Distributive justice: A social-psychological perspective.* New Haven, CT: Yale University Press.

DeVito, J. (1990). *Messages: Building interpersonal communication skills.* New York: Harper & Row.

Dewey, J. (1910). *How we think.* Lexington, MA: D. C. Heath.

Dindia, K. (1997, November). Men are from North Dakota, women are from South Dakota. Paper presented at the Speech Communication Association conference, Chicago.

District updates (2004, Fall). Retrieved April 12, 2005, from http://www.msanetwork.org/district .asp

Dodd, C. (1995). *Dynamics of intercultural communication.* Dubuque, IA: Wm. C. Brown & Company.

Domagalski, T. (1998). *Experienced and expressed anger in the workplace.* Unpublished doctoral dissertation, University of South Florida.

Donnellon, A. (1996). *Team talk.* Boston: Harvard Business School Press.

Donohue, W., & Kolt, R. (1992). *Managing interpersonal conflict.* Newbury Park, CA: Sage.

Dorado, M. A., Medina, F. J., Munduate, L., Cisneros, I. F. J., & Euwema, M. (2002). Computer-mediated negotiations of an escalated conflict. *Small Group Research, 33,* 509–524.

Dorfman, P. W. (2004). International and cross-cultural leadership research. In B. J. Punnett & O. Shenkar (Eds.), *Handbook for international management research.* Ann Arbor: University of Michigan Press.

Dorfman, P. W., Hanges, P. J., & Brodbeck, F. C. (2004). Leadership and cultural variation: The identification of culturally endorsed leadership profiles. In R. J. House, P. J. Hanges, M. Javidan, P. W. Dorfman, & V. Gupta (Eds.), *Culture, leadership, and organizations: The GLOBE study of 62 societies.* Thousand Oaks, CA: Sage.

Dorsey, A., Miller, K., & Scherer, C. (1999). Communication, risk behavior, and perceptions of threat and efficacy: A test of a reciprocal model. *Journal of Applied Communication Research, 27,* 377–395.

Dowd, E. T., Hughes, S., Brockbank, L., Halpain, D., Seibel, C., & Seibel, P. (1988). Compliance-based and defiance-based intervention strategies and psychological reactance in the treatment of free and unfree behavior. *Journal of Counseling Psychology, 35,* 363–369.

Drecksel, G. (1984). *Interaction characteristics of emergent leadership.* Unpublished doctoral dissertation, University of Utah.

Dressler, C. (1995, December 31). Please! End this meeting madness! *Santa Cruz Sentinel,* p. ID.

Drew, J. (1994). *Mastering meetings: Discovering the hidden potential of effective business meetings.* New York: McGraw-Hill.

Dreyfuss, I. (1999, August 30). Sports parents need to keep cool. *Santa Cruz Sentinel,* p. A9.

Driskell, J., Radtke, P., & Salas, E. (2003). Virtual teams: Effects of technological mediation on team performance. *Group Dynamics: Theory, Research, and Practice, 7,* 297–323.

Driskell, J., & Salas, E. (1992, June). Collective behavior and team performance. *Human Factors, 34,* 277–288.

Druskat, V. U., & Wolff, S. B. (1999). Effects and timing of developmental peer appraisals in self-managing work groups. *Journal of Applied Psychology, 84,* 58–74.

Dubrin, A. J., Ireland, R. D., & Williams, J. C. (1989). *Management and organization.* Cincinnati, OH: South-Western.

Dugosh, K. L., Paulus, P. B., Roland, E. J., & Yang, H. (2000). Cognitive stimulation in brainstorming. *Journal of Personality and Social Psychology, 79,* 722–735.

Dunlap, A. (1997). *Mean business: How I save bad companies and make good companies great.* New York: Simon & Schuster.

Durand, D. (1977). Power as a function of office space and physiognomy: Two studies of influence. *Psychological Reports, 40,* 755–760.

Eagly, A. H., & Karau, S. J. (2002). Role congruity theory of prejudice toward female leaders. *Psychological Review, 109,* 573–598.

Eagly, A. H., Karau, S., & Makhijiani, M. (1995). Gender and the effectiveness of leaders: A meta-analysis. *Journal of Personality and Social Psychology, 117,* 125–145.

Eagly, A. H., Makhijiani, M., & Klonsky, B. (1992). Gender and the evaluation of leaders: A meta-analysis. *Psychological Bulletin, 111,* 3–22.

Early, C. (1989). Social loafing and collectivism: A comparison of the United States and the People's Republic of China. *Administrative Science Quarterly, 34,* 555–581.

Efron, S. (1999, October 8). Samples point to wider radioactive impact. *San Jose Mercury News,* p. 6A.

Eisenberger, R., & Armeli, S. (1997). Can salient reward increase creative performance without reducing intrinsic creative interest? *Journal of Personality and Social Psychology, 72,* 652–663.

Eisenberger, R., & Cameron, J. (1996). Detrimental effects of reward: Reality or myth? *American Psychologist, 51,* 1153–1166.

Elley, N. (2001, November/December). Big benefits in small classes. *Psychology Today,* 28.

Emmons, M. (2002, October 12). Winning isn't everything. *San Jose Mercury News,* pp. 1A, 14A.

Emmons, M. (2003, January 6). Giants' snapper: "I screwed it up." *San Jose Mercury News,* p. 7D.

Emmons, M. (2005, April 10). Scholarship pressure

changes youth sports. *San Jose Mercury News,* pp. 1A, 12A–13A.

En-Lai, Y. (2003, July 13). Singapore loosens up to shed its dull image. *San Jose Mercury News,* p. 18A.

Espo, D. (2004, March 28). Social issues split Congress. *San Jose Mercury News,* p. 7A.

Evans, C., & Dion, K. (1991). Group cohesion and performance: A meta-analysis. *Small Group Research, 22,* 175–186.

Fadiman, C. (Ed.). (1985). *The Little, Brown book of anecdotes.* Boston: Little, Brown & Company.

Fairhurst, G., & Sarr, R. (1996). *The art of framing: Managing the language of leadership.* San Francisco: Jossey-Bass.

Fandt, P. (1991). The relationship of accountability and interdependent behavior to enhancing team consequences. *Group and Organization Studies, 16,* 300–312.

Farace, R., Monge, P. R., & Russell, H. M. (1977). *Communicating and organizing.* Reading, MA: Addison-Wesley.

Fausto-Sterling, A. (1993, April). Is nature really red in tooth and claw? *Discover,* 24–27.

Fearing heckling, CHP officer let King bleed. (1993, March 30). *San Jose Mercury News,* p. 3B.

Fenton, B. (2005, June 5). "Chainsaw" to the rescue? Think again! *Fenton Report.* Retrieved June 5, 2005, from http://www.fentonreport.com/ wealth_articles/news/chainsaw_al_dunlap.htm

Fernald, L. (1987). Of windmills and rope dancing: The instructional value of narrative structures. *Teaching Psychology, 14,* 214–216.

Fiechtner, S. S., & Davis, E. A. (1992). Why some groups fail: A survey of students' experiences with learning groups. In A. S. Goodsell, M. R. Maher, & V. Tinto (Eds.), *Collaborative learning: A sourcebook for higher education.* Syracuse, NY: National Center on Postsecondary Teaching, Learning, & Assessment at Syracuse University.

Fiedler, F. (1967). *A theory of leadership effectiveness.* New York: McGraw-Hill.

Fiedler, F., & House, R. (1988). Leadership theory and research: A report of progress. In C. Cooper & I. Robertson (Eds.), *International review of industrial and organizational psychology.* New York: John Wiley & Sons.

Files, J. (2002, November 19). Female leaders make small gains. *San Jose Mercury News,* pp. 1C, 6C.

Filkins, D. (2001, November 13). Letting their hair down. *San Jose Mercury News,* p. 14A.

Finkelstein, K. E. (2001, August 3). Tempers seem to be growing shorter in many jury rooms. *The New York Times.* Retrieved July 11, 2002, from http://www.nytimes.com/2001/08/03/nyregion/03JURY. html?ex_997841696&

Firestein, R. (1990). Effects of creative problem solving training on communication behaviors in small groups. *Small Group Research, 21,* 507–521.

Fisher, B. A. (1986). Leadership: When does the difference make a difference? In R. Hirokawa & M. S. Poole (Eds.), *Communication and group decision-making.* Beverly Hills, CA: Sage.

Fisher, B. A., & Ellis, D. (1990). *Small group decision making: Communication and the group process.* New York: McGraw-Hill.

Fisher, C., & Gitelson, R. (1983). A meta-analysis of the correlates of role conflict and ambiguity. *Journal of Applied Psychology, 68,* 320–333.

Fisher, K. (2000). *Leading self-directed work teams: A guide to developing new team leadership skills.* New York: McGraw-Hill.

Fisher, R., & Brown, S. (1988). *Getting together: Building a relationship that gets to yes.* Boston: Houghton Mifflin.

Fisher, R., & Ury, W. (1981). *Getting to yes: Negotiating agreement without giving in.* New York: Penguin Books.

Fiske, S. T. (1993). Social cognition and social perception. *Annual Review of Psychology, 44,* 155–194.

Fitzhenry, R. (Ed.). (1993). *The Harper book of quotations.* New York: HarperPerennial.

Flippen, A. (1999). Understanding groupthink from a self-regulatory perspective. *Small Group Research, 30,* 139–165.

Flauto, F. J. (1999). Walking the talking: The relationship between leadership and communication competence. *The Journal of Leadership Studies, 6,* 86–97.

Foderaro, L. W. (2003, September 15). Death in frat's hazing ritual shakes a SUNY campus. *The New York Times.* Retrieved May 12, 2005, from http://www.nytimes.com/2003/09/15/nyregion.15HAZI.html?th

Folger, J., Poole, M., & Stutman, R. (1993). *Working through conflict: A communication perspective.* Glenview, IL: Scott, Foresman.

Forsyth, D. (1990). *Group dynamics.* Pacific Grove, CA: Brooks/Cole.

Forsyth, D., Heiney, M., & Wright, S. (1997). Biases in appraisals of women leaders. *Group Dynamics: Theory, Research, and Practice, 1,* 98–103.

Foschi, M., Warriner, G. K., & Hart, S. D. (1985). Standards, expectations, and interpersonal influence. *Social Psychology Quarterly, 48,* 108–117.

Foushee, H., & Manos, K. (1981). Information transfer within the cockpit: Problems in intra-cockpit communications. In C. Billings & E. Cheaney (Eds.), *Information transfer problems in the aviation system (NASA Report No. TP-1875).* Moffett Field, CA: NASA-Ames Research Center.

Foushee, M. (1984). Dyads and triads at 35,000 feet: Factors affecting group process and aircraft performance. *American Psychologist, 39,* 885–893.

Franz, T. M., & Larson, J. R. (2000). The impact of experts on information sharing during group discussion. *Small Group Research, 33,* 383–411.

Freed, A. (1992). We understand perfectly: A critique of Tannen's view. In K. Hall, M. Bucholtz, & B. Moonwomon (Eds.), *Locating power.* Berkeley: Berkeley Women and Language Group, University of California.

French, J., & Raven, B. (1959). The bases of social power. In D. Cartwright (Ed.), *Studies in social power* (pp. 150–167). Ann Arbor, MI: Institute for Social Research.

Friedman, R., Anderson, C., Brett, J., Olekalns, M., Goates, N., & Lisco, C. C. (2004). The positive and negative effects of anger in dispute resolution: Evidence from electronically mediated disputes. *Journal of Applied Psychology, 89,* 369–376.

Furst, S. A., Reeves, M., Rosen, B., & Blackburn, R. S. (2004). Managing the life cycle of virtual teams. *Academy of Management Executives, 18,* 6–12.

Gabrenya, W., Wang, Y., & Latane, B. (1985). Social loafing on an optimizing task: Cross-cultural differences among Chinese and Americans. *Journal of Cross-cultural Psychology, 16,* 223–242.

Galanter, M. (1999). *Cults: Faith, healing, and coercion.* New York: Oxford University Press.

Gammage, K. L., Carron, A. V., & Estabrooks, P. A. (2001). Team cohesion and individual productivity: The influence of the norm for productivity and the identifiability of individual effort. *Small Group Research, 32,* 3–18.

Gamson, W., Fireman, B., & Rytia, S. (1982). *Encounters with unjust authority.* Homewood, IL: Dorsey.

Gardner, L., & Leak, G. (1994). Characteristics and correlates of teacher anxiety among college psychology teachers. *Teaching of Psychology, 21,* 28–32.

Garrett, L. (1994). *The coming plague: Newly emerging diseases in a world out of balance.* New York: Penguin Books.

Garrity, J. (1989, November 20). A clash of cultures on the Hopi reservation. *Sports Illustrated,* 10–16.

Gastil, J. (1994). A meta-analytic review of the productivity and satisfaction of democratic and autocratic leadership. *Small Group Research, 25,* 384–410.

Gayle, B. (1991). Sex equity in workplace conflict management. *Journal of Applied Communication Research, 19,* 152–169.

Gayle-Hackett, B. (1989, February 17). Do females and males differ in the selection of conflict management strategies: A meta-analytic review. Paper presented to the Western Speech Communication Association Convention, Spokane, WA.

Gebhardt, L., & Meyers, R. (1995). Subgroup influence in decision-making groups: Examining consistency from a communication perspective. *Small Group Research, 26,* 147–168.

Geier, J. (1967). A trait approach in the study of leadership in small groups. *Journal of Communication, 17,* 316–323.

Geis, F., et al. (1984). Sex vs. status in sex-associated stereotypes. *Sex Roles, 11,* 771–786.

Gelles, R., & Straus, M. (1988). *Intimate violence: The causes and consequences of abuse in the American family.* New York: Simon & Schuster.

Gelman, D., & Rogers, P. (1993, March 12). Mixed messages. *Newsweek,* 28.

Gerard, H. B., & Mathewson, G. C. (1966). The effects of severity of initiation on liking for a group: A replication. *Journal of Experimental Social Psychology, 2,* 278–287.

Getter, H., & Nowinski, J. (1981). A free response test of interpersonal effectiveness. *Journal of Personality Assessment, 45,* 301–308.

Gibb, J. (1961). Defensive communication. *The Journal of Communication, 11,* 141–148.

Glasner, B. (1999). *The culture of fear.* New York: Basic Books.

Glassman, J. K. (1998, May 29). Put shootings in proper perspective. *San Jose Mercury News,* p. B7.

Glazer, M., & Glazer, P. (1986, August). Whistle-blowing. *Psychology Today,* 37–43.

Gleick, J. (1999). *Faster: The acceleration of just about everything.* New York: Pantheon Books.

Glomb, T. M. (2002). Workplace anger and aggression: Informing conceptual models with data from specific encounters. *Journal of Occupational Health Psychology, 7,* 20–36.

Godar, S. H., & Ferris, S. P. (2004). *Virtual and collaborative teams: Process, technologies and practice.* London: Idea Group Publishing.

Goethals, G., & Darley, J. (1987). Social comparison theory: Self-evaluation and group life. In B. Mullen & G. Goethals (Eds.), *Theories of group behavior.* New York: Springer-Verlag.

Goktepe, J., & Schneier, C. (1989). Role of sex and gender roles, and attraction in predicting emergent leaders. *Journal of Applied Psychology, 74,* 165–167.

Goldhaber, G. (1990). *Organizational communication.* Dubuque, IA: Wm. C. Brown & Company.

Goldstein, S. (1994, April 11). Citadel's lone woman ostracized. *San Jose Mercury News,* p. 13A.

Goleman, D. (1995). *Emotional intelligence: Why it can matter more than I.Q.* New York: Bantam Books.

Goleman, D. (1998). *Working with emotional intelligence.* New York: Bantam Books.

Goleman, D., Boyatzis, R., & McKee, A. (2002). *Primal leadership: Realizing the power of emotional intelligence.* Boston: Harvard Business School Press.

Gomes, L. (1995, March 3). Intuit fesses up again. *San Jose Mercury News,* p. 1C.

Gomez, M. (2003, September 11). Three CCS teams are next to try the impossible. *San Jose Mercury News,* pp. 1D, 9D.

Goodman, E. (2002, September 3). Anxiety reigns as women pull ahead on campus. *San Jose Mercury News,* p. 7B.

Goodstein, L. (1997, March 30). Heaven's Gate had all the classic cult traits, experts say. *The Washington Post,* p. A1.

Goodwin, M. H. (1990). *He said-she said.* Bloomington: Indiana University Press.

Gottman, J. (1994). *What predicts divorce? The relationship between marital processes and marital outcomes.* Hillsdale, NJ: Lawrence Erlbaum.

Gottman, J., & Silver, N. (1994). *Why marriages succeed or fail.* New York: Simon & Schuster.

Gottman, J., & Silver, N. (1999). *The seven principles for making marriage work.* New York: Crown.

Gould, S. (1981). *The mismeasure of man.* New York: W. W. Norton.

Gouran, D. (1981). Cognitive sources of inferential error and the contributing influence of interaction characteristics in decision-making groups. In G. Ziegelmueller & J. Rhodes (Eds.), *Dimensions of argument: Proceedings of the Second Annual Summer Conference on Argumentation.* Annandale, VA: Speech Communication Association.

Gouran, D. (1982a, April). *A theoretical foundation for the study of inferential error in decision-making groups.* Paper presented at the Conference on Small Group Research, Pennsylvania State University.

Gouran, D. (1982b). *Making decisions in groups: Choices and consequences.* Glenview, IL: Scott, Foresman.

Gouran, D. (1983). Communicative influences on inferential judgments in decision-making groups: A descriptive analysis. In D. Zarefsky et al. (Eds.), *Argument in transition: Proceedings of the Third Summer Conference on Argumentation.* Annandale, VA: Speech Communication Association.

Gouran, D. (1986). Inferential errors, interaction, and group decision-making. In R. Hirokawa & M. Poole (Eds.), *Communication and group decision-making.* Beverly Hills, CA: Sage.

Gouran, D. (1988). Principles of counteractive influence in decision-making and problem-solving groups. In R. Cathcart & L. Samovar (Eds.), *Small group communication: A reader.* Dubuque, IA: Wm. C. Brown & Company.

Gouran, D., & Baird, J. (1972). An analysis of distributional and sequential structure in problem solving and informal group discussions, *Speech Monographs, 39,* 16–22.

Green, A. S., & McKenna, K. Y. A. (2002). *The Internet attenuates the effects of social anxiety.* Manuscript submitted for publication, New York University.

Griffin, E. (1994). *A first look at communication theory.* New York: McGraw-Hill.

Griffith, T., & Neale, M. A. (1999). *Information processing and performance in traditional and virtual teams: The role of transactive memory* (Research Paper No. 1613). Stanford, CA: Stanford University Graduate School of Business.

Grusky, O., Bonacich, P., & Webster, C. (1995). The coalition structure of the four-person family. *Current Research in Social Psychology, 2,* 16–28.

Gudykunst, W. (1991). *Bridging differences: Effective intergroup communication.* Newbury Park, CA: Sage.

Gully, S., Devine, D., & Whitney, D. (1995). A meta-analysis of cohesion and performance: Effects of level of analysis and task interdependence. *Small Group Research, 26,* 497–520.

Gumpert, R., & Hambleton, R. (1979, December). Situational leadership: How Xerox managers finetune managerial styles to employee maturity and tasks needs. *Management Review, 9.*

Guzzo, R. A., & Dickson, M. W. (1996). Teams in organizations: Recent research on performance effectiveness. *Annual Review of Psychology, 47,* 307–338.

Ha, K. O. (2005, June 23). In the Philippines, text messaging is c%l. *San Jose Mercury News,* pp. 1B, 2B.

Habitat for Humanity selects Knoxville for milestone 200,000th house built. (2005). Retrieved March 3, 2005, from http://www.habitat.org/newsroom/2005archive/insitedoc008734.htm

Hackman, J. (1987). The design of work teams. In J. Lorsch (Ed.), *Handbook of organizational behavior* (pp. 315–342). Englewood Cliffs, NJ: Prentice-Hall.

Hackman, M., & Johnson, C. (2004). *Leadership: A communication perspective.* Prospect Heights, IL: Waveland Press.

Haleta, L. L. (1996). Student perceptions of teachers' use of language: The effects of powerful and powerless language on impression formation and uncertainty. *Communication Education, 45,* 16–28.

Hall, E. (1981). *Beyond culture.* New York: Doubleday.

Hall, E., & Hall, M. (1987). *Understanding cultural difference.* Yarmouth, ME: Intercultural Press.

Hall, J. A., & Bernieri, F. J. (2001). *Interpersonal sensitivity: Theory and measurement.* Mahwah, NJ: Lawrence Erlbaum.

Hall, J., & Watson, W. (1970). The effects of a normative intervention on group decision-making. *Human Relations, 23,* 299–317.

Halpern, D. (1984). *Thought and knowledge: An introduction to critical thinking.* Hillsdale, NJ: Lawrence Erlbaum.

Hamm, M. (1999). *Go for the goal: A champion's guide to winning in soccer and life.* New York: HarperCollins.

Haney, W. (1967). *Communication and organizational behavior.* Homewood, IL: Irwin.

Hansen, R. S., & Hansen, K. (2005). What do employers really want? Top skills and values employers seek from job-seekers. Retrieved February 22, 2005, from http://www.quintcareers.com/job_skills_values.html

Hare, A. (1994). Types of roles in small groups: A bit of history and a current perspective. *Small Group Research, 25,* 433–448.

Harlan, D. (2001). The Shakers. Retrieved March 5, 2005, from http://religiousmovements.lib.virginia.edu/nrms/Shakers.html

Harmon, A. (2001, September 23). The search for intelligent life on the Internet. *The New York Times.* Retrieved July 12, 2002, from http://www.nytimes.com/2001/09/23/weekinreview/

Harrington, M. (1995). *Women lawyers: Rewriting the rules.* New York: Plume/Penguin Books.

Harris, C. L., & Beyerlein, M. M. (2003). Team-based organization: Creating an environment for team success. In M. A. West, D. Tjosvold, & K. G. Smith (Eds.), *International handbook of organizational teamwork and cooperative working.* New York: John Wiley & Sons.

Hart, J. W., Bridgett, D. J., & Karau, S. J. (2001). Coworker ability and effort as determinants of individual effort on a collective task. *Group*

Dynamics: Theory, Research, and Practice, 5, 181–190.

Haslett, B. B., & Ruebush, J. (1999). What differences do individual differences in groups make? The effects of individuals, culture, and group composition. In L. R. Frey, D. S. Gouran, & M. S. Poole (Eds.), *The handbook of group communication theory and research.* Thousand Oaks, CA: Sage.

Haslett, B., Geis, F. L., & Carter, M. R. (1992). *The organizational woman: Power and paradox.* Norwood, NJ: Ablex Publishing.

Hassan, S. (1988). *Combatting cult mind control.* Rochester, VT: Part Street Press.

Hastie, R., Penrod, S., & Pennington, N. (1983). *Inside the jury.* Cambridge, MA: Harvard University Press.

Hatfield, E., & Sprecher, S. (1986). *Mirror, mirror: The importance of looks in everyday life.* Albany: State University of New York Press.

Hawkins, K. (1995). Effects of gender and communication content on leadership emergence in small task-oriented groups. *Small Group Research, 26,* 234–249.

Heilman, M. E., Wallen, A. S., Fuchs, D., & Tamkins, M. M. (2004). Penalties for success: Reactions to women who succeed at male gender-typed tasks. *Journal of Applied Psychology, 89,* 416–427.

Heim, P. (1992). *Hardball for women: Winning at the game of business.* New York: Penguin Books.

Hellweg, S., Samovar, L., & Skow, L. (1994). Cultural variations in negotiation styles. In L. Samovar & R. Porter (Eds.), *Intercultural communication: A reader.* Belmont, CA: Wadsworth.

Hendra, T. (Ed.). (1982). *Meet Mr. Bomb.* New London, NH: High Meadow Publishing.

Henley, N. (1995). Body politics revisited: What do we know today? In P. Kalbfleisch & M. Cody (Eds.), *Gender, power, and communication in human relationships.* Hillsdale, NJ: Lawrence Erlbaum.

Henningsen, D. D., Cruz, M. G., & Miller, M. L. (2000). Role of social loafing in predeliberation decision making. *Group Dynamics: Theory, Research, and Practice, 4,* 168–175.

Henry, J. (1963). *Culture against man.* New York: Random House.

Hensley, T., & Griffin, G. (1986). Victims of groupthink: The Kent State University Board of Trustees and the 1977 gymnasium controversy. *Journal of Conflict Resolution, 30,* 497–531.

Herbold, S. (1998, May 3). Venture capitalists' slang puts the "go" into "argot." *San Jose Mercury News,* pp. 1A, 26A.

Herek, G., et al. (1987). Decision making during international crises: Is quality of process related to outcome? *Journal of Conflict Resolution, 31,* 203–226.

Hersey, P., & Blanchard, K. (1988; 1996). *Management of organizational behavior: Utilizing human resources.* Englewood Cliffs, NJ: Prentice-Hall.

Hickson, M., & Stacks, D. (1989). *Nonverbal communication: Studies and applications.* Dubuque, IA: Wm. C. Brown & Company.

Hightower, R. T., & Sayeed, L. (1995). The impact of computer mediated communication systems on biased group discussion. *Computers in Human Behavior, 11,* 33–44.

Hirokawa, R. (1985). Discussion procedures and decision-making performance: A test of a functional perspective. *Human Communication Research, 12,* 203–224.

Hirokawa, R. (1987). Why informed groups make faulty decisions: An investigation of possible interaction-based explanations. *Small Group Behavior, 18,* 3–29.

Hirokawa, R. (1992). Communication and group decision-making efficacy. In R. Cathcart & L. Samovar (Eds.), *Small group communication: A reader.* Dubuque, IA: Wm. C. Brown & Company.

Hirokawa, R., & Pace, R. (1983). A descriptive investigation of the possible communication-based reasons for effective and ineffective group decision-making. *Communication Monographs, 50,* 363–379.

Hirokawa, R., & Scheerhorn, D. (1986). Communication in faulty group decision-making. In R. Hirokawa & M. Poole (Eds.), *Communication and group decision-making.* Beverly Hills, CA: Sage.

Hoegl, M., & Parboteeah, K. P. (2003). Goal setting and team performance in innovative projects: On the moderating role of teamwork quality. *Small Group Research, 34,* 3–19.

Hoffer, T. B., Sederstrom, S., Selfa, L., Welch, V., Hess, M., Brown, S., Reyes, S., Webber, K., & Guzman-Barron, I. (2003). *Doctorate recipients* from United States universities: Summary report 2002. Chicago: University of Chicago.

Hofstede, G. (1991). *Cultures and Organizations: Software of the mind.* New York: McGraw-Hill.

Hofstede, G. (2001). *Culture's consequences: Comparing values, behaviors, institutions and organizations across nations.* Thousand Oaks, CA: Sage.

Hogan, R., Curphy, G. J., & Hogan, J. (1994). What we know about leadership: Effectiveness and personality. *American Psychologist, 49,* 493–504.

Hollander, E. (1978). *Leadership dynamics.* New York: Free Press.

Hollander, E. (1985). Leadership and power. In G. Lindzey & E. Aronson (Eds.), *Handbook of social psychology* (pp. 485–537). New York: Random House.

Hollander, E., & Offerman, L. (1990, February). Power and leadership in organizations. *American Psychologist,* 179–189.

Hollingshead, A. (1998). Group and individual training: The impact of practice on performance. *Small Group Research, 29,* 254–280.

Holtgraves, T. (1997). Styles of language use: Individual and cultural variability in conversational indirectness. *Journal of Personality and Social Psychology, 73,* 624–637.

Hong, L. (1978). Risky shift and cautious shift: Same direct evidence on the cultural-value theory. *Social Psychology, 41,* 342–346.

Hoover, N. C., & Pollard, N. J. (2000, August). Initiation rites in American high schools: A national survey final report. Retrieved January 13, 2004, from http://www.alfred.edu/news/html/hazing_study.html

Hotz, R. (1999, October 1). "Dumb" math error blamed for death of Martian probe. *San Jose Mercury News,* p. 1A.

House, R. J. (2004). Illustrative examples of GLOBE findings. In R. J. House, P. J. Hanges, M. Javidan, P. W. Dorfman, and V. Gupta (Eds.), *Culture, leadership, and organizations: The GLOBE study of 62 societies.* Thousand Oaks, CA: Sage.

House, R. J., & Aditya, R. N. (1997). The social scientific study of leadership: Quo vadis? *Journal of Management, 23,* 409–473.

House, R. J., & Javidan, M. (2004). Overview of GLOBE. In R. J. House, P. J. Hanges, M. Javidan, P. W. Dorfman, & V. Gupta (Eds.), *Culture, lead-*

ership, and organizations: The GLOBE study of 62 societies. Thousand Oaks, CA: Sage.

Howell, W. S. (1982). *The empathic communicator.* Belmont, CA: Wadsworth.

Hoyt, C. L., & Blascovich, J. (2003). Transformational and transactional leadership in virtual and physical environments. *Small Group Research, 34,* 678–715.

Huckshorn, K. (1996, March 4). Human rights in Asia: Society comes first. *San Jose Mercury News,* pp. 1A, 15A.

Huguet, P., Charbonnier, E., & Monteil, J.-M. (1999). Productivity loss in performance groups: People who see themselves as average do not engage in social loafing. *Group Dynamics: Theory, Research, and Practice, 3,* 118–131.

Hui, C. H., & Triandis, H. C. (1986). Individualism-collectivism: A study of cross-cultural researchers. *Journal of Cross-Cultural Psychology, 17,* 225–248.

Husband, R. (1992). Leading in organizational groups. In R. Cathcart & L. Samovar (Eds.), *Small group communication* (pp. 464–476). Dubuque, IA: Wm. C. Brown & Company.

Inagaki, Y. (1985). *Jiko hyogen no gijutsu (Skills in self-expression).* Tokyo: PHP Institute.

Infante, D., Rancer, A., & Womack, D. (1997). *Building communication theory.* Prospect Heights, IL: Waveland Press.

Internet usage statistics: The big picture (2005). Retrieved August 19, 2005, from http://www.internetworldstats.com/stats.htm

Irons, E., & Moore, G. (1985). *Black managers: The case of the banking industry.* New York: Praeger.

Isaksen, S. G. (1988). Innovative problem solving in groups. In Y. Ijiri & R. I. Kuhn (Eds.), *New directions in creative and innovative management: Bridging theory and practice.* Cambridge, MA: Ballinger.

Isenhart, M. W., & Spangle, M. (2000). *Collaborative approaches to resolving conflict.* Thousand Oaks, CA: Sage.

Ishii, S., Klopf, D., & Cambra, R. (1984). The typical Japanese student as an oral communicator: A preliminary profile. *Otsuma Review, 17,* 39–63.

Ivanevich, J. M., & Matteson, M. T. (2002). *Organizational behavior and management.* New York: McGraw-Hill.

Jackson, J. M., & Williams, K. D. (1985). Social loafing on difficult tasks: Working collectively can improve performance. *Journal of Personality and Social Psychology, 49*, 937–942.

Jackson, P. (1995). *Sacred hoops: Spiritual lessons of a hardwood warrior.* New York: Hyperion.

Jaksa, J., & Pritchard, M. (1994). *Communication ethics: Methods of analysis.* Belmont, CA: Wadsworth.

James, D., & Clarke, S. (1993). Women, men, and interruptions: A critical review. In D. Tannen (Ed.), *Gender and conversational interaction.* New York: Oxford University Press.

James, D., & Drakich, J. (1993). Understanding gender differences in amount of talk: A critical review of research. In D. Tannen (Ed.), *Gender and conversational interaction.* New York: Oxford University Press.

Janis, I. (1982). *Groupthink: Psychological studies of policy decisions and fiascoes.* Boston: Houghton Mifflin.

Jehn, K. A. (1995). A multimethod examination of the benefits and detriments of intragroup conflict. *Administrative Science Quarterly, 40*, 256–282.

Jehn, K. A., & Weldon, E. (1997). Managerial attitudes toward conflict: Cross-cultural differences in resolution styles. *Journal of International Management, 3*, 291–321.

Jenkins, S. (2003, July 14). Yellow means caution. *San Jose Mercury News*, pp. 1D, 3D.

Jetten, J., Spears, R., & Manstead, A. S. R. (1996). Intergroup norms and intergroup discrimination: Distinctive self-categorization and social identity effects. *Journal of Personality and Social Psychology, 71*, 1222–1233.

Johannesen, R. (1974). The functions of silence: A plea for communication research. *Western Speech, 38*, 20–35.

Johnson, D. W. (2003). Social interdependence: Interrelationships among theory, research, and practice. *American Psychologist, 58*, 934–945.

Johnson, D. W., & Johnson, R. T. (1987a). *Cooperation and competition.* Hillsdale, NJ: Lawrence Erlbaum.

Johnson, D. W., & Johnson, R. T. (1987b). *Learning together and alone: Cooperative, competitive, and individualistic learning.* Englewood Cliffs, NJ: Prentice-Hall.

Johnson, D. W., & Johnson, R. T. (1998). Cooperative learning and social interdependence theory.

In R. Tinsdale et al. (Eds.), *Theory and research on small groups.* New York: Plenum Press.

Johnson, D. W., & Johnson, R. T. (2000, June). Teaching students to be peacemakers; Results of twelve years of research. Retrieved July 22, 2005, from http://www.cooplearn.org/pages/peacemeta.html

Johnson, D. W., & Johnson, R. T. (2003a). Field testing integrative negotiations. *Peace and Conflict: Journal of Peace Psychology, 9*, 39–68.

Johnson, D. W., & Johnson, R. T. (2003b). Training for cooperative group work. In M. A. West, D. Tjosvold, & K. G. Smith (Eds.), *International handbook of organizational teamwork and cooperative working.* New York: John Wiley & Sons.

Johnson, D. W., Johnson, R. T., & Holubec, E. (1986). *Circles of Learning: Cooperation in the classroom.* Edina, MN: Interaction Book Company.

Johnson, S., & Bechler, C. (1998). Examining the relationship between listening effectiveness and leadership emergence: Perceptions, behaviors, and recall. *Small Group Research, 29*, 452–471.

Jones, A. P., Rozelle, R. M., & Chang, W. C. (1990). Perceived punishment and reward values of supervisor actions in a Chinese sample. *Psychological Studies, 35*, 1–10.

Jones, D. (2004, February 20). Contestant Amy Henry shines above the others. *USA Today*, p. 4B.

Jordan, M. H., Field, H. S., & Armenakis, A. A. (2002). The relationships of group process variables and team performance. *Small Group Research, 33*, 121–150.

Ju, L., & Cushman, D. (1995). *Organizational teamwork in high-speed management.* Albany: State University of New York Press.

Judge, C. (1998, July 31). Rookie's father would be proud. *San Jose Mercury News*, p. D8.

Judge, T. A., & Piccolo, R. F. (2004). Transformational and transactional leadership: A meta-analytic test of their relative validity. *Journal of Applied Psychology, 89*, 755–768.

Kalb, C., & McCormick, J. (1998, September 21). Bellying up to the bar, *Newsweek*, 89.

Kampeas, R. (2001, July 17). Government lacks diversity at decision-making levels. *Santa Cruz Sentinel*, pp. A1, A8.

Karakowsky, L., & Siegel, J. P. (1999). The effects of

proportional representation and gender orientation of the task on emergent leadership behavior in mixed-gender work groups. *Journal of Applied Psychology, 84,* 620–631.

Karau, S. J., & Hart, J. W. (1998). Group cohesiveness and social loafing: Effects of a social interaction manipulation on individual motivation within groups. *Group Dynamics: Theory, Research, and Practice, 2,* 185–191.

Kassin, S. (1998). *Psychology.* Upper Saddle River, NJ: Prentice-Hall.

Katz, D. (1982). The effects of group longevity on project communication. *Administrative Science, 27,* 81–104.

Katz, D., & Kahn, R. (1978). *The social psychology of organizations.* New York: John Wiley & Sons.

Katzenbach, J. R., & Smith, D. K. (1993, March–April). The discipline of teams. *Harvard Business Review,* 111–120.

Kelley, T., & Littman, J. (2001). *The art of innovation.* New York: Doubleday.

Keltner, D., Gruenfeld, D. H., & Anderson, C. (2003). Power, approach, and inhibition. *Psychological Review, 110,* 265–284.

Kerber, K. W., & Buono, A. F. (2004). Leadership challenges in global virtual teams: Lessons from the field. *SAM Advanced Management Journal, 69,* 4–11.

Kerr, N., & Bruun, S. (1983). Dispensability of member effort and group motivation losses: Free-rider effects. *Journal of Personality and Social Psychology, 44,* 78–94.

Ketrow, S. M. (1999). Nonverbal aspects of group communication. In L. R. Frey, D. S. Gouran, & M. S. Poole (Eds.), *The handbook of group communication theory and research.* Thousand Oaks, CA: Sage.

Keyton, J., Harmon, N., & Frey, L. R. (1996). Grouphate: Implications for teaching group communication. Paper presented to the Instructional Development Division, Speech Communication Association, San Diego.

Kichuk, S. L., & Wiesner, W. H. (1998). Work teams: Selecting members for optimal performance. *Canadian Psychology, 39,* 23–32.

Killian, L. (1952). The significance of multiple-group membership in disaster. *American Journal of Sociology, 57,* 309–314.

Killion, A. (1996, August 5). VanDerveer ordeal proves worth it for well-drilled team. *San Jose Mercury News,* pp. 1D, 3D.

Killion, A. (2004, August 16). Yet another "wake-up call" won't rouse this U.S. team. *San Jose Mercury News,* pp. 1D, 3D.

Kilmann, R., & Thomas, K. (1977). Developing a force-choice measure of conflict-handling behavior: The MODE instrument. *Educational and Psychological Measurement, 37,* 309–325.

Kirchmeyer, C. (1993). Multicultural task groups: An account of the low contribution level of minorities. *Small Group Research, 24,* 127–148.

Kirchmeyer, C., & Cohen, A. (1992). Multicultural groups: Their performance and reactions with constructive conflict. *Group and Organization Management, 17,* 153–170.

Kirkman, B., & Rosen, B. (1999). Beyond self-management: Antecedents and consequences of team empowerment. *Academy of Management Journal, 42,* 58–74.

Kirkman, B. L., & Shapiro, D. L. (2000). Understanding why team members won't share: An examination of factors related to employee receptivity to team-based rewards. *Small Group Research, 31,* 175–209.

Kirn, W. (1997, October 3). Drinking to belong. *The New York Times,* p. A11.

Klapp, O. (1978). *Opening and closing: Strategies of information adaptation in society.* New York: Cambridge University Press.

Kleiman, C. (1991, July 28). A boost up the corporate ladder. *San Jose Mercury News,* p. 1PC.

Klein, S. (1996). Work pressure as a determinant of work group behavior. *Small Group Research, 27,* 299–315.

Kline, S. L., & Stafford, L. (2004). A comparison of interaction rules and interaction frequency in relationship to marital quality. *Communication Reports, 17,* 11–26.

Kohn, A. (1987, October). It's hard to get left out of a pair. *Psychology Today* 53–57.

Kohn, A. (1992). *No contest: The case against competition.* Boston: Houghton Mifflin.

Kohn, A. (1993). *Punished by rewards.* New York: Houghton Mifflin.

Kolata, G. (1999). *Flu: The story of the Great Influenza Pandemic of 1918 and the search for the virus that caused it.* New York: Farrar, Straus, & Giroux.

Kolb, J. (1997). Are we still stereotyping leadership? *Small Group Research, 28,* 370–393.

Kotter, J. P. (1990). *A force for change: How leadership differs from management.* New York: Free Press.

Kouzes, J. M., & Posner, B. Z. (1987). *The leadership challenge: How to get extraordinary things done in organizations.* San Francisco: Jossey-Bass.

Kouzes, J. M., & Posner, B. Z. (2003). *Credibility: How leaders gain and lose; why people demand it.* San Francisco: Jossey-Bass.

Kramer, M. W., Kuo, C. L., & Dailey, J. C. (1997). The impact of brainstorming techniques on subsequent group processes: Beyond generating ideas. *Small Group Research, 28,* 218–242.

Krauss, R. M., Freyberg, R., & Morsella, E. (2002). Inferring speakers' physical attributes from their voices. *Journal of Experimental Social Psychology, 38,* 618–625.

Kruger, J., & Dunning, D. (1999). Unskilled and unaware of it: How difficulties in recognizing one's own competence lead to inflated self-assessments. *Journal of Personality and Social Psychology, 77,* 1121–1134.

Kruglanski, A. (1986, August). Freeze-think and the Challenger. *Psychology Today,* 48–49.

Kuczynski, A. (2001, August 20). "Best" list for colleges by U.S. News is under fire. *The New York Times.* Retrieved August 20, 2001, from http://www.nytimes.com/2001/08/20/business/media/

Kuhn, T., & Poole, M. S. (2000). Do conflict management styles affect group decision making? Evidence from a longitudinal field study. *Human Communication Research, 26,* 558–590.

Kunkel, A. W., & Burleson, B. R. (1998). Social support and the emotional lives of men and women: An assessment of the different cultures perspective. In D. J. Canary & K. Dindia, *Sex differences and similarities in communication.* Mahwah, NJ: Lawrence Erlbaum.

Kutner, L. (1994, February 20). Winning isn't only thing that counts. *Santa Cruz Sentinel,* p. D2.

LaFasto, F., & Larson, C. (2001). *When teams work best: 6,000 team members and leaders tell what it takes to succeed.* Thousand Oaks, CA: Sage.

Lamb, C. W., Hair, J. F., & McDaniel, C. (2004). *Marketing.* Mason, OH: South-Western.

Lancashire, D. (1970, April 13). When Yoko walked in, McCartney said "O No!" *New York Post,* p. 1.

Landers, A. (1995, February 25). Low income families need fire protection too. *Santa Cruz Sentinel,* p. D5.

Langfred, C. (1998). Is group cohesiveness a double-edged sword? *Small Group Research, 29,* 124–143.

Langlois, J. H., Kalakanis, L., Rubenstein, A. J., Larson, A., Hallam, M., & Smoot, M. (2000). Maxims and myths of beauty? A meta-analytic and theoretical review. *Psychological Review, 126,* 390–423.

Larson, C., & LaFasto, F. (1989). *Teamwork: What must go right, what can go wrong.* Newbury Park, CA: Sage.

Laughlin, P., & Adamopoulos, J. (1980). Social combination processes and individual learning for six-person cooperative groups on an intellectual task. *Journal of Personality and Social Psychology, 38,* 941–947.

Lax, D. A., & Sebenius, J. K. (1986). *The manager as negotiator: Bargaining for cooperation and competitive gain.* New York: Free Press.

Le, P. (1995, October 23). Foundations give schools a growing shot in the arm. *San Jose Mercury News,* p. 1A.

Leak, G. K., & Gardner, L. E. (1992, January). *Teaching anxiety among college psychology teachers.* Paper presented at the Fourteenth Annual National Institute on the Teaching of Psychology, St. Petersburg, FL.

Leana, C. (1985). A partial test of Janis's groupthink model: Effects of group cohesiveness and leader behavior on defective decision making. *Journal of Management, 11,* 5–17.

Leaper, C. (1991). Influence and involvement in children's discourse: Age, gender, and partner effects. *Child Development, 62,* 797–811.

Leathers, D. (1970). The process effects of trust-destroying behaviors in the small group. *Speech Monographs, 37,* 180–187.

Leavitt, H. (1964). *Managerial psychology.* Chicago: University of Chicago Press.

Lee, B. (1997). *The power principle: Influence with honor.* New York: Simon & Schuster.

Lee, M., & Ofshe, R. (1981). The impact of behavioral style and status characteristics on influence: A test of two competing models. *Social Psychology Quarterly, 44,* 73–82.

Leerhsen, C., et al. (1990, February 5). Unite and conquer. *Newsweek,* 50–55.

Levine, J., & Moreland, R. (1990). Progress in small group research. *Annual Review of Psychology, 41,* 585–634.

Levine, S. (1984, August). Radical departures. *Psychology Today,* 20–27.

Lewallen, J. (1972, April). Ecocide: Clawmarks on the yellow face. *Earth,* 36–43.

Lewin, K. (1947). Frontiers in group dynamics. *Human Relations, 1,* 5–42.

Lewin, K. (1953). Studies in group decision. In D. Cartwright & A. Zander (Eds.), *Group dynamics.* Evanston, IL: Row, Peterson.

Lewin, K., Lippitt, R., & White, R. (1939). Patterns of aggressive behavior in experimentally created social climates. *Journal of Social Psychology, 10,* 271–299.

Lewis, R. (1996). *When cultures collide: Managing successfully across cultures.* London: Nicholas Brealey.

Li, C. (1975). *Path analysis: A primer.* Pacific Grove, CA: Boxwood Press.

Lipnack, J., & Stamps, J. (1997). *Virtual teams: Reaching across space, time, and organizations with technology.* New York: John Wiley & Sons.

Lippincott, S. M. (1999). *Meetings: Do's, don'ts, and donuts.* Pittsburgh, PA: Lighthouse Point Press.

Littlejohn, S. (1999). *Theories of human communication.* Belmont, CA: Wadsworth.

Littlepage, G., & Mueller, A. (1997). Recognition and utilization of expertise in problem-solving groups: Expert characterizations and behavior. *Group Dynamics: Theory, Research, and Practice, 1,* 324–328.

Locke, J. (1998). *The de-voicing of society: Why we don't talk to each other anymore.* New York: Simon & Schuster.

Lott, J. R. (2001, June 17). Zero tolerance goes too far. *San Jose Mercury News,* p. 7C.

Lubman, S. (1996, September 15). Volunteers bring schools more than they bargained for. *San Jose Mercury News,* p. 1A.

Lubman, S. (1999, October 13). Nation's response to crisis belies its devotion to detail. *San Jose Mercury News,* p. 21A.

Lulofs, R. (1994). *Conflict: From theory to action.* Scottsdale, AZ: Gorsuch Scarisbrick.

Lumsden, G., & Lumsden, D. (1993). *Communicating in groups and teams: Sharing leadership.* Belmont, CA: Wadsworth.

Lurey, J. S., & Raisinghani, M. S. (2001). An empirical study of best practices in virtual teams. *Information & Management, 38,* 523–544.

Lustig, M., & Koester, J. (2003). *Intercultural competence: Interpersonal communication across cultures.* New York: Longman.

Lutgen-Sandvik, P., Tracy, S., & Alberts, J. K. (2005, February). Burned by bullying in the American workplace: A first time study of U.S. prevalence and delineation of bullying "degree." Paper presented at Western States Communication Association, San Francisco.

Lyman, P., & Varian, H. R. (2003). How much information 2003? Retrieved April 24, 2005, from http://www.sims.berkeley.edu/how-much-info-2003

Lynch, J. J. (2000). *A cry unheard: New insights into the medical consequences of loneliness.* Baltimore: Bancroft Press.

MacIntyre, J. (2005, April 10). Liars at work. *San Jose Mercury News,* p. 3C.

MacNeil, M., & Sherif, M. (1976). Norm change over subject generations as a function of arbitrariness of prescribed norm. *Journal of Personality and Social Psychology, 34,* 762–773.

Majchrzak, A., Malhotra, A., Stamps, J., & Lipnack, J. (2004, May). Can absence make a team grow stronger? *Harvard Business Review,* pp. 131–137.

Mannix, E. A., Thompson, L. L., & Bazerman, M. H. (1989). Negotiation in small groups. *Journal of Applied Psychology, 74,* 508–517.

Man survives stupid arrow stunt. (1993, May 6). *San Jose Mercury News,* p. 9A.

Marcus-Newhall, A., Miller, N., Holtz, R., & Brewer, M. B. (1993). Cross-cutting category membership in role assignment: A means of reducing intergroup bias. *British Journal of Social Psychology, 32,* 125–145.

Mariah "quote" spreads. (1999, February 21). *San Jose Mercury News,* p. 2A.

Marino, V. (2000, November 12). It's all the rage at work, too, *The New York Times,* Money & Business section, p. 3.

Marks, M. (1986, March). The question of quality circles. *Psychology Today,* 36–46.

Markus, M. L. (1994). Finding a happy medium: Explaining the negative effects of electronic communication on social life at work. *ACM Transactions on Information Systems, 12,* 119–149.

Maroda, K. J. (2004). A relational perspective on women and power. *Psychoanalytic Psychology, 21,* 428–435.

Martin, M., & Porter, M. (2006). *DVD and video guide 2005.* New York: Ballantine Books.

Mathison, D. (1987). Sex differences in the perception of assertiveness among female managers. *Journal of Social Psychology, 126,* 599–606.

Matsui, T., Kakuyama, T., & Onglatco, M. L. U. (1987). Effects of goals and feedback on performance on groups. *Journal of Applied Psychology, 72,* 407–415.

Maxwell, J. C. (2001). *The 17 indisputable laws of teamwork: Embrace them and empower your team.* Nashville, TN: Thomas Nelson.

May, M. (2005, February 3). Pledge dies in hazing at Chico fraternity: House was kicked off CSU campus in 2002 for infraction. *San Francisco Chronicle.* Retrieved April 11, 2005, from http://sfgate.com/cgi-bin/article.cgi?f=/c/a2005/02/03/BAGIGB497T1.DTL

May, P. (2002, March 30). Dog owner explains why he showed no remorse. *San Jose Mercury News,* pp. 1A, 18A.

McCauley, C., & Segal, M. (1987). Social psychology of terrorist groups. In C. Hendrick (Ed.), *Review of personality and social psychology: Group process and intergroup relations* (p. 9). Beverly Hills, CA: Sage.

McDaniel, E. (1993, November). *Japanese nonverbal communication: A review and critique of literature.* Paper presented at the Annual Convention of the Speech Communication Association, Miami Beach, FL.

McGrath, J. E., & Hollingshead, A. B. (1994). *Groups interacting with technology: Ideas, evidence, issues, and an agenda.* Thousand Oaks, CA: Sage.

McGregor, D. (1960). *The human side of enterprise.* New York: McGraw-Hill.

McGuinnies, E., & Ward, C. (1980). Better liked than right: Trustworthiness and expertise as factors in credibility. *Personality and Social Psychology Bulletin, 6,* 467–472.

McGuire, P. A. (1998, August). Historic conference focusing on creating a new discipline. *APA Monitor, 29,* 1–15.

McKay, M., Rogers, P., & McKay, J. (1989). *When anger hurts: Quieting the storm within.* Oakland, CA: New Harbinger.

McKenna, K. Y. A., & Green, A. S. (2002). Virtual group dynamics. *Group Dynamics: Theory, Research, and Practice, 6,* 116–127.

McKenna, K. Y. A., Green, A. S., & Gleason, M. (2002). Relationship formation on the Internet: What's the big attraction? *Journal of Social Issues, 58,* 9–31.

McLaughlin, K. (2004, December 24). Couple fulfill wish for a family many times over. *San Jose Mercury News,* pp. 1A, 19A.

McLeod, H., & Cooper, J. (1996, July 31). Politically unplugged. *San Jose Mercury News,* p. 7B.

McLeod, P. L., Lobel, S. A., & Cox, T. H. (1996). Ethnic diversity and creativity in small groups. *Small Group Research, 27,* 248–264.

McMillan, J. J., & Harriger, K. J. (2002). College students and deliberation: A benchmark study. *Communication Education, 51,* 237–253.

McNeil, B. J., Pauker, S. G., Sox, H. C., & Tversky, A. (1982). On the elicitation of preferences for alternative therapies. *New England Journal of Medicine, 306,* 1259–1262.

McNutt, P. (1997, October/November). When strategic decisions are ignored. *Fast Company,* pp. 17–22.

Mead, M. (1961). *Cooperation and competition among primitive peoples.* Boston: Beacon.

Medical mistakes. (2003, January 5). *San Jose Mercury News,* p. 4C.

Meeus, W. H., & Raaijmakers, Q. A. W. (1986). Administrative obedience: Carrying out orders to use psychological-administrative violence. *European Journal of Social Psychology, 16,* 311–324.

Melton, J. G. (1992). *Religious bodies in the United States: A directory.* New York: Garland Press.

Mennecke, B. E., Valacich, J. S., & Wheeler, B. C. (2000). The effects of media and task on user performance: A test of the task-media fit hypothesis. *Group Decisions and Negotiation, 9,* 507–529.

Meyers, R. A., & Brashers, D. E. (1999). Influence processes in group interaction. In L. R. Frey, D. S. Gouran, & M. S. Poole (Eds.), *The handbook of group communication theory and research.* Thousand Oaks, CA: Sage.

Miceli, M. P., & Near, J. P. (1992). *Blowing the whistle: The organizational and legal implications on companies and employees.* New York: Lexington.

Michaelson, L., et al. (1989). A realistic test of individual versus group consensus decision making. *Journal of Applied Psychology, 74,* 834–839.

Milgram, S. (1974). *Obedience to authority.* New York: Harper & Row.

Miller, A. G. (1986). *The obedience experiments: A case study of controversy in social science.* Westport, CT: Praeger.

Miller, C. (1989). The social psychological effects of group decision rules. In P. Paulus (Ed.), *Psychology of group influence.* Hillsdale, NJ: Lawrence Erlbaum.

Miller, K., & Monge, P. (1986). Participation, satisfaction, and productivity: A meta-analytic review. *Academy of Management Journal, 29,* 727–753.

Miller, V. (2005, March 1). Recent Asian bird flu flies under most students' health radars. Retrieved March 4, 2005, from http://www.thehilltop online.com/global_user_elements/printpage .cfm?storyid=880758

Miranda, S. (1994). Avoidance of groupthink: Meeting management using Group Support Systems. *Small Groups Research, 25,* 105–136.

Misra, R. (1980). *The social stratification and linguistic diversity of the Bhojpuri speech community.* Unpublished doctoral dissertation, University of Poona.

Mongeau, P. (1993, February 15). *The brainstorming myth.* Paper presented at the Western States Communication Association Conference, Albuquerque, NM.

Moore, D. W. (2002, May 10). Americans more accepting of female bosses than ever. Gallup Poll News Service. Retrieved February 11, 2004, from http://www.gallup.com/login/?URL_/poll/ releases/pr970829a.asp

Moorhead, G., & Montanari, J. (1986). An empirical investigation of the groupthink phenomenon. *Human Relations, 39,* 399–410.

Moreland, R., & Levine, J. (1987). Group dynamics over time: Development and socialization in small groups. In J. McGrath (Ed.), *The social psychology of time.* Beverly Hills, CA: Sage

Moriarty, T. (1975, April). A nation of willing victims. *Psychology Today,* 43–50.

Morreale, S. (1999, March). Ability to communicate ranked no. 1 by employers. *Spectra, 35,* 10.

Morrison, A., & Von Glinow, M. (1990, February). Women and minorities in management. *American Psychologist,* 200–208.

Moscovici, S., & Mugny, G. (1983). Minority influence. In P. Paulus (Ed.), *Basic group processes.* New York: Springer-Verlag.

Motley, M. (1995). *Overcoming your fear of public speaking: A proven method.* New York: McGraw-Hill.

Moving forward, but still behind. (1999, June 7). *Newsweek,* 32–33.

Mudrack, P., & Farrell, G. (1995). An examination of functional role behavior and its consequences for individuals in group settings. *Small Group Research, 26,* 542–571.

Muir, J. (1992). *C-Span in the communication classroom.* Annandale, VA: Speech Communication Association.

Mulac, A. (1998). The gender-linked language effect: Do language differences really make a difference? In D. J. Canary & K. Dindia (Eds.), *Sex differences and similarities in communication.* Mahwah, NJ: Lawrence Erlbaum.

Mulac, A., & Bradac, J. (1995). Women's style in problem solving interaction: Powerless, or simply feminine? In P. Kalbfleisch & M. Cody (Eds.), *Gender, power, and communication in human relationships.* Hillsdale, NJ: Lawrence Erlbaum.

Mullen, B. (1994). Group cohesiveness and quality of decision making. *Small Group Research, 25,* 189–204.

Murnighan, J. (1978). Models of coalition formation: Game theoretic, social psychological, and political perspectives. *Psychological Bulletin, 85,* 1130–1135.

Myers, D. G. (2003). *Psychology.* New York: Worth.

Myers, D. G., & Bishop, G. D. (1970). Discussion effects on racial attitudes, *Science, 169,* 278–334.

Myers, D. G. (2002). *Intuition: Its power and perils.* New Haven, CT: Yale University Press.

Myers, R. (2000, September 20). Despite prohibitions, school hazing continues. *Christian Science Monitor.* Retrieved May 15, 2003, from http://www.nando.net/24hour/sacbee/opi.../0,1739,50 0260047-500401029-502406989-0,00.html

Myers, R. A., & Brashers, D. E. (1999). Influence processes in group interaction. In L. R. Frey, D. S. Gouran, & M. S. Poole (Eds.), *The handbook of group communication theory and research.* Thousand Oaks, CA: Sage.

Myerson, J. (2001). *IDEO: Masters of innovation.* New York: teNeues Publishing.

Narcisco, J., & Burkett, T. (1975). *Declare yourself.* Englewood Cliffs, NJ: Prentice-Hall.

Neale, M., et al. (1988). *Joint effects of goal setting and expertise on negotiator behavior.* Unpublished manuscript, Northwestern University, Evanston, IL.

Nelson, M. (1998). *Embracing victory: Life lessons in competition and compassion.* New York: William Morrow & Company.

Nickerson, R. S. (1998). Confirmation bias: A ubiquitous phenomenon in many guises. *Review of General Psychology, 2,* 175–220.

Nicotera, A. M. (1995). Conflict and organizations: Communicative processes. Albany: State University of New York Press.

Nicotera, A., & Rancer, A. (1994). The influence of sex on self-perception and social stereotyping of aggressive communication predispositions. *Western Journal of Communication, 58,* 283–307.

Nisbett, R., & Ross, L. (1980). *Human inference: Strategies and shortcomings of social judgment.* Englewood Cliffs, NJ: Prentice-Hall.

Noe, R. (1988). Women and mentoring. *Academy of Management Review, 13,* 65–78.

Noller, P. (1993). Gender and emotional communication in marriage: Different cultures or differential social power? *Journal of Language and Social Psychology, 12,* 132–152.

Northouse, P. (1997). *Leadership: Theory and practice.* Thousand Oaks, CA: Sage.

Nussbaum, B. (2004, May 17). The power of design. *Business Week,* pp. 86–94.

Nye, J. L. (2002). The eye of the follower: Information processing effects on attributions regarding leaders of small groups. *Small Group Research, 33,* 337–360.

Oates, J., & Cullen, D. (2005, February 9). Carly Fiorina quits. *The Register,* p. 13.

Oberg, A. (2003, August 26). From Challenger to Columbia. *San Jose Mercury News,* p. 7B.

O'Brien, T. (1995, November 5). No jerks allowed. *West,* 8–26.

O'Leary, K., Curley, A., & Clark, C. (1985). Assertion training for abused wives: A potentially hazardous treatment. *Journal of Marital and Family Therapy, 11,* 319–322.

Olson, L. N. (2002). "As ugly and painful as it was, it was effective": Individuals' unique assessment of communication competence during aggressive conflict episodes. *Communication Studies, 53,* 171–189.

Orlick, T. (1978). *Winning through cooperation: Competitive insanity, cooperative alternatives.* Washington, DC: Acropolis Books.

Orlitzky, M., & Hirokawa, R. Y. (2001). To err is human, to correct for it divine: A meta-analysis of research testing the functional theory of group decision-making effectiveness. *Small Group Research, 32,* 313–341.

Osgood, C. (1959). Suggestions for winning the real war with communism. *Journal of Conflict Resolution, 3,* 295–325.

Osgood, C. (1966). *Perspective in foreign policy.* Palo Alto, CA: Pacific Books.

Out of "Internet time" (2005, February 12). *San Jose Mercury News,* p. 6B.

Oyserman, D., Coon, H. M., & Kemmelmeier, M. (2002). Rethinking individualism and collectivism: Evaluation of theoretical assumptions and meta-analyses. *Psychological Bulletin, 128,* 3–72.

Parks, C., & Vu, A. (1994). Social dilemma of individuals from highly individualist and collectivist cultures. *Journal of Conflict Resolution, 3,* 708–718.

Pauleen, D. J., & Young, P. (2001). Relationship building and the use of ICT in boundary-crossing virtual teams: A facilitator's perspective. *Journal of Information Technology, 16,* 205–220.

Paulus, P., Dzindolet, M., Poletes, G., & Camacho, M. L. (1993). Perceptions of performance in group brainstorming: The illusion of group productivity. *Personality and Social Psychology Bulletin, 19,* 78–89.

Pavitt, C. (1999). Theorizing about the group communication-leadership relationship. In L. R. Frey, D. S. Gouran, & M. S. Poole (Eds.), *The handbook of group communication theory and research.* Thousand Oaks, CA: Sage.

Pavitt, C., & Curtis, E. (1994). *Small group discussion.* Scottsdale, AZ: Gorsuch Scarisbrick.

Pear, R. (1999, March 15). Clinton seeks to protect whistle-blowers better. *San Jose Mercury News,* p. 4A.

Pearce, C. L., & Sims, H. P. (2002). Vertical versus shared leadership as predictors of the effectiveness of change management teams: An examination of aversive, directive, transactional, transformational, and empowering leader behaviors. *Group Dynamics: Theory, Research, and Practice, 6,* 172–197.

Pearson, J., West, R., & Turner, L. (1995). *Gender and communication.* Dubuque, IA: Wm. C. Brown & Company.

Pennington, N., & Hastie, R. (1990). Practical implications of psychological research on juror and jury decision making. *Personality and Social Psychology Bulletin, 16,* 90–115.

Perret, G. (1994). *Classic one-liners.* New York: Sterling Press.

Perspective. (2000, December 18). *Newsweek,* p. 23.

Pescosolido, A. T. (2001). Informal leaders and the development of group efficacy. *Small Group Research, 32,* 74–93.

Peterson, M. (1997). Personnel interviewers' perception of the importance and adequacy of applicants' communication skills. *Communication Education, 46,* 287–291.

Pettigrew, T., & Martin, J. (1987). Shaping the organizational context for black American inclusion. *Journal of Social Issues, 43,* 41–78.

Phillips, E., & Cheston, R. (1979). Conflict resolution: What works? *California Management Review, 21,* 76–83.

Playing havoc with hormones. (1996, June 7). *San Jose Mercury News,* p. 14A.

Plotz, D. (1997, August 30). Al Dunlap: The chainsaw capitalist. Retrieved January 12, 2002, from http://www.slate.com/Assessment/97-08-30/Assessment.asp

Poll: College students feel pressure to drink. (2000, June 20). *San Jose Mercury News,* p. 9A.

Poole, M. S. (1983). Decision development in small groups III: A multiple sequence model of group decision making. *Communication Monographs, 50,* 321–341.

Poole, M. S., Holmes, M., Watson, R., & DeSanctic, G. (1993). Group decision support systems and group communication: A comparison of decision making in computer-supported and nonsupported groups. *Communication Research, 20,* 176–213.

Poole, M. S., & Roth, J. (1989a). Decision development in small groups IV: A typology of group decision paths. *Human Communication Research, 15,* 323–356.

Poole, M. S., & Roth, J. (1989b). Decision development in small groups V: Test of a contingency model. *Human Communication Research, 15,* 549–589.

Postman, N. (1976). *Crazy talk, stupid talk.* New York: Dell.

Praise thy employee, survey says. (1994, September 13). *San Jose Mercury News,* p. 1E.

Prapavessis, H., & Carron, A. V. (1997). Sacrifice, cohesion, and conformity to norms in sports teams. *Group Dynamics: Theory, Research, and Practice, 1,* 231–240.

Pratkanis, A., & Aronson, E. (2001). *The age of propaganda.* New York: W. H. Freeman & Company.

Pre-employment drug tests ground almost 20% in state. (1990, May 24). *San Jose Mercury News,* p. 1A.

Propp, K. M. (1995). An experimental examination of biological sex as a status cue in decision-making groups and its influence on information use. *Small Group Research, 26,* 451–474.

Propp, K. M. (1997). Information utilization in small group decision making: A study of the evaluative interaction model. *Small Group Research, 28,* 424–453.

Prothrow-Stith, D. (1991). *Deadly consequences.* New York: HarperCollins.

Provine, R. R. (2000). *Laughter: A scientific investigation.* New York: Viking.

Pruitt, D. (1981). *Negotiation behavior.* New York: Academic Press.

Pruitt, D., & Kimmel, M. (1977). Twenty years of experimental gaming: Critique, synthesis, and suggestions for the future. *Annual Review of Psychology, 28,* 363–392.

Pruitt, D., & Rubin, J. (1986). *Social conflict: Escalation, stalemate, and settlement.* New York: Random House.

Purdy, M. (1996, August 1). Don't bow to King Carl. *San Jose Mercury News,* p. 1D.

Put enjoyment ahead of achievement. (1994, February 20). *Santa Cruz Sentinel,* p. D2.

Quattrone, G., & Jones, E. (1980). The perception of variability within in-groups and out-groups: Implications for the law of small numbers. *Journal of Personality and Social Psychology, 38,* 141–152.

Raban, J. (1997, November 24). What the nanny trial tell us about transatlantic body language. *The New York Times,* p. 55.

Rabbie, J. (1993). Determinants of ingroup cohesion and outgroup hostility. *International Journal of Group Tensions, 23,* 309–328.

Radosh, D. (2005, February 28). The pictures: One billion. *The New Yorker,* p. 32.

Rad, P. F., & Levin, G. (2003). *Achieving project management success using virtual teams.* Boca Raton, FL: J. Ross Publishing.

Rahim, M. (1985). Referent role and styles of handling interpersonal conflict. *The Journal of Social Psychology, 12,* 731–745.

Ralston, L. (2001). Campus statistics: Table 3. All undergraduates by ethnicity, fall 1985–fall 2000. Retrieved September 22, 2001, from http://www.chance.berkeley.edu/planning/IC/Campus.Stats/CampStats_F00/CS.F00.Table.F3

Ramirez, L. (1999, August 11). Report: Fewer students take firearms to school. *San Jose Mercury News,* p. 10A.

Rampton, S., & Stauber, J. (2001). *Trust us, we're experts.* New York: Jeremy Tarcher/Putnam.

Rasters, G., Vissers, G., & Dankbaar, B. (2002). An inside look: Rich communication through lean media in a virtual research team. *Small Group Research, 33,* 718–754.

Raush, H., et al. (1974). *Communication, conflict, and marriage.* San Francisco: Jossey-Bass.

Read, P. (1974). Source of authority and the legitimation of leadership in small groups. *Sociometry, 37,* 189–204.

Reddy, M. (2004, May 16). Barbarism theory put into sickening practice in Iraq. *The Age.* Retrieved March 24, 2005, from http://www.theage.com.au/articles/2004/05/15/1084571000862.html?f

Report of the Commission on the Space Shuttle Challenger Disaster. (1986). Washington, DC: Government Printing Office.

Rethinking black leadership. (2002, January 28). *Newsweek,* 42–43.

Riccillo, S., & Trenholm, S. (1983). Predicting managers' choice of influence mode: The effects of interpersonal trust and worker attributions on managerial tactics in a simulated organizational setting. *Western Journal of Speech, 47,* 323–339.

Ridgeway, C. L. (1982). Status in groups: The importance of motivation. *American Sociological Review, 47,* 76–88

Riggio, R. E., Riggio, H. R., Salinas, C., & Cole, E. J. (2003). The role of social and emotional communication skills in leader emergence and effectiveness. *Group Dynamics: Theory, Research, and Practice, 7,* 83–103.

Riley, P. (1994). *The winner within.* New York: Berkley Publishing Group.

Robbins, M. S., Alexander, J. F., & Turner, C. W. (2000). Disrupting defensive family interactions in family therapy with delinquent adolescents. *Journal of Family Psychology, 14,* 688–701.

Robison, J. (2002, September 3). Workplace views: Men and women still miles apart? Gallup Poll News Service. Retrieved January 21, 2003, from http://www.gallup.com/poll/tb/religValue/20020903.asp

Rocheleau, B. (2002). E-mail: Does it need to be managed? Can it be managed? *Public Administration & Management: An Interactive Journal, 7,* 83–116.

Rogelberg, S., & Rumery, S. (1996). Gender diversity, team decision quality, time on task, and interpersonal cohesion. *Small Group Research, 27,* 79–90.

Roland, N., & Mathewson, J. (2002, September 4). Sunbeam ex-CEO "Chainsaw Al" Dunlap settles SEC case. *Bloomberg News,* p. 1.

Romig, D. (1996). *Breakthrough teamwork: Outstanding results using structured teamwork.* Chicago: Irwin Professional Publishing.

Rosenfeld, L. (1983). Communication climate and coping mechanisms in the college classroom. *Communication Education, 32,* 169–174.

Rosenthal, N. (1997, July 15). How to prevent that "us vs. them" feeling within the family. *San Jose Mercury News,* p. 4E.

Ross, L., Amabile, T., & Steinmetz, J. (1977). Social roles, social control and biases in the social perception process. *Journal of Personality and Social Psychology, 37,* 485–494.

Ross, R. (1989). *Speech communication: The speechmaking system.* Englewood Cliffs, NJ: Prentice-Hall.

Rossman, J. (1931). *The psychology of the inventor.* Washington, DC: Inventors' Publishing Company.

Rost, J. C. (1991). *Leadership for the twenty-first century.* New York: Praeger.

Roy, R., & Benenson, J. F. (2002). Sex and contextual effects on children's use of interference competition. *Developmental Psychology, 38,* 306–312.

Rubenstein, M. (1975). *Patterns of problem solving.* Englewood Cliffs, NJ: Prentice-Hall.

Ruggiero, V. R. (1988). *The art of thinking: A guide to critical and creative thought.* New York: Harper & Row.

Ruvolo, C. M., Petersen, S. A., & LeBoeuf, J. N. G. (2004). Leaders are made, not born: The critical role of a developmental framework to facilitate an organizational culture of development. *Consulting Psychology Journal: Practice and Research, 56,* 10–19.

Saint, S., & Lawson, J. (1997). *Rules for reaching consensus.* San Diego: Pfeiffer.

Salazar, A. (1995). Understanding the synergistic effects of communication in small groups. *Small Group Research, 26,* 169–199.

Samovar, L., & Porter, R. (2004). *Communication between cultures.* Belmont, CA: Wadsworth.

Sandoval, R. (1998, July 7). Misery knows no borders. *San Jose Mercury News,* pp. 1C, 4C.

Scandura, R. A., Von Glinow, M. A., & Lowe, K. B. (1999). When East meets West: Leadership "best practices" in the United States and the Middle East. In W. Mobley, M. J. Gessner, & V. Arnold (Eds.), *Advances in global leadership.* Greenwich, CT: JAI.

Schachter, S. (1951). Deviation, rejection, and communication. *Journal of Abnormal and Social Psychology, 46,* 190–207.

Scheer, R. (1983). *With enough shovels: Reagan, Bush and nuclear war.* New York: Vintage Books.

Schittekatte, M., & Van Hiel, A. (1996). Effects of partially shared information and awareness of unshared information on information sampling. *Small Group Research, 27,* 431–449.

Schmidt, S., & Kipnis, D. (1987, November). The perils of persistence. *Psychology Today,* 32–34.

Schultz, B., Ketrow, S., & Urban, D. (1995). Improving decision quality in the small group: The reminder role. *Small Group Research, 26,* 521–541.

Schwartz, S. (1990). Individualism–collectivism: Critique and proposed refinements. *Journal of Crosscultural Psychology, 21,* 139–157.

Seibert, S. (1999). The effectiveness of facilitated mentoring: A longitudinal quasi-experiment. *Journal of Vocational Behavior, 54,* 483–502.

Seligman, J., & Murr, A. (1993, April 12). A town's divided loyalties. *Newsweek,* 29.

Serena Williams interview (2005, May 13). Retrieved May 13, 2005, from http://urbanlegends.about .com/library/bl_serena_williams.htm

Shaffner, G. (1999). *The arithmetic of life and death.* New York: Ballantine Books.

Shaw, M. (1981). *Group dynamics: The psychology of small group behavior.* New York: McGraw-Hill.

Sheldon, K. M. (1999). Learning the lessons of tit-for-tat: Even competitors can get the message. *Journal of Personality and Social Psychology, 77,* 1245–1253.

Shenk, D. (1997). *Data smog: Surviving the information glut.* New York: HarperCollins.

Sheridan, C., & King, R. (1972). Obedience to authority with an authentic victim. *Proceedings of the 80th Annual Convention, American Psychological Association, 7,* 165–166.

Sherif, M. (1966). *In common predicament.* New York: Houghton Mifflin.

Sherif, M., et al. (1988). *The Robbers Cave Experiment.* Middletown, CT: Wesleyan University Press.

Shilling, D. (2000, September). How to find and keep top talent in today's tight labor market. *Medical Marketing & Media, 35,* 125.

Shimanoff, S. B. (1980). *Communication rule: Theory and research.* Beverly Hills, CA: Sage.

Shimanoff, S. (1992). Group interaction via

communication rules. In R. Cathcart & L. Samovar (Eds.), *Small group communication: A reader.* Dubuque, IA: Wm. C. Brown & Company.

Shimanoff, S., & Jenkins, M. (1996). Leadership and gender: Challenging assumptions and recognizing resources. In R. Cathcart, L. Samovar, & L. Henman (Eds.), *Small group communication: Theory and practice.* Dubuque, IA: Brown & Benchmark.

Shirky, C. (1995). *Voices of the Net.* Emeryville, CA: ZD Press.

Shirley, D. (1997). Managing creativity: Inventing, developing, and producing innovative products. Retrieved June 5, 2000, from http://www.managingcreativity.com

Sieburg, E., & Larson, C. (1971). Dimensions of interpersonal response. Paper presented to the International Communication Association, Phoenix, AZ.

Simons, L., & Zielenziger, M. (1996, March 3). Culture clash dims U.S. future in Asia. *San Jose Mercury News,* p. 1A.

Simpson, G. G. (1994). *Alternative medicine: Expanding medical horizons; A report to the National Institutes of Health on Alternative Medical Systems.* Washington, DC: U.S. Government Printing Office.

Sims, R. (1992). Linking groupthink to unethical behavior in organizations. *Journal of Business Ethics, 11,* 651–662.

Singer, M. (1995). *Cults in our midst: The hidden menace in our everyday lives.* San Francisco: Jossey-Bass.

Smith, A., & Williams, K. D. (2004). R U there? Ostracism by cell phone text messages. *Group Dynamics: Theory, Research, and Practice, 8,* 291–301.

Smith, M. (1982). *Persuasion and human interaction: A review and critique of social influence theories.* Belmont, CA: Wadsworth.

Smith, P. (1990). *Killing the spirit: Higher education in America.* New York: Viking.

Smith-Hefner, N. (1988). Women and politeness: The Javenese example. *Language in Society, 17,* 535–554.

Sorensen, S. (1981, May). *Grouphate.* Paper pre-

sented at the International Communication Association, Minneapolis, MN.

Spears, M., Russell, L., & Lee, S. (1990). Deindividuation and group polarization in computer-mediated communication. *British Journal of Social Psychology, 29,* 121–134.

Spitzberg, B., & Cupach, W. (1989). *Handbook of interpersonal competence research.* New York: Springer-Verlag.

Spitzberg, B., & Hecht, M. (1984). A component model of relational competence. *Human Communication Research, 10,* 575–599.

Stahelski, A., & Tsukada, R. (1990). Predictors of cooperation in health care teams. *Small Group Research, 21,* 220–233.

Stanne, M. B., Johnson, D. W., & Johnson, R. T. (1999). Does competition enhance or inhibit motor performance: A meta-analysis. *Psychological Bulletin, 125,* 133–154.

Stanovich, K. (1992). *How to think straight about psychology.* New York: HarperCollins.

Starr, M., & Brant, M. (1999, July 19). It went down to the wire . . . and thrilled us all. *Newsweek,* 46–54.

Stasser, G., & Titus, W. (1987). Effects of information load and percentage of shared information during group discussion. *Journal of Personality and Social Psychology, 53,* 81–93.

Stasser, G., Vaughan, S. I., & Stewart, D. D. (2000). Pooling unshared information: The benefits of knowing how access to information is distributed among group members. *Organizational Behavior and Human Decision Processes, 82,* 102–116.

Stasson, M., & Bradshaw, S. (1995). Explanations of individual-group performance differences: What sort of bonus can be gained through group interaction? *Small Group Research, 26,* 296–308.

State anti-hazing laws (2005, February 3). Retrieved April 11, 2005, from http://www.stophazing.org/laws.html

Stern, A. (1992, May). Why good managers approve bad ideas. *Working Women,* 104.

Stewart, L., Cooper, P. J., Stewart, A. D., & Friedley, S. (1996). *Communication and gender.* Scottsdale, AZ: Gorsuch Scarisbrick.

Stockman, D. (1986). *The triumph of politics: The*

inside story of the Reagan revolution. New York: Avon.

Stogdill, R. M. (1948). Personal factors associated with leadership: A survey of the literature. *Journal of Psychology, 25,* 35–71.

Stogdill, R. M. (1972). Group productivity, drive, and cohesiveness. *Organizational Behavior and Human Performance, 8,* 26–43.

Stogdill, R. M. (1974). *Handbook of leadership.* New York: Free Press.

Stone, B. (2003, October 27). Reinventing everyday life. *Newsweek,* 90–92.

Stone, D., Patton, B., & Heen, S. (1999). *Difficult conversations: How to discuss what matters most.* New York: Viking Press.

Stone, F. (1997, February). We've got to stop meeting like this. *Getting Results . . . for the Hands-on Manager, 42,* 5.

Stout, R. J., Salas, E., & Fowlkes, J. E. (1997). Enhancing teamwork in complex environments through team training. *Group Dynamics: Theory, Research, and Practice, 1,* 169–182.

Straub, D., & Karahanna, E. (1998). Knowledge worker communications and recipient availability: Toward a task closure explanation of media choice. *Organizational Science, 9,* 160–175.

Street, M. (1997). Groupthink: An examination of theoretical issues, implications, and future research suggestions. *Small Group Research, 28,* 72–93.

Sugarmann, J. (2001*). Every handgun is aimed at you: The case for banning handguns.* New York: New Press.

Sulek, J. P. (2004a, November 8). A nod means "I agree" . . . or does it? *San Jose Mercury News,* pp.1A, 9A.

Sulek, J. P. (2004b, December 14). Peterson verdict: Death. *San Jose Mercury News,* pp. 1A, 16A.

Sundell, W. (1972). *The operation of confirming and disconfirming verbal behavior in selected teacher–student interactions.* Doctoral dissertation, University of Denver.

Sundstrom, E., et al. (1990, February). Work teams: Applications and effectiveness. *American Psychologist,* 120–133.

Sunwolf, D. R., & Seibold, D. R. (1999). The impact of formal procedures on group processes, members, and task outcomes. In L. Frey (Ed.), *The handbook of group communication theory and research.* Thousand Oaks, CA: Sage.

Superhuman heroes. (1998, June 6). *Economist,* 10–12.

Suter, E. A. (1994). Guns in medical literature—a failure of peer review. *Journal of the American Medical Association, 83,* 133–159.

Sutton, R. I. , & Hargadon, A. (1996). Brainstorming groups in context: Effectiveness in a product design firm. *Administrative Science Quarterly, 41,* 685–718.

Swezey, R. W., & Salas, E. (Eds.). (1992). *Teams: Their training and performance.* Norwood, NJ: Ablex.

Swim, J. K., & Hyers, L. L. (1999). "Excuse me— what did you just say?": Women's public and private reactions to sexist remarks. *Journal of Experimental Social Psychology, 35,* 68–88.

Swoboda, F. (1999, February 14). Judge fines pilots union. *San Jose Mercury News,* pp. 1A, 28A.

Tang, J. (1997). The Model Minority thesis revisited: (Counter)evidence from the science and engineering fields. *Journal of Applied Behavioral Science, 33,* 291–314.

Tang, S., & Kirkbride, P. (1986). Developing conflict management skills in Hong Kong: An analysis of some cross-cultural implications. *Management Education and Development, 17,* 287–301.

Tannen, D. (1990). *You just don't understand: Women and men in conversation.* New York: Ballantine Books.

Tauer, J. M., & Harackiewicz, J. M. (2004). The effects of cooperation and competition on intrinsic motivation and performance. *Journal of Personality and Social Psychology, 86,* 849–861.

Tavris, C. (1989). *Anger: The misunderstood emotion.* New York: Simon & Schuster.

Tavris, C. (1992). *The mismeasure of women.* New York: Simon & Schuster.

Teamwork characterizes surgical teams that are faster learners of new procedures. (2002, October 22). *Healthcare Review, 15,* 5.

Terdiman, D. (2004, January 22). Gay marriage poll gets annulled. Retrieved January 23, 2004, from http://www.wired.com/news/print/0,1294,61982,00.html

Terry, D. (2000, October 24). Giving gang graffiti the brush-off. *San Jose Mercury News,* p. 17A.

Teubner, G. (2000, November 9). The emergence of control in the flattened organizational structure: Toward a theory of the spiral of control following organizational change. Paper presented at the National Communication Association conference, Seattle, WA.

Thatcher, M. (1993). *The Downing Street years.* London: HarperCollins.

Thomma, S. (2004, June 11). Shock jock aids demos. *San Jose Mercury News,* pp. 3A, 4A.

Thompson, L. F., & Coovert, M. D. (2003). Teamwork online: The effects of computer conferencing on perceived confusion, satisfaction, and postdiscussion accuracy. *Group Dynamics: Theory, Research, and Practice, 7,* 135–151.

Thoms, P., Pinto, J. K., Parente, D. H., & Druskat, V. U. (2002). Adaptation to self-managing work teams. *Small Group Research, 33,* 3–31.

Tjosvold, D. (1986). *Working together to get things done.* Lexington, MA: Lexington Books.

Tjosvold, D., Johnson, D. W., Johnson, R. T., & Sun, H. (2003). Can interpersonal competition be constructive within organizations? *The Journal of Psychology, 137,* 63–84.

Tjosvold, D., & Yu, Z. (2004). Goal interdependence and applying abilities for team in-role and extra-role performance in China. *Group Dynamics: Theory, Research, and Practice, 8,* 98–111.

Toulmin, S., Rieker, R., & Janik, A. (1979). *An introduction to reasoning.* New York: Macmillan.

Townsend, P. (1999a, April 18). Dealing with difficult people. *Santa Cruz Sentinel,* pp. 1C, 2C.

Townsend, P. (1999b, May 23). Some students watch the "in crowd" from afar. *Santa Cruz Sentinel,* pp. A1, A8–A9.

Tran, Q. G. (2001, August 16). Black men in professions earn less than whites. *San Jose Mercury News,* pp. 1C, 4C.

Triandis, H. C. (1990). Cross-cultural studies of individualism and collectivism. In J. Berman (Ed.), *Cross-cultural perspectives* (pp. 41–133). Lincoln: University of Nebraska Press.

Triandis, H. C. (1995). *Individualism and collectivism.* Boulder, CO: Westview Press.

Trompenaars, F. (1994). *Riding the waves of cultures,* Burr Ridge, IL: Irwin.

Tubbs, S. (1984). *A systems approach to small group interaction.* Reading, MA: Addison-Wesley.

Tuck. (1996, September). Brave new meetings, *Presentations,* pp. 28–36.

Tuckman, B. (1965). Developmental sequences in small groups. *Psychological Bulletin, 63,* 384–399.

Tullar, W. L., & Kaiser, P. R. (2000). The effect of process training on process and outcomes in virtual groups. *The Journal of Business Communication, 37,* 408–422.

Turman, P. D. (2003). Athletic coaching from an instructional communication perspective: The influence of coach experience on high school wrestlers' preferences and perceptions of coaching behaviors across a season. *Communication Education, 52,* 73–86.

Turner, M. E., Pratkanis, A. R., Probasco, P., & Leve, C. (1992). Threat, cohesion, and group effectiveness: Testing a social identity maintenance perspective on groupthink. *Journal of Personality and Social Psychology, 63,* 781–796.

Tutzauer, F., & Roloff, M. (1988). Communication processes leading to integrative agreements: Three paths to joint benefits. *Communication Research, 5,* 360–380.

TV or not TV. (1993, April 19). *San Jose Mercury News,* p. 5E.

Tversky, A., & Kahneman, D. (1981, June 30). The framing of decisions and the psychology of choice. *Science,* 453–458.

Uba, L., & Huang, K. (1999). *Psychology.* New York: Longman.

Uranium crew was unaware of atomic risks. (1999, October 23). *San Jose Mercury News,* p. 15A.

Ury, W. (1993). *Getting past no: Negotiating your way from confrontation to cooperation.* New York: Bantam Books.

U.S. Department of Labor. (1991). *Skills and the new economy.* Washington, DC: U.S. Government Printing Office.

Valacich, J., Dennis, A. R., & Connolly, T. (1994). Idea generation in computer-based groups: A new ending to an old story. *Organizational Behavior and Human Decisions Processes, 57,* 448–467.

Valacich, J. S., & Schwenk, C. (1995). Devil's advocacy and dialectical inquiry effects on face-to-face and computer-mediated group decision making. *Organizational Behavior and Human Decision Processes, 63,* 158–173.

Valdez, C. (1983, November 1). Cults focus on identity search. *Western Front,* p. 7.

Vandello, J. A., & Cohen, D. (1999). Patterns of individualism and collectivism across the United States. *Journal of Personality and Social Psychology, 77,* 279–292.

VanDerveer, T., & Ryan, J. (1997). *Shooting from the outside: How a coach and her Olympic team transformed women's basketball.* New York: Avon.

Van de Vliert, E., Euwema, M. C., & Huismans, S. E. (1995). Managing conflict with a subordinate or a superior: Effectiveness of conglomerated behavior. *Journal of Applied Psychology, 80,* 271–281.

Vangelisti, A., Knapp, M., & Daly, J. (1990). Conversational narcissism. *Communication Monographs, 57,* 251–274.

VanLear, C. A., Sheehan, M., Withers, L. A., & Walker, R. A. (2005). AA online: The enactment of supportive computer mediated communication. *Western Journal of Communication, 69,* 5–27.

Van Oostrum, J., & Rabbie, J. (1995). Intergroup competition and cooperation within autocratic and democratic management regimes. *Small Group Research, 26,* 269–295.

Wald, M. L., & Schwartz, J. (2003, July 12). Shuttle probe blames managers, foam equally. *San Jose Mercury News,* p. 8A.

Wallace, P. (1999). *The psychology of the Internet.* New York: Cambridge University Press.

Walther, J. B. (1997). Group and interpersonal effects in international computer-mediated collaboration. *Human Communication Research, 23,* 342–369.

Walther, J. B., & Burgoon, J. K. (1992). Relational communication in computer-mediated communication. *Human Communication Research, 19,* 50–83.

Wanous, J. (1980). *Organizational entry: Recruitment, selection, and socialization of newcomers.* Reading, MA: Addison-Wesley.

Watson, R., Wehrfritz, G., & Hayden, T. (1999, October 11). Can it happen here? *Newsweek,* 44–47.

Watson, W., Michaelsen, L. K., & Sharp, W. (1991). Member competence, group interaction, and group decision making: A longitudinal study. *Journal of Applied Psychology, 76,* 803–809.

Watzlawick, P., Beavin, J. H., & Jackson, D. D. (1967). *Pragmatics of human communication.* New York: W. W. Norton.

Weber, T. (2000, September 26). E-mails too e-motional? Let the computer decide. *Santa Cruz Sentinel,* pp. A1, A5.

Wech, B., Mossholder, K., Streel, R., & Bennett, N. (1998). Does work group cohesiveness afflict individuals' performance and organizational commitment? *Small Group Research, 29,* 472–494.

Weick, K. (1990). The vulnerable system: An analysis of the Tenerife air disaster. *Journal of Management, 16,* 571–593.

Wetzel, P. (1988). Are powerless communication strategies the Japanese norm? *Language in Society, 17,* 555–564.

What employers want vs. what they see in job candidates. (2003). Retrieved June 6, 2003, from http://www.jobweb.com/joboutlook/outlook2.htm

Wheelan, S. A., Davidson, B., & Tilin, F. (2003). Group development across time: Reality or illusion? *Small Group Research, 34,* 223–245.

White, M. M. (2002, September 4). Women to overtake men in management. *Santa Cruz Sentinel,* p. D5.

Who's keeping score? (1999, September 13). *Newsweek,* 56.

Wildschut, T., Insko, C. A., & Gaertner, L. (2002). Intragroup social influence and intergroup competition. *Journal of Personality and Social Psychology, 82,* 975–992.

Wildschut, T., Pinter, B., Vevea, J. L., Insko, C. A., & Schopler, J. (2003). Beyond the group mind: A quantitative review of the interindividual-intergroup discontinuity effect. *Psychological Bulletin, 129,* 698–722.

Williams, K. D., Cheung, C. K. T., & Choi, W. (2000). Cyberostracism: Effects of being ignored over the Internet. *Journal of Personality and Social Psychology, 79,* 748–762.

Williams, K. D., & Karau, S. J. (1991). Social loafing and social compensation: The effects expectations of co-worker performance. *Journal of Personality and Social Psychology, 61,* 570–581.

Williams, K. D., & Sommer, K. L. (1997). Social ostracism by coworkers: Does rejection lead to social loafing or compensation? *Personality & Social Psychology Bulletin, 23,* 693–706.

Wilmot, W., & Hocker, J. (2001). *Interpersonal conflict.* New York: McGraw-Hill.

Wilson, G., & Hanna, M. (1990). *Groups in context.* New York: Random House.

Wilson, R. (2001). Percentage of part-timers on college faculties holds steady after years of big gains. *Chronicle of Higher Education.*

Wiseman, R. (2003). LaughLab. Retrieved April 12, 2004, from http://www.laughlab.co.uk/home.html

Wolf, S. (1979). Behavioral style and group cohesiveness as sources of minority influence. *European Journal of Social Psychology, 9,* 381–395.

Wolkomir, R., & Wolkomir, J. (1990, February). How to make smart choices. *Reader's Digest,* 27–32.

Women CEOs (2005). *Fortune.* Retrieved June 25, 2005, from http://www.fortune.com/fortune/fortune500/articles/0,15114,1046096,00.html?promoid=cnnmoney

Wood, J. T. (1997a). *Communication theories in action: An introduction.* Belmont, CA: Wadsworth.

Wood, J. T. (1997b). *Gendered lives: Communication, gender, and cultures.* Belmont, CA: Wadsworth.

Wood, J. T. (2000). *Relational communication: Continuity and change in personal relationships.* Belmont, CA: Wadsworth.

Wood, J., Phillips, G. M., & Pedersen, D. J. (1986). *Group discussion: A practical guide to participation and leadership.* New York: Harper & Row.

Wood, J. T., & Dindia, K. (1998). What's the difference? A dialogue about differences and similarities between men and women. In D. J. Canary & K. Dindia (Eds.), *Sex differences and similarities in communication.* Mahwah, NJ: Lawrence Erlbaum.

Wooton, J. (1993, September 13). Lessons of Pop Jordan's death. *Newsweek,* 12.

Worthington, D. L., Stallard, M. J., Price, J. M., & Gross, P. J. (2002). Hindsight bias, Daubert, and the silicone breast implant litigation: Making the case for court-appointed experts in complex medical and scientific litigation. *Psychology, Public Policy, and Law, 8,* 154–179.

Wurman, R. (1989). *Information anxiety.* New York: Doubleday.

Young, F. (1965). *Initiation ceremonies.* New York: Bobbs-Merrill.

Yu, X. (1998). The Chinese "native" perspective on Mao-dun (conflict) and Mao-dun resolution strategies: A qualitative investigation. *Intercultural Communication Studies, 7,* 63–82.

Zander, A. (1982). The psychology of removing group members and recruiting new ones. *Human Relations, 29,* 1–8.

Zielenziger, M., & Lubman, S. (1999, October 3). Japan's dislike of quick action proves costly. *San Jose Mercury News,* pp. 1A, 20A.

Zimbardo, P. (1992, 1988). *Psychology and life.* Glenview, IL: Scott, Foresman.

Zornoza, A., Ripoll, P., & Peiro, J. M. (2002). Conflict management in groups that work in two different communication contexts: Face-to-face and computer-mediated communication. *Small Group Research, 33,* 481–508.

Index